Computer Education for Teachers
Integrating Technology into Classroom Teaching

FIFTH EDITION

Vicki Sharp

California State University, Northridge

Boston   Burr Ridge, IL   Dubuque, IA   Madison, WI   New York   San Francisco   St. Louis
Bangkok   Bogotá   Caracas   Kuala Lumpur   Lisbon   London   Madrid   Mexico City
Milan   Montreal   New Delhi   Santiago   Seoul   Singapore   Sydney   Taipei   Toronto

b25131989

The McGraw-Hill Companies

*A Division of The **McGraw-Hill** Companies*
COMPUTER EDUCATION FOR TEACHERS:
INTEGRATING TECHNOLOGY INTO CLASSROOM TEACHING
Published by McGraw-Hill, a business unit of The McGraw-Hill Companies, Inc., 1221 Avenue of the Americas, New York, NY, 10020. Copyright © 2005, 2002, 1999, 1996, by The McGraw-Hill Companies, Inc. All rights reserved. No part of this publication may be reproduced or distributed in any form or by any means, or stored in a database or retrieval system, without the prior written consent of The McGraw-Hill Companies, Inc., including, but not limited to, in any network or other electronic storage or transmission, or broadcast for distance learning. Some ancillaries, including electronic and print components, may not be available to customers outside the United States.

This book is printed on acid-free paper.

1 2 3 4 5 6 7 8 9 0 QPD/QPD 0 9 8 7 6 5 4

ISBN 0 07 288021 X

Publisher: *Emily G. Barrosse*
Senior sponsoring editor: *Allison McNamara*
Senior developmental editor: *Cara Harvey*
Senior marketing manager: *Pamela S. Cooper*
Media producer: *Shannon Gattens*
Project manager: *Jean R. Starr*
Production supervisor: *Janean A. Utley*
Associate designer: *Srjdan Savanovic*
Lead supplement producer: *Marc Mattson*
Associate photo research coordinator: *Natalia C. Peschiera*
Art editor: *Jen DeVere Warner*
Photo researcher: *Natalia Peschiera*
Art director: *Robin Mouat*
Permissions editor: *Marty Granahan*
Cover image: *Gettyimages.com*
Typeface: *9.5/12 Palatino*
Compositor: *Carlisle Communications, Ltd.*
Printer: *Quebecor World Dubuque Inc.*

Library of Congress Cataloging-in-Publication Data

Sharp, Vicki F.
    Computer education for teachers : integrating technology into classroom teaching / Vicki F. Sharp.
        p. cm.
    Includes bibliographical references and index.
    ISBN 0-07-288021-X (softcover : alk. paper)
    1. Education—Data processing. 2. Computers—Study and teaching. 3. Computer-assisted instruction. I. Title.
    LB1028.43.S55 2005
    370'.285—dc22   2004040205

370.285
.S53
2005

www.mhhe.com

This book is dedicated to my husband, Richard Malcolm Sharp, and my son, David Allen Sharp. They are the most important people in my life!

About the Author

Vicki F. Sharp is a professor at California State University and a former elementary school teacher. She received a Ph.D. in Quantitative Research from St. Louis University and a B.A. from Washington University. She teaches math/science methods courses and computer courses, and she supervises student teachers. She has been the author or co-author of more than 33 books, including *Statistics for the Social Sciences* (Little, Brown), the *HyperStudio in an Hour* series, *PowerPoint in an Hour* and *Best Web Sites for Teachers* (ISTE), and the *Make It with Office* series and *Make It with Inspiration* (Visions Technology in Education). She serves as a computer consultant and trainer for software publishers and school districts in southern California. She speaks at computer conventions such as Computer User Educators (CUE) and the National Education Computer Conference (NECC). Her special interests include integrating the computer into the classroom, teacher education, digital photography, and school improvement.

Brief Contents

Contents

Chapter 6

Databases   *118*

Chapter 7

Spreadsheets and Integrated
Programs   *145*

PART 4

What Teachers Should Know About Educational Technology   *385*

Chapter 15

Issues and Research in Educational Technology   *386*

Chapter 16

The Future   *418*

Preface

We have come a long way from the 1940s and 1950s when computers consisted of vacuum tubes, data were recorded on magnetic tapes and magnetic drums, and the machines were used primarily by scientists and engineers. In 1969, when I was working on my Ph.D., I typed cards on a keypunch machine, and the cards were then read by a computer that filled a large room. Then, in 1977, Steve Jobs and Steve Wozniak introduced a fully assembled version of their Apple computer, called the Apple II. I thought this compact desktop computer with its 4K of memory, priced at $1,298, was a marvel. In the early 1980s I wanted to bring computers to teachers, so I bought pocket computers and taught programming off campus. Using the Apple IIe as a demonstration machine, I showed how to use software such as *Lemonade Stand* and used a word processor program called *Bank Street Writer.* At that time, educational software was limited and inadequate, and the focus was teaching the programming language BASIC, followed shortly thereafter by Logo.

Since the mid-1990s, there have been many technological changes, and the computer has emerged as an important tool in society and in education as well. With the production of quality software, the computer's role has changed from a device used for computer programming to an instrument that can efficiently be integrated into the curriculum. Teachers utilize computers for word processing, database management, spreadsheets, graphics generation, desktop publishing, Internet access, and multimedia. Our machines are now smaller, contain gigabyte hard drives, and have gigabyte processing speeds. We use the Internet as a huge library resource, and electronic mail has proliferated. (In fact, we communicate by e-mail to such an extent that I am relieved when our server breaks down.) We are using the Internet more and more for distance learning. Today, computers are being used to help students with special needs realize their potential. In the next ten years, the computer and the Internet will become even more pervasive influences on how we teach and what happens in the classroom. It will be an exciting time for teachers and students, and no one knows what the future will bring. I hope you enjoy this book!

Approach and Features of This Text

Computer Education for Teachers: Integrating Technology into Classroom Teaching is designed to introduce future teachers to computer technology in a meaningful, practical fashion. It is written for undergraduate and graduate students who want an up-to-date, readable, practical, concise introduction to computers for teachers. Covering a large range of topics, this book should help you acquire the knowledge and skills necessary to integrate computers into your classroom in ways that will be of most use to you and of greatest service to your students.

Throughout its four editions, *Computer Education for Teachers* has maintained the key features that contributed to the success of the very first edition:

- **Accessibility:** Readers need not have had any prior experience with computers. The clear, straightforward writing style of the text makes the topics accessible to all.
- **Extensive illustrations:** A wealth of illustrations and screen shots clearly convey the salient features of the latest and best software and help computer novices identify hardware.
- **Learning tools:** Proven learning support features include each chapter's *Introduction, Objectives, Summary, Chapter Mastery Test, Key Terms,* and *Suggested Readings and References.* Practical resources of use to working teachers include evaluation *Checklists, Classroom Lesson Plans, Web Links,* and new *Computer Lab Activities.*
- **Current research:** The inclusion of the latest research on computers provides readers with an understanding of effective and ineffective uses of computer hardware and software and promising new directions for computer use in the classroom.
- **Discussions of advances in computer technology:** These explorations keep readers on the cutting edge of computer knowledge.
- **Internet site listings:** At the end of each chapter, lists of Internet sites provide readers with additional sources of lesson plans, tutorials, historical information, and classroom tools.
- **End-of-chapter references:** These reference lists provide readers with books and articles to launch detailed investigations into many aspects of educational software and hardware and learning theory.

New to the Fifth Edition

Computer Education for Teachers remains true to its original purpose: to provide meaningful and practical guidance in bringing computers into the classroom. However, each edition has refined and updated the text's features to reflect the latest research and technological advances. This fifth edition also offers an even stronger focus on the classroom teacher and what she or he needs to know to put computer technology to work in the classroom. A chapter-opening feature lists practical uses of specific types of computer programs for teachers and K–12 students. This edition features more checklists to help teachers evaluate software. Finally, *Classroom Lesson Plans* have been expanded and now are keyed to standards.

In addition, the organization of this new edition has been streamlined. Four parts highlight key topics: (1) an introduction to computers and educational technology; (2) how to use and select software and hardware; (3) how to integrate educational technology into the classroom; and (4) broader computer-related issues including concerns raised by computer use in the classroom, research findings on computer-based learning, and projections about the future of technology in the classroom.

A New Practice Tool—The Computer Lab CD-ROM

The student *Computer Lab CD-ROM* provides several learning activities per chapter. These activities are designed to encourage practice with different types of applications and technology. In addition, most activities result in a product that can be used in the K–12 classroom.

New Features

The fifth edition of *Computer Education for Teachers* offers numerous new features:

- **An Educational Milestone and Standards chapter:** Chapter 2 briefly reviews the history of the educational use of computers and discusses why and how technology should be integrated into the classroom.
- **A new Hardware Reference Guide for Teachers:** Chapter 3 provides users with a handy listing and explanation of hardware basics.
- **Expanded coverage of the Internet:** Three chapters (9, 10, and 11) now tackle the many pertinent aspects of the Internet in the classroom. Chapter 9 introduces the reader to networking and the Internet. Chapter 10 covers distance learning and Internet-related problems. Finally, Chapter 11 explores how to integrate the Web into the classroom.
- **A revised Special Education chapter:** Chapter 13 provides the most up-to-date information about using technology with children with special needs. The chapter covers hardware, software, federal laws, lesson plans, and ways to integrate the computer into the special education classroom. Additionally, the chapter discusses the implications of IDEA and mainstreaming and inclusion.
- **An expanded and updated Multimedia chapter:** Chapter 8 introduces ways to use the computer to combine text, graphics, and sound into effective presentations.
- **An expanded discussion of ISTE Standards:** The standards are available in full for easy reference on the inside front and back covers. Additionally, ISTE and subject-specific standards are keyed to all of the *Classroom Lesson Plans*.
- **New or expanded chapter learning support tools:** The popular software and hardware evaluation checklists have been expanded. *Study and Online Resources* provide readers with Internet sites that offer opportunities for further exploration of chapter topics. *Computer Lab: Activities for Mastery and Your Portfolio* give readers opportunities to use computer technology and further their mastery over it and chapter concepts.
- **Enhanced art treatment:** More than 150 new illustrations, including screen shots of reviewed software, new tables, and a new two-color design support learning and enhance the reader's experience.

Supplements for Teaching and Learning

This edition of Computer Education for Teachers features new and expanded supplements for course instructors and readers/students.

For the Instructor

Instructors using this book will find additional teaching support in the following supplements:

- The *Instructor's Resource CD-ROM* includes an instructor's manual, test bank, computerized test bank, and *PowerPoint* slides.
- The *Instructor's Online Learning Center,* at **www.mhhe.com/sharp5e**, includes an online version of the instructor's manual, the *PowerPoint* slides, and additional teaching resources.
- Several **course management programs** support the book, including *PageOut, Blackboard,* and *WebCT.*

For the Student

Education students will find their learning supported by three excellent tools:

- The student *Computer Lab CD-ROM* includes several activities per chapter designed to facilitate practice with different types of applications and technology. These step-by-step activities introduce different applications and generate products that can be used in the K–12 classroom.
- The *Online Learning Center* features self-quizzes, a current news feed, links and lesson plans, study tools, recommended software, HTML & LOGO tutorials, and Internet exercises.
- *Folio*Live, an online portfolio tool, guides users in the creation of an electronic portfolio in three easy steps. With this tool, users can create portfolios to demonstrate and archive their mastery of the skills and content taught through *Computer Education for Teachers.*

A Message to Readers

If you would like to see some topic in a future edition or have any comments or questions, please send your thoughts to me at one of the following addresses:

America Online address: VickiFS@aol.com
Internet address: vicki.sharp@csun.edu
University address: Dr. Vicki Sharp, California State University, Northridge, School of
     Education, 18111 Nordhoff, Northridge, CA 91330-8265

Acknowledgments

What a monumental effort this book was. If it were not for some very special people, it would never have been completed.

First, I would like to thank my husband, Dick Sharp, for his invaluable contributions. He not only gave me emotional support, but he also contributed to the writing of this book. He searched for the best websites, wrote descriptions of them, checked the software directory for errors, made phone calls, created the index, and was my severest critic. Furthermore, he is a loving husband and a wonderful father to our son, David.

Second, I would like to thank the terrific Special Education Department at California State University, Northridge. Dr. Sarah Hall not only critiqued chapter 12, but she also created the *Assistive/Adaptive Technology Evaluation Form* and the *Teacher Support Tools Evaluation Form.* The chairperson of the department, Dr. Nancy Burstein, and Dr. Michael Spagna loaned me books and gave me insights into the field of special education. Furthermore, Tobey Shaw, principal and technology coordinator at Frostig Center and a student at CSUN, and Marsha Lifter, writer, lecturer and university teacher at California State University, San Luis Obispo, gave suggestions for chapter 13. I would like to thank Robert A. Sachs, Instructional Technology Application Facilitator—Los Angeles Unified School District C Schools, for his helpful comments on chapter 8.

Third, I want to express my appreciation to Cara Harvey, senior developmental editor at McGraw-Hill, for her suggestions and direction, Allison McNamara, senior sponsoring editor for her insights, and Bob Weiss for his in-depth analysis. The project manager, Jean Starr, is not only a very special person, but she also is a real professional.

I treasure her support and guidance. Finally, Sarah Lane, the best copyeditor in the world, made my writing look better than it deserves to. I am fortunate that she was able to copyedit my book. The McGraw-Hill team is a wonderful group of people to work with and I am proud to be a part of this team.

Fourth, I give a special thanks to Dr. David Moursund, Founder of the ISTE and a professor in the College of Education at the University of Oregon; Janet Caughlin, technology book series writer and speaker; Tony Vincent, handheld expert and fifth-grade teacher; Anthony Nguyen, network administrator at CSUN; and, last but not least, Dr. George Friedman, adjunct professor at USC, formerly research director at the Space Studies Institute, Princeton. David, thank you for the insights on the future of educational technology. Janet and Tony, thank you for sharing your knowledge on handheld computers. Anthony, thank you for your thoughts on wireless networks and distance learning. George, thank you for sharing your experiences on distance learning and giving us some insights into what will happen in the future.

Fifth, I thank all the terrific individuals who critiqued this book and offered many wonderful suggestions that were incorporated into this new edition:

Cindy L. Anderson, National Lewis University
Mandi Batalo, California State University, San Bernardino
Kathy Brandon, Eastern Michigan University
Judy Cestaro, California State University, San Bernardino
Fran Clark, University of Memphis
John Connor, Daytona Beach Community College
David Edybury, University of Wisconsin, Milwaukee
Candace Figg, University of Southwestern Louisiana
Sarah Hall, California State University, Northridge
Heather Koren, East Carolina University
John Langone, University of Georgia
David McCarthy, University of Minnesota, Duluth
Maxine Morris, Pittsburgh State University
Jana Willis, University of Houston, Clear Lake

Last but not least, I thank the many software houses that contributed to the completion of this textbook:

- *Apple Software:* Suman Mariyappa, public relations, and Tim Beeker and Vincent Louque, Mac geniuses
- *AlphaSmart:* Chris Bryant
- *Barnum Software:* Christopher Wright
- *Corel:* Chip Maxwell
- *Don Johnston:* Angie LeBoida
- *Encore:* Jill Griffin
- *Equilibrium:* Dave Pola, corporate communications manager, and Chris Caracci, technical expert
- *FableVision:* Kelly Fischbach, vice president of Educational Publishing
- *FileMaker Inc.:* Stephen F. Ruddock and Kevin Mallon
- *FTC Group:* Mike Kessler and Marsha Kessler
- *Grolier Electronic Publishing:* Veronica Scheer
- *Harmonic Visions:* Joel Brazy
- *Inspiration:* Ava Ryherd, training resource specialist, and Megan Murphy, product manager
- *Knowledge Adventure:* Mary Ann Scovall

- *Logo Computer Systems Inc. (LCSI):* Lea M. Laricci
- *Microsoft:* Irving Kwong
- *Optimum Resources, Inc.:* Christopher J. Gintz, chief operating officer
- *Riverdeep:* Myon (Mike) Puckett, educational sales representative, and Debbie Galdin, public relations
- *Scholastic Software:* Eileen Hilbrand and Veronica Scheer
- *SmartStuff:* Maria Crawford
- *Sunburst Communications:* Christine Pearse, marketing manager
- *Tech4Learning:* Melinda Kolk and David Wagner
- *Terrapin Logo:* Bill Glass
- *T/Maker:* Diane La Mountaine
- *Tom Snyder Productions:* Kim Goodman and Brian L. McKean
- *Ventura Educational Systems:* Fred Ventura
- *Visions Technology in Education:* John Crowdner, president, Ken Harvey, product manager, and Tim Yost, graphics designer
- *Waggener Edstrom:* Sibylle Haupert, account coordinator, Shannon Whiteaker, account coordinator, and Jessica Keller, account coordinator

A very special thanks to Dave Pola (Equilibrium), John Crowder (Visions Technology in Education), and Waggener Edstrom account coordinators Sibylle Haupert, Shannon Whiteaker, and Jessica Keller. These individuals selflessly gave of their time and provided expert advice. *DeBabelizer* (Equilibrium) was used to batch-produce the screen shots and enhance images.

PART I
An Introduction to Computers and Educational Technology

CHAPTER 1

The History of Computers

Computer Literacy

It is only by studying our past that we gain perspective and are able to prepare for the future. In reading this chapter, you will become familiar with some of the major developments in computer technology. You will see that computers were derived from primitive humans' practice of counting with fingers, toes, and rocks. You will learn what led to the development of modern-day computers.

Objectives

Upon completing this chapter, you will be able to do the following:

1. Identify and place in proper sequence five of the major inventions in the history of computing.
2. Discuss succinctly the contributions of each of the following individuals to the field of computing:
   a. Charles Babbage,
   b. Herman Hollerith,
   c. Howard Aiken,
   d. John Atanasoff,
   e. John Mauchly and J. Presper Eckert, and
   f. John Von Neumann.
3. Differentiate among the generations of computers according to their technological advances.

Computers in Education Today

If Rip Van Winkle woke up from his 20-year nap in the middle of a 21st-century classroom, he would be shocked. The modern buildings and the students with their unfamiliar dress, cell phones, tablet PCs, and Personal Data Assistants (PDAs) might make him want to go to sleep again. He would observe students and teachers using computers, digital cameras, scanners, and multimedia projectors. He might see students filming with their camcorders while on a field trip and then, upon their return to the classroom, uploading their films to the World Wide Web for others to see. During his travels, he might witness students logging on to a cyberschool for an online chat, reading lessons on the Internet, talking with classmates through online discussion groups, and delivering presentations via the Web.

When Rip traveled to other schools, he would be in awe of the multitude of electronic devices in use including the electronic tablet, the pocket hard drive, the wireless network, and the interactive whiteboard. A teacher station would be enough to make him think that he was dreaming again. Rip could watch the teacher using an interactive whiteboard to show the entire class what was on her computer, taking the class on virtual online trips to the Getty Museum, the White House, and Carlsbad Caverns.

At this point, Rip might decide he needed a change of scenery and go to visit a rural school district. In this school district he might watch as staff used a video conferencing system to interact with other school districts in the area, sharing curricula. The children at one school might be learning Spanish through video conferencing from an instructor at another. The students could, via video conferencing, take a virtual field trip to Washington, D.C., and a city zoo.

Rip Van Winkle would see things he did not want to see. Not every school he visited would have equal access to technology. He would witness an uneven distribution of funds and budget shortfalls in most school districts. He would note the desperate need for more technology in some classrooms to help underprivileged students enter the workforce.

Rip might realize that many teachers underuse technology because they are not trained to use it. These teachers may have students use the computer only for games as a reward for doing their work. These teachers may have no idea how to show the students how to use an application such as PowerPoint to create a presentation for a science project. They may not even know how to use a digital video camera to tape themselves teaching so that they might improve.

Rip would either be excited by all the new technology or he would yearn for an earlier simpler time. Maybe he would want to find out what led up to all these changes, by taking a trip back in time.

Calculation in Early Times

Primitive humans found it necessary to count, and the natural instruments to use were their fingers. With their fingers, they could show how many animals they had killed on a hunt or the number of people in a village. To indicate large numbers, they used all 10 fingers; since humans have 10 fingers, 10 became the basis of our number system.

As time passed, life became more complex, and people needed a way to keep track of their possessions. They began to use rocks as a way to store information, using one rock to represent each animal they owned, for example. Later, wanting a more permanent record of this information, they carved notches and symbols in stone or wood.

Abacus

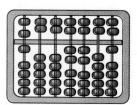

It is believed that people in Babylon started using a primitive abacus for record keeping about 3000 B.C. (Pullan, 1968). The **abacus** was different from any recording device that came before it in that it allowed users to manipulate data. The abacus (Figure 1.1) user manipulates beads in a wood frame to keep track of numbers and place values. Users can perform calculations almost as quickly as they could with a calculator. Of all the early aids to calculation, the abacus is the only one still used today.

Figure 1.1 Abacus

Pioneer Inventors of Calculation Devices

Over time, more calculating devices were invented to make calculations easier and accurate. Most of these calculating devices were arithmetic aids. Numerous inventors of such devices made important contributions with their work to the development of the computer. John Napier, a Scottish mathematician, invented in 1617 what became known as Napier's Rods or Bones. Users could multiply large numbers by manipulating rods. In 1642, Blaise Pascal built a calculating machine (Figure 1.2) that could add and subtract. This machine was the standard until Baron Gottfried Wilhelm Von Leibniz, a German mathematician, designed an instrument called the Stepped Reckoner, which he completed in 1674. Leibniz's machine (Figure 1.3) was more versatile than

Figure 1.2
The Pascaline

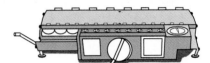

Figure 1.3 Leibniz's Stepped
Reckoner

Pascal's because it could multiply and divide as well as add and subtract. It used cylinders instead of gears to do its calculations. However, Leibniz's most important contribution to the computer's evolution was not his machine but binary arithmetic, a system of counting that uses only two digits, 0 and 1. Leibniz never completed his work on binary arithmetic.[1] It wasn't until 1854, nearly two centuries later, that George Boole devised what became known as **Boolean algebra,** a system of logic based on the binary system. In the late 1930s, inventors built a computer that used this binary system, the standard internal language of today's digital computers.

Though not a calculating device, Jacquard's Loom was the next invention, after the Stepped Reckoner, of great significance in the development of the computer. In 1804, Joseph Marie Jacquard used punched cards to create patterns on fabric woven on a loom. The hole punches directed the threads up or down, producing the patterns. Jacquard's device was the forerunner of the keypunch machine (Figure 1.4).

Figure 1.4 Jacquard's
Loom

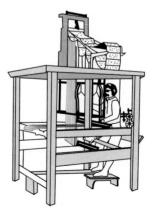

[1]Refer to Chapter 3 for a discussion of binary code.

Beginning of the Computer

Each of these men and each of their inventions brought us closer to the invention of the computer. These devices were capable of performing the same rudimentary functions as the beginning computers. The first individual to work on creating a real computer was Charles Babbage, a Cambridge mathematics professor.

The Analytical Engine

Aggravated by errors in printed mathematical tables, Babbage resigned his position at Cambridge to work on a machine that would perform error-proof calculations. He called this machine the Difference Engine because it worked to solve differential equations. Using government funds and his own resources, he labored on the computer for 19 years but was unable to complete it. Babbage constructed only a few components, and people referred to his engine as *Babbage's Folly.*

After the government withdrew its funding, Babbage proceeded to work on another, more sophisticated version of this machine, which he called the Analytical Engine (Figure 1.5). A close friend of his, Augusta Ada Byron, Countess of Lovelace, the only legally recognized daughter of Lord Byron, tried to help him. She raised money for his invention and wrote a demonstration program for the Analytical Engine. Because of this program, she is considered the first computer programmer, and the programming language **Ada** was named after her.

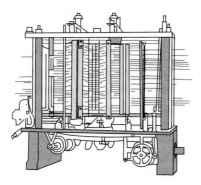

Figure 1.5 Babbage's Analytical Engine

In 1835, Babbage designed a system with provision for printed data, a control unit, and an information storage unit, but the Analytical Engine was never completed because construction of the machine required precision tools that did not exist at the time. For this achievement he is called the "father of computers," and historians have even said that all modern computers were descended directly from Babbage's Analytical Engine. In his day, however, Babbage was considered a failure, and he died in poverty. A mere 19 years later, the punched-card element of the Analytical Engine appeared in a working machine, a tabulator built by Herman Hollerith.

The Tabulating Machine

No history would be complete without a discussion of the American inventor Herman Hollerith. When Hollerith worked at the Census Bureau in the 1880s, he met Colonel John Shaw Billings, who was the director of the division of vital statistics. They became friends and one evening, Billings discussed with Hollerith a hypothetical machine that could do the mechanical work of tabulating the population. Billings envisioned using cards with notches punched on the edges, with the notches representing each individual's description. Hollerith was so fascinated with the idea, he decided to leave his job at the Census Bureau and go to MIT to teach and work on this Tabulating Machine. Hollerith devised several experimental test systems. In 1889, the Census Bureau held a contest for a contract to create such a census-taking machine. Hollerith's innovative Tabulating Machine (Figure 1.6), which relied heavily on Jacquard's punched-card idea, won the contract by a landslide over two competing systems. The census office bought 56 of Hollerith's machines and commissioned him to repair them as needed. Because of Hollerith's invention, the census was completed in just two years, compared to the seven years it took for the 1880 census. Eventually, Herman Hollerith organized his own company called the Tabulating Machine Company. In the 1900s, he leased out his more sophisticated tabulating machines for the census. His business prospered and merged with other companies. The company went through a series of name changes, and the last name change came in 1924 when it became known as International Business Machines, or IBM.

Figure 1.6 Hollerith's Tabulating Machine

Table 1.1 summarizes the achievements of these inventors.

Table 1.1 Computing Devices Before the 20th Century

Inventor	Invention	Year
Unknown	Abacus	≅3000 B.C.
John Napier	Napier's Bones	1617
Blaise Pascal	Pascaline	1642
Gottfried Leibniz	Stepped Reckoner	1674
Joseph Marie Jacquard	Punched Card Loom	1804
Charles Babbage	Analytical Engine	1835
Herman Hollerith	Tabulating Machine	1887

In the 20th century, the Census Bureau bought a machine designed by James Powers to replace Hollerith's machines. Powers founded a company called Powers Accounting Machine Co., which merged with others to become known as Remington Rand and then Sperry Rand. Today, these companies are part of the conglomerate Unisys.

Hollerith's company and Powers's company produced machines that primarily served the business community. The scientific community's need for more complex processing remained unmet.

The Modern Computer

In 1944, the age of the modern computer began. World War II created a need for better data handling that spurred on advances in technology and the development of computers. During the war, a brilliant team of scientists and engineers (among them Alan Turing, Max Newman, Ian Fleming, and Lewis Powell) gathered at Bletchley Park, north of London, to work on a machine that could solve the German secret code. They designed the Colossus, an electronic computer that was used to break the German Enigma cipher. Much of their innovative work remains classified.

Mark I

In 1937, Howard Aiken was to complete his research for his Ph.D. at Harvard. Faced with tedious calculations on nonlinear, differential equations, he decided that he needed an automatic calculating machine to make the chore less arduous. In a memo written in 1937, he proposed to create a computer. Initially, Aiken found little support at Harvard for his machine, so he turned to private industry. IBM was taken with Aiken's idea and agreed to back him in his effort.

Aiken headed a group of scientists whose task was to build a modern equivalent to Babbage's Analytical Engine. In 1943, the Mark I, also called the IBM Automatic Sequence Controlled Calculator, was completed at IBM Development Laboratories at Endicott, New York. It was 51 feet long, 8 feet high, and 2 feet thick; it consisted of 750,000 parts and 500 miles of wire; and it weighed 5 tons. Noisy but capable of three calculations per second, it accepted information by punched cards which it then stored and processed. The results were printed on an electric typewriter.

The first electromechanical computer was responsible for making IBM a giant in computer technology. After the completion of the Mark I, IBM produced several machines that were similar to the Mark I, and Howard Aiken also built a series of machines (the Mark II, Mark III, and Mark IV).

In 1945, the Mark II was housed in a building without air conditioning. Because the computer generated tremendous heat, the windows were left open. One day this giant computer suddenly stopped working, and everyone tried frantically to discover the source of the problem. Grace Hopper and her coworkers found the culprit: a dead moth in a relay of the computer. They removed the moth with a tweezers and placed it in the Mark II logbook.[2] When Aiken came back to see how things were going with his associates, they told him they had had to **debug** the machine, thus coining the term for fixing a computer problem.

---

[2] Today the Mark II logbook is preserved in the Naval Museum in Dahlgren, Virginia.

The ABC

In 1939 at Iowa State University, John Atanasoff designed and built the first electronic digital computer while working with Clifford Berry, a graduate student. Atanasoff and Berry then went to work on an operational model called the ABC, the Atanasoff-Berry Computer. This computer, completed in 1942, used binary logic circuitry and had regenerative memory. No one paid much attention to Atanasoff's computer except John Mauchly, a physicist and faculty member from the University of Pennsylvania. In 1941, he took a train to Ames, Iowa, to learn more about the ABC. Staying five days as Atanasoff's houseguest, he had an opportunity to read Atanasoff's handbook explaining the electronic theories and construction plans of the ABC (Mollenhoff, 1990). Mauchly then returned home to the Moore School of Electrical Engineering at the University of Pennsylvania.

ENIAC

With the start of World War II, the military needed an extremely fast computer that would be capable of performing the thousands of computations necessary for compiling ballistic tables for new Naval guns and missiles. John Mauchly and J. Presper Eckert believed the only way to solve this problem was with an electronic digital machine, so they worked on this project together. In 1946, they completed an operational electronic digital computer called the ENIAC (Electronic Numerical Integrator and Calculator), derived from what Mauchly had gleaned from Atanasoff's unpatented work.[3] The ENIAC worked on a decimal system and had all the features of today's computers. The ENIAC, shown in Figure 1.7, was tremendous in size, filling up a very large room and weighing 30 tons. It conducted electricity through 18,000 vacuum tubes, generating tremendous heat and so had to have special air conditioning to keep it cool.

Figure 1.7 ENIAC

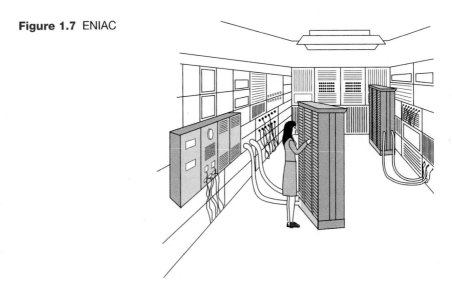

[3]Atanasoff's work was ignored for years; it was rejected by IBM, Remington Rand, and Iowa State. Atanasoff was unheard of until 1973, when he received recognition as one of the fathers of computing. At this time, Sperry Rand brought a suit against Honeywell, and federal district judge Earl R. Larson invalidated the ENIAC patent. Larson said that Eckert and Mauchly had derived some of their ideas from Atanasoff's unpatented work.

This computer operated at a rate that was 500 times faster than any electromechanical computer of the day. A problem that an electromechanical machine would need 30 to 32 hours to calculate this machine solved in three minutes. The ENIAC's limitations were a small memory and difficulty shifting from one program to another, which required rewiring the machine. These problems might have taken years to solve if not for a meeting between Herman Goldstine, a mathematician and liaison officer for the ENIAC project, and John Von Neumann, a logician and mathematician. Because of that meeting, Von Neumann joined the Moore team, which was about to embark on developing a new computer.

The EDVAC

After Von Neumann arrived in Philadelphia, he helped the Moore group with the logical makeup of the EDVAC, the Electronic Discrete Variable Automatic Computer. The Moore team produced a major breakthrough in the form of the stored-program concept. Until this time, a computer stored its program externally, either on plug boards, punched tape, or cards. Mauchly and Eckert discovered that one mercury delay line could replace dozens of vacuum tubes. With this innovation, the EDVAC could store information in memory in the same form as data. Although Von Neumann and his group were credited with using the stored-program concept, theirs was not the first machine to do so.

The UNIVAC and Others

Before 1951, the computer was not manufactured on a large scale. In 1951, with the arrival of the UNIVAC, the era of **commercial computers** began. Only two years later, IBM started distributing its IBM 701, and Burroughs manufactured its E101 and Honeywell its Datamatic 1000. The computers that were developed during the 1940s and 1950s were called *first-generation computers* because they had one common feature, the vacuum tube.

Generations of Computers

Since its inception, the computer has gone through several stages of development. Generally these technological advances are classified by *generations,* a marketing term. Even though there is some overlap among generations it is convenient to view the computer's technological development in terms of this classification.

The First Generation of Computers

The **first generation of computers** began in the 1940s and extended into the 1950s. During this period, computers used **vacuum tubes,** such as the one in Figure 1.8, to conduct electricity. The employment of vacuum tubes made the computers expensive because the tubes, which took up a great deal of space, were continually burning out and having to be replaced. At this time, computers were classified by the main memory storage device they used. The UNIVAC I used an ingenious device called the *mercury delay line,* which relied on ultrasonic pulses. Mercury delay line storage was a reliable device, but it was very slow compared to modern storage devices.

Figure 1.8 Vacuum Tube

During the first generation, pioneering work was done in the area of magnetic storage. Data were recorded on magnetic tapes and magnetic drums, which were used for auxiliary memory. In magnetic tape storage, the data were recorded on tapes similar to the audiocassette tapes used today. Data were held on the tapes in a serial manner, which meant the user could not access the information directly, resulting in slower access time. Similar to magnetic tapes were magnetic drums. These two means of storage were important until magnetic disks appeared in the third generation.

The Second Generation of Computers

Figure 1.9 Transistor

We perceive the **second generation of computers** as beginning when the **transistor** (Figure 1.9) replaced the vacuum tube in the late 1950s. In 1947, John Bardeen, Walter H. Brattain, and William Shockley, a team of physicists working at Bell Labs, invented the transistor. They shared the Nobel Prize for this invention in 1956.

The transistor, an electrically operated switch similar to an old-fashioned relay, was a landmark in the development of the computer. The transistor is created by melting silicon, an element found in common sand. Transistors conduct electricity more efficiently, consume less energy, need less space, and generate less heat than vacuum tubes. In addition, they do not burn out as tubes do. The computer with transistors became smaller, more reliable, faster, and less expensive than a computer with vacuum tubes. Small- and medium-size businesses now found it more economical to buy computers.

Also during this second era of computers, a new form of memory, magnetic-core memory, was developed. This memory permitted data to be retrieved and stored at a millionth of a second.

The Third Generation of Computers

The beginning of the **third generation of computers** is marked by the 1964 introduction of the IBM 360, the computer that pioneered the use of **integrated circuits** on a chip. In that year, computer scientists developed tiny integrated circuits and installed hundreds of these transistors on a single silicon chip, which was as small as a fingertip. The computer became smaller, more reliable, and less expensive than ever before. They were almost a thousand times faster than the first generation of computers, and manufacturers mass-produced them at a low price, making them accessible to small companies. People purchased minicomputers for classrooms, homes, and small businesses.

The integrated circuits were now used as main memory, and magnetic disks replaced magnetic tape as auxiliary memory. These disks allowed information to be retrieved nonsequentially, speeding up access time. Computer terminals flourished, and more and more users began to communicate via these terminals with computers at other locations. In the beginning, the terminal worked like a typewriter, producing a printed output. As time went on, video display terminals replaced punched cards as the means for entering data and programs into the computer.

The 1970s began with the development of **large-scale integration (LSI),** a method that put hundreds of thousands of transistors on a single silicon chip. The chip was as minute as a speck of dust and so delicate that miniature scientific instruments had to be devised to create it. The development of the LSI led to the insertion of computers in cameras, television sets, and cars. Another result of LSI was the personal computer.

The Fourth Generation of Computers

The development of microprocessor technology launched the **fourth generation of computers.** The **microprocessor chip** (Figure 1.10) is a central processing unit, the brains of the computer, built on a single chip.

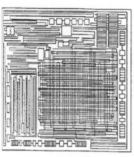

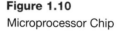
Figure 1.10
Microprocessor Chip

Magnified Chip   Actual Chip Size

Edward "Ted" Hoff designed the microprocessor in 1968 while working at Intel. In 1971, this chip was marketed as the Intel 4004 microprocessor. Intel intended that this chip be used in smaller, less powerful technology, such as calculators because it lacked the power needed to run a microcomputer. However, three years later, Intel introduced its 8080 version, which was capable of running the processing unit of a computer. The journal *Radio Electronics* published an article in 1974 on a home-built computer that used this technology. In June of 1975 *Popular Electronics* ran a story on Altair, a microcomputer that ran on the 8080 chip. The article mentioned that Micro Instrumentation Technology Systems (MITS) was selling kits for this computer. The public response and interest in Altair kits was overwhelming, and they inspired other companies to develop similar products.

Bill Gates and Paul Allen were just college students when they wrote the first BASIC interpreter[4] for the Intel 8080 microprocessor. The language they created, called MBASIC, was licensed to MITS and sold with the Altair computer. In 1975 Bill Gates and Paul Allen founded Microsoft. Years later Microsoft became a leader in programming languages by supplying IBM PCs with DOS (**D**isk **O**perating **S**ystem) and non-IBM PCs with the MS-DOS operating system.

Bill Gates
Paul Allen

[4]Allen Freedman, in *The Computer Desktop Encyclopedia* (New York: American Management Association, 2003), calls this interpreter "a high level programming language translator that translates and runs the program at the same time."

At about the same time that Gates and Allen were launching Microsoft, Steve Wozniak and Steve Jobs were selling from a garage their Apple computers for the price of $666.66. Figure 1.11 shows the Apple I. Wozniak and Jobs placed ads in hobbyist pub-

Figure 1.11 Apple I Computer

Images courtesy of Apple Computers, Inc.

Steve Wozniak and Steve Jobs

lications with the money that they raised by selling their personal possessions. They provided software for their machines free of charge. They achieved a modicum of success, but it was not until they hired professional help and support and in 1977 introduced, in what was a historic moment for computers, a new fully assembled version of their Apple machine called the Apple II, that the Apple took off. The Apple II was the first computer widely accepted by business users because of its spreadsheet simulation program, *VisiCalc*. In addition, it was compact, it came with 4 kilobytes (4K) of memory, it was priced at $1,298, and ran at a clock speed of 1.0.[5]

Four years later, IBM entered the personal computer market with the IBM PC. This computer quickly became a best-seller. Because of IBM's successful entrance in the field, other computer makers chose to capitalize on its popularity by developing their own "clones." These personal computers had many of the same features as the IBM machines and could run the same programs.

With the IBM PC, widespread use of personal computers became a reality. In 1977, computers even began appearing in schools. A time line of the important developments in the history of the modern computer is found on page 13.

The Fifth Generation of Computers

The **fifth generation of computers,** marked from the mid-1990s, heralded superfast computer chips capable of carrying out thousands of operations simultaneously. This generation of computers delivers gigahertz speeds and utilizes millions of transistors. Computers now feature voice recognition, natural and foreign language translation, fiber optic networks, and optical discs. Computers are smaller with increased data storage and gigahertz memory. Many systems now have touch screens and handwriting recognition software that let the user employ a pencil-like stylus as the input device.

[5]Clock speed is the speed of the internal clock of a microprocessor. It is measured in megahertz, and higher clock speed brings gains in microprocessor-intensive tasks (Pfaffenberger, 2000).

Modern Computer Time Line

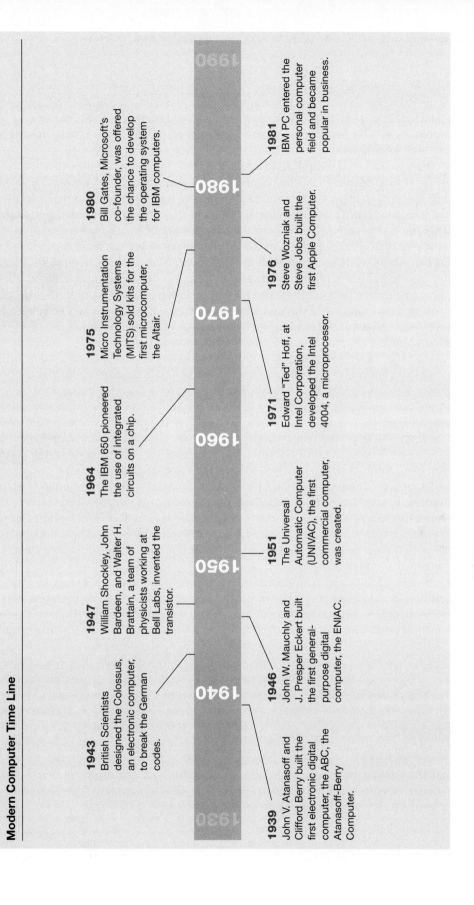

1939
John V. Atanasoff and Clifford Berry built the first electronic digital computer, the ABC, the Atanasoff-Berry Computer.

1943
British Scientists designed the Colossus, an electronic computer, to break the German codes.

1946
John W. Mauchly and J. Presper Eckert built the first general-purpose digital computer, the ENIAC.

1947
William Shockley, John Bardeen, and Walter H. Brattain, a team of physicists working at Bell Labs, invented the transistor.

1951
The Universal Automatic Computer (UNIVAC), the first commercial computer, was created.

1964
The IBM 650 pioneered the use of integrated circuits on a chip.

1971
Edward "Ted" Hoff, at Intel Corporation, developed the Intel 4004, a microprocessor.

1975
Micro Instrumentation Technology Systems (MITS) sold kits for the first microcomputer, the Altair.

1976
Steve Wozniak and Steve Jobs built the first Apple Computer.

1980
Bill Gates, Microsoft's co-founder, was offered the chance to develop the operating system for IBM computers.

1981
IBM PC entered the personal computer field and became popular in business.

1930   1940   1950   1960   1970   1980   1990

Students and teachers are increasingly using computerized electronic organizers such as the Palm. Wearable computers transmit voice and data via a built-in cellular radio. Holographic storage, still at the research stage, could soon be viable. Data storage will eventually rely on laser cards the size of a small plastic credit card that can hold terabytes of information.

This generation of computers is based on logical inference and the extensive use of **artificial intelligence (AI).** Pfaffenberger (2003) describes AI as "a computer science field that tries to improve computers by endowing them with some of the characteristics associated with human intelligence, such as the capability to understand natural language and to reason under conditions of uncertainty." Such machines will shortly be able to reason to the point of making decisions, drawing conclusions, understanding everyday speech, and learning from experience. Already some accomplishments in this area have been achieved: Medical programs aid in diagnosing various diseases. Mining programs help mining companies in their explorations. Educators employ AI in writing assessment engines and smart tutoring systems. Artificial intelligence has been used in board games such as chess and backgammon. Some of the chess and backgammon programs have defeated their creators in tournaments.

In 1950 in an article entitled "Computing Machinery and Intelligence, "Alan Turing proposed a test called the *Imitation Game* or *Turing Test* to determine whether computers can think. According to the Turing Test, if you cannot discern whether a machine or a human is generating conversation over a teletype machine, the computer is reasoning like a human. Some computers are getting close to achieving this standard, and—who knows?—in years to come people might prefer talking to a computer rather than to a person. Computers will communicate in English or Chinese, for example, rather than in a computer language. They will respond to a human voice, not to a keyboard or disk drive. In Stanley Kubrick's film *2001: A Space Odyssey,* the computer HAL understands every word it hears and all the subtleties of human conversation. This thoughtful film predicted much that is a reality today or will become a reality tomorrow. Today, the voice synthesizers that are used in computers sound more human than those used a few years ago. Navigation systems in cars use voice synthesizers to tell us in what direction to travel.

Presently, printers and computers are communicating through wireless networks. In addition, machines employ parallel processing; that is, a computer performs two or more operations simultaneously. Computers come with flat-panel displays that are larger, in color, and detachable. The **Internet,** a worldwide system for linking small computer networks, is exerting an increasingly pervasive influence on our everyday lives. Teachers and students are finding new ways to work from their homes and in schools. Through the use of wireless telecommunication services, they are spending less time in the classroom and more time on the Internet via voice, data, and video conferencing. Teachers and students are using the Internet's research tools, and many communicate through online course software almost exclusively. Exciting new technologies will deliver huge increases in bandwidth capacity, making Internet access occur with lightning-fast speed. With these new developments come new forms of interactive content, realistic 3-D, virtual reality,[6] multiplayer games, and interactive educational video forums. In Chapter 16 we will discuss the many new advances in computer technology and speculate on its future.

---

[6]Virtual reality (VR) is a computer system that can immerse the user in the illusion of a computer-generated world. The user can navigate throughout this world at will (Pfaffenberger, 1997). See Chapter 8 for further discussion.

Table 1.2 highlights the major technological advances in each generation of computers.

Table 1.2 Major Technological Advances of Each Computer Generation

Generation	Years	Technological Advance
First	Early 1950s	Vacuum tube
Second	Mid-1950s	Transistor
Third	Early 1960s	Integrated circuits
Fourth	1970–mid-1990s	Microprocessor
Fifth	Mid-1990s–2000s	AI, Internet, parallel processing, virtual reality

After reading this chapter, Rip Van Winkle might want to know why technology should be integrated into the classroom. He might wonder what educational theorist played an important role in the development of educational technology. What were the important developments in the history of educational computing? What are some of the educational technology standards? These questions and more are explored in Chapter 2.

Summary

The origin of computers can be traced back to inventors who were interested in processing information and developing devices to simplify tedious arithmetic calculations. In the 1800s, Jacquard used punched cards in a loom to produce beautiful patterns, an invention that inspired Charles Babbage. Babbage used the concept of the punched card in his Analytical Engine. Herman Hollerith improved on Jacquard's idea and pioneered processing of statistical data in the 1890 census. Today, statistical data processing is a major application for computers. In the 1900s, inventors constructed the earliest electromechanical computer, quickly replaced by the faster electronic computer.

Subsequent developments were categorized by generations. In the first generation, computers used vacuum tubes to conduct electricity. In the second generation, transistors replaced tubes, which were replaced in the third generation by integrated circuits. The fourth generation saw the advent of large-scale, integrated circuit chips. The fifth generation of computers offers the development of artificial intelligence, computers based on logical inference and parallel processing, and radical changes in the Internet.

Study and Online Resources

*Go to Chapter 1 in the Student Edition of the Online Learning Center at **www.mhhe.com/sharp5e** to **practice with key concepts, take chapter quizzes, read PowerWeb articles** and **news feed updates** related to technology in education, and **access resources** for learning about technology and integrating it into the classroom.*

Click on *Web Links* to link to the following Websites.

The Apple Museum
This site features informative articles, time lines, galleries, and detail of Apple's greatest machines.

Calculating Machines
This site presents the history and classification of mechanical calculating machines. It includes pictures of the machines.

Science: Click-n-Learn

This site gets at the heart of computers, giving detailed descriptions of the insides of a typical CPU. Simply drag your mouse over the exposed skeleton of the computer and click to get full descriptions of the hardware. There are three different knowledge levels for your students to explore; and teachers can benefit from knowing the ins and outs of computers as well.

Computer Museum History Center

This site provides a comprehensive collection of 2,000 computer-related artifacts, including an 1890 Hollerith Census machine, a Cray-3 supercomputer, a World War II ENIGMA device, a see-through Palm Pilot, parts of MIT's Whirlwind computer, and a computer-generated *Mona Lisa*!

John W. Mauchly and the Development of the ENIAC Computer

The world's first electronic digital computer, the Electronic Numerical Integrator and Calculator (ENIAC), was turned on for the first time in 1946. This 30-ton monster was about as powerful as the tiny computers inside today's "singing" greeting cards. The story of ENIAC, as seen by one of its creators, is told at this site.

Historic Computer Images

This site features a photo collection of 200 computer images.

Past Notable Women of Computing

This site offers information on pioneering computing women from Ada Byron King, Countess of Lovelace, to Joan Margaret Winters. The site also includes a photo gallery of women and computers.

Triumph of the Nerds

This companion Website to the PBS television special gives a history of computers. Click on the appropriate link (http://www.pbs.org/nerds/game.html) and you can find a charming guessing game called "Guess the Computer."

Vintage Calculators

This catalog of "old-school" calculators includes the 25-pound Comptometer, the Addiator, and a pinwheel contraption dubbed the Muldivo. All of these models feature actual working gears and levers that can be viewed with the naked eye. When was the last time you fixed your Palm Pilot by replacing a worn washer? You are also invited to browse a time line of calculator history (beginning with the abacus and ending in 1978) and peruse an array of early pocket calculators that appear to be roughly the size of toasters.

World War II Codes and Ciphers

This homespun site was created by Tony Sale, a man instrumental in preserving and restoring the historical collection at Bletchley Park, headquarters of British code breakers during World War II. The site features detailed tutorials for the mathematically inclined and a Bletchley Park photo album.

Yahoo List of Online Computer Museums

Yahoo offers a comprehensive list of computer museums.

Chapter Mastery Test

To the Instructor: *Refer to the Instructor's Manual for the answers to the Mastery Questions. This manual has additional questions and resource materials.*

Let us check for chapter comprehension with a short mastery test. Key Terms, Computer Lab, and Suggested Readings and References follow the test.

1. Discuss briefly the contributions made to the computer field by the following individuals:
   a. Howard Aiken
   b. Charles Babbage
   c. Herman Hollerith
   d. John Atanasoff

2. Identify and place in correct order four of the major inventions in the field of computing.
3. Differentiate the generations of computers by their technological advances.
4. Explain the significance of punched cards and vacuum tubes in the development of early computers.
5. Explain the importance of transistors and microprocessors in the development of modern computers.
6. What was George Boole's lasting contribution to computer history?
7. What computer opportunities would a sixth grader have in 1953 as opposed to a sixth grader in 2004?
8. Why was Hollerith's Tabulating Machine developed for the 1890 census significant for the future of computing?

9. Explain the discovery that made personal computers possible.
10. Explain why Charles Babbage might be considered to have been born at the wrong time.
11. What were some of the problems of first-generation computers?
12. What are Steve Jobs's and Steve Wozniak's major achievements in the computer field?
13. Explain why Ada Lovelace deserves an important place in the history of computers.
14. What spearheaded the development of the electronic digital computer?
15. What are Bill Gates's and Paul Allen's major achievements in the computer field?

Key Terms

Abacus   3
Ada   5
Artificial intelligence (AI)   14
Boolean algebra   4
Commercial computers   9
Debug   7

First generation of computers   9
Fourth generation of computers   11
Fifth generation of computers   12
Integrated circuits   10

Internet   14
Large-scale integration (LSI)   10
Microprocessor chip   11
Second generation of computers   10

Third generation of computers   10
Transistor   10
Vacuum tubes   9

Computer Lab: Activities for Mastery and Your Portfolio

1.1 Interactive Time Line: The Modern History of Computers Test your knowledge of the history of computers with this time line.
1.2 Prepare a paper on the 1973 court trial between Sperry Rand and Honeywell. In this case, Judge Larson ruled that "Eckert and Mauchly did not themselves invent the electronic digital computer, but instead derived the subject matter from one John V. Atanasoff."

1.3 Using a computer time line program such as Tom Snyder's *TimeLiner 5.0,* list at least ten significant computer events from 1863 to 2003.
1.4 Prepare an in-depth research report on the life of an important inventor and his or her contribution to the history of computers.
1.5 Write three biographical sketches on important women in the computer field discussing their achievements.

Suggested Readings and References

Asimov, Isaac. *How Did We Find Out About Computers?* New York: Walker, 1984.

Aspray, William. "John Von Neumann's Contributions to Computing and Computer Science." *Annals of the History of Computing,* 11, no. 3 (1989): 165.

Austrian, G. *Herman Hollerith: Forgotten Giant of Information Processing.* New York: Columbia University Press, 1982.

Bernstein, J. *The Analytical Engine.* New York: Morrow, 1981.

Dunn, Ashley. "UCLA, Hewlett-Packard Scientists' Finding Could Speed up Computing." *Los Angeles Times,* January 3, 2000, p. B5.

Evans, Christopher. *The Micro Millennium.* New York: Viking Press, 1979.

Freedman, A. *The Computer Desktop Encyclopedia.* New York: American Management Association, 2003.

Gardner, David, W. "Will the Inventor of the First Digital Computer Please Stand UP?" *Datamation* 20 (February 1974): 84–90.

Gates, Bill, Nathan Myhrvold, and Peter Rinearson. *The Road Ahead.* New York: Viking Penguin, 1996.

Goldstine, H. *The Computer from Pascal to Von Neumann.* Princeton, N.J.: Princeton University Press, 1972.

Hayes, Frank. "The Story So Far." *Computer World* 36 (September 16, 2002), Issue 38, p. 32.

Hof, Robert D. "The Quest for the Next Big Thing." *Business-Week.* August 18–25, 2003, pp. 91–94.

Holmes, Stanley. "Software Giant Hears Footsteps on Internet." *Los Angeles Times,* December 27, 1999, p. C7.

Levy, Steven. "The Computer." *Newsweek,* February 6, 1998, pp. 28–30.

Macintosh, Allan R. "Dr. Atanasoff's Computer." *Scientific American* 259, no. 2 (August 1, 1988): 90.

Magid, Lawrence J. "The Meanest, Fastest Machine on the Block Isn't for Everyone." *Los Angeles Times,* November 1, 1999, p. C7.

McClosky, Paul. "Tablet PCs Stake out Higher Ed." *Syllabus,* 16, no. 5 (December 2002): 18–20.

McDonald, Glenn, and Cameron Crotty. "The Digital Future." *PC World,* January 1, 2000, pp. 116–134.

Metropolis, N., J. Howlett, and G. C. Rota, eds. *A History of Computing in the Twentieth Century.* New York: Academic Press, 1980.

Mollenhoff, Clark R. "Forgotten Father of the Computer." *The World & I* (March 1990): 319–332.

Molnar, Andrew R. "Computers in Education—a Brief History." *T.H.E. Journal* 24, no. 11 (June 1997): 59–62.

Moore, Johanna D. "Making Computer Tutors More Like Humans." *Journal of Artificial Intelligence in Education* 7, no. 2 (1996): 181–214.

Moreau, Rene. *The Computer Comes of Age: The People, the Hardware, and the Software.* Translated by J. Howlett. Cambridge, Mass.: MIT Press, 1984.

Morrison, P., and E. Morrison, eds. *Charles Babbage and His Calculating Engines.* New York: Dover, 1961.

Naisbitt, John. *Megatrends: Ten New Directions Transforming Our Lives.* New York: Warner Books, 1982.

Naisbitt, John. *Megatrends 2000: Ten New Directions for the 1990s.* New York: Morrow, 1990.

Palfreman, Jon, and Doron Swade. *The Dream Machine.* London: BBC Books, 1991.

Pfaffenberger, Bryan. *Webster's New World Dictionary Computer Dictionary,* 10th ed. New York: Que, 2003.

Pfaffenberger, Bryan, Bill Daley, and Roberta Baber. *Computers in Your Future 2004,* 6th ed. Prentice Hall, 2003.

Port, Otis. "Cheap, Pliable, and Powerful. *Business Week,* August 15, 2003, p. 104.

Pullan, J. M. *A History of the Abacus.* New York: Praeger Publishers, 1968.

Resick, Rosalind. "Pressing Mosaic." *Internet* (October 1994): 81–88.

Ritchie, David. *The Computer Pioneers: The Making of the Modern Computer.* New York: Simon and Schuster, 1986.

Rochester, J., and J. Gantz. *The Naked Computer.* New York: Morrow, 1983.

Smarte, Gene, and Andrew Reinhardt. "15 Years of Bits, Bytes and Other Great Moments: A Look at Key Events in Byte, the Computer Industry." *Byte* 15, no. 9 (September 1, 1990): 369–400.

Takahashi, D. "A Dogged Inventor Makes the Computer Industry Say: Hello, Mr. Chip." *Los Angeles Times,* October 21, 1990, p. C1.

CHAPTER 2

Educational Milestones and Standards

Reflecting on Educational Technology

What is educational technology? Why should technology be integrated into education? What part has education played in the history of computers? What are the current educational milestones? Why are educational technology standards important? What learning theories shed light on how we should use computers in education?

Objectives

Upon completing this chapter, you will be able to do the following:

1. Give three reasons we should integrate technology into education.
2. Identify and place in proper sequence three of the major developments in the history of educational technology.
3. List four ways the computer has changed education.
4. Explain the difference between the teacher-directed approach and constructivism.
5. Be able to identify the ISTE Educational Technology Standards.

Students Can

- do library investigations on the Internet,
- get math tutorial help,
- create electronic portfolios,
- view science simulations,
- write research papers, and
- do desktop publishing.

Teachers Can

- create an electronic spreadsheet grade book,
- find lesson plans and instructional material,
- use technical Internet chat rooms,
- create PowerPoint presentations,
- communicate with students by e-mail, and
- create newsletters for parents.

What Is Educational Technology?

Definitions of *educational technology* abound. Some educators use the term to refer to any media that the teacher can use for classroom instruction, such as visual, audio, or digital media. Other educators use it to refer to the use of a computer or other mechanical or electronic device for teaching and learning (Muffoletto, 1994). For the purpose of this textbook we will take the most general definition, used by the Association for Educational Communications and Technology (AECT): "**Educational technology** is the theory and practice of design, development, utilization, management, and evaluation of processes and resources for learning." In this definition, we can include a wide array of technology including computers, slides, photographs, e-mail, CD-ROMs or DVD-ROMs, the Internet, videotapes, and instructional television.

How Is Technology Integrated into Education?

Technology pervades all of our lives. Look around and you see people talking on cell phones, surfing the Net, and storing data in PDAs. Even 15 years ago, it was rare for people to have computers in their homes. However, today, if you do not have a computer, you are at somewhat of a disadvantage.

The computer has become an indispensable tool. When did you last write a paper by hand? When was the last time you used a card catalog at a library or drew up a worksheet for presenting data calculations? Today, you can find research materials on the Internet. You can perform "if then" calculations using an electronic spreadsheet. You can automatically alphabetize your research paper reference list on the computer.

The research discussed in Chapter 15 shows how the computer is a useful tool for science simulations. Computers can motivate students to learn, and help build math skills. Students can use the Internet as a library resource, investigating everything from critiques of *East of Eden* to essays on the dangers of global warming. Computers can link students at schools around the world. Students can use the computer to write research reports, conduct experiments, and create electronic portfolios for job applications.

Using the computer, a teacher can provide students with different kinds of learning. Teachers can visit Websites to access lesson plans and activities to enhance learning in any subject area. Teachers can use PowerPoint to create presentations to help explain different topics. For example, if a teacher is discussing van Gogh's artwork, she can provide an electronic slideshow of his work with commentary and music. They can have students visit specific Websites and answer questions. They can use drill and practice software programs to help students who are having problems in a particular academic area. Teachers can consult technical chat rooms for help or information about pertinent topics. They can use the computer to create certificates for students and class newsletters.

Finally, administrators can use the computer to create presentations for their planning meetings. They can then display these presentations on a school's Website for teacher viewing and comments. Administrators can create their own Websites, to provide information to students, teachers and parents. They can send teachers e-mail messages about meetings and school programs. Administrators can store important information in electronic databases such as student absenteeism data, current school supply inventories, substitute teacher name and contact information, and access electronic school resources such as CD-ROMs, books, and videotapes. They can create newsletters for teachers, parents, and staff.

Dean Philip Rusche at California State University Uses Technology to Create Presentations

We have just considered only a small percentage of the many ways that technology can enrich our educational experience. Throughout this book, we will consider many more examples of how technology is being used in education. We will also discuss some exciting new possibilities for future uses. First, however, let us examine briefly the history of educational technology.

A Brief History of Computers in Education

Most teachers started to use computers when the microcomputer first appeared in the classroom. However, educational computing had a history that preceded the micro-computer era. The time line on page 23 presents an overview of the developments in educational technology that we'll discuss in this chapter.

Early Developments

The first use of computers in education was primarily in mathematics, science, and en-gineering. Computers replaced the slide rule for solving problems. The oldest tech-nique for learning with a computer was **programmed instruction,** a term coined in 1950 by Harvard psychologist B. F. Skinner. This technology was the forerunner of the computer tutorial.

For this type of instruction, material is broken down into small segments of infor-mation. Students work through the programmed materials at their own rate, and after each step they are tested on their comprehension by answering questions. The students are immediately given the right answer or additional material to help them master the subject. Books, teaching machines, or computers can be used to present this material.

In 1950, the first documented instructional use of the computer occurred at MIT when teachers used a computer flight simulator to train pilots. Nine years later, the first documented instructional use of computers with elementary students occurred in New York City when an IBM computer was used to teach schoolchildren binary arithmetic.

B. F. Skinner

A scarcity of educational software and the inaccessibility of computers to students prompted programmers in the 1960s to design more user-friendly computer languages such as LISP, RPG, APL, SNOBOL, and BASIC. John Kemeny and Thomas Kurtz at Dartmouth College wanted a language that would require minimal instruction and that would be easy to learn in an academic setting. FORTRAN and ALGOL did not

Time Line of Educational Technology

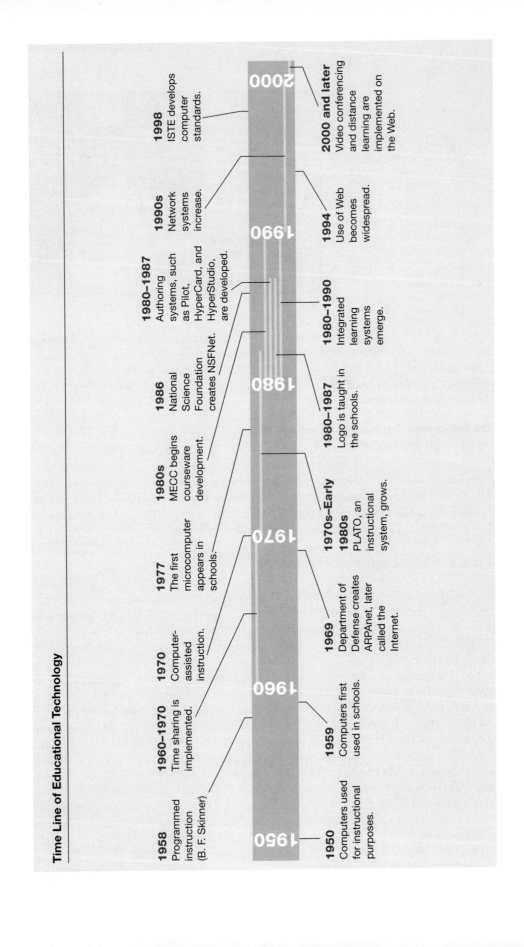

1958
Programmed instruction (B. F. Skinner)

1960–1970
Time sharing is implemented.

1970
Computer-assisted instruction.

1977
The first microcomputer appears in schools.

1980s
MECC begins courseware development.

1986
National Science Foundation creates NSFNet.

1980–1987
Authoring systems, such as Pilot, HyperCard, and HyperStudio, are developed.

1990s
Network systems increase.

1998
ISTE develops computer standards.

1950
Computers used for instructional purposes.

1959
Computers first used in schools.

1969
Department of Defense creates ARPAnet, later called the Internet.

1970s–Early 1980s
PLATO, an instructional system, grows.

1980–1987
Logo is taught in the schools.

1980–1990
Integrated learning systems emerge.

1994
Use of Web becomes widespread.

2000 and later
Video conferencing and distance learning are implemented on the Web.

1950 1960 1970 1980 1990 2000

satisfy these requirements, so Kemeny and Kurtz designed BASIC (Beginners All-Purpose Symbolic Instruction Code), which was a blend of the best of these two languages. In 1964, students at Dartmouth College who sat down at computer terminals were greeted by the famous READY> prompt, beginning an era in which the novice computer user could write and quickly execute simple programs. BASIC was used to create computer-based instructional materials for a variety of subjects at all levels, from elementary school to college.

After BASIC's introduction, word spread about the new language designed for Dartmouth's time-sharing system. **Time-sharing** permitted several students to interact with a machine at the same time. They no longer had to use punched-card machines and enlist the help of programmers who would process their programs only when convenient.

In 1963, Patrick Suppes and Richard Atkinson at Stanford did some research and development on **computer-assisted instruction (CAI)** in reading and mathematics. CAI involves students in instructional activity on a computer. Suppes and Atkinson produced math drill and practice software on mainframe computers.[1] The computer screens would display a problem, the student would respond, and the computer would provide immediate feedback. These self-paced instructional programs freed students from group instruction and encouraged them to take an active role in the learning process. The students mastered the material by drill and practice.

In 1969, the Department of Defense created ARPAnet, which later became known as the **Internet** or the Net. ARPAnet was a large network of computers with links to smaller computer networks. The DOD's major concerns were to ensure mass communication of information while providing for maximum security. (See Chapter 9 for more information.)

In the early 1970s, Seymour Papert, an MIT professor, developed a different approach to computers in education. Papert developed a programming language called Logo to encourage thinking about mathematics. He wanted this language to be accessible to children of all ages. (See the Online Learning Center for an introduction to Logo programming.)

During the 1970s and 1980s, companies such as the Computer Curriculum Corporation (CCC), Control Data Corporation, and IBM emerged as major players in the educational computing field. Stanford University was the first university to use an IBM computer system dedicated to instruction with a programming language called **Coursewriter.** This system featured the first multimedia learning station, which consisted of a cathode-ray tube screen, a microphone, an audiotape player, earphones, and a slide projector. Stanford and other universities were using mainframe systems to teach programming, develop programs, and share programs with other institutions.

Don Bitzer, along with a team of specialists, developed an instructional system called Programmed Logic for Automatic Teaching Operations (**PLATO**). This system featured a terminal with a plasma screen, a specially designed keyboard, and an authoring system called Tutor. This authoring system developed tutorial lessons and complete courses. Other CAI products were Time-Shared Interactive Computer-Controlled Information Television (TICCIT), Program for Learning in Accordance with Needs (PLAN), and Individually Prescribed Instruction (IPI) systems.

With the growth of computer applications such as spreadsheets, educational institutions were able to computerize their administrative activities. They computerized report cards, attendance records, and student and staff records. Because the mainframe

---

[1]Mainframe computers were large computer systems the size of standard classrooms.

systems used by institutions at this time were expensive and complex, the district office would control the hardware and software operation. Interest in computer-assisted instruction began to decline—there seemed to be more potential for using the computer for administrative tasks.

The Time of the Microcomputer

In the early 1970s, computers were so expensive that school districts could only purchase time-shared systems, but use of these systems was restricted. However, with the introduction of the microcomputer, educational computer use was revolutionized. Because of their lower cost and smaller size, microcomputers began appearing in schools, libraries, homes, offices and laboratories. Many universities began telling incoming freshmen to buy their own computers. Teachers organized computer interest groups. In 1979, Dr. David Moursund founded the International Council for Computers in Education (ICCE). (In 1989, ICCE became the International Society for Technology in Education, or ISTE, when it merged with the International Association for Computing in Education.) In that same year, academic groups decided to come together for the first meeting of the National Education Computing Conference (NECC), presently the largest computer conference in the United States. Classroom teachers even began to use their own computers.

Before microcomputers, software came from hardware manufacturers such as IBM. With the advent of the microcomputer, there emerged a new software market that was directed by teachers. The nonprofit Minnesota Educational Computing Consortium (MECC), which had developed a good portion of the mainframe software, began generating software for microcomputers and became a major influence in the software field for education. Other software companies began producing educational software. The MicroSIFT project and the Educational Products Information Exchange (EPIE), as well as professional organizations, magazines, and journals, began to evaluate this software. Eventually, many software evaluation magazines folded because their work was duplicated by schools, many of which had formed committees to evaluate software. Teachers wanted a voice in the design of software, and they were highly vocal in their opinions.

Authoring Systems

Software developers responded to teachers' desire to participate in software design by producing authoring systems such as PILOT and SuperPILOT. These authoring systems were the precursor of modern applications such as *HyperCard, Linkway, HyperStudio, PowerPoint, and Keynote.* (See Chapter 8 for a detailed discussion of these programs.) Over time, interest in this type of software waned as teachers discovered how much time and expertise were needed to develop good courseware. Instead, they felt they could use their time more productively by purchasing predesigned programs. However, teachers needed a way to sift through the many products available, to find the best software. One of their criteria was a strong theoretical base. The teaching that happens in a classroom is based on one or more learning theories, and so software used to support that teaching should also be theory based. Jonassen (1988) discusses learning theories and their application to microcomputer courseware. Learning theories attempt to explain how an individual acquires knowledge and what factors contribute to this learning.

Learning Theories and Technology Integration

Behaviorism, cognitive theory, constructivism, situated cognition, and other theories have been used to investigate the effect of the computer on teaching and learning. Learning theorists have disagreed about what strategies are most useful in achieving educational goals. From this disagreement has evolved a recent interest in two different approaches, teacher directed and constructivist (Roblyer, 2003). The teacher-directed approach is based on the behaviorism learning theory, and the constructivist approach comes from other branches of cognitive learning theory. Since this textbook is not an instructional theory textbook, we will not explore this topic in depth. However, you may want to refer to one of the books listed at the end of the chapter to more comprehensively explore different learning theories.

The Teacher-Directed Approach

The **teacher-directed approach** is derived from the behavioral theories of B. F. Skinner, Edward Thorndike, Richard Atkinson, David Ausubel, Robert Gagné, and Lee Cronbach. These theories position the teacher as the manipulator of the classroom environment and the student as a receptacle for learning. Famous for his work in behavior modification, B. F. Skinner championed programmed instruction, in which lessons and drills are planned in small incremental steps to lessen the chance of incorrect responses on the part of the student. The idea is that the student will learn in a tightly structured environment. The teacher begins with lower-level teaching skills and builds to higher skills systematically. Clearly stated objectives are matched with test items. This approach stresses individual work and emphasizes traditional teaching and assessment methods, such as lectures and worksheets.

During the 1970s and 1980s, when computers first appeared in the classroom, behavioral theories were very popular. Software, which supported such theories, was based on programmed instruction. Today, thousands of educational software programs—such as *High School Advantage 2004* (Encore), *Quarter Mile* (Barnum Software), *Math Blaster: Ages 6–9* (Knowledge Adventure), and *Kaplan SAT, PSAT, & ACT 2004 Edition* (Encore)—are based on the behavioral models of instruction. These programs use drill and practice and tutorial software. They diagnose student skills, monitor student performance, and make changes in instruction when necessary. The software usually generates student and class performance data for teacher use. Advocates of this approach praise the software for its individualized pacing, self-instructional sequences, and remediation, especially useful for a teacher whose time is limited. The software generally makes learning faster, especially of the necessary basic skills. This software performs time-consuming tasks and frees the teacher to handle more complex student needs.

Opponents of this type of software criticize its lack of flexibility and its foundations in preestablished curricula. They say it uses only one type of educational technology, whereas other approaches use a variety such as multimedia and telecommunication.

Constructivism

The **constructivist approach** evolved from the work of developmental theorists such as Jerome Bruner, Jean Piaget, Lev Vygotsky, Seymour Papert, and Howard Gardner. The constructivist feels that learning occurs when the learner controls his or her own acquisition of knowledge. Constructivist models pose problems and involve students in searching for answers through exploration or discovery learning. Assessment involves student portfolios, performance checklists, and tests with open-ended questions and narratives.

Howard Gardner propose the concept of multiple intelligences. He argued there was not one single measure of intelligence, but that humans have a family of seven intelligences. The intelligences are:

Howard Gardner

1. Visual/Spatial intelligence
2. Musical intelligence
3. Verbal intelligence
4. Logical/Mathematical intelligence
5. Interpersonal intelligence
6. Intrapersonal intelligence
7. Bodily/Kinesthetic intelligence

Gardner believed that our educational system was not addressing all the intelligences. He pushed for teachers to break free from the teacher-directed approach's emphasis on testing to focus instead on other sources of information about how students develop skills that are important in real life.

The constructivist model differs widely from the teacher-directed model, especially in its emphasis on group work over individual work. Students play an active rather than passive role, and they work to solve problems through cooperative learning activities.

One of the main technological approaches to constructivist teaching is the computer simulation. The application of simulations can be traced to 17th-century war games in which participants set up mock battles. In the mid-1950s simulations were introduced in business training, and in the 1970s the popular simulation program *Lemonade Stand* by Minnesota Educational Computing Corporation (MECC) was introduced to run on the Apple II computer. Today, programs such as *Roller Coaster* (Microprose), the *Sim* series (*SimCity, The Sims;* Electronic Arts), and others teach complex concepts such as supply and demand by asking players to make decisions about cost, production, price structure, and advertising. A further innovation in this field is virtual reality, in which the student enters an artificial environment, such as in the classic *Myst Masterpiece Edition* (RedOrb).

Other constructivist-based technologies are more recent developments than simulation software. Annotated movies and hypertext, for example, engage students in highly meaningful and active learning.

Advocates of constructivism say that it teaches skills more relevant to students' experiences by anchoring tasks in real-life situations. Students address problems through interactive situations and play active rather than passive roles. They work together in groups to solve problems. This software stresses high-level as well as low-level skills.

Both constructivist and teacher-directed approaches attempt to identify what Gagné (1985) calls the "conditions of learning," or the circumstances that influence learning. Both approaches are based on work done by respected psychologists and learning theorists, and the approaches differ only in the ways they describe the environment in which learning occurs. Table 2.1 compares the characteristics of the teacher-directed model with those of the constructivist model.

Table 2.1 Teacher-Directed Versus Constructivist Instructional Models

Teacher Directed	Constructivist
Is based on worksheets and textbooks	Is based on manipulatives and primary sources
Curriculum is fixed	Curriculum is flexible
Teacher transmits knowledge	Approach develops concepts
Instruction is didactic	Student explores and discovers knowledge
Results in one correct answer	Results in acquisition of large concepts
Stresses individualized work	Stresses cooperative group work
Poses questions for students to answer	Engages students in interactive activities
Is concerned with information acquisition	Is concerned with the process of learning
Assessment is by testing	Assessment is by student products and student observation

Programming and Literacy

The early 1980s saw the emergence of a movement to teach programming, and students learned languages such as BASIC and **Logo.** Apple even built BASIC into the ROM of its computers. Software for students was almost nonexistent, and what was available was expensive; Because BASIC was free, the majority of teachers taught it to their students. There was also a movement to teach Logo in the elementary schools.

Philosophy and Psychology of Programming

Seymour Papert based his philosophy of computer use on the work of Jean Piaget. He expressed his constructivist approach to education in a popular book called *Mindstorms* (1980). Papert discussed his theories on how a computer should be used in the classroom. He felt a computer is best utilized as an aid in the thinking process and not as a piece of hardware that dispenses information. He observed that computer-assisted instruction (CAI) usually meant that the computer was being used to program the child who was the passive receiver of information:

Seymour Papert

> "In my vision, the child programs the computer and, in doing so, both acquires a sense of mastery over a piece of the most modern and powerful technology and establishes an intimate contact with some of the deepest ideas from science, from mathematics, and from the art of intellectual model building" (Papert, 1980, p. 5).

According to Papert, Logo created an environment in which children were free to explore and discover. They could learn geometric concepts, actively test and retest their theories, and develop their intellect. Papert argued that the majority of schools' mathematics programs had nothing to do with reality because the students were taught in a rote, meaningless way. According to Papert, this rote instruction was the reason most children grew up hating and fearing mathematics. Logo combatted this problem by injecting the child into a meaningful mathematics environment.

Furthermore, Papert saw ways that Logo could aid learning across all curriculum areas. For example, in his book he presented the case study of a student named Jenny who had difficulty with English grammar. When she used Logo to generate poetry, she discovered the necessity of knowing the difference between a noun and a verb in order to teach the computer how to write poetry. Jenny did a meaningful activity and learned the material. In the mid-1980s, interest in Logo waned, but the associated view of learning continues.

Integrated Learning Systems (ILSs)

Networking emerged in the 1980s and 1990s when administrators and school districts began to see the value of connecting computers and users. **Networking** consists of connecting a group of computers and peripherals to a communication system. School districts realized that computers networked to a central server could provide instruction more efficiently and at a lower cost than stand-alone machines. To this end, they introduced integrated learning systems (ILSs), which were similar to the drill and practice software developed by Suppes. Because of this trend, teachers had less control of their computers; a technical specialist had to maintain the network systems and fix them when there were problems.

Literacy Movement

In the mid-1980s interest in teaching programming languages declined. Teachers use the computer as a tutor—a way to help students who were academically behind (Molnar, 1978).

In 1986, the National Science Foundation (NSF) created a special network composed of five supercomputers called NSFNet. This network was not for military use but was devoted to research and education. Universities and some secondary schools began to join NSFNet. This network became the major backbone of the Internet.

Accompanying this development was an interest in **computer literacy,** which is the ability to understand and use computers. This interest became so strong in the 1990s that many states required computer literacy courses for prospective teachers.

National Standards

Leading professional groups have developed educational technology standards for teachers, students, programs, and schools. These standards discuss what students should know and be able to accomplish with technology. Furthermore, accreditation standards for teacher education institutions discuss expectations for teacher competency in preparation programs.

In 1998, the International Society for Technology in Education (ISTE), through a National Educational Technology Standards (NETS) project, published a document describing what prospective teachers should know and be able to do with technology. You will find this document at ISTE's Website, http://cnets.iste.org/teachers/t_stands.html. The **ISTE standards** define what prospective teachers should learn and what they should teach. The performance indicators show how prospective teachers will demonstrate that the standard has been achieved. Prospective teachers seeking certification in teacher preparation must meet these educational technology standards.

The National Educational Technology Standards for Students are listed on the back inside cover of this textbook. The National Educational Standards for Teachers are listed on the front inside cover of this textbook.

The Beginning of the World Wide Web

University professors and scientists used the Internet for research and worldwide communication, but it was difficult for the novice to use. It was not until the **World Wide Web** (Web) was developed in 1993 that the Internet opened to all users. The World Wide Web consisted of Internet servers that supported documents formatted in a script called **HyperText Markup Language (HTML).** HTML enables a server to link to other documents, audio, video files, and graphics (Web Webopedia, http://www.webopedia.com/).

In 1989, the European Center for Nuclear Research (CERN) in Geneva developed the Web from a proposal by Tim Berners-Lee. The purpose of the Web was to enable people to share information on nuclear physics. Shortly thereafter, the first command line browser was developed. By 1993, there were 50 Web servers and graphical window browsers.

Marc Andreessen developed one such browser, *Mosaic,* at the University of Illinois's National Center for Supercomputing Applications. *Mosaic,* a software breakthrough, was a navigator tool for interactive material. This software browser allowed users to view pictures and documents by simply clicking on a mouse. A simple interface let users travel through the online world of electronic information along any path they wished in order to discover the wonders contained on the Internet. Educators all over the world quickly became interested in the technology and began to see the potential for this powerful tool.

Distance Learning and Video Conferencing

Distance learning is people participating in educational training at a remote teaching site via a computer. Starting at the turn of the century, people began attending classes and conferences while in the privacy of their own homes. Today, many universities offer distance learning classes and programs or enhance existing offerings with video conferencing. (See Chapters 10 and 15 for more information.)

Summary

Many varying definitions of *educational technology* abound. For the purpose of this text, we will use the ACET definition. The computer has become an indispensable tool. There are many reasons for teachers, students, and administrators to integrate it into schools and the classroom. This chapter discussed some of the uses of computers in education, ranging from using them as research tools to using them to create newsletters. The history of computers in education features numerous important developments such as PLATO, an instructional system, and the widespread use of the World Wide Web. Like a snowball rolling down a hill, expanding as it speeds up, the use of the computer in education is certain to avalanche.

Study and Online Resources

*Go to Chapter 2 in the Student Edition of the Online Learning Center at **www.mhhe.com/sharp5e** to **practice with key concepts, take chapter quizzes, read PowerWeb articles** and **news feed updates** related to technology in education, and **access resources** for learning about technology and integrating it into the classroom.*

Click on *Web Links* to link to the following Websites.

AIL 601: Theories of Learning Applied to Technological Instruction

George E. Marsh II created a course on theories of learning as applied to technological instruction. This site covers Dr. Marsh's course contents. It features extensive information on topics ranging from problem-based learning to a brief history of instructional technology, teaching and learning on the Internet, and distance learning.

ERIC Clearinghouse on Information and Technology

ERIC Clearinghouse on Information and Technology is dedicated to the areas of library and information science and educational technology.

For Parents

This site offers advice on learning and technology from Edmark.

Developing Educational Standards

Developing Educational Standards is an annotated list of Internet sites with K–12 educational standards and curriculum framework documents. It is maintained by Charles Hill and the Putnam Valley Schools in New York.

Educational World's National and State Standards

Education World presents the objectives of the National Education Standards for the major subject areas and provides links to individual departments of education. Click on the icon for http://www.educationworld.com/standards/national/ to find the objectives.

ISTE's National Educational Technology Standards

The National Educational Technology Standards (NETS) Project is an initiative of the International Society for Technology in Education (ISTE) and a consortium of distinguished partners and cosponsors. The site provides online NETS for teachers and students as well as a searchable database of lessons matched to the technology standards.

StateStandards.com

StateStandards.com, a free service from *EdVISION.com,* is a single site for accessing lesson plans based on state curriculum standards. This site offers educational standards for all 50 states and the District of Columbia.

State and National Government Resources

EdVISION.com provides a link to the department of education of each state and the District of Columbia and offers extensive information on content standards and other educational topics.

Chapter Mastery Test

To the Instructor: *Refer to the Instructor's Manual for the answers to the Mastery Questions. This manual has additional questions and resource materials.*

Let us check for chapter comprehension with a short mastery test. Key Terms, Computer Lab, and Suggested Readings and References follow the test.

1. Why did the Internet suddenly become popular?
2. Name two major events that increased the use of the computer in education.
3. Who was B. F. Skinner and what was his contribution?
4. Why did programming suddenly fall out of favor?
5. What were Seymour Papert's major contributions?
6. What are the Educational Technology Standards for teachers, students, programs, and schools?
7. As a student, are you more comfortable with teacher-directed or constructivist strategies?
8. Name three characteristics associated with the constructivist learning model and three characteristics associated with the teacher-directed model.
9. Why did BASIC become so popular in the 1980s?
10. Name two ways that the teacher can integrate the computer into the classroom.

Key Terms

Constructivist
approach 25
Computer-assisted
instruction (CAI) 23
Computer literacy 28
Coursewriter 23

Educational
technology 20
Hypertext Markup
Language (HTML) 29
Internet 23
ISTE standards 28

Logo 27
Networking 28
PLATO 23
Programmed
instruction 21

Teacher-directed
approach 25
Time-sharing 23
World Wide Web 29

Computer Lab: Activities for Mastery and Your Portfolio

2.1 Interactive Time Line: The Modern History of Educational Technology Test your knowledge of the history of educational technology with this timeline.

2.2 Use three magazines to investigate developments in educational computing that occurred during the last five years. Write a brief summary of the findings.

2.3 What are today's schools covering in terms of computer literacy? What are second and seventh graders learning about computer history?

Suggested Readings and References

Bigge, Morris L., and Samuel J. Shermis. *Learning Theories for Teachers,* 6th ed. Boston: Pearson Allyn & Bacon: September 1998.

Bruce, Linda. "The Standards Approach: Planning for Excellence in Distance Education." *Syllabus* 17, no. 2 (September 2003): 29–31.

Gagné, R. *The Conditions of Learning.* New York: Holt, Rinehart and Winston, 1985.

Gardner, Howard. *Frames of Mind: The Theory of Multiple Intelligences.* New York: Basic Books, 1983. The second edition was published in Britain by Fontana Press (1993).

Molnar, Andrew R. "The Next Great Crisis in American Education: Computer Literacy." *AEDS Journal* 12, no. 1 (1978): 11–20.

Muffoletto, R. "Technology and Restructuring Education: Constructing a Context." *Educational Technology* 34, no. 2 (1994): 24–28.

Niemiec, Richard P., and Richard J. Walberg. "From Teaching Machines to Microcomputers: Some Milestones in the History of Computer-Based Instruction." *Journal of Research on Computing in Education* 21, no. 3 (Spring 1989): 263.

Papert, Seymour. *Mindstorms: Children, Computers and Powerful Ideas.* New York: Basic Books, 1980.

Papert, Seymour, and Nicholas Negroponte. *The Connected Family: Bridging the Digital Generation Gap.* Atlanta: Longstreet Press, 1996.

Piaget, J. *The Construction of Reality in the Child.* New York: Basic Books, 1954.

Roblyer, M. D. *Integrating Educational Technology into Teaching,* 3d ed. Columbus, Ohio: Merrill Prentice Hall, 2003.

Strauss, Howard. "Reflections." *Syllabus* 16, no. 9 (April 2003): 41–42.

PART II
Using and Selecting Educational Technology

CHAPTER 3

Getting Started on the Computer

Integrating Computer Hardware into the Classroom

A typical computer system found in any classroom has a monitor, keyboard, mouse, printer, internal disk drive, hard disk drive, CD-ROM drive or DVD drive, modem, and speakers. Before you buy educational software, you should know this and more about computer hardware. In the process of reading the chapter, you will learn how to pick out hardware for the classroom by using specific criteria. You will review a checklist designed to help you select the right computer or monitor for your classroom. Finally, you will learn how to use the Hardware Reference Guide, designed especially for teachers.

Objectives

Upon completing this chapter, you will be able to do the following:

1. Discuss how the basic components of a computer system operate.
2. Describe the major input devices and explain how each works.
3. Describe the major output devices and explain how each works.
4. List the salient features of different printers, monitors, and storage devices.
5. Choose appropriate hardware in terms of established criteria.
6. Explore some useful Internet sites that include online stores, operating system sites, computer terms, and tips and tricks.

What Is a Computer?

A computer is a machine that can handle huge amounts of information at an incredible speed. Computers do not have brains, feelings, or the ability to solve their own problems; they can solve only those problems they have been programmed to solve. A common computer system found in a typical classroom might have a monitor, keyboard, mouse, printer, internal disk drive, hard disk drive, central processing unit (CPU), CD-ROM or DVD drive, microphone, digital camera, modem, and speakers. Figure 3.1 is an example of a computer and its components.

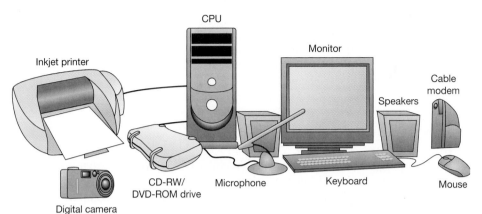

A computer performs four tasks:

1. receiving input such as figures, facts, or sets of instructions;
2. storing information by placing it in its memory;
3. processing the data by acting on the information; and
4. outputting the information by generating the results of the processing.

An example may shed some light on how the computer performs its four basic tasks. Imagine that Professor Friedman is conducting research. She has collected her data carefully and now wants the computer to do some statistical analysis on the data. She installs her statistical program onto the hard drive of her computer. Next, using the keyboard, she enters her data into the spreadsheet of the statistical program and chooses "analysis of variance" from the statistical procedures. The computer stores the data she enters in memory and then processes this information by performing the necessary statistical calculations in its central processing. The professor sees the results of the analysis on the screen or on a printout from the printer.

Elements of a Computer

A computer system consists of a central processing unit and the peripheral devices connected to it, along with the computer's operating system. The central processor, or CPU, is contained on a single chip called a **microprocessor.** The memory, RAM (random access memory), and ROM (read only memory) of the computer are also stored on computer chips.

Computer Chips

A **computer chip** is a silicon wafer, approximately 1/16 inch wide and 1/30 inch thick, that holds from a few dozen to millions of electronic components. The term *chip* is synonymous with *integrated circuit.* Computer chips are encased in plastic to protect them. Metal pins on the chips enable them to be plugged into a computer circuit board. Figure 3.2 shows a chip encased in its plastic protection. If you look carefully at this chip, you can see tiny circuits etched on the metal. The process of putting these circuits on one chip and connecting them together is called **large-scale integration**

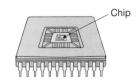

Figure 3.2 Computer Chip Encased in Plastic

(LSI) or **very-large-scale integration (VLSI).** This complex procedure, which involves engineering, plotting, photography, baking, and magnetism, permits silicon chips to be produced in large quantities at a very low cost.

Today, a single chip can hold millions of transistors. With wafer scale integration, eventually these circuits will be built in overlapping layers, and they will hold billions of transistors.

Circuit Boards

In the microcomputer, the RAM chips, ROM chips, CPU chips, and other components are plugged into a flat board called a **printed circuit board** (Fig. 3.3). The other side of this board is printed with electrical conductive pathways among the components. A circuit board in 1960 connected together discrete components; today the boards connect chips that each contain hundreds of thousands and even millions of elementary components (Freedman, 2003).

Figure 3.3 Printed Circuit Board

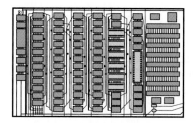

Central Processing Unit

The **central processing unit (CPU),** also called the *processor,* is the computing part of the computer. A personal computer's central processor is contained on a single chip called a *microprocessor,* which is smaller than a fingernail. This unit is essential because it controls the way the computer operates. Whenever a programmer designs software that gives instructions to the computer, it is the processor that executes these instructions. The central processor gets instructions from memory and either carries out the instructions or tells other components to follow the instructions. Then it follows the next set of instructions. This procedure is repeated until the task is completed.

The central processing unit (Figure 3.4) consists of three components: the control unit, the arithmetic unit, and the logic unit. In most microcomputers, the arithmetic unit and the logic unit are combined and are referred to as the **arithmetic logic unit (ALU).**

The **control unit** verifies that the computer carries out instructions, transfers instructions to the main memory for storage, and relays information back and forth between the main memory and the ALU. The arithmetic logic unit carries out all the arithmetic operations and logical decisions. Since the central processing unit can work only on small amounts of information at a time, it needs a way to store information, or memory, while it is not being processed.

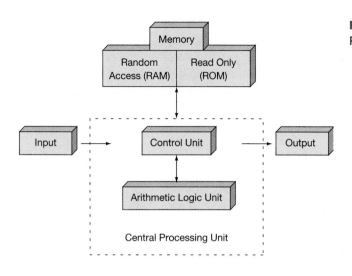

Figure 3.4 Central Processing Unit

Memory

Two types of chips take care of a computer's internal memory: **read only memory (ROM)** chips and **random access memory (RAM)** chips. ROM chips store information permanently in a computer's memory, and this memory supplies the computer with a list of operating instructions. These instructions are burned into the computer during the manufacturing process. ROM is called *nonvolatile memory* because it does not disappear when the computer is turned off. For example, most computers have a program in ROM that uploads the screen symbols, such as a cursor (usually in the form of a blinking square or line). There is nothing an ordinary computer user can do to remove or replace the instructions of ROM. BASIC was stored in the ROM of the Apple II line of computers, and today there are ROM chips in microwave ovens, watches, and calculators.

Unlike the information on ROM chips, the information stored in RAM can be modified; users can write, read, and erase this information. The problem with this type of memory is that it needs a constant power supply so that the data are not lost. RAM is referred to as *volatile memory* because of its temporary nature. Whenever a user turns off the computer, he or she loses whatever information is in RAM. The basic unit for RAM storage is a **byte,** the space available to hold letters, numbers, and special characters.[1] In the 1970s, a computer user normally manipulated thousands of characters at a time so RAM size was measured in **kilobytes,** or thousands of bytes (the symbol for kilobytes is K). For example, a computer that had 512K was capable of holding approximately 512,000 numbers, symbols, and letters.[2] In the early 1980s, computers usually had a memory size of 64K, which was considered more than adequate for a personal computer. Today, RAM size is discussed in terms of **megabytes (MB),** or millions of bytes, and **gigabytes (GB),** or billions of bytes. Tomorrow, RAM will be in trillions of bytes, or **terabytes.**

---

[1]Bytes are discussed in more detail in the *Binary Notation* section of this chapter.
[2]The accurate number is 524,288 (512 × 1,024) because the computer uses powers of 2, and 2^{10} is 1,024. A kilobyte then represents 1,024, or approximately 1,000, bytes.

The amount of RAM chips a computer has determines the amount of information that can be retained in memory, the size and number of programs that can be run simultaneously, and the amount of data that will be processed immediately. Programs vary in their memory requirements; for example, *Inspiration* 7.5 needs 2 MB of RAM to run on a Macintosh with System OS X or later, while 128 MB of RAM is recommended for the Windows XP version of *DeBabelizer*. Fortunately, the RAM size of most computers can be expanded by adding RAM chips.

Binary Notation

All computer input is converted through **binary notation** into binary numbers consisting of two digits, 0 and 1. An instruction that is read as a 1 tells the computer to turn on a circuit, and an instruction read as a 0 tells the computer to turn off the circuit. The digits 0 and 1 are called **bits,** short for *binary* dig*its*. The computer can represent letters, numbers, and symbols by combining these individual bits into a binary code. Each character or letter typed is translated into a byte by turning circuits off and on. This whole procedure happens at lightning speed whenever a user hits a key on the computer keyboard. For example, when the user types the letter Z, the computer translates it into 01011010. When the user types the number 1, it is translated into 00110001. Every character on the keyboard has a different code combination.

Operating Systems

In the early days of computing, a person operated a computer with an elaborate control panel. Later, computer programmers designed a program that would allow the computer to control its own operation. This control program is the **operating system** of the computer, and its major task is to handle the transfer of data and programs to and from the computer's disks. The operating system can display a directory showing the names of programs stored on the disk; it can copy a program from one disk to another; it can display and print the contents of any file on the screen. The operating system controls the computer components and allows them to communicate with each other. There are many other functions that an operating system performs; the computer's system manual enumerates them.

Different computers have different operating systems. The same computer, moreover, may have more than one operating system available to it. For example, the old Apple II computers used DOS 3.3, ProDOS, and OS/GS operating systems (the acronym DOS stands for *disk operating system*). Some other well-known operating systems are MS-DOS, Microsoft Windows 95, Microsoft Windows 2000, UNIX, OS/2, and Macintosh System 6 and System 8. Macintosh OS X is the most recent Apple OS (operating system), and Windows XP is the most recent Microsoft operating system.

Lacking a single standard operating system, all computers are not compatible. Many companies are seeking a solution to this incompatibility problem. *Microsoft Virtual PC for Mac* is a software program that enables a Macintosh computer to run many PC-based operating systems. This economical software product requires plenty of memory and a fast computer to run effectively. The IBM 615-based system runs X86, Macintosh, UNIX, and OS2 software. There are other manufacturers, such as Orange Micro, that produce cards that can be placed inside computers to allow them to run more than one system.

In the past, different models of computers varied in the way their operating systems were supplied to them. Presently, the majority of computers have hard disk drives, and their operating systems are installed from CD-ROM onto the hard disks. Previously, when operating systems were stored on disk, the user would insert the disk into a disk drive, turn on the computer, and wait for it to run a small program usually stored in the ROM of the computer. This program's purpose was to *load* the operating system into the main memory of the computer and then turn over its authority to the operating system. The procedure of starting the computer so that it could load its operating system became known as **booting the system,** because the small program that helped it do this was called a *bootstrap loader,* as the initial loading was analogous to "lifting yourself by your own bootstraps."

Since its inception, the Macintosh's trademark has been its ease of use. It had the most workable operating system, a characteristic that distinguished it from other systems. Practically every Macintosh application program used the same user interface, so the user did not have to relearn commands each time he or she used a different application. The success of the Macintosh interface led Microsoft to introduce its similar interface known as Windows. Both Apple Macintosh OS X–Panther and Microsoft's Windows XP feature **graphical user interfaces (GUIs)** in which the user points with the mouse to a picture or icon to select a program instead of typing commands.

Let us take a look at the opening screens of these particular versions of the Macintosh and Windows operating systems and a third operating system known as Linux.

Macintosh OS X. The new Macintosh operating system referred to as Mac OS X, combines UNIX with the ease of use of the Macintosh. This system has translucent buttons and an aqua interface. At the bottom of the screen, Mac OS X shows icons of folders, applications, documents, storage windows, QuickTime movies, digital images, links to websites, and applications required for instant access (Fig. 3.5). The system's Finder gives users an extremely fast means of finding files, running applications, and communicating with people. This version offers enhanced speech recognition, Internet functionality, and multimedia capabilities.

Figure 3.5 Macintosh Opening Screen

Images courtesy of Apple Computers, Inc.

Windows XP. The Windows XP operating system features the strengths of Windows 2000 Professional, such as standards-based security and reliability, with the best features of Windows 98 and Windows Millennium Edition, such as Plug and Play, easy user interface, and unique support services. The system is built to take advantage of the Internet and provide support for mobile users. As you can see from Windows' opening screen in Figure 3.6, the system eliminates menu clutter.

Figure 3.6 Windows Opening Screen

Screen shot of Windows® used by permission of Microsoft Corporation.

Linux. Linux is a version of UNIX developed by Linus Torvalds at the University of Helsinki in Finland in 1991. Torvalds, a computer science student, turned Minix, a classroom teaching tool, into Linux. Numerous programmers have contributed to this system.

Today, Linux is developed under the GNU General Public License, and its source code is freely available to anyone. This does not mean Linux is free. Companies and developers may charge money for Linux as long as the source code remains available. Linux runs on a variety of hardware platforms including Alpha, PowerPC, ×86 PCs, and IBM's product line. The distribution of Linux along with technical support and training are available for a fee from sellers such as Red Hat Software (www.redhat.com) and The SCO Group (www.sco.com). Linux is a very stable, cost-effective, and secure operating system and that is why it has gained popularity, and its usage is expected to grow. Linux can be used for networking and software development.

VA Linux Systems has a website that discusses Linux (www.linux.com), and Antone Gonsalves has written a good reference text. For further discussion of the Macintosh and Microsoft Windows operating systems, consult operating system manuals or visit the Internet sites listed at the end of the chapter.

Hardware Overview

The **hardware** of a computer system includes the electronic components, boards, wires, and peripherals. Buying hardware for your classroom is a complicated and time-consuming job that requires an examination of many factors.

Before you begin the process of selecting hardware, you first must choose the software that meets the needs of your class. The **software** instructs the computer hardware to perform various tasks. If you have only hardware, you are powerless to accomplish anything with the computer, much as if you had a car without fuel. Selecting software is no easy task either. First you must determine your primary needs and then you must estimate your future needs. For example, you might be satisfied initially with software such as *Ultimate Writing and Creativity Center,* but in time you will require a sophisticated desktop package such as *Quark XPress.* If you want to use such a package or an advanced spreadsheet or statistical software, you will need computer hardware with ample memory.

Regardless of your software needs, however, you will benefit from spending time learning about available hardware, its capabilities, and its functions. Current computer magazines (such as *MacWorld* or *PC Magazine*) will alert you to the latest hardware developments. You can save time and money by being prepared to ask the right questions. We will look at some of the factors that most influence a teacher's or student's hardware decisions. First, we will examine some of the basic hardware equipment available for classrooms. If you want to learn more about any particular device, refer to the *Hardware Reference Guide for Teachers* at the end of this chapter.

Input Devices

An input device gives information to the computer system so that it can perform its tasks. Years ago, the keypunch machine was the major means of input; today, it is the keyboard. However, the keyboard suffers from some drawbacks. It is not ideal for making screen selections. Furthermore, if you are an inexperienced typist, you are more likely to make mistakes when using the keyboard for screen selections. As a result, computer manufacturers have created pointing devices that lessen the need for a keyboard. Today, most computers use both a keyboard and supplemental pointing devices such as the joystick, mouse, trackball, and trackpad.

In addition to pointing devices, many other input devices are used in the classroom. These devices include optical scanning devices that utilize laser capabilities. The laser searches for groups of dots that represent marks, characters, or lines. These input devices differ from each other in terms of the programs used and the way the computers massage the data.

Optical Mark Reader. The **optical mark reader (OMR)** was designed initially to read penciled or graphic information on exam answer sheets. Many schools and school districts use the optical mark reader to grade standardized tests. With the proper software, the OMR will also keep library and attendance records and will report grades.

Scanners. The **scanner** is enjoying popularity in schools because of its affordability and its usefulness in desktop publishing, faxing, and **optical character recognition (OCR).** OCR is machine recognition of typed or printed text. By using OCR software with a scanner, a student can rapidly enter a printed page into the computer. Figure 3.7 shows the results of using the scanner in conjunction with *Omni Page Pro* (ScanSoft), a full-featured optical character recognition software that inputs text. *Omni Page Pro* eliminates the time, expense, and potential errors of typing material to input it. Advanced OCR systems even recognize handwritten text.

Figure 3.7 Omni Page Pro

Used with permission of ScanSoft Software.

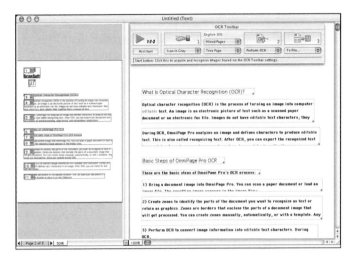

Figure 3.8 Scanned Photograph

Courtesy of Vicki Sharp.

The scanner can also transform images into electronic images. Figure 3.8 is a photograph of my husband and son that was scanned into the computer.

Scanners digitize photographs or line art and store the images as files that can be transferred into paint programs or directly into word processing programs. If you create a newsletter and want to insert a picture into the text, you scan the picture, copy it, and then "paste" it into the document. Scanners used for this purpose come in a variety of forms; the most common in the classroom are flatbed and handhelds. The film scanner is used to a lesser degree.

Scanners differ in **resolution,** or degree of sharpness. The more dots a scanned image contains, the sharper it is. An inexpensive scanner produces images at about 600 dots per inch. The more expensive scanners produce images at high resolution. In the past, most scanners produced black-and-white and halftone images, and color scanners were too expensive for most people. Today, color scanners are commonplace and can be purchased for under $200. Most of them feature 24-bit color, the maximum number of colors supported by most digital systems. In a 24-bit color scanner that offers a resolution of 1,200 dpi, each of the 1,200 pixels uses 24 bits to hold color information (Freedman, 2003).

Digital Cameras. Currently, interest in digital cameras is increasing in schools all over the country. Teachers find having a digital camera in the classroom very useful. The **digital camera** is a quick way to get photos into computer-readable form, which can be used for school reports, desktop publishing, security badges, pictures for Web pages, or parent's notes. Digital cameras make picture taking easy, their image editing programs give users control over pictures, and they eliminate the need to work in a darkroom or drop film off at the local drugstore. You can print one or two shots at a time and not have to wait until your whole roll of pictures is finished.

The only problem with digital cameras is that they cost as much or more than 35-mm single-lens reflex film cameras, and many have simple optics and limited abilities. Digital cameras are still evolving, and every three or four months manufacturers increase resolution, lower price, and reduce size. See Chapter 8 for a lengthy discussion on how to use digital cameras in the classroom.

Video Conferencing or Webcam Cameras.   **Webcams** are small cameras that teachers and students can use to take pictures for newsletters or websites, to make live video, and to take simple e-mail videos and pictures to share with other classes or other school districts. Students can also use these live cameras to see and interact with people and places around the world through a Web browser. An easy way to find live Webcams is by typing "Webcam" in your search engine.

Handheld Computers

Students and teachers are increasingly using electronic organizers, Personal Data Assistants (PDAs), and handheld computers. They have become quite affordable compared to desktop computers. These devices enable you to take notes, conduct scientific data collection and analysis, send and receive faxes, send e-mail, search the Internet, keep a calendar, and collect information from distant databases. Several years ago *Digital Video Magazine* (Figure 3.9) envisioned handheld computers of the future as having picture capabilities so that users could see the person with whom they were communicating. Shortly, handheld organizers *will* have this capability.

Figure 3.9 Next Generation of Computers
Courtesy of *DV Magazine.*

For the education market, some machines provide computer access for every student in the classroom and are quite inexpensive. For example, students can use the AlphaSmart 3000 (Alpha Smart) to do most of their work wherever they happen to be—in a classroom, in the lab, on a field trip, or at home. As we will discover in Chapter 13, at Calahan Elementary school, students use such devices on a daily basis.

AlphaSmart also produces Dana, a combination handheld computer and notebook, which lets users connect wirelessly to the Internet through Wi-Fi (80211b). Users can browse the Web or check e-mail. Dana provides access to thousands of applications, including database, word processing, and spreadsheet applications (see Chapter 13).

Students Using AlphaSmart 3000 in the Classroom.

Buying a Handheld Computer.   Before you buy any handheld computer you must take certain factors into consideration. First, what software does your class need? There are two major operating systems—the Palm OS and the Pocket PC—and they each run different applications. The Palm OS currently runs more applications than does the Pocket PC, but the Pocket PC runs Windows-like applications such as *Microsoft Word*. Second, what can you afford? These handhelds range in price from affordable up to $1,000. Third, is the system pleasing and easy to use? Play with the stylus to see how the touch screen works. How comfortable are you with the handwriting recognition system? Fourth, do you want a color screen? A color display has less of a battery life than a monochrome display. Fifth, what are your resolution needs? Resolution will influence the clarity of the display. Sixth, what accessories do you need? Even though most machines are packaged with rechargeable batteries, you will still need a power source. Look at the different accessories, from carrying cases to foldable keyboards. Seventh, what added features do you want? Pocket PCs enable you to record voice, download books, establish a wireless connection to the Internet, and so on. How do you synchronize or transfer data with your computer? Do you use a serial or USB cable port or infrared?

The Handheld Computer Checklist is a short checklist of what to look for when purchasing a handheld computer.

Handheld Computer Checklist

Operating System
_____ a. Palm OS
_____ b. Pocket PC
_____ c. Other

Software
_____ Meets classroom needs

Cost
_____ a. Basic unit
_____ b. Peripherals

Touch Screen
_____ a. Ease of use
_____ b. Good handwriting recognition
_____ c. High resolution

Display
_____ Monochrome
_____ Color

Battery Life
_____ a. Replaceable (last two or more months)
_____ b. Rechargeable for one or two weeks with a single charge

Handheld Accessories
_____ a. Portable keyboard
_____ b. Carrying case
_____ c. Cables and cradle
_____ d. Car charger
_____ e. Removable storage
_____ f. Other

Features
_____ a. Voice recorder
_____ b. Video player
_____ c. MP3 player
_____ d. E-book player
_____ e. Internet access
_____ f. E-mail capabilities
_____ g. Other

Transfer of Data
_____ a. USB cable
_____ b. Serial cable
_____ c. Infrared
_____ d. Printer

Support
_____ a. Extended warranty
_____ b. Readable manuals
_____ c. Nearby dealer support

Output Devices

One of the most essential output devices is the **printer,** which gives users a permanent record of their work by producing a printout, or hard copy. The three types of printers most often found in the classroom are dot matrix, inkjet, and laser.

For years, the **dot-matrix printer** was the most widely used printer. With the price reduction of laser printers and the advances in inkjet technology, this situation has changed and the dot-matrix printer has disappeared from the majority of classrooms.

Inkjet printers are still slower than good-quality laser printers, but they are faster than most low-cost laser printers. Even though the cost of the color inkjet has been decreasing steadily, there is a significant cost associated with the purchase of the ink cartridges. Because of improvements in technology, color inkjet printers have become popular. These printers start at under $200.

The **laser printer** has become almost as popular as the inkjet because of its price and near-professional quality print. The laser handles graphics beautifully and, for the most part, is very reliable. There are many inexpensive laser printers that print in black and white on the market today. Brother's HL-1440 laser printer costs under $300 and prints 15 pages per minute. The color laser has recently dropped in price (it starts at $700), and when the price of replacement toners improves, this printer will dominate the field.

Screen Displays

The computer could function without peripherals such as digital cameras or speakers, but the monitor is an essential piece of equipment. The two most frequently used types of monitors are the **cathode ray tube (CRT)** monitor and the **liquid crystal display (LCD)** monitor. Teachers and students are constantly using laptops with LCD displays for presentation, networking, and carrying their work with them. In the next few years expect CRT monitors to be replaced by LCD monitors. In the future, other displays such as the organic light-emitting diodes (OLED) display will become popular (see Chapter 16).

Classroom Presentation Devices

The classroom teacher needs a way to use the computer to demonstrate a program or concept to the entire class. Currently, three methods are used: the LCD projection panel, the projector, and the video scan converter.

Liquid Crystal Display (LCD) Projection Panel. The LCD projection panel enables the classroom teacher to use a computer with the entire class. This panel is placed on top of the overhead projector, and it projects the active computer screen on the overhead projector so everyone in the room can see it. Using one computer, the teacher can now show a PowerPoint presentation or demonstrate software use.

Projector. Teachers use the projector to project images from the computer to a screen or television. The LCD projector can connect directly to a school's PC, Mac, VCR, or video source and is an excellent way to demonstrate a software program or show an Internet site.

Video Scan Converter. For teachers working on a budget who want to use already existing equipment, a **video scan converter** is the answer. An ordinary television can be used as a computer display with this technology. A scan converter enables teachers to give presentations, train educators, or show Internet sites.

Storage Devices

The **floppy disk,** introduced by IBM in 1971, was for a long time the most prevalent means of storage. However, this began to change in 1988 with Apple's introduction of the iMac. The iMac was the first personal computer without a floppy disk drive. Today, most new laptop computers come without a floppy drive or they provide it as an external option.

With the advent of Iomega's **Zip disk,** storage media changed forever. The Zip disk became popular because of its ability to store much more data than the floppy disk. The first Zip disks stored 100 MB. Now they store 750 MB.

The latest rage are **USB drives,** which are smaller in size and capable of storing more information than Zip disks. The USB mini flash drives, usually the size of a fat pen, largely fulfill data-exchange needs for USB-equipped PCs. You can easily store digital photos, MP3 files, PowerPoint presentations, and Word documents on them.

The **hard drive** stores huge amounts of data. Teachers can even use portable hard drives as backup. The major flaw with a hard disk is it can wear out in three to five years. The optical disc, which has a 30-year life expectancy, is the hard drive's likely successor. Optical storage currently found in schools consists of compact discs (CDs), compact disc read only memory (CD-ROMs), digital versatile discs (DVD-ROM), and laser discs. CD-Rs (CD-recordable) can be recorded once for archival purposes. DVDs, which holds more information, consist of DVD-Rs (DVD-recordable) and DVD+Rs (DVD+recordable).

Being able to record once, on a CD-R, DVD-R, or DVD+R, is not enough for the consumer. Teachers and students want to be able to use this media as backup but also record on it many times. New technology consists of erasable optical discs. These discs are like floppy disks in that they can be recorded on repeatedly. Three examples of erasable optical discs are CD-Rewriteable (CD-RW), DVD-Rewriteable (DVD-RW), and, DVD+Rewriteable (DVD+RW).

We are now in an era of huge multimedia files and we have a need for more storage. In the classroom, you will find hard drives, Zip disks, USB drives, CD-ROMs, DVDs, laser discs, and CDs. Table 3.1 shows the storage capabilities of these media.

Table 3.1 Storage Capabilities of Current Media*

Compact disc	74 minutes of stereo audio
Floppy disk	Up to 1.44 MB
Hard drive	20 GB and above
Zip disk	Up to 750 MB
USB drive	16 MB to 4 GB presently
CD-ROM	650 MB
DVD-ROM	4.7 to 17 GB
Laser disc	One hour video and digital sound on one side

*For more information on the storage mentioned here see the Hardware Reference Guide for Teachers.

Fax Machine and Modem

The facsimile (fax) machine and the modem are two more input/output devices. The **fax machine** enables users to transmit text and images between distant locations. The **modem** enables two computers to communicate with each other over communications lines, such as telephone lines. Chapter 9 features a detailed discussion of the fax machine and the modem.

Computer Selection Criteria

The following guidelines will help you purchase a desktop, portable, or handheld computer.

Ability to Run Software Applications

The software applications you will be using will determine the computer that you select. You may not be able to buy a certain computer because it does not run the particular software that you need to use in your district. Software programs also have memory and storage requirements as well as additional input/output device needs, which are factors that influence buying decisions. Most computers come bundled with software such as browser or word processing software.

Type of Computer

Is the computer compatible with other computers in the school district? How easy is it to use the equipment? Is the documentation well written? Are the weight and size of the machine important considerations? How durable is the machine? Is it too delicate for classroom use? One of your main decisions is whether to buy a computer equipped with a Windows system or a Macintosh system. The Macintosh is still easier to use, set up, and expand than is a Windows computer. However, Windows computers have a wider selection of peripherals and software. If you are interested in ease of use and expansion, graphics, multimedia, and video, buy a Macintosh; if you need spreadsheets and databases and a wider assortment of peripherals, buy a Windows system.

Memory

A very important consideration during the hardware selection process is the computer's random access memory, the working memory. In the early 1980s, 64K of RAM was considered more than adequate for running educational software. Today, many applications need 32 MB or more of memory, and these memory requirements are continually increasing. For example, *Timeliner 5.0* (Tom Snyder) requires 32 MB to run its Windows version effectively. Every time software publishers upgrade programs, they add more features requiring more memory. The amount of RAM a computer has affects the kind of software it is capable of running. Any new system you are purchasing should have a minimum of 256 MB of RAM. Buy as much RAM as you can afford because you can never have too much.

Expandability

Consider these questions when your computer system is not powerful enough for your needs: Can you upgrade the processor chip? Can the memory of the computer be increased? Can special equipment be added to the machine for the student with disabilities? Is the computer designed so that extra peripherals such as a scanner can be added easily? Does your computer have **expansion slots**? In other words, does your computer have a receptacle inside that will accept expansion boards or printed circuit boards? These boards or *cards,* as they are called, expand the computer's ability so that it can accept other peripheral devices such as sound cards.

Speed

The speed at which a microcomputer accesses its instructions is another important consideration. Speed depends on clock speed and word size. **Clock speed** is the number of electronic pulses per second, measured in megahertz (MHz) up to gigahertz (GHz). The more pulses the computer has per second, the faster it executes the instructions. The clock speed on a microcomputer can vary from 1 MHz to greater than 3 GHz. For example, the old Apple II had a clock speed of 1 MHz. Dell's Dimension 8300 desktop computer has a clock speed of 3.2 GHz. Some programs, such as sophisticated spreadsheet programs, require more speed than others.

Keyboard

You should test out the keyboard feel by sitting at the computer and checking how comfortable it is to type on the keys. Keyboards today have many different ergonomic designs. One computer might have impressive specifications, but typing on its keyboard may be uncomfortable. See if an extended keyboard is available. Extended keyboards have additional keys that can be programmed to perform different functions and numeric pads that speed up number entry.

Hard Disk Space

Like everything else on computers, hard disk space has gotten larger and less expensive. Most new computers are being sold with a minimum of 120 GB. You need a gigantic hard disk if you plan to store digitized photographs or edit videos; the bigger the better!

Video Output

When it comes to the computer monitor, the CRT is the most economical for word processing, spreadsheets, and educational software. The higher the resolution of the screen, the clearer the screen display. Resolution is expressed as the number of linear dots, or **pixels** (picture elements), that are displayed on the screen. The more pixels, the clearer the image or the better the resolution. The size of a monitor screen varies from 5 to 40 inches; usually, a screen displays 24 or 25 lines of text. The size of your monitor should not be smaller than 15 inches; for a few dollars more, you can buy a 17-inch monitor. The dot pitch, which is the smallest dot your monitor displays, should be 0.28 mm or less. The refresh rate, the "rate at which a monitor and video adapter pass the electron guns of a cathode ray tube (CRT) from the top of the display to the bottom" (Pfaffenberger, 1997), should be 85 Hz at the resolution you use. In a couple of years, LCD monitors will be affordable for most schools.

Video RAM (VRAM)

Video RAM, also called **"VRAM,"** is the type of memory used in a display adapter. Video RAM is designed so that it can simultaneously refresh the screen while text and images are drawn in memory (Freedman, 2003). Make sure you have at least 32 MB of graphic memory. If you play multimedia software and video games, 64 MB or 128 MB are preferred.

Sound

The quality of sound is very important for playing musical compositions or educational games. Ask about the number of voices the system has. You should get a minimum of 32 voices. A high-quality sound card can have up to 64 MIDI (Musical Instrument Digital Interface) voices,[3] the "number of musical notes that can be played back simultaneously in a MIDI sound device" (Freedman, 2003). If you want a realistic sound, purchase more voices. Find out the octave ranges of the voices. Most computers offer speech synthesizers capable of pronouncing words.

Peripherals

Study the peripherals that you need and know the features that are available. Read magazines to determine which peripherals are best to purchase. Find out which peripherals have the lowest rate of repair and the fastest access time.

Hardware Reliability and Dealer Support

Are local dealers reputable? Find a local store that can easily service the machine. Does the store give free training on newly purchased machinery? Is there a service contract? Is the equipment warranted for a year, and is there quick turnaround on computer repair? Is the machine relatively easy to operate? Do you need hours to study its thick manuals? For a young student or an easily frustrated adult, these considerations are important. Is there quality documentation for the computer?

Cost

Prices that are quoted by manufacturers are discounted, so check the *Computer Shopper,* the local newspaper ads, and magazines to determine the price structure of a system. Is the machine too costly compared to similar machines? Does the manufacturer include free software? Is there a warranty on the product, on-site repair, or, at the very least, a place to ship the machine for quick repair? For computer equipment it is important to get an extended warranty. The hardware checklist on page 50 should serve as a handy guide for analyzing your hardware needs.

---

[3]"A standard protocol for the interchange of musical information between musical instruments, synthesizers, and computers" (Freedman, 2003).

Hardware Checklist

Directions: Examine the following items and determine which ones you feel are important for your particular class situation. Evaluate the hardware and place an *X* on each line where it meets your needs.

Computer Type _____ **Model** _____ **Manufacturer** _____

Features

_____ 1. Ability to run software
_____ 2. Screen size
_____ 3. Text/graphics display
_____   a. Number of lines
_____   b. Characters per line
_____   c. Resolution
_____   d. Number of colors
_____ 4. Sound
_____   a. Number of voices
_____   b. Number of octaves
_____   c. Loudness
_____ 5. Portability
_____ 6. Keyboard design
_____   a. Number of keys
_____   b. Numeric keypad
_____ 7. Ease of expansion
_____ 8. Color capabilities
_____ 9. Equipment compatibility
_____ 10. Networking
_____ 11. Memory (RAM)
_____ 12. Memory (video RAM)
_____ 13. Hard disk capacity
_____ 14. CD-ROM drive (83, 163, 243, 323, etc.)
_____ 15. Zip drive
_____ 16. DVD drive
_____ 17. CD-RW or DVD-RW drive
_____ 18. Central processing speed

Ease of Use

_____ 1. Easy program loading
_____ 2. Flexibility
_____ 3. Easy equipment setup
_____ 4. Tutorial manual

Consumer Value

_____ 1. Cost of basic unit
_____ 2. Cost of peripherals
_____ 3. Zip drive
_____ 4. Interfaces/cables
_____ 5. Memory expansion
_____ 6. Modem
_____ 7. Monitor
_____   a. Included in price
_____   b. Size
_____ 8. Printer
_____ 9. Other
_____ 10. Software included
_____ 11. Speech synthesizer
_____ 12. Total investment

Support

_____ 1. Service contract
_____ 2. Nearby dealer support
_____ 3. Readable manuals
_____ 4. Tutorial
_____ 5. Index
_____ 6. Warranty period (carry-in or on-site)
_____ 7. Teacher training

Rating Scale

Rate the hardware by placing a check in the appropriate box.
Excellent _____ Very good _____ Good _____ Fair _____ Poor _____

Comments:

Hardware Reference Guide for Teachers

The *Hardware Reference Guide for Teachers* examines a variety of equipment that is summarized in Table R1. Use this brief guide to answer questions in this chapter and broaden your knowledge about hardware devices that are available in the classroom.

Table R1 Classroom Hardware Equipment Summary

Input	Output	Input/output
AlphaSmart 3000	Cathode ray tube monitor	Compact disc
Digital camera	Dot-matrix printer	CD-ROM disc
Flatbed scanner	Inkjet printer	CD-R disc
Film scanner	Laser printer	CD-RW disc
Handheld computer	LCD monitor	DVD-ROM disc
Handheld scanner	LCD projection panel	DVD+R or DVD-R disc
Joystick	Projector	DVD+RW or DVD-RW disc
Keyboard	Scan converters	Fax machine*
Mouse		Floppy disk
Optical mark reader		Hard disk
Touchpad		Laser disc
Trackball		Modem*
Webcam		Optical disc
		USB drive
		Zip disk

*See Chapter 9 for a discussion of fax machines and modems.

Input Devices

AlphaSmart 3000

The AlphaSmart 3000 is produced by Alpha Smart, Inc. This device works with virtually any Macintosh or PC running any application. Weighing 2 pounds, these rugged units have a word processor and spelling checker. The AlphaSmart prints directly to the printer and downloads files to the computer. Furthermore, there are features for special needs: sticky keys, which stay down when you press them; key repeat control; and four keyboard layouts.

AlphaSmart 3000
Courtesy of AlphaSmart, Inc.

Digital Camera

The digital camera records images in a digital format. The main difference between the digital camera and the standard camera is the medium that is used to capture images. The digital camera uses a charge-coupled device (CCD) which the computer reads, while the traditional camera uses film. A digital camera uses a floppy disk, flash memory card, write-once CD, or writeable CD for storage. Every camera has a maximum resolution, such as $1,600 \times 1,200$ pixels, and a fixed number of colors that can be represented. The images are transferred to the computer with a serial or universal serial bus (USB) cable or by the storage medium itself if the computer has a corresponding reader.

Canon Digital Camera

Flatbed Scanner

ArtToday.com.

Flatbed Scanner

A flatbed scanner easily scans documents, books, or periodicals. You simply open the lid of the scanner and place the materials on the "bed." It is more versatile than a hand scanner, but it is more expensive. A flatbed scanner can adequately scan film if the model used comes with a transparency adapter.

Film Scanner

ArtToday.com.

Film Scanner

The film scanner is designed for scanning slides, film, or other transparent materials. This scanner delivers resolutions that range from 1,000 to 4,096 dots per inch, and it can read 16.8 million colors. You want a minimum resolution of 1,200 dpi optical resolution to scan film.

Palm Tungsten T

Courtesy of Palm Computing, Inc.

Handheld Computer

Handheld computers are small mobile computers that accept input through a penlike instrument called a *stylus* with which you write on the computer's screen. These handheld computers typically use one of two operating systems: Palm OS or Pocket PC. The Palm, formerly known as the *Palm Pilot,* is a leader in the field. The company's latest handheld is the Palm Tungsten T. The Tungsten T handheld handles a wide range of multimedia and wireless capabilities. This handheld has built-in Bluetooth technology which enables you to access mail and connect to the Internet over a compatible mobile phone. Besides this, the Tungsten T personal organizer offers a new color screen and a built-in voice recorder.

Handheld Scanner

ArtToday.com.

Handheld Scanner

A handheld scanner fits in the palm of your hand. You slide it across an image or document slowly, at the rate of about an inch every 10 seconds. It works well on 4-inch columns, but it is not able to scan an entire line of text in a single pass. The only alternative is to stitch or paste the material together, which is time-consuming but does produce acceptable results.

Joystick

ArtToday.com.

Joystick

The **joystick** is a pointing device that consists of a rod mounted in a base with one or two buttons. Using the stick, you are able to move objects around the screen in all directions. The joystick is generally used for video games or computer-assisted design (CAD) programs.

Keyboard

The computer **keyboard** is similar to that of a standard typewriter, but it includes extra keys such as function keys and a numeric pad. To the right is a standard keyboard with a numeric pad on the right for quick data entry.

Computer Keyboard

Courtesy of Nova
Development Corporation.

Mouse

Originally designed by Xerox, the **mouse** was popularized by the Apple Macintosh computer. The original mouse was a palm-size box with a button on it. It was connected to the computer by either a cable or a wire. Today, the mouse comes in different shapes and sizes, some are cordless, and they can have from one to three buttons. The mouse can have two different internal mechanisms: mechanical or optical. The mechanical mouse has a rubber-coated ball on the bottom of its case; when you move the mouse, the ball rotates. The optical mouse shows its position by detecting reflections from a light-emitting diode[4] that aims the beam downward. This mouse usually required a special pad to reflect the beam correctly. However, Apple's Pro mouse, based on high-precision tracking, does not require a special pad.

Mouse

Courtesy of Apple Computer.

The movement of the mouse is represented by a cursor or blinking light on the screen. If you move the mouse to the right, the cursor moves to the right. If you push the mouse's button, the cursor is positioned at that particular location. Furthermore, the mouse can be used to select items from a pull-down menu, to delete and insert text, and to draw or paint when used with paint or draw software such as *Corel Draw*. The mouse is easy to use and install; however, it is awkward for delicate drawing, and it requires space.

Optical Mark Reader

The optical mark reader (OMR) is special scanning equipment that reads pencil or pen marks placed in predetermined positions on specially marked documents. This device is frequently used to read answer sheets, surveys, and forms. Lamps furnish light that reflects from test paper. The amount of reflected light is measured by a photocell. When a mark is made on a sheet of paper, it blocks light from reflecting. The Scanmark's optical mark reader compares the pattern of marks on test papers with the correct pattern stored in the computer's memory.

Optical Mark Reader

Courtesy of Scanmark's
ES 2010.

Touchpad

The **touchpad** is a pressure-sensitive pad that is smaller, more accurate, thinner, and less expensive to build than the trackball. You slide your finger over this pad the same way you would move a mouse. The faster your fingers travel on the pad, the greater the distance you will cover on the computer screen. You can also tap on the pad's surface instead of pushing the touchpad keys.

Touchpad

ArtToday.com

[4]A diode, an electronic component that acts primarily as a one-way valve, is used as a temperature or light sensor (Freedman, 2003).

Trackball

Trackball

An alternative device that is stationary and requires less desk space is the trackball. The **trackball**, which performs the same tasks as the mouse, operates with a rotating metal ball inset in a small, boxlike device. It does not require a desktop. With your fingers, you roll the exposed part of the trackball, producing cursor movement on the screen. This device was very popular in portable computers until Apple introduced the touchpad.

Output Devices

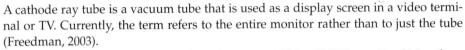

Red, Green, and Blue
(RGB) Monitor
© The Sony Multiscan.

Cathode Ray Tube (CRT) Monitors

A cathode ray tube is a vacuum tube that is used as a display screen in a video terminal or TV. Currently, the term refers to the entire monitor rather than to just the tube (Freedman, 2003).

The best of the CRT monitors is the **red, green, and blue (RGB) monitor.** Using three electronic guns, this monitor generates three colors. It is the most expensive monitor and produces the sharpest images because it uses separate video signals for each of the three guns. The RGB monitor generates a better image than the television, which merges the three colors together.

Dot-Matrix Printer

The dot-matrix printer is an impact printer that produces characters and graphic images by striking an inked ribbon with tiny metal rods called *pins.* When the movable print head with its pins is pressed against ribbon and paper, it causes small dots to print on the paper (see below). The print quality depends on the number of pins the printer has; for example, a 24-pin printer produces better-looking characters than a 9-pin printer.

Dot-Matrix Printer

ClickArt Images © 1995
T/Maker Company.

Letter **A** on a Dot-
Matrix Printer

Inkjet Printer

ArtToday.com

Inkjet Printer

The inkjet printer uses a nozzle to spray a jet of ink onto paper. These small, spherical bodies of ink are released through a matrix of holes to form characters. Inkjet printers produce high-quality output, have few moving parts, and are quiet because they do not strike the paper with metal parts.

Laser Printer

The laser printer operates like a copying machine but with one important difference. The copying machine produces its image by focusing its lens on paper, but the laser printer traces an image by using a laser beam controlled by the computer. Laser printers produce text and graphics with high resolution; however, the print quality is not as high as that obtained by a phototype machine used by commercial textbook publishers.

Laser Printer
Courtesy of Brother.

Liquid Crystal Display (LCD) Monitor

The most common flat-screen displays are liquid crystal displays (LCDs). The LCD is created by positioning a liquid crystal material between two sheets of polarizing material squeezed between two glass panels. This display depends on reflected light, so the viewing angle is important; the image can disappear with the wrong angles and with inadequate adjustment of the contrast controls. Used in calculators, watches, and laptops, LCD technology is also becoming popular for flat-panel desktop monitors. The LCD flat panels not only take up less space, but they also resist glare, use less energy, and emit less radiation.

There are two types of LCDs: the *active matrix* and the *passive matrix*. In the active matrix display (TFT), each of the screen's tiny electrodes has its own transistor. The passive matrix display (DSTN, CSTN, etc.) has only a single transistor that controls an entire column of the display's electrodes. The active matrix is superior in contrast and resolution and has a broader viewing angle, but it is much more expensive. LCD panels have always been available for laptops. The latest Apple Powerbook notebook which has an LCD of 17 inches is shown at the right.

Apple Powerbook G4 with LCD Monitor
Courtesy of Apple Computer.

Liquid Crystal Display (LCD) Projection Panel

The LCD panel is a projector that receives computer output and displays it on a liquid crystal screen placed on top of an overhead projector. The overhead becomes the projector, displaying the programs that the computer generates on a larger screen for an entire class to see. Different manufacturers make panels in different sizes.

Projector

A projector is an optical instrument that can be hooked up to your computer to project an enlarged computer image on a screen or television set. These projectors start at $2,000. The InFocus projectors are compact, are portable, and have a zoom lens. For teachers who need a lightweight traveling projector, the LP130 weighs only 3 pounds and is high quality.

LP130 InFocus Projector
Courtesy of InFocus.

Video Scan Converter

Another name for a scan converter is *analog-to-digital converter.* This device converts the video output of a computer to a standard television signal. FOCUS Enhancements offers a series of video scan converters that accomplish this simply and inexpensively, costing about $150 to $275. The TView Gold video scan converter connects almost any computer, is both Mac and PC compatible, and has pan, zoom, and freeze capabilities.

TView Gold Scan Converter
Courtesy of FOCUS Enhancements.

Input/Output Devices

Compact Disc (CD)

Introduced in 1983, the CD is a digital audio disc that is 4.75 inches in diameter and contains up to 74 minutes of hi-fi stereo sound. The CD-ROM evolved from this CD.

Compact Disk (CD-ROM)

CD-ROM (Compact Disk–Read Only Memory). CD-ROMs store text, graphics, and hi-fi stereo sound in a digital format. The CD-ROM is similar to the music CD, but it uses a different tracking system. A CD-ROM handles at least 650 MB of data—the equivalent of 250,000 pages of text, four hundred 3½-inch high-density floppy disks, or fifteen 40-MB hard disks. This medium is invaluable for storing large volumes of data such as the *Grolier Electronic Encyclopedia.*

CD-R. Using a form of CD technology, the CD-R (CD-recordable) can be recorded on a single time. Teachers and students can use CD-Rs to make backup recordings of their work for archival purposes or to make a master disc for their class. If you have a 40× recorder, recording 74 minutes takes only a couple of minutes.

CD-RW. The development of the CDR (CD-rewritable) gave users a way to back up their work. The CD-RW let you erase, add files, and rewrite this disc 1,000 times. The CD-RW has six layers, with an outer layer that is the same as a CD-ROM. The drives are slower and are designated by three numbers, such as 8×4×32×. The first number refers to the writing speed of the CD-R, the second number is the rewrite speed of the CD-RW, and the last number is the reading speed of the CD-ROM media.

DVD-ROM. DVD-ROMs (digital versatile discs) are the same overall size as a CD-ROM but have significantly higher capacities because they are double sided. DVD-ROMs read CD-ROM media as well as their own discs. A DVD-ROM can hold from 4.7 to 17 GB of information using this double-sided technology. DVD-ROMs also come in recordable versions.

DVD+R and DVD–R. Like CD-Rs, DVD+Rs and DVD–Rs can only be recorded on one time. DVD–R and DVD+R are now in competition to set an industrial standard. They accomplish the same purpose, but they use different technologies. For more information, visit the Tech Encyclopedia at CPM Net's site at http://www.techweb.com/encyclopedia/.

DVD+RW and DVD–RW. DVD technology also developed a way not only to play, but also to record and erase and rerecord data on its compact discs. DVD–RW (DVD-read write) and DVD+RW are two different rewritable discs that record data and movies. DVD–RW and DVD+RW both hold 4.7 GB and can be rerecorded 1,000 times.

Floppy Disk

Floppy Disk

ArtToday.

In the 1970s, IBM introduced the 8-inch floppy disk (diskette) for data storage. This disk was replaced by the 5¼–inch disk, which was subsequently replaced by the 3½–inch disk. This disk consists of a circular piece of plastic, oxide-coated matter enclosed in a protective jacket that is similar in appearance to an audiocassette tape. When the disk is placed in a disk drive, it rotates inside its jacket, thus allowing data to be stored on it and viewed later.

Hard Disk

The **hard disk**, positioned in a sealed unit, is made of metal and covered with a magnetic recording surface. The read/write head, an electronic device that electromagnetically records and reads information from the disk, travels across this surface via an air cushion, without touching the disk. This disk is fixed or removable and can hold anywhere from 20 GB to 1 TB of information. This is a much greater storage capacity than that of a 3½–inch floppy disk, which typically holds 1.44 MB of information. Hard disk storage capacity is the amount of room on the hard disk and should not be confused with RAM, the amount of memory necessary to run a program. Presently, the 120 GB hard disk is commonplace, and by the year 2004 you will see drives that offer 10 times this amount of storage.

Hard Disk
ArtToday.com

Laser Disc

A **laser disc** is a read-only optical disc that stores and retrieves still and moving pictures, sound, or color. This disc looks like a large CD, holds from 30 minutes to 2 hours of video, and provides direct access to any location on its disc. Many laser disc systems were introduced in the 1970s. The laser disc has become increasingly scarce in the classroom with the introduction of CD-ROMs and DVDs.

Optical Disc

An **optical disc,** a direct-access disc, has information recorded on it with a laser beam that burns pits into its surface. Another laser beam reads back information that it detects from these pits. These optical discs are recorded at the time of manufacture and cannot be erased. The optical disc is less likely than other discs to become defective due to heat and magnetic fields.

USB Drive

Sony Micro Vault
Courtesy of Sony.

The USB drive consists of a memory card that plugs into your computer's USB port. The storage of the USB drives varies from 32 MB to 4 GB. These small USB devices fit in a shirt pocket and operate in a fashion similar to that of a disk drive.

Video Conferencing or Webcam Cameras

Logitech Camera
Courtesy Logitech.

The webcam video camera captures images and sends them to be displayed on a Web site. The camera is connected to a video capture card that resides in the computer. There are hundreds of these webcams that enable students to video conference over the Web. These inexpensive cameras may cost as little as $50. They usually have built-in microphones, and they have an easy way to capture still pictures and moving images for your presentations. Logitech offers a series of these cameras.

Zip 750 Disk

Zip Disk

The Zip disk is a flexible tapelike material encased in a firm plastic cover. The disk is small and removable. The Zip disk stores data in the same way as the hard disk: It spins on a surface that can be magnetized or demagnetized. The number of tracks that are on a disk is a function of how accurately the disk is constructed, how fast the disk spins, how sensitive the disk is to magnetization, and so forth.

Summary

In education, the student uses the computer to perform three functions: logic comparisons, arithmetic operations, and storage and retrieval. The computer accomplishes these functions at high speed, storing huge amounts of data in a binary format. The central processing unit, the brain of the computer, controls what is happening; an arithmetic logic unit (ALU) performs the arithmetic and logic operations; and primary memory, ROM and RAM, store all data and instructions necessary for operation. ROM, read only memory, cannot be changed and is hardwired into the machine. RAM, random access memory, is temporary memory that stores data and programs that need processing. Because of its erasable characteristics, RAM allows a program to be executed as many times as the user needs. Since RAM is temporary, disks are very important permanent storage media. The operating system, the control program that handles the transfer of data and programs to and from computer disks, makes it possible to enter and run programs.

Every computer has input, output, and input/output devices that add functionality to the machine. This chapter has explored the functions of the major input, output, and input/output devices: keyboards, mouses, trackballs, touchpads, optical readers, and scanners. The two most important output devices are the printer, which produces a hard copy of work, and the screen display, which shows the information on the screen. The display screens discussed were the liquid crystal display (LCD) and the cathode ray tube (CRT). The printers discussed were dot matrix, inkjet, and laser. The dot matrix printer has a print head with wires to create its characters; the inkjet printer sprays ink; and the laser printer uses a process similar to photocopying. We discussed and compared floppy disks, hard disks, optical discs, and the USB drive. We also considered criteria for hardware selection. At the end of the chapter, the *Hardware Reference Guide for Teachers,* provides detailed information about many types of hardware.

Study and Online Resources

Go to Chapter 3 in the Student Edition of the Online Learning Center at **www.mhhe.com/sharp5e** to **practice with key concepts, take chapter quizzes, read PowerWeb articles** and **news feed updates** related to technology in education, and **access resources** for learning about technology and integrating it into the classroom.

Click on *Web Links* to link to the following Websites.

Apple Computer

Apple's home page consists of a range of items—reviews, news, products, and downloads.

Educational Resources

Educational Resources, in operation since 1985, offers more than 5,000 software titles, supplemental software, and mixed-media curriculum courseware, as well as peripherals and accessories.

Foldoc Free Online Dictionary of Computing

The *Free Online Dictionary of Computing* (FOLDOC) is a searchable database with more than 13,000 entries, and it is still growing. You can search it by using a search engine or by clicking on an alphabetical index.

Learning Services

Learning Services has been in operation for more than 20 years, and it features over 5,000 software titles. It offers supplemental software and mixed-media curriculum courseware, as well as peripherals and accessories.

MacFixIt

Created in 1996 by Ted Landau, this site brings together experts who discuss conflicts and fixes for things connected to the Macintosh.

Microsoft

Microsoft's home page contains an assortment of items ranging from news to downloads to product information.

PC-Mac Connection

Mac and PC Connection Inc. is a mail order company that offers more than 100,000 brand-name products at competitive prices.

PC-Mac Warehouse (CDW)

Mac and PC Warehouse Inc. is a mail-order company that offers brand-name products at competitive prices.

Windows 95 and 98 Tips and Tricks

This site is dedicated to helping you navigate through the Windows 98 operating system. It contains Windows 98 tips and tricks.

Windows 2000 Tips and Tricks

This site is dedicated to helping you navigate through the Windows 2000 operating system. It contains Windows 2000 tips and tricks.

Windows XP Tips

Windows XP Tips is dedicated to news, downloads, drivers, links, and tips for Windows XP.

Computer Lessons for Kids and Small Adults

Computer Lessons for Kids and Small Adults offers easy-to-understand lessons on the parts and operating systems of a personal computer.

Hardware Central

This site features the latest in hardware news and reviews.

PC Webopedia

This is a resource for information about PCs. It contains definitions of 2,000 computer terms, with links to sites related to each term.

PC Webopedia's Hardware Companies

This site links to leading PC hardware companies.

Tip World

This site provides daily free e-mail tips for the Windows and the Mac OS operating systems and for keeping your hardware humming along.

What's in That Box?

This site is a presentation on what is in your computer and how it works.

Yahoo! Hardware

This site offers an extensive list of links to hardware company products, from the ill-fated Amiga to the highly successful iMAC computer.

Kingston Technology

This site has everything you ever wanted to know about computer memory. See table of contents on the left panel in blue.

Chapter Mastery Test

To the Instructor: *Refer to the Instructor's Manual for the answers to the Mastery Questions. This manual has additional questions and resource materials.*

Let us check for chapter comprehension with a short mastery test. Key terms, Computer Lab, and Suggested Readings and References follow the test. Consult the *Hardware Reference Guide for Teachers* as well as the chapter for answers to these questions.

1. Compare and contrast RAM and ROM.
2. Explain how the different components of a central processing unit work.
3. What is an operating system and what function does it perform?
4. Discuss the microprocessor, the CPU, and memory and explain how they function independently and as a complete unit.

5. Why is it important to have enough RAM for your computer?

6. Define and explain the following terms: *bit, byte, kilobytes,* and *megabytes.*

7. What does "to boot a computer" mean?

8. Explain what an optical disc is and what distinguishes it from a floppy disk.

9. Why are erasable optical discs the wave of the future?

10. What is a digital camera and what are three uses for it in the classroom?

11. Explain the difference between a CD-ROM and a DVD-RAM.

12. Name two input and two output devices. Explain how each works.

13. Name four factors to consider when examining hardware.

14. Compare a laser printer with an inkjet printer.

15. What is a scan converter and how would you use it in the classroom?

Key Terms

Arithmetic logic unit (ALU) 36
Binary notation 38
Bit 38
Booting the system 39
Byte 37
Cathode ray tube (CRT) 45, 54
Central processing unit (CPU) 36
Circuit boards 36
Clock speed 48
Computer chip 35
Control unit 36
Digital camera 42, 51
Dot-matrix printer 44
Expansion slots 47
Fax machine 46

Floppy disk 45
Gigabyte (GB) 37
Graphical user interface (GUI) 39
Hardware 40
Hard disk 57
Inkjet printer 45
Joystick 52
Keyboard 53
Kilobyte (K) 37
Large-scale integration (LSI) 35
Laser disc 57
Laser printer 45
Liquid crystal display (LCD) 55
Liquid Crystal Display Projection Panel 45

Megabyte (MB) 37
Microprocessor 36
Modem 46
Mouse 53
Operating system 38
Optical character recognition (OCR) 41
Optical disc 46
Optical mark reader (OMR) 41
Pixel 48
Printed circuit board 36
Printer 44
Projector 45
Random access memory (RAM) 37
Read only memory (ROM) 37

Red, Green, and Blue (RGB) monitor 54
Resolution 42
Scanner 41, 52
Software 41
Terabyte 37
Touchpad 53
Trackball 54
USB drive 46
Very-large-scale integration (VLSI) 36
Videoconferencing cameras 43
Video RAM (VRAM) 49
Video scan converter 45
Webcam 43
Zip disk 46

Computer Lab: Activities for Mastery and Your Portfolio

3.1 Putting the Computer Together Test your knowledge of computer hardware by "putting together" a computer.

3.2 Hardware Review Test your visual recognition of computer hardware.

3.3 Visit a computer store and compare the output of laser and inkjet printers. Report on the differences.

3.4 Take a field trip to a school that uses digital cameras and report how they are incorporated in student writing projects.

3.5 Using a digital camera, illustrate a book report or a creative story.

3.6 Prepare and illustrate a report discussing the different storage technologies.

3.7 Write a paper on the history of computer memory and in this paper explain the following:

a. how data is stored in the computer,
b. the speed and cost of memory, and
c. the limitations and advantages of the system used.

3.8 At the library, find a recent article on microchips and discuss recent developments in this technology.

3.9 Compare and contrast two operating systems.

3.10 Interview a local school district and write a report on how the district uses computers.

3.11 Visit a computer retail store and write a report on the different hardware devices that could enrich the use of computers in the classroom.

3.12 Using a program like Tom Snyder's *Timeline 5.0,* prepare a time line on the evolution of the computer.

3.13 Have the students use the Hardware Checklist on page 50, and go online to make a hypothetical purchase of a computer system.

Suggested Readings and References

American National Standards Institute. *American National Standard Code for Information Interchange.* New York: ANSI, 1986.

Barr, Christopher. "First Sub-Mini Hard Disk." *PC Magazine* 11, no. 1 (January 14, 1992): 30.

Batane, Tshepo. "Technology and Student Collaboration." *T. H. E. Journal* 30, issue 3 (October 2002): 16.

Bruder, Isabelle. "Schools of Education: Four Exemplary Programs." *Electronic Learning* 10, no. 6 (March 1991): 21–24, 45.

Fasimpaur, Karen. "The Power of Handheld Computers in Education." *Media & Methods* 39, issue 1, (September–October 2002): 16.

Flanagan, Patrick. "The 10 Hottest Technologies in Telecom." *Telecommunications* 31, no. 5 (May 1997): 25–28, 30, 32.

Freedman, Alan. *Computer Desktop Encyclopedia.* Pennsylvania: The Computer Language Company, 2003.

Fritz, Mark. "DVD Dream." *Presentations,* March 2000, 38–45.

Gonsalves, Antone. "The Linux Alternative." *Teaching and Learning* 23, no. 8 (March 2003): 9–12.

Goodman, A. *The Color-Coded Guide to Microcomputers.* New York: Barnes and Noble, 1983.

Keller, Jeff. "This Month in Digital Cameras." *Macworld* 20, issue 2 (February 2003): 48.

Laurie, Peter. *The Joy of Computers.* Boston: Little Brown, 1983.

Maran, Ruth. *Windows 98 Simplified.* Foster City, Calif.: IDG 3-D Visual Series, Worldwide, Inc., 1998.

Maran, Ruth. *Teach Yourself Visually: Windows XP.* Foster City, Calif.: IDG 3-D Visual Series, Worldwide, Inc., 2003.

Maran, Ruth. *Teach Yourself Visually: Mac OS X 10.2 Jaguar.* Foster City, Calif.: IDG 3-D Visual Series, Worldwide, Inc., 2002.

Murray, Charles J. "LCD Monitors Grow Wider, Smarter." *Electronic Engineering Times,* issue 1256 (February 10, 2003): 65.

Pfaffenberger, Bryan. *Webster's New World Dictionary.* New York: Webster New World Book, 2003.

Pfaffenberger, Bryan. *Linux Command: Instant Reference (Command Reference).* New York: Sybex, 2003.

Pownell, David, and Gerald D. Bailey. "The Next Small Thing." *Learning and Leading with Technology* 27, no. 8 (May 2000): 47–49.

Randall, Neil. "Setting up a Webcam." *PC Magazine,* April 18, 2000, 138–140.

Reed, Sandy. "Microsoft to Launch Its Windows 2000 to a More Skeptical Marketplace." *InfoWorld* 22, no. 6 (February 7, 2000): 77.

Richman, Ellen. *Spotlight on Computer Literacy.* Rev. ed. New York: Random House, 1982.

Robertson, S. "The Use and Effectiveness of Palmtop Computers in Education." *British Journal of Educational Technology* 28, no. 3 (July 1997): 177–189.

Schumacher-Rasmussen, Eric. "HP in Hot Water over DVD+RW Drives." *EMedia* 15, issue 5 (May 2002): 11.

Stone, M. David. "Color Laser Printers for Less than $1,000." *PC Magazine* 21, issue 21 (December 3, 2002): 43, chart 2c.

Takezaki, Noriko. "Mobile Computing and the Internet." *Computing Japan,* October 1997, 31–33.

Tomlinson, Howard. "Educational PDA Games Engage Students, Teach Essential Language Skills." *T.H.E. Journal,* September 2003, 2–44.

"Trends in Computer Hardware." *Media & Methods* 37, issue 5 (March/April 2001): 28.

Trosko, Nancy. "Making Technology Work for Your Students." *Technology Connection* 4, no. 2 (April 1997): 20–22.

Turner, Sandra, and Michael Land. *Tools for Schools,* 2d ed. Belmont, Calif.: Wadsworth, 1996.

CHAPTER 4

Word Processing

Integrating Word Processing into the Classroom

Word processing is the most popular computer application. Students at all grade levels can use word processing software to create book reports, lab sheets, letterhead stationery, and flyers. In the lower grades students can use large-size fonts to create stories, alphabet books, and journals. Teachers can have students write letters to people in the class and across the country. This chapter will discuss how to select a word processor for the classroom. We will consider the general features of a word processor. A checklist will help you choose the right word processor. Exercises will help you integrate word processing into the classroom. You will become familiar with Internet sites that provide creative writing tips, forums, writing clubs, and lesson plans.

Objectives

Upon completing this chapter, you will be able to do the following:

1. Define the term *word processor.*
2. Describe the features and functions of a word processor.
3. Demonstrate how a word processing program operates.
4. Evaluate word processing software based on standard criteria.
5. Utilize and create a repertoire of word processing activities for the classroom.
6. Evaluate a word processing program utilizing the criteria given in this book.
7. Explore the offerings of Internet sites on word processing, which range from creative writing tips to lesson plans.

Students Can

- create a research report,
- prepare a resume,
- design letterhead stationery,
- create a Web page, and
- create a flyer.

Teachers Can

- create a certificate,
- create a brochure,
- design place cards for the classroom,
- create a newsletter,
- make a book report form, and
- write a mail merge letter for the parents.

Word Processing in the Classroom

In a 1991 study of teachers' perceptions of computer needs, word processing was ranked the primary need for students and teachers (Woodrow, 1991). Pfaffenberger (2003) noted that word processing programs are the most widely used computer application in the office, home, and classroom.

In the classroom, teachers and students can use word processing programs for varied and different uses.

Historical Background

In 1961, IBM introduced the elite Selectric typewriter, a fast electric model with changeable print balls, typefaces, and type sizes. Ten years later, Wang Laboratories inaugurated its Wang 1200, a small-screen typing workstation capable of reading output and storing information on a cassette tape. System users could retrieve documents whenever needed and could edit text. Several years later, Wang expanded and improved the 1200 by developing a disk storage system that could store approximately 4,200 pages.

The computer did not feature disks as a workable storage medium until 1976, when Digital Research Corporation introduced the Computer Program Management (CP/M) operating system. Three years later, Seymour Rubenstein created *WordStar,* a word processor for the CP/M operating system. In 1980, Alan Ashton and Bruce Bastian produced *WordPerfect,* another word processor for the Data General minicomputer. Dedicated word processors, machines designed solely for word processing, soon dominated the office market.

Word processing took a leap forward in 1981, when IBM introduced its personal computer, the PC. Simultaneously, Unlimited Software announced the first piece of software to run on this new machine: a word processor program called *EasyWriter.* A few months before the announcement about *Easy Writer,* Lifetree Software developed a program called *Volkswriter.*[1] The years between 1981 and 1985 saw a flurry of word processing program introductions: *MacWrite* (Apple), *Microsoft Word* (Microsoft Corporation), *Bank Street Writer* (Scholastic), *PFS Write* (Software, Inc.), and *AppleWorks* (Apple). *AppleWorks,* introduced in 1983, was an integrated program combining word processor, database, and spreadsheet. In the 1980s, helpful features such as a spell checker, mail merge, font capabilities, and an electronic thesaurus were introduced to such programs. With graphical user interface (GUI) systems, such as those on Macintosh computers and personal computers that ran Windows, programs could now display different types of fonts and font size choices on the screen as well as handle simple desktop publishing functions such as creating newsletters.

The 1980s marked the beginning of a trend away from stand-alone word processing programs toward comprehensive products incorporating several software tools in one package. In the education field these packages are popular because they are economical, beating the cost of the tools purchased separately. Manufacturers began

---

[1]Lifetree is now called Writing Tools Groups, a subsidiary of Wordstar International.

selling two types of these packages: integrated programs such as *AppleWorks* and *Microsoft Works* and suites such as *WordPerfect* and *Microsoft Office*. An **integrated software package** usually consists of a word processor, a spreadsheet, a database, graphic tools, and communication software. A **software suite** usually contains additional programs and comes in a variety of combinations tailored to meet the needs of the educator or businessperson.

What Is a Word Processor?

A **word processor** is a software program designed to make the computer a useful electronic writing tool for editing, storing, and printing documents. Before the computer, the typewriter was the principal tool used for writing reports, and a typist had to take great pains to avoid making mistakes because correcting and revising were tedious tasks. Word processing programs enable users to make changes quickly and efficiently simply by pressing a few keys on the keyboard. Users can easily save a document on a disk, make multiple copies, and store disks for safekeeping.

In the past, businesses used computers that were designed primarily for word processing (**dedicated word processors**). These machines had a special keyboard with keys programmed to perform such tasks as underlining and italicizing. These machines were inexpensive and perfectly adequate for typing projects. Today's businesses require more sophisticated word processing capabilities as provided by microcomputers. The majority of these computers are networked so that programs and correspondence can be handled electronically.

Today, when writers discuss word processing they usually are talking about personal computers with word processing software. Such software programs are for sale at local software stores usually on CD-ROM. The buyer installs the program on a computer and can then create documents, edit text, underline, and delete.

Components of Word Processing

A word processor usually involves interaction among the components shown in Figure 4.1. Through the software, the user types in text on the keyboard, views it on the monitor, changes it as necessary, saves the document on the hard drive or to a Zip disk or flash drive, and prints it on the printer.

Figure 4.1 Word Processing Components

Dell Computers, HP Printer

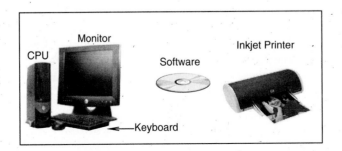

The word processing packages on the market today come with every imaginable feature. Among these programs are word processors well suited for classroom use. For elementary school students, software reviewers recommend programs such as *Write:OutLoud, Clicker 4, Kid Works Deluxe,* and *Storybook Weaver Deluxe* because they have fewer features and are easier to use. The features in most programs for children include *delete,* which removes unwanted text, and *insert,* which inserts lines or passages. *Writer's Companion, AppleWorks, Microsoft Works, WordPerfect,* and *Microsoft Word* are for the junior high, high school, and college students, and they are more complicated, offer multiple features, and occupy more disk space and memory. A case in point is *Microsoft Word,* which contains many desktop publishing features, macros, charting tools, and custom toolbars.

General Word Processing Features

Most word processors feature *cursor control, word wrap,* and *page breaks.*

Cursor Control

A **cursor** is a blinking (usually white) block of light that shows the position of a character. The computer user positions the cursor where he or she wants to correct text or enter text. The equivalent on a typewriter is the place on the paper where the next keystroke will strike. As you type, the cursor stays just ahead of the last character you have typed. The cursor can move one character at a time, line by line, or over a block of text. You can also move it with the mouse.

Word Wrap

Word wrap lets you type as much as you want without paying attention to the end of lines. When you reach the right-hand margin, the cursor automatically moves to the beginning of the next line; you do not have to hit the return key. If the word you are typing does not fit at the end of a line, word wrap automatically moves it to the next line. You need to hit the return key only to start a new paragraph or to move down a line.

Page Breaks

Most word processors display some mark on the screen that tells where the pages in the document break. Before printing your document you can use this feature to check to make sure there are no bad breaks, such as those that strand a single word on a page.

Standard Editing Features of a Word Processor

Word processors vary in their editing capabilities, and some are more powerful than others. However, they all usually have the same basic editing features: *insert, delete, find and replace, cut, paste, copy,* and *drag-and-drop.*

Insert

The **insert** function allows you to insert lines of text, words, and paragraphs anywhere in the document.

Delete

The **delete** function allows you to erase words, lines, or paragraphs of text. After you delete the material, the text closes up around the remaining space.

Find and Replace

The **find and replace** function (Figure 4.2) in *Microsoft Word* allows you to search a document for a word or phrase and replace it with another. For example, if you have misused the word *their,* you can instruct the computer to find every incident of *their* so you can replace it with *there.* This feature also allows you to conduct a global search and replace. So you might tell the computer to change automatically all instances of the name Sarah to Sara, for example.

Figure 4.2 *Microsoft Word XP* Replace Function

Screen shot of *Microsoft*® *Word XP* used by permission of Microsoft Corporation.

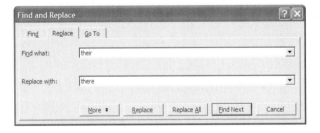

Cut and Paste

With the **cut and paste** feature the user selects letters, words, or blocks of text and removes them from their location and then "pastes" them in a new location. This is how it works:

1. Highlight the text that you want to move.

2. Use the cut function to delete the specified portion of text.

3. Position the cursor where you want the material to be placed and then instruct the computer to paste or insert. The text will arrange itself automatically with proper spacing.

Copy

The **copy** function works similarly to cut and paste. With this feature you make a copy of what you want elsewhere and then you paste it in a new location.

Drag and Drop

With the **drag-and-drop** feature, you use the mouse to select a small block of text. Then, while pressing the mouse button, you can drag the text to a new location. This function is very handy for moving text short distances within a document.

Spelling Checkers

The spelling checker checks the spelling of the words in your document against those in a dictionary that is stored on the hard disk drive. If a word in the document does not appear in the dictionary, the spelling checker will display the word in question and give you the opportunity to override the query or select an alternative. In an *AppleWorks 6.0,* document shown in (Figure 4.3), the word *looks* is misspelled; the spelling checker suggests many alternatives and highlights the most likely. You can add any words you wish to the spelling checker's dictionary. Once you have added a word, the spelling checker will no longer question that particular spelling. The good spelling checker lets you see the misspelled word in the context of your document. Advanced spelling checkers can correct misspellings automatically the next time they appear.

Figure 4.3
AppleWorks 6.0 *Spell Checker*

Images courtesy of Apple Computers, Inc.

Grammar Checkers

Grammar checkers are built into a word processing program. They help with grammar, style, punctuation, and even spelling errors. The grammar checker identifies problems such as incorrect verb tense, lack of subject-verb agreement, and misuse of specific words. It will also check for inconsistencies, awkward phrases, clichés, and wordiness. After it identifies the problem, it suggests corrections and provides an online tutorial explaining the grammar rule that applies. Usually, you make the correction with a click of the mouse. You have the option of rewriting the incorrect sentence or leaving it just as it is.

In *Microsoft Word's* Spelling and Grammar dialog box (Figure 4.4) under the heading *Subject-Verb Agreement* the pertinent part of the writer's document appears. Under *Suggestions* is the word *are*, the correction. A dialog box explains the error. In this case, the user takes the suggestion by clicking on *Change*. If the user had not liked the suggestion, he or she could have clicked on *Ignore Once* or *Ignore Rule*. The *Next Sentence* button lets the writer skip the sentence entirely. Even though there have been advances in recent years, grammar checkers are still in the process of evolving.

Figure 4.4 *Microsoft Word XP* Grammar Checker

Screen shot of *Microsoft® Word XP* used by permission of Microsoft Corporation.

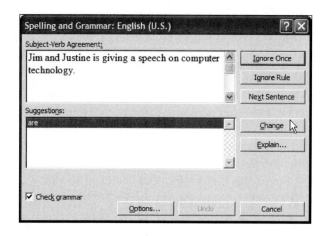

Thesaurus

The **thesaurus** has the capacity to generate synonyms for any word that it has in its dictionary. For example, if you want a different word for *peculiar*, *WordPerfect's* thesaurus lists such words as *odd, curious, strange, unusual*, and *funny*. Figure 4.5 shows the *WordPerfect* thesaurus screen. The user selects the word that he or she wants to use—in this case *curious*—and clicks *Replace*. The program automatically substitutes the new word.

Figure 4.5
WordPerfect 9
Thesaurus

WordPerfect 9 Copyright © 1999 Corel Corporation and Corel Corporation Unlimited. All rights reserved.

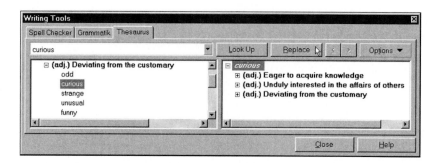

Saving and Printing

Word processors let you save a document in different file formats. This feature enables you, for example, to save a file in a format that a different word processing program can open. This is useful if you are exchanging documents with people who use different software. You can also save your document as a Web page. Figure 4.6 shows some of the file formats that are available in Microsoft Word.

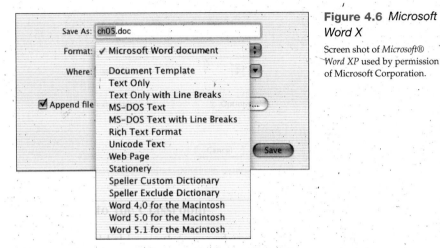

Figure 4.6 *Microsoft Word X*

Screen shot of *Microsoft® Word XP* used by permission of Microsoft Corporation.

All word processing programs allow you to print documents either in color or in black and white. There are many printing options, ranging from different layouts to different image quality.

Standard Formatting Functions

Besides being able to edit your document, you must also be able to format it. Formatting involves making the text appear a certain way on the printed page by adjusting margins, tabs, text justification, header size and font, and line spacing, among other things.

Margins

The **margin** is the spacing between the edge of the page and the main text area. A *margin* is set for an entire document, whereas an *indent* is set for individual paragraphs. Margins can be adjusted easily to meet your needs.

Tabs

Tabs are similar to the tabs on a typewriter, which position text precisely within a line in a document or within a column in a table. When you press the tab key, the cursor moves across the page quickly to set adjustable tab points.

Justification

Justification aligns the margins of text. Text can be aligned along the left side or the right side of a page, it can fill the type space to align both left and right, or it can be centered. In left-justified text (Figure 4.7A), the left margin is aligned and the right margin is uneven. This is the most common type of justification, and word processing programs usually have this as their default. In right-justified text (Figure 4.7B), the right margin is aligned and the left margin is uneven. Full-justified text (Figure 4.7C) is aligned along both margins. The computer achieves this alignment by adding space between words in a line of text to extend it. In center-justified text (Figure 4.7D), all the lines of text are centered on the page. This type of justification is often used to make headings more attractive on a page.

Figure 4.7
Justification Types

A. Left-Justified Text

Suddenly this giant computer stopped working, and everyone was frantically attempting to discover the source of the problem.   Grace Hopper and her coworkers found the culprit was a dead moth in a relay of the computer. They removed the moth with a tweezer and placed it in the Mark II logbook.

B. Right-Justified Text

Suddenly this giant computer stopped working, and everyone was frantically attempting to discover the source of the problem.   Grace Hopper and her coworkers found the culprit was a dead moth in a relay of the computer. They removed the moth with a tweezer and placed it in the Mark II logbook.

C. Full-Justified Text

Suddenly this giant computer stopped working, and everyone was frantically attempting to discover the source of the problem.   Grace Hopper and her coworkers found the culprit was a dead moth in a relay of the computer. They removed the moth with a tweezer and placed it in the Mark II logbook.

D. Center-Justified Text

Suddenly this giant computer stopped working, and everyone was frantically attempting to discover the source of the problem.   Grace Hopper and her coworkers found the culprit was a dead moth in a relay of the computer. They removed the moth with a tweezer and placed it in the Mark II logbook.

Headers and Footers

A **header** is text that appears at the top margin of each page of manuscript, and a **footer** is text that prints in the bottom margin of a page of manuscript. Headers and footers usually include descriptive text, such as page numbers, titles, and dates. Word processing programs enable the user to specify what goes into the header and footer of a document.

Line Spacing

Line spacing is the amount of space between lines of text. You can make text single spaced, one and one-half spaced, or double-spaced with the line spacing function.

Superscripts and Subscripts

Superscripts and subscripts are used in mathematical formulas and as footnote markers. The 8 in 2^8 is a superscript; the 1 in A_1 is a subscript. Word processing programs enable you to make a letter, number, or symbol super- or subscript, and most provide an automatic footnote feature for which you can adjust the style of footnote.

Page Numbering

Many word processors offer automatic numbering functions. These number the pages in a document. You can instruct the computer to start numbering a document with a particular number. For example, you might want an appendix to begin on page A-1.

Font

Font is a term that refers to the appearance of a typed character, including its typeface, its pitch, its point size, and its style. **Typeface** refers to the design of a character, such as Geneva or Palatino. **Pitch** represents the number of characters per inch. **Point size** is the height of a character. **Style** refers to whether a character is roman, italicized, boldface, or underlines. Programs vary in the number of fonts that can be used. Figure 4.8 shows examples of different type faces, pitches, sizes, and styles that can be generated on a computer. Fonts can be printed as bit map, in a pattern of dots, or as outlines defined by a mathematical formula.

Font Styles And Sizes

Flora Medium 9 Point Plain
New York 10 Point Bold
Courier 14 Point Shadow
Palatino 18 Point Bold
Helvetica 24 Point Italic

Figure 4.8 Font Choices

Advanced Word Processing Features

Many word processors have advanced features that range from desktop publishing capabilities to graphic organizer functions. *Microsoft Word* offers essential desktop publishing features with which students and teachers can create graphics and produce elegant newspapers from scratch. In addition, Microsoft comes with a series of newsletter templates that help students produce a newsletter. This particular word processor can perform many of the functions of a desktop publishing program.

Writer's Companion (Visions Technology in Education) is a combination graphic organizer, word processor, and desktop publishing program (Figure 4.9). This program is also an instructional tool that helps students learn how to use it. Students brainstorm, organize, and sequence their work. When they are satisfied, they produce a rough draft. Final drafts can include graphics and sound. If students want to e-mail their stories to others, *Writer's Companion* will automatically create a Web page to facilitate such sharing.

Figure 4.9 *Writer's Companion*

Reprinted with permission of Visions Technology in EducationTM.
www.ToolsforTeachers.com.

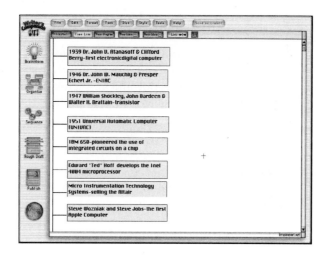

Table 4.1 summarizes some of the advanced word processing features that you can find in word processing programs.

Table 4.1 Advanced Word Processing Features

Feature	Description
AutoCorrect	When you type words, the AutoCorrect feature automatically corrects common spelling, typing, and grammatical errors.
AutoFormat	The AutoFormat feature automatically applies formatting to the text. For example, it can convert a Web address to a hyperlink or number a list.
Change tracking	This feature lets you color code changes you make to a text so you and others can see how you changed it. It also lets you add comments without changing the document.
Charts	With this feature you can create charts and insert them in the document.
Columns	The majority of word processors enable you to create columns of text (such as in a newspaper), but the advanced ones enable you to wrap words to the next line within the column.
Desktop capabilities	With such capabilities you can resize, rotate, and scale graphic objects. You also can create borders.
Endnotes	This enables you to compile your footnotes at the end of a document, as endnotes.
Equation editor	With this feature you can generate complex equations using special math symbols: $$\frac{-b \pm \sqrt{b^2 - 4ac}}{2a}$$

Table 4.1 *Continues*

Feature	Description
Footnotes	This feature will insert footnotes at the bottom of pages.
Glossaries	This feature creates a list of the terms and definitions you select.
Graphic organizer	With this feature, you can outline and use symbols and graphics.
Graphic import	Using this feature, you can insert images in different graphic formats such as PICT, GIF, PCX, BMP, or EPS into a document.
Hyperlinks	You can create hyperlinks that enable a reader of a document to jump to another location in the document or to a Web page. Here is an example: http://www.csun.edu/
Indexes	An index feature enables you to create automatically an index of key words with the page numbers on which they appear.
Macros	This feature enables you to record a series of keystrokes or menu selections and then allocate to them a key or name combination. For example, you could record a macro that would insert a picture when you press the F1 key. The macro would enable you to perform this function more quickly than using menu selections.
Mail merge	Mail merge creates a personalized document by inserting information such as a recipient's name and address into a form letter.
Math computations and sorting	You can use this feature to perform simple math calculations on columns of numbers and then sort the columns.
Outlining	This feature creates headings for key ideas.
Speech recognition	Using this function, you can speak into the computer and your words will be displayed on the screen as text.
Style sheets	Once a document is created, you can reuse its format by storing fonts, tabs, margins, and so on in a style sheet file.
Table of contents	By assigning codes to words in the document, you can have the word processor generate a list of major headings with page numbers.
Tables	By simply typing in the number of rows and columns you want, you can create a table like this one.
Templates	A template is a formatted document designed for a specific use. For example, a word processor might come with a resume template or a fax cover sheet template.
Voice annotation	You can use this feature to add sound comments to a text.
Web page creation	Many word processors help you create Web pages.
Windows	This feature allows you to work on two or more documents at the same time by showing them in different windows on the screen.
Wizards	A wizard leads you through the process of creating a document in a step-by-step fashion.

Evaluation of Word Processing Programs

Word processing programs have so many features that it is difficult for the beginner to tell a good program from an inferior one. It takes time to explore the programs and evaluate them. The computer you are using also limits you. Old computers more than likely will not work with the latest word processing package. For this reason, before you begin your exploration of software, consider your computer's capabilities.

Hardware Compatibility

Check out the computers that are available at your school. For example, do you have old Apple IIes, Macintosh G5s, or IBM compatibles? How much memory do these machines have: 64 MB, 256 MB, or 2 GB of RAM? What is the computer's processor speed? How much storage space does the hard disk drive contain? What other peripherals or external devices are available? Does the school district have a CD-ROM, DVD-ROM player, or a scanner? After you are knowledgeable about your hardware and you have examined the different word processing features, you are ready to consider a software program's instructional design.

Instructional Design and Features

For the lowest grade levels, a word processor should offer at least the following functions: insert, delete, center, underline, double space, save text, and print. A word processor program should be easy for a student to learn and not require hours of instruction.

Write:OutLoud is a talking word processor that provides auditory feedback for students with or without learning disabilities. Students hear the words, letters, or sentences as they type them. The program includes a talking spelling checker and a toolbar. It also features large font sizes to make the letters easier to read. *Write:OutLoud* displays its functions at the top of the screen (Figure 4.10), which is ideal for beginners because it saves them from having to remember the functions. For example, to print a document, the user chooses the printer icon on the toolbar; to save work, he or she chooses the floppy disk icon on the toolbar. This word processor is a perfect example of a picture- or icon-based application.

Figure 4.10
Write:OutLoud

Used with permission of Don Johnston Incorporated, 26799 W. Commerce Dr., Volo, IL 60073, Phone: 800-999-4660, 847-740-0749, Fax: 847-740-7326, Web: www.donjohnston.com, E-mail: info@donjohnston.com.

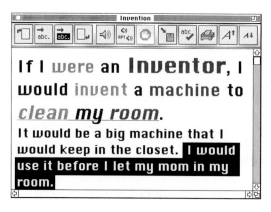

AppleWorks 6.0 features a starting point (Figure 4.11) dialog box that makes it easy for the novice to begin using the program. The program also offers a very useful help

Figure 4.11
AppleWorks 6.0
Startup Screen

Images courtesy of Apple
Computers, Inc.

function, a spelling checker, a thesaurus, hypermedia functions, a presentation package, and desktop capabilities. In one version of *AppleWorks 6.0,* the major functions appear at the top of the screen.

In your search for a word processor, examine only those with easy-to-remember keys for functions. Find out how the word processor carries out simple functions such as underlining or boldfacing.

In the higher-grades, students make considerable use of word processing, so they need a more sophisticated word processor like *WordPerfect* (Corel Corp.). This program includes many advanced features but is simple to use. For example, the program enables a user to click a button to select a specific margin justification (Figure 4.12).

Figure 4.12
Justification Buttons

WordPerfect® *9.* Screen shot is copyright © 1999 Corel Corporation and Corel Corporation Unlimited. All rights reserved. Reprinted by permission.

Ease of Use

You should make sure that using the word processing program's functions, such as centering, boldfacing, and italicizing, is effortless. Take the program for a test drive and see how much you can learn in an hour. The program's features are immaterial if the program is difficult to learn. Can a person in a reasonable amount of time learn to use this program?

Clicker 4, for grades K–6 (Crick Software, Figure 4.13) is exceptionally easy to use. Most instructions appear on the top of the screen, so teachers do not have to read a large manual. Every step of the way icons suggest the function of each button. For example, users choose the printer button to print a document and a disk button to save a document.

Figure 4.13 *Clicker 4*

© 2004 Riverdeep Interactive Learning Limited, and its licensors.

Also, users click words and pictures at the bottom of the screen to help them write. Are there help screens that tell the student what to do each step of the way? Is there a tutorial disk or manual that guides the user through the program? Can you set up the printer easily and is it ready to print immediately? Is there a spelling checker, grammar checker, or thesaurus? Even the more sophisticated word processors such as *Microsoft Word* or *WordPerfect* display these icons at the top of the screen, so you can just click on them. Is there good online help? The majority of software programs include online help, which you access by clicking help on the menu bar. Most programs also include many safety features to protect you from making a mistake, such as by mistakenly deleting a document.

Safety Features

A program should come with enough safety devices to prevent the user from making errors. It is important to have as many of these safeguards as possible, especially when you are about to save material. These safeguards consist of queries to warn both the novice and advanced user about what they may be on the verge of doing. Many word processing programs try to protect against data loss by automatically saving material intermittently. Other programs remind the user to save. *Microsoft Word XP* displays the screen in Figure 4.14 when the user is about to quit an application without saving the

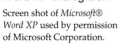

Figure 4.14 *Microsoft Word XP* Dialog Box

Screen shot of *Microsoft® Word XP* used by permission of Microsoft Corporation.

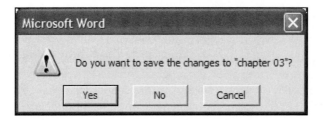

changes. The user then has three options: not to save, to cancel, or to save. Another important safety feature is the **undo** feature, which reverses the last action performed on the document. *Nisus, Word,* and *WordPerfect* advanced-level word processing programs feature unlimited **undos.**

Consumer Value

Software is expensive, and for teachers cost is often a consideration. Consider any **public domain software** package that can be purchased for a minimal price and duplicated as often as needed, as long as it offers the features you need. There is one catch: The program cannot be sold to anyone. **Shareware** is inexpensive software that is copyrighted but that you can try before you buy it. Usually, commercial software is more expensive, but there are exceptions. Even though public domain and shareware is inexpensive, you generally do not receive the same quality of technical support with it that you get from a vendor of commercial packages.

Support

Support refers to personal as well as written help from the software company. Can you call a technician at the software company to get immediate help or must you sift through a series of messages and wait an unbearable amount of time? Is the technical support toll-free or does it require a pay call? Are you charged for the amount of time you are on the telephone with the technician? Is there a yearly fee for unlimited support, and is it reasonable? Is the manual readable, and does it include activities, lesson plans, and an index? The new and revised advanced programs are packaged with all three. Is there a website on the Internet that provides support?

Recommended Software

For a listing of recommended word processing programs, go to the Online Learning Center.

Word Processing Program Checklist

As you can see, a teacher looking for a classroom word processing program must weigh many factors. Choosing software for the classroom is a five-step process: (1) determine the hardware compatibility; (2) study the program's features; (3) consider its instructional design; (4) evaluate its ease of use; and (5) measure its cost effectiveness and technical support. Use the Word Processing Program Checklist form on page 78 to guide you through the process.

Integrating a Word Processor into the Classroom

Teachers as well as students can use the word processing program in a variety of ways. The teacher can use it to prepare lesson plans, worksheets, memos, lab sheets (Figure 4.15), book report forms, assignment sheets, course syllabi, and other instructional materials. They can create quizzes, tests, and different types of evaluation forms. Furthermore, they can write letters and create weekly newsletters for parents.

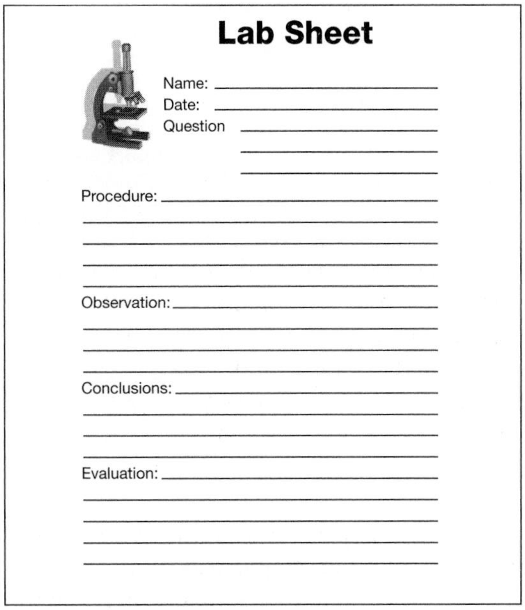
Lab Sheet

Name: ______

Date: ______

Question ______

Procedure: ______

Observation: ______

Conclusions: ______

Evaluation: ______

Figure 4.15 Word Processing Document

ClickArt Images © 1995 T/Maker Company.

Word Processing Program Checklist

Directions: Examine the following items and determine which ones you feel are important for your class situation. Place an X on each line for which the software meets your needs.

Product Name _____ **Manufacturer** _____ **Grade Level** _____

Hardware
_____ 1. Computer processor speed
_____ 2. Computer compatibility
_____ 3. CD-ROM or DVD capabilities
_____ 4. Monitor resolution
_____ 5. Hard disk space required
_____ 6. Memory needed
_____ 7. Printer compatibility
_____ 8. Microphone

General Features
_____ 1. Cursor control
_____ 2. Word wrap
_____ 3. Page breaks

Standard Editing Features
_____ 1. Cut and paste
_____ 2. Copy
_____ 3. Drag and drop
_____ 4. Find and replace
_____ 5. Insert and delete
_____ 6. Spelling checker
_____ 7. Grammar checker
_____ 8. Thesaurus
_____ 9. Saving and printing

Standard Formatting Functions
_____ 1. Automatic page numbering
_____ 2. Font
_____   a. Typeface
_____   b. Pitch
_____   c. Point size
_____   d. Style
_____ 3. Headers and footers
_____ 4. Justification
_____ 5. Line spacing
_____ 6. Margins
_____ 7. Superscripts and subscripts
_____ 8. Tabs
_____ 9. Underlining

Advanced Features
_____ 1. AutoCorrect
_____ 2. AutoFormating
_____ 3. Automatic indexing
_____ 4. Change tracking
_____ 5. Charting

_____ 6. Columns
_____ 7. Desktop publishing capabilities
_____ 8. Endnotes
_____ 9. Equation editor
_____ 10. Footnoting
_____ 11. Glossary
_____ 12. Graphic organizer
_____ 13. Hyperlink creation
_____ 14. Importing of different graphic file formats
_____ 15. Macros
_____ 16. Mail merge
_____ 17. Math computations and sorting
_____ 18. Outlining
_____ 19. Speech recognition
_____ 20. Style sheets
_____ 21. Table of contents
_____ 22. Tables
_____ 23. Templates
_____ 24. Voice annotation
_____ 25. Web page creation
_____ 26. Windows
_____ 27. Wizards

Safety Features
_____ 1. Undo last move(s)
_____ 2. Warning questions
_____ 3. Automatic save

Ease of Use
_____ 1. Help screens
_____ 2. Online tutorial
_____ 3. Printer setup
_____ 4. Talking processor

Support Features
_____ 1. Technical support
_____ 2. Tutorial material
_____ 3. Readable manual
_____   a. Activities and lesson plans
_____   b. Tutorial
_____   c. Index

Consumer Value
_____ 1. Cost
_____ 2. Free technical support
_____ 3. Guarantees

Rating Scale
Rate the word processor by placing a check in the appropriate line.
Excellent _____ Very good _____ Good _____ Fair _____ Poor _____

Comments:

Students at all grade levels can use word processing software to create an assortment of projects. In the lower grades, they can create large-font stories, alphabet books, and journals. Students can create classroom reports, outlines, flyers, book reports, and lab reports with tables and graphs. Furthermore, students can create a class newspaper using clip art or create their own letterhead stationery. After their letterhead stationery has been designed, students can use the software to write letters to people in the class, across the country, or around the globe. Finally, they can use the word processor to edit, using grammar and spelling checking and an electronic thesaurus.

Classroom Lesson Plans

I. TRAVELING ABROAD

Subject

Social Studies

Grade(s)

4 and up

Objective

Students will use the word processor to create a travel brochure like the one shown in Figure 4.16.

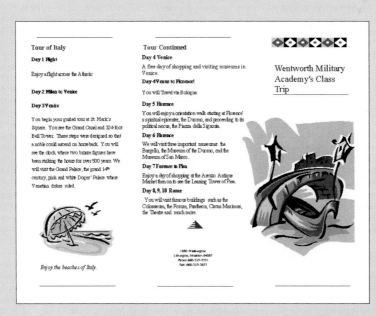

Figure 4.16 Travel Brochure, *Make It with Office XP,* by Vicki F. Sharp.

Reprinted with permission of Visions Technology in EducationTM.
www.ToolsforTeachers.com.

Standards

- National Council for the Social Studies Curriculum Standards 3
- ISTE NETS for Students 1, 3, 4, 5

Materials

You will need a word processing program such as *Microsoft Word* and one or more computers.

Procedures

1. Divide the class into small groups.
2. Explain to students that they will create a travel brochure about a country they have visited or a country that they would like to visit.
3. Instruct students to create their brochures in such a manner that anyone who reads them will want to visit the countries advertised.
4. Ask students to use the Internet or print resources to research the country and collect facts and images.
5. Have groups use a word processor to create their brochure's.
6. When all groups are done, discuss how effective each brochure is in publicizing the country chosen.

Variation

The brochure can cover any topic, and students can work independently.

II. NEWSLETTER

Subject

English

Grade(s)

2 and up

Objective

Students will use a word processor to create a newspaper.

Standards

- NCTE English Language Arts Standards 4, 5, 7, 8, 12
- ISTE NETS for Students 1, 2, 3, 4, 5

Materials

You will need a word processing program such as *Writer's Companion*, *AppleWorks*, or *WordPerfect* and one or more computers.

Procedures

1. Divide the class into small groups.
2. Meet with students to discuss what the newspaper will cover.
3. Have students make a list of topics.

4. Ask each group to choose a leader and divide their tasks. One person might write a gossip column, another might handle sports, and another might cover world news, for example.
5. Have students use a word processor to produce the newspaper (see Figure 4.17 for an example).

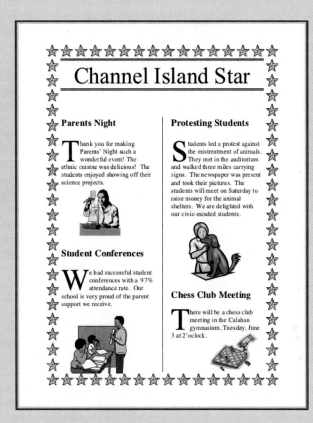

Figure 4.17
Newspaper, *Make It with Office XP*, by Vicki F. Sharp.

Reprinted with permission of Visions Technology in EducationTM. www.ToolsforTeachers.com.

Variation

The newspaper can cover a multitude of topics, from famous historical figures or current political leaders to scientific inventions.

III. WRITING A WACKY STORY

Subject

English

Grade(s)

2 and up

Objective

Students will improve their writing skills and, in the process, use the cut and paste and find and replace functions.

Standards

- NCTE English Language Arts Standards 4, 5, 6, 12
- ISTE NETS for Students 1, 2, 3, 4

Materials

You will need a word processing program such as *Writer's Companion, AppleWorks*, or *WordPerfect* and one or more computers.

Procedures

1. Have each student independently create a random sentence for a story file.
2. Instruct each student to write his or her sentence on a piece of paper.
3. Ask students to examine the sentences of two classmates, correcting grammar errors.
4. Next instruct the students to enter, one at a time, their sentences into the computer.
5. When the sentences are entered, have students separate them by a line and number them in the order they are entered.
6. Ask the last student to enter his or her sentence to save the entire file of sentences under a name such as *Story 1*.
7. Go around the room asking students to call out random numbers no higher than the number of sentences that were recorded for *Story 1*.
8. Call up *Story 1* on the computer and record at the top of the screen the random sequence of numbers the students gave.
9. Have the students take turns using the find and replace function to locate the sentences in the random sequence and using the cut and paste function to move the sentences into the order of the random sequence.
10. Print out a copy of the ordered sentences for each student. During independent work time, ask the students to make stories out of their sentences, without changing the order of sentences, by adding sentences or words.
11. Ask students to share their finished stories.

Example

Use the find and replace and cut and paste functions to create a story from the sentences that follow. Arrange the sentences in the following sequence: 1 4 8 2 3 5 6 9 7.

1. Do not judge food on calories alone.
2. The professor was frustrated with the paperwork he had to turn in next week.
3. The student was eagerly awaiting an exciting lecture on computers.
4. The wind blew a bee into the room.
5. "Don't forget to pick up the groceries at the store," said Paul.
6. "Did the emergency rations arrive?" asked Maria.

7. There were many children on the playground.
8. The centerfielder could not catch the ball.
9. The sound came from another room.

Do not judge food on calories alone. This is what the professor was saying as the wind blew a bee into the classroom. I was daydreaming as usual, watching the baseball team. The centerfielder could not catch the ball. The professor banged on the board. I looked up. He seemed crabby. I think he was frustrated with the paperwork he had to turn in next week. He called on Dewayne. The student was eagerly awaiting an exciting lecture on computers but instead he was invited up to the board to solve a complicated problem. I went back to daydreaming. There was something I was supposed to do after class. Suddenly I remembered. While I was brushing my teeth that morning, my roommate made a grocery list. "Don't forget to pick up the groceries at the store," said Paul as I ran out the door. Then at the bus stop, I ran into my friend Maria, who was heading up an earthquake disaster team. She was talking to someone else on the disaster team. "Did the emergency rations arrive?" asked Maria. As Dewayne tried to solve the problem, I decided I would donate some of my groceries to Maria's earthquake relief efforts. An explosion interrupted my daydreaming. The sound came from another room, the chemistry lab. Dewayne still wasn't finished. I looked back out the window. There were many children on the playground.

IV. FORTUNE COOKIE WORD PROCESSING

The idea for this activity came from a 1996 *Learning and Leading with Technology* article written by R. Reisman.

Subject

English

Grade(s)

2 and up

Objective

Students will improve their word processing skills by creating a booklet of sayings. In the process, they will learn about themselves and each other.

Standards

- NCTE English Language Arts Standards 4, 5, 12
- ISTE NETS for Students 1, 2, 3,

Materials

You will need a word processing program such as *Writer's Companion*, *AppleWorks*, or *WordPerfect* and one or more computers.

Procedures

1. Buy fortune cookies and have the class eat them and then discuss what the sayings mean.
2. Divide the class into small groups.
3. Have each group create some fortune cookie sayings on the computer and print them out.
4. After the class is through, have the students cut these sayings into strips and put them in a hat.
5. Randomly hand out a saying to each student in the class.
6. Ask students to share their sayings with the whole class and tell if they think the sayings are true of them.
7. Have the students use an art program to depict the meaning of their sayings.
8. Finally, have the whole class use a word processing program to publish the class sayings in a class booklet.

V. UNSCRAMBLE THE STORY

Subject

English

Grade(s)

2 and up

Objective

Students will improve their reading comprehension and learn how to use a word processor's copy and paste function.

Standards

* NCTE English Language Arts Standards 3, 6
* ISTE NETS for Students 1, 6

Materials

You will need a word processing program such as *Writer's Companion, AppleWorks,* or *WordPerfect* and one or more computers.

Procedures

1. Choose a story that the students are currently reading.
2. Type the story or part of the story into the computer. You might choose "The Hare and the Tortoise,"[2] one of Aesop's Fables, as follows:

---

[2]From *The Children's Treasury,* Paula S. Goepfert, ed. New York: Gallery Books, 1987, p. 229.

The Hare and the Tortoise

A hare was once boasting about how fast he could run when a tortoise, overhearing him, said, "I'll run you a race." "Done," said the hare and laughed to himself, "but let's get the fox for a judge." The fox consented and the two started. The hare quickly outran the tortoise, and knowing he was far ahead, lay down to take a nap. "I can soon pass the tortoise whenever I awaken." But, unfortunately, the hare overslept. When he awoke, though he ran his best, he found the tortoise was already at the goal. *Slow and steady wins the race.*

3. Save this story under *Hare/Tortoise.*
4. Now use the cut and paste functions on the word processor to scramble the story. The scrambled Tortoise and Hare story might look like this:

The Scrambled Hare and the Tortoise

The hare quickly outran the tortoise, and knowing he was far ahead, lay down to take a nap. "Done," said the hare and laughed to himself, "but let's get the fox for a judge." *Slow and steady wins the race.* The fox consented and the two started. But, unfortunately, the hare overslept. When he awoke, though he ran his best, he found the tortoise was already at the goal. A hare was once boasting about how fast he could run when a tortoise, overhearing him, said, "I'll run you a race." "I can soon pass the tortoise whenever I awaken."

5. Save this scrambled fable under *AERH*, which is *Hare* scrambled.
6. Load *AERH* into each student's computer.
7. Ask students to use their word processors to arrange the story correctly.
8. Record each student's score by writing down the time taken to complete the activity and the number of sentences arranged correctly.

Variation

1. Divide the class into two teams, Team A and Team B.
2. Instruct Team A to scramble a story.
3. Instruct Team B to rearrange the story.
4. Determine Team B's score by calculating the time it takes the team to rearrange the story and the number of sentences correct on completion.
5. Then have the teams swap roles.

VI. WEB PAGE

Subject

English

Grade(s)

2 and up

Objective

Students will gain practice creating simple Web pages. They will create a Web page similar to the one shown in Figure 4.18.

Figure 4.18 Web Page, *Make It with Office XP*, by Vicki F. Sharp.

Reprinted with permission of Visions Technology in EducationTM. www.ToolsforTeachers.com.

Standards

- NCTE English Language Arts Standards 3, 4, 5, 6, 7, 8, 12
- ISTE NETS for Students 1, 2, 4

Materials

You will need a word processing program such as *Writer's Companion, AppleWorks,* or *WordPerfect* and one or more computers.

Procedures

1. Give the class pointers on how to plan and create a Web page.
2. Show different Web page examples.
3. Have students discuss which pages they consider excellent and the reasons for their choices.
4. Ask students to create their own Web pages using the word processor. The Web pages can be on any topic.

Summary

This chapter traced the historical beginnings of word processing and showed how word processing has come a long way from the Wang 1200. We examined the merits of the word processor over the standard typewriter. We discovered how easy it is for users to change and edit documents with word processors. We became familiar with the basic features of word processing and gained insight into what features to consider when selecting a word processor. The chapter presented a checklist and evaluation scale to facilitate this decision-making process, along with specific ideas on how to incorporate the word processor into the classroom. Six word processing activities covered a range of curriculum areas. Be sure to review the annotated list of award-winning word processing programs located under **Recommended Software** on the Online Learning Center.

Study and Online Resources

Go to Chapter 4 in the Student Edition of the Online Learning Center at www.mhhe.com/sharp5e to **practice with key concepts, take chapter quizzes, read PowerWeb articles** *and* **news feed updates** *related to technology in education, and* **access resources** *for learning about technology and integrating it into the classroom.*

Click on *Web Links* to link to the following websites.

Aaron Shepard's RT Page
Aaron Shepard's *Reader's Theater Editions* provide scripts for getting the creative juices going.

Aha! Poetry
This site features poems in progress and encourages the viewer to add to, comment on, or finish the poems. You can also begin a new poem and have others add to it.

AskERIC Computer Science Lesson Plans
This site offers a collection of technology lesson plans for grades K–12.

Carol Hurst's Children's Literature Website
This site is packed with hundreds of teaching suggestions for integrating writing into the curriculum using children's books.

Children's Literature Web Guide
David K. Brown, Doucette Library librarian at the University of Calgary, has collected extensive resources to facilitate and encourage the writing process. For example, the *More Links* section contains hundreds of links to the pages of well-known children's authors and to teacher resources.

Interactive Poetry Pages
This site is a link from a larger site that features many forums for poetry.

KidNews: Kids' Writing from Practically Everywhere
KidNews gathers different forms of writing. Submissions from kids around the world include news, features, creative writing, pen pals, and book reviews.

Melisa C. Michaels
The author of the Skyrider science fiction series offers writing tips, samples from her novels, short stories and poems, and story starters.

NativeTech: Poems and Stories
The site, accompanied by illustrations, includes poetry shaped by Native American experiences. The poems feature imagery of nature, animals, and the seasons and are divided into sections called "Beavers and Beyond" and "Medicine Dreams."

North Carolina Department of Instruction: Computer Skills Lesson Plans
Computer Skills Lesson Plans contains a table of lesson plans on keyboarding, word processing, and other applications.

Scholastic Lesson Plans and Reproducibles
Scholastic provides a rich collection of lesson plans that range from pre-K to 8th grade.

Sheldon Oberman's Writing and Storytelling
Sheldon Oberman, a Canadian children's author, presents a wealth of writing ideas and resources from warm-up exercises to descriptive character sketches.

Teachers @Random
This site offers instructional ideas for a wide range of novels indexed by grade, theme, and curriculum subject. It also includes author biographies.

The Write Site
This site presents an interactive language arts and journalism project for middle schools. It includes information on how to conduct research and develop one's own personal writing style.

The Young Writers Club
At this site, students can join a free online writers' club, read other kids' work, and take part in contests and activities. They can also submit their writing to the site.

Chapter Mastery Test

To the Instructor: *Refer to the Instructor's Manual for the answers to the Mastery Questions. This manual has additional questions and resource materials.*

Let us check for chapter comprehension with a short mastery test. Key terms, Computer Lab, and Suggested Readings and References follow the test.

1. What is word processing and why is it important in education?
2. What distinguishes a typewriter from a word processor?
3. Identify and describe five features that are common to all word processors.
4. Discuss three different ways a word processor would be useful in the classroom.
5. Select two standard editing features and justify their use.
6. Explain the concept of line justification as it relates to the computer and give two examples.
7. Discuss the factors involved in selecting a word processor for a school district. The Online Learning Center presents an annotated list of word processing software.

8. Define the following terms:
   a. font,
   b. copy and paste,
   c. mail merge,
   d. drag and drop, and
   e. find and replace.
9. What safety features should be included in a word processor and why?
10. Evaluate a real or hypothetical word processing software program based on the criteria used in this chapter.
11. Choose three advanced word processing features and explain how you would use them in a high school classroom.
12. If you were buying a word processing program for use in an elementary school, what three features would be essential in your selection and why?
13. Compare two word processors on the basis of their features; then review each one separately.
14. Americans generally use word processing software more than Europeans do. Explain why you think this situation will or will not change.
15. Explain why templates have become a highly popular word processing tool.

Key Terms

Copy 66
Cursor 65
Cut and paste 66
Dedicated word
   processors 64
Delete 66
Drag-and-drop 67
Equation editor 72
Font 71
Footer 70

Grammar checkers 67
Graphic organizer 73
Header 70
Insert 66
Integrated software
   package 64
Justification 69
Macro 73
Margin 69
Pitch 71

Point size 71
Public domain
   software 76
Replace 66
Spelling checker 67
Shareware 76
Software suite 64
Style 71

Tabs 69
Thesaurus 68
Typeface 71
Undo 76
Wizards 73
Word processor 64
Word wrap 65

Computer Lab: Activities for Mastery and Your Portfolio

4.1 Footnotes and Bibliographic Styles Learn how to cite information found on the Internet.
4.2 Create Genre Signs and Book Slips Create genre signs and book slips in your classroom library.
4.3 Create a Certificate Make a certificate for any occasion.
4.4 Create a piece of letterhead stationery. Write another member of the class using the stationery.

4.5 Use a word processing template to prepare a resume.
4.6 Create a flyer publicizing a hypothetical product that you want to sell.
4.7 Create a form letter and then do a mail merge for a small group of students in the class.
4.8 Write a research report with footnotes and bibliography.

Suggested Readings and References

Allen, Philip A. "Adult Age Difference in Letter-Level and Word-Level Processing." *Psychology and Aging* 6, no. 2 (June 1, 1991): 261.

Bahr, Christine M. "The Effects of Text-Based and Graphics-Based Software Tools on Planning and Organizing of Stories." *Journal of Learning Disabilities* 29, no. 4 (July 1996): 355–370.

Balajthy, E. "Keyboarding, Language Arts, and the Elementary School Child." *Computing Teacher,* February 1988, 40–43.

Bangert-Drowns, Robert L. The word processor as an instructional tool: A meta-analysis of word processing in writing. *Review of Educational Research* 63, issue 1, (Spring 1993): 69–93.

Boone, R. *Teaching Process Writing with Computers.* Eugene, Ore.: ISTE, 1991.

Bowman, Marcus. "Children, Word Processors and Genre." *Scottish Educational Review* 31, no. 1 (May 1999): 66–83.

Bracey, Gerald W. Word processing and writing: A summary: *Phi Delta Kappan* 75, issue 3 (November 1993): 272.

Campbell, George. "Get Their Attention with Voice Attachments." *PC World* 18, no. 3 (March 2000): 265.

Cerrito, Patricia. "Writing Technology and Experimentation to Explore the Concepts of Elementary Statistics." *Mathematics and Computer Education* 28, no. 2 (Spring 1994): 141.

Coats, Kaye, et al. "Ideas from Teachers! Writing Notebook." *Creative Word Processing in the Classroom* 7, no. 4 (April–May 1990): 40–41.

Cochran-Smith, Marilyn. "Writing Processing and Writing in Elementary Classrooms: A Critical Review of Related Literature." *Review of Educational Research* 61, no. 1 (Spring 1991): 107.

Daiute, C. *Writing and Computers.* Reading, Mass.: Addison-Wesley, 1985.

Drumm, John E., and Frank M. Groom. "Teaching Information Skills to Disadvantaged Children." *Computers in Libraries* 19, no. 4 (April 1999): 48–51.

Greenleaf, Cynthia. "Technological Indeterminacy: The Role of Classroom Writing Practices and Pedagogy in Shaping Student Use of the Computer." *Written Communication* 11, no. 11 (January 1, 1994): 85.

Howell, R., and P. Scott. *Microcomputer Applications for Teachers.* Scottsdale, Ariz.: Gorsuch, 1985.

Howie, S. H. *Reading, Writing, and Computers: Planning for Integration.* Needham Heights, Mass.: Allyn & Bacon, Longwood Division, 1989.

Jarchow, E. "Computers and Computing: The Pros and Cons." *Electronic Education,* June 1984, 38.

Joslin, E. "Welcome to Word Processing." *Computing Teacher,* March 1986, 16–19.

Laframboise, Kathryn L. "The Facilitative Effects of Word Processing on Sentence-Combining Tasks with At-Risk Fourth Graders." *Journal of Research and Development in Education* 24, no. 2 (Winter 1991): 1.

Land, Michael, and Sandra Turner. *Tools for Schools,* 2d ed. New York: Wadsworth Publishing Company, 1996.

Langone, John. "The Differential Effects of a Typing Tutor and Microcomputer-Based Word Processing on the Writing Samples of Elementary Students with Behavior Disorders." *Journal of Research on Computing in Education* 29, no. 2 (Winter 1996): 141–158.

Levy, Michael C., and S. Ransdell. "Computer-Aided Protocol Analysis of Writing Processes." *Behavior Research Methods, Instruments, & Computing* 26, no. 2 (May 1, 1994): 219.

MacArthur, Charles A. "Using Technology to Enhance the Writing Processes of Students with Learning Disabilities." *Journal of Learning Disabilities* 29, no. 4 (July 1996): 334–354.

MacArthur, Charles A. "Word Processing with Speech Synthesis and Word Prediction: Effects on the Dialogue Journal Writing of Students with Learning Disabilities." *Learning Disability Quarterly* 21, no. 2 (Spring 1998): 151–166.

Marcus, Stephen. "Word Processing: Transforming Students' Potential to Write." *Media and Methods* 27, no. 5 (May 1, 1991): 8.

Milone, Michael N. *Every Teacher's Guide to Word Processing: 101 Classroom Computer.* Englewood Cliffs, N.J.: Prentice Hall, 1985.

Montague, Marjorie, and Fionelle Fonseca. "Using Computers to Improve Story Writing." *Teaching Exceptional Children* 25, no. 4 (Summer 1993): 46–49.

Morton, L. L. "Lab-Based Word Processing for the Learning-Disabled." *Computers in the Schools* 8, no. 1/3 (1991): 225.

Nichols, Lois Mayer. "Pencil and Paper Versus Word Processing: A Comparative Study of Creative Writing in the Elementary School." *Journal of Research on Computing in Education* 29, no. 2 (Winter 1996): 159–166.

Owen, Trevor. "Poems That Change the World: Canada's Wired Writers." *English Journal* 84, no. 6 (October 1995): 48–52.

Pfaffenberger, Bryan. *Webster's New World Dictionary of Computer Terms,* 10th ed. New York: John Wiley & Sons, Inc., 2003.

Porter, Rebecca. "Word Versus WordPerfect: Word-Processing Software on Trial." *Trial* 36, no. 3 (March 2000): 55.

Poulsen, Erik. "Writing Processes with Word Processing in Teaching English as a Foreign Language." *Computers & Education* 16, no. 1 (1991): 77.

Reissman, R. "Computerized Fortune Cookies: A Classroom Treat." *Learning and Leading with Technology* 23, no. 5 (1996): 25–26.

Robinette, Michelle. "Top 10 Uses for ClarisWorks in the One-Computer Classroom." *Learning and Leading with Technology* 24, no. 2 (October 1996): 37–40.

Roblyer, M. D. "The Effectiveness of Microcomputers in Education: A Review of the Research from 1980–1987." *T.H.E. Journal,* September 1988, 85–89.

Schramm, Robert M. "The Effects of Using Word Processing Equipment in Writing Instruction." *Business Education Forum* 45, no. 5 (February 1, 1991): 7.

Schumm, Jeanne Shay, and Linda Saumell. Word processor: Their impact on process and product. *Journal of Reading* 37, issue 3, (November 1993): 190.

Sharp, Vicki. *Make It with Microsoft Office 2001 (Macintosh).* Eugene, Ore.: Visions Technology in Education, 2001.

Sharp, Vicki. *Make It with Microsoft Office 2000 (Windows).* Eugene, Ore.: Visions Technology in Education, 2001.

Sharp, Vicki. *Make It with Microsoft Office XP (Windows).* Eugene, Ore.: Visions Technology in Education, 2003.

Sharp, Vicki. *Make It with Microsoft Office X (Macintosh).* Eugene, Ore: Visions Technology in Education, 2003.

Solomon, Gil L. "Four Tips for More Efficient Word Processing." *Family Practice Management* 6, no. 8 (September 1999): 54.

Stone, M. David. "Choose Your Words." *PC Magazine* 19, no. 6 (March 21, 2000): 113.

Varblow, Judy. "Reading, Writing, and Word Processing: An Interdisciplinary Approach." *Balance Sheet* 72, no. 2 (Winter 1990): 22.

Woodrow, Janice F. J. "Teachers' Perceptions of Computer Needs." *Journal of Research on Computing in Education* 23, no. 4 (Summer 1991): 475–493.

Zorko, Leslie J. "Creative Writing: A Comparison Using the Computer vs. Handwriting." *National Association of Laboratory Schools Journal* 18, no. 2 (Winter 1993): 28.

CHAPTER 5

Desktop Publishing

Integrating Desktop Publishing into the Classroom

Desktop publishing is the second most popular computer application. In classrooms, students can use desktop software to create a variety of projects such as minibooks, book reports, yearbooks, newsletters, posters, and flyers. Teachers can use a desktop publishing program to create awards, worksheets, signs, flyers, and posters for classroom display. This chapter will discuss how to select a desktop publishing program for the classroom and the general features of a desktop publishing program. A checklist will help you choose the right desktop publishing software, and exercises will help you integrate desktop publishing into the classroom. Finally, we will examine Internet sites that feature tutorials, software tips, design basics, and classes for learning desktop publishing.

Objectives

Upon completing this chapter, you will be able to do the following:

1. Explain what desktop publishing is.
2. Describe the features of desktop publishing.
3. Demonstrate how a desktop publishing program operates.
4. Evaluate different desktop publishing packages using standard criteria.
5. Create and apply a repertoire of desktop publishing activities in the classroom.
6. Discuss three guidelines for desktop publishing.
7. Use in the classroom desktop publishing articles, tips, tutorials, and lesson plans from Internet sites.

Students Can

- create a class newspaper,
- design cards for other students,
- design posters and fliers,
- create a banner for the class,
- create a school yearbook,
- make a personal résumé, and
- design science experiment sheets.

Teachers Can

- create a school newspaper,
- create a brochure for the school,
- design an award or certificate,
- create flash cards or vocabulary cards,
- create a layout for the school yearbook, and
- create a letter to the parents.

Word Processing Versus Desktop Publishing

Many of the word processing programs we studied in Chapter 4 had desktop publishing capabilities. Users could manipulate text, add graphics to the text, and lay out the text and graphics. These programs included graphic fonts as well as a variety of different type sizes. The distinction between desktop publishing and word processing has certainly become blurred.

Although the majority of word processing programs are capable of performing some desktop publishing functions, the strength of such programs is text manipulation. Word processing programs outshine desktop publishing programs when it comes to checking spelling and grammar, changing margins, performing global replace and find searches, and setting tabs for an entire document. The strength of desktop publishing programs, on the other hand, is graphic design, or the ability to combine text and graphics to communicate effectively. A desktop publishing program gives the user more control over a document's design than does a word processing program. These programs offer more features, tools, and color palettes.

Historical Background

In Europe before the 1400s, troubadours traveled from place to place, transmitting information orally. They would sing ballads or recite poems to broadcast the news or gossip of the day. Few people could read or write, and books were scarce because they had to be handwritten.

Figure 5.1 Early Printing Press

© Dubl-Click Software, Inc.

Then around 1450, Johannes Gutenberg revolutionized communication with the invention of **movable type.** Modifying a winemaker's press to hold type, he poured hot metal into molds from which he created letters, numbers, and symbols. He set this type and engravings on the bed of the press, inked the surface, and covered it with a sheet of paper. When he cranked the handle of the press, the pressure of the plate created an image on the paper (Figure 5.1).

Gutenberg's printing innovation gave more people the opportunity to read by making books more available. Even though Gutenberg's methods were refined over time, the basic concept behind his press remained unchanged for 400 years.

In the late 1880s, Ottmar Mergenthaler invented the **Linotype machine** the first successful automated typecasting machine. This mechanical type-composing machine enabled the operator to cast an entire line of type at once by using a keyboard. It was first used to typeset the *New York Tribune* in 1886. A year later, Tolbert Lanston invented the **Monotype machine,** which produced three characters of set type a second and was widely used for books.

The Linotype and Monotype, along with hand-set type, dominated typesetting until Intertype introduced the first phototypesetting machine in 1950. Phototypesetting replaced cast type because of its low cost, faster speed, and flexibility. Phototypesetting used film to reproduce type and images on metal plates that could then be inked for reproduction on paper.

The search for higher typesetting speeds resulted in the development in the mid-1960s of a method that stores characters in electronic digital format. Computer-typesetting equipment generates letterforms as nearly invisible dots. This invention led the way for desktop publishing (DTP), a term coined by Paul Brainerd of Aldus Software.

What Is Desktop Publishing?

Desktop publishing (DTP) is probably the second most popular use of computers in schools next to word processing (Kearsley, Hunter, and Furlong, 1992). Desktop publishing uses the personal computer (in conjunction with specialized software) to combine text and graphics to produce high-quality output on either a laser printer or a typesetting machine. The elements of this multistep process, which involves different types of software and equipment, are as follows (see Figure 5.2):

1. Input your material using the keyboard, a scanner, a Zip disk, a CD-ROM, or a video digitizer. Also input illustrations from clip art, from a drawing or painting program, or from a program such as *SnagIt* (TechSmith Corporation), which captures images on the computer screen.
2. Lay out the text and graphics on the screen, revising and refining the material using the DTP's capabilities.
3. At this point, you have two choices: to print the finished document on a laser printer or, for better quality, to print it on a typesetting machine.
4. After obtaining proofs, make further changes and corrections and ready the final copy for printing or instruct the typesetter to do so.

Desktop publishing has become an all-encompassing term. It can refer to 14 Macintosh computers connected to a magazine's editorial and design departments; to an IBM user running *Print Shop 15* (Riverdeep) to produce a newsletter on an inkjet printer; or to an 8 year old creating a sign about a lost pet. DTP is no longer the exclusive property of the skilled technician or computer programmer. With a desktop publishing program, you can design a business newsletter, create a banner, or produce a school newspaper.

In the past, each student working on the high school or college newspaper was assigned a different task. Typically, there was a designer, a writer, an illustrator, a typesetter, and a paste-up artist. Now DTP makes it possible for one person to perform all these functions. DTP permits a student to

1. create on-screen layouts,
2. select among different typefaces or fonts,

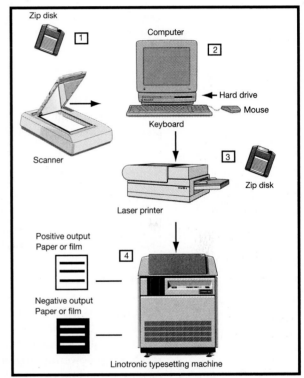

Figure 5.2 Desktop Publishing Process

From Crisp: Desktop Design 1st edition by LAMAR. © 1991. Reprinted with permission of Course Technology, a division of Thomson Learning: www.thomsonrights.com. Fax 800-730-2215.

3. justify text and lay out multiple columns,
4. insert art and text on the same page, and
5. print camera-ready copy.

There are many advantages to preparing student publications this way. DTP offers great flexibility in designing graphics and headlines and gives the user a great deal of control over the final product. DTP is a more versatile, faster, and less expensive way to produce publications than the traditional methods because fewer people need to be involved and fewer revisions are necessary.

As recently as 1985, there were few DTP programs, and the available ones, *Page-Maker* (Adobe) and *Ready Set Go* (Manhattan Graphics), were designed only for the Macintosh computer. Today, there are more programs to choose from, and they exist for all computers. The software and hardware that the student needs for DTP range in price from inexpensive to very expensive. If you want to print an informal newsletter, you might use a program such as *Print Shop 15* (Riverdeep) or *Microsoft Publisher* and a simple color inkjet printer. You also might use an advanced word processing program with desktop features like *Microsoft Word* or *AppleWorks*. If you are responsible for a business presentation, you might use expensive scanning equipment with programs such as *Adobe InDesign, Adobe PageMaker,* or *QuarkXPress* (Quark). Although the resolution from a laser printer is not as high as that from professional typesetting equipment, the resulting copy would be exceptional.

Desktop programs differ in degree of complexity, cost, and features. Let us explore some of the basic characteristics of these programs.

Basic Desktop Publishing Features

Although desktop programs differ in their sophistication, all of them offer the ability to (1) do page layout, (2) do word processing, (3) create style sheets and templates, (4) create and manipulate graphics, (5) manipulate the page view, and (6) create Web pages.

Page Layout

Page layout is the process of arranging various elements on a page. The process involves setting page margins, selecting page and column width and the number of text columns, and positioning graphics and text.

The most powerful programs, such as *Adobe PageMaker* and *QuarkXPress,* allow the greatest control in page design; however, these programs are sophisticated and come with a steep learning curve. Less powerful programs, such as *Print Shop 15* and *Microsoft Publisher* (Windows version), offer a wide variety of templates and wizards and require less learning time. *Microsoft Publisher* (Windows version) includes designs for flyers, newsletters, calendars, and award certificates (Figure 5.3). Once you select a template design, you can make all kinds of modifications to it with a click of the mouse. For example, you can choose among a variety of fonts and colors. This program includes websites and e-mail wizards and Design Sets. *Microsoft Publisher* is more complicated than *Print Shop 15,* but it lacks some of the more sophisticated features of *PageMaker* or *QuarkXPress.*

Word processing programs such as *Microsoft Word, WordPerfect, AppleWorks,* and *The Student Writing Center* (Riverdeep), include sufficient desktop capabilities to fulfill the desktop publishing needs of students from age 10 and up. Finally, programs such as

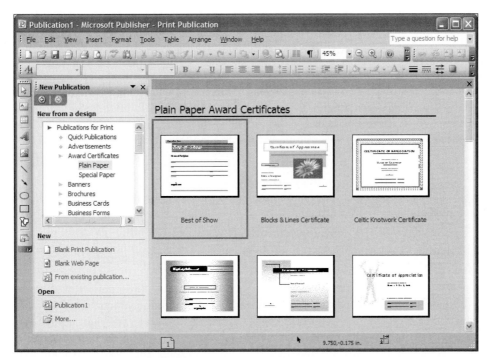

Figure 5.3 *Microsoft Publisher 2003* (Windows Version) Screen

Screen shot of *Microsoft® Publisher 2003* used by permission of Microsoft Corporation.

Storybook Weaver Deluxe (Riverdeep) and *The Ultimate Writing & Creativity Center* (Riverdeep) meet the needs of younger users. *Storybook Weaver Deluxe* features hundreds of graphics and sound effects from which students choose to create a story with music and sound effects. Students can then hear the text in either Spanish or English. *The Ultimate Writing & Creativity Center,* for users ages 6 to 10, creates reports, signs, journals, storybooks, and newsletters. Reports are limited to one-column pages, and newsletters consist of two or three fixed columns of text and a heading region that extends across the full width of the page. This program can read documents aloud and enables students to add animation.

In *PageMaker,* you determine the page size, set the margins, and choose the number of columns and the width of each column. *PageMaker's* master pages enable you to design a template for a document with measuring rulers and guides to help with the placement of graphics and text on each page. Like the majority of DTP programs, *PageMaker* shows a reduced-size view of a page or page spread so you can see it all at once on screen. Many present programs can resize, reshape, and reposition text or graphics, and they all feature automatic page numbering.

Most page-layout programs are based on **frames.** Frames are boxes that contain text or graphics. They have resize handles for stretching and resizing. If you want to put text into a document, you may place it on the base page, an immovable frame that covers the entire page. Alternatively, you may draw a frame with the help of a screen ruler. Once the frame is defined, you can import text or graphics into it. You also can stack frames or create captions that overlay illustrations. The desktop publishing program should allow you to create as many frames as you want and to put them anywhere on the page, stacking them and adjusting them as necessary. If you link text frames, you can add text to the first one, and it will overflow into other text frames, which is useful for newspaper layouts involving articles that continue from a column on one page to a column on another.

Word Processing

Word processor power varies among desktop publishing programs, but all DTPs can edit and format text to some degree.

Editing.   The majority of DTP packages enable you to enter text, edit it, and import documents from other programs. The typical word processing functions are *delete, insert,* and *copy.* The majority of DTP programs also offer a spelling checker and a thesaurus. High school students require *move, search,* and *replace* functions as well.

Formatting.   Formatting features, such as *type size, font,* and *typeface,* determine how a page will look. The more control you have over the text, the more professional looking your document. Many DTP programs enable you to center or align text along uniform margins, and some programs enable you to define the space between letters,[1] words, and lines to improve the readability and appearance of the document.

Style Sheets and Templates

A **style sheet** stores formatting that you can repeat throughout a document. For example, you might design a style sheet that puts page numbers in the right corner, two inches from the top of the page. Once you have created the style sheet, all pages in your document will automatically have page numbers in the right corner. On your style sheet, you can set margins, type style, line spacing, headers, footers, and quotation style for your entire document.

Figure 5.4 shows the dialog box you would use to define a style. In this example, the style selected is *Body text,* and it is defined as Times at 12 points, with automatic leading, flush left justification, a 0.333 first indent, and automatic hyphenation. To apply

Figure 5.4 *PageMaker* Dialogue Box

Used with permission of Adobe Systems Incorporated. Adobe and Pagemaker are either registered trademarks or trademarks of Adobe Systems Incorporated in the United States and/or other countries.

---

[1]*Kerning* is the adjustment of spaces between pairs of characters, so that the characters print in a visually appealing manner.

this style you would select the text you wanted to apply it to and click on *Body text* in the *Style* dialog box. The style sheet then automatically would be applied to the selected text. It would look like this:

> "The longest running-computer crime. Double-entry inventory control at Saxon Industries. A Fortune 500 company that reported profits of $7.1 million and $5.3 million in 1979 and 1980, respectively, it went bankrupt in 1982. A bogus inventory record was maintained by computer by Saxon's Business Products Division. It was used to inflate the company's annual revenues. The double books were kept for thirteen years, and the crime might never have been revealed if the company had been profitable. Saxon was $53 million in the hole when it went under" (Rochester and Gantz, 1983, p. 117).

Quite a few DTP programs feature their own style sheets, and others enable you to import style sheets from other programs. Many DTPs provide **templates,** which are pre-designed "molds" into which you can "pour" your text, and some companies enable you to create your own templates. Templates are time-savers because the user does not have to establish styles. The classroom template in Figure 5.5 is from *Microsoft Publisher* (Windows). This program is packaged with a multitude of templates for different uses.

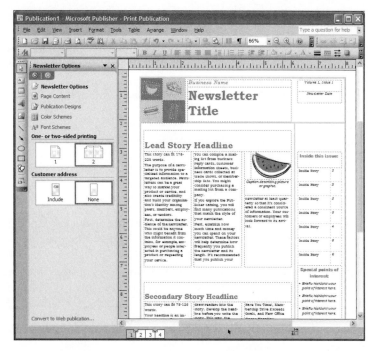

Figure 5.5 *Microsoft Publisher* Newsletter Template

Screen shot of *Microsoft® Publisher* used by permission of Microsoft Corporation.

Graphics

Desktop publishing programs enable you to add different types of pictures or graphics to text either by drawing them or by importing them. Even though graphics can be created in DTP programs, these programs rarely offer full-featured graphic capabilities. Typically, you need to create a graphic in a draw or paint program and then import it into the publishing program.

Tools

A desktop program usually features a variety of tools (Figure 5.6) for manipulating text and graphics:

- The item tool 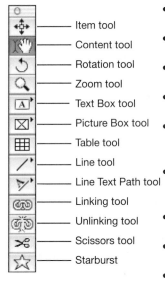 moves boxes, items, or lines on a page.

- The content tool manipulates the content within a box.

- The rotation tool rotates an item.

- The zoom tool enlarges or reduces the document view.

- The text box tool draws rectangle text boxes that are used to hold text. By clicking on this Tool, you have access to other text box tools.

- The picture box tool creates a rectangle box. By clicking on this tool, you have access to other picture box tools.

- The table tool creates tables.

- The line tool draws lines at any angle.

- The line text path tool will create text at any angle. This tool also gives access to other text path tools.

- The linking tool connects text boxes, permitting the flow of text from one box to another.

- The unlinking tool breaks the connection between these text boxes.

- The scissors tool cuts line segments.

- The starburst tool draws stars.

    Generally, DTPs feature tools for customizing artwork; reducing, enlarging, rotating, or flipping a drawing; zooming in for detail; and editing graphics, pixel by pixel. With some programs you can trace edges and change perspective, which is useful in producing halo effects around graphics, in outlining type, or even in converting silhouettes to simple outline form. With a DTP, you can crop or trim away part of an image and use it as a separate graphic. You can also repeat or duplicate an image. Figure 5.7 shows the

Figure 5.6 Tools from *QuarkXPress™*

Quark, QuarkXpress and other Quark, Inc. trademarks are the property of Quark, Inc. and all applicable affiliated companies. Portions © 2000 Quark, Inc. All rights reserved.

Figure 5.7 Dolphin Border Pattern

ClickArt Images © 1995. T/Maker Company.

same dolphin image duplicated in a regular border pattern. Make sure your DTP program includes a **text wrap** feature to take care of any graphic overlay problems caused by importing. This feature will wrap lines of text around a graphic without covering it.

Page View

After your page layout is completed, you will want to see how it looks before printing out the document. *The Student Writing Center* shows in reduced size what the page will look like. High-end programs such as *QuarkXPress* and *Pagemaker* give you a full range of **page view** magnifications.

Web Page Creation

Programs such as *QuarkXPress* and *Microsoft Publisher* offer Web capabilities. *QuarkX-Press* enables you to create Web documents with hyperlinks. These Web documents can then be exported as HTML documents and posted on the Web. They also can be edited in other programs such as *Dreamweaver.* Quark exports Web document pictures in JPEG, GIF, or PNG formats. Less difficult programs such as *Microsoft Publisher* feature website wizards that help you build Web pages.

Now that you have some idea of what the basic features of a desktop publishing program are, let us explore how to use a desktop publishing program.

Learning to Use a Desktop Publishing Program

This section gives an overview of how a desktop publishing program operates. It should not serve as a substitute for a program's operation manual. For illustrative purposes, we will use *Microsoft Publisher,* a good middle-school desktop program that offers many more advanced features than *The Ultimate Writing & Creativity Center,* a DTP program for grades 2 to 5. We will consider how *Microsoft Publisher* creates a layout, adds text and graphics, and produces a printout.

When you open *Microsoft Publisher* you are asked to select the type of publication from a list. You can create a document from scratch or you can use a "Wizard" or template to speed up the procedure. In Figure 5.8, *Newsletters* print template has

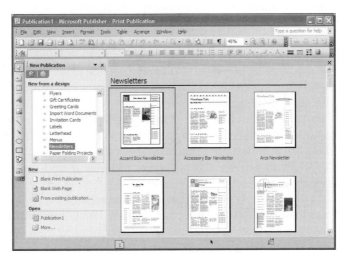

Figure 5.8 *Microsoft Publisher 2003* Newsletter Layouts

Screen shot of *Microsoft® Publisher 2003* used by permission of Microsoft Corporation.

been selected. You next select a newsletter design, in this case Accent Box News-letter. The dialog box now changes and the left side of the screen gives different op-tions for this newsletter design (Figure 5.9), ranging from page content to font

Figure 5.9 *Microsoft Publisher* Newsletter Options

Screen shot of *Microsoft® Publisher* used by permission of Microsoft Corporation.

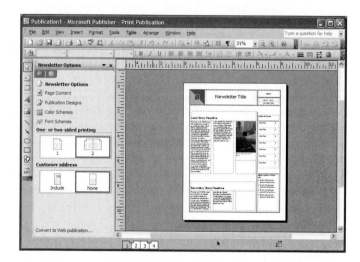

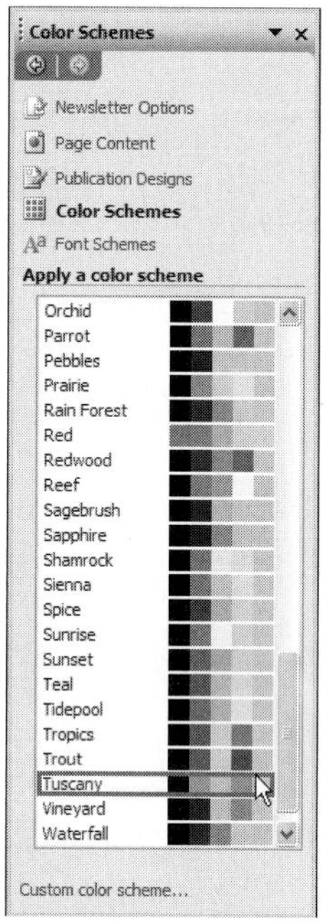

Figure 5.10
Microsoft Publisher 2003 Color Schemes

Screen shot of *Microsoft® Publisher* 2003 used by permission of Microsoft Corporation.

Figure 5.11 *Microsoft Publisher 2003* Picture Frame with Handles

Clip Art from *Microsoft® Publisher* used by permission of Microsoft Corporation.

schemes. If you decide to change the colors in your newsletter, you must select the color schemes option. In Figure 5.10, the Tuscany color scheme has been selected. If you want, you can experiment with different color schemes. While creating your newsletter, you also can change the margins, column size, borders, and page num-bers style. *Publisher* features layout rulers, drawing tools, work areas, and storage areas.

When you are ready to write text or import text and pictures into the document, you need to decide whether to use the program's word processing functions or to do your word processing in another program and then import the text into *Publisher*. For *Microsoft Publisher,* it is usually best to import your text in the form of text frames that can be moved as a complete unit. *The Student Writing Center* imports text from word processing documents in a **text-only format,** which means the imported text loses its formatting.

You may want to add graphics to illustrate a story; this usually means defining spaces or frames for the graphics. In *Microsoft Publisher,* you insert the picture you select from the Clip Gallery or from a separate file, that you scan or import from a digital camera, or that you import from another program. The picture then appears with eight frame handles around it (Figure 5.11). You can use the handles to resize it, move it, rotate it, or turn it sideways. *Microsoft Publisher's* Clip Gallery features hundreds of pictures covering a range of subjects; you also can import pictures from other clip art collections or pictures that you created with paint programs (unlike *The Student Writing Center,* this particular program includes painting and graphics tools of its own).

As you experiment with layout and importing of art, you frequently need to view the entire page. Activate the page preview function to display the document in a re-duced size that fits on screen, as shown in Figure 5.12. Many DTP programs include a zoom feature that enables you to see a close-up of small sections of the document.

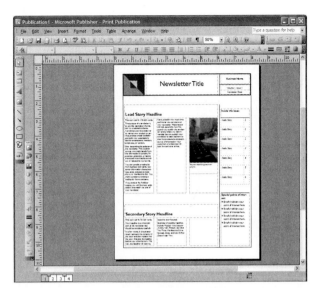

Figure 5.12 *Microsoft Publisher 2003* Page Preview Function

Screen shot of *Microsoft® Publisher 2003* used by permission of Microsoft Corporation.

The last step is to print the document either on an inkjet or a laser printer. The laser printer produces a very professional quality copy, but this output does not approach the resolution of that produced by a professional typesetting machine.

As you can see, using a program like *Microsoft Publisher* is not difficult. This program is appropriate for junior high and high school. *Microsoft Publisher* is less expensive and does not have all the features of a professional program such as *QuarkXPress*, which is more suitable for serious high school and college students. *QuarkXPress* is a more sophisticated program with which you have to make more decisions that are not as clearly defined. For example, when you open the program, the tool palette appears and you have to know to use the file menu to choose a new project. When the dialog box in Figure 5.13

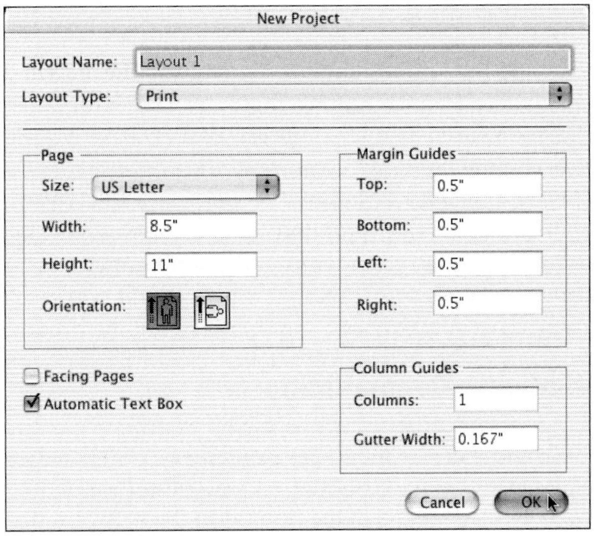

Figure 5.13 *QuarkXPress™* Dialog Box

Quark, QuarkXpress and other Quark, Inc. trademarks are the property of Quark, Inc. and all applicable affiliated companies. Portions © 2000 Quark, Inc. All rights reserved.

appears, you have to be knowledgeable enough to make choices about such items as number of columns, gutter width, and page size. You then import text and graphics into your blank document. After you are finished creating your document, you can view it in different ways such as a thumbnail sketch, at 50 percent of actual size, at 200 percent of actual size, or in a presized window (Figure 5.14).

Figure 5.14
QuarkXPress™ Preview Screen

Quark, QuarkXpress and other Quark, Inc. trademarks are the property of Quark, Inc. and all applicable affiliated companies. Portions © 2000 Quark, Inc. All rights reserved.

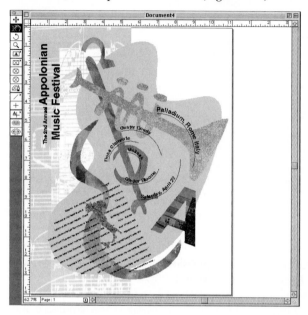

Although using a DTP program seems like a straightforward process, compatibility problems between programs will often arise. Some programs are much easier to use than others and import graphics easily, and others offer more flexibility and painting and drawing tools but are more difficult to use.

How to Choose a Good Desktop Publishing Program

Many desktop publishing packages are on the market today, and they come with every imaginable feature. Among these are DTP programs that lend themselves easily to classroom use, such as *Storybook Weaver Deluxe, Print Shop 15* (Windows), *EasyBook Deluxe* (Sunburst), *The Ultimate Writing & Creativity Center, The Student Writing Center, Microsoft Publisher* (Windows version), and *Kid Works Deluxe* (Knowledge Adventure).

To choose a DTP program for the classroom, (1) examine the program hardware compatibility; (2) consider the program's general features; (3) study the program's instructional design; (4) investigate how easy it is to use the package; (5) evaluate the program's cost effectiveness; and (6) check out the program's technical support.

Hardware Compatibility

Find out what computers are available at your school and whether they are Windows-based PCs or Macintoshes. Are these computers new and running the latest systems, or are they dinosaurs that are limited in the software they can run? How much memory does each machine have: 64 MB, 2 GB, or more? How large are their hard drives: 6 GB or 120 GB? What are the computers' processing speeds? What type of backup storage is available: a 750 MB Zip drive, a 2.2 GB ORB removable media drive, or something else? What other equipment is available: video digitizers, printers, multipage monitors, modems, CD-recordable drives or DVD-recordable drives, or scanners?

General Features

Next, consider the features of each program. How many columns can you create for a document? (*PageMaker* creates 20 columns, *The Student Writing Center* creates a maximum of 9 columns, and *The Ultimate Writing & Creativity Center* creates only 2 or 3 fixed columns.) Is the program a what-you-see-is-what-you-get (WYSIWYG) program? Can you enlarge or shrink the graphics you import? If you make a mistake, can you easily change it? When you load a program into the computer, what is displayed on the screen? Is there an untitled document with tools or an endless series of screens? How difficult is it to change the fonts and italicize or boldface the text? How many fonts are included, and can you mix type and font styles and sizes anywhere on the page? How easy is it to insert art in the document? What graphic formats does the program handle? What graphics tools are supplied to change the artwork that was imported or created? How extensive are the word processing features? Does the program have a find and replace feature; the ability to copy, cut, and paste text; and a spelling checker and thesaurus?

There are a myriad of features to consider, but the most important question to ask is, Which features are necessary? In choosing a computer for the elementary school child, the goal should be to find a product that produces pleasant results. The high school student or novice requires more features and more versatility.

Instructional Design

A desktop publishing program design should be straightforward. Programs with a menu bar displayed at the top of the screen are ideal for beginners who do not then have to memorize the different functions. *The Ultimate Writing & Creativity Center* (Figure 5.15) features such a menu bar. It clearly displays the choices that are available in this program.

Figure 5.15 *The Ultimate Writing & Creativity Center* Menu Bar

© 2004 Riverdeep Interactive Learning Limited, and its licensors.

Menu bars make it easy for any novice to change the font, add a picture, or use the printer. The advantages of programs such as *Print Shop 15* and *Microsoft Publisher 2003* are the flexibility of their design and the many options available for the user. *Print Shop 15* comes with an excellent manual and is easy to learn. *Microsoft Publisher* features a great on-screen tutorial that guides users step-by-step.

In looking at instructional design, you should ask the following questions: Is it a simple matter to make changes? Can you easily delete, add, or insert text? How fast is the general performance? (A program that is very slow can waste time—an annoyance if you are in a hurry to complete a job. For example, *Newsroom,* one of the first DTP programs for the elementary school, was a slow and cumbersome program.) How quickly can you change fonts, font style, line spacing or leading, and paragraph justification? What flexibility does the program have in printing a newspaper? How easy is it to access the program functions? (Programs such as *Microsoft Publisher 2003* feature keyboard shortcuts for many of their functions, so it is not necessary to use their pull-down menus.)

Ease of Use

The program must be easy to learn and must use simple English commands. Ask the following questions: Can a student in approximately 60 minutes learn to use this program? Do help screens inform users what to do each step of the way, and are they easily accessible? Is there a menu bar across the screen so users do not have to memorize the different functions? Does a tutorial disk or manual take students through the program? How difficult is it to figure out how to print a document? Can the printer be set up quickly? Is the program tedious to use because of too many help prompts and safety questions? Is there an automatic save feature?

Consumer Value

Cost has to be a major consideration in choosing a program for the classroom. *The Ultimate Writing & Creativity Center* can be purchased for around $48, whereas programs such as *PageMaker* and *QuarkXPress,* even with academic pricing, cost hundreds of dollars. To determine a program's value, ask the following questions: Does the program include templates and graphic art? (*The Writing Center, Print Shop 15,* and *Microsoft Publisher 2003* provide templates and art, which makes these programs better value for the money.) Are on-site licenses, lab packs, or networked versions available? (Software companies, at a special price, offer on-site licenses so that you can freely copy the software for in-house use. Other manufacturers distribute lab packs that enable you to purchase software at a reduced price. Finally, many manufacturers offer networked versions of the software so that a set of software can be shared among many computers.)

Support

Is the documentation accompanying the program helpful or bulky and unreadable? Can you call someone to get immediate help on the telephone, or must you wade through a series of messages and wait an unbearable amount of time? (Many software companies now tell you how many customers are in "line" before you and how long the wait is. When the wait is too long, some manufacturers ask you to leave your number and promise to call you back.) Do you have to pay a yearly fee or a fee per incident to get technical support? Is customer support available toll free or must you pay long-distance rates? Does a tutorial accompany the software package? Is the tutorial in manual form, is it on disk, or does it come both ways? (Many manufacturers provide both to simplify learning of their programs.) Is the manual readable and does it feature activities, lesson plans, and an index? How easy is it to get a refund or a new disk if the disk is defective? Is it easy to get an update to bug-riddled software?

Recommended Software
Desktop Publishing Programs

For a listing of recommended desktop publishing software, go to the Online Learning Center.

Desktop Publishing Program Checklist

Before selecting a desktop publishing program, consider the pupils' needs in the classroom. Determine what features meet these needs. Next, examine one of these programs using the sample checklist and evaluation rating instrument on page 105. After using this checklist a couple of times, you should be able to make a more informed decision when selecting software.

Desktop Publishing Program Checklist

Directions: Examine the following items and determine which ones you feel are important for your class situation. Place an X on each line for which the software meets your needs.

Product Name _____ **Manufacturer** _____ **Grade Level** _____

Hardware
_____ 1. Memory needed
_____ 2. Computer compatibility
_____ 3. Printer compatibility
_____ 4. Hard drive space
_____ 5. Computer processing speed

Features
_____ 1. Comprehensive undo
_____ 2. Page size selection
_____ 3. Adjustable column size
_____ 4. Page preview
_____ 5. Graphics
_____   a. Ruler guides
_____   b. Resize, position, crop
_____   c. Flip, rotate, invert
_____   d. Graphic importing
_____   e. File formats (EPS, Pict, GIF, JPEG, etc.)
_____ 6. Wraparound graphics
_____ 7. Word processing
_____   a. Insert and delete
_____   b. Find and replace
_____   c. Cut and paste
_____   d. Spelling checker
_____   e. Thesaurus
_____   f. Tabs
_____   g. Automatic pagination
_____   h. Hyphenation
_____ 8. Typesetting
_____   a. Variety of type sizes
_____   b. Different type styles
_____   c. Variety of fonts
_____   d. Kerning (spacing between letters)*
_____   e. Margin setting
_____ 9. Drawing/painting tools

Design
_____ 1. Speed of execution
_____ 2. Ease of graphics insertion
_____ 3. Simple saving function
_____ 4. Easy printing procedure
_____ 5. Number of columns possible
_____ 6. Type of page layout
_____ 7. Method of graphic importing
_____ 8. Formatting within program

Ease of Use
_____ 1. On-screen help
_____ 2. Tutorial disk
_____ 3. Easy printer setup
_____ 4. Minimal learning time
_____ 5. Automatic save

Consumer Value
_____ 1. Cost
_____ 2. Templates
_____ 3. Clip art included
_____ 4. Lab pack
_____ 5. Networked version
_____ 6. On-site license

Support Features
_____ 1. Technical
_____ 2. Tutorial material
_____ 3. Readable manual
_____   a. Activities
_____   b. Lesson plans
_____   c. Index
_____   d. Money-back guarantee

Rating Scale
Rate the desktop publishing program by placing a check on the appropriate line.
Excellent _____ Very good _____ Good _____ Fair _____ Poor _____

Comments:

Kerning is the adjustment of space between pairs of characters, so that the characters print in a visually pleasing manner.

Integrating Desktop Publishing into the Classroom

Teachers and students can use desktop publishing programs to produce a multitude of projects. Teachers can create worksheets, signs, flyers (Figure 5.16), posters, or other

Figure 5.16 Clip Art

Clip Art from *Microsoft® Word* used by permission of Microsoft Corporation.

graphic-based materials to display in the class. They can create a class newsletter to send home to parents. In addition, teachers can make brochures to promote extracurricular activities at the school. Students can use desktop publishing software to create minibooks, book reports, yearbooks, product advertisements, newsletters, posters, and flyers.

Desktop Publishing Programs for the Classroom

Let us quickly review a few desktop publishing programs in terms of age-level suitability. *Storybook Weaver Deluxe, The Ultimate Writing & Creativity Center, Kid Works Deluxe,* and *The Imagination Express Series* (Riverdeep) are early grade programs with desktop publishing features. *Storybook Weaver Deluxe* enables children to design and publish their own illustrated books. The children can choose from hundreds of graphics to illustrate their books. With *The Ultimate Writing & Creativity Center,* children can produce reports, newsletters, storybooks, and signs. The children can add animations to their stories, and the program has the ability to read documents aloud. With *Kid Works Deluxe,* a child can create stories with graphics. *The Imagination Express Series* offers rudimentary word processing features and bare-bones page-layout capabilities. Nevertheless, children can use it to create interactive stories by selecting background, scenery, and characters; by recording dialogue; and by adding text and sound effects. These programs have very limited word processing and picture handling features, but they are superior programs for the primary grades because of their low learning curve.

The Student Writing Center and *Print Shop 15* are more advanced and suitable for the middle grades because of their better picture handling and increased word processing capabilities. Although these programs offer improved features, they are by no means fully functioning desktop publishing programs. *The Student Writing Center* offers basic word processing features with a spelling checker. This program enables students to combine graphics and text to produce newsletters, book reports, research papers, journals, letters, résumés, and signs. With *Print Shop 15* (Windows), students can make banners, certificates, greeting cards, newsletters, brochures, postcards, and more. Students can incorporate headers and footers into documents and edit their work using a spelling checker and thesaurus. When students graduate from this type of program, they might try programs such as *Microsoft Publisher 2003,* which fill a void by providing additional drawing tools and word processing and page-layout features that are useful for the junior high school and high school student.

Finally, at the advanced high school, college, and adult level, professional programs such as *Adobe PageMaker* and *QuarkXPress* offer a multitude of features, file-handling capabilities, and flexibility. They are very expensive, but academic versions exist for these products.

Design and Layout Tips

When you look at a well-designed page you do not notice the separate elements but instead view the page as a whole. On this type of page the text and graphics are arranged attractively. In order to design this type of document you have to be cognizant of certain principles governing space, color (light and dark), and lines. A successful layout is the result of choices about balance, alignment, proximity, contrast, repetition, and white space. Is there a difference between headlines and subheadlines? Do narrow columns feature smaller type? Did you limit your use of white text on black, using it only to emphasize a letter or one word? If you boxed your text did you make sure you had large enough margins around the words so that they did not appear crowded? Did you restrict your use of fancy or unusual type to headlines only?

What follows are design guidelines for desktop publishing projects:

1. Spend time planning and collecting the items that will be included in your project.
2. Make a sketch or a rough layout.
3. Review what will be communicated. Who is the audience? What approach will be best for communicating the message? Be flexible and willing to experiment.
4. Look for consistency on each page of the document and check for balance of design.
5. Add interest when it is needed.
6. Organize a page around a dominant visual.
7. Pay close attention to borders and margins.
8. Provide a dramatic graphic for the front page.
9. Use forceful headlines to organize the writing.
10. Add emphasis to the work. For example, use a large type size to emphasize important ideas when needed. When necessary, vary the type style by using boldface or italics. Use blank spaces to make the designs stand out. Highlight the ideas with artwork, but do not overdo it. Help the reader's eyes focus on a particular part of the page.
11. Be careful not to clutter the page with too many elements. At the same time, use a variety of items to avoid boring the audience.
12. Do not use too many typefaces because it detracts from the general feeling of the writing.

13. Select typefaces that are easy to read, such as Times. Avoid typefaces such as Tekton.
14. Make type large enough so that any student can read it.
15. Use white space to focus attention on areas that contain information.
16. Make the design fit the content of the document.
17. Make sure the information is easy to find and not buried. Have it flow from the upper left corner to the right.
18. Balance related columns and facing pages. Make sure that facing pages and columns are aligned within approximately one or two lines of each other.
19. Make the size of the components on the page match the size of surrounding components.
20. Face artwork into the text.
21. Check the work thoroughly before printing out copies. Look at a printout to detect where finishing touches are needed.
22. When possible, place titles below illustrations and guide the reader with headings.
23. Do not overuse pictures and elaborate graphics. Remember, they are to convey information but not distract the reader.
24. Avoid excessive underlining, lines composed of leftover single words, unequal spacing, and cramped logos.

The books and articles in the suggested readings will provide more information about design.

Classroom Lesson Plans

I. NEWSLETTER DESIGN

Subject

English

Grade(s)

4 and up

Objectives

Students will learn some preliminary organizational skills and produce a simple picture with a few lines of text.

Standards

- NCTE English Language Arts Standards 4, 5, 6, 12
- ISTE NETS for Students 1, 3

Materials

You will need a desktop publishing program such as *Microsoft Publisher* and one or more computers.

Procedures

1. Ask students to bring newsletters, newspapers, and magazines to class. Distribute these items around the class.
2. Divide the class into groups of five and have each group clip text and pictures from the newspapers and magazines.
3. Next, instruct each group to choose a picture and a line or two of text and put them together to communicate a message. Students might choose a headline from an article, a graphic from an advertisement, and a line of text from an article, for example.
4. Now have each group use the desktop publishing program to translate its paste-up representation into print. Students will have to make some substitutions depending on the graphics available with their desktop publishing program.
5. End the process by having each group display its final design and discuss it with the entire class.

II. STUDENT STORIES

Subject

English

Grade(s)

4 and up

Objective

Students will learn some preliminary DTP skills.

Standards

- NCTE English Language Arts Standards 4, 5, 6
- ISTE NETS for Students 1, 3

Materials

You will need a desktop publishing program such as *Microsoft Publisher* and one or more computers.

Procedures

1. Ask each student in the class to write a story.
2. Discuss each story with the student and, as a class, make recommendations on how to improve it.
3. Have the students use their scissors to revise their stories.
4. Next, instruct each student to use the DTP program to enter his or her story into the computer.
5. Print out copies of each child's story for the entire class.
6. Divide the class into groups and have each group read and discuss the stories.

III. MATH STORIES

Subject

Math-Problem Solving

Grade(s)

2–6

Objective

Students will learn how to write math word problems using their DTP program.

Standards

- National Council of Teachers of Mathematics Standards: 1, 2, 6
- ISTE NETS for Students 6

Materials

You will need a desktop publishing program such as *Microsoft Publisher* and one or more computers.

Procedures

1. Distribute a math story similar to the one shown in Figure 5.17.

Figure 5.17 *Math Story*
© Dubl-Click Software Inc.

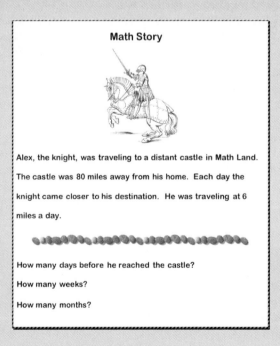

Math Story

Alex, the knight, was traveling to a distant castle in Math Land. The castle was 80 miles away from his home. Each day the knight came closer to his destination. He was traveling at 6 miles a day.

How many days before he reached the castle?

How many weeks?

How many months?

2. Ask the students to read and solve the word problems found in the story.
3. Next, ask students to write their own stories and related word problems.

4. After the students have finished writing their story problems, they should take turns entering these stories into the computer.
5. Have the students lay out and illustrate their stories with clip art, scanned images, or their own art created in a drawing program.
6. Use the printed stories as a math test for class.

IV. SCIENCE EXPERIMENTS

Subject

Science

Grade(s)

5 and above

Objective

Students will design their own science lab sheet and experiment.

Standards

- National Science Education Standards A1, A2
- ISTE NETS for Students 1, 3, 5, 6

Materials

You will need a desktop publishing program such as *Microsoft Publisher* and one or more computers.

Procedures

1. Help the students design individual experiments related to an overall classroom science topic.
2. Show students some sample lab sheets similar to the one in Figure 5.18.

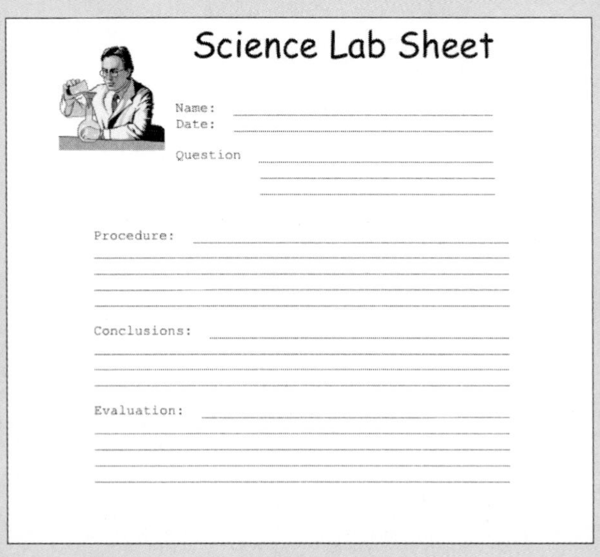

Science Lab Sheet

Name: _____
Date: _____

Question _____
_____
_____

Procedure: _____
_____
_____
_____

Conclusions: _____
_____
_____

Evaluation: _____
_____
_____
_____

Figure 5.18 Lab Sheet

Clip Art from *Microsoft® Word* used by permission of Microsoft Corporation.

3. Ask students to use the DTP to design lab report forms for their experiments.
4. Have students conduct their experiments using their own lab reports. After the experiments, discuss how the students could modify their reports for the next experiment.

V. HISTORY FIGURES

Subject

History

Grade(s)

5 and up

Objective

Students will create professional-looking stationery. In the process, they will learn how to write a grammatically correct letter and at the same time learn something about a historical figure.

Standards

- National Council for the Social Studies Curriculum Standards IIB and IVD
- ISTE NETS for Students 1, 3, 5

Materials

Students should have access to a desktop publishing program and clip art.

Procedures

1. Bring to class sample letterhead stationery such as that shown in Figure 5.19. If the desktop publishing program you are using includes letterhead templates, show these templates to the class.

Figure 5.19 WordArt
Stationery

Screen shot of *Microsoft*®
WordArt used by permission
of Microsoft Corporation.

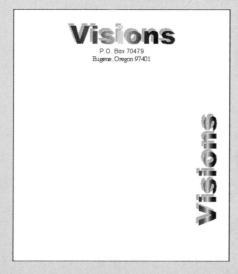

2. Ask each student to design his or her own stationery.
3. Discuss the results in class.
4. Next, have each student write a letter as a historical figure such as Abraham Lincoln or Clara Barton. When the students write this letter, they must talk about some of the problems the individual is facing.
5. Next, have the students choose appropriate pictures to illustrate their letters. Talk about the importance of visual appeal and pictures that correlate with the time period.
6. The students should then check their work for grammar and spelling errors and historical accuracy.
7. Discuss the letters in class.

VI. NEWSLETTER PRODUCTION

Subject

English

Grade(s)

5 and up

Objective

Students will produce a newsletter for the class using word processing, page layout, and graphics programs.

Standards

- NCTE English Language Arts Standards 4, 5, 6, 7
- ISTE NETS for Students 1, 3, 5
- National Council for the Social Studies Curriculum Standards VIA and VIC

Materials

Students should have access to a desktop publishing and graphics program.

Procedures

1. Bring to class sample newspapers and newsletters and distribute them to everyone.
2. Divide the students into work groups and assign each group a different writing task. For example, one group might write a news article on dolphins, another group might write an editorial on a controversial issue, and a third group might be responsible for a gossip column or movie reviews. Discuss with the students the process followed by journalists. Instruct them to determine who, what, why, where, and when in their reporting.
3. Have each work group write and revise its story.
4. Next, have the students write headlines and choose the pictures they want to use to illustrate their articles. Talk about the importance of visual appeal. Discuss how to be bold with headlines and how to place pictures effectively. The students

should plan their placement of articles early in the process. Check their work for grammar and spelling errors. Use the sample from *PageMaker* in Figure 5.20 as a model.

Figure 5.20 Sample from *PageMaker*

Used with permission of Adobe Systems Incorporated. Adobe and Pagemaker are either registered trademarks or trademarks of Adobe systems Incorporated in the United States and/or other countries.

Volume 2 Number 15 • April 25, 1992

Hill Resort to Open in Early May

Smooth Hill Resort, Hilson Properties' latest in a collection of comfortable family vacation spots, will open its doors in May of this year. Located in the Mustang River Valley, the resort is surrounded by the Hoosik Hills, which offer a variety of vacation activities year-round.

Smooth Hill Resort is reminiscent of a southern mansion, with tall white columns and gingerbread eaves, surrounded by manicured lawns and graceful willows. The resort features 180 spacious one- and two-bedroom units. Each unit sports 1-1/2 baths, 2 closets, cable TV, and a fully-equipped kitchen with dishwasher and full-sized refrigerator. Extra beds are available. Four restaurants offer variety: The Hilltop, for gourmet dining, The Captain's Table for family dining, and two snack bars, one at poolside. The resort offers child care references all year round. A small shopping arcade will meet the needs of most vacationers, including a drug store, clothing stores, and gift shop.

In the summer, vacationers can walk along 8 miles of marked nature trails that offer valley views. Nearby streams offer trout fishing with equipment rental available at the main lodge. Swimmers will find Smooth Hill's 2 swimming pools suitable for all family members, the olympic-sized pool for adults, and a smaller pool for children.

In the winter, the hiking trails become cross-country

An entrance reminiscent of a Southern mansion welcomes visitors to Smooth Hill.

skiing routes with three levels of difficulty clearly marked. Activities for children include cross-country ski lessons, and the annual Snow Castle Contest. Smooth Hill is located within an hour's drive a 2 major downhill ski areas.

For reservations at Smooth Hill, call Getaway at (555) 555-5555. Special introductory vacation packages available.

Weekend Scuba Diving in Niagara Falls

Fred and Harriet Brown were a just another professional couple until a recent vacation experience transformed their lives. "We had fallen into the patterns of suburban life—the same schedule, day in and day out; housework on the weekends. . .we never envisioned the impact this experience would have upon our lives," they told us excitedly.

Waterfall Scuba Diving is not new to the sporting world, although recent technological breakthroughs, such as oxygen tanks and diving helmets, have propelled the sport into an entirely new dimension. Early, more primitive,

forms involved holding one's breath while plunging over the falls in a wooden barrel reinforced with steel rings. Although a favorite activity among thrillseekers, this version of the sport soon lost popularity, probably due to a steady decrease in the number of available participants.

The recent fitness craze has transformed the tourist of the past, who was satisfied at merely gazing at the falls from a safe distance or remaining sedentary on a tour boat, into an active participant. Fred and Harriet now claim, "You haven't seen the falls until you've seen them from inside."

Weekend packages are available through the Great Adventure Travel Agency, including weekend accommodations for two, a hearty meal plan, scuba gear rental, and a hospitalization plan. For more information on this new sport, please contact Getaway at (555) 555-5555.

5. Ask students to use the DTP program to enter into the computer their articles for the paper. Make sure students view the entire document repeatedly to check its visual appeal.
6. After everyone is satisfied with the product, print out a copy. For later editions of the paper, rotate the tasks of the different groups in the class.

ADDITIONAL ACTIVITIES

The list of DTP activities is almost endless. Students can write historical, autobiographical, art, sports, or science newsletters. Find out where your students' interests are and capitalize on those interests. They can design awards, flyers, progress reports, questionnaires, and outlines for book reports. A sample award sheet created with *Microsoft Publisher* is shown in Figure 5.21.

Figure 5.21 *Microsoft Publisher* Award Sheet

Screen shot of *Microsoft®
Publisher* used by permission
of Microsoft Corporation.

Summary

The computer has changed the steps involved in publishing a newsletter, magazine, or book. What was done mechanically is now handled electronically. Desktop publishing has altered the way school newspapers, business newsletters, and advertisements are produced.

This chapter traced the historical beginnings of desktop publishing. In the process, we considered the merits of desktop publishing. We discovered how easy it is for a user to produce a newsletter or lab report with one of these programs. We became familiar with the basic features of desktop publishing and gained insight into what features to consider when selecting a program. A checklist and evaluation scale presented in this chapter facilitate this decision-making process. The chapter also offered specific ideas on how to incorporate DTPs into the classroom. We considered six DTP activities that cover a range of curriculum areas. Be sure to review the annotated list of award-winning desktop publishing programs located under **Recommended Software** on the Online Learning Center.

 ## Study and Online Resources

Go to Chapter 5 in the Student Edition of the Online Learning Center at **www.mhhe.com/sharp5e** to **practice with key concepts, take chapter quizzes, read PowerWeb articles** and **news feed updates** related to technology in education, and **access resources** for learning about technology and integrating it into the classroom.

Click on *Web Links* to link to the following websites.

About.com's Desktop Publishing Page
This site is an excellent starting place for articles about getting started in desktop publishing, design basics, software tips and tutorials, and classes for learning DTP.

About.com's Desktop Publishing Lesson Plans
This site features DTP lesson plans for the K–12 classroom involving brochures, résumés, and business cards and includes step-by-step instructions.

Desktop Publishing.com
The site is a premiere resource for clip art, desktop publishing, fonts, Web authoring, and information about uploading your page to the Internet. Also offered are free website templates enabling you to build your home page in minutes using either Navigator or Explorer.

Desktop Movies in Education
Desktop movies (digital video) allow you to develop stunning projects and activities with video (and audio)—right from your Macintosh. This capability can further the learning, creative, and communication environments of the K–12 classroom.

Desktop Publishing
Dr. Robert S. Houghton of Western Carolina University in Cullowhee, North Carolina, provides basic information about desktop publishing. The site places special emphasis on a tutorial for using a "fast-publish" desktop application and on

tutorials teaching the capture and manipulation of images for newsletters and many other applications.

dtp-aus.com
This site offers free online publishing tutorials for learning HTML and DTP.

Desktop Publishing Resources
The Davis School District, in Farmington, Utah, presents a collection of desktop activities and ideas.

DTP Zone
DTP Zone features a collection of tips and tricks for various DTP software programs including *PageMaker, Photoshop, Coreldraw,* and *Freehand.*

Mary Finlay's Desktop Publishing Course
Mary Finlay, a technology teacher at Adlai E. Stevenson High School in Lincolnshire, Illinois, presents the basics of desktop publishing.

Microsoft Publisher
Microsoft Publisher 2002 helps you easily create, customize, and publish materials such as newsletters, brochures, flyers, catalogs, and websites. You can publish on your desktop printer or directly to the Web.

Chapter Mastery Test

To the Instructor: *Refer to the Instructor's Manual for the answers to the Mastery Questions. This manual has additional questions and resource materials.*

Let us check for chapter comprehension with a short mastery test. Key Terms, Computer Labs, and Suggested Readings and References follow the test.

1. What is desktop publishing? Explain its importance in education.
2. Explain the difference between a word processing program and a desktop publishing program.
3. Name and describe three features of a desktop publishing program.
4. Discuss a few general rules to follow when creating a newsletter or advertisement using desktop publishing software.

5. What five DTP features are critical in producing a school publication? Explain why.
6. Discuss three uses of DTP programs in the classroom.
7. Does DTP software make the traditional methods of producing newsletters and books obsolete? Justify your answer.
8. What is a layout? Briefly discuss why it is important to take considerable time when creating a layout.
9. Explain in general terms the way a newsletter might be produced with a DTP program.
10. Briefly trace the history of DTP from inception to the present.
11. What are some of the software, hardware, and design requirements of a typical DTP program?

Key Terms

Desktop publishing (DTP) 93	Linotype machine 92	Page layout 94	Templates 96
Frames 95	Monotype machine 93	Page view 98	Text-only format 100
	Movable type 92	Style sheet 96	Text wrap 98

Computer Lab: Activities for Mastery and Your Portfolio

5.1 Create a Small-Book Make a small-book for a specified reading level.

5.2 Create an "Introducing the Teacher" Brochure Create a brochure about yourself and your teaching philosophy to hand out at parent night or send home on the first day of school.

5.3 Create a Template Create templates for transparency masters, student worksheets, signs, newsletters, flashcards, and more.

5.4 Develop a lesson plan using a DTP program.

5.5 Describe one DTP activity and show how a teacher can use it in a classroom situation.

5.6 Examine two DTP programs and compare their strengths and weaknesses.

5.7 Learn more about DTP by interviewing someone who uses a program. Have the individual demonstrate three or four features of the program. Identify any feature that is too complicated and then discuss some way of reducing the difficulty.

5.8 Read two articles about one DTP program and then use the program. Next, prepare a report that might persuade a school district to buy this program. In the presentation, discuss the benefits of using a DTP program.

Suggested Readings and References

Berman, Michael. "A New Desktop Publishing Contender." *Journal of Commerce* 423, no. 29671 (March 8, 2000): 6.

Braun, Ellen. "Word Processing, Desktop Publishing Share Features." *Office* 117, no. 5 (May 1, 1993).

Breen, Christopher. "Desktop Publishing for the Home." *PC World* 17, no. 1 (January 1999): 77.

Clark, Sandra. "Desktop Publishing: Alive, Well & Growing." *Media and Methods* 27, no. 3 (January 1, 1991): 42.

Ekhaml, Leticia. "Creating Better Newsletters." *School Library Media Activities Monthly* 12, no. 9 (May 1996): 36–38.

Ellis, Robert. "Creating a Studio Newsletter." *Clavier* 35, no. 3 (March 1, 1996): 27.

Fraser, Bruce. "Print Publishing Secrets." *Macworld* 19, issue 1 (January 2002): 74–76.

Goldsborough, Reid. "Making Documents Look Good: Eight Tips." *Reading Today* 16, no. 4 (February/March 1999): 11.

Guthrie, Jim. "Designing Design into an Advanced Desktop Publishing Course (A Teaching Tip)." *Technical Communication: Journal of the Society for Technical Communication* 42, no. 2 (May 1995): 319–321.

Hartley, James. "Thomas Jefferson, Page Design, and Desktop Publishing." *Educational Technology* 31, no. 1 (January 1, 1991): 54.

Kaye, Joyce Rutter. *Graphic Idea Resource: Layout: Working with Layout for Great Design.* Boston: Rockport Publishers: February 1998.

Krause, Jim. *Layout Index: Brochure, Web Design, Poster, Flyer, Advertising, Page Layout, Newsletter, Stationery.* Boston: North Light Books: January 2003.

Kramer, Robert, and Stephen A. Bernhardt. "Teaching Text Design." *Technical Communication Quarterly* 5, no. 1 (Winter 1996): 35–60.

Lamar, Laura. *Desktop Design.* Los Altos, CA.: Crisp Publications, 1990.

Luisa, Simone. "New Desktop Publishing Packages Heat up the Rivalry." *PC Magazine,* vol. 21, issue 7 (April 9, 2002): 32–34.

Lumgair, Christopher. *Teach Yourself Desktop Publishing.* New York: McGraw-Hill/Contemporary Books: January 7, 2001.

Maxymuk, John. "Using Desktop Publishing to Create Newsletters, Handouts, and Web Pages: A How-to-Do-It Manual." *How-to-Do-It Manuals for Librarians* 74 (1997).

McCracken, Harry. "Publishing's Cheap with Print Shop and Canon." *PC World* 17, no. 11 (November 1999): 108.

Mendelson, Edward. "Publishing the Easy Way." *PC Magazine* 16, no. 4 (February 18, 1997): 60.

Min, Zheng, and Roy Rada. "MUCH Electronic Publishing Environment: Principles and Practices." *Journal of the American Society for Information Science* 45, no. 5 (June 1994): 300–309.

Navarrete, Angela. "Complete Publisher '99." *PC World* 17, no. 4 (April 1999): 84.

Peterson, Nancy. "101 Expert Tips." *MacUser* 13, no. 8 (August 1997): 52.

Popyk, Marilyn K. "If Gutenberg Could See Us Now: Teaching Desktop Publishing." *Balance Sheet* 71, no. 3 (Spring 1990): 5.

Power, Brenda, "Strengthen Your Parent Connection." *Instructor* 109, no. 3 (October 1999): 30.

Sharp, Vicki. *Make It with Microsoft Office X (Macintosh).* Eugene, Ore.: Visions Technology in Education, 2003.

Sharp, Vicki. *Make It with Microsoft Office XP (Windows).* Eugene, Ore.: Visions Technology in Education, 2003.

Sutton, Jayne O. "Stepping up to Desktop Publishing." *Secretary* 57, no. 3 (March 1, 1997): 14.

Thompson, James A. "Producing an Institutional Fact Book: Layout and Design for a User-Friendly Product." *New Directions for Institutional Research* 91 (Fall 1996): 49–62.

Valle, Dwight, "Tools for Schools." *FamilyPC* 5, no. 8 (September 1998): 60.

Williams, Robin. *The Non-Designer's Design Book,* 2d ed. San Francisco: Peachpit Press: September 15, 2003.

Woody, Leonhard, Kyla K. Carlson, and Joel Enos. "Better Letters in Word." *PC Computing* 12, No. 6 (June 1999): 230.

CHAPTER 6

Databases

Integrating Databases into the Classroom

Teachers can use a database to prepare classroom materials, locate instructional resources, motivate students, locate student records, and send personalized letters to parents. Students can use a database to engage in higher-level thinking, develop research skills, and manage information. This chapter will examine how to select a database program for the classroom and consider the general features of a database program. A checklist has been designed to help you choose the right database software. Furthermore, exercises will help you integrate the database into the classroom. You will become familiar with Internet sites that include tutorials, software tips, and discussion forums.

Objectives

Upon completing this chapter, you will be able to do the following:

1. Explain what a database is and name its basic components.
2. Describe the basic features of a database.
3. Evaluate database software according to standard criteria.
4. Create and utilize a repertoire of database activities for the classroom.
5. Explain three methods of organizing data within a database.
6. Describe three different types of databases.
7. Explore relevant Internet site tutorials and searchable databases.

Teachers Can

- create a parent address/phone list,
- create a mail merge document for letters sent home,
- create a classroom inventory,
- create a weekly progress report,
- design a database for classroom management with students' reading levels, discipline problems or health problems, and schedules, among other things.

Students Can

- design an opinion survey database,
- create a dictionary of spelling words,
- construct a database of presidents of the United States,
- create a database of planets, animal groups, and rocks and minerals,
- develop research skills by using a database to search for information, and
- create a database of world events.

What Is a Database?

We are constantly bombarded with information in the workplace, at home, or at school. John Naisbitt in his book *Megatrends* writes, "We are drowning in information but starved for knowledge" (1982, p. 24). Since teachers cannot possibly retain all this information in memory, it is imperative that they develop skills in finding and interpreting data. Students also must master skills of organizing, retrieving, manipulating, and evaluating available information.

A **database** is a collection of information organized according to some structure or purpose. An all-encompassing term, *database* describes anything from an address book, recipe box, dictionary, or file cabinet to a set of computerized data files with sophisticated data relationships. To understand what a database is, you must be familiar with three terms: file, record, and field:

- **File:** A file is a collection of information on some subject. For example, a class studying birds may place all its information on this topic in a file labeled *birds.*
- **Record:** A record contains the information about one entry in a file. In our example of birds, a record would be information about a particular bird, such as the *hummingbird.*
- **Field:** Within a record there exist fields or spaces for specific information. The fields set aside for the hummingbird might include *beak type, scientific name, habitat,* and *migration patterns.*

The file cabinet, or database, in Figure 6.1 contains files that store information in a systematic way. A principal using this file cabinet at Clayton High School might

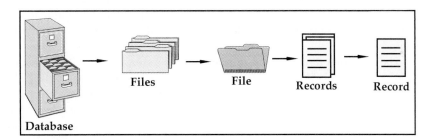

Figure 6.1 How a Database Works

© 2004 Riverdeep Interactive Learning Limited, and its licensors.

take a stack of files from the student information drawer. She searches through the files for the senior class file. This file contains a number of records, including John Doe's record. She scans the record for John Doe's telephone number. The record is organized into five fields, or categories of information (Figure 6.2): name, address,

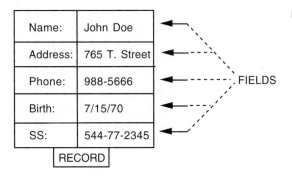

Figure 6.2 Fields

Name:	John Doe
Address:	765 T. Street
Phone:	988-5666
Birth:	7/15/70
SS:	544-77-2345

RECORD

FIELDS

telephone number, birth date, and Social Security number. She gets John's phone number from the telephone field.

In an electronic database, the information is similarly stored but on a disk. Figure 6.3 shows seven individual student records in *AppleWorks.* After she designs the format, or template, the record is automatically saved. Her record template is shown in Figure 6.3.

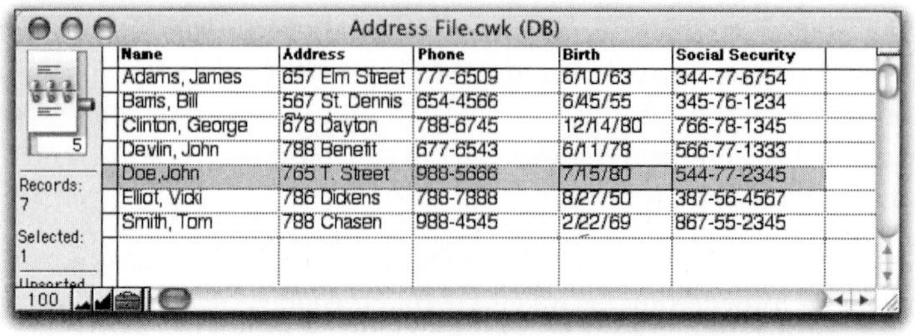

Figure 6.3 Sample Database

Images courtesy of Apple Computers, Inc.

Name	Address	Phone	Birth	Social Security
Adams, James	657 Elm Street	777-6509	6/10/63	344-77-6754
Barris, Bill	567 St. Dennis	654-4566	6/45/55	345-76-1234
Clinton, George	678 Dayton	788-6745	12/14/80	766-78-1345
Devlin, John	788 Benefit	677-6543	6/11/78	566-77-1333
Doe, John	765 T. Street	988-5666	7/15/80	544-77-2345
Eliot, Vicki	786 Dickens	788-7888	8/27/50	387-56-4567
Smith, Tom	788 Chasen	988-4545	2/22/69	867-55-2345

Advantages of an Electronic Database

The computerized database has many advantages over the file cabinet. Every database has a method of organization that enables a person to retrieve information using some keyword. For example, the database in Figure 6.3 arranges the address file alphabetically. The problem with the nonelectronic listing of this information is it cannot easily be modified; after too many changes, the sheets of paper become unreadable and need retyping. This is not the case with an electronic database in which the information is stored on disk.

The computer database also minimizes data redundancy; that is, the same information is available in different files. When a clerk searches through a file cabinet, he has to use his fingers to locate key files, which can take a long time. The electronic database user can generate reports, retrieve files, sort data in a variety of ways, edit, and print information with more flexibility and at faster speeds than can the file clerk. Furthermore, electronic files cannot easily be misplaced, and data can be shared easily among individuals. In addition, a user can execute a file search with incomplete information. With only the first half of a name and a brief description, for example, the police can use a database to search for a suspect. The only disadvantages to using a database are the time and effort expended in learning how to use it and the need to convert existing written files into the electronic format.

Computerized databases are used daily in government, occupational, and professional agencies. Teachers and students can choose among virtually thousands of repositories of information, such as Educational Resources Information Clearinghouse (ERIC), for their research work. ERIC, the primary database for teachers, is the basic indexing and abstracting source for information about education. For example, a student searching for *problem solving* in *primary math* would input these keywords to locate abstracts from recent papers on this topic.

Whenever there is a large amount of information to be managed, there is a need for **database management system** software. This software controls the storage and organization of data in a database.

How a Database Works

We will use *FileMaker Pro* as an example of how an electronic database operates, but this discussion should not substitute for *FileMaker Pro*'s documentation. Imagine that a teacher needs to keep track of the software she has accumulated haphazardly in a closet. The teacher wants to create a database to make order of this chaos. This particular database consists of one file simply labeled *Software,* which represents the software collection. The teacher must first determine the number of fields for the record. She designs a record based on library referencing techniques that includes five fields: Title, Subject, Company, Copies, and Grade Level. In Figure 6.4 the first

Figure 6.4 Selecting a Field

Copyright © 1994-2002 FileMaker, Inc. All rights reserved. Used with permission. FilMaker is a trademark of FileMaker, Inc., registered in the U.S. and other countries.

field the teacher creates is *Title.* After she designs the format, or template, the record is automatically saved. Her record is shown in Figure 6.5.

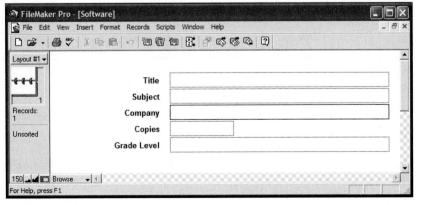

Figure 6.5 Sample Record

Copyright © 1994-2002 FileMaker, Inc. All rights reserved. Used with permission. FilMaker is a trademark of FileMaker, Inc., registered in the U.S. and other countries.

The next step is to enter the record data for each piece of software in the closet. A completed software file record is shown in Figure 6.6. The field *Title* has the entry

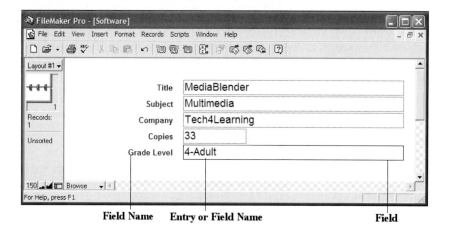

Field Name   Entry or Field Name   Field

MediaBlender, the field *Subject* has *Multimedia,* and the field *Company* has *Tech4Learning.* As the teacher enters the information, she has the option of adding or changing it. When one record is completed, she generates another. The teacher continues filling in records until she decides to stop or reaches the storage capacity of the particular database file program. When the task is finished, she has a database file that lists 10 records for the software file (Figure 6.7).

Title	Subject	Company	Copies	Grade Level
AppleWorks	Integrated Program	Apple	33	5-12
Grolier Multimedia	Reference	Scholastic	7	4-12
Inspiration	Concept Mapping	Inspiration	30	4-Adult
Math Blaster Deluxe	Math	Knowledge Adventure	4	3-5
MediaBlender	Multimedia	Tech4Learning	33	4-Adult
Oregon Trail 5	Social Studies	Riverdeep	3	5-12
Print Shop	Desktop Publishing	Riverdeep	12	4-Adult
Science Seekers	Science	Tom Snyder	14	5-8
Stickybear Reading	Reading	Optimum Resource	35	K-3
Ultimate Writing &	Desktop Publishing	Riverdeep	7	2-5

Now that the database is completed, the teacher can use it.

Retrieving Information

One of the major tasks of any database is to retrieve information. This can be accomplished in a variety of ways:

1. You can retrieve an entire file by listing this file on the screen or printing it out.
2. You can retrieve only a few field headings, such as *Title* and *Subject* (Figure 6.8).

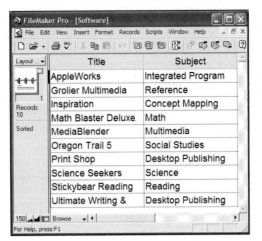

3. You can use a field to search for one record in the database. For example, you might type *Ultimate Writing & Creativity Center* in the *Title* field. Figure 6.9 shows this retrieved record.

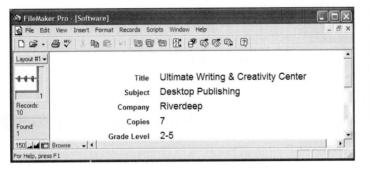

4. You can retrieve a record using more than one criterion, such as the company name and the grade level, by using **Boolean operators.**[1] For example, in this next search, the teacher uses the Boolean operator *and* to search for software that meets two criteria: (1) is a desktop publishing program and (2) has at least two copies available. The result of this search (Figure 6.10) generates two programs: *Print Shop* and *The Ul-*

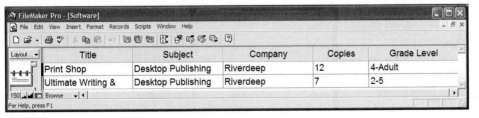

timate Writing & Creativity Center. The Boolean operator *or* enables the teacher to find records that meet the requirements of either criterion. In this instance, either a desktop publishing program or software with at least two copies available is acceptable.

[1]In arithmetic, the primary operations are *add, subtract, multiply,* and *divide,* but in Boolean logic, the primary operations are *and, or,* and *not.*

5. You can search for a record with **data strings.** There are times when the database user wants to search for a record and is not sure how to find it. For instance, suppose the teacher cannot remember the name of a publisher but recalls that it begins with *Sun*. A data string is a subset of the characters within a field. *Sun* and *burst* are data strings for the publisher *Sunburst*. To find the Sunburst publisher, the teacher need only type *Sun* as the field name to distinguish the choice from information in other records. This type of search is often called a **wildcard search.** The search usually uses symbols to represent any value. For example, an asterisk (*) will act as a wildcard character, and the word *Sun** will return documents with the words *Sunburst, Sunfield,* or *Sunland,* depending on what publishers are in the database. This type of wildcard use is the most common and is known as *right-hand truncation.*

Sorting Information

The other important function of a database program is sorting, the ability to arrange the records in a file so that the values in a field appear in alphabetical, numerical, or chronological order. Any field can be sorted, and sorting is done by field type. If the field has characters in it, it is sorted alphabetically, A to Z or Z to A. If the field is numeric, it is sorted lowest to highest or highest to lowest. Finally, a user can sort a field chronologically by date or time.

Types of Databases

Today not many database programs are available for the classroom. The programs available vary in price and capabilities. Some database programs are single purpose, whereas others are integrated. The *single-purpose program* performs database functions exclusively. It is primarily used in business contexts that require a database that is powerful and can hold many records. An example of a stand-alone program that is appropriate for education is *FileMaker Pro* (FileMaker, Inc.). *Microsoft Access,* a program often used in high schools, is sold as a part of the *Office Suite.* The *integrated program* offers other capabilities such as telecommunication, charting, word processing, and spreadsheet creation. An example of this type of database is *AppleWorks.*

Database software programs employ different methods of data organization. These include hierarchical, network, *HyperCard* (Apple), free-form or encyclopedia, relational, and flat-file databases.

Hierarchical Databases

The **hierarchical database** was one of the first methods of database organization developed for the computer. The majority of operating systems, including DOS, Windows NT, Windows XP, and Macintosh OS, use this file system to store data and programs. This database stores information in a top-to-bottom organization. Data are accessed sequentially through this database. In other words, you start at the top and proceed through the hierarchical levels. The database organizes data into a series, with the most general grouping first and the subgroups next. Each subgroup branches downward and can link only to the parent group. For example, a professor who wants to access a student's record must move first through the university, then the college, and then the departmental data before accessing the record of the particular student. There are two disadvantages to such a database. First, you cannot easily locate records in different sections or subgroups of the database. In the example just given, if you wanted to access another student's record, you would have to start all over again by moving first to the university level; there are no shortcuts. This method can be inefficient and time-consuming. Second, the hierarchical database requires a complete restructuring each time the user adds a new field. On the positive side, once the data are set up, searching is fast and efficient because you do not have to search through all the records; you just search through specific groups.

Network Databases

The **network database** works the same as a hierarchical database except that it permits a record to belong to more than one main group. This database is superior to the hierarchical database because it allows the user access to multiple data sets. Data can be accessed with speed and ease through different types of sources. However, networked databases still require every relationship to be predefined, and the addition of any new field requires a complete redefinition of the database.

Free-Form Database

A **free-form,** or **encyclopedia, database** enables the user to access data without specifying data type or data size. In this type of database, the user does not search for data in a field but instead uses a keyword or keywords. The software then searches all its text entries for matches. The advantage of an encyclopedia database is that a user who forgets the exact title of an article can find the article with only a single relevant word (Figure 6.11).

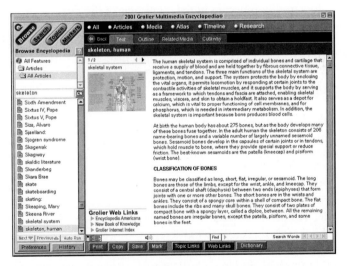

Figure 6.11 Grolier Multimedia Encyclopedia

Many of the Internet search engines use keyword searches. The main application of the free-form database is the online encyclopedia. The encyclopedia database maintains a large collection of information that is subject oriented. For example, an education database may group files according to different issues in education. You can then search by categories. Many of these databases are collections of data from other large free-form databases, giving users access to vast amounts of information. Typically these databases include such topics as news, microcomputer information, magazine articles, and medical information. *News* would enable you to access current news articles, newspapers, and information from news wire services. *Microcomputer information* would contain data from popular computing magazines. *Magazine articles* would enable you to access thousands of periodicals that focus on specialized areas such as medicine, education, and business. *Medical information* would give you access to medical journals.

HyperCard Databases

HyperCard, a multimedia program, played an important role in changing the way databases are used in education. *HyperCard* was the first program to integrate data organization with graphics. Using *HyperCard,* the teacher and student can create individual cards or screens of data with both text and graphics. They can then link these cards to produce a stack, or group of cards. The *HyperCard* stack is equivalent to a database. In education, the ability to create cards, link these cards, and produce instructional data is a very potent tool. We will explore other programs of this nature such as *HyperStudio* (Sunburst), *MediaBlender* (Tech4Learning), *Leonardo's Multimedia Toolbox* (NEC), and *eZediaMX* (eZedia, Inc.) in Chapter 8.

Relational Databases

A **relational database** enables the user to work with more than one file at a time. It helps eliminate data redundancy. For example, a department chair might need several different files, such as test scores and transcript data for a particular student. If each of these files is a separate electronic file, the chair would have to duplicate information for each file to make it understandable. The relational database removes this problem by linking separate files or even entire databases through a common key field such as the student's Social Security number. In relational databases, changes made in one file are automatically reflected in the other files of the record. The product *dBase* (Borland International) is a classic example of this type of database. This database is very useful for the administration of elementary, high school, and college records. However, the majority of classroom teachers have little need for this type of database software.

Flat-File Database

Classroom teachers want a simple, straightforward way of entering their data, and the **flat-file database** fulfills this requirement. It works with only one data file at a time, and offers no linking to other data files. This database does not permit multiple access to data files or advanced questioning techniques. There is variation among flat-file databases, but generally they do not allow merging with other application programs.

In the past, the administrative office of a school district was the only place in the district that needed a database; the office was where student records, personnel files, and school resources were kept. Recently, however, classroom teachers are using computerized databases to keep track of students' progress and to store anecdotal comments on individual students. Furthermore, students are using prepared databases such as the *Encyclopedia Britannica Deluxe* which includes a Word Atlas, and the *New Millennium World Atlas Deluxe* (Rand McNally, Figure 6.12). These databases provide users with a vast amount of geographic, historic, and demographic information. The *New Millennium World Atlas Deluxe* includes detailed three-dimensional maps and information on the role of geography in important world events. A notebook feature organizes historic, scientific, cultural, and wildlife information into presentations and school reports. There is a powerful search tool, along with Internet links to thousands of sites and geographic articles covering most important events.

The database is the perfect tool for teaching higher-level critical thinking skills, such as the ability to hypothesize, draw inferences, and use Boolean logic. Imagine that stu-

Figure 6.12 *New Millennium World Atlas Deluxe*

© Rand McNally. Printed with permission.

dents in a class are instructed to search a hypothetical database for the names of students who took Dr. Gallio's computer class. After the students develop a strategy, they perform the search and find out who the students are. The teacher then asks them to hypothesize how many female students received As in the computer class. This time their strategy is more complex, as they are looking for names of people who meet two criteria: (1) students who are female and (2) students who received an A. Following this search, the students are asked to draw inferences about the results of the search and conduct further searches to see if there is any correlation among other items.

Besides helping with higher-level thinking, a database can help students learn content material in any of the curriculum areas. Many databases on the Internet cover specific academic areas. An excellent federal government site is *Digital Classroom* (http://www.archives.gov/digital_classroom/index.html). If students understand how to manipulate a database, they can gain deeper insight into any field of study; they can find patterns, draw relationships, and identify trends.

Today, students can use database files that they create themselves or files prepared by teachers or software houses. It is often more beneficial for students to enter their research into a design created by their teacher. The mastery of databases takes longer than the mastery of word processing because, to learn databases, students need a good deal of hands-on experience and varied types of assignments.

The manuals supplied with databases include instructions on how to manipulate data, student worksheets, and suggested activities. Although schoolchildren cannot understand the logic behind database programs, they can understand some essential concepts such as record, field, and search. Nevertheless, it may be wise to save the complex searching for the junior high school students.

How to Choose a Database for the Classroom

There are many questions to ask when choosing a database program. For example, you will want to know how limited the program is in its ability to search. Can you easily add or change the data in the files? If there is a prepared database with the product, is the content proper for students? Is the information accurate? What is the quality of the documentation? How easy is the program to use? Let us examine these factors more closely for the purpose of understanding how to make more informed decisions.

The database packages on the market today offer every imaginable feature, some more appropriate for classroom use than others. The more popular programs for schools include *FileMaker Pro, Microsoft Works* (Windows only), *AppleWorks,* and *Microsoft Access.* Generally, these classroom-appropriate databases come with fewer features and are easier to use than programs such as *dBase 2.*

To choose a database program for the classroom you must consider six factors: (1) hardware compatibility, (2) general features, (3) instructional design, (4) ease of use, (5) consumer value, and (6) support.

Hardware Compatibility

Check out the computer that your school is using. Is it an old Apple IIe, a Sony with a Pentium IV chip, or a Macintosh with a G5 chip? How much memory does it have: 64K, 2 GB, or more? (Some database programs need a huge amount of computer memory.) How large are their hard drives: 80 GB or 1 TB? What type of backup storage is available? What printers will work with this database program?

General Features

The most common functions provided by database programs are (1) sorting data, (2) changing or updating data, (3) searching for specific information, (4) deleting and adding information in the file, and (5) printing.

Sorting.   **Sorting** is the ability to arrange the records in different ways. Programs should enable you to name the field type easily and do the sort quickly. At the very least, the program should perform the following: (1) an alphabetical sort from A to Z or Z to A, in any appropriate character field, (2) a numeric sort from lowest to highest and highest to lowest, in any numeric field, and (3) a chronological sort from earlier to later. No matter what program you choose, you should be able to sort to the screen and the printer.

Changing and Updating.   Every database can update and change a file. The questions that must be asked are the following: How difficult is it to accomplish this task? Is it easy to find the record and change it? How hard is it to add a record to the file, and is it a drawn-out procedure?

Searching or Retrieving.   Database programs vary in the type of search criteria used to find forms in a file. For instance, there may be exact matches, partial matches, numeric matches, and numeric range matches. In an exact match, the program looks for the forms that exactly match the search criteria. An exact match for Florence Singer is Florence Singer or FLORENCE SINGER; Mrs. Florence Singer; Singer, Florence; and FlorenceSinger are not matches.

All database programs have exact matches, and many database programs have partial matches. You would use a partial match when unsure of how the information was entered into the database or when interested in locating different records with the same information. For instance, you might be able to find Florence Singer's file by just typing in *Florence* or *Singer.* Or, you would use a partial match to find the records containing the names of students with computer experience.

The more advanced the database, the more exotic the features. *FileMaker Pro* (Filemaker Publishing Corporation), an advanced program for Windows and Macintosh, does quite a few numeric searches. This program enables you to look for items less than, greater than, or equal to a given number. If you want to find the records for all children who were born later than 1982, you would enter Year: >1982. This program also has a numeric range match feature that enables you to search for numbers within a certain range. For instance, you might search for dates within the range of 1988 to 2004.

The database program should let you search using multiple criteria as well. For instance, you might want to search for the names of students eligible to take your advanced computer course. You would use two criteria: (1) students who are in 11th grade and (2) students who have computer experience. At the end of your search, the computer would generate the names of students who fit these qualifications.

Searching a file in some database programs can change the file if you are not careful. Because of this problem, it is desirable to choose a program in which the *search* feature is separate from the *add* feature. The ideal program has a way to lock files so they will not be accidentally erased.

Deleting and Adding.   The database program should enable you to add information to or delete it from a record or field with minimum trouble. When you add a new field to one record, you want the new field to be added to all the records.

Printing.   Your program should allow you to print a neat report. The instructions for this task should be easy to follow, and the printout should show the data fields that you select for the report.

Advanced Features

Some programs enable you to design the way the data will be displayed. Some perform mathematical calculations on data. Database programs do not perform the complex functions of a spreadsheet, but they will total simple columns of numbers or compute student averages. Most database programs show the final list or report on the screen before it is printed. With *FileMaker Pro, AppleWorks, Microsoft Works* (Windows only), *FoxPro* (Microsoft), and *Microsoft Access* you can select fields for different records and display them on the screen all at once. Some programs enable you to publish their database on the Web, and other programs enable you to store a picture with each record. The advanced student can merge data from a database document with a word processing document to produce a customized letter or report. With the **mail merge** function, the computer will automatically place a name, address, and grade from the database into the word processing document's form letter. To produce a mail merge document, start by writing a basic form letter, the general text you want to send each person on your mailing list. In this letter do not include the name or address of the recipient or grades because these items will be inserted automatically from a mailing list. In their place insert placeholders, or merge fields, that tell your word processor where to put the items. Next, click on a mail merge tool. Select the list you want to merge, and the word processor will print one personalized letter for each record received from your mailing list.

Flexibility

The key to the success of database programs is their flexibility. How easy is it to make changes, and how easy is it to add a field or add information to a field in the database program? When you do, do you lose the information that already exists in the field? Does the database program make you start again when you want to make changes? What is the search speed of the program? What flexibility is there in printing a report? Can you be selective in printing certain columns or are you forced to print all the items as shown on the screen? What is the limit of the database? With *FileMaker Pro* you theoretically can have 100 fields on a page and a file size of 2 GB. Is there a size limitation for the information in each field? *FileMaker Pro* allows 6,400 characters per page or field, and *AppleWorks* allows a total of 1,005 characters, including the field name. Database programs vary in the kinds of searches they are capable of accomplishing—what type of searches do you require? Can you conduct Boolean searches? Does the searching technique fit the skills you are emphasizing in the classroom?

Ease of Use

A major concern in buying a database program is how easy the program is to learn. Its features are immaterial if it is difficult to comprehend. A database program should require minimum learning time. The program that displays a menu bar at the top of the screen is ideal for beginners because users do not have to memorize the different functions. *AppleWork*'s database is very popular because of its design and its collection of templates (Figure 6.13) that help you use the product quickly. The templates can be modified easily to suit your own needs. Just add or modify fields, layouts, or text when necessary.

Figure 6.13
AppleWorks Template

Images courtesy of Apple
Computers, Inc.

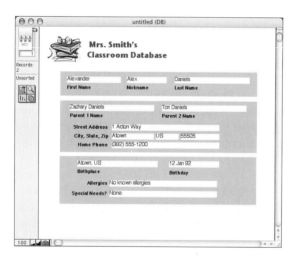

Before buying a program ask some questions: Can you learn in a reasonable amount of time to use this program? Is there a tutorial disk that takes the user through the program? (*AppleWorks* uses simple English commands and offers online help to teach you the program step by step.) Do help screens tell the user what to do each step of the way? Can you access these help screens whenever you need them? Are there menu bars across the screens so users do not have to memorize the different functions? Is the printer set up easily, and can you be ready to print immediately? Are there too many help prompts and safety questions?

Recommended Software
Database Programs

For a listing of recommended Database Programs, go to the Online Learning Center.

Consumer Value

Because software is expensive, cost is a major consideration. Since public domain software costs very little, it is a natural alternative to commercial software. For example, free software can be obtained in California through the California State Department of Education. Commercial software is more expensive, but many programs are worth the cost. Many software companies sell one disk that you can use to load the software on all your computers. Other companies offer an inexpensive on-site license that enables you to make as many copies as you need. Some companies offer lab packs of a large quantity of software at a reduced price.

Support

Support may be the thing that stands between a good program and your ability to use it. Can you call someone on the telephone at the software company and get immediate help, or must you wade through a series of messages and wait an unbearable amount of time? (As mentioned previously, many publishing houses will tell you how many customers are in line before you and how long you must wait.) Is the technical support available toll free? (Many companies are charging a fee for technical support.) Does the software package offer tutorial lessons to help the beginner learn the program? Is the manual readable and does it have an index? Does the program feature templates or computer-based files? Do the software producers offer data files for various content areas?

Before selecting the software, decide which features are important for your particular class. Next, examine one of these programs using the sample checklist and evaluation rating instrument in the Database Program Checklist form on page 132.

Integrating the Database into the Classroom

Teachers can use databases to help locate instructional material and to meet students' needs among many other things. For example, a teacher may categorize in a database the books and resources in the classroom. The teacher then can easily search this database for instructional material to motivate the class. The teacher might create a database to store student information such as birthdays, reading levels, special medication, learning problems, students' favorite hobbies, and people with authorization to pick up a student from school. The teacher could use an address database to personalize letters to parents.

Students can use databases for a multitude of classroom tasks. In language arts students might use a database to write book reports. For data fields, the students would include *Title, Author, Type of Book, Setting, Main Character,* and *Summary.* After the books are catalogued, students might search for books that meet their interests. A synonyms database could help students write poetry. Other language arts ideas for database files are diaries, famous quotes, funny stories, legal terms, novelists, and parts of speech.

Social studies is the perfect curriculum area to use databases. Students might create databases on countries, states, or famous people such as Albert Einstein, U.S. presidents, African-American politicians, and inventors and their inventions. There are all sorts of "Who Am I?" games that can be executed in the classroom (see the lesson plan activities at the end of the chapter).

In science, databases may be created for animal groups, birds, insects, snakes, plant groups (flowers, vegetables, trees), and rocks and minerals. Furthermore, students might create databases for food groups, calories, nutrients, amphibians, animal behavior, chemical compounds, chemical elements, fish, gems, geological formations, planets, poisons, and antidotes.

Database Program Checklist

Directions: Examine the following items and determine which ones you feel are important for your class situation. Place an X on each line for which the software meets your needs.

Product Name _____   **Manufacturer** _____   **Grade Level** _____

Hardware
- _____ 1. Memory needed
- _____ 2. Computer compatibility
- _____ 3. Printer compatibility
- _____ 4. Hard drive capacity
- _____ 5. Processing speed

Features
- _____ 1. Selection of field types
- _____ 2. Sorting
  - _____ a. Alphabetic
  - _____ b. Numeric
  - _____ c. Chronological
  - _____ d. Reverse order
  - _____ e. To screen and printer
- _____ 3. Changing and updating
- _____ 4. Searching
  - _____ a. Alphabetic
  - _____ b. Numeric
  - _____ c. And-or
  - _____ d. Using multiple criteria
- _____ 5. Deleting and adding fields
- _____ 6. Printing
- _____ 7. Calculation
- _____ 8. Mail merge
- _____ 9. Copy and paste
- _____ 10. Capacity to generate reports
- _____ 11. Publishing your database on the Web

Flexibility
- _____ 1. Speed of search
- _____ 2. Ease of changing fields

- _____ 3. Ease of adding new fields
- _____ 4. Size requirements
  - _____ a. Field size
  - _____ b. Characters per field
  - _____ c. Number of records in a file
- _____ 5. Display vs. printing
  - _____ a. Can display selected fields
  - _____ b. Selective printing

Ease of Use
- _____ 1. Help screens
- _____ 2. Tutorial disk
- _____ 3. Easy printer setup
- _____ 4. Automatic save
- _____ 5. Warning question

Consumer Value
- _____ 1. Cost
- _____ 2. Lab packs or on-site licensing

Support
- _____ 1. Technical
- _____ 2. Tutorial material
- _____ 3. Lab packs
- _____ 4. Templates
- _____ 5. Prepared software
- _____ 6. Readable manual
  - _____ a. Activities
  - _____ b. Lesson plans
  - _____ c. Tutorial
  - _____ d. Index

Rating Scale
Rate the database program by placing a check on the appropriate line.
Excellent _____ Very good _____ Good _____ Fair _____ Poor _____

Comments:

In the arts, students might use databases on artists, classical music, famous works of art, musical instruments, and popular music. Students might add pictures to any database to make it easier for the visual learner.

Teacher Practice Activities

The following exercises can be used in conjunction with any database. If a computer lab is not available, just follow this section to get an idea of what kinds of activities can be used in the classroom. The first exercise is a step-by-step introduction to a database program.

Database 1

1. Open your database program.
2. From the main menu, select the option that creates a file and gives the file a name, such as *Class*.
3. Type in the following field names: *Teacher, Students, Room, Grade,* and *Gender.* Correct any mistakes made.
4. Using the add-a-record function, type the information shown in Table 6.1 for each record.

Table 6.1 Practice Data

Teacher	Students	Room	Grade	Gender
Smith	23	21	K	Male
Adams	16	14	4	Female
Gramacy	17	25	3	Female
Witham	33	29	1	Female
Youngblood	21	24	K	Male

5. Add another record to the list: *Teacher,* Sharp; *Students,* 20; *Room,* 12; *Grade,* 3; and *Gender,* Female.
6. Change the name *Smith* to *Small* and his room number *21* to *24* and the name *Adams* to *Allen* and the number of students she has from *16* to *28*.
7. Next, delete the *Gramacy* record.
8. Alphabetize the list of records A to Z in the *Teacher* name field. The list should now look like the one shown in Table 6.2.

Table 6.2 Revised Data

Teacher	Students	Room	Grade	Gender
Allen	28	14	4	Female
Sharp	20	12	3	Female
Small	23	24	K	Male
Witham	33	29	1	Female
Youngblood	21	24	K	Male

9. Print out the results.
10. Next, numerically sort the field *Grade* from highest to lowest.
11. Search for the following records:
   a. Youngblood (type the name *Youngblood* in the *Teacher* field);
   b. Allen; and
   c. the kindergarten records (type *K* in the field *Grade*).

The program should find *Small* and *Youngblood.* The database shows the records that match the specifications you type. If there is no record, the program usually displays a 0. You also get a 0 if you spell the record name differently from the way it was spelled in the original entry in the database.

12. Search for records using two criteria: (a) teachers who are male and (b) teachers who have exactly 21 students. Type *21* for the *Students* field and *Male* for the *Gender* field. For this search, there is only one record: *Youngblood.*
13. Find the male kindergarten teachers' records. Type *K* for the *Grade* and *Male* for *Gender.* In this case, there are two teachers who fit these criteria: *Small* and *Youngblood.*
14. If the database program has a greater than (>) or less than (<) feature, find the following records:
   a. all the teachers who have a class size greater than 20;
   b. the male teachers who have 23 or more students; and
   c. the female teachers who have 18 or more students.

Database 2

For practice, create another database. Type in the following field names: *Student, Gender, Hair color,* and *Birth date.*

1. Using the add function, type the information shown in Table 6.3 for each record.

Table 6.3 Student Data Sheet

Pupil	Gender	Hair Color	Birth Date
Smith, Joan	Female	Brown	1975
Lorenzo, Max	Male	Black	1977
Chen, Mark	Male	Black	1978
Sharp, David	Male	Brown	1977
Schainker, Nancy	Female	Red	1976
Edwards, Bobbie	Female	Blond	1979
Lopez, Mary	Female	Black	1980
Jefferson, LeMar	Male	Black	1979
Jung, Nicky	Female	Red	1979

2. Change the field name *Pupil* to *Student.*
3. Next, change David Sharp's birth date to 1950, Nicky Jung's description to *Male* with *Black* hair, and Bobbie Edwards's *Hair color* to *Red.*
4. Add the following file: *Student,* Lee, Bessie; *Hair color,* Brown; *Gender,* Female; *Birth date,* 1980.

5. Alphabetize the list A to Z in the *Student* field and print out the list.
6. Find the following files:
   a. David Sharp;
   b. all students who are female;
   c. students who have red hair;
   d. students born after 1950;
   e. students born before 1977; and
   f. all students who are female and have red hair.

Classroom Lesson Plans

I. PLANETS

Subject

Science

Grade(s)

5–12

Objective

Students will use a database program to create a scientific database like the one in Table 6.4.

Table 6.4 Planet Data

Planet	Diameter (miles)	Distance from Sun (millions of miles)	Satellites	Rings	Atmosphere	Rotation Around the Sun	Rotation on its Own Axis
Earth	7,926.2	92.9	1	0	Water (70%), air, and solid ground	365.2 days	23 hrs, 56 min, 4 sec
Jupiter	88,736	483.88	16	1	Colored dust, hydrogen, helium, methane, water, and ammonia	12 Earth years	9 hrs, 55 min
Mars	4,194	141.71	2	0	Carbon dioxide (95%)	687 Earth days	24 Earth hrs, 37 min, 23 sec
Mercury	3,032.4	36	0	0	Helium (95%) and hydrogen	88 Earth days	59 Earth days
Neptune	30,775	2,796.46	8	4	Hydrogen, helium, methane, and ammonia	165 Earth years	16 hrs, 7 min
Pluto	1,423	3,666	1	?	Methane	248 Earth years	6 days, 9 hrs, 18 min
Saturn	74,978	887.14	19	1,000	Hydrogen and helium	29.5 Earth years	10 hrs, 40 min, 24 sec
Uranus	32,193	1,783.98	17	11	Hydrogen, helium, and methane	84 Earth years	17 hrs
Venus	7,519	67.24	0	0	Carbon dioxide (95%), nitrogen, sulfuric acid, other elements	225 Earth days	243 Earth days

Standards

- National Science Education Standards A1, A2, C3, D1, D2
- ISTE NETS for Students 1, 3, 4, 5

Materials

You will need a database program such as *Microsoft Access* or *FileMaker Pro* and one or more computers.

Procedures

1. Divide the class into small groups.
2. Ask each group of students to create a scientific database. Give them a list of topics from which to choose, such as *planets, dinosaurs, and presidents.*
3. Have the students research their topics using books or the Internet.
4. Instruct each group to create cards that look like the one in Figure 6.14.

Figure 6.14 Planets Database

Screen shot of *Microsoft®* *Access* used by permission of Microsoft Corporation.

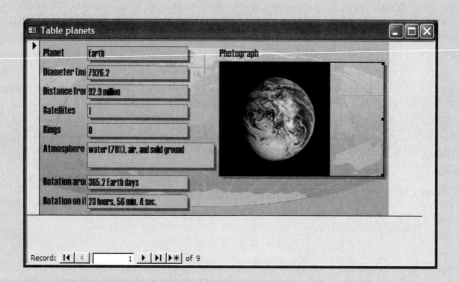

5. Each group should make up a list of 10 questions for their database.
6. After the databases are created, have the groups exchange questions and databases.
7. Give the class a time limit to find answers to their 10 questions.

II. DOING A BOOK REPORT

Subject

Language Arts

Grade(s):

2–6

Objectives

Students will create a database book report file, learn to sort alphabetically, and read a book.

Standards

- NCTE English Language Arts Standards 2, 3, 5, 6
- ISTE NETS for Students 1, 3, 5, 6

Materials

You will need the Book Report Form, a database program (*FileMaker Pro, Microsoft Access, AppleWorks, Microsoft Works,* etc.), and one or more computers.

Procedures

1. Have each student read a book.
2. After the reading assignment is finished, have each student complete the book report form (shown in Table 6.5).

Table 6.5 Book Report Form

Student's name _____
1. Author:
2. Title:
3. Type of book:
4. Setting:
5. Main character of the story:
6. Summary of the story:

3. Instruct students to input their information under each field name on the same data file disk. This activity requires a database program that has a *Comment* field. If the database program does not have this feature, eliminate this field name.
4. After this task has been completed, have the students do the following:
   a. Search for books they might like to read, using the search function.
   b. Print out a list of all the books in the database.
   c. Sort the database alphabetically by title and print out the list.
   d. Sort the database file alphabetically by author and print out the list.
   e. Find out how many students read baseball stories or biographies by using the find function of the database program.

III. FINDING OUT ABOUT DINOSAURS

Subject

Science

Grade(s)

5–8

Objectives

Students will create a dinosaur database, learn about dinosaurs, sort alphabetically, practice using Boolean operators, and sort by number.

Standards

- National Science Education Standards A1, A2, C1, C3
- ISTE NETS for Students 1, 3, 4, 5, 6

Materials

You will need the Dinosaur Database Form, a database program (*FileMaker Pro, Apple-Works, Microsoft Works,* etc.), and one computer or more.

Procedures

1. Have each student read about a dinosaur.
2. After the reading assignment is completed, have each student fill out the dinosaur database form shown in Table 6.6.

Table 6.6 Dinosaur Database Form

Name	Habitat	Food	Feet	Armored

3. Instruct each student to enter his or her information on the same data file disk. Table 6.7 shows a sample Dinosaur Database Form that has been completed.

Table 6.7 Sample Dinosaur Database Form

Name	Habitat	Food	Feet	Armored
Ankylosaurus	Land	Plants	4	Yes
Tryannosaurus	Land	Meat	2	No
Brachiosaurus	Water-Swamp	Plants	4	No
Apatosaurus	Water-Swamp	Plants	4	No
Corythosaurus	Water-Swamp	Plants	2	No
Diplodocus	Water-Swamp	Plants	4	No
Iguanodon	Land	Plants	2	No
Protoceratops	Land	Plants	4	Yes
Stegosaurus	Land	Plants	4	Yes
Coelophysis	Land	Meat	2	No

4. After this task has been completed, have the students do the following:
 a. Sort the file by the number of feet in the field, highest to lowest.
 b. Using the Boolean operator *and,* find out if there are any two-legged plant eaters and any four-legged meat eaters.
 c. Sort alphabetically by name and print out the list.

Variation

Have students add fields such as *Weight, Height,* and *Nickname* and sort the fields by (1) length (lowest to highest), (2) weight, and (3) characteristics.

IV. STATE SHEET

Subject

Social Studies

Grade(s)

3–8

Objectives

Students will create a geographical data file for each state, learn geographical information about each state, sort the data alphabetically, and search using the Boolean operators *and* and *or.*

Standards

* National Council for the Social Studies Curriculum Standards 3, 5
* ISTE NETS for Students 1, 3, 4, 5

Materials

You will need the State Geographical Sheet, a database program (*FileMaker Pro, AppleWorks, Microsoft Access, Microsoft Works,* etc.), and one or more computers.

Procedures

1. Have each student in the class choose a state to research.
2. Have the students use reference books or the Internet to complete the State Geographical Sheet shown in Table 6.8.

Table 6.8 State Geographical Sheet

Field Name	Data
1. Location (Midwest, Northeast, etc.)	
2. Size (Square Miles)	
3. Natural resources	
4. Climate	
5. Terrain (Desert, Mountains, etc.)	

3. Have the students enter the proper information under each field name on the data file disk.
4. After this task has been completed, have the students independently use the search function to answer *Who am I?* questions such as those shown in Table 6.9.

Table 6.9 Who Am I? Questions

1. I am a small state.
2. I am known for my mountains.
3. I have red clover flowers.

V. STATES

Subject

Social Studies

Grade(s)

4–12

Objectives

Students will create a state data file, learn statistical information about the United States, sort alphabetically, and search using the Boolean operators *and* and *or*.

Standards

- National Council for the Social Studies Curriculum Standards 3, 5
- ISTE NETS for Students 1, 3, 4, 5

Materials

You will need the State Data Sheet, a database program (*FileMaker Pro, AppleWorks, Microsoft Works, Microsoft Access,* etc.), and one computer or more.

Procedures

1. Have each student in the class choose a state to research.
2. Have the students use encyclopedias or the Internet to complete the State Data Sheet shown in Table 6.10.

Table 6.10 State Data Sheet

Field Name	Data
1. Capital	
2. Population	
3. Number of representatives in Congress	
4. Year of statehood	

3. Have the students enter the proper information under each field name on the same data file disk.
4. After this task has been completed, have the students independently use the search function to carry out the following tasks:
   a. Search for the states that have populations over 2 million.
   b. Find the last state that was added to the United States.
   c. Sort the records according to population from lowest to highest.
   d. Sort the records alphabetically by the name of the state and print out a list.
   e. Sort the states by population and print out a list.
5. Next, divide the class into two teams and collect each team's State Data Sheet.
6. Read aloud one of the State Data Sheets without revealing the name of the state.
7. Ask Team One to try to figure out what state the data sheet describes.
8. Ask Team Two to check Team One's answer by using the computer. If Team One has answered correctly, it scores a point.
9. Read another data sheet.
10. Ask Team Two to try to identify the state and Team One to check Team Two's answer. The first team to reach 10 points wins.

VI. MUSIC

Subject

Arts

Grade(s)

3–12

Objectives

Students will learn how to create a database by cataloging their own music CD collection or the school's CD collection and they will find information using certain criteria.

Standards

- ISTE NETS for Students 1, 2, 3, 5

Materials

You will need a database program (*FileMaker Pro, AppleWorks, Microsoft Works,* etc.) and one or more computers.

Procedures

1. Ask the class to decide which fields they are going to use to create their database. For example, they could use *Artist, Title, Description, and Style of music.*
2. Have the students create their own database using their CD collection at home or school.
3. After the databases are created, have the students do the following:
   a. Find their favorite performer.
   b. Find the CDs that are rock and roll.
   c. Find female vocalists only.
   d. Find male vocalists only.
4. Next, have each student share his or her database with another member of the class.

Summary

The database is an effective manager of information and a powerful tool for learning in the classroom. With a database, students can look for relationships among data, test hypotheses, and draw conclusions. This chapter discussed the merits of an electronic database and its basic features. We examined a database checklist evaluation form and learned how to introduce the database to the class. Classroom activities covered a range of curriculum areas. Be sure to review the annotated list of award-winning database software in the Online Learning Center.

 # Study and Online Resources

*Go to Chapter 6 in the Student Edition of the Online Learning Center at **www.mhhe.com/sharp5e** to **practice with key concepts, take chapter quizzes, read PowerWeb articles** and **news feed updates** related to technology in education, and **access resources** for learning about technology and integrating it into the classroom.*

Click on *Web Links* to link to the following websites.

About.com's Database for Beginners

Database for Beginners provides *Access* and *FileMaker Pro* tutorials and explains how the contents of organized data can easily be accessed, managed, and updated.

Access All Areas (A3)

Access All Areas provides help for *Microsoft Access* users. The site includes basic database information, reviews, and discussion forums.

Activity Search

The Education Place Activity Search, sponsored by Houghton Mifflin, is a searchable database of over 500 original K–8 classroom activities and lesson plans for teachers in all subject areas.

Digital Classroom

The federal government's National Archives and Records Administration (NARA) offers a searchable database of historical documents useful for Social Studies teaching.

FileMaker Today

This popular *FileMaker Pro* users site offers free *FileMaker Pro* training, templates, plug-ins, and the latest news from the FileMaker community. It also features the FileMaker Cafe, a *FileMaker Pro* question-and-answer forum.

Introducing *AppleWorks 6*

This site offers information on the latest version of *AppleWorks,* which features word processing, spreadsheet, database, presentation, and drawing and painting capabilities.

Tammy's Technology Tips for Teachers

This site shows how to use a database and other computer tools to make classroom management tasks easier.

What is?com

This site includes thousands of explanations of computer and software terms including *relational* and *object-oriented databases.*

Chapter Mastery Test

To the Instructor: *Refer to the Instructor's Manual for the answers to the Mastery Questions. This manual has additional questions and resource materials.*

Let us check for chapter comprehension with a short mastery test. Key Terms, Computer Lab, and Suggested Readings and References follow the test.

1. What is a database and how can it be used in the classroom?
2. Define the following: *file, record,* and *field.*
3. Name and describe two ways of sorting data.
4. What differentiates a file cabinet from a database?
5. What are three ways you would use a database to help your teaching?
6. Discuss the factors involved in selecting a database for a school district.
7. Name and describe three ways of searching for a file.
8. When should a student use a wildcard search?
9. Explain three methods of organizing data within a database.
10. What is a relational database?
11. Name two common functions of a database.
12. What is a free-form database?

Key Terms

Computer Lab: Activities for Mastery and Your Portfolio

6.1 **Create a Parent Database**   Create a database of parent information. Run reports, make queries, print address labels, and more.

6.2 **Create a Field Trip Information Database**   Create a database of information on cultural, scientific, and civic institutions in your area that might make for interesting trips or that might send educators to your school.

6.3 **Create a Library Database**   Create a database of information about the books in your classroom library.

6.4 Create a database file on famous composers.

6.5 Examine three database programs and compare their different features.

6.6 Choose a grade level and create a database activity for it.

Suggested Readings and References

Adams, Sharon, and Mary Burns. ERIC ED428759 *Connecting Student Learning and Technology.* 1999.

Anders, Vicki, and Kathy M. Jackson. "Onliners. CD-ROM—The Impact of CD-ROM Databases upon a Large Online Searching Program." *Online* 12, no. 6 (November 1, 1988): 24.

Antonoff, Michael. "Using a Spreadsheet as a Database." *Personal Computing,* 1986, 65–71.

Bachor, D. G. "Toward Improving Assessment of Students with Special Needs: Expanding the Database to Include Classroom Performance." *Alberta Journal of Educational Research* 36, no. 1 (March 1, 1990): 65.

Barbour, A. "A Cemetery Database Makes Math Come Alive." *Electronic Learning,* February 1988, 12–13.

Bensu, Janet. "Use Your Database in New Ways." *HR Magazine* 35, no. 3 (March 1, 1990): 33.

Bergen, Doris. "Differentiating Curriculum with Technology-Enhanced Class Projects. Technology in the Classroom." *Childhood Education* 78, no. 2 (Winter 2001–2002): 117–118.

Bernard, Deborah F., and Yolanda Hollingsworth. "Teaching Web-Based Full-Text Databases." *Reference & User Services Quarterly* 39, no. 1 (Fall 1999): 63.

Bock, Douglas B. "Solving Crime with Database Technology." *Journal of Systems Management* 39, no. 10 (October 1, 1988): 16.

Braun Jr., Joseph A. "Ten Ways to Integrate Technology into Middle School Social Studies." *Clearing House* 72, no. 6 (July 1999): 345–351.

Byers, John A. "Database Program to Manage Slides and Images for Teaching and Presentations." *Educational Media International* 36, no. 1 (March 1999): 77–80.

Caughlin, Janet. *Access Workshop for Teachers.* New York: Scholastic Books, 2002.

Coe, Michael. "Keeping up with Technology." *Computing Teacher* 18, no. 5 (February 1991): 14–15.

Davey, Claire, and Adrian S. Jarvis. "Microcomputers for MicroHistory: A Database Approach to the Reconstitution of Small English Populations." *History & Computing* 2, no. 3 (1990): 187.

Dunfey, J. "Using a Database in an English Classroom." *Computing Teacher* 12, no. 8 (1984): 26–27.

"Electronic Databases." *Media & Methods* 36, no. 4 (March/April 2000): 39.

Ennis, Demetria. "Interdisciplinary Database Activities for Fifth Graders at Tomas Rivera." *Journal of Computing in Childhood Education* 8, no. 1 (1997): 83–88.

Epler, D. M. *Online Searching Goes to School.* Phoenix, Ariz.: Oryx Press, 1989.

Fagan, Patsy J., and Ann D. Thompson. "Using a Database to Aid in Learning the Meanings and Purposes of Math Notations and Symbols." *Journal of Computers in Mathematics and Science* 8, no. 4 (Summer 1989): 26.

Ferraro, Joan M. "Teacher Education Reform: An ERIC Bibliography." *Journal of Teacher Education* 50, no. 4 (September/October 1999): 315.

Flynn, Marilyn L. "Using Computer-Assisted Instruction to Increase Organizational Effectiveness." *Administration in Social Work* 14, no. 1 (Winter 1990): 103.

Hane, Paula J. "New FileMaker Pro 6 Provides Integrated XML Support." *Information Today* 19, issue 8 (September 2002): 37–40.

Hannah, L. "The Database: Getting to Know You." *Computing Teacher,* June 1987, 16–23.

Hodson, Yvonne D., and David Leibelshon. "Creating Databases with Students." *School Library Journal* 32 (May 1986): 12–15.

Hunter, Beverly. "Problem Solving with Databases." *Computing Teacher* 12 (1985): 20–27.

Kearsley, G., B. Hunter, and M. Furlong. *We Teach with Technology.* Wilsonville, Ore.: Franklin, Beedle, & Associates, 1992.

LaBare, Kelly M., and R. Lawrence Klotz. "Using Online Databases to Teach Ecological Concepts." *American Biology Teacher* 62, no. 2 (February 2000): 124–128.

Lathrop, Ann. "Online and CD-ROM Databases in School Libraries: Readings." *Libraries Unlimited,* Database Searching Series no. 2 (1989): 361–366.

Levetan, Janice. "Apples and Oranges and Lemons?" *Online Elementary Periodical Indices Library Talk* 12, no. 4 (September/October 1999): 38.

McIntyre, D. R., Pu Hao-Che, and Francis G. Wolff. "Use of Software Tools in Teaching Relational Database Design." *Computers & Education* 24, no. 4 (1995): 279.

Mittlefehlt, Bill. "Social Studies: Problem Solving with Databases." *Computing Teacher* 18, no. 5 (February 1991): 54–55.

Mohan, C., and H. Pirahesh. "Parallelism in Relational Database Management Systems." *IBM Systems Journal* 33, no. 2 (1994): 2.

Naisbitt, J. *Megatrends.* New York: Warner, 1982.

O'Leary, Mick. "Online Comes of Age." *Online* 21, no. 1 (January–February 1997): 10–14, 16–20.

Peck, Jacqueline K., and Sharon V. Hughes. "So Much Success from a First-Grade Database Project!" *Computers in the Schools* 13, no. 1–2 (1997): 109–116.

Rae, John. "Getting to Grips with Database Design: A Step-by-Step Approach." *Computers & Education* 14, no. 6 (1990): 281.

Scharberg, Maureen A., and Oran E. Cox. "Creating and Using a Consumer Chemical Molecular Graphics Database: The 'Molecule of the Day.' " *Journal of Chemical Education* 74, no. 7 (July 1997): 869.

Sharp, Vicki. *Make It with Office XP.* Visions Technology in Education, 2003.

Smith, Nancy H. G. "Teaching Teachers to Search Electronically." *Book Report* 11, no. 3 (November/December 1992): 23.

Wakerfield, A. P. "Creating and Using a Database of Children's Literature." *Reading Teacher* 48, no. 4 (December/January 1994–1995): 366–367.

Watson, J. *Teaching Thinking Skills with Databases.* Eugene, Ore.: International Society for Technology in Education, 1991.

Weib, J. H. "Teaching Mathematics with Technology: Data Base Programs in Mathematics Classrooms." *Arithmetic Teacher* 37, no. 5 (January 1990): 38–40.

CHAPTER 7

Spreadsheets and Integrated Programs

Integrating Spreadsheets into the Classroom

An electronic spreadsheet is faster and more flexible than the traditional methods of numerical calculation and data prediction. Teachers can use a spreadsheet as a grade book or for classroom budgets, attendance charts, surveys, and checklists. Students can use a spreadsheet to create time lines, game boards, or graphs and to keep track of classroom experiments. This chapter will discuss how to select a spreadsheet program for the classroom and the general features of a spreadsheet program. A checklist has been designed to help you choose the right spreadsheet software. Exercises will help you integrate the spreadsheet into the classroom. In addition, we will discuss integrated software programs, software suites, and you will become familiar with Internet sites that include tutorials, software tips, lesson plans, and discussion forums.

Objectives

Upon completing this chapter, you will be able to do the following:

1. Define *spreadsheet, integrated software, software suite, cell, windowing, macro,* and *logical functions.*
2. Describe the basic features and functions of spreadsheets and integrated programs.
3. Discuss ways of integrating the spreadsheet into the classroom.
4. Evaluate different spreadsheet software programs based on standard criteria.
5. Utilize and create a repertoire of spreadsheet activities for the classroom.
6. Explore at relevant Internet sites spreadsheet information, tutorials, tips, and discussion forums.

Teachers Can

- calculate and enter student grades,
- create charts and graphs,
- create lesson planners,
- construct game boards,
- create seating charts,
- create inventories,
- develop rubrics, and
- set up schedules.

Students Can

- track results of science experiments,
- find area and perimeter,
- create time lines and charts,
- keep track of their own grades,
- plan a budget,
- calculate data and store equations and numbers, and
- analyze statistics for team sports.

What Is a Spreadsheet?

Yearly, people across the United States prepare their income tax forms. College students often request government loans, and families determine their budgets and predict their annual expenses. The businessperson keeps a record of transactions to determine profits and liabilities, and the scientist performs mathematical calculations on experimental data. A teacher enters pupils' test scores and assignments, performs calculations, and makes inferences about the numerical data. To accomplish their various tasks, these people use worksheets or electronic spreadsheets. A **spreadsheet** is "a graphical representation of an accountant's worksheet, replete with rows and columns for recording labels (headings and subheadings) and values" (Pfaffenberger, 2000).

Historical Overview

The spreadsheet is one of the earliest applications of the microcomputer. In the early 1970s, it was primarily hackers and hobbyists who used the microcomputer. This all changed when Dan Bricklin, a Harvard student, and Robert Frankston, an MIT student, combined efforts to create the first spreadsheet, *VisiCalc*, introduced in 1979. *VisiCalc*, primarily designed for microcomputers, had a small grid size and limited features. Because the Apple Computer was the only computer that could run *VisiCalc*, it became the first computer to be accepted by business users. *VisiCalc* served as a prototype for many other programs, such as *LogicCalc* and *Plannercalc*, designed for microcomputers. Within a decade, spreadsheets improved vastly, offering more features (such as the ability to create graphic displays), faster execution speeds, and a larger grid size.

   In 1982, *Lotus 1-2-3* (Lotus Development) initiated a new generation and became the leading spreadsheet. It was the first integrated spreadsheet, meaning that it combined several different programs so that information could be presented in different formats. Later versions of spreadsheets had extended capabilities: a communication component, expanded spreadsheet size, and word processing. The word processor feature enabled the user easily to explain the figures presented in the spreadsheet, and the communication component enabled computers to communicate with each other over telephone lines.

Components of a Spreadsheet

Every electronic spreadsheet is organized in a similar manner with two axes: rows and columns. Figure 7.1 shows *Microsoft Excel*'s blank spreadsheet (Windows version). The letters across the top are used to identify the columns, and the numbers along the side identify the rows.[1] The intersection of each row and column forms a

[1]Spreadsheets can differ in the system used to label rows and columns.

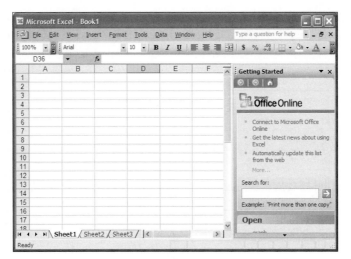

Figure 7.1
Spreadsheet from
Microsoft Excel 2003
(Windows Version)

Screen shot of *Microsoft® Excel*
used by permission of
Microsoft Corporation.

box, called a **cell.** A cell is identified by its column letter and row number. For example, in Figure 7.2, cell A1 is in the top left corner, and cell B1 is one cell to the right. To

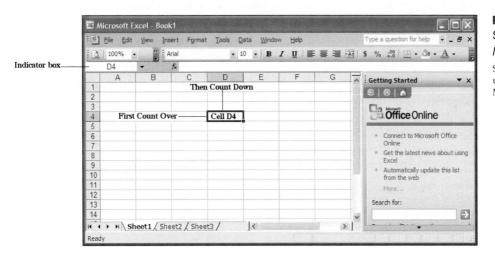

Figure 7.2
Spreadsheet Cells from
Microsoft Excel 2003

Screen shot of *Microsoft® Excel*
used by permission of
Microsoft Corporation.

locate cell D4, you would count over to column D and then count down four cells to row 4. You would select cell D4 by clicking the cursor in its box. When selected, a cell shows a heavy border, and its name appears in the indicator box above the A label. Three types of information can be entered into any single cell: number, text, or formula. The ability to enter formulas onto the spreadsheet makes it a powerful tool for business, science, and education.

How a Spreadsheet Operates

For illustrative purposes, let us use *Microsoft Excel 2003* (Windows version) and a grade book example, a popular educational use of the spreadsheet.

To use a *manual* spreadsheet for grade records, you would enter the students' names and their test scores. Imagine there are nine students and three test scores (Figure 7.3).

Figure 7.3 Teacher's Grade Roster

Screen shot of *Microsoft® Excel* used by permission of Microsoft Corporation.

Name	Test 1	Test 2	Test 3	Total	Average
1. Adams, Jayne	78	86	88	252	84
2. Bannon, John	95	88	85	268	89
3. Bentley, David	91	93	93	277	92
4. Brown, Melissa	77	67	77	221	74
5. Fink, Karen	95	94	96	285	95
6. Johnson, Alex	83	84	83	250	83
7. Kelly, Jim	77	58	74	209	70
8. Romero Scott	87	78	96	261	87
9. Schainker, Holly	88	98	88	274	91

Next, using paper, pencil, and a calculator, you would add Jayne Adam's scores, obtaining a total of 252. You would record the answer in the total column and then divide this total by 3 for an average of 84. You would continue this manual procedure for each subsequent student. If you made an error or changed a score, you would have to recalculate everything.

An *electronic* spreadsheet offers many advantages over a manual one. When you open *Microsoft Excel,* you see a blank spreadsheet (see Figure 7.1). You enter the headings *Name, Test 1, Test 2, Test 3,* and *Average.*[2] Then you type the nine pupils' names, last name first, and their respective test scores. While entering this information, you can easily make changes, corrections, deletions, or additions. You also can use the sort function to alphabetize automatically the list of students by last name. When you are finished, your screen resembles the one in Figure 7.4.

Figure 7.4 Gradebook Roster in *Microsoft Excel 2003*

Screen shot of *Microsoft® Excel* used by permission of Microsoft Corporation.

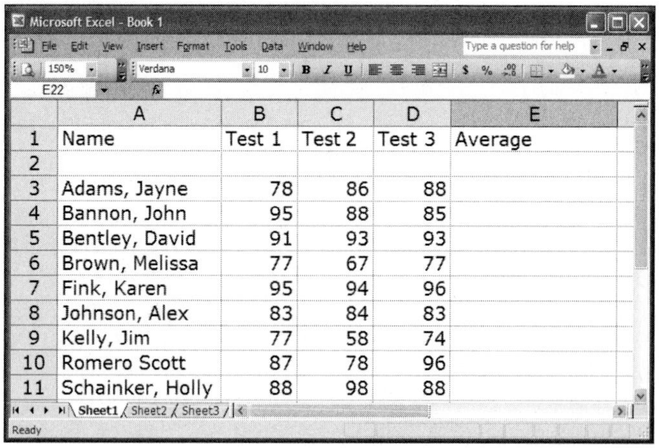

	A	B	C	D	E
1	Name	Test 1	Test 2	Test 3	Average
2					
3	Adams, Jayne	78	86	88	
4	Bannon, John	95	88	85	
5	Bentley, David	91	93	93	
6	Brown, Melissa	77	67	77	
7	Fink, Karen	95	94	96	
8	Johnson, Alex	83	84	83	
9	Kelly, Jim	77	58	74	
10	Romero Scott	87	78	96	
11	Schainker, Holly	88	98	88	

[2]It is unnecessary to create a total column in this electronic spreadsheet, as the program keeps track of totals for averaging purposes.

The beauty of any spreadsheet is that each cell serves as an individual calculator that performs computations quickly and accurately. For example, to determine each student's average score, select cell E3 and type, in *Microsoft Excel*'s formula tool bar, =(B3+C3+D3)/3. The spreadsheet calculates the mean for numbers 78, 86, and 88 and records the answer 84 instantaneously in cell E3. (The equal sign that begins the formula (B3+C3+D3)/3 tells the computer to compute an average from cell B3 to D3; see Figure 7.5.)

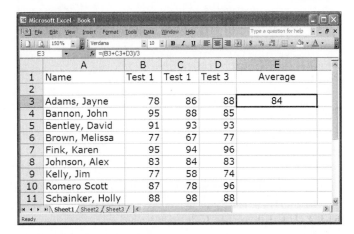

Figure 7.5 Gradebook Roster with Average from *Excel 2003*

Screen shot of *Microsoft® Excel* used by permission of Microsoft Corporation.

To calculate the averages for the remaining pupils, you would not have to rewrite the formula, since every spreadsheet has a way of copying the original formula. In *Microsoft Excel,* you could use the fill handle to select cells E3 through E10 by dragging the small box in the bottom right corner of the dark border surrounding cell E3 (see Figure 7.5). The rest of the students' averages would automatically be displayed in the appropriate cells, as shown in the highlighted cells in column E of Figure 7.6.

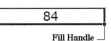

Fill Handle

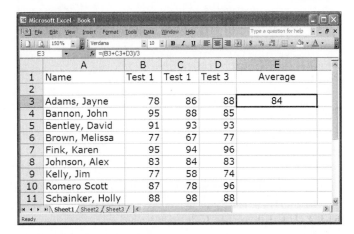

Figure 7.6 *Microsoft Excel 2003* Completed Roster

Screen shot of *Microsoft® Excel* used by permission of Microsoft Corporation.

Microsoft Excel features more than 230 functions, or shortcuts, that save you from typing in formulas. A **function** is a built-in software routine that performs a task in the program. To apply the average function to the cell, click on *Edit formula* (=) in the formula toolbar and then select the average function from the pull-down menu that appears (Figure 7.7).

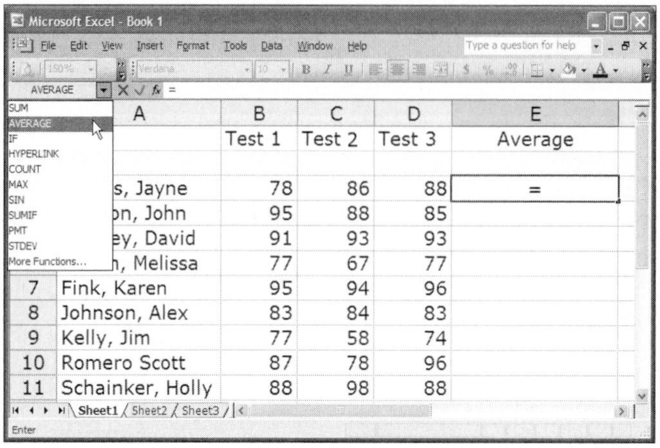

Figure 7.7 Average Function from *Microsoft Excel 2003* (Windows Version)

Screen shot of *Microsoft® Excel* used by permission of Microsoft Corporation.

Every spreadsheet has its own collection of built-in functions, ranging from *sum* to *average* to *sine*. These functions make the use and application of formulas quick and easy. You simply select the function, and it is pasted into the spreadsheet. *AppleWorks* offers more than 100 built-in functions; *Cruncher 2* (Knowledge Adventure) comes with 23. Generally, the more built-in or predetermined functions, the more versatile the spreadsheet.

Why Use an Electronic Spreadsheet?

There are many reasons for a teacher to choose a computerized spreadsheet over a manual worksheet. The electronic spreadsheet is faster and more flexible than the traditional methods of numerical calculation and data prediction, permitting you to change the information on the screen as often as you want. A noncomputerized spreadsheet with a matrix of more than 25 rows and columns is cumbersome, whereas a computerized spreadsheet with a matrix of thousands of data entries performs instant calculations. Furthermore, on a computerized spreadsheet you can access any number instantaneously, simply by pressing a key or two. Another major feature of a spreadsheet is its ability to recalculate; that is, when you change the number in a cell, the spreadsheet automatically recalculates the other values. The recalculation feature of an electronic spreadsheet enables you to employ **what-if analysis** strategies, which are used to answer questions such as "What would happen if Elena scored a 90 on this exam instead of a 60?" Another question commonly asked by students is "What grade will I achieve in the course if I earn an 80 on the final exam?" Homeowners might ask, "If the interest rate drops from 8 to 6 percent, what will my mortgage payments be?" As a spreadsheet user, you would only have to enter the score or rate to see the effects or answers immediately.

There are still more advantages to the electronic spreadsheet. It enables you to display and print the output in many visually appealing ways. Also, as long as you enter the formula correctly, your data will be accurate. Spreadsheets have the invaluable copy function, with which you effortlessly repeat a formula once it has been defined. Clearly, the electronic spreadsheet has enormous advantage over a manual spreadsheet in terms of saving time and increasing productivity.

Basic Features of a Spreadsheet

Protected and Hidden Cells

Many spreadsheets have built-in safeguards to protect a group of cells from being altered or erased. For example, you may have a formula that you want to keep safe from accidental erasure or deletion. Even when you remove this cell protection so that you can view the data, there may be a command you can give to prevent accidental erasure of data. In addition to this option, some spreadsheets allow you to take confidential information and hide it from view, even blocking it out in your printed reports. On a good spreadsheet, you should be able to retrieve easily the information from these hidden cells. Some spreadsheets require users to employ a secret password to access data.

Logical Functions

Powerful spreadsheets include **logical functions** that evaluate whether a statement is true or false. For example, imagine a teacher created a grade book spreadsheet with four exam grades and an average score for each student. He now wants to invite into honors math only those students who received averages of 97 or above. Since the first average is in cell F4, he would enter a formula in G4 and repeat this formula for every student's score. With the spreadsheet program *Lotus 1-2-3,* this formula would read as follows: @If(F4>96,100,0).

The formula makes a 100 represent the honors class and a 0 represent the standard class. When the spreadsheet does its calculation, it checks to see whether the value entered (F4) is greater than 96, and if it is, the spreadsheet will print the first option (100) in cell G4. If the average in F4 is lower than 96, the spreadsheet will print the second option (0) in G4. All the students with 100s meet the requirements for honors class.

Predetermined Functions

The majority of spreadsheet programs come with a range of built-in mathematical functions including simple statistics, logarithmic functions, financial functions, and trigonometric functions. These **predetermined functions** are ready-made formulas that enable you to solve problems quickly.

Date and Time Function

The date and time function is another advanced feature. It automatically calculates how many days have elapsed between two dates in spreadsheet cells.

Macros

Macros are a group of routines or commands combined into one or two keystrokes. You can play these routines back at the touch of a key or two. This is how it works. First, you determine what key(s) you want to use, such as key F12. Then, you decide what the key will generate; for instance, F12 could generate a name, address, and telephone number. Finally, you program the macro so that, when F12 is pressed, it automatically enters the name, address, and telephone number in the chosen cell. Some macros execute their commands to a certain point, wait for the input, and then continue with the command execution.

Graphing

Many spreadsheets generate bar or pie graphs based on data entered. The more advanced spreadsheets can generate dozens of different types of charts and feature all sorts of design options. These graphs are great visual aids because, as the data change, you can see the corresponding changes in the graphs.

Memory

When you enter data into a spreadsheet, you want to know how much memory remains so that you do not run out at a crucial point. A spreadsheet that has a running indicator of the memory available is better than one that simply flashes a message once the program is out of memory.

Cell Names

Some programs enable you to label the cells with words instead of simple, short cell addresses. For instance, if you record profit in Column C, Rows 3 through 15, you can tell the program to label these cells *Profit.* Then you can use the name *Profit* in any formula that refers to this range.

Windows

When you work on a large spreadsheet, you cannot see the whole spreadsheet on the screen but must use the cursor to scroll among sections. If you need to compare figures on different screens, it is helpful to be able to split the screen into two or three sections, each windowing a different part of the work, so that you can see your current location in the spreadsheet, see the effect your work has on cells in different locations, and easily compare figures from different sections. If the spreadsheet does not have a split-screen option, it may come with the ability to set fixed titles. A fixed title option enables you to keep designated rows and columns permanently on the screen, even as you scroll through sections.

Attached Notes

Some spreadsheets can attach notes to cells, much as you would attach sticky notes to your written work.

Editing and Sorting

When you make a mistake, the spreadsheet should offer a simple way of correcting the error. You should be able to insert and delete rows and columns. You should be able to widen or narrow the spreadsheet's columns quickly to meet your entry requirements. After the information is edited to your satisfaction, you should be able to sort it alphabetically and numerically.

Copying Command

The copying command on a spreadsheet copies the contents of a group of cells from one column to the cells in another, replicating formulas, values, and labels. The ability to copy and move from one location to another saves time on data entry. For instance, instead of retyping a formula, you quickly can copy it from one cell in the spreadsheet and then paste it into any other cells in which you need to use the same formula (see Figure 7.6).

Templates

It is very useful to have ready-to-use templates (see Chapter 5). A template is simply a spreadsheet that contains no data but comes with selected functions for certain cells. You fill the appropriate cells of this spreadsheet with your own data. When you enter data in cells for which formulas are selected, the computer makes the calculations and the results are displayed in the appropriate cells. When you are finished, you save this altered spreadsheet under another name so that the template can be used for another spreadsheet. You can also create your own templates.

Online Help

Online help allows you to get help from the computer while using the program.

Formatting

Many spreadsheets come with formatting capabilities that enable you to align numbers and text labels or apply different fonts and type styles. *Microsoft Excel* has an AutoFormat feature with which you can apply built-in table designs to give your spreadsheet a professional look. This AutoFormat feature uses distinctive formats for different elements of the table.

Advanced Features of a Spreadsheet

The more powerful spreadsheets can link with other spreadsheets so they can perform complex calculations. Linking spreadsheets allows you to get information from one spreadsheet and pull it directly into your current sheet (this complicated feature is not meant for novices).

Many spreadsheet programs come with database capabilities. With such capabilities, you can sort a set of rows numerically or alphabetically and choose items that match particular criteria. These programs offer tools to maintain lists. For example *Excel's List Manager* maintains simple databases with rows and columns that represent fields and records within a frame. *Lotus 1-2-3* has database capabilities, but these functions are not comparable to those of a database program; what they offer is a spreadsheet approach to database functions. It is better to use a database program if your list is very large and you need more complex features.

Many spreadsheets feature desktop publishing tools that enable you to shade boxes, vary fonts, add pictures and logos, and print sideways. (Generally, printing is limited to 80 columns, or 136 if you use compressed type.)

The most advanced spreadsheets offer special fonts, multiple dimensions, sound, and add-on software. These spreadsheets have Internet capabilities that enable you to save your data to a website by converting the worksheet to HTML format (see Chapter 11). When you save the worksheet this way, you can see it in your Web browser. In addition, many spreadsheet programs enable you to add **hyperlinks** to your worksheet. This means that when you click on specific text or graphics you are sent to a specific Web page, a file on your disk, or a file on a local network.

How to Select a Good Spreadsheet for the Classroom

Spreadsheets were originally designed for adults, but a handful of programs are suitable for the classroom. *Cruncher 2.0* is for grades 3 and up, and the high schools utilize *Microsoft Works, AppleWorks, Lotus 1-2-3 Millennium Edition, Microsoft Excel 2003* (Windows), *Microsoft Excel X* (Macintosh), or *Quattro Pro* (Corel).

Choosing spreadsheet software for the classroom is a six-step process: (1) determine the hardware compatibility; (2) study the program's features; (3) test how easy it is to use the program; (4) examine the program's built-in functions; (5) investigate the program's consumer value; and (6) check out the technical support.

Hardware Compatibility

You need to determine what computers are available in the school: old Apple IIGs, Windows-based machines, or Macintosh G5's? How much memory do these machines have? Is there enough memory to accommodate the spreadsheets the students are using?

General Features

Determine how the labeling is done on the spreadsheet. Can you easily center the labels or move them to the left or right? How does the spreadsheet handle decimal points and dollar signs? If you make a mistake, can you effortlessly modify the cell or cells? Can the width of the columns be adjusted easily? Can you protect the cells from being erased accidentally? Can you hide certain cells and not print them out? How does the spreadsheet show negative values? How many predetermined functions does the spreadsheet have? Does it have a date and time function? Can you easily calculate how many days have passed between two dates entered in the spreadsheet? Does the spreadsheet include macros? Can you generate bar or pie graphs? How does the spreadsheet indicate the amount of memory it has left? Does the spreadsheet have windows so that you can split the screen into two or three sections, each displaying a different part of the work? Can you link this spreadsheet with other spreadsheets or arrange the information in the spreadsheet alphabetically or numerically? Does the spreadsheet have enough columns and rows to meet the classroom needs? What special functions do the students need to use in the class? For example, when students use the spreadsheet, is it to calculate sums, averages, or standard deviations?

Ease of Use

The spreadsheet is much more difficult to use than a database program because it involves working with numbers and formulas. Therefore, it is imperative that you choose a spreadsheet program that gives online help that can be accessed quickly. *Cruncher 2.0* fits these criteria with a step-by-step tutorial and online help. Figure 7.8 shows a screen

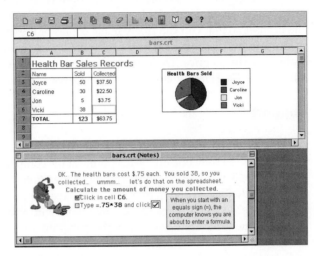

Figure 7.8 *Cruncher 2.0*

Reprinted with permission of Davidson and Associates.

from this tutorial. *AppleWorks,* an integrated program, includes a word processor, spreadsheet, database, drawing capabilities, painting features, and presentation capabilities. The program enables the student quickly to build graphs, slide shows, and pictures. It is packaged with clip art images, sounds, movies, and templates (Figure 7.9) that duplicate what students are learning in school.

Figure 7.9 *AppleWorks*

Images courtesy of Apple Computers, Inc.

When considering ease of use, ask these questions: How fast can you edit the cells and enter the data? Can you smoothly delete and insert rows or columns? Is it hard to copy formulas from one row to another? How do you move the cursor from one cell to another?

Consumer Value

Software is expensive, so cost is an important consideration. *Cruncher 2.0* costs under $100, but *Microsoft Excel* sells for more than $250. Some software companies offer on-site licenses so that you can freely make copies of the software for in-house use. Other manufacturers distribute lab packs that enable you to purchase multiple copies of software at a reduced price. There are quite a few shareware spreadsheet programs; for examples, see *The Spreadsheet Page* at http://www.j-walk.com/ss/.

Support

A software company's willingness to support its product is an extremely important factor. Can you call someone on the telephone at the company and get immediate help? Do you have to spend excessive time waiting on the phone? Is the technical support toll free or are you charged by the minute? Do you have to pay a yearly fee to receive any type of assistance? Does the software package come with a tutorial? Is the manual readable? Does it come with an index? Does the program have templates? Use the following checklist when selecting a spreadsheet.

Before selecting the software, decide which features are important for your particular class. Next, examine one of these programs using the sample checklist and rating instrument in the Spreadsheet Checklist form on page 157.

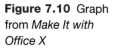

Recommended Software
Spreadsheet Programs

For a listing of recommended Spreadsheet Software, go to the Online Learning Center.

Integrating a Spreadsheet into the Classroom

The spreadsheet can be used as a grade book or for classroom budgets, attendance charts, lesson plans, surveys, seating charts, rubric development, checklists, or displaying test scores graphically (Figure 7.10). The spreadsheet is not only a management

Figure 7.10 Graph from *Make It with Office X*

Reprinted with permission of Visions Technology in EducationTM. www.ToolsforTeachers.com.

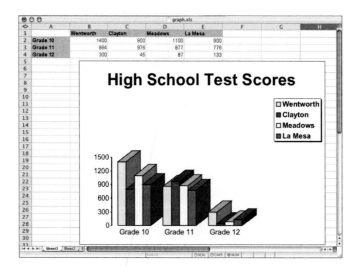

Spreadsheet Checklist

Directions: Examine the following items and determine which ones you feel are important for your class situation. Place an X on each line for which the software meets your needs.

Product Name _____ **Manufacturer** _____ **Grade Level** _____

Hardware
_____ 1. Memory needed
_____ 2. Computer compatibility
_____ 3. Printer compatibility
_____ 4. Hard disk space

Features
_____ 1. Protected cells
_____ 2. Hidden cells
_____ 3. Sorting
_____   a. Alphabetical
_____   b. Numerical
_____ 4. Windowing
_____ 5. Macros
_____ 6. Formulas
_____ 7. Logical operators
_____ 8. Fixed titles
_____ 9. Transfer to word processing
_____ 10. Link to other spreadsheets
_____ 11. Integration with database
_____ 12. Name ranges
_____ 13. Graphing
_____ 14. Flexibility of printing
_____ 15. Manual recalculation
_____ 16. Sound
_____ 17. Internet capabilities
_____ 18. Deleting and adding columns

_____ 19. Changing column width
_____ 20. Copying labels and formulas
_____ 21. Formatting of cells
_____ 22. Erasure
_____ 23. Date and time
_____ 24. Memory tracking

Ease of Use
_____ 1. Help screens
_____ 2. Tutorial disks
_____ 3. Quick printer setup
_____ 4. Easy editing of cells
_____ 5. Simple command names
_____ 6. Quick cell movement
_____ 7. Warning questions

Consumer Value
_____ 1. Cost
_____ 2. On-site license
_____ 3. Lab packs
_____ 4. Network version

Support
_____ 1. Technical
_____ 2. Tutorial material
_____ 3. Readable manual
_____ 4. Templates

Rating Scale
Rate the spreadsheet program by placing a check on the appropriate line.
Excellent _____ Very good _____ Good _____ Fair _____ Poor _____

Comments:

tool; it is also a tool for learning in the classroom. Spreadsheets can be used to supplement instruction in a variety of curriculum areas.

The teacher can use a spreadsheet as a study aid for history, for physics experiments, and for accounting problems. Teachers can improve learning by using spreadsheets to demonstrate numerical concepts such as percentages, multiplication, and the difference between electoral votes and popular votes. Using the spreadsheet, teachers can generate graphs to illustrate abstract concepts. Teachers can have the class keep track of a stock portfolio's performance with a spreadsheet. The spreadsheet can aid teachers in preparing class materials or completing calculations.

Students can use the spreadsheet to create time lines, game boards, and graphs or to solve problems, keep track of classroom experiments, explore mathematical relationships, and delve into social studies or scientific investigations. Students can test various hypotheses and conduct what-if analyses. They can calculate averages and standard deviations for statistics problems and even keep track of their grades. They can also create their own what-if questions to see what scores they need to raise their grades. They can use a spreadsheet to determine how much water and money are wasted by a dripping faucet. Furthermore, they can calculate the time to travel between cities by different means of transportation or they can explore relationships in the chemical periodic chart. They can convert Fahrenheit to Celsius temperatures, compare characteristics of the major groups of vertebrates or invertebrates, and compare the climates of several countries. Students can learn about the weather and use the spreadsheet to store data about such items as temperature, precipitation, and barometer readings. They can use a spreadsheet for comparison shopping, calculating the expense of keeping a pet, calorie counting, calculating income tax returns, figuring baseball statistics, and creating a budget (Figure 7.11). They can keep track of money from fund-

Figure 7.11 Budget from *Make It with Office X*

Reprinted with permission of Visions Technology in EducationTM. www.ToolsforTeachers.com.

	A	B January	C February	D March	E April	F May	G June
3	Budget						
4	Income	$ 6,000	$ 6,000	$ 6,500	$ 7,000	$ 6,000	$ 6,500
5	Food	$ 400	$ 440	$ 500	$ 375	$ 330	$ 300
6	Telephone	$ 120	$ 130	$ 145	$ 150	$ 110	$ 123
7	Utilities	$ 250	$ 200	$ 155	$ 145	$ 150	$ 200
8	Rent	$ 1,800	$ 1,800	$ 1,800	$ 1,800	$ 1,800	$ 1,800
9	Automobile Loan	$ 200	$ 200	$ 200	$ 200	$ 200	$ 200
10	Insurance	$ 1,500	$ -	$ -	$ -	$ -	$ -
11	Entertainment	$ 200	$ 300	$ 350	$ 200	$ 240	$ 240
12	Clothes	$ 300	$ 200	$ 500	$ 200	$ 100	$ 85
13	Medical Bills	$ 50	$ 500	$ 75	$ 20	$ 10	$ 45
14	Savings	$ 400	$ -	$ 300	$ 500	$ 600	$ 700
15	Total Expenses	$ 5,220	$ 3,770	$ 4,025	$ 3,590	$ 3,540	$ 3,693
16	Balance	$ 780	$ 2,230	$ 2,475	$ 3,410	$ 2,460	$ 2,807

raising activities such as magazine drives. You can use the spreadsheet to perform activities that range from statistics management to energy consumption calculation to simple science experiments.

Teacher Practice Activity

The following exercises are meant to be used in conjunction with any spreadsheet. If a computer lab is not available, simply read through this section to get an idea of how you would set up a spreadsheet. The first exercise introduces you step-by-step to a spreadsheet program.

1. Open the spreadsheet program.

2. Create a new file and give it the name *Grade Book*.

3. Begin by entering labels across the first row of the spreadsheet. Starting at cell B1, type the following labels: *Exam 1, Exam 2, Exam 3, Exam 4, Exam 5.* Place the label *Exam 1* in cell B1, *Exam 2* in C1, *Exam 3* in D1, *Exam 4* in E1, and *Exam 5* in F1. Leaving cells A1 and A2 empty, put the label *Pupils* in cell A3. These labels will describe the contents of the cells. The spreadsheet should look similar to the one in Figure 7.12, which is in *Microsoft Excel*.

	A	B	C	D	E	F
1		EXAM 1	EXAM 2	EXAM 3	EXAM 4	EXAM 5
2						
3	PUPILS					
4						

Figure 7.12 *Microsoft Excel* Spreadsheet

Screen shot of *Microsoft® Excel* used by permission of Microsoft Corporation.

4. Starting at A5, enter the pupils' last names: A5, *Smith;* A6, *Sharp;* A7, *Garcia;* A8, *Raj;* A9, *Friedman;* A10, *Washington;* A11, *Reilly;* A12, *Hughes;* A13, *Sherrin;* and A14, Jones.

5. Using the sort or arrange function, alphabetize the names and align each name on the left side of the cell.

6. Now enter the data in the grade book. Enter Friedman's Exam 1 score as *89* in cell B5, his Exam 2 score as *46* in cell C5, Exam 3 as *69* in D5, Exam 4 as *74* in cell E5, and Exam 5 as *35* in cell F5. Now continue entering the exam scores for the remaining students; the spreadsheet should look like the one in Figure 7.13.

	A	B	C	D	E	F
1		EXAM 1	EXAM 2	EXAM 3	EXAM 4	EXAM 5
2						
3	PUPILS					
4						
5	FRIEDMAN	89	46	69	74	35
6	GARCIA	45	23	75	75	34
7	HUGHES	89	43	67	67	34
8	JONES	99	45	75	75	40
9	RAJ	98	50	73	73	39
10	REILLY	56	50	67	67	32
11	SHARP	98	45	72	71	39
12	SHERRIN	78	46	73	72	34
13	SMITH	99	45	74	74	40
14	WASHINGTON	87	45	72	72	34
15						

Figure 7.13 *Microsoft Excel* Spreadsheet with Grades

Screen shot of *Microsoft® Excel* used by permission of Microsoft Corporation.

7. Next, type the label *AVERAGE* in cell G1. You want to enter a formula to calculate the average score for Friedman's five exams. Begin by putting the cursor on cell G5 and type the formula. There will be a variation in these formulas; for instance, if you are using *AppleWorks,* the formula is =AVERAGE(B5:F5). In *Microsoft Excel,* the formula is =AVERAGE(B5:F5). After you enter the formula, the average (62.6) should appear instantly in cell G5.

8. Next, use the copy or fill function to calculate the averages for the remaining students (Figure 7.14).

Figure 7.14
Calculating Averages in *Microsoft Excel*

Screen shot of *Microsoft® Excel* used by permission of Microsoft Corporation.

	A		G
1			AVERAGE
2			
3	PUPILS		
4			
5	FRIEDMAN		62.6
6	GARCIA		50.4
7	HUGHES		60
8	JONES		66.8
9	RAJ		66.6
10	REILLY		54.4
11	SHARP		65
12	SHERRIN		60.6
13	SMITH		66.4
14	WASHINGTON		62
15			

9. Learn how to save the data on the formatted disk and print them out for inspection.

Classroom Lesson Plans

SPEED AND DISTANCE

Subject

Math/Science

Grade(s)

5 and up

Objectives

Students will learn about speed and how to use a spreadsheet to do simple calculations.

Standards

- National Council of Teachers of Math Standards 1, 2, 6, 9
- National Science Education Standards A1, A2
- ISTE NETS for Students 1, 3

Materials

You will need a spreadsheet program such as *AppleWorks, Excel, Cruncher 2.0,* or *Quattro Pro.*

Procedures

1. Discuss how fast an automobile can travel and the relationships among distance, miles, and time.
2. Have the students create a spreadsheet similar to the one in Figure 7.15.

	A	B	C
1	RATE	TIME	DISTANCE
2	25	0.5	
3	30	1	
4	35	2	
5	40	2	
6	45	3	
7	50	3	
8	55	4	
9	60	5	
10	65	6	
11	70	7	

Figure 7.15 Speed Spreadsheet in *Microsoft Excel*

Screen shot of *Microsoft® Excel* used by permission of Microsoft Corporation.

3. Next, pose the following question: What is the distance covered when traveling so many hours at a given speed?
4. Have the students type a formula in cell C2 that multiplies cell A2 by cell B2. Then copy this formula for cells C3 to C11.
5. After the students have accomplished this, have them examine the results and determine the answers to questions that you and they pose. If there are not enough computers, let the students use their calculators and a pencil and paper to complete this task.

Variations

You can generate other spreadsheets that would enable students to answer the following questions:

1. How much time does it take to travel a specified number of miles at a certain speed?
2. At what speed must you travel to go 300 miles in 5 hours?

II. EXPENSE TRACKING

Subject

Math

Grade(s)

5 and up

Objective

Students will use a spreadsheet to keep track of expenses.

Standards

- National Council of Teachers of Math Standards 1, 2, 6, 9
- ISTE NETS for Students 1, 3

Materials

You will need a spreadsheet program such as *AppleWorks, Excel, Cruncher 2.0,* or *Quattro Pro.*

Procedures

1. Discuss the following problem with the students: The $10 Computer Club is having a fund-raiser to buy software for its club. The cost of the software is $700, and the club members expect to sell three raffle tickets apiece. They are selling these tickets for $3 each. Figure 7.16 shows how many tickets each student in the club sells.

Figure 7.16 Ticket
Sales Spreadsheet

	A	B	C	D	E	F	G	H	I
1	$10 CLUB			DAYS OF THE WEEK					AVERAGE
2		1	2	3	4	5	6	7	
3									
4	1. Adams	6	4	6	2	3	4	5	
5	2. Barrett	5	4	4	5	0	0	3	
6	3. Devlin	5	2	6	2	6	1	2	
7	4. Johnson	2	1	4	4	2	1	3	
8	5. Mason	3	0	0	0	10	0	2	
9	6. Carcia	1	2	3	4	3	2	1	
10	7. Youngblood	2	3	4	5	5	7	8	
11	8. Sands	1	3	2	5	0	4	3	

2. Have each student create the same spreadsheet and then finish the data by calculating the average for each student.
3. Tell the students to use the logical function to determine how many club members sold six or more tickets on a daily basis. Was the $10 Computer Club able to buy its software?

Variation

1. Change the totals in the spreadsheet for any two students not selling at least three raffle tickets daily to three raffle tickets and record the value the spreadsheet recalculates.
2. Have the students compute the averages again for the raffle ticket price raised to $5.

III. FAMILY AND CONSUMER EDUCATION

Subjects

Home Economics and Math

Grade(s)

7 and up

Objective

Students will use a spreadsheet to keep track of their expenditures for six months.

Standards

- National Council of Teachers of Math Standards 1, 2, 6, 9
- ISTE NETS for Students 1, 3, 6

Materials

You will need a spreadsheet program such as *AppleWorks, Excel, Cruncher 2.0*, or *Quattro Pro.*

Procedures

1. Have each student record in a spreadsheet expenditures for the 10 items shown in Figure 7.17 during a six-month period.

◇	A	B	C	D	E	F	G
1		January	February	March	April	May	June
2	Expenses						
3	Food						
4	Telephone						
5	Utilities						
6	Rent						
7	Automobile Loan						
8	Insurance						
9	Entertainment						
10	Clothes						
11	Medical Bills						
12	Savings						

Figure 7.17
Expenditures
Spreadsheet

2. Have students use the sum formula to total each column.
3. Ask them to add an additional column to keep track of six-month totals.
4. Change values in the completed spreadsheet so that the students can answer what-if questions such as "If I cut down on my entertainment, how much more can I save a year?"

Variation

From the savings row, create a spreadsheet that shows how much an initial deposit of $200 would grow at different interest rates and at different intervals of time.

IV. THE PENDULUM

Subjects

Science and Math

Grade(s)

5 and up

Objectives

Students will practice predicting, changing variables, and estimating and learn how to use a formula in a spreadsheet.

Standards

- National Council of Teachers of Math Standards 1, 2, 3, 4, 6, 9
- National Science Education Standards A1, A2, B1, B2
- ISTE NETS for Students 1, 3, 4, 5, 6

Materials

You will need string, thumbtacks, weights, and a spreadsheet program like *AppleWorks*, *Excel*, *Cruncher 2.0*, or *Quattro Pro*.

Procedures

1. Before beginning, make sure students understand how the pendulum works.
2. Have each student experiment with different weights, lengths, and amplitude values. The objective is to determine what affects the pendulum's period. A period is simply the time it takes the pendulum to swing from point A to point B and then back to point A again.
3. Ask each student to create a table like the one in Table 7.1.

Table 7.1 Pendulum Investigations

Length	Weight	Amplitude	Period

4. Have students use a formula to figure each period for the pendulum.

V. THE ELECTION

Subjects

Social Studies and Math

Grade(s)

4 and up

Objectives

Students will learn about elections and in the process how to use a spreadsheet to add and figure percentages.

Standards

- National Council of Teachers of Math Standards 1, 6, 8
- National Council for the Social Studies Curriculum Standards 3, 6
- ISTE NETS for Students 1, 3, 4

Materials

The students will have to make voting booths and have access to a spreadsheet program such as *Excel* or *Cruncher 2.0.* They will need ballots and tallies for each voting booth.

Procedures

1. Before beginning, make sure students understand the election process.
2. Have the students nominate candidates for president of the room or school.
3. Conduct an election with voting booths.
4. Have students create a spreadsheet similar to the one in Figure 7.18.

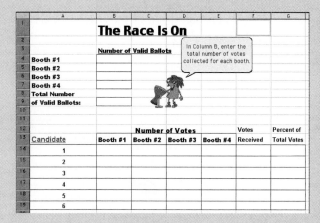

Figure 7.18 *Cruncher 2.0* Race Spreadsheet

Used by permission of Knowledge Adventure/Havas Interactive.

5. Have students write the candidates' names and tally the votes.
6. Have students enter the number of valid ballots that were cast.
7. Have student use the sum function to calculate the total number of valid ballots.
8. Have student use the percent function to calculate the percentage of the total vote that each candidate received.
9. Pose questions such as the following: Was the election close? What percentage of the total votes did my candidate earn? How many votes were there all together?

Integrated Programs

Previously, we discussed three popular applications of the computer: the word processor, the database, and the spreadsheet. Each application was dedicated to a separate task: The word processor created and edited documents, the database organized information, and the spreadsheet worked with numerical data.

Once you are comfortable with these individual programs, you may require software that allows for the free interchange of data among programs. For example, you may need to take budget information stored in the spreadsheet and transfer it to a letter that you are writing on the word processor. Regardless of the software you have, you can accomplish this task by going through seven laborious steps: (1) write the report on the word processor, leaving space for the spreadsheet table; (2) print a hard copy of the report; (3) close the word processing application and open the spreadsheet; (4) enter data into the spreadsheet's cells and manipulate it; (5) generate a printout of this spreadsheet; (6) use scissors to cut the spreadsheet printout and paste the results onto the word processor hard copy; (7) photocopy the report. Cutting and pasting among applications in this way is very time-consuming.

Stand-alone programs are generally not capable of communicating with other applications. There are many aspects of programming that limit the ability of these programs to address one another, and one important limitation is the differences among their command structures. For example, the *Cruncher 2.0* spreadsheet cannot electronically transfer information into the *AppleWorks* word processor because of their different commands.

The **integrated program,** on the other hand, includes in its most common configuration a word processor, a database, and a spreadsheet that can communicate with one another. *Lotus 1-2-3,* a pioneer in its field, was developed in the early 1980s as a spreadsheet. It was one of the first programs to offer as a part of its design a database with some graphics capabilities. After the success of *Lotus 1-2-3,* many programs followed its example. *SuperCalc 3* integrated database, spreadsheet, and graphics. *Microsoft Works* combined spreadsheet with file management and word processing. Integrated programs such as *Microsoft Works* expanded to include more applications such as a calendar maker and an address book. *AppleWorks* (Figure 7.19), another popular inte-

Figure 7.19
AppleWorks Starter Screen

Images courtesy of Apple Computers, Inc.

grated program, offers word processor, spreadsheet, database manager, painting, drawing, and presentation capabilities.

The applications of an integrated program share a similar command structure. Because of this similarity of command structure across the various applications, the program is easy to learn. Since each module is a component of one program, data are transferred seamlessly. You can effortlessly combine tables with text, for example. Finally, integrated programs cost much less than the total price of several stand-alone programs.

Nevertheless, some integrated programs have disadvantages. They typically need more memory, and the applications usually offer fewer functions than comparable stand-alone programs.

Alternatives to Integrated Programs

Some alternatives to integrated programs exist:

1. You can use the stand-alone program as it is and cut and paste when necessary. If you are fortunate, your stand-alone program may come with all the database or word processing capabilities that you require, even if they are limited.

2. You can retype your data into the separate applications. This sounds like a reasonable alternative, but it requires much typing and opens your data to errors. Also, anytime you change a number in one application, you will have to remember to change it in the other applications.

3. You can file share, which permits access to the files of the other programs. Because there is little standardization among the files of programs, these files cannot be directly read. If you want to read them, you need a special translator program like *MacLink Plus* (DataViz) for the Macintosh or *Conversions Plus* (DataViz) for Windows. These translator programs enable you to input a file of one type, make it conform to the file structure of another type, and then output this transformed file. Unfortunately, these translator programs are not available for all software programs, and sometimes in the process of transforming the data the formatting may be lost.

If you do not need to transfer data among applications, a basic stand-alone application that fits your computer needs should suffice. However, if you are going to need to transfer information from one application to another, you should buy an integrated software package or perhaps try a software suite.

Software Suites. In the 1990s software companies started a new trend with the introduction of software suites. A **software suite** is a package of individual programs designed to work together to share data easily and quickly. A suite consists of stand-alone applications that are otherwise sold individually. Each application works together through special links that create a mock integration. Four popular examples of suites are *Corel WordPerfect Office, Microsoft Office 2003, Microsoft Office X* (Macintosh version), and *Lotus SmartSuite.* A suite costs less than the total of the individual stand-alone applications and offers more features. For example, *Corel WordPerfect Suite* includes the following software: *WordPerfect, Quattro Pro, Corel Presentations, Trellix 2, Corel Print Office,* and *Corel Central* as well as hundreds of templates, hundreds of fonts, and thousands of clip art images. You can install the entire suite or only the programs that you want.

There are many similarities between an integrated package and a suite. Both enable you to run many programs at once, and they are designed to work together. An integrated program and a suite feature a **clipboard,** a place to store text, graphics, audio, and video clips. You use this clipboard to move data among the programs of the suite or integrated program applications. You copy the data to the clipboard and then paste it into the other applications. Both integrated programs and suites enable you to write more sophisticated reports and papers because they give you access to a variety of programs.

The main difference between a software suite and an integrated program is that the suite's components are full-featured programs and not limited versions. These applications usually started as independent programs that were popular before being combined in a suite. In most cases, a suite is very economical, because software vendors use it to induce people to buy their products. It serves as a marketing strategy for preventing the user from switching to a new product.

On the negative side, the various components in a suite do not work as smoothly as the applications on an integrated program. There are very high hardware requirements to run a suite. The hard disk space, the memory, and the speed of the computer should all be taken into consideration. A suite like *Microsoft Office X* requires more than 180 MB of hard disk space. This would not be a problem for modern computers, but old relics that are often found in poorer elementary schools might have some problems. It is preferable to have a more powerful computer to take full advantage of the programs' capabilities. Mastering a suite is definitely harder than mastering an integrated program. Expect to spend considerable time and effort if you want to learn more than just the basics.

Recommended Software
Integrated Programs

For a listing of recommended integrated programs, go to the Online Learning Center.

When you scrutinize an integrated program or suite you are concerned with the same features as you would be when considering separate applications. You should consider the same questions: How rapidly does the database sort? How much time is needed to load a file? How quickly does the spreadsheet calculate? How many columns and rows can you create using the spreadsheet document? Does the word processor have a thesaurus or grammar checker? You should find out how quickly and easily each module in the integrated package or software suite shares data.

Summary

The electronic spreadsheet, which consists of a matrix of rows and columns intersecting at cells, was developed to handle complicated and tedious calculations. In this chapter, we became familiar with the basic features of a spreadsheet and discussed which features to consider when buying a spreadsheet program for the classroom. We also explored activities for introducing the spreadsheet to students.

In addition, we examined the integrated software package, a group of programs that freely exchange data with each other. In their most common configuration today, these integrated programs include a word processor, database, spreadsheet, telecommunication module, drawing module, and graphics module. Additionally, we discussed the software suite, a bundling of linked stand-alone programs. Be sure to review the annotated list of award-winning spreadsheet and integrated programs under **Recommended Software** on the Online Learning Center.

Study and Online Resources

Go to Chapter 7 in the Student Edition of the Online Learning Center at **www.mhhe.com/sharp5e** to **practice with key concepts, take chapter quizzes, read PowerWeb articles** and **news feed updates** related to technology in education, and **access resources** for learning about technology and integrating it into the classroom.

Click on *Web Links* to link to the following websites.

Dan Bricklin's Website
This site, maintained by Dan Bricklin, a co-creator of *VisiCalc,* contains historical information about *VisiCalc,* the first computer spreadsheet program.

Excel 101
Excel 101 is a tutorial offering general information on using *Microsoft Excel* as well as specific instruction on formulas and formatting.

Mathematics and Spreadsheets
The forum site offers basic information for using spreadsheets in education, grades 8–12. See also the lesson plan ideas in Margaret Sinclair's *Using Spreadsheets to Solve Algebraic Problems* and Suzanne Alejandre's *Graphs.*

Microsoft Excel
The Microsoft site for *Excel* provides information about the product as well as how-to articles and tips for using it. The Microsoft education site lists tutorials including *Excel XP.*

Microsoft Office Template Gallery
Microsoft Office Template Gallery contains hundreds of templates for résumés, cover letters, legal documents, and much more. You can browse by category or search to find the template you need.

Productivity in the Classroom
The site provides a variety of lessons and activities for integrating technology into the classroom using Microsoft software such as *Excel.*

Robert's Online Spreadsheet!
Dr. Robert Lum offers a free Web-based spreadsheet program.

Spreadsheet Lesson Plans
The North Carolina Department of Education offers spreadsheet lesson plans for middle grades.

The Spreadsheet Page
This extensive site provides information about spreadsheets of all types and includes downloads, tips, and FAQs, with special emphasis on *Microsoft Excel.*

Using Spreadsheets to Keep Track of Students' Grades
This is a basic guide explaining the tasks for setting up a spreadsheet to keep a record of students' grades.

Chapter Mastery Test

To the Instructor: *Refer to the Instructor's Manual for the answers to the Mastery Questions. This manual has additional questions and resource materials.*

Let us check for chapter comprehension with a short mastery test. Key terms, Computer Lab, and Suggested Readings and References follow the test.

1. What is a spreadsheet?
2. Give an example of each of the following terms: (a) macro, (b) cell, (c) logical functions, (d) predefined functions, (e) windows.
3. What is the advantage of being able to copy a formula in a spreadsheet?
4. Choose two important features of a spreadsheet and show how they can be utilized in the classroom.
5. Discuss the factors involved in selecting a spreadsheet for a school district.
6. Explain the advantage of a spreadsheet over a calculator.
7. Give an example of a situation in which an integrated software program has an advantage over a stand-alone program.
8. Describe the advantage of using what-if analysis with a spreadsheet. Name some applications in which this type of comparison would be important.
9. Explain and suggest reasons for the popularity of software suites.
10. If you were buying an integrated program, what are some features you would look at before buying?

Key Terms

Cell   147
Clipboard   167
Function   149
Hyperlinks   154

Integrated program
   165–166
Logical functions   151

Macros   151
Predetermined
   functions   151

Software suite   167
Spreadsheet   146
What-if analysis   150

Computer Lab: Activities for Mastery and Your Portfolio

7.1 Create a Classroom Budget Planner   Chart expenses for art materials, bulletin boards, holiday decorations, and so on.
7.2 Create a Gradebook   Keep track of student grades in all subjects.
7.3 Create a Day Planner   Keep track of daily class schedules, assembly times, prep periods, and so on.
7.4 Develop a spreadsheet activity for the classroom.
7.5 Create a spreadsheet similar to the grade book example given in this chapter, but for this example have 12 students take three exams and a final. Calculate the final exam as 40 percent of the grade and the other three exams as 20 percent each.
7.6 Prepare a review comparing three spreadsheets.
7.7 Use a spreadsheet to compare the expenses with a devised budget.
7.8 Outline in a lesson plan format three different ways a spreadsheet would be useful in the classroom.
7.9 Prepare a report on integrated programs, comparing their strengths and weaknesses.
7.10 List the different ways an integrated program would be useful in the school district office.

Suggested Readings and References

Abramovich, Sergei, and Peter Brouwer. "Revealing Hidden Mathematics Curriculum to Pre-Teachers Using Technology: The Case of Partitions." *International Journal of Mathematical Education in Science & Technology* 34, issue 1 (January 2003): 81–95.

Abramovich, Sergei, and Wanda Nabors. "Spreadsheets as Generators of New Meanings in Middle School Algebra." *Computers in the Schools* 13, no. 1–2 (1997): 13–25.

Ageel, M. I. "Spreadsheets as a Simulation Tool for Solving Probability Problems." *Teaching Statistics* 24, issue 2 (Summer 2002): 51–55.

Arad, O. S. "The Spreadsheet Solving Word Problems." *Computing Teacher* 14, no. 4 (December/January 1986–1987): 13–15, 45.

Aranbright, Deane E. "Mathematical Applications of an Electronic Spreadsheet." *Computers in Mathematics Education.* Reston, Va.: NCTM 1984 Yearbook, 1984.

Beigie, Darin. "Investigating Limits in Number Patterns." *Mathematics Teaching in the Middle School* 7, issue 8 (April 2002): 438–443.

Berglas, Anthony, and Peter Hoare. "Spreadsheet Errors, Risks and Technique." *Management Accounting: Magazine for* 77, no. 7 (July/August 1999): 46.

Berit Fuglestad, Anne. "Spreadsheets as Support for Understanding Decimal Numbers." *Micromath* 13, no. 1 (1997): 6.

Birmingham, Stephen. "Spreadsheets at the Beach." *Wall Street Journal Eastern Edition,* June 25, 1999, W9.

Black, Thomas R. "Simulations on Spreadsheets for Complex Concepts: Teaching Statistics." *International Journal of Mathematical Education in Science & Technology* 30, no. 4 (July/August 1999): 473.

Bourgeois, Michelle. "The Cruncher 2.0." *T.H.E. Journal* 27, no. 1 (August 1999): p. 52.

Brooks, Lloyd D. *101 Spreadsheet Exercises for Lotus 1-2-3 and Other Spreadsheet Software,* 2d ed. New York: Macmillan/McGraw-Hill, 1992.

Brown, J. M. "Spreadsheets in the Classroom." *Computing Teacher* 14, no. 3 (1987): 8–12.

Brown, J. M. "Spreadsheets in the Classroom Part II." *Computing Teacher* 14, no. 4 (February 1987): 9–12.

Brown, Graeme. "Spread It on thick." *Times Educational Supplement,* issue 4478 (April 26, 2003): 26–28.

Burns, Mary. "Beyond Show and Tell: Using Spreadsheets to Solve Problems" 31, no. 2 (2003): 22–27.

Carter, Ashley J. R. "Using Spreadsheets to Model Population Growth, Competition and Predation in Nature." *American Biology Teacher* 61, no. 4 (April 1999): 294.

Cooke, B. A. "Some Ideas for Using Spreadsheets in Physics." *Physics Education* 32, no. 2 (March 1997): 80–87.

DeMarco, Neil. "Numbers Tell Their Own Story." *Times Higher Education Supplement,* issue 1536 (May 3, 2002): 10–12.

Drier, Hollylynne Stohl. "Teaching and Learning Mathematics with Interactive Spreadsheets." *School Science and Mathematics* 101, no. 4 (April 2001): 170–179.

Gruet, Marie-Anne, Anne Philippe, and Christian P. Robert. "MCMC Control Spreadsheets for Exponential Mixture Estimation." *Journal of Computational and Graphical Statistics* 8, no. 2 (June 1999): 298.

Haugland, Ole Anton. "Spreadsheet Waves." *Physics Teacher* 37, no. 1 (January 1999): 14.

Holmes, Elizabeth. "The Spreadsheet—Absolutely Elementary!" *Learning and Leading with Technology* 24, no. 8 (May 1997): 6–12.

Hunt, William J. "Technology Tips: Spreadsheets—A Tool for the Mathematics Classroom." *Mathematics Teacher* 88, no. 9 (1995): 774–777.

Karlin, M. "Beyond Distance-Rate/Time." *Computing Teacher,* February 1988, 20–23.

Leonhard, Woody. "Excel Power Tips." *PC Computing* 12, no. 1 (January 1999): 264.

Lesser, Lawrence M. "Exploring the Birthday Problem with Spreadsheets." *Mathematics Teacher* 92, no. 5 (May 1999): 407.

Loeffler, Louis. "The Cruncher 2.0." *T.H.E. Journal* 27, no. 1 (August 1999): 54.

Luehrmann, Arthur. "Spreadsheets: More Than Just Finance." *Computing Teacher* 13 (1986): 24–28.

Manouchehri, Azita. "Exploring Number Structures with Spreadsheets." *Learning and Leading with Technology* 24, no. 8 (May 1997): 32–36.

Pfaffenberger, Bryan. *Webster's New World Computer User's Dictionary,* 8th ed. New York: Macmillan, 2000.

Ray, Beverly. "PDAs in the Classroom: Integration Strategies for K–12 Educators." *International Journal of Educational Technology* 3, no. 1 (November, 2002).

Riley, Kyle. "Using Spreadsheets to Estimate the Volatility of Stock Prices." *Mathematics and Computer Education* 36, no. 3 (Fall 2002): 240–246.

Sharp, Vicki. *Make It with Microsoft Office X (Macintosh).* Eugene, Ore.: Visions Technology in Education, 2003.

Sharp, Vicki. *Make It with Microsoft Office XP (Windows).* Eugene, Ore.: Visions Technology in Education, 2003.

Smith-Gratto, Karen, and Marcy A. Blackburn. "The Computer as a Scientific Tool: Integrating Spreadsheets into the Elementary Science Curriculum." *Computers in the Schools* 13, no. 1–2 (1997): 125–131.

Walkenbach, John. "Surprise, Surprise! Excel Can Handle Fractions." *PC World* 18, no. 5 (May 2000): 254.

Warner, C. Bruce, and Anita M. Meehan. "Microsoft Excel as a Tool for Teaching Basic Statistics." *Teaching of Psychology* 28, no. 4 (August 2001): 295–298.

CHAPTER 8

Multimedia

Using Multimedia to Integrate the Computer into the Classroom

Students learn better when they are involved in the learning process. This involvement increases as more of the senses are used in acquiring information. Multimedia provides an interactive, multisensory learning experience, which motivates the learner and improves the quality of learning. Using this technology, students can have a more exciting and interesting school experience. Students can create electronic portfolios using programs such as *eZediaMX, PowerPoint, Keynote, Kid Pix,* or *AppleWorks.* They can use a digital camera and programs such as *Photoshop Elements* to edit their digital images and print them, e-mail them, or post them on the Web. This chapter will provide suggestions on how to use multimedia in the classroom to help students better accomplish their educational objectives. You will become familiar with Internet sites that include software tips, multimedia resources, tutorials, design basics, and lesson plans.

Objectives

Upon completing this chapter, you will be able to do the following:

1. Define *multimedia.*
2. Explain the terms *hypermedia* and *hypertext.*
3. Discuss the origins of hypermedia.
4. Identify several major contributors to the field of hypermedia.
5. Explain the basic features of programs such *as eZediaMX, Keynote,* and *PowerPoint.*
6. Discuss the digital camera and how it can be used to create multimedia presentations.
7. Discuss some of the issues surrounding hypermedia.
8. Describe *QuickTime, morphing, warping,* and *virtual reality.*

Students Can

- create writing projects,
- design electronic portfolios,
- research curriculum topics,
- show a slideshow on the Internet,
- create interactive storybooks, and
- write biographies of famous leaders.

Teachers Can

- present lectures,
- introduce new math concepts,
- review historical material,
- show a famous painter's artwork,
- prepare a Web page tutorial, and
- create a presentation on the human body.

What Is Multimedia?

We are bombarded with the term **multimedia** everywhere we travel: on television, at the shopping mall, in newspapers, and in educational circles. What does this ubiquitous and elusive term really imply? Is it just a catchword tossed about, or does it have a specific meaning? In general and in this textbook, *multimedia* refers to communication of more than one media type, such as that involving text, audio, graphics, animated graphics, and full-motion video.

Multimedia is not a new concept. For years, teachers have made presentations using different kinds of media. Traditionally, they have used slides, movies, cassette players, and overhead projectors to enrich lessons. Now, however, teachers may employ personal computer and hard disk storage to combine these different media sources in their teaching. A computer-based method of presenting information, multimedia emphasizes interactivity (Pfaffenberger, 2003). Computers offer input and output devices, such as CD-ROM, DVD-ROM, and stereo sound.

Historical Perspective

In the professional literature, words closely related to multimedia are *hypertext* and *hypermedia*. Hypertext originated more than 50 years ago. Vannevar Bush, an electrical engineer and Franklin Delano Roosevelt's first director of the Office of Scientific Research and Development, is given credit for first proposing the idea of a hypothetical machine, predating computers, that would mimic the mind's associative process. In 1945, Bush described a workstation called a *memex* that imitated the linking and retrieval functions of the human mind. Influenced by Bush's associative linking and browsing concepts, Douglas Engelbard conducted research at the Stanford Research Institute in 1960 that led to several significant inventions, including the mouse, an online work environment now named Augment, and the concept of a "viewing filter." With a viewing filter, users could quickly view an abstract of a document or file, thus being able to scan a database for important information (Fiderio, 1988).

These developments were important, but it was Ted Nelson who took the critical step in the development of multimedia. Around 1965, he coined the term **hypertext,** meaning nonsequential writing, and he developed the writing environment called *Xanadu* that enables a user to create electronic documents and interconnect them with other text information. Through this endeavor, Nelson was attempting to make literary works available electronically. (Each time a user accessed text through this system, Nelson was paid a royalty.)

Hypertext and Hypermedia

In hypertext, text, images, sound, and actions are linked together in nonsequential associations so the user can browse through related topics in any order. At the center of this system is linking. No document or bit of information exists alone; each document contains links to other related documents. Figure 8.1 illustrates the nonlinearity of hypertext.

An example of hypertext is a computer glossary from which a user can select a word and retrieve its definition. This definition is linked to other words, and the user can move from it to other, related terms.

Hypermedia is nearly synonymous with *hypertext;* it emphasizes the nontextual components of hypertext. Hypermedia uses the computer to input, manipulate, and

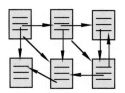

Figure 8.1 The Nonlinearity of Hypertext

output graphics, sound, text, and video as part of a system. The different forms of information are linked together so that the user can move from one to another. When a teacher uses hypermedia, the computer directs the action of devices such as a video camera, videodisc player, CD-ROM or DVD-ROM player, tape recorder, VCR, scanner, video digitizer, audio digitizer, or musical keyboard. Figure 8.2 shows an example of a hypermedia workstation.

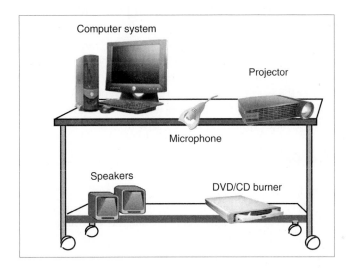

Figure 8.2 Using Technology in the Classroom— Hypermedia Workstation

Dell, Infocus, LACIE.

A computer and a monitor are the basic equipment necessary for a hypermedia presentation, with the computer acting as a controller and the monitor displaying images. Depending on the sophistication of their equipment, teachers can add a variety of devices and software programs to enhance the hypermedia creation (Figure 8.3).

Figure 8.3 Equipment Used with Presentations

Copyright 2001 www.arttoday.com (scanner and video camera); digital camera courtesy of CUSA; video digitizer courtesy of Freedman, Desktop Encyclopedia, 2000.

For example, they can use the digital camera to take pictures and the video camera to film a scene while the videocassette player records a television program. The scanner adds graphics or text, the audio digitizer transfers sound, and the video digitizer transfers noncomputer media such as photos or videotape. The video digitizer enables the user to convert an analog signal generated by a video camera, television tuner, videocassette player, or videodisc player into a digital signal. When this happens, the student or teacher can manipulate these digital images on the computer and incorporate them into a presentation.

Figure 8.4
FlexCam-iCam

VideoLabs.

A quick way to get slides into your presentation is to use photo-CD technology. This technology was developed by the Eastman Kodak Company to make it easier on individuals who wanted to scan color slides or negatives into a photo-CD. The user simply takes slides or negatives to a service that puts the images on a photo-CD at a reasonable cost.

Students creating presentations for biology can use a FlexCam-iCam (Videolabs) camera (Figure 8.4) to project images from a microscope to a television or computer. With the right accessories, they can capture images for their multimedia presentation. Teachers can also use art programs such as *CorelDraw* or *Kid Pix Deluxe 3* (Riverdeep) to enhance artwork, a musical keyboard to provide customized musical accompaniment, and a laser printer to produce high-quality images. Hypermedia components range from sound-enhanced documents that will play on any computer to *PowerPoint* presentations that include sound, animation, and color.

Hypermedia Authoring Tools

One objective of this chapter is to provide an overview of hypermedia authoring tools and programs and how they operate. While you cannot expect to become a hypermedia-programming expert based on the information in this chapter, you can consider the possibilities of hypermedia. Hypermedia authoring tools prepare students for the information-intensive society of the future in which hypermedia publishing may eliminate publishing as we know it.

HyperCard

One of the first implementations of hypermedia and the best-known one was **Hyper-Card,** developed by Bill Atkinson at Apple Computer. Atkinson created *HyperCard* in 1987 to run on the Macintosh computer. At that time, *HyperCard* became almost synonymous with *hypermedia,* although it is important to remember that not all hypermedia used *HyperCard.*

HyperCard was an authoring tool that enabled users to organize information, browse through it, and retrieve it. Information was stored in the form of on-screen *cards* (rectangular boxes on the screen) that contained text, graphics, sound, and animation. You could browse through the cards with the help of buttons, or "hot spots," that you clicked (Figure 8.5). The cards, which were displayed one at a time, were organized in

Figure 8.5 Elements of a Card

Images courtesy of Apple Computers, Inc.

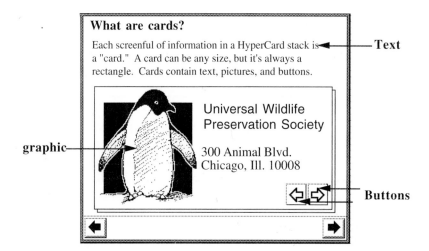

stacks, much in the same way you would organize a Rolodex or flipchart. *HyperCard* came with ready-made stacks, but the program also enabled teachers and students to create their own.

Many other authoring tools developed for hypermedia performed the same functions as *HyperCard,* such as, *LinkWay* for MS-DOS machines and *TutorTech* for Apple II. Although these programs represented a major step forward, they had limited use. Even though using them was not as difficult to learn as a programming language, creating stacks still required considerable time.

HyperStudio

When Roger Wagner produced *HyperStudio* for the Apple IIGS, hypermedia took a giant leap forward. *HyperStudio* had many of the *HyperCard* features and functions, but *HyperStudio*'s simplicity made it more suitable for most teachers and students. *HyperStudio* did not require scripting (programming) because all its major functions were already built into the software program itself. *HyperStudio*'s built-in features included CD-ROM support, animation, and scrolling. Advanced users could still program with *HyperStudio* by using a scripting language called *HyperLogo.*

HyperStudio, like *HyperCard,* displayed its information in the form of **cards** (Figure 8.6) that contained text, graphics, sound, and animation. These cards also

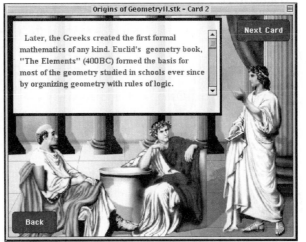

Figure 8.6
HyperStudio 4 Card

Used by permission of Knowledge Adventure/Havas Interactive.

included **buttons** with which the user could navigate through the cards and perform actions such as playing video and accessing websites (Figure 8.7). The cards were

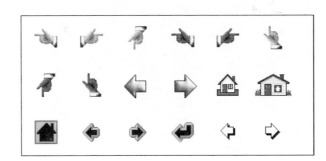

Figure 8.7
HyperStudio 4 Buttons

Used by permission of Knowledge Adventure.

organized in **stacks** (Figure 8.8), and *HyperStudio* came with ready-made stacks, but the program also enabled teachers and students to create their own.

Figure 8.8
HyperStudio 4 Stack

Used by permission of
Knowledge Adventure.

A new version of *HyperStudio* (Sunburst/ER) is currently under development.

PowerPoint

PowerPoint (Microsoft), a presentation tool for all age levels, enables users to turn ideas into powerful presentations. The program comes with instant layouts, on-screen directions, and tool tips to help users make compelling multimedia presentations. *PowerPoint*, unlike *HyperStudio*, displays its information in the form of **slides** that contain text, graphics, sound, and animation. By examining the *PowerPoint* (Microsoft) presentation in the following figures closely, you will gain an understanding of what is involved in working with this presentation tool. This Web page slide show guides students in planning a Web page and explains the factors to consider when judging a Web page.

Slide 1 (Figure 8.9) is the title screen with text, clip art, sound, and a button. The clip art, text, and button are all animated, appearing on screen one by one. When the button in the bottom right corner is pressed, the next slide is shown. Slide 2

Figure 8.9
PowerPoint Slide 1

Reprinted with permission of
Visions Technology in
EducationTM.
www.ToolsforTeachers.com.

(Figure 8.10) shows the steps the teacher feels are important in planning a Web page. This slide contains text, bullets, a video movie, and buttons. When the slide comes on

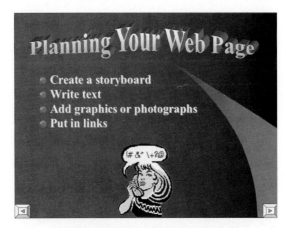

Figure 8.10
PowerPoint Slide 2

Reprinted with permission of Visions Technology in EducationTM. www.ToolsforTeachers.com.

the screen, a voice reads the text, a movie plays, and each point is made with the teacher's mouse click. The left arrow button takes users back to Slide 1, and the right arrow button plays a sound clip and then takes users to Slide 3. Slide 3 (Figure 8.11) contains animated text, graphics, and buttons. The text explains how to evaluate a website.

Figure 8.11
PowerPoint Slide 3

Reprinted with permission of Visions Technology in EducationTM. www.ToolsforTeachers.com.

When the teacher clicks the right arrow button, Slide 4 (Figure 8.12) appears. This slide contains an imported picture of the author and two hyperlinks, one to an e-mail

Figure 8.12
PowerPoint Slide 4

Reprinted with permission of Visions Technology in EducationTM. www.ToolsforTeachers.com.

address and the other to a site. The right arrow button takes the user to the last slide (Figure 8.13). Slide 5 ends the show with music and applause.

Figure 8.13
PowerPoint Slide 5

Reprinted with permission of Visions Technology in EducationTM.
www.ToolsforTeachers.com.

As you can see, *PowerPoint* is a versatile product, and the kinds of slide shows a teacher and student can create are endless. From this example, you can envision the amount of time, effort, and creativity involved in creating only five slides.

Keynote

Keynote is an extremely easy to use presentation program for Apple computers. Using this program you can create compelling presentations, with beautiful charts and tables (Figure 8.14). The program features layered graphical elements, and fantastic transitions

Figure 8.14 Pie chart from *Keynote*

Images courtesy of Apple Computers, Inc.

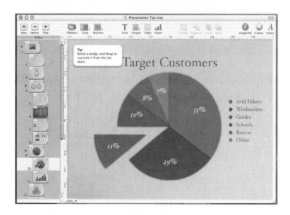

move the user from one slide to another. *Keynote* comes with professionally designed images and themes. You do not have to start all over when you use *Keynote* because you can import most file types into the program. You can even paste data from *Excel* documents into your *Keynote* charts and tables.

eZedia MX

eZedia MX (Macintosh and Windows) is a multimedia authoring tool with which students or teachers can create digital résumés, yearbooks, research reports, multimedia slide shows, and portfolios (Figure 8.15). These projects then can be included on

Figure 8.15 Teacher Portfolio

Reprinted by permission of eZedia Inc.

CD-ROMs, shown with projectors, or posted on websites. Students can also use this tool to develop travel journals, create storyboards, and make class albums. *eZedia MX* is an intuitive program; its simple drag-and-drop interface does not require scripting or programming. With this program, users can incorporate graphics, animations, movies, sound, text, virtual reality, and MP3s in their projects. Students have the ability to do sound mixing and fading as well as video editing.

MediaBlender

MediaBlender (Tech4Learning) is a multimedia-authoring tool that runs on your computer, or you can access it online at tech4Learning.com/mediablender/. Figure 8.16 shows a tide pool hypermedia presentation created with *MediaBlender.* It can be found

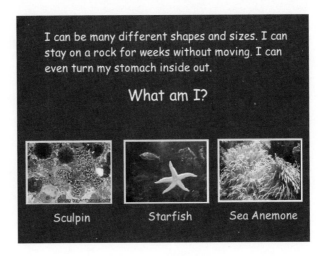

Figure 8.16 MediaBlender

Images used by permission of Tech4Learning, Inc.

online at http://tech4Learning.com/mediablender/samples.html. This particular project was designed to test students' knowledge of animals in a tide pool. Using this online feature students and teachers can easily share their creations.

MediaBlender comes with its own media library loaded with hundreds of copyright-free photos, sounds, movies, animations, and illustrations. The program features integrated paint tools that are easy to use and a very simple interface.

Other Programs

Table 8.1 displays an additional seven authoring programs.

Recommended Software
Multimedia Programs

For a listing of recommended multimedia software, go to the Online Learning Center.

Table 8.1 Additional Hypermedia Programs

Program	Publisher	Description
AppleWorks	Apple	Integrated program with slide presenter that can include QuickTime movies and sound
Create Together	Bytes of Learning	Wizards with different fill-in-the-blank templates, encyclopedias, interactive games, and hyperlinked or linear presentations
Kid Pix Deluxe 3	Riverdeep	Voice painting, photo editing, art tools, realistic sound effects, digital storybooks, comic books, e-mail drawings, and multimedia movies
Leonardo's Multimedia Toolbox	Riverdeep	300 interactive project templates and enhanced toolsets including animation, video editing, and sound editing
MovieWorks	Interactive Solutions	Tools to create QuickTime movies, videos, text, graphics, and animation
MP Express	Bytes of Learning	Intuitive floating palettes and a publisher-supplied collection of multimedia resources
VideoBlender	Tech4Learning	Videos, sounds, pictures, and text that can be combined to create digital movies, video portfolios, and video stories

Classroom Suggestions for Using Hypermedia

Students and teachers have a rich selection of software and hardware to choose from when developing first-class hypermedia presentations. Students can write and illustrate stories that combine text with graphics. They can create their own book reports, research presentations, tours, historical portraits, travelogues, animal reports, world events chronologies, and even school yearbooks. Students can create science presentations on a variety of different topics including chemistry, plants, animals, and rockets. For example, a student might want to generate a presentation on the different parts of the human body. One of the slides might look similar to the one in Figure 8.17. In the process of creating

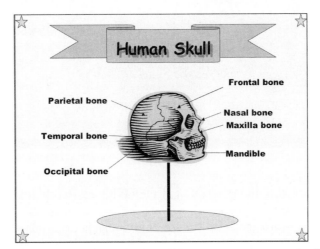

Figure 8.17
PowerPoint XP

Reprinted with permission of Visions Technology in EducationTM. www.ToolsforTeachers.com.

this presentation, the student would learn how to use the hypermedia program's drawing tools, print the slide on a transparency, and use the class overhead projector. This very same presentation could then be saved as a Web page for all students to access.

With a program such as *PowerPoint* or *Keynote* students can even create organizational charts and Jeopardy™-like games. They may create interactive books on African wildlife, for example. One student might create a presentation on a lion to be included in the book. In this multimedia presentation, he would discuss where the lion lives, what it eats, and how it tracks, and he could illustrate this presentation with photographs, music, narration, and a table of contents.

Teachers can generate slide shows on a range of topics from Beethoven to cell mitosis, all accompanied by music, sound effects, and digitized human voices. Using camcorders, teachers can prepare interesting film clips of field trips or school events. A presentation can be combined with computer graphics, photographs, animation, sound, and music. Teachers or students can then add computer titles and credits to their videotapes.

A teacher could create a slide show to enable students to browse through the permanent collection of the National Gallery of Art in Washington, D.C. She could import color images of the different works of art from the gallery onto the slides and record a narration about each painting. Students in her class could move through the gallery at their leisure, clicking buttons to move on to new paintings or to return to ones they had already seen. They also could click buttons to take a tour through the French countryside that inspired Monet's work or to listen to a concert of the music of composers such as Debussy who were contemporaries of some of the artists represented in the gallery.

A teacher might create a presentation that teaches a foreign language or a training module on how to use a digital camera. A teacher may even want to create a digital photo album (Figure 8.18) for an open house. For such an on-screen presentation, each student's photo would appear with music, text, and dazzling effects.

Figure 8.18 Photo Album in *PowerPoint*

Reprinted with permission of Visions Technology in EducationTM. www.ToolsforTeachers.com.

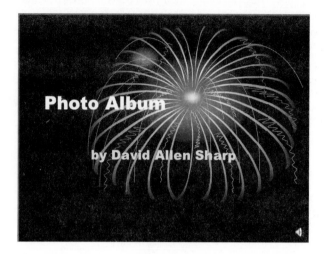

Guidelines for Creating a Multimedia Presentation

To plan a good presentation or multimedia stack, it is useful to follow some guidelines:

1. Consider your teaching objectives. What should users learn? What will they do?
2. Plan ahead. Do a sketch or rough layout of the slides or cards in your stack. Review what is to be communicated. Who is the audience? What approach will best express your message? You should be willing to experiment and be flexible.
3. Look for consistency on each card or slide and check for balance of design. Add interest when it is feasible and organize a card or slide around a dominant visual image. Be sure not to clutter a card or slide with too many elements.
4. Look at the format of your cards or slides. Pay close attention to borders and margins. Provide a dramatic graphic for the title card.
5. Add emphasis to the work. For example, use a large font size to call attention to important ideas. When needed, vary the type style by using boldface or italics. Use blank spaces to make designs stand out. Highlight the objects on the page with artwork, but do not overdo it. Help the reader's eyes focus on a particular part of a card or slide.
6. Do not use too many fonts because that detracts from the general message a card is communicating.
7. Use color wisely. Avoid clashing colors; work with complementary ones instead.
8. If you are only working in black and white, try to avoid too much white space. If this is unavoidable, surround the area with gray or black space.
9. Check your work thoroughly before showing or printing out copies of your work. Use the Computer Multimedia Checklist form to help you evaluate your multimedia projects.
10. Have students or other intended audience members preview your work. Watch their reactions. Do they learn what you intended? Are they able to navigate your stack successfully?

Computer Multimedia Project Checklist

Directions: Examine the following items and determine which ones you feel are important for your class situation. Place an X on each line for which the project meets the criteria.

Title _____ Date _____ Subject Area _____

Grade Level _____ Length _____

Audience _____ Objectives _____ Prior Knowledge _____

Content

_____ 1. Is current
_____ 2. Is accurate
_____ 3. Is clear and concise
_____ 4. Matches curriculum
_____ 5. Has no bias or objectionable language
_____ 6. Has clear directions
_____ 7. Contents include graphics, text, sound, and visuals

Graphics, Sound, and Visuals

_____ 1. Each slide has text and graphics appropriate to the content.
_____ 2. Buttons on each card work appropriately.

_____ 3. Graphics and sounds are not distracting.
_____ 4. Screens are neither cluttered nor barren.
_____ 5. Special effects are used appropriately.
_____ 6. Buttons and sounds associated with buttons are appropriate.

Fonts

_____ 1. There are not too many fonts or type sizes.
_____ 2. Font shadowing and outlining are not overdone.
_____ 3. Type is large enough for reading when projected.

Rating Scale

Rate the multimedia presentation by placing a check on the appropriate line.
Excellent _____ Very good _____ Good _____ Fair _____ Poor _____

Comments:

Pros and Cons of Hypermedia

Before concluding our exploration of hypermedia authoring tools, let us consider some of the benefits and drawbacks of this technology. Hypermedia as entertainment may effectively mesmerize its audience with spectacular presentations. A student viewing a hypermedia presentation—replete with text, graphics, film clips, still photographs, animation, sound effects, and moving maps—is very likely to be an involved student! One of the teacher's first responsibilities is to motivate students to learn, and the hypermedia presentation achieves this motivation. Students using hypermedia products are not passive receptacles of knowledge; rather, they are actively engaged in their learning, making decisions about how to proceed. The technology facilitates the development of research skills and encourages cooperative learning and problem solving. Reluctant readers are motivated to read, and inquisitive students have the freedom to explore topics independently. All students are able to acquire depth of knowledge on whatever stack, folder, or assortment of screens they are using.

Rehbein, Hinostroza, Ripoll, and Alister (2002); Myers, and Beach (2001); Lu, Wan, and Liu (1999); and Dede (1994) see this tool as serving a purpose beyond the creation of simple presentations, offering new methods of structured discovery, generating significantly better scores on remote association of concepts, addressing varied learning styles, motivating students, and applying pattern recognition techniques to help students master higher-order thinking skills. Swan and Meskill (1996) showed how hypermedia tools supported the teaching and acquisition of critical thinking skills in language and reading. Richard Mayer (1999) reviewed evidence from more than 40 studies that multimedia learning environments can promote constructivist learning that facilitate problem-solving transfer. Turner and Dipinto (1992) discuss how the hypermedia environment encourages students to be introspective and imaginative. According to Bill Gates (1995), hypermedia authoring may play a major role in preparing students for the intensive information world of the future.

Researchers such as Roblyer (1999) and Marchionini (1988) feel there are important contributions that hypermedia systems offer educators. First, they give students quick and easy access to large amounts of information in a variety of formats. Learners can easily use this diverse material stored in a compact form to follow national paths among items, or they may create their own interpretations. Second, the environment offers a high level of learner control because users may choose predetermined paths through the lesson or paths that suit individual interests and abilities. Third, hypermedia gives teachers and students an opportunity to change roles, in that students can use the technology to make presentations and teach one another, and teachers can learn from the technology's offerings about students' interests and abilities.

Obviously, hypermedia has great potential, but there are problems that must be addressed. One key question concerns the overburdened teacher's responsibility in this process: How is a teacher going to find the time to master hypermedia and devise hypermedia presentations? The average time required to put together a quality hypermedia presentation is between 20 and 50 hours. Who is going to train teachers to use hypermedia programs? Training requires funds and a commitment from school districts. Although there is general agreement that this medium stimulates in-depth knowledge, whether it fosters breadth of knowledge is yet to be determined. Also unclear are the implications of random learning, possible when students determine their own programs. Another problem according to Roblyer, Edward, and Havriluk (1997) is that students need sufficient online time, and their computers must be configured for hypermedia authoring; that is, they must have the capacity for digitized sound or input video. Finally, some critics question the value of hypermedia, claiming that it is all form and little substance. Teachers who prepare these presentations do spend inordinate amounts of time and energy so that their presentations will look professional, but perhaps this time is being diverted from substantive learning. A presentation ending with a barrage of images that have a limited connection with a topic may be a way of ensuring emotional involvement, but the cost may be a loss of real learning. Fiderio (1988); Stanton and Baber (1992); Roblyer, Edward, and Havriluk (1997); Dillon and Gabbard (1998); Shapiro (1998); and Chen (2002) describe some of the negatives of hypermedia as a technology:

1. Users need guidance because they can become lost in obscure links when they explore various databases.
2. Students may be attracted to tangential topics and be diverted away from subject matter that is relevant.
3. Teachers also may have difficulty breaking the information into smaller, more organized components.

4. The cost of hardware and the large memory requirements of hypermedia may make hypermedia prohibitively expensive for many schools. (Recently, this problem has been alleviated by the lower cost of equipment.) Some critics caution teachers not to substitute hypermedia for books and the library.

In conclusion, hypermedia is so embryonic a technology that research on its roles in classrooms is inconclusive and minimal (Weinberg, 2002; Roblyer, 1999; Madian, 1995; and Toomey and Ketterer, 1995). Do the benefits outweigh the problems? In the end, each individual educator must decide whether to embrace this technology, adopt selected hypermedia software, or cautiously await further developments.

Multimedia Software

As evidenced by the software catalogs, almost every software program incorporates some form of multimedia. In fact, just about every program mentioned in this book has some multimedia elements. Let us examine three of these programs to discover what makes them particularly useful in a classroom setting.

Inspiration

Multimedia visual mapping programs such as *Inspiration* for students in grades 4 and up and *Kidspiration* (Inspiration Software) for students in grades K–3 are perfect for planning a multimedia presentation, creating stories, organizing information, developing understanding of concepts, and expressing and sharing ideas. Figure 8.19 is a book analysis of *The Outsiders* by S. E. Hinton created with *Inspiration*. Through the process of creating this diagram, the student gathers all the information needed to write

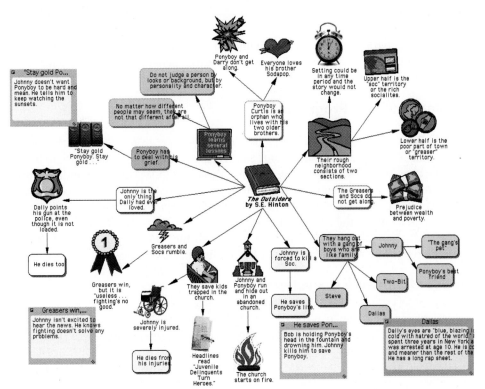

Figure 8.19 Book Analysis of *The Outsiders*, in *Inspiration 7.5*

Diagram created using *Inspiration*® by Inspiration Software®, Inc.

an in-depth book report. At the same time the student is creating this visual map, he is simultaneously creating an outline (Figure 8.20), which will aid in the writing process. This outline can be transferred to *AppleWorks* or *Microsoft Word*.

Figure 8.20 Outline for *The Outsiders*, in *Inspiration 7.5*

Created using *Inspiration*® by Inspiration Software®, Inc.

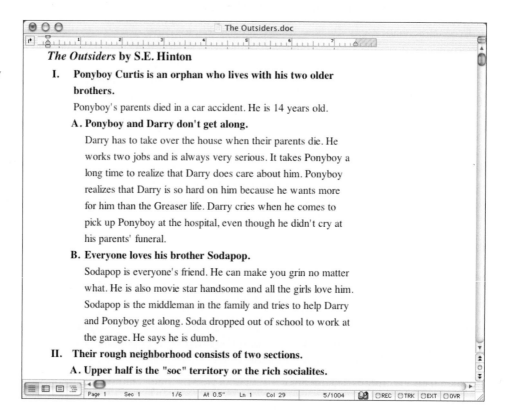

Using this program across curriculum lines, students can brainstorm, create concept maps, make graphic organizers, design storyboards, generate cause and effect diagrams, and prepare outlines.

Scholastic Series Programs

The Scholastic series programs *What's the Big Idea Ben Franklin? Where Do You Think You're Going, Christopher Columbus?* and *Shh! We're Writing the Constitution!* are based on books by popular award-winning authors. These CD-ROMs offer a wonderful way to explore social studies themes as required by the National Social Studies Curriculum Standards. Each program features a Learning Cube as its main menu. From this cube, users can go to any of the chapters in the programs. Students can see and hear entertaining videos or take audiovisual side trips with the Video Explorer. Each lesson comes with three games that help check and reinforce what the student has learned.

Grolier Multimedia Encyclopedia

General reference tools such as the *Grolier Multimedia Encyclopedia* can address any area of the curriculum. With this tool students can access such items as multimedia maps, explanatory illustrations and videos, animation, sound explanations, and time lines. Users are able to access audiovisual essays that combine photos, music, and narration to give comprehensive overviews of subjects such as the human body or space exploration.

Videos document historic events such as Dr. Martin Luther King Jr.'s "I Have a Dream" speech. Students can travel along a time line from prehistoric times to the present.

You can see that current educational programs have come a very long way from the static drill and practice texts of the 1970s. These new programs push technology to new heights with their multimedia features and their lifelike animations.

Multimedia Technology

Multimedia software caters to the needs of users of a wide variety of technology. It also makes such technology accessible to people in a wide variety of settings, including educational settings. Let us examine some of the most common technological tools used by multimedia software.

Digital Cameras

Pictures are a perfect way to add interest to a presentation. With the advent of inexpensive digital cameras (Chapter 3), teachers do not have to run to the local film development store but can instantly develop their own pictures.

There are many important considerations when purchasing a digital camera for your school; we will examine only a few here.

First, consider the camera's *image quality*. The more expensive cameras have the higher image quality. One factor that determines image quality is pixel density or pixel depth. Current digital cameras are capable of storing 8 million pixel images. Another factor that determines image quality is the quality of the lens system, which varies with the type of camera you buy.

Second, consider *camera use*. Buying the most expensive camera could be overkill when all you want to do is put images on a Web page or print to an inexpensive low-resolution printer.

Third, consider how the camera stores images and transfers images to the computer. Since teachers and students need a quick and easy way to transfer images to the computer, CD-R media or flash memory cards might be the preferred methods.

After you take pictures, you can use a program such as *Adobe Photoshop Elements* (Macintosh and Windows), *ImageBlender* (Macintosh and Windows), or *iPhoto* (Macintosh) to modify the images (see Chapter 14 for a discussion of art programs). A fun classroom activity is to give the class a picture and have the students modify it to your specifications. For example, I gave the class a picture of my son who thinks he is a punk rocker (Figure 8.21).

Figure 8.21 Before and After

Courtesy Tim Yost

Using *Photoshop Elements,* the class removed David's beard and earrings, fixed his slightly closed eye, changed his complexion, and gave him a better haircut.

After a digital picture is modified to your liking, you can then incorporate it into a multimedia presentation. You can also incorporate pictures into a classroom newspaper, slide show, or written report.

ImageBlender (Tech4Learning) is an image editor for the novice. Using *ImageBlender,* students and teachers can painlessly edit images. They can quickly crop an image; add a drop shadow, border, or bevel; and share images with fellow teachers, students, and Internet users. *ImageBlender* is easy to use with its intuitive graphic tools and multitude of interesting effects. This product lets the user make slide shows and enhance them with sound. *ImageBlender* comes with a Storybook Maker (Figure 8.22) compo-

Figure 8.22
Storybook Maker,
ImageBlender

Images used by permission of
Tech4Learning, Inc.

nent with which the teacher or student can create stories accompanied by recorded sound, backgrounds, and narration. These storybooks are automatically saved in HTML. Once you have placed a story on the Web and turned on the text-to-speech feature, the Web browser will read the story to the viewer. Tech4learning has a wonderful Web page loaded with images and terrific lesson plans and activities. Visit it at http://www.tech4learning.com/.

Video Editing Technology

Video editing involves integrating multimedia elements such as text, video, and audio into a presentation and then changing these elements to improve the presentation. Video editing includes cutting out unnecessary parts of an audio or video, recording dialogue, adding video and audio transitions such as fades, and creating a more finished product. *Adobe Premiere* is a full-featured video editing package that is daunting for the beginner. Several companies have created easy-to-use video editing applications for the classroom. Apple's *iMovie3* (Figure 8.23) is a relatively simple to use digital video editing software application that works on the new Macintosh computers. This program features convenient pull-down menus and icons that represent familiar tools and objects. It gives the student the ability to cut and paste video clips. Ulead's *Video Studio* uses a time-line or storyboard interface. For the time-line interface the student lays out the video clips chronologically. With the storyboard interface, the user orders and reorders video clips by dragging and dropping.

Figure 8.23 *iMovie3*
Images courtesy of Apple
Computers, Inc.

When working on video, it is important to have good storage and also a fast way to transfer data. FireWire (IEEE 1394), a high-speed serial bus or pathway, enables the user to connect up to 63 devices at speeds ranging from 100 to 400 Mbits/sec. (The second version of FireWire [IEEE 1394b] provides 800 to 3,200 Mbits/sec speeds). FireWire is widely used for attaching digital cameras and other devices to the computer (Freedman, 2003).

Music Technology

After years of silence, the Internet is coming alive with sound and music. Students are getting their music from a variety of sources, giving small bands opportunities they never had before. Teachers can easily make collections of music, adding richness to their history and cultural discussions.

Compression Technology. In the early days of computing, it would take forever to download a music file, because of the speed of the Internet connection and the size of the music files. Most people today have fast connections to the Internet and the ability to download music files quickly with audio compression technology.

Compression technology eliminates 50 to 95 percent of file size in a matter of seconds without losing data. **MPeg Audio Layer3 (MP3)** is an audio compression technology that produces CD-quality sound while providing almost the same fidelity. This technology enables people to download quality audio from the Internet quickly. In about five minutes, an hour of near–CD-quality audio can be downloaded. After the MP3 file is downloaded it is played through software such as *WinAmp3* or *iTunes* or players such as the *iPod* (Apple), which is attached to the computer by USB or FireWire cable.

Among the many programs available for creating classroom collections of music are *WinAmp3* (Nullsoft; http://www.winamp.com) and *iTunes* (Apple; http://www.apple.com). These media players enable you to play MPEG-4 audio, MP3, Wav, and other audio formats; build custom playlists; and track your music by artist, track, song, music style, or whatever is important to you.

iPod. The iPod (Figure 8.24) is a lightweight digital music player that is capable of holding 10,000 songs and downloading music at lightning speed. The iPod includes a

Figure 8.24 iPod
Images courtesy of Apple
Computers, Inc.

hard drive capable of holding 40 GB. This digital player works in conjunction with *iTunes Music Store* where students can preview, buy, and download music. The iPod can then make unlimited playlists and burn individual songs to a CD.

MIDI (Musical Instrument Digital Interface). **Musical Instrument Digital Interface (MIDI)** is "A standard protocol for the interchange of musical information between musical instruments, synthesizers, and computers" (Freedman, 2003). For multimedia presentations, MIDI has become widely used as background music. Many teachers have downloaded MIDI files to provide sound for their PowerPoint presentations. If a computer has a MIDI interface, students can record sounds created on their synthesizer and change these sounds to make new ones, by, for example, changing them from B Major to D Major.

Sound Editing Technology

If you are working with sound, you need a sound-editing program such as *Sound Companion* (FTC Publishing) (Figure 8.25). Students and teachers can use this program to enhance their multimedia presentations. First, you open a sound file on

Figure 8.25 *Sound Companion*

Used with permission of FTC Publishing.

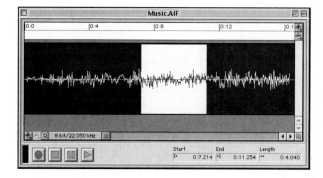

your computer. Then you can easily cut, copy, and paste audio segments from and to the file. *Sound Companion* can also apply sound effects such as echoes and fade in and out to an audio file. You can also record new sounds through a microphone. This program is a gem because it is reasonably priced and very easy to use.

Video and Sound Players

Apple was the first to integrate motion video into its operating system through *QuickTime* in Mac OS System 7. (The Windows options are presently called *Audio–Video Interleaved* (AVI) and *QuickTime for Windows.*) **QuickTime** is a video and sound player used to display miniature motion picture sequences in a screen window. A *QuickTime* file can contain all kinds of digital media. Any application that is compatible with *QuickTime* can play video, sound, and animation within its program. *QuickTime* is also used on the Web to provide Web pages with animation and video. *QuickTime* users also can create, edit, publish, and view multimedia content. With *QuickTime,* students and teachers can create and edit their own movies and incorporate them in *PowerPoint* or *Keynote* presentations.

No special hardware is required to play *QuickTime* videos. Early versions of this software produced low-resolution video quality, and the viewing window was small. Additionally, the quickness of video playback was dependent on the computer used. Another drawback was the large video file size required to transport and store these files. Computers are now faster and have large hard disk storage space to accommodate these large file sizes. *QuickTime* 6.5 (Apple) improves the compression rate (lessens the storage space) of these multimedia files, has better quality video and audio, and has quick playback.

QuickTime VR, an extension of *QuickTime,* enables the user to view and create videos in 3-D space. Videos are created from renderings or multiple still shots taken from all sides. The images are then fastened together into one continuous file. Thus, viewers are able to see around an object in 360 degrees, with seamless pan and zoom abilities. In addition, viewers are able to interact with the videos.

The first product that used this technology was *Star Trek: The Next Generation Interactive Technical Manual.* Some current programs that use *QuickTime VR* are *Oregon Trail* (Riverdeep), *eZediaMX* (eZedia, Inc.), and *HyperStudio 4.5* (Sunburst). Students may be able to use *QuickTime VR* to create walk-through presentations of their schools or sites of interest.

Morphing and Warping Technology

Morphing programs animate a picture sequence by gradually blending one image into another. An example of morphing is the shape-shifting security guard in *Star Trek: Deep Space Nine* or the evil terminator in *Terminator 2: Judgment Day.* I used *Morph Version 2.5,* a program by Gryphon, to morph a picture of my son, David, at 5 years old into a picture of him at 10 years old. This five-second video clip shows his transformation over the five-year period. Figure 8.26 shows four still pictures from this

Figure 8.26 *Morph Version 2.5*

Used by permission of Knowledge Adventure/Havas Interactive.

transition. The morphing software accomplishes the smooth transformation by matching a series of central points set in the beginning image to points in the ending image. In my short film, I selected the nose in the first image as a central point to be matched to the location of the nose in the last image. I kept adding these central points until the important features such as the mouth, eyes, ears, and head shape were charted. When the points are established, the morphing software sends the dots that are charted in the beginning image to their final location in the ending image, blending their shapes and colors.

The more points you add in morphing, the smoother the transition from one figure to the other. The traditional animation techniques that were perfected in the 1940s required 30 to 35 hand-drawn images to animate a figure for a single second on screen. Today, a morphing program relieves artists from performing this type of tedious detailed work and also generates a remarkable effect.

Warping is a completely different type of special effect from morphing. In warping, the key points of one image are used to create an effect that does not involve the blending of two images. By adjusting these main points, you push the selected points of the original image into a different shape. The final image is stretched so as to look completely different from the original one. For example, a rounded human face could be stretched into a narrow face, with pointed jaw and bulging eyes. In the movie *The Mask,* warping was used to stretch Jim Carrey's face whenever he put on the mask. The *Mona Lisa*'s face in Figure 8.27 is warped using *Kai's Power Goo* (Corel). With this program, the user can create liq-

Figure 8.27 Warping in *Kai's Power Goo*

Used with permission from MetaCreations Corporation, formerly MetaTools.

uid images and manipulate them by smearing, smudging, stretching, and fusing them. You can superimpose these images and blend parts of one image with another to create a third image.

As motivational devices, morphing and warping have some practical classroom applications. Students can experiment with different images and then copy and paste them to illustrate a story or report. They can create a morphed movie or warped picture for a hypermedia presentation. For example, students might show cell division or plant growth by morphing different pictures together. They might morph pictures of their parents to create new offspring or pictures of themselves and their grandparents to see how they might age.

Virtual Reality

The supreme achievement in multimedia is **virtual reality (VR).** Many authorities in the field consider William Gibson's depiction of cyberspace in his book *Neuromancer* to be the ultimate example of VR. In this book, cyberspace is described as the sum of all interconnected telecommunication networks in this future world (Gibson, 1984). People use this network by plugging their minds into it.

A more down-to-earth explanation of VR is a three-dimensional, interactive simulation. Participants in a computer-generated VR environment can manipulate what they see around them. In VR, users are electronically immersed in a simulated environment, in which they use their sight, hearing, and touch in all three dimensions to manipulate that environment. Participants wear headgear in which computer-generated images are sent to small screens placed before their eyes and to headphones in their ears. The headgear permits users to block out all actual stimuli to concentrate solely on the simulated stimuli. Participants also wear gloves or bodysuits equipped with sensors that communicate changes in body position to the computer, which then communicates the changes to the headgear (Figure 8.28).

Imagine that you are entering a simulation of the Tate Gallery. You look into one of the exhibit rooms. All around you are paintings and sculptures. As you turn your head, the screens in your headgear adjust to show you what you would be seeing in the actual gallery. If you walk forward, the screens will change again to simulate your movement. As you ap-

Figure 8.28 Virtual Reality

Photo by Kathie Koenig-Simon, http://www.nist.gov/public_affairs/gallery/labphim.htm.

proach the security guard to ask her a question, her voice becomes louder and louder in your headphones. When you raise your hand to point at one of the paintings, you see a simulated hand on your headgear screen. When you pick up one of the sculptures to examine it from different angles, the screen shows your hands and the different views of the sculpture, and your headphones transmit the angry voice of the security guard.

Virtual reality has found its way into research labs, business, the dentist's office, the military, and video arcade games. In some video games, you direct the action of the game with the movements of your own body, wearing headgear, gloves, and a bodysuit. In 1994, the first virtual reality wedding took place in a computer simulation of the lost city of Atlantis. The couple, Monika Liston and Hugh Jo, was married at the CyberMind Virtual Reality Center in San Francisco, where Liston works. The bridegroom, bride, and minister wore helmets with small built-in eye-level monitors; handheld controllers allowed them to move their virtual reality parts. Guests could view the ceremony on three large TV screens (Snider, 1994).

Fakerspace Systems' CAVE products are now used to simulate a virtual reality environment in order to test the design of a new building or to train people how to operate a Caterpillar bulldozer. This virtual reality system uses projectors to display images on three or four walls and the floor. Special glasses make everything appear as 3-D images and also track the path of the user's vision (Freedman, 2003).

In education, virtual reality's potential has yet to be explored. What is certain is that this potential is tremendously exciting; virtual reality technology will enable students to interact more fully with information being presented in all subject areas. Students with physical disabilities could benefit from VR by immersing themselves in different environments in which they have full abilities. Students and teachers could conduct experiments and experience situations that otherwise might be too costly or dangerous. Imagine networking an educational virtual reality system worldwide in real time. It would be a wonderful way to foster positive interaction among people of different cultures. Consider the usefulness of a virtual reality tour of London. Or your students could don helmets and fly the first spaceship to the moon or enter the human bloodstream to look at the heart.

In a physical education class, students could use a simulation to practice pitching to an all-star batter. In a science class, they could explore the laws of physics in a virtual world by testing how changes in gravitational forces affect virtual objects. In a language arts class, students could be visited by a virtual Mark Twain who could talk to

Recommended Software

Multimedia Software

For a listing of recommended Multimedia Software, go to the Online Learning Center.

them about his books and even answer the students' questions. A student violinist might even practice with the world's finest virtual orchestra and receive individualized tutoring. These are but a few of the options that will be available to educators in the near future. The biggest impediment to this advancement in technology is cost. Still, a future with virtual reality holds much promise for educators.

Classroom Lesson Plans

I. ORGANIZING YOUR THOUGHTS

Subject

Language Arts

Grade(s)

2 and up

Objective

Students will learn how to map their life visually using a software program such as *Kidspiration* or *Inspiration* (Figure 8.29).

Figure 8.29 Life Map in *Inspiration 7.5*

Used by permission of Inspiration Software, Inc.

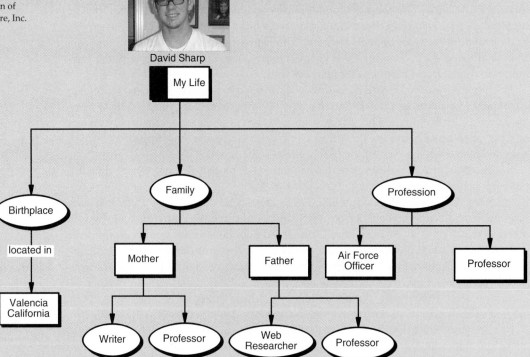

Standards

- NCTE English Language Arts Standards 1, 4, 5, 6, 12
- ISTE NETS for Students 1, 2, 3, 4, 5

Materials

You will need a program that does graphic organizing such as *Kidspiration* or *Inspiration* and one or more computers.

Procedures

1. Have the students write about themselves, their friends, their families, and their future goals.
2. Ask the students to take digital pictures of themselves, use the scanner to scan pictures they already have, and bring in clip art for their autobiographies.
3. Have the students work in teams to experiment with *Kidspiration* or *Inspiration.*
4. Next, ask each student to use *Kidspiration* or *Inspiration* to create a visual map of her or his life.

Variation

Have the students write about what they will be doing 10 years from now. They can take digital pictures of themselves and change them to make themselves appear older.

II. ANIMAL RESEARCH

Subject

Science

Grade(s)

4 and up

Objectives

Students will learn how to work with a software program such as *HyperStudio, PowerPoint, Keynote,* or *MP Express* and create a presentation in some subject area.

Standards

- National Science Education Standards A1, A2, C1
- ISTE NETS for Students 1, 2, 3, 4, 5

Materials

You will need a multimedia program such as *HyperStudio, PowerPoint,* or *Keynote.*

Procedures

1. Divide the students into small groups.
2. Have each group choose an animal to read about and research.
3. Ask the students to go on the Internet to find information about this animal. They can copy pictures of their animal and download sounds.
4. Have the students plan their stacks together.
5. Have the students in each group write a description of the animal and about where it lives, its enemies, its reproduction, its eating habits, and its prospect for survival in the future.
6. Finally, tell the students to create their slides or stacks and then have them share their presentations with the class.

III. TRAVELING TO A COUNTRY

Subjects

Social Studies and Language Arts

Grade(s)

4 and up

Objective

Students will use a software program such as *HyperStudio, PowerPoint, Keynote, MP Express*, or *Kid Pix Deluxe 3* to create a presentation about a country they would like to visit.

Standards

- National Council for the Social Studies Curriculum Standards 1, 3
- NCTE English Language Arts Standards 1, 4, 5, 6, 8, 12
- ISTE NETS for Students 1, 2, 3, 4, 5, 6

Materials

You will need a multimedia program such as *HyperStudio, PowerPoint*, or *Keynote* and a word processing program such as *Microsoft Word* and access to the Internet.

Procedures

1. Divide the students into small groups.
2. Have each group choose a country it would like to visit.
3. Have the students work in groups to research this country, finding out about the country's climate, people, money, language, and famous sites. They can go on the Internet or use books from the library for their research.
4. After this task is completed, have students create an itinerary for their country.
5. Ask students to use the Internet to find out the cost of hotels and airline tickets.
6. Next, have students plan their stacks together, collecting pictures of their country and downloading sounds and movies.

7. Have students use a multimedia software program such as *PowerPoint* to create their presentations.

8. When the presentations are finished, ask students to show their presentations to the class.

Variation

The students could use a word processing program such as *Microsoft Word* to produce brochures.

IV. MATH CONCEPTS

Subject

Math

Grade(s)

2–8

Objective

Students will use a software program such as *HyperStudio, PowerPoint, eZediaMX, MP Express,* or *Kid Pix Deluxe 3* to create a presentation that illustrates mathematical terms such as *fractions* and *percent* (Figure 8.30).

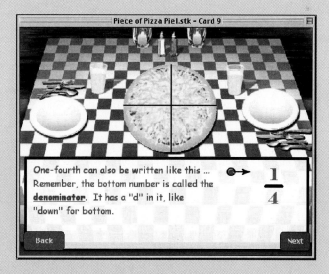

Figure 8.30 Fractions and Percent, in *HyperStudio 4.0*

Used by permission of Knowledge Adventure/Havas Interactive.

Standards

- National Council of Teachers of Math 8, 9, 10
- ISTE NETS for Students 1, 2, 3, 4

Materials

You will need a multimedia program such as *HyperStudio, PowerPoint,* or *Keynote.*

Procedures

1. Divide the students into small groups.
2. Have each group devise a definition for each mathematical term.
3. Ask students to plan their stacks together, collecting pictures and downloading sounds.
4. Have students use a multimedia software program such as *PowerPoint* to create their slides.
5. When the slides are finished, ask students to share their presentations with the class.

V. FAMOUS GENERALS

Subject

Social Studies

Grade(s)

4 and up

Objective

Students will use a software program such as *HyperStudio, PowerPoint, eZediaMX, MP Express,* or *Kid Pix Deluxe 3* to create a stack about famous generals of the Civil War.

Standards

- National Council for the Social Studies Curriculum Standards 1, 2, 3
- ISTE NETS for Students 1, 2, 3, 4, 5

Materials

You will need a multimedia program such as *HyperStudio, PowerPoint,* or *Keynote* and a word processing program such as *Microsoft Word* and access to the Internet.

Procedures

1. Divide the students into small groups.
2. Have each group choose a general.
3. Have the students work in groups to research the general, finding out about his life. They can go on the Internet or use books from the library or a multimedia encyclopedia to do their research.
4. After this task is completed, have the students create an outline.
5. Next, ask students to plan their presentation together, collecting pictures and downloading sounds and movies.
6. Have students use a multimedia software program such as *eZediaMX* to create their presentations.
7. When the presentations are finished, ask students to present their work to the class.

Summary

Hypermedia is the use of a computer to input, manipulate, and output graphics, sound, text, and audio in the presentation of information. In this chapter, we learned how hypermedia authoring tools such as *HyperStudio, eZediaMX, Keynote,* and *MP Express* operate and how they may be used as tools for instruction. We examined some of the unique multimedia software, the special effects that are available for the classroom, and some suggested activities for multimedia software. We explored five practical activities for use in the classroom, examined a checklist for evaluating a multimedia presentation, and considered some guidelines for creating a presentation. The Online Learning Center, under **Recommended Software,** includes an annotated list of multimedia software.

 Study and Online Resources

Go to Chapter 8 in the Student Edition of the Online Learning Center at **www.mhhe.com/sharp5e** *to* **practice with key concepts, take chapter quizzes, read PowerWeb articles** *and* **news feed updates** *related to technology in education, and* **access resources** *for learning about technology and integrating it into the classroom.*

Click on *Web Links* to link to the following websites.

African Studies Center
The African Studies Center at the University of Pennsylvania provides a wide variety of K–12 multimedia resources for exploring the historic and cultural diversity of sub-Saharan African people.

Apple's *iMovie*
Apple provides information at this site about its *iMovie* software for making desktop movies.

Ask Jeeves for Kids
Ask Jeeves for Kids enables you to search for thousands of filtered educational websites including multimedia resources. By entering *New Resources,* you will find the National Geographic for Kids site and *Scholastic News'* educational site for teachers and kids, which contains news, popular culture items, games and quizzes, and many other multimedia references for grades K–12.

BBC Schools Online
BBC offers a wealth of online multimedia resources in reading, math, history, and other subject areas for primary, middle, and high school students. To find other interactive activities, be sure to visit the *Education* and *Learning Zone* links.

The *Britannica Concise Encyclopedia*
This is a rich source of answers to questions about the full range of human knowledge, with more than 25,000 alphabetical entries covering the arts, business, computers, geography, history, literature, medicine, philosophy, politics, and popular culture.

Children's Educational Software
Children's Educational Software sells a great number of K–12 multimedia products online.

Columbia Encyclopedia 6th edition
The *Columbia Encyclopedia* 6th edition site contains nearly 51,000 entries on a variety of topics, with more than 80,000 hypertext cross-references.

ExploreMath.com
This site offers free course pages for teachers and multimedia mathematical activities for students studying algebra, geometry, and other high school math subjects.

Harcourt Brace School Publishers Learning Site
Click on the site map to find a wealth of interactive activities for grades 1–8, including an animated math glossary as well as a multiplication mystery.

HyperStudio
Knowledge Adventure provides information about *HyperStudio* software, consisting of multimedia-authoring tools enabling students to create interactive reports by mixing digital sources such as clip art, text, photos, video, sounds, animation, and narration. The site includes a showcase section where you can share and view other projects, discussion forums where you can learn more about this hypermedia program, and free training materials.

iLife
iLife features the latest versions of Apple's *iMovie, iPhoto, iTunes,* and *iDVD.* It contains lesson ideas to help you and your students make the most of digital movies, photos, and music in school projects and classroom presentations.

Inspiration Software
Inspiration Software is a visual idea development tool that creates and updates diagrams, flow charts, and other concept maps for educational purposes. The site has examples, tutorials, templates, and tips.

Interactive Solutions' *MovieWorks*

MovieWorks software, developed by Interactive Solutions, is a tool for making a *QuickTime* movie, video, or multimedia presentation.

Jac-Cen-Del Elementary

The Jac-Cen-Del Elementary School in Osgood, Indiana, showcases student-created projects (classroom activities) that use multimedia software. To learn about other schools integrating software in the classroom, visit Buddy Picks.

Kid Pix

The Learning Company (Riverdeep) provides information about its multimedia *Kid Pix* software. The site includes an online painting program.

Leonardo Software

Leonardo Software offers over 100,000 sound effects corresponding to everything from aardvarks to zeppelins on compact disc.

The Library of Congress

The U.S. government's Library of Congress provides a wealth of multimedia materials to enrich the K–12 social studies curriculum.

Listen.com

Listen.com is your guide to online music, offering reviews and links to music by more than 160,000 artists in 500 genres. The site helps you find the music of your favorite artist and every type of music on the Internet, including legal downloadable files such as MP3s and streaming audio and video.

Math Forum's Internet Mathematics Library

The Math Forum provides a comprehensive collection of sites offering downloadable material and software to enhance the teaching of K–12 math.

McGraw-Hill School Division

This K–8 educational publisher of textbooks and multimedia software provides Web-linked lesson plans for all major subject areas.

Microsoft *PowerPoint*

Microsoft *PowerPoint* is a software tool for creating presentations, organizing and formatting your materials, illustrating your points with images or clip art, and showcasing your presentations over the Web. The site includes how-to articles, tips and tricks, as well as support services.

MP3.com

MP3.com offers thousands of free downloadable songs. The songs come from different musical styles from all over the world. The site also features comprehensive hardware and software reviews, musical greeting cards, breaking digital music news, and more!

Multimedia Physics Studios

Tom Henderson of Glenbrook South High School in Illinois provides a collection of GIF animations with accompanying explanations of major physics concepts. The animations cover common physics principles discussed in a first-year high school physics course.

SafeKids.com

Larry Magid's site provides a safe-surfing haven for software, videos, links, and other multimedia resources. To find these resources, scroll to the *safety quiz* and click on *links* and *safe searching.*

SimScience

SimScience provides multimedia learning modules using computer simulations for grades K–12. It covers the science topics of *membranes, fluid flow, cracking dams,* and *crackling noise.*

Smile! Digital Cameras Can Make Your Day

Teachers are discovering valuable uses for digital cameras that make their own professional lives easier. Included on this site are more than three dozen easy activities for using digital cameras in the classroom.

SRA

SRA, a division of McGraw-Hill, provides teachers with hundreds of curriculum-aligned websites and multimedia demonstrations and students with websites, interactive math games, and science animations.

Yahoo! Music

Yahoo's directory contains all the information you could want about music, including MP3s, music you can listen to online, and other music topics. It also offers hundreds of streaming audio and video downloads.

Here are some additional digital camera sites that are loaded with classroom activities and teaching tips.

1001 Uses for a Digital Camera

http://pegasus.cc.ucf.edu/~ucfcasio/qvuses.htm

Digital Cameras Enhance Education

http://members.ozemail.com.au/~cumulus/digcam.htm

Digital Gadgets

http://school.discovery.com/schrockguide/gadgets.html
http://www.wacona.com/digicam/digicam.html#Lesson

Using Digital Cameras In the Classroom

Digitals Camera in the Class
http://www.techteachers.com/digitalcameras.htm

Using a Digital Camera
http://emints.more.net/info/digitalcamera/

Chapter Mastery Test

To the Instructor: *Refer to the Instructor's Manual for the answers to the Mastery Questions. This manual has additional questions and resource materials.*

Let us check for chapter comprehension with a short mastery test. Key Terms, Computer Lab, and Suggested Readings and References follow the test.

1. What is *hypermedia*?
2. What are two advantages of using your own authoring tool for a hypermedia presentation?
3. Who invented *HyperCard* and why was it so revolutionary?
4. Define the following hypermedia terms: *cards, stacks,* and *buttons.* Give an example of each.
5. What is the major disadvantage of using programs such as *Keynote* or *eZediaMX*?
6. Discuss how you would use the button function in a *HyperStudio* or *PowerPoint* program.
7. In preparing your multimedia presentation for class, name two mistakes that you want to avoid.
8. If you were to evaluate a multimedia presentation, what criteria would you use and why?
9. Describe a multimedia program for each of the following subject areas: social studies, language arts, science, music, and mathematics. Use the Computer Lab CD-ROM to help you with your selection.
10. If you were to buy two multimedia programs, which two would you choose? What are the reasons for your choices?
11. Discuss the advantages and disadvantages of multimedia productions in the school setting.
12. Define *virtual reality* and discuss some of its implications.
13. Explain how morphing and warping work.
14. What is a *video digitizer*?
15. When purchasing a digital camera for your school what factors should you consider before making the purchase?

Key Terms

Buttons 176	Morphing 192	Musical Instrument Digital	Stacks 176
Cards 175	MPeg Audio Layer 3	Interface (MIDI) 190	Video editing 188
HyperCard 174	(MP3) 189	*QuickTime* 190	Virtual reality (VR) 192
Hypermedia 173	Multimedia 172	*QuickTime VR* 191	Warping 191–192
Hypertext 172		Slides 176	

Computer Lab: Activities for Mastery and Your Portfolio

8.1 Message Design Primer This primer illustrates design heuristics regarding capturing an audience, layout, typography, image, and color.

8.2 Multimedia Evaluation Scenarios Using the checklist included in the text, evaluate a sample multimedia program or application for possible use in the classroom.

8.3 Learn a hypermedia application (such as *PowerPoint, eZediaMX,* or *MediaBlender*) and write a short report describing its strengths and weaknesses.

8.4 Explain a mathematical concept by generating your own slide show, using software such as *Kid Pix Deluxe 3.*

8.5 Tape record an interview on some important topic. Write a script using the speaker's words and add your own synchronized sound effects. Using one of the hypermedia authoring tools, create a presentation from this interview.

8.6 Record an interesting event or trip with a camcorder and combine this with animation, speech, and music, using one or more of the software programs discussed in this chapter.

Suggested Readings and References

Adams, P. E. "Hypermedia in the Classroom Using Earth and Space Science CD-ROMs." *Journal of Computers in Mathematics and Science Teaching* 15, no. 1–2 (1996): 19–34.

Bagui, S. "Reasons for Increased Learning Using Multimedia." *Journal of Educational Multimedia and Hypermedia* 7, no. 1 (1998): 3–18.

Baker, Richard L., and Michael C. Blue. "The Cost-Effective Multimedia Classroom." *T.H.E. Journal* 27, no. 1 (August 1999): 46.

Bornman, H., and S. H. von Solms. "Hypermedia, Multimedia, and Hypertext—Definitions and Overview." *Electronic Library* 11, no. 4–5 (1993): 259–268.

Boyle, T. *Design for Multimedia Learning.* London: Prentice Hall, 1997.

Brewer, Stephen. "Software." *Family PC* 7, no. 7 (July 2000): 72.

Brownstein, Mark. "Batter up for Broadband." *Byte Special Report,* October 1997, 71–74.

Bruder, Isabelle. "Multimedia—How It Changes the Way We Teach and Learn." *Electronic Learning* 11, no. 1 (September 1991): 22–26.

Brunner, C. "Judging Student Multimedia." *Electronic Learning* 15, no. 6 (1996): 14–15.

Buckleitner, Warren. "Classrooms Without Walls." *Instructor (1999)* 110, no. 2 (September 2000): 91.

Bull, Glen, Gina Bull, and Aileen Nonis. "Intent Scripting with HyperStudio." *Learning and Leading with Technology* 24, no. 8 (May 1997) 40–43.

Carr, Tracy, and Asha K. Jitendra. "Using Hypermedia and Multimedia to Promote Project-Based Learning of At-Risk High School Students." *Intervention in School and Clinic* 36, no. 1 (September 2000): 40.

Carroll, John M. "Designing Hypermedia for Learning." *American Journal of Psychology* 106, issue 4 (Winter 1993): 616–621.

Cates, Ward Mitchell, and Susan C. Goodling. "The Relative Effectiveness of Learning Options in Multimedia Computer-Based Fifth-Grade Spelling Instruction." *Educational Technology Research and Development* 45, no. 2 (1997): 27–46.

Cochran, David, and Robb Staats. *HyperStudio Express 3.1.* New York: Glencoe/McGraw-Hill, 1999.

Dede, Christopher J. "The Future of Multimedia: Bridging to Virtual World." *Educational Technology* 32, no. 5 (May 1992): 54–60.

Dede, Christopher. "Making the Most of Multimedia." *Multimedia and Learning: A School Leaders Guide.* Alexandria, Va.: NSBA, 1994.

D'Ignazio, Fred. "A New Curriculum Paradigm: The Fusion of Technology, the Arts, and Classroom Instruction." *Computing Teacher,* April 1991, 45–48.

D'Ignazio, Fred, and Joanne Davis. "What I Did Last Summer 21st Century Style." *Learning and Leading with Technology* 24, no. 8 (May 1997): 44–47.

Dillon, Andrew., and Ralph. Gabbard. "Hypermedia as an Educational Technology: A Review of the Quantitative Research Literature on Learner Comprehension, Control, and Style." *Review of Educational Research* 68, issue 3 (Fall, 1998): 322–349.

Eddings, Joshua. *How Virtual Reality Works.* Emeryville, Calif.: Ziff-Davis Press, 1994.

Fiderio, Janet. "Grand Vision." *Byte* 13, no. 10 (October 1, 1988): 237–242.

Finkel, LeRoy. *Technology Tools in the Information Age Classroom.* Wilsonville, Ore.: Franklin Beedle and Associates, 1991.

Fleck, Tim, et al. *HyperStudio for Terrified Teachers.* Huntington Beach, Calif.: Teacher Created Materials, 1997.

Florio, Chris, and Michael Murie. "Authoritative Authoring: Software That Makes Multimedia Happen." *NewMedia* 6, no. 12 (September 9, 1996): 67–70, 72–75.

Freedman, Alan. *Computer Desktop Encyclopedia.* Point Pleasant, Pa.: The Computer Language Company, 2003.

Gates, Bill. "Multimedia Revolution Is Here. Life On-Line." *Gainesville* (Florida) *Sun,* May 15, 1995, 7.

Gibson, William. *Neuromancer.* New York: Ace Books, 1984.

Goolkasian, Paula. "Getting Started with Multimedia." *Behavior Research Methods, Instruments, & Computers* 28, issue 2 (May 1996): 279.

Gratton, Marilyn. *Microsoft Powerpoint 2000: One Step at a Time.* New York: IDG Books Worldwide, 2000.

Green, Tim, and Abbie H. Brown. "Multimedia Projects in the Classroom: A Guide to Development and Evaluation." *MultiMedia Schools* 9, no. 4 (September 2002): 20–24.

Guglielmo, Connie. "Multimedia Makers Get Point, Click." *Macweek* 5, no. 18 (May 1991): 22.

Hoffman, Joseph L., and David J. Lyons. "Evaluating Instructional Software." *Learning and Leading with Technology* 25, no. 2 (October 1997): 52–53.

Holsinger, Erik. *How Multimedia Works.* Emeryville, Calif.: Ziff-Davis Press, 1994.

Johnson, Stuart J. "Multimedia: Myth vs. Reality." *InfoWorld* 12, no. 8 (February 19, 1990): 47–52.

Lifter, M., S. I. Kessler, M. Adams, and J. Patterson. *Multimedia Projects for Kid Pix.* Bloomington, Ill.: Family Time Computing, 1998.

Lu, Gang, Hongwen Wan, and Shouying Liu. "Hypermedia and Its Application in Education." *Educational Media International* 36, no. 1 (March 1999): 41–45.

Madian, Jon. "Multimedia—Why and Why Not?" *Leading and Learning* 22, no. 7, (2003): 16.

Marchionini, G. "Hypermedia and Learning: Freedom and Chaos." *Educational Technology* 28, no. 11 (1988): 8–12.

Mayer, Richard E. "Multimedia Aids to Problem-Solving Transfer." *International Journal of Educational Research* 31, no. 7 (1999): 611–623.

McBride, Karen, and Elizabeth DeBoer Luntz. *Help! I Have HyperStudio. Now What Do I Do?* Eugene, Ore.: Visions Technology in Education, 2001.

Milheim, William D. "Virtual Reality and Its Potential Application in Education and Training." *Machine-Mediated Learning* 5, no. 1 (1995): 43–55.

Milligan, Patrick, and Chris Okon. "Mastering Multimedia." *MacUser,* October 1994, 82–88.

Milton, Karen, and Pattie Spradley. "A Renaissance of the Renaissance—Using HyperStudio for Research Projects." *Learning and Leading with Technology* 23, no. 6 (March 1996): 20–22.

Monahan, Susan, and Dee Susong. "Author Slide Shows and Texas Wildlife: Thematic Multimedia Projects." *Learning and Leading with Technology* 24, no. 2 (October 1996): 6–11.

Moran, Tom. "QuickTime VR: A New Spin." *MacWorld,* October 1994, 34–35.

Moreno, Roxana, and Richard E. Mayer. "Learning Science in Virtual Reality Multimedia Environments: Role of Methods and Media." *Journal of Educational Psychology,* vol. 94, no. 3 (September 2002): 598–610.

Needleman, Raphael. "'Action' Takes the Pain out of Creating Presentations." *InfoWorld* 13, no. 32 (August 12, 1991): 1, 91.

Nelson, Theodore H. *Dream Machines: New Freedoms Through Computer Screens—A Minority Report.* Chicago: Hugo Books Service, 1974.

Oliver, Kevin, and Michael J. Hannafin. "Student Management of Web-Based Hypermedia Resources During Open-Ended Problem Solving." *Journal of Educational Research,* vol. 94, no. 2 (December 2000): 75–92.

Olsen, Gary. *Getting Started in Multimedia Design.* Cincinnati: North Light Books, 1997.

Pfaffenberger, Bryan. *Webster's New World Dictionary of Computer Terms,* 8th ed. New York: IDG Books Worldwide, 2000.

Pfiffner, Pamela. "Welcome to QuickTime's Virtual Reality." *MacUser,* September 1994, 31.

Porter, Anne E. "Scavenged Idea and Virtual Hypermedia." *Computing Teacher,* May 1991, 38–40.

Rehbein, Lucio, Enrique Hinostroza, Miguel Ripoll, and Isabel Alister. "Students' Learning through Hypermedia." *Perceptual & Motor Skills* 95, issue 3 (December 2002): 795.

Roblyer, M. D., J. Edward, and Mary Anne Havriluk. *Integrating Educational Technology into Teaching.* Upper Saddle River, N.J.: Prentice Hall, 1997.

Roblyer, M. D. "Our Multimedia Future: Recent Research on the Impact of Multimedia on Education." *Learning & Leading with Technology.* Eugene, Ore.: ISTE, 1999.

Shapiro, Amy M. "Promoting Active Learning: The Role of System Structure in Learning from Hypertext." *Human–Computer Interaction* 13, no. 1 (1998): 1–35.

Sharp, Vicki. *HyperStudio 3.2 in an Hour (Windows and Macintosh Version).* Eugene, Ore.: ISTE, 1999.

Sharp, Vicki. *Make It with Inspiration.* Eugene, Ore.: Visions Technology in Education, 2003.

Sharp, Vicki. *Make It with Office, 97, 2000, XP (Windows Version), 98, 2001, X. (Macintosh Version).* Eugene, Ore.: Visions Technology in Education, 2004.

Sharp, Vicki. *PowerPoint 97 in an Hour (Windows Version).* Eugene, Ore.: ISTE, 1999.

Sharp, Vicki. *PowerPoint 98 in an Hour (Macintosh Version).* Eugene, Ore.: ISTE, 1999.

Smith, Irene, and Sharon Yoder. *Inside HyperStudio: Scripting with HyperLogo.* Eugene, Ore.: ISTE, 1997.

Snider, Mike. "In the Heart of Cyberspace." *USA Today,* August 19, 1994, 1.

Song, Chiann–Ru. "Literature Review for Hypermedia Study from an Individual Learning Differences Perspective." *British Journal of Educational Technology* 33, issue 4 (September 2002): 435.

Stamp, Dave, Bernie Roehl, and John Eagan. *Virtual Reality Creations.* Corte Madera, Calif.: Waite Group Press, 1994.

Stanford, Alan. "It's Time for Quicktime." *MacHome,* May 1998, 18–20.

Stanton, Neville, and Chris Baber. "An Investigation of Styles and Strategies in Self-Directed Learning." *Journal of Educational Multimedia and Hypermedia* 1, no. 2 (1992): 147–167.

Stefananc, S., and L. Weiman. "Macworld Multimedia: Is It Real?" *MacWorld,* April 1990, 116–123.

Swan, Karen, and Carla Meskill. "Using Hypermedia in Response-Based Literature Classrooms: A Critical Review of Commercial Applications." *Journal of Research on Computing in Education* 29, no. 2 (Winter 1996): 167–195.

Swartz, James D., and Tim Hatcher. "Virtual Experience: The Impact of Mediated Communication in a Democratic Society." *Educational Technology* 36, no. 6 (November–December 1996): 40–44.

Toomey, R., and K. Ketterer. "Using Multimedia as a Cognitive Tool." *Journal of Research on Computing in Education* 27, no. 4 (Summer 1995): 472–483.

Turner, S. V., and V. H. Dipinto. "Students as Hypermedia Author: Themes Emerging from a Qualitative Study." *Journal of Research on Computing Education* 25, no. 2 (1992): 187–199.

Vaughan, Tay. *Multimedia: Making It Work,* 4th ed. New York: Osborne McGraw-Hill, 1998.

Wagner, Nancy. "Get-Acquainted Slide Show." *Instructor (1999)* 110, no. 2 (September 2000): 28.

CHAPTER 9

Telecommunications and the Internet

The Internet in the Classroom

Marianne Brooker's class at Calahan Elementary School working on the Internet.

The worldwide Internet population was over 600 million in 2002. It is projected to reach over 900 million in 2005. Having access to the Internet means that you could tap into thousands of databases and talk electronically with experts all over the world on any subject. Students can explore this giant library with millions of sites and obtain information on any curriculum area, participate in online discussion groups, download lecture notes, and do research. They can create their own Web pages to showcase and share information. This chapter will introduce you to telecommunication and the Internet. Exercises will help you integrate the Internet into the classroom. We will examine Internet sites that include articles on the Internet's origins, online encyclopedias, and online dictionaries.

Objectives

Upon completing this chapter, you will be able to do the following:

1. Describe *networking* and explain how it operates.

2. Discuss the Internet's historical background.
3. Explain the issues to consider when using the Internet.

Students Can

- research for projects,
- do homework and seek tutorial help,
- take practice quizzes,
- participate in collaborative science investigations, and
- video conference with other students.

Teachers Can

- post exams online,
- find lesson plans and instructional material,
- share common problems with other teachers,
- work on collaborative projects, and
- communicate with e-mail and video conferencing.

What Are Telecommunications and Networking?

Telecommunications is the electronic transmission of information including data, television pictures, sound, and facsimiles. In order to transmit information electronically, you must connect one computer to another, using hardware and software. In the majority of cases, the hardware consists of equipment that sends the data over some type of communications line, such as a telephone line. This equipment includes a modem, telephone lines, and a computer. The software controls the flow of data.

With this equipment, you can communicate with a friend in St. Louis, Missouri, or Paris, France, and send and receive anything from a manuscript to a simple message. A homebound child can interact with a teacher in the classroom, an office worker at home can interact with colleagues at work, and a doctor can access a remote computer for research data.

The reasons for using telecommunications are convincing:

1. it is expedient and efficient,
2. it decreases air pollution from auto emissions,
3. it saves time and money,
4. it enables people to work from home, and
5. it facilitates distance learning in which students can share information and computer research findings with students and teachers all over the world.

Networking is another way that computers communicate with each other. In a network, numerous computers are connected together. A computer network generally requires one or more computers and a **file server,** which is a computer with a large data capacity that serves as a repository for information. The file server directs the flow of information to and from the computers in the network. You also need a network card, if the networking capabilities are not built or plugged into the computer, and cables, wires, hookups, and operating system software (available from companies such as Novell, Apple, and Microsoft) that gives access to the file server. Besides this special software and equipment, you need "networkable" software that runs on the network. In addition, a network needs a variety of devices to connect parts of the network and handle traffic among the various components. A **hub** is a central connecting device that joins communication lines together on a network. **Switches** and **routers** are devices used to organize the traffic along the correct pathway. They forward this information from one network to another. A network can have a permanent connection such as a cable or a temporary connection made through the telephone or another communication device.

The computer's network cable connection can be either copper or fiber optic. The more expensive fiber optic cables, a transmission medium consisting of glass fibers, transmit digital signals in the form of pulses of light produced by a laser. Using this type of cabling, the network can handle more messages simultaneously than it could with copper wiring or coaxial cable. Heinich et al. (2002) explain that "two glass optical fibers can handle 6,000 telephone conversations at a time, a task that would take 250 copper wires."

Networks

Local area networks (LANs), wide area networks (WANs), and telephones are three types of networks. LANs provide communication within a local area, usually within 200 or 300 feet, such as in an office building. A school might have its card catalog stored on a file server's hard disk, accessible by other computers throughout the building through a LAN. WANs provide communication for a larger area and require miles of communication linkage. A telephone network connects computers via telephone. The only difference between a WAN and a telephone network is the fact that the telephone's communication is intermittent, but the wide area network communicates all the time. Networks not only use cables but are also being connected without wires.

Wireless Networks

A **wireless network** enables you to transmit data "between computers, servers, and other network devices without the use of a physical cable or wire" (Freedman, 2003). The different means used to provide wireless transmission are infrared, cellular, microwave, and satellite. Presently, infrared transmission is being used in small networks of either one room or to connect computers from room to room. This type of transmission has become popular in the classroom, because it is very easy to install. In using this type of network, all the user has to worry about is making sure the signal is not blocked from the computers or deflected. Current portable computers have infrared transceivers so they can send files to their printer, a desktop computer, or a handheld computer.

Apple's *Airport Extreme Wireless* is an example of a wireless technology that uses radio signals to communicate and does not require an unobstructed line of sight to make a connection. *Airport Extreme* also delivers fast, affordable wireless technology to the home or classroom without cables or complicated networking hardware. With this software, students can go on the Internet wirelessly with their iBook, iMac, PowerBook, or Power Mac G5 at home, in the classroom, or in the dorm. As many as 50 Macintosh, and Windows users in a single network can be online simultaneously surfing on different websites, accessing e-mail, and exchanging files through one Internet service account. They can communicate up to 150 feet away, and the communication is fast, at 54 megabits per second (Mbps). *Airport Wireless* Internet access requires an *Airport Extreme* Card, an *Airport Extreme* Base Station (Figure 9.1), and In-

Figure 9.1 Apple's *Airport Extreme* Wireless Technology

Images courtesy of Apple Computers, Inc.

ternet access. Some Internet service providers (ISPs) are not compatible with *Airport*, and range may vary with the site conditions.

Another example of a wireless network comes from Bluetooth Special Interest Groups (http://www.bluetooth.com). *Bluetooth* is short-range radio communication, which uses radio waves that can transmit through walls and nonmetal objects. This technology enables a variety of devices, such as laptops, PCs, phones, personal data assistants (PDAs) (Chapter 3), and printers, to communicate with each other without cables. A small group of users can also use this technology to create their own personal area network. Data can be sent from 750 Kb to 1 Mb per second across distances of up to 100 meters.

Wireless Networks in the Schools

Anthony Nguyen, a network administrator at California State University, Northridge, feels that in the near future, we will see wireless networks gaining even more ground in the schools. The wireless network eliminates expensive cabling and adds flexibility, permitting users to move the machines freely around a room and eliminating the cost of running cables throughout a building.

Having wireless-network access could eliminate the cost of upgrading computer equipment: Some colleges provide wireless-network access but leave it to students to purchase the laptop computers with wireless-network cards to use the network. For example, California State University, Northridge is moving in the direction of providing wireless Ethernet service for all students, faculty, and staff. Using wireless networking, students and faculty can access this network from different areas of the campus. The network relies on wireless access points (base stations) that are connected to the server. These base stations transmit radio frequency over the campus. When a user leaves the transmitting area of one station, he or she enters that of another. As the cost of wireless decrease and the speed of computers increases, wireless networks will proliferate in schools across the country. That is when we will see the possibility of every classroom being connected to the Internet.

Network Arrangements

The three most commonly known network arrangements are the ring, the star, and the shared bus. The **ring network** is a communication network that connects devices such as computers in a closed loop or ring. This network does not rely on a file server or central computer, so if one computer goes down in the system, the others still operate (Figure 9.2). This configuration is found in university administrative offices in which each computer performs when needed and each computer has its own software.

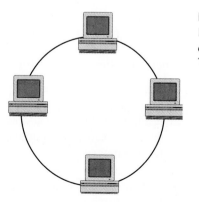

Figure 9.2 Ring Network

ClickArt Images ©1995 T/Maker Company.

In the second arrangement, the **star network** (Figure 9.3), a file server is connected with several computers or terminals. The star network becomes inoperable if

Figure 9.3 Star Network

ClickArt Images ©1995 T/Maker Company.

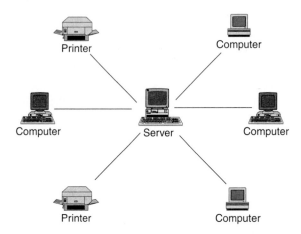

the file server fails because it has in its memory all the data that the other computers use for processing. A school computer center might use this type of network for its card catalog.

In the third arrangement, the **shared-bus network** (Figure 9.4), a single bidirectional cable acts as a "bus line" to carry messages to and from devices. Each stop along the line has its own address, so a problem at one stop will not cause a problem throughout the

Figure 9.4 Shared-Bus Network

ClickArt Images ©1995 T/Maker Company.

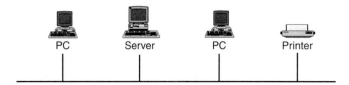

network (Pfaffenberger, 2002). Information is stored in a central computer. To avoid the data collisions that occur when two or more stops, or nodes, try to use the line at the same time, bus networks use collision detection. Small local area networks use this configuration because it is an easy system to set up and use.

Advantage of a Network

A network offers the following advantages:

1. It establishes communication among computers and is especially helpful when people work on different floors or in different buildings.
2. It improves the speed and accuracy of communication, preventing messages from being misplaced and automatically ensuring total distribution of key information.
3. It saves money because users share software and equipment such as word processing programs and laser printers.
4. A network enables users to share files with one another, which makes it suitable for class research.

Disadvantages of a Network

A network presents the following potential disadvantages:

1. The costs of networking entail hardware, computer training, and maintenance, which can be high.
2. Networking requires expertise that may not always be readily available, and school districts must consider the frustration level of teachers faced with the extra burden of learning a new system.
3. It is difficult to find competent technicians to repair this equipment, and teachers who come to rely on their computers may be at a loss if the system crashes.
4. The necessary networking software is not always available.
5. The user must be mindful of system security; an unauthorized individual can access all information if the network is unprotected.

The Internet

The **Internet** is a large network that links smaller computer networks in more than 100 countries (Freedman, 2003). Having access to the Internet means that you can tap into thousands of databases and talk electronically with experts worldwide on any known subject. You can find jobs, communicate with teachers for educational planning, work out technical problems, sell products, conduct research, and find medical articles.

Historical Background of the Internet

In 1969, the Department of Defense created the Internet for military research purposes. It wanted to connect the Pentagon with defense researchers in academia and business. The department's major concerns were to ensure mass communication of information while providing for maximum security. The original network was called ARPAnet because the Advanced Research Projects Agency designed it. The goal was to build a decentralized network that would run even if nuclear war destroyed a portion of it. This network would continue to function during a disaster because it did not rely on a single pathway for data transmission. The Department of Defense experimented with different ways of sending the data efficiently. Eventually, researchers devised a protocol (rules for transmitting and receiving data) called the Internet protocol, or IP, to be used along with transmission control protocol, or TCP. This standardized format enabled computers to communicate with each other on the network.

In its first few years, this electronic highway provided a way of exchanging electronic mail service and linking online libraries to government agencies and universities. These agencies served as testers for the network's integrity. In the early 1980s, the original ARPAnet divided into two networks, ARPAnet and Milnet. The connection between the networks was called the Defense Advanced Research Projects Agency, or DARPA Internet. In a short time, the name was shortened to the *Internet.*

In 1986, the National Science Foundation encouraged nondefense use of the Internet by creating a special network called NSFNet, which connected five new supercomputing centers across the country. Universities all over the country then started connecting into NSFNet. As the United States continued to develop its national and local networks during the 1980s, other countries did the same. This gave rise to connections among different national networks. As time passed, more countries joined the Internet to share its rich resources. By the late 1980s, students could gain Internet access when they registered at their colleges.

Since the Internet has become easier to use, more individuals and businesses have accessed it. In 1991, only 376,000 computers were registered on the Internet, but only a year later this number had increased to 727,000. The number of Internet users varies depending on how researchers define Internet use. For instance, some researchers count Internet surfers at age 2, but other researchers count Internet surfing starting at age 18. According to NUA Internet Surveys, as of 2002 there were 605 million Internet users all over the world. One estimate is that the number of Internet users around the world will reach 943 million by 2005 (Nua.com). This growth is a far cry from the unenthusiastic reaction that U.S. Congressman Al Gore received in the 1980s when he called for the creation of a national network of "information highways" (Laquey and Ryer, 1992).

Recent Growth of the Internet

For many years people used command-line UNIX utilities to interact with the Internet. For example, they might have used an FTP (file transfer protocol) program to download their files, and a telnet, a terminal emulation program, to log onto a computer in the Internet. This type of usage made the Internet difficult for the novice. However, Swiss researchers developed the **World Wide Web,** a system that enables the user to move smoothly through the Internet, jumping from one document to another (see Chapter 11). Software tools called *browsers* were developed that made access to Internet resources uncomplicated.

In the last half of the 1990s, two developments led to a surge in the Internet's growth. First, with the new graphics-based Web browsers such as Microsoft's *Internet Explorer* and *Netscape Navigator,* the World Wide Web exploded. Students and teachers found the Web easy to use, and it was no longer the private domain of scientists and hackers. Delphi was the first online service to offer access to the Web. Simultaneously, new Internet service providers offered access to individuals and companies. Internet service providers (ISPs) such as the award-winning Microsoft Software Network (MSN) provided Internet access and e-mail, and EarthLink Network, the world's largest independent ISP, provided network access and home pages. Many school districts gave students free ISP connection. Some commercial ISPs provide free connections to users. Liquid Slate lists such free Internet service providers (http://www.liquidslate.com/).

The second development was the proliferation of e-mail, which made the Internet more popular. As online services such as America Online and CompuServe connected to the Internet, the Internet came to function as a central gateway linking users of different services.

Internet 2

Because of the Internet's congestion, academic and scientific users of the Internet are again developing their own network. Led by 205 universities, **Internet 2** is an association that works together with government and industry to develop advanced network applications and technologies. Internet 2 is designed primarily to exchange multimedia data, real-time, at high speeds.

If you want to learn more about this network visit the association's home page at http://www.internet2.edu/.

Connecting to the Internet

To access the Web, you need a connection to the Internet and a computer that is powerful enough to handle the memory requirements for most browsers, such as a computer running Windows with at least a Pentium processor or a Macintosh computer running System 7 or higher. You will be happier with at least 256 MB of RAM. You will need a modem, or digital subscriber line (DSL), or an integrated services digital network (ISDN), or a satellite data service.

The Modem

A **modem** enables two computers to communicate over some type of communications line, such as a telephone line. There are two types of modems: internal and external. Internal modems reside in the computer and are plugged into an open slot. They do not require any special cabling, nor do they take up any extra desk space. External modems (Figure 9.5) are separate units that sit outside the computer and are connected to the telephone jack with a telephone cable. External modems usually have diagnostic lights so users can monitor what is transpiring. This type of modem is portable and easily accessible for repair.

    Modem is a contraction of MOdulator/DEModulator. The modem *modulates* the computer output to an acceptable signal for transmission and then *demodulates* the signal back for computer input. The modem on the transmitting computer converts the digital signals to modulated, analog signal tones and transmits them over the telephone lines. The receiving computer's modem transforms the incoming analog signals back to their digital equivalents in order to understand them. Figure 9.6 illustrates this modem-to-modem transmission.

Figure 9.5 External Modem

Figure 9.6 Modem-to-Modem Transmission

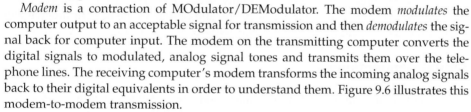
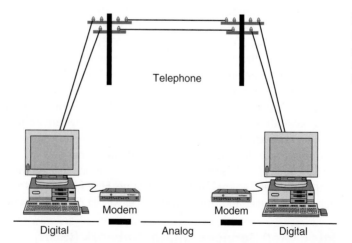

Telephone

Modem   Modem

Digital   Analog   Digital

    The software that is required to operate a modem is usually included in the operating system. In Windows, the dial-up networking "Make New Connection" wizard takes you through the steps of setting up your modem. Macintosh provides a similar wizard with its operating system.

    The power of your modem compared to the power of your personal computer is antiquated. Using a modern modem with today's Power G5 Macintosh machines or Windows Pentium IV machines is like trying to power a race car with a lawn mower engine. Modems are certainly faster than they used to be, but due to larger downloading and more complexity, the modem feels slower or as slow. The villain responsible is the **bandwidth,** or the amount of data that can be transmitted through the computer network in a certain time period. An analogy would be the amount of water than can flow through pipes of different sizes. New technologies promise to increase bandwidth capacity.

Currently, 56 Kbps internal modems come standard with computers. They achieve their speed using the regular phone line. These modems are probably the last of their kind. They are half as fast as the ISDN modem, but lower monthly charges for using the 56 Kbps service make them attractive. A drawback is that you need a good-quality phone line in your house, or you have to be within a mile or two of a phone company's switch, which means that rural areas do not have access to 56 Kbps services. Furthermore, you need an Internet service provider (ISP) that offers hardware support for this kind of modem.

A **cable modem** enables you to connect to the Internet with the same cable that attaches to a standard television set. The cable modems offered by many cable companies provide shared point-to-point transmission. Cable modems offer a greater bandwidth (the amount of data transmitted in a fixed time period) than DSL. Even though this is the case, a cable modem is limited by the amount of use of the line, because the cable line is shared among many users. The speeds for cable vary, and heavy downloads are faster when few people are online. In the near future, we will see faster cable modems.

Digital Connections

Digital subscriber lines (DSLs) and cable modems are different technologies, but both provide dedicated multimegabit connections to a service, and they are both always on, unlike dial-up modems. DSL is a digital point-to-point technology that offers high-speed transmission over standard copper telephone wiring. Downloading occurs at speeds up to 8 Mbps. DSL can carry both voice and data signals at the same time, in both directions. There are many versions of DSL with varying transmission speeds. The percentage of homes in the United States with **broadband,** or high-speed–transmission Internet access is expected to increase from 5 percent in 2000 to 66 percent in 2008, according to a study by the investment bank Goldman Sachs. Broadband growth will be driven by an increase in consumer adoption of cable modem and DSL technology (Deveaux, 2000). Recently, companies providing DSL have been competing with cable companies to provide faster service.

A benefit of DSL is that you can use the phone at the same time you use the Web, so you do not need a separate telephone line. However, DSL speeds are tied to the distance between the user and the central office. Also, DSL may not be available in your area.

Integrated Services Digital Network (ISDN)

The **integrated services digital network (ISDN)** was designed in the early 1980s as a replacement for analog telephone service. This service uses high-speed digital phone lines offered by the phone companies in most urban areas. The connection can range from 64 to 128 Kbps. When ISDN burst on the scene, it was difficult to order, and it was particularly difficult to install the hardware. Moreover, ISDN is not universally available in the United States, and the combination of per-call connect charges and per-minute billing on data calls makes it expensive. Therefore, interest in this technology has diminished.

Satellite Data Service

Satellite data service uses a satellite dish to connect your computer to the Internet. A satellite data service can provide speeds of 400 Kbps for downloading. Computers connect to this service via an analog modem, and the installation charges are high. Of the technologies briefly described here, it is impossible to know which will dominate in the years to come. However, it is certain that the connection speeds will be faster, and more users will be using high-speed digital lines.

Internet Service Providers (ISPs)

An ISP is an organization that provides access to the Internet. A customer is usually charged a fixed amount of money per month, but there can be other charges involved. Small service providers usually just give access to the Internet, whereas large service providers such as America Online (AOL) provide forums, services, and proprietary databases as well.

In the early years of the Internet, online services were only self-contained organizations that offered databases, resources, and e-mail. For example, DIALOG (a Thompson company), Genie (now defunct), and CompuServe Interactive Services (acquired by AOL) existed as self-contained services. After the Internet became popular, the different services provided access to their particular databases and general Internet access to Internet service providers.

A full-service provider such as America Online gives members access to the Internet as well as to special content including e-mail, instant messaging, chat rooms, customized news information, financial information and stock quotes, movie information, maps and driving directions, and local entertainment information (Figure 9.7).

Figure 9.7 America Online

Reprinted by permission of AOL.

America Online (AOL) is the world's largest online information service with over 35 million members (Freedman, 2003). Microsoft Network (http://essentials.msn.com/access/) is another large popular service provider. There are many smaller ISPs that offer e-mail and full-scale Internet access but fewer special services such as members-only chat rooms and news. Subscribers to these ISPs can access some specialized members-only services through their browsers, such as *Netscape*.

Several resources can help you find an ISP to fit your needs. If you already have access to the Internet through an online service, you can check out a list of providers at http://www.thelist.com/. *The List* enables you to search for providers by country, state, or area code. In the *ISP Directory of Internet Access* (http://findanisp.com/) you can find dial-up or other Internet access services in the United States, organized by local phone calling areas. Another place to find information about ISPs is in the local Yellow Pages. You might also contact a local computer user group.

Internet Resources

The resources available through a connection to the Internet range from e-mail to searchable databases. We will discuss electronic mail and a few other resources in this chapter. In Chapter 11, we will discuss the World Wide Web.

Electronic Mail

Electronic mail, or **e-mail,** can be used to send messages to individuals at local or distant locations in a matter of seconds. What makes this system unique is the fact that the message recipient does not have to be present to receive a message. A host computer stores in memory any messages received; when the recipient logs on to the system, the screen displays a message informing him or her about the mail. There are many additional advantages to e-mail. You can quickly address an issue via e-mail without time-consuming social interaction. E-mail also conquers the problems of long-distance communication. People all over the world can easily communicate with each other instantly. E-mail can generate answers quickly and inexpensively.

A typical e-mail address has two parts: (1) the user's identification followed by the *at* symbol, @, and (2) the domain information consisting of the site name and type of organization. For example, the author's e-mail address is vicki.sharp@csun.edu. The user's name identified in this example is *vicki.sharp.* The site name or domain name is *CSUN* (California State University, Northridge), and the domain type is *edu* (educational institution). Other domain types are government organization (*gov*), nonprofit organization (*org*), and commercial organization (*com*). In the year 2000 the exponential growth of the Internet required the addition of new domain types such as *name, museum,* and *biz.*

Electronic mail did not develop as rapidly as its innovators thought it would. There were two impediments to quick development. First, people were accustomed to fax machines (Figure 9.8), which scan a piece of paper and convert its image into coded form for transmission over the telephone system; at the other end, a fax machine reconverts the transmitted code and prints out a facsimile of the original sheet of paper. This device does not require a computer or special knowledge in order for people to exchange information quickly. The second impediment was the existence of many incompatible, inadequately connected electronic mail systems. The Internet has solved the incompatibility problems of electronic mail systems. Figure 9.9 shows an electronic mail message sent via America Online.

E-mail applications are integrated into browsers such as *Netscape.*[1] Furthermore, stand-alone commercial e-mail programs such as *Eudora Pro* (Qualcomm) are loaded

Figure 9.8 Fax Machine

Some images © 2003–2004 www.clipart.com.

---

[1] *Netscape* is now part of America Online, which is one of the most popular Internet service providers in the world. The *Netscape* browser does not come packaged with many IBM-compatibles. To use it you have to download it from the Netscape Website.

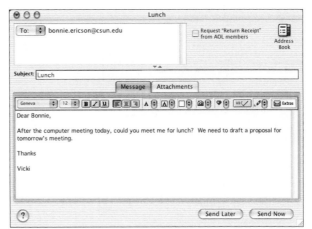

Figure 9.9 E-mail Message on America Online

Reprinted by permission of AOL.

with features. Students who need fewer bells and whistles can download a freeware program (software that is disseminated without a charge) such as *Eudora Light* or *Pegasus* (David Harris, publisher) and use this program without restrictions. Both programs include basic components such as sending and receiving messages, forwarding, replying, and setting up an address book. In addition, there are free Web-based mail services such as *Yahoo! Mail* and *Hotmail. Yahoo! Mail* enables the user to navigate by pointing and clicking. In addition, it offers nice features such as a signature file and mail filters. *Hotmail,* one of the newest members to the Microsoft Network, besides being easy to use includes an antivirus scanner provided by McAfee. The *Free Email Address* site reviews some of these e-mail services (http://www.free-email-address.com/). *Gaggle.Net* is a monitored Internet e-mail service for children. The advertising-supported version of Gaggle is free (http://www.gaggle.net/learn.html). Teachers can sign up entire classes to use it.

Chat Rooms

The **chat room** is a discussion by keyboard on a specific topic. The chat takes place in real time; that is, it occurs instantly. When you type a text message on the computer screen your words are seen on the screen by other people in the chat room. Chat rooms are available from services such as America Online, websites such as *Yahoo!*, and the Internet relay chat system.

Instant Messaging

Instant messaging is a feature enabling two or more people to swap messages in real time. In addition, instant messaging systems enable users to transfer files, and some systems enable users to send messages even if they are not online.

In 1996, Israel based ICQ introduced instant messaging. Shortly after its introduction Instant Messaging became very popular with students, teachers, and businesses. Three major services that offer this system are Yahoo! Messenger, AOL's Instant Messenger (AIM), and Microsoft's MSN Messenger.

With instant messaging you can share photos and sounds with friends. If you set up a buddy list (Figure 9.10) of the names of people you want to send messages to, when people on your list log on to the Internet with the Instant Messaging software you are

Figure 9.10 Yahoo! Messenger Buddy List

Reproduced with permission of Yahoo! Inc. © 2004 by Yahoo! Inc. YAHOO! And the YAHOO! Logo are trademarks of Yahoo! Inc.

notified that they are online. When they log off, you are also notified. With a Web cam and a headset (Figure 9.11), you can chat with friends by speaking and seeing them

Figure 9.11 Web Cam and Headset

Sony webcam image courtesy of Sony Electronics Inc. Clip art—some images © 2003–2004 www.clipart.com.

What follows is an example of an instant messaging session between my son and me (Figure 9.12).

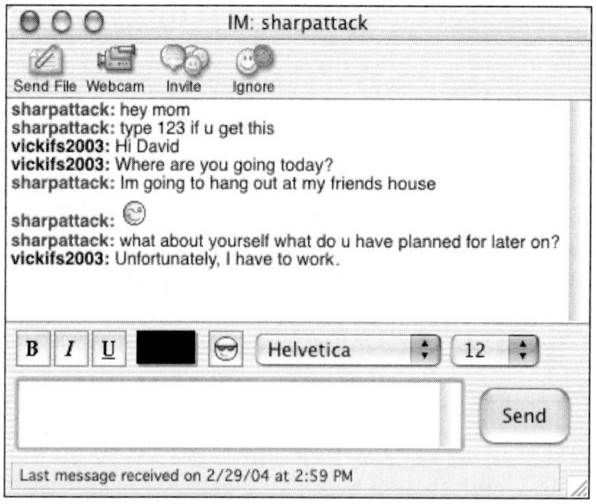

Figure 9.12 Yahoo! Instant Messenger

Reproduced with permission of Yahoo! Inc. © 2004 by Yahoo! Inc. YAHOO! And the YAHOO! Logo are trademarks of Yahoo! Inc.

Internet Relay Chat (IRC)

Internet relay chat (IRC) is computer conferencing on the Internet. IRC channels on a wide range of topics take place on IRC servers around the world. After you join a channel, your messages are broadcast to everyone listening on that particular channel.

Additional Resources

The Internet offers the additional resources found in Table 9.1.

Table 9.1 Internet Resources

Archie server	Archie server helps you find a file stored at an anonymous FTP site.
bulletin board system (BBS)	A central computer used as a source of information for an interest group is a BBS. BBSs were used to distribute drivers and shareware before the Web became popular. They are presently used in remote areas where there is less Internet access.
file transfer protocol (FTP)	An FTP is a transfer protocol used to transmit files over the Internet. It is a tool for copying files containing text, pictures, sounds, and computer programs.
finger service	Finger service finds out information about another Internet user, including the name of the person behind the user identification name (userid).
gopher	Gopher displays a simple series of menus through which you can access any type of textual information on the Internet.
listserv	listserv is an e-mail account that resides on a special server with subscribers. When a person sends a message to the e-mail account, every subscriber receives a copy of the message.
multiple user dimension (MUD)	An MUD is a program that involves rudimentary virtual reality, similar to Dungeons and Dragons. You participate by taking on a role and exploring it in interactions with others.
newsgroup	Newsgroups are Internet discussion groups that focus on a particular topic. Newgroups are like public bulletin boards where you can read messages that others have written and write your own thoughts. An example of a website with a wide variety of newsgroups is e-groups at http://www.egroups.com.
telnet	Telnet is a software utility that enables you to log on to a remote computer.
usenet	Usenet is a place for discussion groups. Through this network, individual articles can be distributed throughout the world.
wide area information service (WAIS)	WAIS accesses databases that are distributed around the Internet. For example, you can use it to access ERIC (Education Resources Information Clearinghouse). By specifying a list of keywords to use in a search, you are telling WAIS what databases to search. WAIS then searches every article in all the databases that you select. You can then view or print out the list of articles found in the search.
World Wide Web	The World Wide Web (WWW) is a collection of computers containing documents accessed with special software that enables users to view text, graphics, video, and photos and to link to another document on the Web. (See Chapter 11.)

Netiquette

Getting along in the electronic environment is called **netiquette.** Here are a few suggestions for online behavior:

1. Keep your messages to the point and brief.
2. Do not use ALL UPPERCASE LETTERS; this is considered shouting.
3. Never criticize a person's writing or spelling.
4. Do not overreact to items you see online.
5. Do not send excessive messages to multiple groups (cross-posting), in disregard of the members' interests.
6. Do not post items that are offensive.
7. Use discretion by not getting too personal with anyone.
8. Do not lie about your identity.

You can find further suggestions on netiquette at the Netiquette Home Page (http://www.albion.com/netiquette/) and at The Net: User Guidelines and Netiquette—Index (http://www.fau.edu/netiquette/net/).

Integrating the Internet into the Classroom

The Internet is becoming a pervasive influence on our lives. In 1994, only 35 percent of public schools had access to the Internet. In 2002, 99 percent of U.S. public schools had access to the Internet. The ratio of students per instructional computer in public school is approximately 4.8 to 1 (National Center for Education Statistics, http://nces.ed.gov/).

The Internet offers some exciting possibilities for the classroom. Because teachers and students have access to this huge library of information, teachers need to develop skill for determining the most relevant and best quality information. Here are a few suggestions on how to enhance the students' learning experiences:

1. Students can conduct online research using databases and online resources. They can find information and visual and auditory data on topics such as whales, pandas, educational statistics, laws, teenage smoking, and the Civil War.
2. The class can track current events through online magazines and newspapers. Students are no longer limited to hometown newspapers and magazines. Access to the Internet gives students access to critical stories in a variety of places. Students can compare local newspaper stories with what is being written by national and world news organizations.
3. New and experienced teachers can access databases of lesson plans, teaching methods, and instructional approaches. Students can find information on what to teach, hands-on experiments, drama techniques, and lesson plans.
4. Students can even access information on job possibilities, job contacts, and résumé preparation.

Classroom Lesson Plans

I. E-MAIL

Subject

Language Arts

Grade(s)

2 and up

Objective

Students will e-mail letters to other students.

Standards

- NCTE English Language Arts Standards 4, 5, 12
- ISTE NETS for Students 1, 2, 3, 4

Materials

You will need a computer, a word processing program, and a connection to the Internet.

Procedures

1. Introduce the students to telecommunications.
2. Demonstrate how the computer, software, modem, and printer work.
3. Discuss terms such as *bulletin boards* and *electronic mail*.
4. Show examples of completed pen pal letters.
5. Have students type and transmit letters to students at another school, using the Internet.

II. ECONOMICS

Subject

Math

Grade(s)

5 and up

Objective

Students will improve their research skills and learn about the Stock Exchange.

Standards

- National Council of Teachers of Math 1, 5, 8, 10
- ISTE NETS for Students 1, 2, 4, 5, 6

Materials

You will need a computer with access to the Internet.

Procedures

1. Teach a unit on the stock market.
2. Have students research a minimum of six stocks (three for the New York Stock Exchange and three for the NASDAQ).
3. Have students use the library and the Internet to find information.
4. Give the students $3,000 in play money to make pretend purchases.
5. Have the students maintain a stock portfolio for the entire semester.
6. At the end of the semester, ask students to write reports using graphs, charts, and spreadsheets to describe the results of their purchases.

III. CHEMICAL AND PHYSICAL WEATHERING

Subject

Science

Grade(s)

4 and up

Objective

Students will identify and explain causes of chemical and physical weathering.

Standards

- National Science Education Standards A1, A2, D1, D3
- ISTE NETS for Students 1, 2, 4, 5, 6

Materials

You will need a computer with access to the Internet.

Procedures

1. Teach a unit on current environmental issues.
2. Have students measure local rainfall and its acidity level.

3. Access the Internet and have students use it to discover patterns of acidity in the rainwater across the continent.
4. Ask students to post their results online for other schools to use.
5. Have students download information from other students and draw maps and charts.

IV. LESSON PLANS

Subject

General

Grade(s)

9 and up

Objective

Using the Internet, students will find online activities or lessons.

Standards

* ISTE NETS for Students 1, 2, 4, 5

Materials

You will need a computer and access to the Internet.

Procedures

1. Have the students search the Internet for useful sites.
2. Ask students to choose a lesson plan for a specific topic in a subject area that consists of an online interactive activity.
3. Have students print the lesson plan and discuss or demonstrate it to the class.

V. PRESIDENTS

Subject

Social Studies

Grade(s)

4 and up

Objective

Students will learn about the American presidency by searching a site such as *The American Presidency,* found at http://gi.grolier.com/presidents/.

Standards

- National Council for the Social Studies Curriculum Standards 3, 4, 5, 6
- ISTE NETS for Students 1, 2, 4, 5

Materials

You will need a computer and access to the Internet.

Procedures

1. Discuss in class how to search the site.
2. Divide the students into small groups.
3. Next, have the students use *The American Presidency* site or one like it to make up questions on the presidency.
4. Have the groups exchange questions and tell them to find the answers in a 15-minute time period. (Vary the time period according to the number and complexity of questions.)
5. The first group that answers the question correctly earns the same number of points as the number of groups that there are. The second group to finish earns one less, and so on.
6. Have the groups exchange questions again and continue the activity until every group has seen all the questions.
7. The winner is the group with the most points.

VI. FAMOUS ART TREASURES

Subject

Art

Grade(s)

6 and up

Objective

Students will use a site such as *Treasures of the Louvre*, located at http://www.paris.org/Musees/Louvre/Treasures/, to learn about the different art treasures found in a museum.

Standards

- ISTE NETS for Students 1, 2, 4, 5, 6

Materials

You will need a computer and access to the Internet.

Procedures

1. Discuss some of the art treasures that people see in the Louvre.
2. Divide the students into small groups.
3. Have each group research on the Internet at the museum a treasure that is located and write a description of this art object.
4. In class, have each group discuss the art treasure it researched.
5. Each week e-mail a set of clues to each group to help them find a particular art treasure.
6. The first group to come up with the answer gets a point.

Summary

In this chapter, we discussed the Internet, the mother of networks, in detail, including its history and the many resources it offers. We discussed e-mail and netiquette. Finally, we examined six classroom activities.

Study and Online Resources

Go to Chapter 9 in the Student Edition of the Online Learning Center at **www.mhhe.com/sharp5e** to **practice with key concepts, take chapter quizzes, read PowerWeb articles** and **news feed updates** related to technology in education, and **access resources** for learning about technology and integrating it into the classroom.

Click on *Web Links* to link to the following websites.

Barry's Clip Art Server
Barry's Clip Art Server contains thousands of images, all free for download.

Bluetooth
This is the official Bluetooth site, containing news, special events, special interest groups, and developer information. The site explains how to use Bluetooth technology, how it works, and what its various products are.

Britannica.com
The Britannica.com site brings you the best websites, leading magazines, related books, and the complete encyclopedia.

Education Week—on the Web
This site is for people interested in education reform, schools, and the policies that guide them. *Education Week,* published by Editorial Projects in Education, also includes extensive education information on every state and the District of Columbia.

FamilyEducation.com
This site provides useful information and interactive communication tools to help busy parents help their children succeed. It includes school resources, quizzes, polls, discussion groups, and articles on parenting and education subjects. It also contains a network of local school websites, with school calendars and community-level information fostering parent-school connection.

Internet Dictionary
Internet Dictionary is a collection of terms pertaining to the Internet.

Internet Society
The Internet Society article topics range from Internet history makers to the World Wide Web past, present, and future.

The List
This ISP buyer's guide enables you to search for providers by country, state, or area code.

Chapter Mastery Test

To the Instructor: *Refer to the Instructor's Manual for the answers to the Mastery Questions. This manual has additional questions and resource materials.*

Let us check for chapter comprehension with a short mastery test. Key Terms, Computer Lab, and Suggested Readings and References follow the test.

1. How did the Internet begin and what led to its growth?
2. Define *networking*.
3. Discuss the advantages and disadvantages of using networking in the classroom.
4. Describe the Internet and discuss three of its resources.
5. Explain the differences among e-mail, chat room, and instant messaging.
6. What is the World Wide Web and why is it an invaluable resource?
7. Distinguish between 56 Kbps modems and cable modems.
8. What is Internet 2 and why was it necessary?
9. What are some advantages of a wireless network?

Key Terms

Archie server 217
Bandwidth 212
Broadband 212
Bulletin board system
    (BBS) 217
Cable modem 212
Chat room 215
Digital subscriber lines
    (DSLs) 212
E-mail 214
File server 205
File transfer protocol
    (FTP) 217

Finger service 217
Gopher 217
Hub 205
Instant messenging 216
Integrated Services Digital
    Network (ISDN) 212
Internet 209
Internet relay chat
    (IRC) 217
Internet service provider
    (ISP) 213
Internet 2 210
Listserv 217

Local area networks
    (LANs) 205
Modem 211
Multiple user dimension
    (MUD) 217
Netiquette 218
Networking 205
Newsgroup 217
Ring network 207
Routers 205
Satellite data service 213
Shared-bus network 208

Star network 208
Switches 205
Telecommunications 205
Telnet 217
Usenet 217
Wide-area information
    service (WAIS) 217
Wide area networks
    (WANs) 205
Wireless network 206
World Wide Web
    (WWW) 217

Computer Lab: Activities for Mastery and Your Portfolio

9.1 Understanding the Internet Take a quiz to test your knowledge of Internet-related terms.

9.2 E-mail someone in your class or at another school.

9.3 Take a field trip to a school that uses networking. Find out what type of network and what software are being utilized and how students are using networking in the

classroom. Evaluate this school's program, listing its strengths and weaknesses.

9.4 Examine the different online services and compare their costs and benefits.

Suggested Readings and References

Andrews, Paul. "A Tech Rebirth?" *U.S. News & World Report* 134, issue 1 (January 13, 2003): 28–31.

Brown, Eric. "The Wireless Web." *Entrepreneur* 28, no. 7 (July 2000): 36.

Charp, Sylvia. "Technology for All Students." *T.H.E. Journal* 30, issue 9 (April 2003): 8.

Coffee, Peter. "Internet's 20th Anniversary Is Not Worth All the Hype." *eWeek* 20, issue 2 (January 13, 2003): 53–54.

Craig, Dorothy, and Jaci Stewart. "Mission to Mars." *Learning and Leading with Technology* 25, no. 2 (October 1997): 22–27.

Davis, Bob. "Internet in Schools: A National Crusade Backed by Scant Data." *Wall Street Journal Eastern Edition,* June 19, 2000, A1.

Davitt, John. "Need a Lesson Plan? Just Browse the Web." *Times Educational Supplement,* March 14, 1997, Computers Update, 10.

Desposito, Joseph. *Que's Computer Buyer's Guide.* Carmel, Ind.: Que Corporation, 2000.

Deveaux, Sarah, "Cable vs. DSL Is No Battle," *InfoWorld,* July 11, 2000, http://www.infoworld.com.

Dixon, Robert S. "Internet Videoconferencing: Coming to Your Campus Soon!" *Educause Quarterly* 23, no. 4 (2000): 22–27.

Duffy, Bob. "Buttoning Down the Content Explosion." *Electronic Library* 15, no. 3 (June 1997): 227–229.

Dyril, Odvard, E. "Stats Making News." *Technology and Learning* 18, no. 7 (March 1998): 64.

Eklund, John, and Peter Eklund. "Collaboration and Networked Technology: A Case Study in Teaching Educational Computing." *Journal of Computing in Teachers Education* 13, no. 3 (April 1997): 14–19.

Fletcher, Geoffrey H. "Igniting the Internet Revolution." *T.H.E. Journal* 30, no. 4 (November 2002): 1–23.

Fraser, Bruce. "Digital Cameras Coming into Focus." *MacWeek* 11, no. 31 (August 8, 1997): 11.

Freedman, Alan. *Computer Desktop Encyclopedia.* Pennsylvania: The Computer Language Company, 2003.

Globus, Sheila. "Good, Bad and Internet." *Current Health 2,* vol. 28, issue 6 (February 2002): 13–15.

Gowan, Michael. "The Future Web." *PC World* 19, issue 4 (April 2001): 105–117.

Harris, Judy. "Ridiculous Questions! The Issue of Scale in Netiquette." *Learning and Leading with Technology* 25, no. 2 (October 1997): 13–16.

Heinich, Robert, Michael Molenda, James D. Russell, and Sharon Smaldino. *Instructional Media and the New Technologies Instruction,* 7th ed. New York: Merrill/Prentice Hall, 2002, 296.

Kirk, Rea. "A Study of the Use of a Private Chat Room to Increase Reflective Thinking in Pre-Service Teachers." *College Student Journal* 34 (March 2000): 115.

Kurland, Daniel, Richard Sharp, and Vicki Sharp. *Introduction to the Internet for Education.* Belmont, Calif.: Wadsworth, 1997.

Laquey, Tracy, and Jeanne Ryer (foreword by Al Gore). *Internet Companion.* Boston, Mass.: Addison-Wesley, 1992.

Lindroth, Linda. "Internet Connections." *Teaching Pre K–8* 27, no. 4 (January 1997): 62–63.

Minkel, Walter. "The Chat's Out of the Bag." *School Library Journal* 46, no. 2 (February 2000): 33.

Molnar, Andrew R. "Computers in Education: A Brief History." *T.H.E. Journal* 24, no. 11 (June 1997): 59–62.

Morse, David. *Cyber Dictionary.* Boston: Knowledge Exchange, 1997.

Odvard, Dyrli. "The Internet Grows Up." *Technology and Learning* 17, no. 6 (March 1997): 42–47.

Peha, Jon M. "Debates via Computer Networks: Improving Writing and Bridging Classrooms." *T.H.E. Journal* 24, no. 9 (April 1997): 65–68.

Pfaffenberger, Bryan. *Webster's New World Computer User's Dictionary,* 10th ed. New York: Macmillan, 2002.

Ralston, Anthon, and C. L. Meeks, eds. *Encyclopedia of Computer Science.* New York: Petrocelli, 1976.

Resick, Rosalind. "Pressing Mosaic." *Internet,* October 1994, 81–88.

Roberts, Nancy, George Blakeslee, Maureen Brown, and Cecilia Lenk. *Integrating Telecommunications into Education.* Englewood Cliffs, N.J.: Prentice Hall, 1990.

Schwartz, John. "Decoding Computer Intruders." *New York Times* 152, issue 52463 (April 24, 2003): E1.

Selway, Mark. "Netiquette for Beginners." *Accountancy: International Edition,* April 1999, 47.

Simkin, Mark G., and Robert H. Dependahl. *Microcomputer Principles and Applications.* Dubuque, Iowa: Wm. C. Brown Publishers, 1987.

Sisneros, Roger. "Telecomputing Takes the Mystery out of On-Line Communication." *Telecomputing,* Spring 1990, 15–22.

Sullivan, Brian. "Netiquette." *Computerworld* 36, issue 10, (March 2, 2002): 48.

Turner, Sandra, and Michael Land. *Tools for Schools,* 2d ed. Belmont, Calif.: Wadsworth, 1997.

Van Horn, Royal. "Technology." *Phi Delta Kappan* 81, no. 10 (June 2000): 795.

Weise, Elizabeth. "Successful Net Search Starts with Need." *USA Today,* January 24, 2000, 3D.

Wilkerson, George J. "Teaching Composition via Computer and Modem." *Teaching English in the Two-Year College* 22, no. 3 (October 1995): 202–210.

Withrow, Frank B. "Technology in Education and the Next Twenty-Five Years." *T.H.E. Journal* 24, no. 11 (June 1997): 59–62.

Woolley, Scott. "Wider-Fi." *Forbes* 171, issue 8 (April 14, 2003): 201–205.

Zepke, Nick, and Linda Leach. "Appropriate Pedagogy and Technology in a Cross-Cultural Distance Education Context." *Teaching in Higher Education* 7, no. 3 (July 2002): 309–321.

CHAPTER 10

Distance Learning and Internet-Related Issues

Distance Learning and the Classroom

Distance learning offers stay-at-home women a great opportunity for an education. The Internet also offers a cunning person the opportunity to steal your identity. And it offers a virus the opportunity to infect your computer files. In this chapter, you will learn about distance learning and also about all sorts of Internet-related problems such as Internet crime, spam, plagiarism, and copyright infringement. Exercises will help you integrate the Internet into the classroom. Finally, you will become familiar with Internet sites that include articles on distance learning and information about topics ranging from desktop video conferencing to identity theft.

Objectives

Upon completing this chapter, you will be able to do the following:

1. Discuss distance learning and its implications for education.
2. List the advantages and disadvantages of distance learning.
3. Describe Internet issues such as ethics violation, crime, viruses, plagiarism, and copyright infringement.
4. Explain what video conferencing is and how it is being used.

Distance Education and Distance Learning Defined

In the past, experts made a distinction between distance education and distance learning. **Distance education** referred to institutions or instructors delivering knowledge using telecommunication or remote capabilities. **Distance learning** referred to students "obtaining education and training from a remote teaching site via TV or computer" (Freedman, 2003). In other words, distance education was about the instructor, and distance learning was about the student. These terms have since become interchangeable.

Figure 10.1 Distance Learning

Used by permission of ArtToday.com, Inc.

A Short History of Distance Education

Before we discuss distance education any further, let us look at its historical background. The first attempt at distance education was through correspondence.

Correspondence Education

In 1873, Ann Ticknor made an important contribution to distance learning by establishing the Society to Encourage Studies at Home in Boston. In a 24-year period, the Society provided correspondence instruction to 10,000 women of all social classes (Nasseh, 1997). From 1883 to 1891, Chautauqua College of Liberal Arts granted academic degrees to students who successfully finished work by correspondence (Nasseh, 1997).

Correspondence learning grew in acceptance, and the National University Extension Association (NUEA) was created in 1915. The NUEA widened the focus of distance education with its concern for issues such as acceptance of credit, transferring of credit, and standards for correspondence instructors (Nasseh, 1997). There was now a need for research to justify distance education. In 1933, the University of Chicago conducted a study that suggested that distance education should be done on an experimental basis. The students used self-study instructional material that was sent to them via the mail. They did their assignments, and when they finished they mailed the work back to the teacher. A local proctor gave exams to the students, and the results were mailed to the teacher. A teacher's job was to develop materials and select books. A student's job was to learn the material. There was not much interaction between the teacher and student, only in the form of mailed-in questions and answers. However, the delay between question and answers made this type of interaction very difficult.

Distance Learning Technologies

Through the years, distance education has changed as technology has evolved. We have come a long way from the first attempt at distance education. Correspondence is still used today, but the audiocassette, videocassette, and CD-ROM among other things are used to supplement the printed text.

Radio

The federal government granted radio broadcasting licenses to universities, colleges, and school boards from 1918 to 1946. Radio seemed to be ideal for distance learning because it was able to reach a large geographical area at a low cost. Also, it provided a uniform message to a diverse audience. It was especially useful in curriculum areas with emphasis on voice, such as music or language arts. Unfortunately, radio broadcasts had a fixed schedule, and the communication was limited to one direction, from the teacher to the student. By 1940 there was only one college-level credit course offered by radio, and it did not attract any students (Nasseh, 1997). It was the experimentation with radio that led to the development of educational television in the 1950s.

Television

Educational television grew at a slow pace because of teacher resistance. Teachers felt that television in the classroom was expensive, and television by itself could not address the different conditions necessary for student learning. It was not until the 1960s and 1970s that this situation changed (http://www.pbs.org/als/dlweek/resources/).

Because of the success of Britain's Open University, a university that offered courses using distance learning, a new respect for this kind of learning emerged. The British Open University courses combined television broadcast, radio broadcast, correspondence work, and summer school work. This university published its own course materials. The students met with counselors at local student centers. Tutors taught students in the evenings and weekends and graded the students' assignments. Lecturers designed the courses, set up exams, and made broadcasts (Hawkridge, 2003).

Soon open universities appeared in other countries. In 1971 the first United States open university began at New York State's Empire State College (NYSES). This school made higher-education degrees accessible to students unable physically to attend the traditional campus courses. The program used study guides, radio and television broadcasts, audiotapes, telephone conferences, and correspondence materials.

More research and experimentation in distance education followed. In the late 1970s and early 1980s, microwave networks developed and costs improved. In the 1980s and 1990s women's participation in distance learning spurred its growth. With women's role in the family and society changing and women participating in large numbers in the job market, the need for more educational opportunities for women grew. Since it was harder for women to attend classes because of family obligations, distance learning emerged as a viable way to get an education.

Telephone

Audio teleconferencing uses the telephone to connect individuals or groups at two or more locations. Participants can use a speakerphone or additional equipment such as a microphone, amplifier, and speakers to communicate across distances. This technology made it possible for a person to give a lecture to classrooms across the country all at once. When time and cost are factors, this audio teleconferencing method is also an effective way to conduct a meeting, give simple instructions, or conduct an interview. The only drawback to this type of technology is that it uses only audio.

Video

Video can be delivered over distances using cable, television, satellite, microwave transmission, and closed circuit. There are different levels of video: Some is one-way video with audio, some is one-way video with two-way audio, and some is two-way video with audio.

Television usually consists of one-way transmission of information. Today, schools use programs developed by the Public Broadcasting System and CNN's Newsroom and their local stations to reach a mass audience; the disadvantages of these programs are that there is no flexibility when it comes to broadcast time, and there is a lack of interaction between the instructor and learner. To solve the latter problem, the instructor might add a simple telephone connection or a speakerphone to link the two locations. Students can then call the instructor with questions.

The closest thing to face-to-face instruction in a classroom is two-way interactive video. The sending and receiving parties have cameras, video monitors, and microphones. The transmission is by cable, fiber optic, microwave, or digital-grade telephone lines that link the sites together. There are many experiments in this type of instruction in K–12 schools.

This technology is still young, and the video compression, which is needed to support two-way interactive video, can still cause some problems with picture quality. This system can be difficult and expensive to operate.

Computers

Learners can use CD-ROMs and instructional software to take a course for credit. For this type of course, the student relies on still pictures and graphics along with audio teleconferencing over the Internet. With the proper equipment, students also make telephone calls over the Internet. This method is less expensive than a normal telephone call. Unfortunately, this technology is still new, and the audio quality is not good. Furthermore, the computer can be used as a slide projector to present text and graphics.

The teacher can supplement these computer devices for distance learning with mail, computer conferencing, chat rooms, and the Web. With e-mail, students can contact the teachers personally and individually. With computer conferencing, two or more individuals and even all the members of a class can communicate with each other no matter where they are located. The computer conference is an ongoing conversation among individuals who can leave the conversation when they want and not miss anything. To interact in real time, students use a chat function. Students can use chat rooms to interact with students at another school or talk to experts in the field of science or math (Figure 10.2).

With the computer, students can more easily communicate with instructors, and instructors can be more accessible and responsive to students' questions. More and more schools and universities are developing two-way audio and video capabilities for distance education.

Figure 10.2 Students Working on a Distance Learning Project

Used by permission of ArtToday.com, Inc.

Desktop Video Conferencing

Video conferencing enables you to be in two places at the same time. Instead of moving large sums in an armored car, a bank can relay video messages on how much money it wants to transfer. A teacher can confer with an ill student at home without leaving the classroom. A businessperson can attend a long-distance conference without leaving the office. Around 1992, video conferencing equipment cost $100,000, filled a room, and required satellite hookups and expensive data lines (Leeds, 1994). Today the industry is expanding because of better data compression, miniaturization, lower costs, wider availability of digital telephone lines, and faster processors.

Nevertheless, video conferencing is still difficult to configure, provides marginal video and audio quality, and lacks compatibility between systems. Currently, video conferencing can be done only by people who use the same system.

Because of technological improvement, desktop video conferencing is becoming common in schools and classrooms across the United States. If you have the proper hardware and software, you can engage in **desktop video conferencing.** You need a network or modem connection, speakers, microphone, video camera, and computer. You can use software such as White Pine's *CU-SeeMe, Yahoo! Messenger, iChat* AV

(Figure 10.3), or Microsoft's *NetMeeting.* When you use *iChat* AV with the *iSight* camera, you and another person are able to talk to and see each other as if you were in the same room. (Apple's *iSight* camera is a combination camera and microphone.)

Figure 10.3 Teachers Having a Video Conference

For a student at home this is a great convenience; he or she can communicate with a teacher to get an explanation of a problem. This technology is also a great asset for a student with hearing difficulties. Not only can the student read the text spoken by the teacher but he or she also can read the lips of the teacher. Unfortunately, there are drawbacks to this software. It requires a lot of bandwidth, and transmission can be slow and jumpy. You need special high-speed connections for it to work well. The demand for higher bandwidth is increasing, however, so this problem should be resolved shortly.

Even with its drawbacks desktop video conferencing is becoming quite popular in the classroom. It is not uncommon to find a microphone and video camera and speakers at a classroom computer station. The teacher can use a liquid crystal display (LCD) projection panel connected to the computer to make it possible for a group of people to see the screen.

During desktop video conferencing participants can share data and documents. One tool used for such sharing is the **electronic whiteboard.** Similar to a blackboard, an electronic whiteboard displays what is written on it to people sitting before it. It can also transmit its contents electronically for viewing at another location.

Different Approaches to Distance Learning

Some independent study courses rely on computer-based student contact and feedback. Some distance learning programs have students communicate with teachers through electronic mail, attend some class sessions, and meet in small groups on the weekend. Some undergraduate and graduate degree programs rely on cable networks, providing video courses accompanied by a textbook and other materials.

You may wonder what approach to distance learning is the most effective. Regardless of the technology used, the best approach focuses first on the needs of the students, the content requirements, and the constraints of the situation. The delivery system is secondary. Good printed instructional materials such as readings and a syllabus can give the students most of what they need. Technology can then be used to provide face-to-face or voice-to-voice interaction, access to experts in the field, student feedback, information about assignments, and audiotaped or videotape lectures on topics that require an explanation.

The Future of Distance Education

As the number of individuals using the Internet increases, more people will be engaging in distance education. Presently, distance education is being used in medicine, law, education, and business. For years, doctors, lawyers, and engineers have used it to continue their educational studies. Many of these professionals are too busy in their work to participate in classroom study, and they find home study their only option. Distance learning also reaches students who are in remote, rural locations. Some schools may not be able to spend money on a teacher to teach an advanced physics or chemistry course, and distance learning addresses this problem. Additionally, learners who are homebound due to serious illness or physical disability may not be able to travel to educational institutions. Furthermore, through distance learning technology the teacher can bring experts or special individuals into a classroom. Distance learning can also link two classrooms so that students can communicate with each other.

Throughout the United States, professors are engaging in electronic instruction. Higher-education institutions have used distance education to reach a diverse audience that would not be accessible through traditional classroom instruction. Many universities are offering degrees via the Internet. Duke University and the University of Maryland are offering master's degree programs entirely through the Internet (Molnar, 1997). In 1999, the Georgia Institute of Technology began offering courses over the Internet that could be applied toward a Master of Science degree in Mechanical Engineering. The University of Illinois at Champaign–Urbana (UICU) offers any student in the state the chance to take engineering courses without having to attend classes on campus. UICU students take exams, receive class assignments, are graded on their work, and engage in discussions with their teachers and classmates electronically, accomplished with conferencing software. At Curtain University in Australia, teachers use distance learning to reach students in Western Australia. In 1996, the Hudson, Massachusetts, Public School System and the Concord Consortium started one of the first pre–college-level virtual schools, "The Virtual High School." TEAMS distance learning, a service of the Los Angeles County Office of Education (LACOE), brings learning opportunities to K–8 students, teachers, and parents across the United States through nationally televised satellite broadcasts and the Internet.

According to Anthony Nguyen, a network administrator at California State University, Northridge, online learning is becoming increasingly popular. Nguyen believes that this is related to the explosion of network bandwidth via high-speed connection at home, such as DSL or cable. Today, online instructional materials are loaded with multimedia, such as sound and movie clips, which can make learning more interesting. Moreover, the influx of students in higher-education institutions is outpacing the growth of the infrastructures of many colleges. This leaves colleges no choice but to open up a virtual campus, teaching through telecommunications and other methods such as the Internet, print-based instruction, and satellites. Private higher-education institutions are particularly eager to implement online education because they can use it to recruit more students and offer instruction at lower cost. Public institutions, in turn, have been forced to jump in to stay competitive and to retain their students. The same trend is now happening in high schools and even at middle schools in some rural areas.

The two major players providing software to facilitate the distance learning setup are WebCT (http://www.webct.com) and Blackboard (http://www.blackboard.com). WebCT offers a free download and trial of its software. Once you upload your courses online, you pay a license fee based on your projected enrollments. Blackboard offers free course setup on its server with a limited storage space. If you go beyond that limit, you have to pay a fee. You can also buy its software to install on your server. Blackboard's long customer list is available at http://company.blackboard.com/customers.cgi. Many of those customers are K–12 schools. A newcomer in the field is Metacollege (http://www.metacollege.com/), which offers marketing schemes similar to Blackboard's.

Dr. George Friedman, adjunct professor in the School of Engineering at the University of Southern California, is also research director at the Space Studies Institute at Princeton and is a founder, fellow, and former president of the International Council on Systems Engineering. He retired in 1993 as corporate vice president of engineering and technology at the Northrop Corporation. This is what Friedman had to say about the future of distance education:

> Presently, American children are scoring quite poorly on worldwide tests in science and mathematics. Paradoxically, they are enormously computer literate; often shamefully outdistancing even their well-educated parents. The opportunity here is to devote this computer literacy—and great desire to play and compete on the computer—to an effective educational tool which can increase their test scores not only in science and math but in ALL subjects, academic or not. This will not be easy, but reasonable extrapolations of computerized instruction, expert systems, other domains of artificial intelligence, and virtual reality can motivate, interest, and teach our children the necessary life and work skills in a far more effective environment than the present classroom. An important part of this plan is to employ the communication technologies necessary for distance education, so that rather than the students and professors being trapped in an inflexible classroom, the students, instructors, educational institutions, and coursework are distributed throughout a dynamic cyberspace where learning is conducted at any time and any place.
>
> This concept of a dynamic educational cyberspace is being pursued by USC and the U.S. Air Force in their new strategy of providing graduate education—at the master of science level—to large populations of engineers engaged in careers in either industry or at the Department of Defense. The graduate students being served by either USC or the Air Force Institute of Technology are an extremely busy, mobile, and geographically dispersed population. An initial step in the distance education of these groups was to provide small studios collocated with the workplace where students would view televised lectures, which would otherwise be impossible to attend. Typically, for any of Dr. Friedman's lectures, over 80 percent of the students are viewing and listening to him from remote sites across all four time zones in the United States. Questions and discussion are handled by telephone in these cases. USC is well into the next phase, which requires only that each student have a laptop computer with Internet access. The student can download all the lecture material prior to the start of the class. In addition to viewing the lecture in real time as well as using telephonic discussions, the student has the option of viewing the lecture at a later, perhaps more convenient time, and if he or she wishes, of replaying the lecture many times. If further discussion is required to understand any given concept, then one-on-one dialogues via e-mail, fax, or phone can follow. Student feedback strongly indicates that this mode of asynchronous dialogue is superior to the hurried interchanges that normally occur during class discussions or even office hours. A

further reinforcement of this mode of education is the evolution of the engineering of large complex systems via the use of wide bandwidth networking, data sharing, discussions, and decision making.

Drawbacks of Distance Education

The main drawback of distance education is that its technology is expensive. Two-way interactive can be very costly because the equipment needed is expensive and the cost of connecting two sites can be quite high. The cost of transmitting over telephone lines is high because of the huge bandwidth that the signal requires.

Another disadvantage is that the technology is difficult to set up. Video conferencing requires an expert to coordinate personnel, vendors, technicians, and the telephone company. Extensive planning—scheduling of equipment and rooms—is needed. The rooms have to be planned in advance, and the equipment must be checked.

In addition, people need to learn how to use this technology. Teachers need to redesign their lessons and activities to take advantage of distance learning technology, but first they need to be trained. A lot of work is involved in distance learning, and only those who are able to expend the extra time, effort, and resources should undertake it. The quality of distance learning depends on the instructor's attitude and preparation.

Another problem that occurs is the misuse of the technology. An instructor may not use it to its full potential because of a lack of training. A poor technician might unfavorably influence the educational environment by building anxiety in the students and failing to help the teacher.

Frequently, equipment problems cause delays in instruction. Poor sound or audio quality can impede learning and teaching. Severed connections can frustrate all participants.

Finally, a series of drawbacks involve more subtle concerns. The advantage of eye-to-eye contact is limited in or missing from a distance learning context. Preparing for a distance learning course requires more time and effort on the part of the teacher. Furthermore, teaching a distance-learning course usually does not help a teacher get promotion or tenure. Not all subjects are best taught through distance education, and not all students are suited for this type of learning.

Despite its drawbacks, the trend toward distance education continues. In the process, the way we view the traditional school may change forever. Technology will certainly change the way students learn and the time they spend in the school building. See Chapter 15 for a discussion of the research in distance education.

Internet Problems

Computers have benefited us in many ways. Computers have improved education, medical care, and business operations. Computers have also helped artists be more creative and enabled factories and businesses to operate more efficiently and effectively.

As we have just seen in our discussion on distance learning, no advance comes without disadvantages. In this section, we will examine some of the problematic issues associated with using the Internet. We will talk about Internet security, spam, safety concerns, invasion of privacy, crime, identity theft, plagiarism, and copyright infringement.

Internet Security Problems

There are quite a few security drawbacks on the Internet. People can use it to steal information. Some companies have had clients' correspondence violated. It is for this reason that Chrysler, Chevrolet, and Ford will not send designs over the Internet. Even though data are encrypted or encoded, it is difficult to verify a user's identity. Experts such as Taso Devetzis, a Bellcore lab researcher who does encryption work on the Internet, feels that the Internet is still not 100 percent secure.

Because of security problems, many school districts are using a security system called a **firewall** to protect their schools' networks against threats from hackers from other networks. A firewall is usually a combination of software and hardware that prevents computers in a school's network from communicating directly with computers outside the network.

Spam

On May 3, 1978, Gary Thuerk became the first person to send **spam.** He sent an e-mail ad to 600 people over a network of university and government computers (Streitfeld, 2003). According to the *Wall Street Journal,* the amount of spam sent in 2003 was estimated at 76 billion spam e-mails.

Anyone using e-mail has been personally affected by spam. My spam messages outnumber my legitimate e-mails. Just yesterday, I received 225 e-mail messages. The majority of these messages were spam, ranging from pornography to advertisements for miracle pills, phony degrees, pyramid schemes, and low-interest loans and mortgages to chain letters. Oh, I forgot. I also received a Nigerian-based e-mail that informed me how I would receive a share of an unclaimed fortune. I have not bought my multimillion-dollar estate yet.

According to a report compiled by Senator Charles Schumer's office, the number of junk e-mails sent in one year in New York City alone is eight million (D'Errico, 2003). Schumer and others are trying to get legislature passed that would alleviate this situation. Recently, EarthLink won a $16.4 million suit against a sender of junk e-mail (Swartz and Davidson, 2003). Soon, it will be common for the courts to impose civil penalties on spammers. Industry groups will find more ways to block, authenticate, or otherwise filter bulk mailers. But all of these remedies may not solve the problem right away because there are so many groups that have an investment in this issue.

Until this problem is cleared up, you need to safeguard your e-mail addresses, use the delete key, and complain to your ISPs and e-mail service. You will need to learn to use your browser's filtering feature or buy a spam-filtering product such as *SpamKiller* by McAfee or *Spam Sleuth* by Blue Squirrel. This software will filter out from your mailbox most spam.

Safety Concerns

Filtering and monitoring software helps ensure a safer online experience by blocking access to inappropriate sites. Filtering programs include *Cyber Patrol* (SurfControl, Inc.), *Net Nanny* (Net Nanny Software International), and *Cyber Snoop* (Pearl Software). With *Cyber Patrol,* the teacher can customize lists of sites appropriate for individual students. *Cyber Patrol* also comes with an extensive array of fully researched websites that are updated on a daily basis. *Net Nanny* keeps a list of multiple users. It is a very user-friendly product. It maintains a list of approved and blocked websites. Furthermore, users can view full website lists. Finally, *Cyber Snoop* (Figure 10.4) keeps track of Internet activities so you know when users are online. This Windows program captures the full text of chats and messages that are received and easily enables users to block unwanted con-

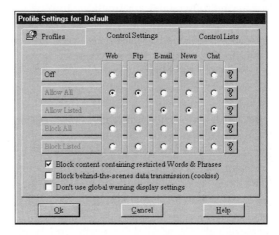

Figure 10.4
CyberSnoop

Reprinted with permission from Pearl Software.

tent while directing students to desirable sites. This program's features include time controls, unlimited user profiles, and report generation.

In addition to software programs, there are search engines such as *Ask Jeeves for Kids* (http://www.ajkids.com) and *Yahooligans.com* (http://www.yahooligans.com) that are specially designed for students. These databases contain no sex or pornography sites.

Privacy Violation

The concern for privacy is an issue that is not unique to computerized systems, but such systems increase the likelihood that an individual's privacy will be invaded. Computerized systems have proliferated in recent years, and these systems contain many different types of information. If a person lives in the United States, his or her name appears in federal, state, and local government data banks and in many private-sector files.[1] The Internal Revenue Service keeps records on everyone who files tax returns. State and local governments maintain files concerning taxes and law enforcement; public and private institutions keep records on students' educational performance; and medical data banks store medical records. It is hard to determine exactly who has what information and how this information will be used.

The Society for Human Resource Management (SHRM; http://www.shrm.org/) conducted a survey of more than 500 members of primarily human resource professional organizations. One startling finding was that 36 percent of the organizations providing e-mail to customers look at their employees' e-mail records for business purposes or security, and 75 percent of those polled felt that employers should have the right to read company-provided e-mail. Personal information such as addresses, telephone numbers, and maps to homes is accessible through the Internet. A technology called a **cookie** keeps records of the online activities on your hard drive. A cookie gives the server the name of the site you visited and information about your choices, and when you return to the site, it requests information from your cookie file and gathers even more data on your habits.

---

[1]A data bank is an electronic storehouse for data.

With so many different types of computerized systems, financial or academic indiscretions of 10 years ago may return to haunt you. Information that you provided for one purpose may be used for another. The computer poses a threat to our privacy, and we should be concerned about the possibility of unauthorized persons or groups gaining access to personal information simply by entering a system. By looking at statements of charges from Nordstrom's, Ticket Master, Toys'R' Us, Apple Computers, and Foreign Automotive Services, a "computer detective" can deduce that you like to go shopping in an upscale store, go to the theater, have children, and own a computer and a foreign automobile. If bills are examined over an extended period, a personal, psychological, and economic profile can be developed, and this information could be used to swindle you out of huge sums of money—or even to blackmail you.

Another concern regarding invasion of privacy is computer record matching, the comparison of files stored in different governmental agencies on the same individual. Law enforcement agencies use computer matching to find a criminal by comparing the Medicare files and Social Security benefits files to identify individuals who are believed deceased but are still receiving Social Security checks. Supporters of this use of the computer argue that people who break the law should be punished, and this procedure saves the taxpayers money. Opponents argue that it uses information for a purpose different from what was originally intended. If the people who supplied the information thought that it would be used against them, they might falsify data or not supply the needed information, impeding the operation of the asking agencies and costing the taxpayers money.

In the 1970s and 1980s, a series of laws was enacted to protect privacy by controlling the collection and dissemination of information. The Freedom of Information Act (1970) gave individuals access to information about themselves collected by federal agencies. (Unfortunately, the government can still continue to collect information and, under many circumstances, can refuse to release it or release only edited versions.) The Privacy Act of 1974 stated that data collected for one purpose could not be used for another. This restriction only applied to federal agencies. The Family Education Rights and Privacy Act (1974) regulated access to public and private school grades and anecdotal records stored on computer. Because of this law, parents or the student could gain access to the student's records, and unauthorized parties were blocked from this information. Finally, the Comprehensive Crime Control Act (1984) made it illegal for private individuals to modify, destroy, disclose, or use information stored in a government computer.

Viruses and Worms

Another harmful force in computing today is the **virus,** a set of instructions that infects computer files by duplicating itself. A malicious individual writes a code and buries it in an existing program. When the program is loaded into the computer, the virus attaches itself to other programs that are on the person's computer. This creates a chain reaction. When a person installs an infected program on his or her computer or downloads an infected program from the Internet, the person also installs the virus.

Computers can become infected electronically when a hacker creates a virus and sends it over the phone lines to a local network. Since the network is connected to thousands of computers, the infection is carried to all the connected computers. When the virus arrives at each of these computers, it performs the assignment it was created to do. E-mail attachments have become a quick way to spread viruses. In 2000, federal agencies experienced attacks by malicious e-mails spreading the "I LOVE YOU" virus. At least 14 agencies were affected, including the CIA and the Department of Energy. Strange as it may seem, an industry group had warned about the "I LOVE YOU" and "Love Letter" e-mail viruses, but there was an eight-hour delay before this information was given to federal agencies. This virus was so destructive that it cost an estimated $15 billion worldwide.

A virus program can be nearly harmless, simply producing an obscene or silly message unexpectedly on the computer screen. But it also can be a very destructive force, wiping out huge amounts of data. For example, a recent version of a popular utility program contained a virus that destroyed all the data on the user's hard disk. (Of course, the company that created the program rectified the situation by shipping a new version without the virus.) A virus can also find bank accounts with certain names and give the owners large sums of money.

Viruses are very hard to detect because they can be programmed to wreak havoc immediately or to lie dormant until a given future date. Viruses that are programmed to go off at a certain time are called *time bombs.* For example, the famous Michelangelo virus, named after the artist, activated itself on Michelangelo's birthday.

Another enemy of the computer user is the **worm,** which is sometimes confused with a virus. The virus is a piece of code that adds itself to other programs and cannot run independently. A worm is "a destructive program that replicates itself throughout disk and memory, using up the computer's resources and eventually putting the system down" (Freedman, 2003). After the worm is finished with its work, the data usually are corrupted and irretrievable. A famous example, called the Internet Worm, occurred on November 2, 1988. This program, authored by Robert T. Morris, a graduate student in computer science at Cornell, was responsible for disrupting the operations of between 6,000 and 9,000 computers nationwide.

In early August of 2003, the SoBig.F computer worm infected computers by filling e-mail in-boxes and jamming networks. SoBig.F sent e-mail messages to personal computers with titles like "Thank you! Your details," "Re: Your application," "Re: Wicked screensaver," and "Re: That movie," with each message containing an attachment. This computer mass-mailing worm was designed to turn machines into robots capable of delivering spam to thousands of machines. In one day, my husband received 8,500 e-mail messages as a result of this worm.

A large industry of virus protection software such as Symantec's *Norton AntiVirus* and McAfee Security's *Virex* (Figure 10.5) has come into existence to combat the different

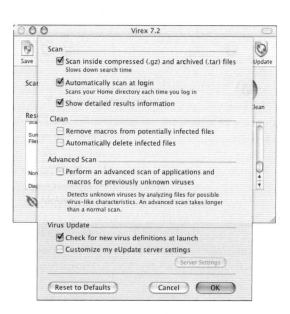

Figure 10.5 *Virex*

types of viruses. The software scans for viruses, repairs damaged files, and prints status reports. McAfee recently reported that there are over 81,000 viruses, and the number is growing at an unprecedented rate (http://vil.nai.com/). Unfortunately, these antivirus programs are imperfect at best, because new, undetectable viruses pop up all the time. In 1986 there was only one unknown virus. Presently, between 10 and 15 new viruses are discovered every day. (Symantec's AntiVirus Research Center, http://www.sarc.com/). Thank goodness most are low-level threats. The WildList Organization keeps track of viruses all over the world. Their Web page is found at http://www.wildlist.org.

The best protection against virus infection involves taking certain precautions. Table 10.1 shows some of these safety tips. Some warnings about computer viruses

---

Table 10.1 Precautions Against Viruses

Frequently back up your hard disk.

Download into a single computer as opposed to a networked system.

Use virus protection programs to check every piece of software for a virus before loading it into your computer's memory.

Always lock your USB drive or zip disk so that they cannot be destroyed.

Do not open attachments unless you know the sender, because of the viruses that can be attached to what is now considered "regular" e-mail.

---

are hoaxes. In 1997, many people received a warning that said, "Beware of e-mail bearing the title Good Times." It went on to say, "Don't open this message; delete it immediately. If you read the message it will unleash a virus that will damage your computer hard drive and destroy your computer." The warning then told people to e-mail their friends to tell them about this threat. Even some of the experts were scared, and big corporations fell for the hoax. In reality, the e-mail did not contain a computer virus but instead a self-replicating e-mail virus. People were tricked into replicating the e-mail message. Another popular hoax, sent by e-mail to Windows user, told the receiver that an infected computer file had been downloaded on their computer. The hoax gave directions on how to delete the file. If the unsuspecting person deleted the file, they unknowingly deleted a valid part of the Windows operating system.

Crime

According to InterGOV International, computer crime could cost as much as $50 billion per year (http://www.intergov.org/public_information/general_information/latest_web_stats.html). Criminals steal computers from people's homes and department stores, manipulate financial accounts, break into secret governmental computer files, and even use computer online services to lure young people to their homes. In a report by IDC, the cost of protecting against Web penetration is expected to increase to $700 million in 2006 from 65 million in 2001 (IDC, 2003; http://www.idc.com/).

In the early 1980s, there were no clear laws to prevent individuals from accessing military computers or White House computers. Ian Murphy, a 24-year-old hacker called *Captain Zap,* changed this situation when he and three companions used a home computer and telephone lines to hack into electronics companies, merchandise order records, and government documents. A **hacker** is a computer programming expert or someone who illegally accesses and tampers with computer files. The group was caught and indicted for receiving stolen property. Murphy was fined $1,000 and sentenced to jail for two and one-half years.

After this case, legislators spent several years in research and discussion. The culmination of their efforts was the Computer Fraud and Abuse Act of 1986, "a U.S. federal law that criminalizes the abuse of U.S. government computers or networks that cross state boundaries" (Pfaffenberger, 1997). Fines and prison sentences are given for illegal access, theft of credit data, and spying. The case of Herbert Zinn, a high school dropout, was the first to test this law. He was convicted on January 23, 1989, under the Computer Fraud and Abuse Act, of breaking into AT&T and the Department of Defense systems. He destroyed $174,000 worth of files, copied programs worth millions of dollars, and published passwords and ways to circumvent computer security systems. Because Zinn was not yet 18, he was sentenced to only nine months in prison and fined $10,000. However, if Zinn had been 18, he would have received a 13-year prison sentence and a fine of $80,000. The same year, Kevin Mitnick broke into Digital Equipment Corporation's computer network. He was caught and sentenced to a year in jail.

Kevin Mitnick

http://www.discovery.com/area/technology/hackers/zero.html

In 1994, a gang of Russian hackers, led by Vladimir Levin, broke into Citibank's computers and made unauthorized transfers totaling more than $10 million from customers' accounts. Citibank recovered all but $400,000, and the hackers were arrested at Heathrow Airport in 1995. Two years later, Levin was extradited to the United States where he was sentenced to three years in prison. He had to return his share of the robbery, $240,015, to Citibank.

Some hackers perpetrate criminal violations for simple amusement. The members of the 414 Club, a well-known hackers' organization,[2] made a game out of accessing private computer files. By the time the FBI apprehended them in 1983, they had broken into many different business and government computers. And more recently, a hacker accessed Microsoft's source code (programming instructions), and the FBI was called to help find the culprit (InfoWorld, 2003).

Vladimir Levin

http://www.discovery.com/area/technology/hackers/levin.html

Unfortunately, hacking is now associated with theft and fraud, but this was not always the case. In the beginning, the majority of computer hackers were not considered crooks or pranksters but computer geeks who had a curiosity about how things operated. Some of these programmers created "hacks"—programming shortcuts to complete computing tasks faster. The best-known hack was created in 1969 when Dennis Ritchie and Ken Thompson, two employees at Bell Labs' think tank, came up with a standard operating system called UNIX. Today, hacking is more prevalent than ever, but the hackers have gone underground because of fear of prosecution.

As you have probably surmised, only estimated statistics on computer crime are available. Many people are unaware that their rights have been violated by crime, because their data were transferred electronically. In addition, individuals who are aware hesitate to take claims to court because of the inevitable exposure of their

---

[2]The FBI called the hackers the 414 Club because their area code was 414.

private lives. Furthermore, companies prefer to handle computer crime internally to avoid embarrassment and unfavorable publicity.

Identity Theft

Identity theft is the stealing of a person's identity by using his or her Social Security number, driver's license, or other types of identifications. The thief uses the information to purchase items, open new charge accounts, and access the person's existing accounts. The thief charges items and runs up large bills. The thief can commit all sorts of crimes using the person's identity without the person's knowledge. In many cases it is extremely difficult for the victim to prove that he or she was not the one who ran up charges or committed a crime.

The Federal Trade Commission reported that in the last five years, 27.3 million Americans have been victims of identity theft. This crime cost consumers $5 billion, and businesses lost $48 billion. If you want to prevent this from happening to you do the following: (1) make sure your passwords are not easy to guess or obtain; (2) be careful to make physical access to your computer hard; (3) be careful who you are talking to on the Internet; and (4) update your antivirus program and run firewalls for protection. You can report cases of identity theft through the FTC's identity theft website at http://www.consumer.gov/idtheft (Rupley, 2003).

Plagiarism on the Internet

Webster's New World College Dictionary defines **plagiarism** as the taking of ideas, writings, and so on from another and passing them off as one's own. Plagiarism via the Internet is an escalating problem. It is very easy for a student to copy information and then paste it into a document. Prior to the Internet, it was easier to check whether a student's work was plagiarized. A teacher had only to research in the library or textbooks. Today, students have access to a gigantic amount of information. Teachers do not want to spend hours looking at websites to find out if a paper has been plagiarized. Unethical students are violating copyright at the elementary, high school, and college levels. Eighty percent of college students admit to cheating, and 90 percent believe that students who cheat are not caught and that when they are they are not properly disciplined. *Education Week* published a national survey that showed that 54 percent of students admitted that they had plagiarized at least once via the Internet (http://www.plagiarism.com).

In 1996, Turnitin.com was one of the first sites to help educators combat digital plagiarism. To use Turnitin.com, the teacher must register for the service and submit a request for a quote. The cost varies depending on the institution or school. Instructors create a profile, class list, and assignments. The students also create a profile and enroll in their instructor's class. After the registration is complete, the students can submit their papers to the site, or the teacher can collect the students' papers and submit them all at once to the site. Turnitin then analyzes the student work by comparing it to billions of pages of content found via the Internet (http://www.Turnitin.com). Then Turnitin gives the teacher an evaluation similar to the one in Figure 10.6.

To avoid plagiarism, you must give credit for a person's theory, opinion, idea, graphic, drawings, or statistics. You must give credit for anything that is spoken or written by another individual or that you paraphrase from what they said or wrote. Refer to the Internet sites on plagiarism at the end of the chapter.

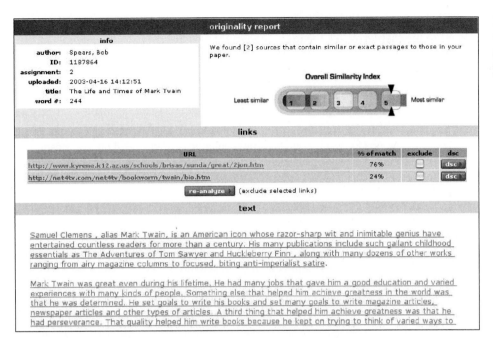

Figure 10.6 Turnitin Originality Report

Screen shot courtesy of iParadigms, developers of Turnitin.

Copyright Infringement

According to *Webster's New World College Dictionary* **copyright** is "the exclusive right to the publication, production, or sale of the rights to literary, dramatic, musical, or artistic work, or the use of a commercial print or label, granted by law for a specified period of time to an author, composer, artist, distributor, etc." In short, copyright gives the author the right to do the following:

- reproduce the work,
- permit copies to be made by others,
- prepare derivative works, and
- publicly display the copyrighted work (Brewer, 2003).

When students copy information from the Internet, they should cite it, whether it is an e-mail message, a photograph, a video file, a music file, an audio file, or content from a website. Students should check the fine print on websites before borrowing their content. When in doubt, students should cite work.

Copyright laws not only protect against downloading material from the Internet, but they also protect books, videos, newspapers, reference materials, magazines, and software. Teachers should understand the Copyright Act of 1976 and be able to explain the concept of fair use, which refers to the guidelines that regulate how educators can copy and otherwise use copyrighted materials for nonprofit educational purposes in their classrooms. To determine whether a use would constitute infringement of the copyright law, the teacher should look at the

1. purpose and character of the use,
2. nature of the copyrighted work,
3. portion used of the work, and
4. effect of the use on the marketplace.

What this all means is tread carefully when dealing with copyrighted material. (At the end of the chapter, check the useful copyright websites.)

Summary

In higher education the Internet is being used more and more for distance education, which has become a key in improving instruction and classes. There are many reasons for this trend, from an increase in homebound students to a shortage of teachers. The Internet is also used for less-noble purposes. Computers are involved in new types of crime as well as some variations on traditional crimes. We discussed such Internet crime and Internet security problems, spam, safety concerns, invasion of privacy, identity theft, plagiarism, and copyright infringement. The chapter discussed the website Turnitin where teachers can check to see if students' papers are plagiarized.

Study and Online Resources

Go to Chapter 10 in the Student Edition of the Online Learning Center at **www.mhhe.com/sharp5e** *to* **practice with key concepts, take chapter quizzes, read PowerWeb articles** *and* **news feed updates** *related to technology in education, and* **access resources** *for learning about technology and integrating it into the classroom.*

Click on *Web Links* to link to the following websites.

Computer Crime
Law Enforcement with Cliff Brinson links to over 700 sites on computer crime that range from fighting Internet crimes to computer crime research resources.

Consumer.net
Consumer.net provides extensive information on Internet privacy, cookies, junk mail, and other privacy and security issues.

CyberCriminals Most Wanted
CyberCriminals Most Wanted covers hundreds of issues on computer fraud and security, from e-mail to shopping.

Cybercitizen Partnership
The Cybercitizen Partnership for parents and teachers provides information on responsible computer use.

Desktop Video Conferencing
Desktop Video Conferencing is a research project from the College of Education at the University of Missouri—Columbia. This site includes frequently asked questions, hardware and software, information on how to set up a two-way conference, and links to Web resources.

Internet Fraud Watch
This site offers news, updates, and advice from the National Fraud Information Center.

Internet Do's and Don'ts
Internet Do's and Don'ts explains to youths that vandalism in cyberspace is the same as old-fashioned wrongdoing. Ethics and cybercrime topics covered are computer law and online cheating. This page is part of the *Department of Justice Web Page for Kids!*

Internet ScamBusters
This site provides information to help you avoid getting ripped off by Internet scams, fraud, misinformation, and hyperbole.

Microsoft's Security and Privacy Web page
Microsoft's Security and Privacy Web page is the place to visit for the latest tips on protecting your PCs from viruses and other threats. Recent virus alerts and the latest patches and security filters are posted on the site regularly. The site offers newsgroups and chat networks for discussing security issues, and visitors can sign up for e-mail alerts with the latest security updates. The site also gives detailed instructions on how to check for and install an Internet firewall to protect against Internet threats, and it provides security resources for IT professionals. In addition, educators can purchase from the site classroom posters that advocate safe practices.

PBS Campus
Launched by the Public Broadcasting Service, PBS Campus enables users to search for college courses offered via distance learning, identify and contact colleges, as well as learn about other education options.

Safeguarding the Wired Schoolhouse
Safeguarding the Wired Schoolhouse is a must-see for educators and other decision makers. Keeping students safe on the Internet is a concern in every wired school. This site offers excellent information on how best to manage the content that students are able to access. The site presents a checklist of

questions that teachers should ask when making content management decisions. The *Other Resources* section includes links to some of the best sites on the Internet about child safety, acceptable use policies, filtering, and content management.

Safe & Smart: Research and Guidelines for Children's Use of the Internet
The National School Boards Foundation released these findings from its major national survey on online safety; the report includes data, implications, resources, and guidelines for school leaders and parents.

Distance Learning Sites
About.com
About.com contains a variety of information on distance learning. The site includes discussion groups and chat rooms, educational materials, a distance learning glossary, magazine journals and newsletters, and admission procedures and strategies.

Distance Education Clearinghouse
This site features a wealth of information including research, statistics, a glossary, journals and organizations, and technology. One of this site's most popular features is a section devoted to current news items and headlines related to distance education.

Distance Learning on the Net
Distance Learning on the Net, created by Glenn Hoyle, includes descriptions of distance education websites, along with links to further distance learning and education resources on the Internet.

Distant Learning Resource Network
The Distance Learning Resource Network (DLRN) is the dissemination project for the U.S. Department of Education Star Schools Program. This site contains information about distance learning, other distance learning programs, Web-based instruction, news and publications, literature reviews and reports, and other resources.

Resources for Distance Learning
Professor Charles Darling at Capital Community College in Hartford, Connecticut, maintains this extensive list of resources on distance learning.

The Online Degree
This terrific site has researched online schools and identified the best. Listed are those schools with their URLs and nice descriptions.

Virus Protection Sites
F-Secure Computer Virus Info Center
This center enables you to search a database to find a particular virus. In addition, it lists viruses alphabetically, with examples. You can also check for news and updates on virus protection.

IBM's Anti Virus Online
IBM's Anti Virus Online site contains a database of viruses and a glossary to help you with the jargon. You can even search for viruses by alternative names. There is a test to see how well your virus protection is working.

MacAfee Virus Information Center
This site lists more than 81,000 viruses. Here you can learn about major threats and new ones. The site lists virus removal procedures.

Symantec
Symantec's site is a very informative site that lists known viruses and hoaxes. At this site, you can learn how to remove viruses from your computer and where you can send a suspected threat to be evaluated.

Virus.com
Virus.com is a global resource for virus protection. This site has up-to-date news, discussion forums, a listing of recent viruses and hoaxes, a virus search engine, informative articles, and much more.

Chapter Mastery Test

To the Instructor: *Refer to the Instructor's Manual for the answers to the Mastery Questions. This manual has additional questions and resource materials.*

Let us check for chapter comprehension with a short mastery test. Key Terms, Computer Lab, and Suggested Readings and References follow the test.

1. What does copyright give to its creator and what is *plagiarism*?
2. What are some of the advantages and disadvantages of distance education?
3. Discuss two issues related to computer privacy.
4. Discuss the AT&T case and Herbert Zimm and explain why it was important.

5. Why are computer viruses destructive? List some precautions you can take to prevent one from infecting your computer system.

6. What is *spam* and why is it causing havoc?

7. What happens when you are a victim of identity theft?

8. What is a *computer cookie* and why should we be concerned about what it does?

Key Terms

Cookie 235
Copyright 241
Desktop video
   conferencing 229

Distance education 226
Distance learning 226
Electronic
   whiteboard 230

Filtering and monitoring
   software 234
Firewall 234
Hacker 239

Plagiarism 240
Spam 234
Virus 236
Worm 237

Computer Lab: Activities for Mastery and Your Portfolio

10.1 Understanding Copyright Laws Use this exercise to determine your understanding of copyright law.

10.2 Research an example of a recent computer crime and prepare a short report. In this report, describe (a) what happened, (b) how the crime was discovered, and (c) how the crime could have been prevented.

10.3 Prepare a report on two types of computer viruses. Explain how they affected your computer and how they were discovered.

10.4 Find three current examples of how computers were used to invade a person's privacy. How could these violations have been prevented?

Suggested Readings and References

Altschuler, Glenn C., and Ralph Janis. "Promise and Pitfalls in Distance Education for Alumni." *Chronicles of Higher Education* 46, issue 41 (June 16, 2000): PB8.

Brewer, Tony. *Technology Integration in the 21st Century Classroom.* Eugene, Ore.: Visions Technology in Education, 2003.

Brown, Joan Marie. "Technology and Ethics." *Learning and Leading with Technology* 24, no. 6 (March 1997): 38–41.

Cavanaugh, Terence, and Catherine Cavanaugh. "Educational Applications for Digital Cameras." *Technology Connection* 4, no. 6 (November 1997): 22–33.

Dede, Chris. "The Evolution of Distance Education: Emerging Technologies and Distributed Learning." *American Journal of Distance Education* 10, no. 2 (1996): 4–36.

D'Errico, Richard. "Slam Spam, Propose Solutions." *Business Review,* May 19, 2003.

Dyrli, Odvard Egil. "Online Privacy and the Cookies Controversy." *Technology and Learning,* March 1997, 20.

Freed, Ken. "Financial Opportunities in Educational Television." *Financial Times Media & Telecoms.* London, 1999.

Freedman, Warren. *The Right of Privacy in the Computer Age.* New York: Quorum Books, 2003.

Friedlander, Emily. "Access Denied." *FamilyPC* 7, no. 7 (July 2000): 28.

Gomes, Lee. "Internet Relay Chat Is Suspected Launch Pad of Web Hackers." *Wall Street Journal Eastern Edition,* February 14, 2000, B6.

Hawkridge, David. "The Human in the Machine: Reflections on Mentoring at the British Open University." *Mentoring & Tutoring: Partnership in Learning* 11, issue 1 (April 2003): 15–25.

Kanabar, Dina, and Vijay Kanabar. "A Quick Guide to Basic Network Security." *Computers in Libraries* 23, issue 5 (May 2003): 25–27.

Kandra, Anne. "Don't Let Them Steal Your Good Name." *PC World* 20, issue 10 (October 2002): 43–46.

Kaufman, Roger, and Ryan Watkins. "Assuring the Future for Distance Learning." *Quarterly Review of Distance Education* 1, no. 1 (Spring 2000): 59–68.

Kennedy, David M. "Dimensions of Distance: A Comparison of Classroom Education and Distance Education." *Nurse Education Today* 22, no. 5 (July 2002): 409–416.

Leeds, Mathew. "Desktop Videoconferencing." *MacWorld,* November 1994, pp. 87–92.

Livingston, Brian. "There's Life Left in IIS." *InfoWorld,* January 2003.

Menn, Joseph. "Virus Fails to Hit Microsoft, But Users Are Not So Lucky." *Los Angeles Times,* Saturday, August 16, 2003, Business Section, C1, C3.

Merritt, Mark. "Videoconferencing." *Presentation,* June 2000, 72–74.

Mikat, Richard P. "Desktop Video Conferencing." *Journal of Physical Education, Recreation and Dance* 70, no. 7 (September 1999): 9.

Nasseh, Bizhan. "A Brief History of Distance Education," 1997. <http://www.seniornet.org/edu/art/history.html> (March 2001).

Pfaffenberger, Bryan. *Webster's New World Dictionary of Computer Terms,* 6th ed. New York: Que, 1997.

Rubenking, Janet. "Identity theft: What, me worry?" PC Magazine, March 2, 2004, 75–77.

Rupley, Sebastian. "Identity Theft: The Scary Truth." *PC Magazine,* September 3, 2003.

Schwartz, Jon, and Paul Davidson. "Spam Thrives Despite Effort to Screen It Out." *USA Today,* May 8, 2003.

Shiver Jr., Jube. "Teenager Charged in Blaster Attacks." *Los Angeles Times,* August 31, 2003, Business Section, C1, C2.

Streitfeld, David. "Opening Pandora's In-Box." *Los Angeles Times,* May 11, 2003.

Tunstall, Jeremy. *The Open University Opens.* London: Routledge, 1974, vii–xx.

Tweney, Dylan. "Distance Learning Is No Substitute for Real-World Education." *InfoWorld Magazine,* May 17, 1999.

Van Horn, Royal. "The Electronic Classroom and Video Conferencing." *Phi Delta Kappan* 80, no. 5 (January 1999): 411.

Watkins, Ryan, Roger Kaufman, and Ingrid Guerra. "The Future of Distance Learning: Defining and Sustaining Useful Results." *Educational Technology* 41, no. 3 (May–June 2001): 19–26.

PART III

Integrating Educational Technology into the Classroom

CHAPTER 11

Integrating the World Wide Web (WWW) into the Classroom

Integrating the Web into the Classroom

There are many ways to integrate the World Wide Web into the classroom. One way is to build a Web page using HTML. In creating this Web page, students can learn about any academic subject and simultaneously express themselves through the Web page. Students can learn to use a search engine to find specific information. Teachers can have students team with each other and do WebQuests on a variety of topics such as "What would Abraham Lincoln think about how teenagers live today?" In this chapter you will learn about the criteria for selecting websites. In addition, you will read about some useful Web utility programs, and you will review an excellent collection of Web lesson plans. Finally, you will become familiar with Internet sites that include information about search engines, tutorials, lesson plans, and activities and tips.

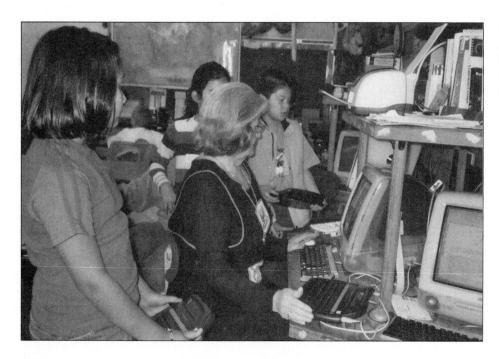

Searching on the Web—Marianne Brooker's Class, Calahan Elementary School, Northridge, California

Objectives

Upon completing this chapter, you will be able to do the following:

1. Name two search engines and describe their strengths.
2. Develop some strategies for searching.
3. Identify four criteria for selecting websites.
4. Describe Web building software.
5. Follow guidelines for Web page design.
6. Explain what a WebQuest is and why it is useful in the classroom.

What Is the World Wide Web (WWW)?

The World Wide Web is "an Internet service that links documents locally and remotely." (Freedman, 2003). These documents or Web pages reside on a Web server. This server distributes Web pages and other files through the Internet. When you access a **website,** the first page of the site is referred to as the **home page.** Using software called *browsers,* such as *Microsoft Internet Explorer* or *Safari,* you access these Web pages. Each website has its own unique **Uniform Resource Locator (URL),** or address, to help you locate it. For example, when you type the URL http://www.paris.org/Musees/Louvre/Treasures/ in Microsoft's *Internet Explorer*'s address text box (Figure 11.1) and then press enter, after a few seconds the home page corresponding to the URL, the Treasures of the Louvre, appears.

Figure 11.1 *Internet Explorer's* Address Text Box

Screen shot of *Microsoft® Internet Explorer* used by permission of Microsoft Corporation.

You are now ready to explore links, or connections to other Web pages. On this page, specific items are underlined. These underlined items are called *links* (Figure 11.2). The

Figure 11.2 Treasures of the Louvre

From www.parispages.com. Louvre artwork as follows: The Venus de Milo © Musée du Louvre The Joconde © Leonardo da Vinci/Musée du Louvre. Statuette of a Man © Musée du Louvre. Standing Lion © Musée du Louvre. The Winged Victory of Samothrace © Musée du Louvre. Voltaire © Jean-Baptiste Pigalle/Musée du Louvre. Frontal view of a man's head (c) Andrea del Sarto/Musée du Louvre. Eagle of Sugerius © Musée du Louvre. Screen shot of *Microsoft® Internet Explorer* used by permission of Microsoft Corporation.

World Wide Web gets its name from these links, which are like threads in a spider's web. Links, or *hot spots*,[1] are underlined words that are displayed in a different color or pictures that are boxed by a colored border. When you click on a live link, the cursor (or arrow) becomes a hand, and you can jump to another page, whether on the same computer or on another computer on the other side of the world.

The size of the text on the Web page as well as the color of the links can be changed using the preferences or view menu. This type of modification helps the individual who is colorblind or has trouble seeing small print.

A Brief History

Before the World Wide Web came into existence, people used text commands to communicate on the Internet. In 1989, Tim Berners-Lee, who worked at the European Particle Physics Laboratory, wrote a proposal that led to the development of the World Wide Web. A year later, he wrote a point and click hypertext editor, called *WorldWideWeb*, which ran on the Next computer. He also created the first Web server, a computer that stored and distributed Web pages or Web documents.

In 1991, a math student by the name of Nicola Pellow created a browser that would work on any device (Berners-Lee, 2003). By the beginning of 1992, there were 50 Web servers and a browser called Voila X Window, which gave the Web graphical capabilities.

Simultaneously, Marc Andreessen developed **Mosaic** at the University of Illinois's National Center for Supercomputing Applications (NCSA). *Mosaic* was a software browser that enabled the user to view pictures and documents on the Internet by simply clicking on a mouse. At the time, Jim Clark, founder of Silicon Graphics Inc., decided not to license the source code of *Mosaic* but instead hired some of NCSA's programmers to reengineer a *Mosaic*-like browser. Marc Andreessen and Jim Clark formed a partnership they called Netscape Communications Corporation. They produced *Netscape Navigator*, which was a higher-performance World Wide Web browser offering multiple and simultaneous image loading. This browser was faster than *Mosaic* and much simpler to use. It also was more advanced than other browsers in the way it handled graphics (Morgenstern, 1995). In a short period of time, more browsers were developed, such as Microsoft's *Internet Explorer*; these browsers made it unnecessary to learn the Unix commands that people had previously used on the Internet. By the start of 1995, there were nearly 10,000 websites, and by 2002, there were more than 29,123,261 registered domain names (http://www.registeryourdn.com/useful_info.html).

Finding a Web Page

When teachers or students want to visit a site, they usually type its URL in a browser window. But what happens when the browser cannot locate the address? One way to handle this problem is physically to modify the URL to get the page you desire. For example, when you try to call up the *Medical Matrix* home page at http://www.medma-

---

[1]A location on the computer screen, usually inside a hypermedia program, that causes an action when a person uses his or her mouse to click it.

trix.org/SPages/Patient_Education_and_Support.stm, you get an error message. Try deleting the final segment (Patient_Education_and_Support.stm) and press *Return* or *Enter.* Continue removing segments from the URL up to the forward slashes until it works. For this example, the functional URL is http://www.medmatrix.org/ (to access this particular site you must register).

If this method of trying to find the URL does not work, try using a search engine to find the site.

Search Engines

Because the Web has millions of searchable pages, finding information is a difficult task. **Search engines** are software programs that help you locate information in a database on the Internet (Morse, 1997). Search engines have been around for years, but they have only come to the forefront since the explosion of the World Wide Web. Search engines locate Web pages on a subject or locate a specific page when you are lacking its URL. To use a search engine, type a word or phrase called a *keyword* or *search term* in the search engine's text box. For example, you might type *Fort Sumter* as your searching term. The search engine then returns results in the form of links to relevant sites. Well-known search engines are *About.com, Excite, Google, HotBot, Yahoo!, Lycos, Open Directory,* and *AltaVista.* The kind of search site you use depends on the information you need. *Yahoo!,* launched in 1994, was the first major online Web-based subject directory and search engine to gain attention.

Many of the search engine sites automatically send **spider programs** out on the Web to collect the text of the relevant Web pages. These spiders are automated electronic software programs that follow the links on a page and put all the text into one huge database. You then search this database when you use the site. Some search engines are combination directories and search engines. **Metasearch engines** do nothing but search other sites. For example, an excellent metasearch engine is *Metacrawler.* These sites simultaneously bring you the results from many search engines. Many sites have become **portals,** sites that do not link to other sites but contain the information you seek. For a list of all major search engines, how they work, and their significant features, visit http://www.searchenginewatch.com. Table 11.1 on page 252 lists some popular search engines that enable you to look for any topic.

How to Search

To be a good searcher, you must have the mind of a detective and think creatively. After all, the Internet is a big database with thousands of links that vary in quality. The search tool you choose is determined by what you are trying to find. If you just want to browse, directories such as *Yahoo!* are a good place to begin. If you are a beginner and want to ask a simple question, *Ask Jeeves* might be very useful. If you need a special type of database, try *Open Directory* (http://dmoz.org). Finally if you are doing advanced searches, begin with *Google.*

Here are a few general rules to follow when you search:

1. Narrow your search and avoid thousands of unnecessary results or hits. When using *Yahoo!,* for example, click the advanced search link and try using an exact phrase match. After you get your results, you can scroll to the bottom of the page and click on other search engines that are listed.

Table 11.1 Popular Search Engines

Search Engine	URL	Description
About.com	http://about.com/	Real people offer expert guidance on the Internet's best. They search in a wide range of subject areas.
AltaVista	http://www.altavista.com/	AltaVista is a database of Internet resources including World Wide Web pages and some Usenet newsgroups.
Ask Jeeves	http://www.ask.com/	Ask Jeeves asks you to type in an actual question. The software identifies a varietyof possible answers to your question. A kid's version called Ask Jeeves for Kids is available at http://www.ajkids.com/.
Dogpile	http://www.dogpile.com	Dogpile searches 26 databases simultaneously and supports Boolean searches.
Excite	http://www.excite.com	Excite collects the "most popular," frequently accessed Internet sites. It is unique because it searches by concept.
Fast Search	http://alltheweb.com	Fast Search has one of the largest indexes of the Web. The site is also known as All The Web.
Google	http://www.google.com	Google searches for sites based on popularity, and these sites are ranked by how many sites have links to them.
Google Web Directory	http://directory.google.com	Google Web Directory is a database of sites organized by subject categories. This directory has over 1.3 billion pages and is considered the largest database.
HotBot	http://www.hotbot.lycos.com	Lycos Network's HotBot provides a number of search options and ranks search results by relevancy.
ixquick	http://ixquick.com	ixquick brings forth the best engines on the Internet and merges the results. It removes redundancies and puts the results into a grouping.
KidsClick!	http://www.kidsclick.org/	KidsClick!, created by a group of librarians, shows students sites for grades K–8.
LookSmart	http://www.looksmart.com/	LookSmart is a searchable, category-based Web directory.
Lycos	http://www.lycos.com	Lycos is a cross between Yahoo! and AltaVista. It also enables you to search for images.
MetaCrawler	http://www.metacrawler.com	MetaCrawler searches many search engines quickly and at the same time. It also offers the winning MiniCrawler, which performs searches in a window on the desktop.
Open Directory Project	http://dmoz.org	Open Directory Project is one of the most comprehensive search engines, with millions of sites.
Yahoo!	http://www.yahoo.com	Yahoo! is a popular hierarchical directory. A kid's version called Yahooligans is available at http://www.yahooligans.com.
Web Crawler	http://www.webcrawler.com	Web Crawler searches content areas and is also a Web directory.

2. When searching, avoid generic or commonly used words. For instance, a search for the *Civil War* is too general and will deliver a tremendous number of matches. In *Google,* for example, using the search term *Civil War* on January 24, 2004, delivered 6,780,000 pages. By limiting the search to *Civil War, Merrimac,* you will be given only 8,490 pages.

3. Most search engines enable you to link your search terms with words such as *and, or,* or *minus* (−) as well as to search for phrases by placing the words in quotation marks, which causes the engine to search for *all* the terms enclosed in the quotation marks. For example, searching for "Harry Truman and Pearl Harbor," would give you only information that addressed both Truman *and* Pearl Harbor. If you replace *and* with *or,* the search would be directed to identify either one topic or the other. If you replace the *and* with the minus sign (no spaces), the engine will find the pages that contain references to Harry Truman but not to Pearl Harbor. The connnectors vary with the search engines. Check your search engine's help page for more tips and tricks.

4. Use wildcards if the search engine allows it. Wildcards will turn up results on all terms containing the wildcard. For example, surg* will yield results on *surgery, surgeries,* and *surgical.*

5. Enter singular terms. Many search engines will find the substring and include plural terms in the results.

The following three sites give you tips and tricks for searching:

- The University of California at Berkeley recommends specific search tools and search strategies, including advance-searching techniques. Go to http://www.lib. berkeley.edu/TeachingLib/Guides/Internet/ToolsTables.html.
- The University of South Carolina's BareBones 101 (http://www.sc.edu/beaufort/ library/bones.html) offers a basic Web search tutorial, including definitions, search strategies, and specific information about top directories and search engines.
- *Awesome Library* (http://www.awesomelibrary.org/help.html) shows simple as well as advanced searching techniques.

Multimedia Via the Internet

With the explosion of the World Wide Web came a surge in the number of websites created by individuals and organizations. Website authors included graphics, animations, and sounds in their sites. Students and teachers used visual images to communicate in distance learning, including clip art, animations, photos, and scans on their Web pages. Students shot movies with their camcorders and downloaded these movies to the Internet. Users of all ages began using the Web to listen to music. With this increase in users and usage came an increase in Internet multimedia applications. We will review some here.

Streaming Video

Streaming video is a compressed movie sent in real time via the Internet. The receiving users can play these streaming movies with a streaming video player such as *RealVideo* or *QuickTime.* Streaming video begins playing as soon as you start to download. The quality of the movie depends on the speed of the computer connection.

Videomaker's site on streaming video, found at http://www.streamingvideos.com, gives complete answers to frequently asked questions about streaming video.

Streaming Audio

Streaming audio is one-way audio transmission over the data network. *Real One* is a multimedia player that plays streaming audio and streaming video in real time.

Plug-ins

Web browsers come with plug-in extensions for video, audio, telephony, 3-D animations, and video conferencing. A **plug-in** is a separate program that works with a browser to enhance its capabilities. Table 11.2 lists popular plug-ins.

Table 11.2 Some Popular Plug-ins

Name	Website	Description
Acrobat Reader	http://www.adobe.com/	Displays and prints *Adobe Acrobat* documents (PDF files).
Apple QuickTime	http://www.apple.com	Plays animation, music, MIDI, audio, video, and VR panoramas and objects.
Flash Player	http://www.macromedia.com	Displays animation and graphics.
RealJukebox	http://www.real.com	Plays MP3 files.
RealOne (formerly *RealPlayer*)	http://www.real.com	Plays audio and video.
Shockwave	http://www.macromedia.com	Plays interactive games, multimedia, and streaming audio and displays graphics.

Website Evaluation

Sifting through sites on the Internet is a complex process; it is important to be able to distinguish a good website from one that is mediocre. Users must be cautious, because anyone can have a Web page and include on it information that is inaccurate, false, or just plain fantasy. The following criteria will help you evaluate websites.

Download Time

Does the home page download fast enough to use during full-class instruction? Does this page download efficiently enough to keep the students focused during small-group and independent study? Does the page download too slowly because it has too many graphics?

Navigation Ease

Are your students able to move easily from page to page? Is the page designed in such a way that the students do not get confused or lost? Are the links and descriptions clearly labeled so the students have no trouble keeping at task? Do the majority of the links work?

Appearance

Is the home page's design attractive and appropriate for students? Is the students' first impression positive, and will they be motivated to return repeatedly? Is the design clear so that the students can explore the page effectively? Are the screens easy to read?

Graphics, Videos, and Sounds

Do the graphics, videos, and sounds have a clear purpose, and are they appropriate for the intended students? Do the graphics, videos, and sounds help the students reach their objectives? Do they enhance the content?

Content

Does the site offer information that meets the learning objective? Is this information clearly labeled and accurate? How is the site organized? Is the information at an appropriate grade level, and can the student easily understand it? Are the related links worthwhile and appropriate? Is the content free of bias and stereotype? Does the site provide interactivity that increases its instructional value?

Currency

Is the site updated on a regular basis?

Credibility

Is the site a trustworthy source of information? Does it provide author and source citations as well as a contact person to answer students' questions?

Now you have an idea of what is important when examining a website on the Internet. You might want to reproduce the checklist form on page 256 and use its criteria to rate a site to see if it meets your curriculum objectives.

Integrating the Web into the Classroom

In this section, you will find websites that are particularly useful for teachers and students. They cover all curriculum areas and include an excellent collection of lesson plans. The sites were chosen for their currency, ease of use, comprehensiveness, and organization. They met the criteria listed in the form on page 256. The sites are updated frequently and contain the latest information. Many of the sites are award winners and have been cited for their authoritative and reliable information.

Website Checklist

Site Title: _____ Grade Level and Class: _____

Subject: _____ Objective: _____

URL (address): _____ URLs for Individual Site Pages (addresses): _____

Evaluate the website according to the following criteria. Circle the number that you feel the site deserves, 5 being outstanding and 1 being unacceptable.

Download Speed

Quickly loads text	5	4	3	2	1
Quickly loads graphics	5	4	3	2	1

Navigation Ease

Easy moves from link to link	5	4	3	2	1
Links are clearly labeled	5	4	3	2	1
Links to other sites operate effectively	5	4	3	2	1
Links provided for backward and forward movement	5	4	3	2	1
Provides an adequate number of links	5	4	3	2	1
Links are apropos and helpful	5	4	3	2	1

Appearance

Visual appeal	5	4	3	2	1
Clarity	5	4	3	2	1

Content

Information meets objectives	5	4	3	2	1
Is clearly organized and labeled	5	4	3	2	1
Is linked to worthwhile sites	5	4	3	2	1
Is accurate and useful	5	4	3	2	1
Provides interactivity	5	4	3	2	1

Is free of bias and stereotype	5	4	3	2	1
Site author is clearly identified	5	4	3	2	1
Offers sufficient worthwhile information	5	4	3	2	1
Is authoritative	5	4	3	2	1
Is readable by students at grade level	5	4	3	2	1
Enables students to collaborate with other sites	5	4	3	2	1
Teachers can share with others	5	4	3	2	1

Graphics, Videos, and Sounds

Use is clearly identified	5	4	3	2	1
Have a clear purpose and are appropriate	5	4	3	2	1
Aid students to achieve objectives	5	4	3	2	1
Are relevant for the site	5	4	3	2	1
Graphics enhance content	5	4	3	2	1
Currency (frequency of updating)	5	4	3	2	1

Credibility

Author and source are cited	5	4	3	2	1
Contact person provided	5	4	3	2	1

Add the total number of points that the site earns to determine the overall rating.

Overall Rating: _____

Rating Scale

_____ 150–133 points: This site is of sound content, and I can let the students freely explore.

_____ 132–111 points: This site contains good instructional material, but the students will need very specific instructions to explore the site.

_____ 110–94 points: This site contains some worthwhile information, but students will need more specific links and a list of bookmarks along with frequent discussions to progress.

_____ 93–63: Although some useful information exists at this site, the best way to use this site is through whole-class instruction and guiding the students.

_____ 62–52: This site contains some useful information, but other sites would be more appropriate, and I must supervise the students.

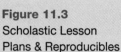

Websites to Use in the Classroom

MULTISUBJECT

Scholastic's Teacher Section

http://teacher.scholastic.com/

Scholastic provides standards-based lesson plans and reproducible materials for grades Pre-K–8. Click *Online Activities* for Web-based, ready-to-use curriculum materials. The science lesson plan seen in Figure 11.3 (http:// www.scholastic.com/magicschoolbus/

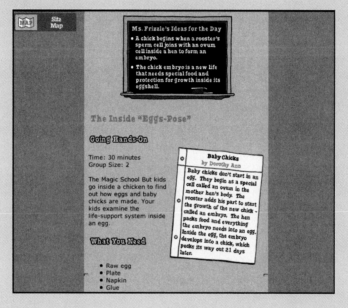

Figure 11.3
Scholastic Lesson
Plans & Reproducibles

From Scholastic.com/
magicschoolbus/teacher.
Copyright © 2004 by
Scholastic Inc.

Used by permission. The
Magic School Bus is a
registered trademark of
Scholastic Inc.

games/teacher/eggs/index.htm) is an example of what you find at this site. Use the site's search engine to find a specific lesson plan.

CanTeach

http://www.canteach.ca/

CanTeach offers hundreds of lesson plans, thousands of links, and tons of other resources for elementary school teachers. The physical science lesson plan "Making a Pinhole Camera #2" is shown in Figure 11.4 (http://www.canteach.ca/elementary/ physical4.html).

Figure 11.4 *CanTeach*

Used by permission of
CanTeach. Visit us at
http://www.track0.com/
canteach/elementary/
physical14.html or
http://www.track0.com/
canteach/.

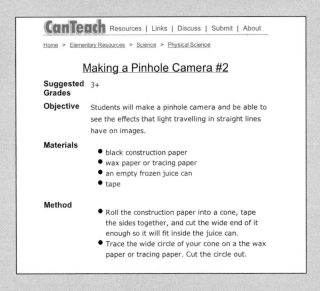

LANGUAGE ARTS

Pals Activities

http://pals.virginia.edu/scores/Activities/activity.cfm?type=edit&what=Activity& id=26&subcategoryID=7

This site offers an assortment of activities for reinforcing readiness reading skills. Concepts covered are letter sounds, alphabet recognition, word concepts, word recognition, rhymes, beginning sounds, and blending. For beginning sounds, one of the game activities is the "Follow-the-Path Game" shown in Figure 11.5.

Figure 11.5 PALS
Website

Reprinted with permission
from the PALS office at the
University of Virginia and the
Virginia Department of
Education.

Lesson Plans from *The Teacher's Desk*

http://www.teachersdesk.org

The Teacher's Desk contains a collection of over 150 language arts lesson ideas for grades 5–6 including the vocabulary activity "Translating Fairy Tales" shown in Figure 11.6. Click on *Spelling* to find this activity.

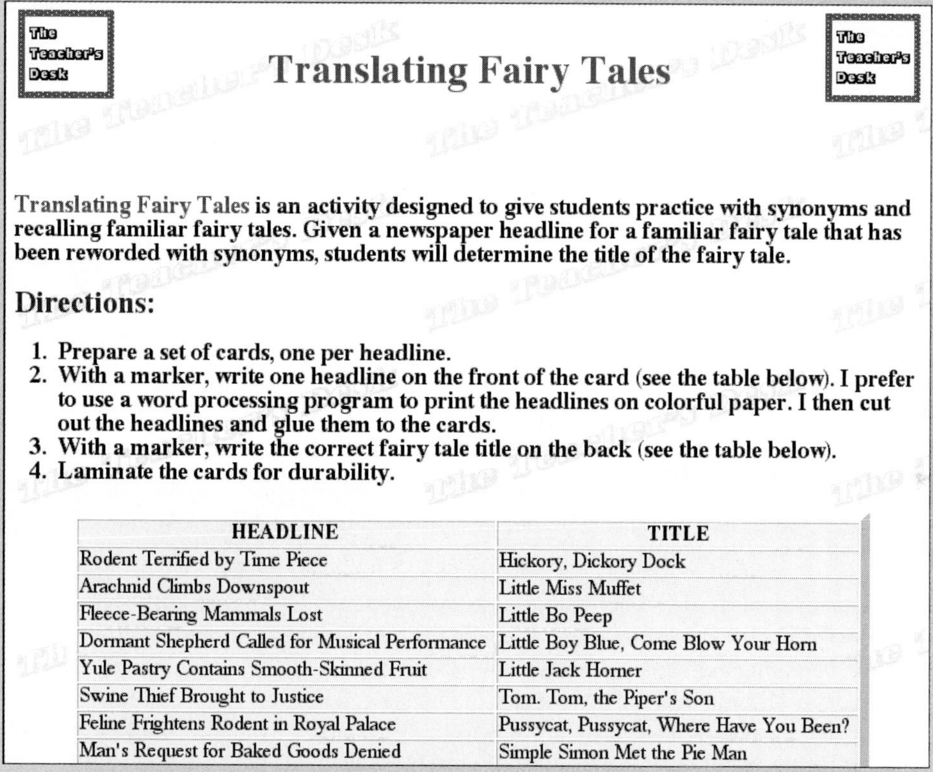

Figure 11.6 *The Teacher's Desk*

Reprinted by permission. Visit us at http://www.knownet.net/~ackley/vocabtale.htm.

The Teacher's Desk

Translating Fairy Tales

Translating Fairy Tales is an activity designed to give students practice with synonyms and recalling familiar fairy tales. Given a newspaper headline for a familiar fairy tale that has been reworded with synonyms, students will determine the title of the fairy tale.

Directions:

1. Prepare a set of cards, one per headline.
2. With a marker, write one headline on the front of the card (see the table below). I prefer to use a word processing program to print the headlines on colorful paper. I then cut out the headlines and glue them to the cards.
3. With a marker, write the correct fairy tale title on the back (see the table below).
4. Laminate the cards for durability.

HEADLINE	TITLE
Rodent Terrified by Time Piece	Hickory, Dickory Dock
Arachnid Climbs Downspout	Little Miss Muffet
Fleece-Bearing Mammals Lost	Little Bo Peep
Dormant Shepherd Called for Musical Performance	Little Boy Blue, Come Blow Your Horn
Yule Pastry Contains Smooth-Skinned Fruit	Little Jack Horner
Swine Thief Brought to Justice	Tom. Tom, the Piper's Son
Feline Frightens Rodent in Royal Palace	Pussycat, Pussycat, Where Have You Been?
Man's Request for Baked Goods Denied	Simple Simon Met the Pie Man

---

CyberGuides: Teacher Guides and Student Activities

http://www.sdcoe.k12.ca.us/score/ cyberguide.html

CyberGuides are supplementary, standards-based, Web-delivered units of instruction centered on core works of literature. Each *CyberGuide* contains a student and teacher edition, standards, a task, a method for completion, teacher-selected websites, and a rubric. A sample lesson plan for the book *The Door in the Wall* is seen in Figure 11.7 (http://www.sdcoe.k12.ca.us/ score/door/doortg.html).

The story "The Door in the Wall" takes place in the Middle Ages. Life during this time period is revealed through the experiences of Robin, a 10-year-old boy who hopes to become a knight. After becoming ill and losing the use of his legs, he struggles to overcome his handicap and proves himself a hero.

Figure 11.7 *The Door in the Wall*

San Diego County Office of Education.

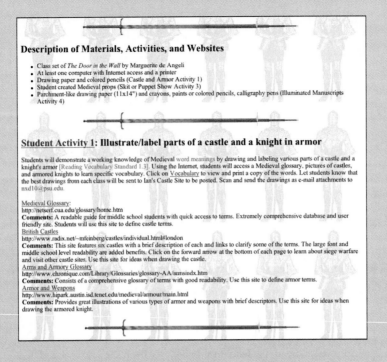

MATH

SCORE Mathematics Lessons

http://score.kings.k12.ca.us/

SCORE Mathematics Lessons reflect California's and the National Council of Teachers of Mathematics' standards. Excellent sample lesson plans are "What's My Number?" (http://score.kings.k12.ca.us/lessons/100board.html) and "Shopping for Toys" (http://score.kings.k12.ca.us/lessons/shop4toy.htm). For "What's My Number?" students seek information on the Internet to find facts needed to arrive at a number on the 100 board, a number known only to the author. Students use the information to work math problems. In "Shopping for Toys" (Figure 11.8), students have won a $100 gift cer-

Figure 11.8 *SCORE Mathematics*

Used by permission of Kings County Office of Education. Visit us at http://www.score.kings.k12.ca.us/lesson/shop4toy.htm.

tificate and can spend up to that amount to buy some toys. They then make a display consisting of drawings of some of the toys they chose and a few sentences explaining why they chose those toys. They answer teacher-made questions and fill in their order forms.

MathStories

http://www.mathstories.com/

This website has more than 8,000 word problems classified according to grade level and topics. The worksheets can support any math lesson, and teachers can make copies of these sheets. Figure 11.9 reproduces "Planets/Scientific Notation," a word problem sheet for grade 7 or 8. This site is a subscription-based site and charges a yearly subscription.

Figure 11.9
MathStories.com™
Used with permission.

MathStories.com™

Copyright © 1999 Math Stories . com , Inc, 2416 Ramke Place , Santa Clara, California 95050 . All Rights Reserved.

Sheet # 43/Planets/Scientific Notation

Name: _____ Date_____

Fill the following table.

Planet	Average Distance From the Sun (in km)	Express in Scientific Notation
Mercury	58,000,000 .	
Venus	108,000,000 .	
Earth	150,000,000 .	
Mars	228,000,000 .	
Jupiter	778,000,000 .	
Saturn	1,429,000,000 .	
Uranus	2,875,000,000 .	

TeAch-nology the Web Portal for Educators

http://www.teach-nology.com/

TeAch-nology.com provides free access to 19,000 lesson plans and 5,600 printable worksheets. This site also includes teacher downloads, rubrics, teacher tools, educational games, teaching tips, current education news, and WebQuests. On the left-hand side, under *Top Areas,* click on *Lesson Plan Center.* Then click on *Economics* to see a variety of lesson plans. Click on the lesson entitled "Crude Awakenings" (Figure 11.10).

Figure 11.10 "Crude Awakening" Lesson Plan

Copyright © 2004 by The New York Times Co. Reprinted with permission.

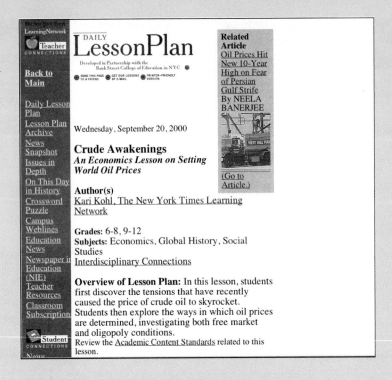

Math Forum Internet Mathematics Library

http://mathforum.org/library/resource_types/lesson_plans/

This immense collection offers hundreds of topics from many sources, including Suzanne Alejandre's *Understanding Algebraic Factoring* (Figure 11.11, http://mathforum.org/alejandre/algfac.html).

Figure 11.11 Understanding Algebraic Factoring

Reprinted by permission of The Math Forum, Swarthmore College.

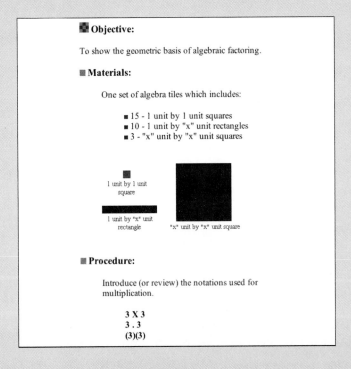

SOCIAL STUDIES

Archiving Early America

http://www.earlyamerica.com/

This site links to many primary sources of historical documents and portraits from 18th-century America. It includes portraits of famous 18th-century figures, original historical documents with abstracts, and chapters from books such as *The Autobiography of Benjamin Franklin*. It also has a script that scrolls to what happened on a particular day in history. Click on *World of Early Americans* to see documents such as *The Declaration of Independence* (Figure 11.12).

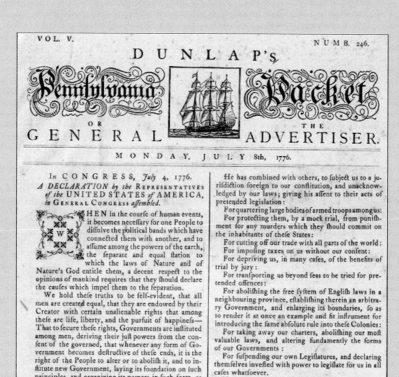

Figure 11.12

Archiving Early America

Copyright, Archiving Early America—http://earlyamerica.com. Reprinted with permission.

Shotgun's Home of the Civil War

http://www.civilwarhome.com/

This site contains a range of information on Civil War battles, Civil War biographies, Civil War medicine, Civil War potpourri, essays on the Civil War, letters about the Civil War, and much more. Click on *Civil War Biographies* to find the biography on Ulysses Simpson Grant shown in Figure 11.13. The biographical information covers the subject's participation in the Civil War, and in many instances pictures are included.

Figure 11.13
Shotgun's Home of the
Civil War

Text excerpted from *Who Was
Who in the Civil War* by Stewart
Sifakis. Published by Facts on
File, 1988. Screen capture from
www.civilwarhome.com.

Ulysses Simpson Grant
(1822-1885)

The best evidence of the changes that had occurred in warfare from
Jomini to Clausewitz can be found in the campaigns of Robert E. Lee and
Ulysses S. Grant. The latter was born Hiram Ulysses Grant in Ohio but
through confusion at West Point he became Ulysses Simpson Grant.
Appointed to the military academy, he found it distasteful and hoped that
Congress would abolish the institution, freeing him. He excelled only in
horsemanship for that he had displayed a capability early in life and
graduated in 1843, 21st out of 39 graduates. Posted to the 4th Infantry,
since there were no vacancies in the dragoons, he served as regimental
quartermaster during most of the Mexican War. Nonetheless he frequently
led a company in combat under Zachary Taylor in northern Mexico.

He came to greatly admire his chief but was transferred with his
regiment to Winfield Scott's army operating from the coast. He received

WPI Military Science

http://www.wpi.edu/Academics/Depts/MilSci/BTSI

This site features detailed descriptions of the historic battles of Lexington, Concord, and
Breed's Hill/Bunker Hill and the events that led to our Revolutionary War (Figure 11.14).

Figure 11.14
Worcester Polytechnic
Institute, Military
Science

Reprinted with permission.

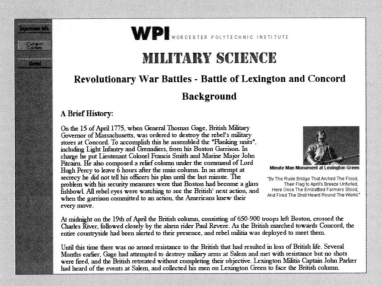

SCIENCE

CEEE GirlTECH Lesson Plans

http://teachertech.rice.edu/Lessons/index.html

GirlTECH has offered Internet science and math lesson plans for grades 7–12 since
1995. Use the site's search engine to find the lesson plan you want. An excellent chemistry lesson activity, "It's ELEMENTary!" investigates the properties and characteristics

of elements and promotes the understanding of the periodic table (Figure 11.15, http://users.ev1.net/~vklawinski/ptinternetact.htm).

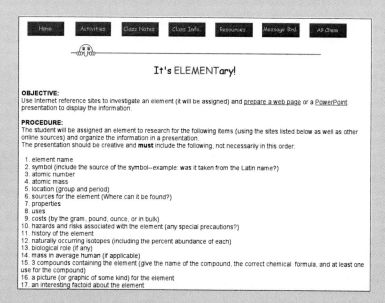

Figure 11.15 It's ELEMENTary!

Used by permission of Radica USA; for more information contact Lori Dawn Howl at ldhowl@radicausa.com.

It includes an interactive quiz, links to other resources, a description of the project, project requirements, and Internet links that will enable the student to access the information needed to complete the project.

SCORE Science

http://scorescience.humboldt.k12.ca.us/

Click on *Lessons Search* to find a collection of lesson plans and activities organized by grade level and subject for grades K–12. An excellent example is "Newton's Laws," which explains clearly everything you have ever wanted to know about Isaac Newton and Newton's Laws (Figure 11.16, ttp://www.ced.appstate.edu/whs/goals2000/projects / 97 / michael /michael.htm).

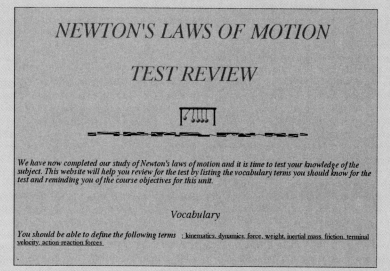

Figure 11.16 Newton's Laws

Used by permission of Humboldt County Office of Education.

I Can Do That!

http://www.eurekascience.com/ICanDoThat/

I Can Do That! is an amusing site that helps students learn about DNA, RNA, cells, protein, cloning, and other biotechnology topics (Figure 11.17).

Figure 11.17 *I Can Do That!*

Reprinted by permission of Eureka! Science Corp.

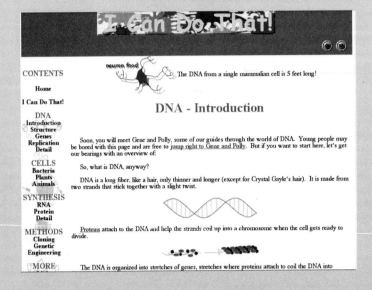

Rock Hound

http://www.fi.edu/fellows/payton/rocks/index2.html

Learn about different types of rocks and rock collecting and take a safety quiz from Rocky the Rock Hound (Figure 11.18) at this site. To find other science lesson plans, visit the parent site, *The Franklin Institute Online Fellows Wired@School* (http://www.fi.edu/ fellows/).

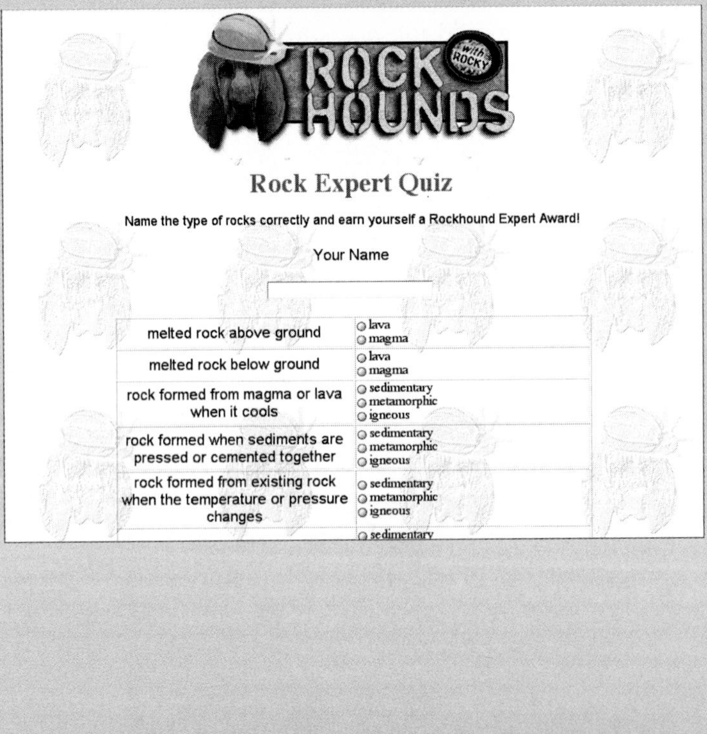

Figure 11.18 Rocky the Rock Hound

Used by permission of The Franklin Institute Science Museum. Please visit us at http://www.fi.edu/ educators.html.

Newton's Apple

http://www.tpt.org/newtons/

This site contains a complete collection of teacher's guides, seasons 9 through 15, from the TV show *Newton's Apple.* All the guides are organized by topic and show number. Try the sample lesson plan on the human eye and some fun experiments shown in Figure 11.19 (http://www.tpt.org/newtons/tryits/14/sciencetryits.html). For a complete collection of Science Try-Its, visit http://www.tpt.org/newtons/tryits/index.html.

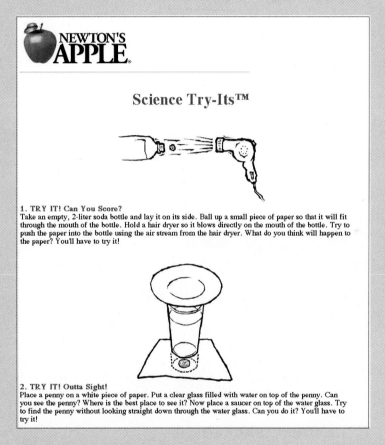

Figure 11.19 Science Try-Its™

Reprinted courtesy of Twin Cities Public Television, Inc.

AskERIC Lesson Plans

http://www.askeric.org/cgi-bin/lessons.cgi/Science/Biology

This site has a large collection of lesson plans contributed by teachers for grades K–12. Topics include agriculture, biological and life sciences, earth science, physical sciences, space science, and technology. Click on *science* and you find the excellent lesson plan on Photosynthesis/Cell Respiration/Enzymes/Light shown in Figure 11.20. Along with this lesson plan comes a downloadable PowerPoint presentation.

Figure 11.20 ERIC
Lesson Plans

Educator's Reference Desk,
"Jeopardy PowerPoint" Lesson
Plan by Aubrey Melton,
http://www.eduref.org.
Reprinted with permission.

Jeopardy PowerPoint: Photosynthesis / Cell Respiration / Enzymes / Light

An Educator's Reference Desk Lesson Plan

Submitted by: Aubrey Melton
Email: amelton@bigfoot.com
School/University/Affiliation: University of Michigan – Flint

Date: February 5, 2003

Grade Level: 8, 9, 10, 11

Subject(s):

● Science/Biology

Duration: 55-60 minutes

Description: A PowerPoint Jeopardy–like game that can be used as a review of biology concepts.

Goals: Michigan State Standards – Science Benchmarks :
Organization of Living Things

● All students will use classification systems to describe groups of living things; compare and contrast differences in the life cycles of things; investigate and explain how living things obtain and use energy; and analyze how parts of living things are adapted to carry special functions.
● Benchmark: III.2.H3 – Explain the process of food storage and food use in organisms.

Classroom Lesson Plans

I. COMBINING GEOGRAPHY WITH ART

Students will learn how to use a map site such as *MapQuest* (http://www.mapquest.com) and a drawing or painting program such as *Corel Draw* or *AppleWorks*. They will find a map at *MapQuest* that covers an area they would like to visit. Next, they will copy and paste this map into their paint or draw program. Finally, they will add text, arrows, and pictures to illustrate their map.

II. WEATHER TRACKERS

Students will use an Internet weather site such as *Weather.Com* (http://www.weather.com) to track the weather conditions around the world. They can create charts and graphs using a program such as *Excel*. Finally, they will discuss the results with their classmates.

III. WACKY STORIES

Students will make up a list of words to be used at *Education Place's Wacky Web Tales* site (http://www.eduplace.com/tales/index.html). This site will generate wacky stories, or "mad libs." Students can then share their funny stories with their classmates.

IV. HISTORY PUZZLES

Students will use a puzzle site such as *PuzzleMaker* (http://www.puzzlemaker.com) to create a crossword puzzle for their history vocabulary words. They will then exchange puzzles to see if their classmates can solve them. They can also use one of many crossword puzzles from the existing database.

V. BUILDING A HOME PAGE

Students will make their own home pages using an existing Web page builder such as *GeoCities* at http://www.geocities.yahoo.com.

VI. SCAVENGER HUNT 1

Students will form groups to make up a scavenger hunt in science, social studies, music, art, or science. Their objective is to find a picture of a hawk or find out who the first American woman astronaut was. Next, students will exchange their scavenger hunts and search online for the required answers.

Variation

Students can use a scavenger hunt online to see who can solve it the fastest. For example, if they are studying black history month they might use *Dr. Martin Luther King, Jr., Scavenger Hunt* (http://users.massed.net/~tstrong/Martin.htm).

VII. SCAVENGER HUNT 2

Subject

All subjects

Grade(s)

Varied

Objective

Students will find factual information about topics ranging from history to current events.

Standards

National Council for the Social Studies Curriculum Standards 1, 3
ISTE Nets for Students: 1, 2, 3, 4, 5

Materials

You will need a computer, a communications package, a modem, and access to the Internet.

Procedures

1. Discuss different searching techniques with the students.
2. Have the students form small groups.
3. Using the Scavenger Hunt form in Table 11.3 have the students find the answer to each question by searching the specific site.

Table 11.3 Scavenger Hunt Form

1. What is Michigan's state tree?
   http://www.michigan.gov/
2. What animal made Jane Goodall famous?
   http://www.janegoodall.org
3. Why do leaves change color in the fall?
   http://www.sciencemadesimple.com/
4. Who was the first American woman astronaut to orbit the earth?
   http://www.nauts.com/
5. Which president served the shortest term in the White House?
   http://www.whitehouse.gov/history/presidents/
6. What was the name of the Supreme Court decision that overturned legalized segregation?
   http://www.infoplease.com/history.html
7. What is the currency in Zambia?
   http://www.xe.com/ucc/
8. In what year was the last star sewn on our present-day flag?
   http://www.ushistory.org/betsy/
9. How many immigrants were processed at Ellis Island from 1892 to 1924?
   http://www.ellisisland.org/
10. Starting from the foot of the pedestal, how many steps must you climb to reach the torch of the Statue of Liberty?
    http://www.nps.gov/stli/

4. When the students are finished, have them compare answers.

WebQuests

In 1995, at San Diego State University, Professor of Educational Technology Bernie Dodge developed and coined the concept **WebQuest** while teaching preservice teachers. He gave the students a format for online lessons that would foster high-order thinking. Shortly thereafter, Tom March, working as a fellow for Pacific Bell, developed the first WebQuest. Dr. Dodge's format for Web-based lessons was later published in *The Distance Educator Journal* (http://edweb.sdsu.edu/courses/edtec596/about_webquests.html). This paper, "Some Thoughts About WebQuests," defined a WebQuest as "an inquiry-oriented activity where most or all of the information that the students use comes from the Web."

The WebQuest can take a single class session or be a month-long unit. It usually involves a group of students who divide their labor. The lessons consist of materials selected by the teachers and used by the students. WebQuests can be done on a variety of topics that are not well defined and that require creativity and problem-solving skills. Some examples are "What was it like to live during the American Revolution?" "What would Benjamin Franklin think about how teenagers live today?" WebQuests are not meant to prompt simple recall but foster inquiry and logical constructivism incorporating collaborative learning.

What you need to create a WebQuest is the ability to design a Web page with links. Of course, if you are not talented this way, there are plenty of templates available on the Web. A server is not necessary, because you can copy the WebQuest on the hard drive. If you see a WebQuest that you want to use, you can use a program such as *Grab-a-Site 5.0* (Blue Squirrel) to load it on your hard drive. (Naturally, you need to get the author's permission to grab the page.)

In a WebQuest there are six important components: (1) introduction, (2) task, (3) process, (4) resources, (5) evaluation, and (6) conclusions. The *introduction* gives students background information and assigns roles for them to play. For example, a student might be a member of a research team or an astronaut. The teacher also gives students an overview of the learning objectives. The *task* tells the students what they will accomplish by the end of the WebQuest. For example, using *Planetary WebQuest* (Figure 11.21, http://teacher.esuhsd.org/webquests/webquests/planetary.html), stu-

Figure 11.21
Planetary WebQuest
© Bernie Dodge.

dents analyze the different planets and decide which planet to colonize. At the end of the assignment, each team has to identify the planets, give general physical characteristics, and evaluate its sources. The *process* consists of the step-by-step instructions the students go through to accomplish the task that is set. The *resources* section should consist of a list of resources, either printed or bookmarked websites that the students need to complete the task. The resources are either listed separately or embedded in the process section. The students can also use other resources such as videos, audiocassettes, or maps. Each WebQuest must have some method for *evaluation.* The method should be fair and consistent for the tasks set. Finally, the *conclusion* component has students discuss what they discovered and the teacher summarize what has transpired.

Since the beginning of WebQuests, teachers, curriculum specialists, and teacher educators at the university level have used Bernie Dodge's *WebQuest Page* (http://edweb.sdsu.edu/webquest/webquest.html) as a source of material and ideas. Over time, the *WebQuest Page* has grown and developed links to WebQuests all over the world. Thousands of teachers have created WebQuest lessons on the Web. To find them, simply search with any search engine by typing in the search term *WebQuest.* Your search may turn up the WebQuest lesson *Mathart* (Figure 11.22), which

Figure 11.22 *Mathart*
© Bernie Dodge.

connects geometry with art (http://u2.lvcm.com/esullivan/webquest.html), or *Eco-Quest: Desert Edition* (http://members.aol.com/QuestSite/1/), an interactive WebQuest designed for teachers in search of middle school science curricula. It is structured to introduce students to Internet research and multimedia design. In addition, Bernie Dodge has developed an excellent index of lessons (http://www.macomb.k12.mi.us/wq/webqindx.htm). These WebQuests were created during a three-day in-service in the summer of 1997. Lesson topics range from clouds to Johnny Tremain. You can find more excellent WebQuest lessons at edHelper.com (Figure 11.23).

Figure 11.23
edHelper.com
Reprinted with permission.

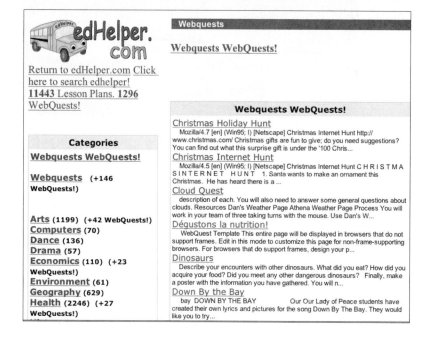

This site has a collection of over 1,200 WebQuests. These lessons cover a variety of topics from exploring China to global warming. Kathy Schrock's Guide for Educators (http://school.discovery.com/schrockguide/webquest/webquest.html) includes excellent WebQuests created by students and teachers and links to other sites. Finally, Welcome WebQuests (http://www.techtrekers.com/webquests/) contains WebQuests from all curriculum areas. The WebQuest topics include art and music, careers, ESL, social studies, Spanish, and much more.

Weblogs

A **Weblog** is a personal online diary (Bull, Bull, and Kajder, 2003). Weblogs are usually referred to as *blogs.* In 1999 to create a blog you needed to be able to program using HTML. Today, companies such as *Blogger* (Figure 11.24) and *Live Journal* offer free blog

Figure 11.24 Blogger

Reprinted with permission of Google, Inc.

publishing. Blogger (http://www.blogger.com) is free, but students must register with an e-mail address. During the registration process they name their site. They work from online templates and then write what they want. Whenever a student logs on, a window appears to which the user can add a journal entry. When the student is done, the entry is posted and can be viewed at the site. A Weblog is a very motivating activity encouraging students to write, experiment with new ideas, and expand their horizons. Students can use their blog as a response journal, to share comments and feedback with other students. They can use it as a public forum for discussing issues with a community of students. They can use the blog as a private place to write down their ideas.

Blogger offers the user audio-posting service through which a journaler can phone in a posting. Users can also insert audio and pictures to make their blogs more interesting.

Web Page Creation

With the growth of the Internet, computer-literate people everywhere have expressed themselves by creating Web pages. The building of Web pages has increased exponentially, and these pages range from the informative to the ridiculous. Because of the popularity of Web pages, many programs were designed to create them. Using HTML was difficulty for the ordinary computer user, so software companies produced Web publishing programs that had a simple graphical interface for Web pages and that automatically generated the HTML code. Word processing programs such as *Word Perfect* and *Microsoft Word* (Figure 11.25) enable you to create a Web page and export it as HTML.

Figure 11.25 *Make It with Office XP*

Reprinted with permission of Visions Technology in EducationTM. www.ToolsforTeachers.com.

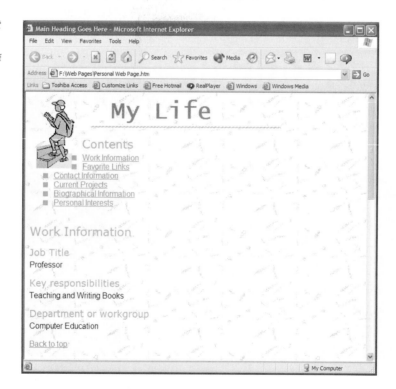

Programs such as *Web Workshop 2.0, Web Workshop Pro* (Sunburst), and *Microsoft FrontPage* work similarly to a word processor, offering a menu bar and toolbar with which users can create the page as if they were viewing it through a Web browser. Tags[2] are inserted automatically, so knowledge of HTML is not necessary. *Web Workshop* (Figure 11.26) is perfect for the beginning student, grades 2 to 8. It contains clip art, familiar paint tools, and a simple interface that makes it easy for the student to create a Web page. All the student does is select backgrounds, add text, and place pictures with a click of the mouse. To create a link, students select an item and type in a World Wide Web address. This software is a perfect choice for the first-time Internet user.

Web Workshop Pro is for the older students, from grades 6 to 12. This website design software provides tools and templates that prompt students to think about the content and function, purpose, and navigability of their site. There is free one-step publishing on Sunburst's website.

[2]Code that is used in HTML and is surrounded by the < and > symbols.

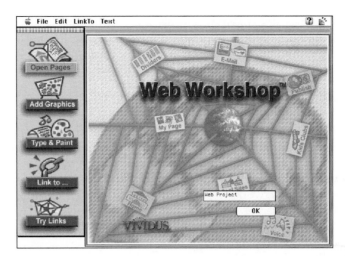

Figure 11.26 *Web Workshop*

Used by permission of Sunburst Communications (800) 321-7511.

In the same manner, *Microsoft FrontPage* enables you to create full-featured Web pages without having to know anything about HTML or URLs. The software is simple, and you can quickly add frames and tables to your Web page.

As a part of the *Netscape Communicator* browser, *Netscape Composer* is a simple to use website builder, and it is free. Higher-level programs such as *Dreamweaver MX* (Macromedia) or *GoLive Studio* (Adobe) are for the advanced student. *Dreamweaver MX* and *GoLive Studio* enable you to create professional websites. They feature visual layout tools and extensive code editing.

HTML editors are less intuitive but are available as shareware programs that can be purchased for a fraction of the cost of the others. Programs of this kind include *Hot Dog* (Sausage Software), *HTML Editor* (Rick Giles), and *PageSpinner* (Jerry Aman, Optima System). In addition to these Web page creators, there are organizer programs such as *Inspiration,* and presentation programs such as *Microsoft PowerPoint* and *Apple's Keynote* that have HTML features built into their programs. Furthermore, sites such as Yahoo's! *GeoCities* (http://geocities.yahoo.com/) enable you to build your own Web pages. You can use page wizards at these sites to create a Web page in a matter of minutes. You simply answer a few questions, and the wizard builds the page according to your answers (Figure 11.27). The

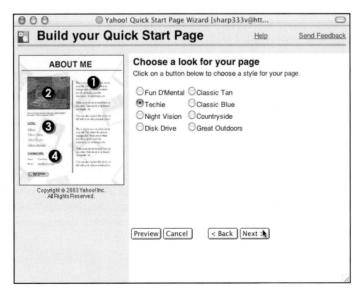

Figure 11.27 *Quick Start* Web Page Wizard

Reproduced with permission of Yahoo! Inc. © 2004 by Yahoo! Inc. YAHOO! And the YAHOO! Logo are trademarks of Yahoo! Inc.

wizard creates a professional-looking page. In addition, you can create pages from scratch using a page builder. With a page builder, you drag and drop items. If you are a purist and want to work close to the code, you will have to learn hypertext markup language (HTML).

Hypertext Markup Language (HTML)

Hypertext Markup Language (HTML) is the formatting language behind the documents that you see on the World Wide Web. Some browsers, such as *Netscape,* come with an option that enables you to view the HTML source code for any existing Web page. You use HTML tags to mark up text so that it can be read by your browser locally or over a network. *NSCA Beginner's Guide to HTML* (http://archive.ncsa.uiuc.edu/General/Internet/WWW/HTMLPrimerAll.html) should further help you understand Web page creation.

In the **Online Learning Center** is a brief guide that will give you some of the basics for creating an HTML document.

Java

Whereas HTML is a document display format that is constantly being changed to make it accomplish more, **Java** is a full-blown programming language. Using Java, a person can write a program that will work on any computer that can run a Java interpreter, which is built into the majority of browsers today. Using Java you can create **applets,** or small computer programs, that provide a specific function such as displaying a scrolling, or ticker tape, message, a clock, or a calculator. Java is important because it has the potential to power a new generation of devices that might make today's desktop personal computers obsolete (Hiltzik, 1997).

JavaScript

JavaScript is a scripting language developed by Netscape Communications for publishing on the World Wide Web. According to Gesing and Schneider (1997), "scripting languages combine tools from programming languages to make them more concise and usable." JavaScript's purpose is to expand the functionality of Web pages, and it is written as part of an HTML document. By using JavaScript, you are able to customize a Web page, depending on your browser; check for mistakes in a form before the form is submitted; get visual feedback on your actions; create animations; and offer interactive features on your Web pages.

Guidelines for Creating a Web Page

Before creating your own Web page, read through the following guidelines:

1. Plan ahead; that is, decide what type of information you want to put on the Web. Then outline your ideas, write your text, and revise it. You need to present the information in a logical order and make every word count. Be sure to run your spelling checker and carefully proofread.

2. Organize your information. Create a sketch so you can see where you will place your text and graphics. In other words, storyboard your ideas. You can use a concept mapping program such as *Inspiration* (Inspiration Software, Inc.) for this purpose.

3. To help you decide where you want to place your navigational buttons,[3] create a map and experiment by putting these buttons in different locations on the map. Rather than spending time scrolling, your reader should be able to jump easily from one location to another.

4. Read your home page carefully. Does it communicate well, set a good tone, and catch people's attention? Good first impressions count in Web pages as well as in life.

5. Use graphics wisely to enhance content. Do not overload your page with pictures; no user enjoys long waits for graphics to load. Use an **interlaced GIF,** which displays graphics with one set of alternative lines at a time. (GIF stands for *graphic interchange format.*)

6. Be sure your site contains appropriate, relevant, timely, and engaging material.

7. Check the information on your site for reliability.

8. Be careful not to clutter the page with too many elements. Use of too many typefaces detracts from the general feeling of the writing.

9. Break up your text so it is more readable.

10. Keep the content interesting by using a variety of items so as not to bore the audience.

An example of a good website is *Cells Alive!* (Figure 11.28, http://www.cellsalive.com/). This site is a primer on cellular biology featuring a fascinating collection of pictures and animations with clear explanations. You can actually see how penicillin destroys bacteria and can view microscopic parasites.

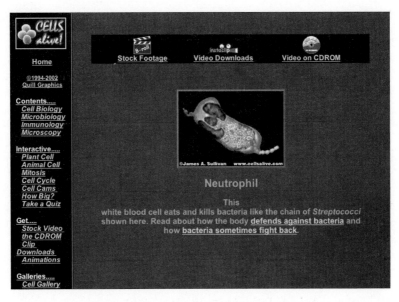

Figure 11.28 *Cells Alive!*

Used with permission of CELLS *alive!*

---

[3]A location on the computer screen, usually inside a hypermedia program, that causes an action when a person uses his or her mouse to click on it.

Web Development Tools

Since Web page creation has become such a popular phenomenon, a cottage industry has developed around it. Web animation programs such as flash and image editing programs such as *ImageBlender* and *VideoBlender* are being used more and more in the schools.

Macromedia Flash (Figure 11.29) is a well-known creator of animations. This program integrates video, text, audio, and graphics into a Web presentation. Flash produces interactive movies that enable you to play sounds, type text into interactive forms, create

Figure 11.29 *Flash*

Used with permission of Macromedia.

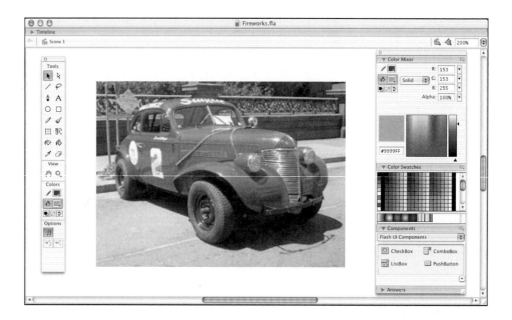

links to URLs, and much more. *Flash* has its own language called *ActionScript*. This program comes with a set of tutorials that show the interested user how to create professional-looking animations in no time at all.

Tech4Learning (http://www.tech4learning.com/) produces two programs that are ideal for website development: *ImageBlender* and *VideoBlender*. *ImageBlender* (Figure 11.30) is a great tool for editing images for Web pages and multimedia projects. This program supplies an assortment of graphic effects and paint tools and enables you to save slide shows in HTML.

Figure 11.30 *Image Blender*

Images used by permission of Tech4Learning, Inc.

VideoBlender enables you to import media from a variety of sources. You can access thousands of copyright-friendly images, play multiple videos, and combine video and graphics in one scene. After you finish a movie you can share it with other students on the Internet or on a CD-ROM.

Web Utilities

Some Web utilities that teachers find very useful are off-line browsers and **URL managers.** With an **off-line browser,** students can examine websites without an Internet connection. With a good URL manager, the teacher or student can organize URLs so they can easily find them when they want. Table 11.4 shows a few of these programs.

Table 11.4 Web Utilities

Title, Publisher	Description
URL Manager Pro, Kagi Shareware by Alco Blom	This utility is a professional **bookmark manager** for the Macintosh. *URL Manager Pro* enables you to organize and collect URLs in a hierarchical manner, organize bookmarks between folders with drag and drop, and access URLs on the Web.
URL Manager, Vince Sorensonby	This program is a professional bookmark manager for Windows.
Grab-a-Site 5.0, Blue Squirrel	*Grab-a-Site 5.0* enables you to save websites to your hard drive. It works on numerous Windows operating systems. This utility is ideal for browsing off line.
WebWacker 4.0, Blue Squirrel	*WebWacker* is an off-line browser for the Macintosh that saves websites to a hard drive.

Subscription-Based Sites

Subscription-based websites such as *Learning.com, NetTrekker, QuickMind Online, Waterford,* and *Knowledgebox* contain lesson plans, state standards, and tutorials. They are aligned with ISTE's National Educational Technology Standards (NETS) and also reinforce the state core curriculum standards. The sites usually have a trial period, and they cost from $1,000 to $1,200 a year for a class.

Learning.com

http://learning.com/

Learning.com website's *EasyTech* is a subscription-based service that provides online instruction for grades K–8. This service integrates technology into the classroom and reinforces core curriculum concepts. It covers the national technology standards and enables teachers to use their own states' core curriculum standards. Through interactive online tutorials, students learn to use word processing, database, spreadsheet, and presentation software. They learn by using these applications as tools in core curriculum areas such as science, language arts, social studies, and math. *EasyTech* come, with free phone and e-mail support as well as a management system with which teachers can assign lessons and assess how well students are achieving the educational objectives. The teacher is provided with class reports, student reports, and lesson reports.

Waterford Early Reading Program, Waterford Reading and Math, and KnowledgeBox

http://www.pearsondigital.com

Pearson Digital Learning (formerly Electronic Education) builds critical thinking and learning skills at grades Pre-K–6. Pearson produces *Waterford Early Reading* and *KnowledgeBox*. *Waterford Reading and Math* are under development. These online products were created by professional educators.

Waterford Early Reading is individualized computer instruction that enables the student to move at his or her own pace. The curriculum covers phonemics, phonics, vocabulary, fluency, and comprehension. There are three levels, and each level gives daily instruction and additional material that can be used at home. *KnowledgeBox* (Figure 11.31) is a learning system for reading/language arts, math, social studies, and science. *Knowlegebox* offers interactive games, multimedia lessons, and dynamic video for

Figure 11.31
KnowledgeBox

Used with permission of
Pearson Digital Learning.

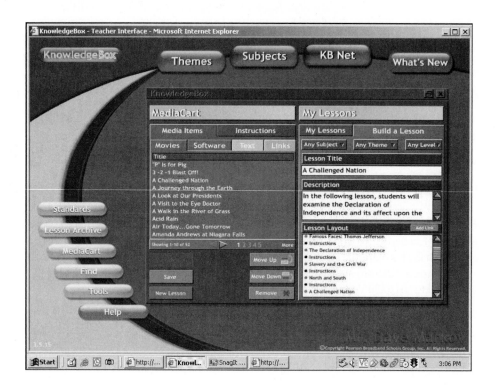

grades K–6, all based on state's standards. Using your mouse, you can select multimedia components that are organized by subject or theme and create lessons to meet the state and national standards. *Knowledgebox* delivers digital video, interactive software, animation, and digital text.

QuickMind.net

http://www.quickmind.net/

Created by Sunburst, *QuickMind* is a site for grades K–12. *QuickMind* is a database that contains a rich variety of resources and tools with which teachers and students can share, print e-mail, publish or download. Teachers can create tests, Web projects, math and science activities, and crossword and word search puzzles. Teachers can enter their own content and assign their tests or activities to students in their class. Teachers can also access community databases for other existing projects across the United States.

netTrekker

http://www.nettrekker.com/frontdoor/

netTrekker is a search engine for schools that gives easy access to 180,000 K–12 online educational resources that are aligned with every state's standards. Each site is rated (Figure 11.32) by educators and librarians and comes with its own individual de-

Figure 11.32
netTrekker

Used with permission of netTrekker, the trusted search engine for schools.

scription. This is a safe way for students to search the Web, because they can be sure that the sites contain only academic content that is organized around the K–12 curricula. Using *netTrekker* you can access your state's standards; find online lesson plans, learning exercises, and websites; as well as use interactive history time lines.

Summary

In this chapter, we discussed the World Wide Web, and especially Web page creation, hypertext markup language (HTML), and guidelines for creating a website. In the process, we discussed some useful Web utilities such as *Grab-a-Site 5.0* and *URL Manager Pro.* We examined the WebQuest and considered some examples. Furthermore, we looked at the various search engines and explored a few pointers on how to search. We examined criteria for selecting websites and a website evaluation scale. Finally, we considered ways to integrate the Web into the classroom.

 # Study and Online Resources

*Go to Chapter 11 in the Student Edition of the Online Learning Center at www.mhhe.com/sharp5e to **practice with key concepts, take chapter quizzes, read PowerWeb articles** and **news feed updates** related to technology in education, and **access resources** for learning about technology and integrating it into the classroom.*

Click on *Web Links* to link to the following websites.

Blackboard
The CourseSites channel, a free service, enables instructors to add an online component to their classes or even to host an entire course on the Web. Without knowing any HTML, instructors can quickly create their own learning materials, class discussions, and tests online. There are many ways a teacher can incorporate searching into the classroom.

Britannica
This is the best tutorial on how to search. Click on *Search Tips* to find helpful suggestions.

Concept to Classroom
At the Concept to Classroom site, you can learn how to use WebQuests to teach your students to think critically about information on the Internet. Students can also learn how to design their own WebQuests here.

Creating a Web Page
Marshall Elementary School provides HTML tutorials, guidelines, resources, free home pages, editors, graphics, and much more.

Evaluating Websites: Criteria and Tools
This site discusses factors to consider when you evaluate a website. The site contains Web links, Web reviews, and rankings.

How to Create Web Pages
This is a list of sites that will help you learn how to create Web pages.

How to Search the Web: A Guide to Search Tools
This site, created by Terry A. Gray, discusses search engines such as *AltaVista, Excite, WebCrawler, Lycos,* and *Yahoo!* It features searching tips, useful articles, and a summary chart.

HTML Writers Guild Website
The *HTML Writers Guild* provides resources, support, representation, and education for Web authors at all skill levels.

Kathy Schrock's Guide for Educators—Critical Evaluation Surveys
Kathy Schrock has designed a series of evaluation surveys, one each at the elementary, middle, and secondary school levels.

On-Line Practice Modules
This site was created by Susan Brooks and Bill Byles from the Memphis City Schools. You will find here a collection of tutorials for teachers or students in grades K–12. These tutorials

give instructions in software programs such as *Microsoft Office Suite* and *Inspiration.* In addition, there is a tutorial for creating a WebQuest.

Open Directory
The *Open Directory* is a comprehensive Web directory, relying on a vast army of volunteer editors.

Practical Guide to HTML Publishing and Resources
This site lists HTML books, basics, editors, resources, and graphics.

Researching the Web and Web Page Creation
This site contains a variety of sites that help you search the Web, create Web pages, and evaluate what you find.

Teacher'sFirst.com
Teacher'sFirst.com has a nice collection of Web resources and lessons for the K–12 teacher. If you click on *Site Resources* you will be able to find a Web tutorial on WebQuests. TeachersFirst's Webquest 101 tutorial is where you learn the basics of WebQuest design, as well as search strategies.

The Good, The Bad & The Ugly
Susan Beck's comprehensive site features evaluation criteria with samples, suggestions, and a bibliography.

Want to Make Your Own Home Page?
This site is designed for the absolute beginner. It tells you everything you need to know to start creating your own home page.

WebQuest Central
From the Educational Network, WebQuest Central contains a collection of WebQuest units, lessons, and sites.

The WebQuest Page
The creator of WebQuest, Dr. Bernie Dodge, has designed this site to serve as an extensive resource for individuals who are using the WebQuest model to teach. This site provides excellent examples and collected materials.

Yahoo!Groups (formerly egroups)
Yahoo!Groups enables anyone to create a special-interest group on the Internet with its own e-mail address and website. With this free service, you can discuss issues on a specific topic of interest to the group, stay in touch with your classmates, and share information.

Yahoo! WebQuests
Yahoo's! directory has hundreds of examples of WebQuests that can be used in K–12 classrooms.

Chapter Mastery Test

To the Instructor: *Refer to the Instructor's Manual for the answers to the Mastery Questions. This manual has additional questions and resource materials.*

Let us check for chapter comprehension with a short mastery test. Key Terms, Computer Lab, and Suggested Readings and References follow the test.

1. Identify four criteria for selecting websites.
2. Offer a few generalized suggestions for searching the Web.
3. Explain what a *search engine* is and give an example.
4. Give three general rules to follow when creating a Web page.
5. What is the World Wide Web and why is it an invaluable resource?
6. Give an example of a browser and explain why you need to use one.
7. Name two ways you can use websites in the classroom.
8. What is HTML?
9. What is a WebQuest and why is it valuable for students?
10. Define the following terms: *home page* and *URL*.
11. What are *streaming audio* and *streaming video* and how are they being used on the Web?
12. How can you use a Weblog as a motivating activity?

Key Terms

Applets 276
Home page 249
Hypertext markup language
    (HTML) 276
Interlaced GIF 277
Java 276

JavaScript 276
Metasearch engines 251
Mosaic 250
Off-line browsers 278
Plug-in 254
Portals 251

Search engines 251
Spider programs 251
Streaming audio 254
Streaming video 253
Uniform resource locator
    (URL) 249

URL managers 278–279
Weblog 273
WebQuest 270–273
Website 249

Computer Lab: Activities for Mastery and Your Portfolio

11.1 Internet Searching Strategies   Test your understanding of how to search the internet.

11.2 Create a Teacher Web Page   Create a Web page for your classroom.

11.3 Create a Student Web Page   Use these directions to help your students create Web pages.

11.4 Use the website evaluation form to rate five websites.

11.5 Investigate five different search engines and explain the advantages and disadvantages of each one.

11.6 Create a simple Web page that
    a. displays a graphic,
    b. has a link, and
    c. has text.

11.7 Create multimedia projects or reports on the Web using applications such as *PowerPoint*. Some invaluable telecommunications tutorials accompany products such as *Microsoft Works* and *AppleWorks*.

Suggested Readings and References

Bakken, Jeffrey P., and Gregory F. Aloia. "Evaluating the World Wide Web." *Teaching Exceptional Children* 30, no. 5 (May/June 1998): 48.

Berners-Lee, Tim, with Mark Fischetti. *Weaving the Web: The Original Design and Ultimate Destiny of the World Wide Web.* New York: HarperCollins Publishers, 2000.

Bond, Jill D., ed. *Internet Yellow Pages,* 6th ed. Indianapolis, Ind.: New Riders Publishing, 1997.

Bull, Glen, Gina Bull, and Tim Sigmon. "Interactive Web Pages." *Learning and Leading with Technology* 24, no. 6 (March 1997): 22–27.

Bull, Glen, Gina Bull, and Sara Kajder. "Writing with Weblogs (Reinventing Student Journals)." *Learning and Leading with Technology* 31, no. 1 (September 2003): 32–35.

Bunz, Ulla. "Web Site Creation as a Valuable Exercise: Seven Steps to Communicating Significance Online." *Technology Teacher* 62, issue 5 (February 2003): 7–10.

Cafolla, Ray, and Richard Knee. "Creating World Wide Web Sites." *Learning and Leading with Technology* 24, part I (November 1996): 3–9.

Carr, Stephen. "Putting It All Together." *Education Week* 17, no. 11 (November 10, 1997): 16–18.

Carroll, Sean. "How to Find Anything Online." *PC Magazine,* vol. 22, issue 9 (May 27, 2003): 80–82.

Craig, Dorothy, and Jaci Stewart. "Mission to Mars." *Learning and Leading with Technology* 25, no. 2 (October 1997): 22–27.

Dyril, Odvard E. "Stats Making News." *Technology and Learning* 18, no. 7 (March 1998): 64.

Freedman, Alan. *Computer Desktop Encyclopedia.* Point Pleasant, Penn.: Computer Language Company, 2003.

Frye, Nickola, and Michael Wise. *Integrated Classroom Curriculum Series.* Visions Technology in Education, 1999–2000. (This series covers teaching units in math, science, social studies, and other areas. There is a CD-ROM included that gives activities, games, and quizzes.)

Gants, David L. "Peer Review for Cyberspace: Evaluating Scholarly Web Sites." *Chronicle of Higher Education* 45, no. 3 (October 9, 1999): B8.

Gesing, Ted, and Jeremy Schneider. *Java Script for the World Wide Web.* Berkeley, CA: Peachpit Press, 1997 (p. 3).

Glossbrenner, Alfred, and Emily Glossbrenner. *Search Engines for the World Wide Web.* Berkeley, Calif.: Peachpit Press, 1998.

Hahn, Harley. *Harley Hahn's Internet & Web Yellow Pages 2003.* New York: Osborne/McGraw-Hill, 2003.

Harris, Judy. "Ridiculous Questions! The Issue of Scale in Netiquette." *Learning and Leading with Technology* 25, no. 2 (October 1997): 13–16.

Hiltzik, Michael Al. "Microsoft: Internet Explorer." *Los Angeles Times,* December 12, 1997, 1.

Junion-Metz, Gail. "Surf For." *School Library Journal* 46, no. 2 (February 2000): 35.

Kelly, Rebecca. "Working with WebQuests." *Teaching Exceptional Children* 32, no. 6 (July/August 2000): 4.

Kobler, Ron, ed. *PC Novice Guide to the Web.* Lincoln, Neb.: PC Novice, 1997.

Kraynak, Joe. *Que's Official Internet Yellow Pages.* New York: QUE, 2003.

Kurland, Daniel, Richard Sharp, and Vicki Sharp. *Introduction to the Internet for Education.* Belmont, Calif.: Wadsworth, 1997.

Laquey, Tracy, and Jeanne Ryer (foreword by Al Gore). *Internet Companion.* Boston: Addison-Wesley, 1992.

Leebow, Ken, Randy Glasbergen (ill.), and Paul Joffe (ed.). *300 Incredible Things to Do on the Internet,* 3d ed. Mass Market Paperback, 1999.

Levine, Martin G. "Social Studies Web Sites for Teachers and Students." *Social Studies Review* 36, no. 2 (Spring–Summer 1997): 95–98.

Lynch, Patrick J., and Sarah Horton. *Web Style Guide: Basic Design Principles for Creating Web Sites.* New Haven, Conn.: Yale University Press, 1999.

McCollum, Kelly. "Bookmark." *Chronicle of Higher Education* 46, no. 31 (April 7, 2000): A47.

McCracken, Harry. "Search Engines with a Soul." *PC World* 18, no. 6 (July 2000): 43.

Metcalfe, Bob. "Cable TV Modems Are Finally Delivering the Net to Homes and Small Offices." *InfoWorld* 20, no. 5 (February 2, 1998): 107.

Morse, David. *Cyber Dictionary.* Boston, Mass.: Knowledge Exchange, 1997.

Panepinton, Joe. "Family Parents' Guide to the Web." *Family PC,* February 1997, 42–60.

Pfaffenberger, Bryan. *Webster's New World Dictionary.* New York: Que, 2003.

Randall, Neil. "Design Web Pages with Office 2000." *PC Magazine* 19, no. 5 (March 7, 2000): 122.

Ryder, James Randall, and Tom Hughes. *Internet for Educators.* Columbus, Ohio: Merrill, 1997.

Salpeter, Judy. "Industrial Snapshot: Where Are We Headed." *Technology and Learning* 17, no. 6 (March 1997): 22–32.

Santo, Christine. "Ultimate Guide to the Web." *FamilyPC,* October 1997, 64–80.

Sharp, Richard, Vicki Sharp, and Martin Levine. *Best Math and Science Web Sites for Teachers.* Eugene, Ore.: ISTE, 1997.

Sharp, Vicki. *Netscape Navigator 3.0 in an Hour.* Eugene, Ore.: ISTE, 1996.

Sharp, Vicki F. "Prospecting for Science Sites on the Internet." *CSTA Journal,* Fall 1996, 26–34.

Sharp, Vicki, Richard Sharp, and Martin Levine. *Best Web Sites for Teachers,* 5th ed. Eugene, Ore.: ISTE, 2002.

Sheppard Jr., Nathaniel. "Building Your Place on the Web." *Emerge* 10, no. 8 (June 1999): 32.

Slater, James, and Brian Beaudrie. "Doing the Real Science on the Web." *Learning and Leading with Technology* 25, no. 4 (December/January 1997–1998): 28–31.

Sosinsky, Barrie, and Elisabeth Parker. *The Web Page Recipe Book.* Upper Saddle River, N.J.: Prentice Hall, 1996.

Stilborne, Linda, and Ann Heide. *The Teacher's Complete and Easy Guide to the Internet.* Ontario, Canada: Trifolium Books, 1996.

Turner, Marcia Layton, and Audrey Seybold. *Que's Official Internet Yellow Pages: Milennium Edition.* Carmel, Ind.: Que Education and Training, 2000.

Turner, Sandra, and Michael Land. *Tools for Schools.* Belmont, Calif.: Wadsworth, 1997.

Weinstein, Peter. "Tools for Becoming a Power Browser." *Technology and Learning* 20, no. 8 (March 2000): 49.

Williams, Robin. The Non-Designer's Web Book, 2d ed. Berkeley, Calif.: Peachpit Press, 2000.

Williams, Robin, and Dave Mark. *Home Sweet Home Page.* Berkeley, Calif.: Peachpit Press, 1996.

Williams, Robin, John Tollett, and Dave Rohr. *Web Design Workshop.* Berkeley, Calif.: Peachpit Press, 2001.

Withrow, Frank B. "Technology in Education and the Next Twenty-Five Years." *T.H.E. Journal* 24, no. 11 (June 1997): 59–62.

Yahoo! Editors. "Anatomy of a Web Site." *Yahoo Internet Life* 4, no. 2 (February 1998): 75–76.

CHAPTER 12

Selecting Technology and Integrating It into the Classroom

Integrating Software into the Classroom

Math software such as *Quarter Mile* can help a student improve his or her computational skills. When the computer is used as an instructional tool, students develop in curriculum areas such as math, language arts, science, and social studies. This chapter will discuss computer-assisted instruction and computer-managed instruction. We will examine criteria for selecting software for the classroom and learn different ways of using educational software in the school. Furthermore, the chapter will present examples of lesson plans that can be used in a variety of situations and review Internet sites containing a rich assortment of lesson plan content, software reviews, shareware, educational resources, and links to software publishers and reviews.

Objectives

Upon completing this chapter, you will be able to do the following:

1. Differentiate between *computer-assisted instruction* and *computer-managed instruction*.
2. Define these software terms: *public domain, shareware, drill and practice, problem solving, simulation,* and *games*.
3. Name and discuss the criteria for selecting quality software.
4. Evaluate a piece of software based on standard criteria.
5. Create a plan for organizing a software library.
6. Identify useful lesson plans and Internet sites.

Computer-Assisted Instruction

In previous chapters, we considered the computer as a productivity tool in the classroom—its uses as a word processor, database, spreadsheet, and desktop publisher. This chapter will focus on the computer as an instructional tool, or tutor.

The computer has many purposes in the classroom, and it can be utilized to help a student in all areas of the curriculum. **Computer-assisted instruction (CAI)** refers to the use of the computer as a tool to facilitate and improve instruction. CAI programs use tutorials, drill and practice, simulation, and problem-solving approaches to present topics, and they test students' understanding. These programs enable students to

Teacher is helping student use a math tutorial

progress at their own pace, assisting them in learning the material. The subject matter taught through CAI can range from basic math facts to more complex concepts in math, history, science, social studies, and language arts.

Historical Background

In 1950, MIT scientists designed a flight simulator program for combat pilots, the first example of CAI. Nine years later, IBM developed its CAI technology for elementary schools, and Florida State University offered CAI courses in statistics and physics. About the same time, John Kemeny and Thomas Kurtz at Dartmouth College created **Beginner's All-Purpose Symbolic Instruction Code (BASIC),** which provided a programming language for devising CAI programs.

In the early 1960s, CAI programs ran on large mainframe computers and were primarily used in reading and mathematics instruction. Computer programmers also produced simulation programs, modeled after real-life situations. Unfortunately, most of this early software was tedious, long on theory and short on imagination, and lacking in motivating sound and graphics.

The invention of the microcomputer led to the development of improved instructional software and, indirectly, to the resurgence of interest in classroom computer use because of public demand and the competition among companies. Today, software companies employ teams of educators to enhance their products, and textbook publishers are involved in producing software.

Types of CAI

Computer-assisted instruction facilitates student learning through various methods. CAI can provide the student with practice in problem solving in math; it can also serve as a tutorial in history and provide further drill and practice in English. Let us look at the different types of CAI: (1) tutorial, (2) simulation, (3) drill and practice, (4) problem solving, and (5) instructional games.

Tutorial Programs

A **tutorial**'s job is to tutor by interactive means—in other words, by having a dialogue with the student. The tutorial presents information, asks questions, and makes decisions based on the student's responses. Like a good teacher, the computer decides whether to move on to new material, review past information, or provide remediation. The computer can serve as the teacher's assistant by helping the learner with special needs or the student who has missed a few days of school. The computer tutorial is very efficient, because it gives individual attention to the student who needs it. In addition, the student using this software can progress at his or her own pace. A good tutorial is interesting and easy to follow; it enhances learning with sound and graphics. It has sound educational objectives, is able to regulate the instructional pace, and provides tests to measure the student's progress.

CAI tutorials are based on the principles of programmed learning: The student responds to each bit of information presented by answering questions about the material and then gets immediate feedback on each response. Each tutorial lesson has a series of frames. Each frame poses a question to the student. If the student answers correctly, the next frame appears on the screen. Educators disagree about the arrangement of these frames. Some educators are proponents of the linear tutorial, and others prefer the branching tutorial. The **linear tutorial** presents the student with a series of frames that supply new information or reinforce the information learned in previous frames. The student has to respond to every frame in the exact order presented, and there is no deviation from this presentation, but the student does have the freedom to work through the material at his or her own speed. The **branching tutorial** offers more flexibility in the way the material is covered. The computer decides what material to present to each student. The pupil's responses to the questions determine whether the computer will review the previous material or skip to more advanced work.

There are many tutorial programs, spanning the gamut of software. Encore Software produces *Math Advantage 2004.* The program covers 10 core math subjects: prealgebra, algebra I, algebra II, geometry, geometry II, trigonometry (Figure 12.1),

Figure 12.1 *Math Advantage 2004—* Trigonometry

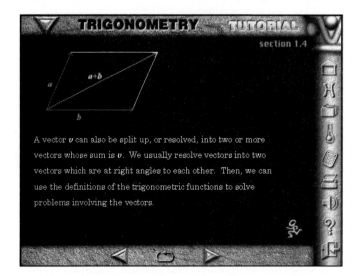

pre-calculus, calculus, statistics, and business math. It features animated examples, narrated text, quizzes, games, and a problem generator with which a user can get unlimited practice with problem sets within each subject area. The in-depth tutorials offer a hint system, step-by-step problem solutions, and real-life examples of math applications. Encore also publishes *Elementary Advantage, Middle School Advantage,* and *High School Advantage.* These programs are comprehensive core curriculum educational suites that help students in subject areas that range from math to world history. Additional programs that help high school or college-level students learn biology, chemistry, and physics are *BioTutor, ChemTutor,* and *Physics Tutor* (Interactive Learning, Inc.). These programs cover the full curriculum for a first or second course in these subjects. While working on these tutorials, the students are given immediate feedback at each step. *Mavis Bacon Teaches Typing Deluxe 15 EEV,* produced by Riverdeep, is an excellent typing tutorial that improves students' typing speed and accuracy. The *Learn About* science series (Sunburst) for elementary students provides simple tutorials that teach about plants, dinosaurs, weather, animals, and the human body. In *Learn About the Human Body* (Figure 12.2), students see inside the human body, study the major systems, learn how systems work together, and discover ways to stay fit.

Figure 12.2 *Learn About the Human Body*

Information from "Learn About Life Science: The Human Body" used with permission from Sunburst Technology Company. Copyright © 2002 by Sunburst Technology Company. All rights reserved.

Simulation Programs

In **simulation** programs, students can experience real-life situations without having to risk the consequences of failure. Students can experiment with dangerous chemicals on the computer screen, for example, and not be in danger from the actual chemicals. For laboratory simulations, there is no expensive lab equipment to buy, and students can observe the results without waiting a long time. Moreover, students can repeat experiments easily as often as they wish. Many educators feel that a well-designed simulation software affords students the opportunity to learn in more realistic situations than can otherwise be set up in a classroom.

A classic example of a simulation program is *The Oregon Trail* (Riverdeep). In the fifth edition (Figure 12.3), students try to survive various conditions and hardships as they travel along the Oregon Trail. They make significant decisions about resting, hunting,

Figure 12.3 *The Oregon Trail*, 5th ed.: *Pioneer Adventures*

© 2004 Riverdeep Interactive Learning Limited, and its licensors.

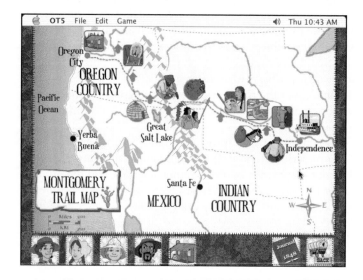

crossing rivers, and avoiding starvation, exposure, and death. In the process, the class gains an understanding of what it was like to be a settler of European descent during the pre–Gold Rush years between 1840 and 1848. The enhanced educators' version gives the user a progress report.

Edmark (Riverdeep) has two interesting science simulations for grades 6 to 12. They are *Virtual Labs: Light* and *Virtual Labs: Electricity. Virtual Labs: Light* enables students safely to run virtual laser experiments that would be dangerous and impractical to run in the real world. The students use virtual lasers and other optical tools to learn about the nature of light, mirrors, reflection, and more. In the same vein, *Virtual Labs: Electricity* (Figure 12.4) is a simulation program with which students do experiments in a lab or create their own electricity experiments without the hazards inherent in playing with electricity. This is a great program for hands-on learning in science. The students experiment, develop problem-solving skills, and improve their prediction skills.

Figure 12.4 *Virtual Labs: Electricity*

© Riverdeep Interactive Learning Limited.

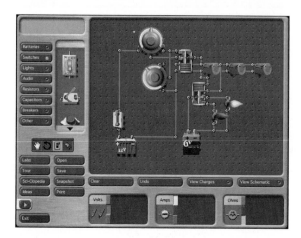

The *Decisions, Decisions* series (Tom Snyder Productions) offers well-executed simulation social studies software programs. The series includes titles such as *Constitution, Revolutionary Wars, Immigrants, Violence in the Media,* and *Drinking and Driving.* There is an online version of the *Decisions, Decisions* series, with a different controversial topic to debate each month. For example, in *Gun Control,* students play the role of a senator and debate an upcoming bill (http://ddonline.tomsnyder.com/). *Decisions, Decisions* offers this service free for 30 days; after that the user must subscribe.

Drill and Practice Programs

In 1963, Patrick Suppes and Richard Atkinson produced **drill and practice software** on a mainframe computer. The computer screen displayed a problem, the student responded, and the computer provided immediate feedback. The learner stayed with the problems until reaching a certain level of proficiency and then moved on to a more difficult level. With the arrival of the microcomputer in the 1970s, this drill and practice software began to be produced widely in all subject areas. It was so popular that 75 percent of the educational software developed at this time was drill and practice. In the 1980s, many educators argued that drill and practice software was being overused. They believed that the computer should be used to encourage higher-level thinking and not as an electronic workbook. Today's drill and practice programs are more sophisticated, offer greater capabilities, and are accepted in the schools. Most educators see the value of a good individualized drill and practice program; this software frees the students and the teacher to do more creative work in the classroom. Many of these programs serve as diagnostic tools, giving the teacher relevant data on how well the students are doing and what they need to work on. The programs also provide immediate feedback for students, allowing them to progress at their own speed and motivating them to continue.

Drill and practice software differs from tutorial software in a key way: It helps students remember and utilize skills they have previously been taught, whereas a tutorial teaches new material. Students must be familiar with certain concepts prior to working drill and practice programs in order to understand the contents.

The typical drill and practice program design includes four steps: (1) the computer screen presents the student with questions to respond to or problems to solve; (2) the student responds; (3) the computer informs the student whether the answer is correct; and (4) if the student is right, he or she is given another problem to solve, but if the student responds with a wrong answer, he or she is corrected by the computer. Figure 12.5 illustrates the four steps.

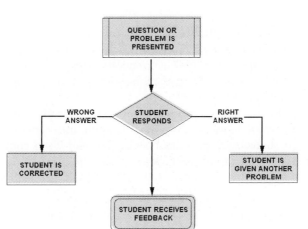

Figure 12.5 Drill and Practice Program Steps

The computer program can handle incorrect responses in several different ways. The computer display might tell students to try the problem again. If they keep giving the wrong answer, the computer gives the right answer and then proceeds to the next problem. The computer might ignore all keys pressed except the right one or even beep when students try to type another response. It might display the answer that should have been typed. It might give students a hint when they respond incorrectly and a better hint if they miss the answer again. After three or four hints, it shows the right answer. Finally, it might give students additional information to help them respond to a question. This type of drill and practice program is similar to a tutorial program.

Many drill and practice programs motivate students with their ingenious use of graphics and sound. Some programs are games in which players are rewarded points for the correct answers. An example of an addictive drill and practice program is *The Quarter Mile*. Barnum Software produces a series of these math programs that focus on a range of topics from whole numbers to equations for grades K–9. *The Quarter Mile* is designed so that users are in a competitive drag race with themselves. Students can opt to race "wild running horses" (Figure 12.6) instead of cars. When they answer a

Figure 12.6 *The Quarter Mile*

Used with permission of Barnum Software.

problem correctly, the car leaves the starting line at 65 miles per hour. Thereafter, the car accelerates by 5 mph with each correct answer, racing against an exact video replay of their own five best previous races. The car goes faster and faster as the racer accelerates to the accompanying sound effects, giving users the thrill of watching their improvement.

Today, quite a few science software programs offer drill and practice components. *GeoSafari Animals* (Educational Insights Interactive) uses a game show format with questions based on animal trivia. *GeoSafari Plants* contains 15 activities on topics such as the human skeleton, rocks, minerals, space travel, and trees. *GeoSafari Geography* (Educational Insights Interactive) is a drill and practice program that contains multiple-choice quizzes that help with all sorts of geography subject matter such as memorizing the state capitals or learning where states are. In Figure 12.7, the state highlighted is Washington, and the student has clicked on the correct answer.

Figure 12.7 *GeoSafari Geography*

Used by permission of Educational Insights.

Problem-Solving Programs

Problem-solving skills are necessary in a complex world, and a good way to develop these skills is to use problem-solving programs. Teachers like this type of software because it teaches students to test hypotheses and take notes. Similar to simulation programs, problem-solving programs easily can be used with only one computer and as many as 30 students. The whole class can be involved in critical thinking and making inferences. The critical thinking needed for problem solving can be practiced in any content area. Problem-solving programs emphasize cooperation and are suitable for small groups or individual students. This type of software gives students more freedom to explore than does drill and practice software.

A variety of computer programs focus on higher-level thinking. Riverdeep produces *ClueFinders Reading Adventures Ages 9–12, ClueFinders 4th Grade Adventures with A.d.a.p.t, Where in the USA is Carmen Sandiego?*, and *Where in the World Is Carmen Sandiego? Treasures of Knowledge EEV.* This last program is a problem-solving program whose objective is to recover a stolen treasure from Carmen Sandiego and her cohorts. In Figure 12.8, a shopkeeper has told the student that Carmen is at the Shinto shrine. The student then uses the program's search feature to find that the Shinto shrine is located in Japan. In the process of using this program, students must solve puzzles, travel to different countries, learn about each country, identify important sites, and read historical information about explorers and ancient civilizations.

Intellectum Plus (http://www.mathandscience4u.com/) produces a series of interactive problem-solving programs centering on elementary physics concepts such as force, motion, and friction. These programs are appropriate for junior high school students to adults. The software is based on advanced problem-solving methodologies incorporating

Figure 12.8 *Where in the World Is Carmen Sandiego? Treasures of Knowledge EEV*

© 2004 Riverdeep Interactive Learning Limited, and its licensors.

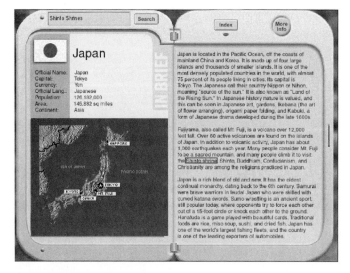

artificial intelligence features. Intellectum has launched an Internet portal through which it offers its curriculum-based software such as *PhysicaElementa* (Figure 12.9).

Figure 12.9
PhysicaElementa—Measurements and Units

Reprinted by permission of Intellectum Plus, Inc. Screen shot of *Microsoft® Internet Explorer* used by permission of Microsoft Corporation.

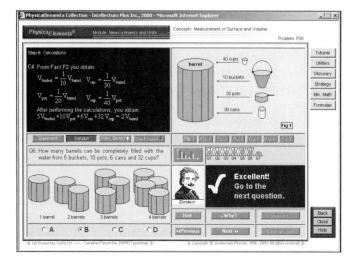

Game Programs

Game programs for the computer usually involve fantasy situations with some sort of competition. Game programs are classified as either entertainment or educational software. The educational programs have specific learning objectives, with the game serving as a motivational device, whereas the major goal of the entertainment programs is amusement. Educational software offers a range of learning outcomes; entertainment software has little academic value except in teaching game strategy.

Most CAI programs use a game format that ranges from drill and practice to logic. For example, *Reader Rabbit Learn to Read with Phonics* (Riverdeep) is an early reading program that helps students learn letters and sounds and read words and sentences. In Figure 12.10 the student must help the rabbit climb the wall by creating compound words.

Figure 12.10 *Learn to Read with Phonics*

© 2004 Riverdeep Interactive Learning Limited, and its licensors.

The program *VisiFrog* (Ventura Educational Systems) helps students master the anatomy of a frog. This program accomplishes this purpose with interactive games. The program uses detailed graphics to represent the skeletal system, nervous system, cardiovascular system, reproductive system, and musculature. In Figure 12.11, the student types in the proper part to earn points, in this case *small intestine.*

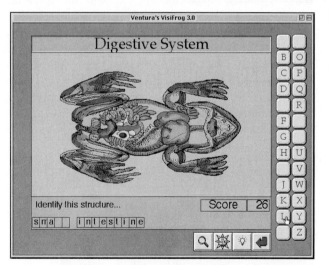

Figure 12.11 *VisiFrog*

Used by permission of Ventura Educational Systems, Grover Beach, CA 93483-0425. www.venturaes.com

Because computer games are very popular, many educators think that CAI programs should be designed as games. A good educational game involves the active physical and mental participation of the players. Graphics, fast motion, and sound effects are used to enhance the program, not to detract from its educational value.

Most CAI programs incorporate more than one type of software in their design. For example, a program that is a tutorial may have a drill and practice element, and a simulation may have a game as an integral part of its program. The main element of *The*

Oregon Trail is simulation; its game component is a hunting game. Now that we have looked at the different types of CAI, let us look at some of the educational software programs that are available for grades K–12.

Subject Area Software

Recommended Software

Subject Area Arts Programs

For a listing of recommended subject area Art programs, go to the Online Learning Center.

There are thousands of quality educational software programs. These programs are typically designed for specific areas of the curriculum.

Art Software

An example of a first-rate program that teaches students about artistic masterpieces is *The World's Greatest Museum* (Voyager/Grolier). This program showcases 150 masterpieces of painting and sculpture, from prehistoric drawings to contemporary art. The art is chosen from 70 of the most famous museums in the world. In addition, *Master-Stroke* (Clearvue) introduces students to some of the works and drawing techniques of Old Masters, ranging from Rembrandt to Van Gogh, with six tutorials that cover topics such as color, composition, and animation.

Mathematics Programs

Recommended Software

Math Programs

For a listing of recommended math programs, go to the Online Learning Center.

The research literature offers no apparent agreement on how best to use computer software for improving math skills or for developing higher-order thinking. In 2000, the National Council for Teachers of Mathematics (NCTM) published its extensive standards for using technology. See the NCTM site for information on these standards at http://www.nctm.org/standards/. Even with these standards, teachers must decide how to use math software according to their own classroom needs. They might choose a math drill and practice program such as *MindTwisters* (Riverdeep), which focuses on math facts, rounding, measuring, counting money, and telling time. They may instead want the class to work on a math simulation program such as *Hot Dog Stand Top Dog* (Sunburst). With the program, students experience what it is like to be in the real world when they operate a hot dog stand in competition with computer-generated vendors. Students try to outperform their competitors by selling the most food to different types of customers. Using this program (Figure 12.12) students grades 3 through 8 learn how to con-

Figure 12.12 *Hot Dog Stand Top Dog*

Information from "Hot Dog Stand Top Dog" used with permission of Sunburst Technology Company. Copyright © 2002 by Sunburst Technology Company. All rights reserved. Netscape browser reprinted by permission of AOL.

duct research, how to calculate probability and statistics, business math money management, how to read charts and graphs, and much more. With a connection to the Internet students can post their scores on the Web. The class can work on this program as a group, or the class can be divided into smaller groups that compete against each other.

Music

Recently there has been a resurgence in music programs. Current programs give instruction in playing music, in music appreciation, and in composition and music theory. *Piano Discovery System* (Jump! Music) and *eMedia Intermediate Guitar Method* (eMedia) offer comprehensive, guided instruction in piano and guitar. Clearvue offers comprehensive music CD-ROMs on different musical periods, composers, and instruments. Still other music programs are sing-along adventures; they enable students to experiment with music, explore musical elements, and practice on musical instruments. *Play Music* (Notation Technologies) enables beginning students to play, e-mail, and print their own sheet music.

The award-winning *Music Ace* and *Music Ace 2* (Harmonic Vision) are programs that introduce students to music fundamentals. *Music Ace 2*, the second in the series, introduces advanced concepts such as standard notation, rhythm, melody, and harmony in an engaging format. There are 24 lessons, 2,000 musical examples, 24 games, and a composition tool. The interactive lessons come before each set of games. In Figure 12.13 the student is hearing an excerpt from Beethoven's Sonata Number 8, *Pathetique.* After listening, she chooses the correct tempo of the piece, in this case slow tempo.

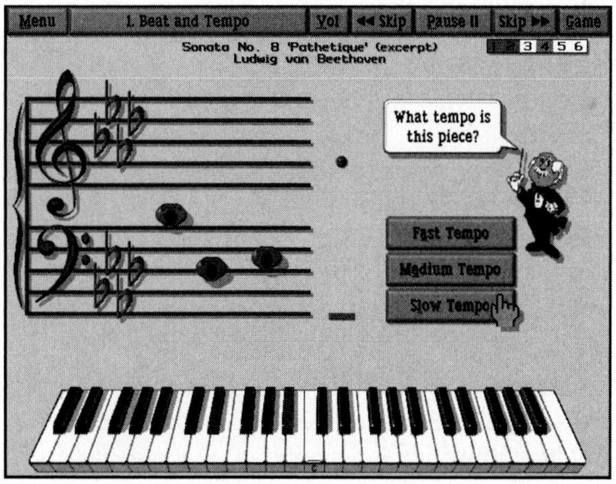

Figure 12.13
Music Ace 2

Music Aces 2. © The McGraw-Hill Companies, Inc. Reprinted with permission.

Science Programs

In many elementary schools, science programs are limited to requiring memorization of textbook facts; teachers have not had the time or money to collect the necessary materials for exciting hands-on science lessons. Furthermore, the breadth of a science class has depended on a teacher's interests and specific areas of expertise. Because of their general lack of knowledge in science, some teachers have ignored many science topics, and most elementary students have received very little science education. Experimentation has occurred primarily in the high school science lab, an experience usually reserved for college-bound students.

The computer has begun to change this unfortunate situation. The science investigation skills of classifying, synthesizing, analyzing, and summarizing data are skills that the computer is designed to reinforce. The computer cannot replace the actual science laboratory, but it can simulate complex, expensive, and dangerous experiments, saving time and money. Because there is a renewed interest in science education, more schools are incorporating the computer into the science curriculum, and science software is flourishing.

There are good science tutorials that are readily available, especially at the upper elementary, high school, and college levels. At the high school or college level, *BioTutor*, *ChemTutor* (Figure 12.14), and *Physics Tutor* (Interactive Learning, Inc.) help students

Figure 12.14
ChemTutor

ChemTutor® Excalibur for Interactive Learning, Inc. (www.highergrades.com). Reprinted by permission.

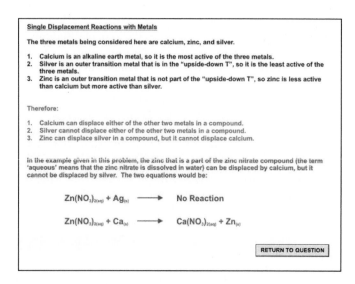

Single Displacement Reactions with Metals

The three metals being considered here are calcium, zinc, and silver.

1. Calcium is an alkaline earth metal, so it is the most active of the three metals.
2. Silver is an outer transition metal that is in the "upside-down T", so it is the least active of the three metals.
3. Zinc is an outer transition metal that is not part of the "upside-down T", so zinc is less active than calcium but more active than silver.

Therefore:

1. Calcium can displace either of the other two metals in a compound.
2. Silver cannot displace either of the other two metals in a compound.
3. Zinc can displace silver in a compound, but it cannot displace calcium.

In the example given in this problem, the zinc that is a part of the zinc nitrate compound (the term 'aqueous' means that the zinc nitrate is dissolved in water) can be displaced by calcium, but it cannot be displaced by silver. The two equations would be:

$$Zn(NO_3)_{2(aq)} + Ag_{(s)} \longrightarrow \text{No Reaction}$$

$$Zn(NO_3)_{2(aq)} + Ca_{(s)} \longrightarrow Ca(NO_3)_{2(aq)} + Zn_{(s)}$$

RETURN TO QUESTION

learn biology, chemistry, and physics. These programs cover the full curriculum for a first or second course in these subjects. (See the Online Learning Center for more science programs.)

Recommended Software

Social Studies Programs

For a listing of recommended social studies programs, go to the Online Learning Center.

Social Studies Programs

Social studies software excels at presenting current and historical events that foster class discussion and student decision making. Using **application software,** students can integrate other information into the social studies program. Students can use word processors to write about any subject, spreadsheet and graphics programs to analyze statistical data and to display pertinent information, and database programs to retrieve data and analyze the information. For example, students using the social studies program *New Millennium World Atlas* (Rand McNally) access detailed maps and comprehensive statistics and information. Students can use the software to form patterns and see relationships. Teachers can use programs such as *TimeLiner 5.0* (Tom Snyder Productions) to create time lines for any subject (see Chapter 14).

A unique program called *Talking Walls* (Riverdeep) helps students in grades 4–8 explore the stories behind the world's most spectacular walls to see how these barriers have influenced history. Based on a book by Margy Burns Knight, this software links cultural and historical facts in a collection of stories of 14 famous walls. In the example in Figure 12.15, the student is learning about the Great Wall of China. Students can view pictures, time lines, and videos to learn about the culture that created the particular

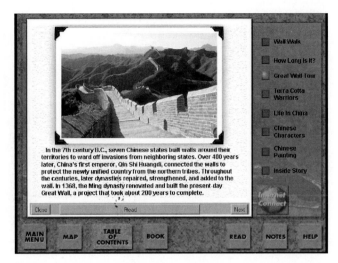

Figure 12.15 *Talking Walls*

© Riverdeep Interactive Learning Limited.

wall they are studying. If the classroom has an Internet connection, students can link to the material that is associated with the content of the program. *Talking Walls* has a research component through which students can take notes, save, and print them. The second program in the series is called *Talking Walls: The Stories Continue.*

Language Arts and Reading Programs

Because of the multitude of good language arts programs, it is often easier to integrate language arts programs into the curriculum than any other types of programs. Refer to the Online Learning Center for an annotated listing of helpful programs. Language arts programs are subdivided into many categories: writing, spelling, grammar, reading (including reference tools), and more.

To improve spelling, there are programs that involve everything from sea animals, magic castles, and gulping frogs to jungle adventures and penny arcade activities. There are also a variety of grammar programs such as *School House Rock: Grammar Rock* (Riverdeep), a drill and practice program, that contains videos on grammar from the ABC television program, and *Grammar for the Real World* (Knowledge Adventure), a simulation program that teaches grammar, sentence structure, punctuation, and spelling.

Reading programs range from elementary phonics instruction and basic comprehension to literature analysis. Two programs that help students master basic phonics concepts are *3D Froggy Phonics* (Ingenuity Works) and *Stickybear Phonics 1, 2 and 3* (Optimum Resources). Optimum Resources has an excellent high school comprehension series for grades 9–12. The topics for the high school series include history, cars, fashion, and famous people. For the high school level the literature ranges from Shakespeare to Steinbeck. *Literature: The Time, Life, and Works* series (Clearvue/eav) includes such authors as *Chaucer, Thomas Hardy, Wordsworth, Dickens,* and *Shakespeare.*

Furthermore, there are test-specific programs such as *Kaplan's SAT & PSAT ACT 2004 Edition* (Encore Software). These tutorial programs use a step-by-step approach to

Recommended Software

Language Arts and Reading Programs

For a listing of recommended language arts and reading programs, go to the Online Learning Center.

help secondary students master the strategies for dealing with the SAT, PSAT, and ACT tests. The programs cover all pertinent subject areas (Figure 12.16), and they review ba-

Figure 12.16 *Kaplan's SAT & PSAT ACT 2004 Edition*

Adapted from *Higher Score SAT & PSAT ACT 2004 Edition* Software. Reprinted by permission of Kaplan Test Prep and Admissions.

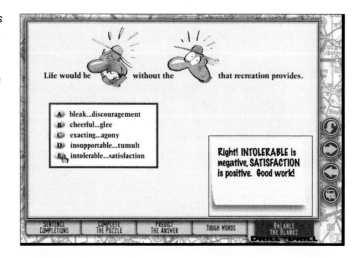

sic skills using multimedia lessons. Students are able to see their scores improve and track their progress against the scores of last year's freshman class. Finally, there are reference tools such as *Encarta Reference Library Educator Edition 2004* (Windows only) and *World Book 2004. Encarta Reference Library Educator Edition 2004*, designed for older students, includes the *Encarta Encyclopedia,* the *Encarta World dictionary,* a thesaurus, the *Encarta Interactive World Atlas,* quotations, *Encarta Researcher,* and a statistics center.

Applications for Students with Special Needs

Recommended Software
Programs for Students with Special Needs

For a listing of recommended software for students with special needs, go to the Online Learning Center.

Much of the software that has been discussed can be used with students who have special needs. The computer is patient, always waits for a response, and repeatedly gives the same explanation; thus, it is an ideal tool for individualization and remediation. Furthermore, the teacher can add special hardware devices to the computer to overcome the physical limitations of the student with learning disabilities. For example, the instructor can install a special communication board that will respond to a student's spoken command. Students who have to stay at home can enjoy all the benefits of CAI with a terminal or modem connected to the school computer. Computer software houses offer programs for the hearing impaired that feature sign language or closed captioning. (Refer to Chapter 13, which is dedicated to special education.)

Computer-Managed Instruction

In this section, we will examine **computer-managed instruction (CMI).** CMI differs from CAI in that it focuses on the needs of the teacher, helping him or her manage the learning of students.

The computer in CMI manages instruction; keeps track of student test scores, attendance records, and schedules; and offers diagnostic-perspective instruction in all curriculum areas. CMI makes the teaching environment more organized and productive, enabling the teacher to individualize instruction. It directs students so that they can proceed at their own pace, and it supervises instruction by assigning certain books and particular tapes at the right times. When the students finish their work, the computer tests them and gives further assignments. The computer grades the tests and records scores so that the teacher can see and evaluate the students' progress.

CMI is based on the underlying concept that all children can learn if they proceed at their own pace and are given the proper instructions and materials. CMI can be a comprehensive program for one or more areas of the curriculum. Many computer-managed instruction programs are based on a pretest, diagnosis, a prescription, instruction, and a posttest. At the beginning of most CMI programs, the student takes a pretest on the computer. If the computer survey indicates an area of need, the student is given the appropriate test to pinpoint the area of weakness. If questions are missed on this exam, a prescription is given. If the student fails again, he or she must see the teacher. The teacher can customize the program, omitting tests for individuals in the class. The teacher can also select remediation assignments and decide when the testing ends. The instructor can call up records, class lists, tests, and status reports on individuals and can generate class reports, group reports, and graph reports.

CMI is being incorporated into the latest CAI. For example, Sunburst's *Math Arena Advanced* features a teacher management tool that enables the teacher to customize the students' experience and track their performance and progress. *Kaplan's SAT & PSAT ACT 2004 Edition* (Encore) tutorial program offers test-taking tips, tests, and an analysis of test-taking skills. Numerous Riverdeep programs such as *PrintShop, Mavis Bacon Teaches Typing,* and *Oregon Trail* have CMI components.

Computer-managed instruction increased in popularity as a result of the No Child Left Behind Law signed by President Bush in 2002. This law emphasized accountability and testing. The law's purpose was to close the achievement disparity between disadvantaged students and their peers by proposing stronger accountability, local control, teaching methods that have worked, and more options for parents (http://www.nochildleftbehind.gov/). Software companies are trying to meet this challenge by offering integrated learning systems (ILS).

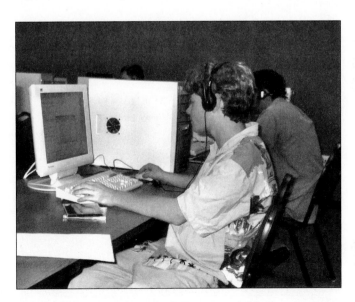

Student using an integrated learning system

Integrated Learning Systems (ILS)

Integrated learning systems (ILS) are a combination of computer-managed instruction and computer-assisted instruction. The software companies call ILS a one-package educational software solution to teachers' problems because it generates diagnostic data and instruction based on this data, monitors the students' performance, and makes changes in instruction when needed. In most cases, the software companies offer this instruction online through the Internet. ILS usually requires its own file server (computer) to store the different types of software (tutorial, drill and practice, etc.) and the individualized instruction software that keeps track of the students' progress.

Companies such as Curriculum Advantage and Riverdeep have developed these kinds of programs. Curriculum Advantage's *ClassWorks High School* open learning system combines software with management tools and integration help. *ClassWorks High School* is designed for grade 9–12 students. It focuses on pre-algebra, algebra, geometry, and English language arts. This open learning system helps the teacher test, evaluate student progress, and prescribe work. The teacher views a record of students' progress and is able to customize lessons with placement, assessment, and instruction tailored to students' needs. In addition, the teacher can effortlessly change lesson plans and learning levels.

Similarly, Riverdeep recently developed *Math Skill Navigator* and *Language Arts Navigator* to fulfill the math and language arts requirements for high school students. *Math Skill Navigator* reinforces key math skills for grades 9–12, and *Language Arts Navigator* for grades 9–12 reinforces key language arts, reading, and writing skills. These programs feature progress reports, quizzes, practice tests, and resource materials. They are computer-managed systems that help students in grades 9–12 prepare for the standardized tests they encounter in high school. The programs give initial skills assessment tests to determine each student's level of achievement. Figure 12.17 shows a student taking the brain scan test in *Math Skills Navigator.* From the results of this test

Figure 12.17 *Math Skills Navigator*

© 2004 Riverdeep Interactive Learning Limited, and its licensors.

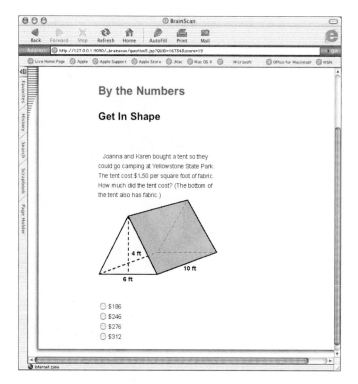

the program generates a study plan, customized lesson plans, and assignments. The student then uses the online tutorials to improve his or her score. This content is correlated with the NCTM standards and helps the student pass the exit exams.

In theory, ILS programs are sound, but in practice they pose some real problems. A common complaint is the difficulty of setting up the management module for students. It takes time to enter each student's name and define tasks, a job that normally would occur over a span of months. With an ILS, however, it has to be accomplished immediately. The ILS systems have moved toward more user-friendly software, but many programs are still difficult to use. Some researchers feel that use of ILS results in a decrease in the interaction between student and teacher (Coburn et al., 1982). Another frequent teacher complaint is the quality of the software. The ILS tests basic skills only, using such instruments as multiple-choice and true/false questions. Another complaint is the cost, which can be exorbitant; in addition, such systems may require considerable access to computers. Even though this individualized instruction motivates the students at the beginning it soon loses its appeal (Healy, 1998). Finally, there is some question about the capability of the computer to correctly assess students' performance and provide the appropriate prescription for learning. Unfortunately, ILS has not been researched adequately, and its results are inconclusive (Patersonet et al., 2003; Carter and Lyle, 2001–2002; Estep et al., 1999–2000; Miller, 1997; Healy, 1998).

Public Domain Software, Freeware and Shareware

Most software programs discussed in this book are commercial. The commercial programs can be expensive, especially in multiple copies. Fortunately, there is an alternative to commercial software: public domain software. **Public domain software** can legally be copied and shared with other users with no restrictions on use. Public domain is not copyrighted, and its authors choose not to seek formal rights or royalties. Users pay a one-time postage and handling fee. The software is distributed by electronic bulletin board services (BBSs) and software vendors, downloaded through a commercial service such as America Online (AOL) or from the Internet. User groups pass around public domain software to their members. The quality of this software varies considerably. There are very useful public domain programs, but you have to choose carefully and wisely; professional programmers and teachers write these programs in their free time.

Freeware

Freeware is like public domain software because the user obtains it without a charge. However, the company that developed the software retains the ownership. Because they own the product, they have the option of releasing a new version and charging a fee. When this happens, the program is no longer freeware but becomes a commercial software package.

Shareware is software that is distributed on a trial basis through websites, BBSs, online services, mail-order vendors, and user groups. Users try the program to see if it fits their needs. In most cases the program has a 30-day tryout period, and some of the program's functions are disabled. If, after looking over the software, the parties involved wish to use the product, they must register with the owner of the product and pay a fee. In return for the fee, the user usually gets documentation, technical support, and free updates. There are tens of thousands of shareware programs; some are terrific, others mediocre. Two excellent sites for shareware software are *Tucows* at http://www.tucows.com and *CNET Shareware.com* at http://shareware.cnet.com.

Software Selection: A General Guide

In prior chapters, we examined different application software such as word processing and desktop publishing programs and learned how to evaluate these programs by using appropriate criteria. Now we will look at some general principles that apply to evaluating any software program. Choosing good software is an eight-step process: (1) specify the software needs of your population; (2) locate the software; (3) research hardware compatibility; (4) examine the program's contents; (5) look at instructional design; (6) check out how easy the program is to learn; (7) evaluate the program in terms of consumer value; and (8) investigate the technical support and cost.

Identify the Software Needs of Your Population

To make a wise decision, it is essential to know the learning/curriculum objectives that you wish to accomplish. After you have determined what these objectives are, you can better determine the software needs of your population. Ask the following questions: What type of program will best meet these objectives? Does the class need a math drill and practice program to reinforce some math skill? Does the group need a tutorial program to learn something already taught? What is the grade and ability level of the software program? How sophisticated should this software be? For example, should the program be a simple desktop publishing program for a school newsletter or a heavy-duty desktop publishing program for a professional publication? After making these decisions, list the features the classroom requires. If you are teaching first grade, you might want a word processor that produces a nice assortment of interesting large fonts. If you are working with high school students, you might want a sophisticated word processor that has an outliner.

Locating Software

Recommended Software
Mail-Order Sources

For a listing of recommended mail-order software sources, go to Appendix B on page 451.

The major sources of software information are journals, indexes, educational organizations, magazines, software house catalogs, and the Internet. A fast way to locate software is through catalogs such as *Learning Services, Educational Resources, Software Express,* and *CCV Software.* These catalogs include program descriptions and often tell you the names of the company's best-selling programs. The companies operate via mail order and offer discounted prices. Professional journals and periodicals in the field publish numerous reviews. For example, the *Arithmetic Teacher* publishes reviews on math software, and the *Journal of Learning Disabilities* prints occasional reviews of software for students with learning disabilities. Other magazines such as *T.H.E. Journal, Electronic Learning, Learning, Leading with Technology,* and *Journal of Special Education* review software. Furthermore, there are many specialized resources such as *Only the Best Educational Software and Multimedia,* published by the Association for Supervising and Curriculum Development, Complete Sourcebook on Children's Interactive Media published by Active Learning Associates, Inc., and the *Educational Software Preview Guide,* published by the International Society for Technology in Education. On the Internet there are sites that focus on reviewing software such as *Children's Software Re-*

vue, School House Software Reviews, and *Techlearning.com.* At the end of this chapter are listed Internet sites that rate software.

Regardless of the source you use, you should read several reviews of a software program to get different perspectives. Often there is disagreement among reviewers on what constitutes "good" software because every reviewer has a priority. For example, Reviewer A may feel that ease of use is the most important factor, but Reviewer B might be concerned with features. Also, look at advertisements for new products. You can see what new products are available just by scanning the magazine ads or asking the manufacturers to send a more detailed list. You might want to call the manufacturer of the product directly to find out about some features. Software developers such as Sunburst send preview copies if you guarantee their safe return. Many software publishers let you download demonstration copies of their software from the Internet or order a demonstration CD by telephone. After a trial period of 30 or 60 days users have a good idea if they want to buy the program.

There are other sources for previewing software: university software libraries, state departments of education, and software clearinghouses. And always keep in mind any computer enthusiast acquaintance or friend who may have used a product. *Microsoft Word* may be a hot-selling program, but by talking to a friend who is actually using it, you might learn it is not right for your particular situation. Computer user groups recommend good software, demonstrate it at their meetings, and answer questions. At the very least, these groups put you in touch with people who have the software, and they generally keep abreast of new developments in the field.

After you have properly researched different types of software, you will be ready to visit the computer store or go online to examine the software package. Make sure the store is reputable and reliable, and ask about its policy on defective disks and returns. When examining a program, check the version number to be sure it is not an old version that has been languishing in the store. Make sure the version is compatible with the computer that you are using. For example, your old Pentium II processor may not run program X, which requires a computer having at the minimum a Pentium IV processor. Also, inspect the package to see if it is a teacher's version or a consumer version. The consumer edition may be less expensive, but it usually does not come with a backup disk or an activity book.

Hardware Compatibility

Ask the following questions: Do the computers at the school have enough memory to run most programs? The more memory the computer has the better it is for running programs. How many gigabytes is the hard drive? What type of backup storage do the machines have? Do they have Zip drives or high-speed FireWire hard drives? How fast is the CD-ROM or DVD-ROM drive? Is it a CD-rewritable drive or a DVD-rewriteable drive? Most software programs today are in the CD-ROM format, but this will change as more machines are packaged with DVD drives. Does the software program you want to buy need more RAM to run faster and more efficiently? Is it a networkable program? What are the video-RAM requirements? What equipment is necessary? Does the program require a digital camera or a microphone? What type of printers does the program support?

Program Content

First, ask these questions: What are the objectives of this program? Do these objectives match my curriculum objectives? Are these objectives clearly stated? Does the program meet these objectives? Many programs are not logically organized and lack a theoretical base. The objectives do not have to be seen on the computer screen. However, they should be found in the documentation that accompanies this software package.) Next, ask these questions: How appropriate is the program for the students? What knowledge or skills must a student possess to utilize this software program? Are the graphics and skills required reasonable for this grade level? (Be careful not to buy a program that is too easy or hard for the class.) Is the vocabulary appropriate for the grade level? (Many publishers supply readability scores that can serve as a benchmark.) How accurate is the material presented in the program? Is the program free of unnecessary computer jargon, and are the spelling and grammar correct? If it is a historical program, are the data accurate? How much time is needed to run the program? What about the program's transmitted values? Is the program free from prejudices or stereotypes? Is the program violent in nature? Is the program sensitive to moral issues? Does the program insult or talk down to the user?

Instructional Design

Many important factors relate to program design. These include learner control, reinforcement, sequencing, flexibility, and appearance.

Learner Control. Who controls the software program, the student or the computer? Can the student move back and forth in the lesson easily? Can the student quickly return to the previous frame? Can the student escape to the menu whenever he or she wants? Can the student control the speed of the program? Does the program move the academically advanced students forward to more difficult problems, or does the level of difficulty remain the same? (It is important to be able to use the program at more than one ability level.) How easy is it for the student to exit the program or to restart an activity?

Reinforcement. How are the students reinforced? The reinforcement should be delivered in a positive way. The software should be encouraging and not degrading. There should be little reinforcement for inappropriate responses. Some programs have reinforcement for wrong answers that is more rewarding than the reinforcement for right answers. Does the program vary the reinforcement? Is the feedback active, passive, or interactive? (A student receives passive feedback when the program simply states that the answer is wrong or right. The student receives active feedback when animation appears on the screen such as a rabbit doing a jig.)

Sequencing. Is the instructional sequence appropriate? Does it start from the simple idea and move to the complex?

Flexibility. You should be able to adapt the program for small and large groups. You also should be able to modify the program to meet the individual needs of the students in the classroom. For example, *Fraction Operations* (Sunburst) enables you to change fractions that appear in each multimedia activity. Does the program provide a record of the student's progress?

Program Appearance. Does the program have colorful graphics, animation, and sound? Does the sound motivate the students or does it interfere with their learning? Are the graphics distracting or helpful? How is the screen laid out? Is it crowded or well organized? Is the full power of the computer being used? Are there too many instructions on the screen?

Ease of Use

Is the program easy to learn? Can the student immediately load the program and use it? Does the program use simple English commands? Can the student access a help screen whenever it is needed? Does a tutorial disk or manual take the user through the program? Is the printer easy to set? Can the student answer a few questions and then be ready to print immediately? Are there help prompts and safety questions? Is there an automatic save feature? What happens when the student hits a wrong key? Must the student reload the program or does the software crash? Does the program have error messages so that the student can correct problems? Are the directions clear and concise? Can the student follow the directions on the screen without going to the documentation that accompanies the software? Are the instructions brief and to the point?

Consumer Value

Cost is a concern because some software can run into the thousands of dollars. You have to decide whether that $395 word processor is really better than the $50 one. Are all the features found in that $395 package worth the cost? (Find out if a discount house or mail-order firm carries the software at a considerable savings; see Appendix B for a list of recommended mail-order sources.) Is the software protected? Do you have to type in a serial number or find a code word in the manual or use the original disk to install? For a reduction in software price per computer, you can order lab packs, a networkable version of the software, or a **site license. Lab packs** are multiple copies of a program with one set of documentation. **Networkable software** can run over a network without a reduction in performance. You simply install the program on a single file server at one school site with a varying number of computers connected. If you buy a site license, the teacher at a site can make a number of copies of the software from the original.

Support

How good is the technical support? Can you call someone immediately to get help, or must you wait forever on the telephone? Do you have to make five or six menu choices and then get a recorded message that sends you online? Is the telephone call toll free or is it a long-distance call? Does the company charge by the minute for technical help? Is there a tutorial with the software package? Is the tutorial on a disk or in book form? (Many manufacturers provide both to simplify learning their program.) Is the manual readable, with activities and lesson plans? (The documentation should be written for the target audience.) Is this publisher reputable? Will the company still be in business when you are having trouble with the software product? If you happen to get a defective disk, will the publisher replace it?

Shopping for software is an involved process. Use the software checklist on page 308 to evaluate software.

Even if software purchased meets high standards, it can have its intent subverted when used. Purchasing software is not the only consideration; teachers must be given instruction and help in incorporating it into the classroom.

Software Program Checklist

Directions: Examine the following items and determine which ones you feel are important for your class situation. Place an X on each line for which the software meets your needs.

Product Name _____ **Manufacturer** _____ **Grade Level** _____

Subject Area _____ **Skill Level** _____

Program Type
_____ 1. Drill and practice
_____ 2. Tutorial
_____ 3. Simulation
_____ 4. Educational game
_____ 5. Problem solving
_____ 6. Teacher management
_____ 7. Other _____

Hardware Compatibility
_____ 1. Memory needed
_____ 2. Computer compatibility
_____ 3. Printer compatibility
_____ 4. Hard disk space
_____ 5. CD-ROM drive speed
_____ 6. DVD drive
_____ 7. Peripherals
_____ 8. Other

Program Content
_____ 1. Objectives met
_____ 2. Vocabulary appropriate
_____ 3. Material accurate
_____ 4. Free of bias or stereotype
_____ 5. Motivational
_____ 6. Grade-appropriate skills

Instructional Design
_____ 1. Learner control
_____ a. Speed control
_____ b. Program movement
_____ 2. Reinforcement
_____ 3. Sequencing
_____ 4. Flexibility

_____ 5. Appearance
_____ a. No distracting sound/visuals
_____ b. Animation/sound/graphics
_____ c. Uncluttered screen
_____ d. Material clearly presented
_____ e. Product reliability

Ease of Use
_____ 1. Easy program installation
_____ 2. Simple screen directions
_____ 3. On-screen help
_____ 4. Tutorial manual—hard copy
_____ 5. Easy printer setup
_____ 6. Students can use without help
_____ 7. Students can review directions on demand

Consumer Value
_____ 1. Cost
_____ 2. Extra programs
_____ 3. Lab packs
_____ 4. Network version
_____ 5. Site license

Support
_____ 1. Free technical help
_____ 2. Toll-free number
_____ 3. Readable manual
_____ a. Activities
_____ b. Lesson plans
_____ c. Tutorial
_____ d. Index
_____ 4. Money-back guarantee
_____ 5. Defective disk policy

Rating Scale
Rate the program by placing a check on the appropriate line.
Excellent _____ Very Good _____ Good _____ Fair _____ Poor _____

Comments

Reasons for Poor Software Quality

Hardware manufacturers frequently rush out their new products while they are still unfinished and bug ridden. For example, a few years ago computers with Intel's Pentium chip had a flaw that resulted in inaccurate calculations. Software quality varies as well. In the past, a lack of sophistication in software development frequently led to errors in programs. Today, the most common reasons for poor-quality software are greed, technical incompetence, and lack of instructional design.

Greed

Some computer developers deliberately turn out products prematurely to keep up with the competition or beat it into the marketplace. They rely on clever advertising, catchy titles, and deceptive marketing to get the public to buy their products, which are so faulty that they need many revisions to run properly. The public buys these bug-ridden programs and unknowingly becomes a beta tester for the final product.

Technical Incompetence

Because hardware manufacturers are constantly turning out new machines, software manufacturers expend a great amount of effort just keeping up. Many of the new machines are not compatible with current software. (The manufacturer usually makes some minor modification that prevents the existing software from working on the machine.) The software developer is then faced with angry customers who cannot understand why their programs are not working. The developer has to make modifications and send out revised versions to all customers, an expensive proposition. To save money, many manufacturers post updates to their products on the Internet. Another common problem occurs when Apple or Microsoft updates its operating system. When this happens a user will find that a peripheral, such as a printer or scanner will not work.

Lack of Instructional Design

Many programs have good graphics and sound and are attractive. However, despite their slick appearance, these programs often have little value because they are not based on sound educational theory. It is therefore important that educators become involved in the process of software development. Incorporating learning theory is a crucial part of the instructional design of any first-rate classroom software package. Many educational programs offer nothing different from what might be found in a workbook. Why spend thousands of dollars producing a software program when all a teacher has to do is buy a workbook? The software program should offer much more than a standard textbook or workbook.

Guidelines for Setting up a Software Library

Once you have the software, the most important job still remains ahead. Every teacher needs guidelines on how to organize a software collection. What follows is one approach to software organization:

1. Consult your school librarian for information on cataloging and advice on timesaving techniques.

2. Choose the location for the collection wisely. It could be a classroom, library, or media center. The more central the location, the easier the access.

3. Use a database software program to keep a record of the software. Alphabetize the software by title, subject, type, age, and so on and simultaneously make an annotated listing of the software.

4. Catalog the software. There is no standardized procedure, but one of the simplest and most effective ways is to color-code the software and documentation by subject area. For example, math software might be labeled with blue stickers or kept in blue folders. If you have a large software collection, use the Dewey Decimal System and the Sears List of Subject Headings.

5. Decide how the software is to be stored. Will you use hanging file folders, file cabinets, stands, or plastic containers?

6. Protect the collection. Make security arrangements and store disks, CD-ROMs, and DVD-ROMs vertically in containers. Protect these discs from dust, dirt, and strong magnetic fields.

7. Separate the computer discs from the documentation and serial numbers for security reasons.

8. Devise a set of rules for software use. For example, forbid food or drinks in any of the computer labs. Not only can food and drink cause damage to the computer, but they also can entice ants. Place software in its designated container.

9. Create a policy and procedures manual that handles the following issues:
   a. Who is responsible for this collection?
   b. What procedures will be used to evaluate, select, and catalog this software?
   c. How will the software be checked out?
   d. How will a teacher verify that the software is workable?
   e. How will the teacher report technical problems?

Organizing and maintaining a software library is a monumental task that requires someone to be in charge of it on a full-time basis. After this library is established, schools can benefit by devising a review procedure so that a continually growing library of software reviews can be developed and made available to all teachers.

Classroom Lesson Plans

I.   MATH FOR THE REAL WORLD

Subject

Math

Grade(s)

6–8

Objective

Students will improve their math skills by using a math simulation program such as *Math for the Real World* (Knowledge Adventure) or *Hot Dog Stand Top Dog* (Sunburst).

Standards

- National Council of Teachers of Math 1, 6, 8, 9
- ISTE NETS for Students 1, 3, 6

Materials

You will need a program such as *Hot Dog Stand Top Dog* or *Math for the Real World.*

Procedures

1. Using a math simulation program, work through a problem with the whole class.
2. Next, divide the class into four or five small groups.
3. Ask each group to elect a leader, keyboarder, and recorder.
4. Have each group take a turn on the computer to see how much money it can earn.
5. At the end of the day, ask each group to discuss how well it did. Also, have group members establish a goal for the next day or session.
6. Ask students to keep a written record of their activities and progress.
7. Have groups rotate roles.
8. Move among the groups asking questions and helping when appropriate.

II. ANIMAL BOOK

Subject

Science

Grade(s)

1–3

Objective

Students will use a product such as *EasyBook Deluxe* (Sunburst) or *Kreative Komix* (Visions Technology in Education) to create an electronic book.

Standards

- National Science Education Standards A1, A2, C1, C2, C3
- ISTE NETS for Students 1, 2, 3, 4, 5

Materials

You will need a book-making program such as *EasyBook Deluxe* or *Kreative Komix.*

Procedures

1. Explain how to use the software program.
2. Have the students use books or the Internet to study a subject such as plants or dinosaurs.

3. Have students create books about what they have learned.
4. When the students have completed the assignment, have them share their electronic books with the class.

III. WRITING AN ARTICLE

Subject

Social Studies and Language Arts

Grade(s)

4 and up

Objective

Students will use an electronic encyclopedia such as *World Book* or *Encarta*, to create articles for a newspaper.

Standards

- National Council for the Social Studies Curriculum Standards 1, 3
- NCTE English Language Arts Standards 1, 3, 4, 5, 6, 7, 8, 12
- ISTE NETS for Students 1, 2, 3, 4, 5

Materials

You will need access to the Internet, an electronic encyclopedia such as *World Book* or *Encarta*, and a publishing program such as *Microsoft Publisher*.

Procedures

1. Divide the class into small groups.
2. Have each member of the group determine what famous person he or she wants to research. For example, a student might choose Abraham Lincoln or Harriet Tubman.
3. Have each student use an electronic encyclopedia to research the chosen person and write an article about the times in which this person lived.
4. Have the group then create a newspaper with its articles using a publishing program such as *Microsoft Publisher*.
5. At the end of the assignment, have the groups come together and share newspapers.

IV. MY STORY

Subject

Language Arts

Grade(s)

2 and up

Objective

Students will use a multimedia story-writing program such as *Kreative Komix* (Visions Technology in Education) to create a book report.

Standards

- NCTE English Language Arts Standards 1, 4, 5, 6, 12
- ISTE NETS for Students 1, 2, 3

Materials

You will need a writing program such as *Kreative Komix* or *Microsoft Publisher* and one or more computers.

Procedures

1. Have students read a book and then talk about the elements that shape the story.
2. Next, ask students to write down a summary of the events.
3. Show the students how to use the software to insert text and graphics.
4. Have students print hard copies of their reports and present them in class.
5. As a class, discuss the reports and offer suggestions for change.

V. MAKING MUSIC

Subject

Music

Grade(s)

2 and up

Objective

Students will identify musical notes.

Standards

- ISTE NETS for Students 1, 2, 3

Materials

You will need a program such as *Making Music* and one or more computers.

Procedures

1. Draw eight bars on the board to represent a scale.
2. Turn the computer monitor away from the students and have a student play six random notes.
3. Ask the students to listen carefully to the sounds and draw the bars and notes that represent the sound patterns.

4. Do this two more times so that the students can check their work.

5. Now turn the monitor toward the class and play the pattern. Have them compare their patterns to the ones that are being played.

Summary

The computer has many invaluable uses in all areas of the curriculum. Computer-assisted instruction (CAI) software uses the computer as a tool to improve instruction, provide the student with practice in problem solving, serve as a tutor, and supply drill and practice. Computer-managed instruction (CMI) assists the teacher in managing learning. We consid-ered eight criteria to apply when choosing software. We ex-amined a software evaluation form (checklist) to aid in soft-ware selection. We considered reasons for poor-quality software, and guidelines for setting up a software library. On the Online Learning Center is a comprehensive and anno-tated list of award-winning programs.

Study and Online Resources

Go to Chapter 12 in the Student Edition of the Online Learn-ing Center at www.mhhe.com/sharp5e *to **practice with key concepts, take chapter quizzes, read PowerWeb articles** and **news feed updates** related to technology in education, and **access resources** for learning about technology and in-tegrating it into the classroom.*

Click on Web Links to link to the following websites.

Art

The Art Room

The Art Room features a variety of classroom projects for grades 3–12 in the *Doorway* section. This section also presents other useful art activities, including the *Artifacts Center.*

AskERIC Lesson Plans

AskERIC Lesson Plans provides more than 40 lesson plans for students in grades K–12. Areas include art history and vi-sual arts.

Collections

These two sites present famous paintings by acknowledged masters.

Emmett Scott's Arts & Activities

This site, for grades K–5, provides step-by-step instructions for drawing cartoons, as well as special tricks for creating them.

Joseph Wu's Origami Page

This is the ultimate origami site, with extensive resources and information for K–12 teachers.

Kennedy Center's ArtsEdge

The Kennedy Center's ArtsEdge provides a forum where teachers and students can share information and ideas that support the arts in the K–12 curriculum.

Museo del Prado

Museo del Prado offers information about the museum itself, a quick tour of 49 of its best-known works of art, a tour of its currently featured exhibit, and links to other museums on the Web. A Spanish-language version is available.

Software

About.com's Shareware/Freeware-Educational Software

This site provides links to software publishers, a multimedia tutorial, and an archive of previous features.

Children's Software Revue

Former teachers started Children's Software Revue. They publish a well-known magazine called *Children's Software Revue,* which contains authoritative reviews and ratings as well as helpful articles, tips, and spotlights on each school subject. You can browse their site for news, sample articles, and recommended software by age group and category. There are in-depth reviews of over 5,800 titles of the latest children's educational software.

CNET Download.com's Home and Education

The Computer Network (CNET) is an index of Macintosh- and PC-compatible educational software (freeware, shareware, demos) available for download. The site includes program descriptions, reviews, and links to FTP sites. Users may search by keyword, browse by subject area, or view the newest, most popular, or highest-rated titles. Categories are *kids, language, literature, mathematics, miscellaneous, science,* and *teaching tools.*

CNET Shareware.com
The Computer Network offers a searchable shareware database of software files for Windows and Macintosh platforms.

Education World: Technology in the Classroom
This site offers a number of articles and tips for purchasing and using software and the Internet in the K–12 classroom. They range from *Online Encyclopedias* to *Software Bargains for Teachers!*

Game's Zone KidZone
The GZKidZone helps students find information about children's software. The main purpose of this site is to educate parents and students on what is available in the software market.

Kids Domain
Kids Domain is an educational site for children aged 2 to 12, parents, and teachers. This site includes sections with games and activities, stories, jokes and riddles, contests, and downloads. In addition, the site features software reviews and craft and activity ideas.

SafeKids.Com
SafeKids.Com contains suggestions on how to make your experience online productive.

School House Software Reviews
This site contains professional reviews of the latest educational software for children and adults. School House Software Reviews is updated several times a week.

Simply the Best
Simply the Best is a collection of the best shareware, music, metasearches, and so on.

SuperKids Educational Software Review
SuperKids contains educational software for Macs and PCs, a buyers' guide, and discounts for online orders. There are software reviews by parents, teachers, and students.

Techlearning.com
Techlearning.com features a searchable database of reviews of educational software, taken from the print journal for K–12 educators.

Tucows
The Tucows site offers more than 30,000 software titles in libraries located around the world.

Yahoo! Directory of Children Software
Yahoo!'s directory contains an array of safe sites for children.

General Curriculum and Math Sites
What follows is an annotated list of top-rated Internet sites you can use in all curriculum areas. These curriculum sites range from math lesson plans to science resources.

Academy Curriculum Exchange
Academy Curriculum Exchange offers lesson plans for grades K–12 in a variety of subject areas. To find more than 50 plans for math, click these links: *Elementary School, Intermediate School,* or *High School.*

AskERIC Lesson Plans: Math
AskERIC Lesson Plans: Math provides a collection of math lesson plans contributed by teachers for grades K–12. Topics include algebra, applied math, arithmetic, functions, geometry, measurement, and probability. Each lesson plan features an overview, purpose, objectives, activities, and resource materials.

The Electric Teacher
The Electric Teacher, created by teacher Cathy Chamberlain, provides a rich assortment of ideas for integrating technology into the curriculum. Categories for resources include *community resources, thematic resources, literacy and technology, K–12 teacher resources,* and *education listservs and collaboration sites.* Tutorials help teachers incorporate *Word, Excel, PowerPoint,* and *FrontPage* into the regular classroom. The site also includes a tutorial on the basic use of the Internet, sample lessons, tips for taking quality photos, and help for working with graphics.

Science Sites
Activity Search
Activity Search, from Houghton Mifflin, features a curriculum database K–8 teachers can search for science lesson plans/activities and other subject areas by grade level. Activities can also be browsed by theme.

Double Helix Science Experiments
CSIRO provides a collection of over 100 science experiments for grades 3–8.

Social Studies Sites
Academy Curricular Exchange
Academy Curricular Exchange includes over 200 social studies lesson plans for elementary, intermediate, and high school students.

Awesome Library Social Studies Lesson Plans
This site presents a large number of links to a variety of lesson plans representing all areas of the K–12 social studies curriculum.

Education World: Lessons to Celebrate Black History Month!
This site contains 10 classroom activities, other online resources, and award-winning sites for celebrating Black History Month.

Mr. Donn's Ancient History Page
Mr. Donn's ancient civilization lesson plan and information resource covers ancient Mesopotamia, Egypt, Greece, Rome, China, and ancient civilizations.

Language Arts Sites
AskERIC Lesson Plans: Language Arts
AskERIC Lesson Plans: Language Arts provides a collection of nearly 100 language arts lesson plans contributed by teachers for grades K–12. Topics include *literature, writing composition, reading,* and *spelling.* Each lesson plan features an overview, purpose, objectives, activities, and resource materials.

A to Z Teacher Stuff
A to Z Teacher Stuff provides hundreds of lesson plans and thematic activities for teaching children's literature in the elementary school. The site also includes *LessonPlanz.com,* a search engine with over 4,000 lesson plans.

Cool Teaching Lessons and Units
Richard Levine provides an extensive collection of WebQuests and lesson plans.

IN TIME (Integrating New Technologies into the Methods of Education)
IN TIME provides research, information, and videos about integrating technology into proven research-based methods of teaching and learning. Videos show teachers integrating technology into their classrooms. Search videos by title, content area, grade level, learning element, and 10 other criteria. Lesson plans are available for download. A substantial *Help* section is available for all sections of the site—including for downloading necessary plug-ins and accessing lesson plans. If you need more excellent sites with ideas for integrating technology in the K–12 classroom, browse the *Education World* directory at http://www.educationworld.com/awards/past/topics/ed_tech.shtml.

Music Sites
Children's Music Web Guide
The Children's Music Web Guide, created by Monty Harper, contains a searchable and browsable database of hundreds of children's music sites for grades K–12. Categories include elementary education, fun, live music, media, music education, musicians/bands, resources, and songs.

GEM: Subject Arts—Music Pre-K to 12
The Gateway to Educational Materials (GEM), sponsored by the U.S. Department of Education, provides a collection of art and music lesson plans and instructional resources for grades pre-K–12.

Internet Music Resource Guide
Internet Music Resource Guide features links to a variety of music resources, including bands and artists, magazines, and search sites.

K–12 Resources for Music Educators
This site contains important resources for music educators and students in all areas of the music curriculum.

Yahoo! Classical Composers
This site introduces students in grades 5–12 to hundreds of composers from the Baroque period to the 20th century. Select a musical period and click on a composer's name to find biographical information, pictures, and descriptions of the composer's work.

Chapter Mastery Test

To the Instructor: *Refer to the Instructor's Manual for the answers to the Mastery Questions. This manual has additional questions and resource materials.*

Let us check for chapter comprehension with a short mastery test. Key Terms, Computer Lab, and Suggested Readings and References follow the test.

1. Name two advantages of using drill and practice software to learn mathematics.
2. Suggest two ways social studies software can be used to teach U.S. history.
3. Should the teacher use language arts software to improve writing skills? Give reasons to support your position.

4. What methods can a teacher use to improve problem-solving skills on the computer?

5. Explain how students might use the computer in gathering, organizing, and displaying social studies information. Include two titles of exemplary software.

6. What are the advantages of using computer math manipulatives over traditional math manipulatives?

7. What is the most critical step in the evaluation of software? Explain its importance.

8. Discuss three criteria that a teacher should consider when choosing software for the classroom.

9. What is the main difference between *shareware* and *public domain software*?

10. Why is feedback a crucial element to consider when evaluating software?

11. Should the student or the computer control the direction of a program? Explain.

12. What is the major difference between a drill and practice program and a tutorial program?

13. Define *simulation program* and give an example.

14. Can a problem-solving program also be a simulation program? Explain in detail.

15. Give the paradigm for the typical drill and practice program design.

16. What is the major difference between computer-managed instruction and computer-assisted instruction?

17. Discuss two reasons for poor-quality software.

18. What are important considerations for setting up a software library?

Key Terms

Application software 298
Beginner's All-Purpose Symbolic Instruction Code (BASIC) 287
Branching tutorial 288
Computer-assisted instruction (CAI) 286

Computer-managed instruction (CMI) 300
Drill and practice software 291
Freeware 303
Integrated learning systems (ILS) 302

Lab packs 307
Linear tutorial 288
Networkable software 307
Public domain software 303

Shareware 303
Simulation 289
Site license 307
Tutorial 288

Computer Lab: Activities for Mastery and Your Portfolio

12.1 **Create an Interactive Time Line** Use one of several applications to create an interactive time line to use in your classroom.

12.2 **Learning About Genre** Use this activity with your students to create genre signs for the classroom library.

12.3 **Books I've Read** Use the activity with your students to create a database of books they have read.

12.4 **Benjamin Franklin's Gulf** Benjamin Franklin recorded the water temperature every day in his journeys across the Atlantic and discovered the Gulf Stream. Re-create Franklin's efforts.

12.5 Review a software program using the guidelines that were given in this chapter.

12.6 The software evaluation form that was used in this chapter was of a general nature. Develop a software checklist for a drill and practice software program in the area of math or science.

12.7 Using the Recommended Software found on the Online Learning Center or a software directory, locate several math software packages for an eighth-grade class. Make a list.

12.8 Find a published review on a software program in the school's collection. Test out the product to determine the validity of the review. Write your own review.

12.9 Visit a school that uses computers and a variety of computer programs. Write a brief report on the criteria used by the school in selecting its software.

12.10 Discuss the problems inherent in language arts software given the existing curriculum. Research the topic to support your discussion.

Suggested Readings and References

Association for Educational Communications and Technology. *Tech Trends Media Reviews.* Columns that have in-depth evaluations of educational multimedia (1-800-347-7834).

Baker, Elizabeth. "Integrating Literacy and Technology: Making a Match Between Software and Classroom." *Reading & Writing Quarterly* 19, issue 2, (April 2003): 193–198.

Becker, H. "Mindless of Mindful Use of Integrated Learning Systems." *International Journal of Educational Research* 21, no. 1 (1994): 65, 79.

"Best Products of 2003." *PC Magazine* 22, issue 1 (January 2003): 92–104.

"Best Software." *PC World* 20, issue 7 (July 2002): 89–91.

Beltrame, Julian. "Making Music Together on Web Becomes Reality." *Wall Street Journal,* July 6, 2000, B1.

Branzburg, Jeffrey, and Susan McLester. "Advice for Picking out Great Software." *Technology and Learning* 20, no. 3 (October 1999): 44.

Buckleitner, Warren, ed. "The Elementary Teacher's Sourcebook on Children's Software." *Children's Software Revue* 10 (Spring 2002).

Buckleitner, Warren, ed. *Children's Software Revue* 11, no. 3 (May/June 2003).

Carter, Carolyn M., and Lyle R. Smith. "Does the Use of Learning Logic in Algebra I Make a Difference in Algebra II?" *Journal of Research on Technology in Education* 34, no. 2 (Winter 2001–2002): 157–161.

Cassidy, Jacquelyn A. "Computer-Assisted Language Arts Instruction for the ESL Learner." *English Journal* 85, no. 8 (December 1996): 55–57.

Coburn, Peter, et al. "How to Set up a Computer Environment." *Classroom Computer News* 2, no. 3 (January–February 1982): 29–31, 48.

Cohen, Steve, Richard Chechile, and George Smith. "A Method for Evaluating the Effectiveness of Educational Software." *Behavior Research Methods, Instruments, and Computing* 26, no. 2 (May 1, 1994): 236.

Dede, C. "A Review and Synthesis of Recent Research in Intelligent Computer-Assisted Instruction." *International Journal of Man-Machine Studies* 24, no. 4 (1986): 329–353.

Estep, S., W. McInerney, and E. Vockell. "An Investigation of the Relationship beween Integrated Learning Systems and Academic Achievement." *Journal of Educational Technology Systems* 28, no. 1 (1999–2000): 5–19.

Gonce-Winder, C., and H. H. Walbesser. "Toward Quality Software." *Contemporary Educational Psychology* 12, no. 10 (July 1987): 19–25.

Harrison, Nancy, and Evelyn M. Van Devender. "The Effects of Drill-and-Practice Computer Instruction on Learning Basic Mathematics Facts." *Journal of Computing in Childhood Education* 3, nos. 3–4 (1992): 349–356.

Healy, J. M. *Failure to Connect: How Computers Affect Our Children's Minds—for Better and Worse.* New York: Simon and Schuster, 1998.

Hough, Bradley W., and Margaret W. Smithey. "Creating Technology Advocates: Connecting Preservice Teachers with Technology." *T.H.E. Journal* 26, no. 8 (March 1999): 78.

Goyne, June S., Sharon K. McDonough, and Dara D. Padgett. "Practical Guidelines for Evaluating Educational Software." *Clearing House* 73, no. 6 (July/August 2000): 345.

Ivers, Karen S. "Desktop Adventures: Building Problem-Solving and Computer Skills." *Learning and Leading with Technology* 24, no. 4 (December–January 1996–1997): 6–11.

Johnson, Judi Mathis, ed. *Educational Software Preview Guide 2000.* Eugene, Ore.: International Society for Technology in Education (ISTE), 2000.

Kafai, Yasmin B., Megan L. Franke, and Dan S. Battery. "Educational Software Reviews under Investigation." *Education, Communication & Information* 2, issue 213 (December 2002): 163–181.

Kassner, Kirk "One Computer Can Deliver Whole-Class Instruction." *Music Educators Journal* 86, no. 6 (May 2000): 34.

Klinger, Mike. "The One-Computer Music Classroom." *Teaching Music* 3, no. 3 (December 1995): 34–35.

Kultgen, Sherri. "Computer Portfolios." *Arts and Activities* 125, no. 4 (May 1999): 20.

Lindroth, Linda. "Hot Websites." *Teaching Journal PreK–,* vol. 34, issue 4, (May 2004): 22–24.

McMillen, Linda, et al. "Integrating Technology in the Classroom." *Language Arts* 74, no. 2 (February 1997): 137–149.

Miller, H. L. "The New York City Public Schools Integrated Learning Systems Project." *International Journal of Educational Research* 27, no. 2 (1997): 91–183.

Netochka, Nezvanova. "A Musical Instrument in Perpetual Flux." *Computer Music Journal* 24, no. 3 (Fall 2000): 38.

Only the Best Educational News Service. Alexandria, Va.: Association for Supervising and Curriculum Development (31250 North Pitt Street, Alexandria VA 22314-1453).

Paterson, Wendy A., Julie Jacobs Henry, Karen O'Quin, Maria Ceprano, and Elfreda V. Blue. "Investigating the Effectiveness of an Integrated Learning System on Early Emergent Readers." *Reading Research Quarterly* 38, issue 2 (April–June 2003): 172–175.

Reed, W. Michael. "Assessing the Impact of Computer-Based Writing Instruction." *Journal of Research on Computing in Education* 28, no. 4 (Summer 1996): 418–437.

Roblyer, M. D., Jack Edwards, and Mary Anne Havriluk. *Integrating Educational Technology into Teaching.* Upper Saddle River, N.J.: Merrill-Prentice Hall, 2003.

"Six Strategies for Raising a Scientist." *Software Revue* 8, no. 4 (2000): 12–16.

Schackner, Bill. "Colleges Byte Back When Music Software Jams Networks." *Black Issues in Higher Education* 17, no. 6 (May 11, 2000): 28.

Schlenker, Richard M., and Sara J. Yoshida. "Integrating Computers into Elementary School Science Using Toothpicks to Generate Data." *Science Activities* 27, no. 4 (Winter 1990): 13.

"The 18th Annual Editors' Choice Awards." *Macworld* 20, issue 2 (February 2003): 79–85.

Voas, Jeffrey A. "New Generation of Software Quality Conferences." *IEEE Software* 17, no. 1 (January/February 2000): 22.

Vockell, Edward, and Robert M. Deusen. *The Computer and Higher-Order Thinking Skills.* Watsonville, Calif.: Mitchell Publishing, 1989.

CHAPTER 13

Computers in Special Education

Integrating the Computer into the Special Education Classroom

Technology can help students with disabilities realize their potential. The computer can help such students achieve equal access to the general education curriculum. This chapter will provide guidelines on how the teacher can help students accomplish these educational goals. We will examine examples of hardware devices that make it easier for students with special needs to function successfully in regular classroom settings. We will also explore some ways in which the classroom teacher can use computer software to help students with disabilities learn. Furthermore, the chapter will present examples of lesson plans that can be used in a variety of situations and Internet sites containing a rich assortment of content.

Objectives

Upon completing this chapter, you will be able to do the following:

1. Describe three hardware devices that can be used by individuals with disabilities to increase access and function.
2. Name three software programs that are available for individuals with special needs.
3. Discuss some of the important laws passed for special education.
4. Discuss some of the problems and issues involved in special education.
5. Utilize or (or adapt) activities to increase integration of students with special needs in the classroom.
6. List some excellent Internet sites on special education that range from lesson plans to organizations.

Students with Disabilities

All students display some differences in terms of physical characteristics: Some are tall, others short; some are thin, others heavy; some wear glasses, others do not. Students also differ in learning ability. Some students differ from the average to such an extent that specialized education or adapted programs are necessary to meet their needs. The

CHIME Charter School, Woodland Hills, California. Students are working together in an inclusive setting

term **exceptional children** refers to students who have physical disabilities or sensory impairment, students who have behavior and/or learning problems, or students who are gifted or have special talents (Heward, 2002).

The major disability categories recognized by the school districts are learning disabilities, deaf/hearing impairments, speech or language impairments, visual impairments, other health impairments, orthopedic impairments, mental retardation, emotional disturbance, autism, traumatic brain injury (Smith, Polloway, Patton, and Dowdy, 2001). We will only cover some of these categories.

Learning Disabilities

More than half of the students who receive special education services have learning disabilities (Fuchs and Fuchs, 1998; Henley, Ramsey, Algozzine, 2003). The learning disabilities category includes more students than all the other categories combined (Smith, Dowdy, Polloway, and Blalock, 1997). As defined by the U.S. Department of Education, a learning disability is "a disorder in one or more of the basic psychological processes involved in understanding or using spoken or written language, which may appear as an impaired ability to listen, think, speak, read, write, spell, or do mathematical calculations."

For students with learning disabilities, there is a wide assortment of assisted technology products that can help them improve their skills. For example, when students have difficulty reading, they can use programs such as the *Start-to-Finish Books, Simon Sounds It Out* (Don Johnston), *Edmark Reading Program Series,* and *Sound Reading CD-Teens, 20's and Beyond* (Sound Reading Solutions.) These programs enable students to hear whole passages that are highlighted or to click on individual words. The programs feature comprehension checks, voice, and corrective feedback to help the student. The words and sound are pronounced and accompanied by colorful pictures. In many of the programs, students can record words and listen for evaluation.

An area that causes students problems is writing. Using organizers with speech capabilities such as *Kidspiration* and *Inspiration* (Inspiration, Inc.) and word processors with organizers such as *Draft: Builder* (Don Johnston) and *Writer's Companion* (Visions Technology in Education) helps students outline and organize their writing. Talking word processors such as *Write:Outloud* and *Kurzweil 3000* help students self-correct, set level of speech feedback, and spell check. In addition, these programs enable the student to adjust how the screen looks. This is an important consideration because, with fewer items on the screen, students can more easily focus on their writing. *Dragon Naturally Speaking* (ScanSoft) enables students to dictate their compositions.

Many students with learning disabilities have trouble with telling time, counting coins, and making change. They can use talking calculators such as *Programming Concepts* and *Coin-U-Lator* (Figure 13.1) that teach students coin counting. In addition, they can use software programs such as *Edmark Telling Time* (Riverdeep), *Making Change* (Attainment), and *IntelliMathics* (Intellitools) for problem solving. These programs generate word or number problems and come with full auditory support.

In our discussion thus far we have talked about hardware and software devices that help students with learning disabilities do their academic work. But there is an obvious free option found in our very own computers. Today, computer makers incorporate computer accessibility options into their operating systems.

The location of this feature is dependent on the operating system of your computer. For the Mac OS (Figure 13.2), the feature is found in the *Preferences,* whereas for the

Figure 13.1
Coin-U-Lator

Reprinted with permission of PCI Educational Publishing.

Figure 13.2
Macintosh OS Universal Access Settings

Images courtesy of Apple Computers, Inc.

Windows XP, the feature is found in the *Control Panel* (Figure 13.3). The computer includes options for the mouse and input devices other than the keyboard, and there are also display, sound, and speech options.

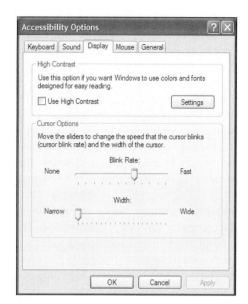

Figure 13.3 *Windows XP* Accessibility Options

Screen shot of *Microsoft®Windows XP* used by permission of Microsoft Corporation.

Students with Low Vision and Students Who Are Blind

For the student with visual impairment, a standard monitor that can display large type enables the student to read three large lines at a time. Most computers come with the option to switch from black text on a white background to white text on a black background or to change it to gray scale; these features can enhance the visibility of what is on the screen. In addition, a standard zoom feature or advanced screen magnification programs such as *ZoomText* (Windows; Ai Squared) or *inLarge* (Macintosh; Synapse Adaptive) can enhance readability.

Usually, this type of student will be able to use a standard keyboard, but some students may do better with large keytop labels. Standard printers can print out in large size to improve readability. A Braille embosser can print material from the computer in Braille.

Speech Synthesis. Optical character recognition software can convert printed documents into an electronic format, which can then be read aloud with a speech synthesizer. Many products today use **speech synthesis** or computer-generated speech. For example, automobile computers audibly remind drivers to shut the door or fill the tank. Speech synthesis is very helpful for students who are visually impaired.

However, students with disabilities are no longer trapped in front of the computer screen to use speech synthesis, Programs such as NextUp.com's *TextAloud MP3* and Fonix Corporation's *iSpeak* save files in MP3 or WAV formats. Students can then download their files to an MP3 player or personal digital assistant with sound capabilities.

Screen reading programs such as IBM's *Home Page Reader (HPR)* make the Internet more accessible to visually impaired students. *Home Page Reader* enables the student to access the Web quickly and easily by requesting a specific URL. Working in conjunction with IBM *ViaVoice Outloud* text-to-speech synthesizer, the program reads the contents of the website. Text-speech products such as the *CAST eReader* (Cast Products) read content from word processors, the Internet, and scanned and typed text. Using a simple interface, the student has no trouble navigating and manipulating Web page elements or reading e-mail.

Students with low vision or students who are blind can also use speech synthesis technology to read books and access Braille services online. A free text-to-speech application is available at http://www.readplease.com/.

Voice Recognition. Voice recognition software enables users to communicate with the computer through a microphone. The computer then follows their instructions by pulling down a menu or typing text. Everyone's computer fantasy is to be able to dictate a command to the computer through a microphone and have the computer execute the command on the screen. For years, starship captains have been talking to their computers on TV. In the real world, this technology is still in its infancy.

Voice recognition software works by converting the spoken word into binary patterns that are computer recognizable; essentially, it understands human speech. You can enter data or issue simple commands through the system simply by speaking. *Dragon Naturally Speaking* (ScanSoft) is a speech-recognition product that enables users to talk at a natural pace; their words appear on the screen spelled correctly. Visually impaired students as well as students who cannot type or use handheld devices can benefit from such software. They can create documents, browse the Web, e-mail, and navigate the desktop. Eventually, voice recognition may relegate the mouse and keyboard to the storage bin. As voice recognition systems improve, the visually impaired will attain complete accuracy in their documents when they dictate to the computer.

Adaptive Devices for the Blind. Blind students can use Braille printers, a standard keyboard with Braille key labels, or a **refreshable Braille display.** A refreshable Braille display can be added to a computer system to translate text on the screen into Braille. The display is flat and designed to be placed underneath the keyboard. There are mechanical pins that raise and lower for each eight-dot Braille cell. The text that is typed is on a single-line display, which follows the movements of the cursor (Figure 13.4).

Figure 13.4
Refreshable Braille Display, Alva Access Group
http://www.aagi.com/.

Students with Hearing and Speech Impairment

For the student who is deaf or hard of hearing, visual output on the screen replaces sound. The standard flash option can be selected to alert a user when a sound occurs. For example, instead of emitting audible beeps, the monitor blinks. Software programs for the hard of hearing should have captions for spoken elements. People with hearing impairments can learn to speak by matching words displayed on a screen with the sound waves for each word. As the Internet has grown, more hearing-impaired individuals use online mail programs instead of specially designed telephones for the deaf (TTY). Currently, Web caption editors, such as *MAGpie* (National Center for Accessible Media), can write video captions in different formats.

Health Problems

Students who are hospitalized or at home can have easy access to their teachers through the Internet. Using a video camera, they can talk to and see their teachers. They can thus feel some personal connection to the teacher and ask questions that trouble them. The beauty of this arrangement is that the teacher can give the student an automatic response. With video conferencing, students also can talk to their fellow classmates and thus feel some personal connection with the classroom environment. Using the Internet, they can send e-mail and get instant messages and access an unlimited library. In the privacy of their house or hospital room they can view online videos on pertinent topics, research reports, or visit online museums. These are but a few of the ways that the computer can help the student with disabilities communicate.

Adaptive Technology

The computer has become a natural tool to help the special education student access a general education curriculum. The computer can help the student by acting as a tutor. It can help the student more easily express his or her ideas to the outside world. Using the computer, the student with special needs is often motivated to spend more time working on an instructional assignment and doing well in school. The computer is very patient and private, so the student is not embarrassed to try or to fail. Students with disabilities enjoy the control they can exert over the rate at which they learn; such students often have the experience of having little control over their learning environment. Special education students receive recognition from the outside world when they achieve something on the computer. Furthermore, the computer increases such students' chances of expressing themselves musically or in words. Students with disabilities who received instruction on computers when they were young can shine when using a computer. They can model skills for other students, boosting their own self-esteem.

The computer can speak for those who cannot speak and generate text for those who cannot move their arms. It can help those with low vision by magnifying text. It can read to the blind and help them communicate more easily. Students who are hearing impaired can easily communicate via e-mail and can participate in chat rooms.

For the student with disabilities to get the full benefits of the computer, certain modifications may be needed for the hardware or software. More than 50 million Americans have some type of disability, necessitating some adaptation of hardware or software for them to use computer technology (Kamp, 1999). **Adaptive or assistive technology** devices are defined as "any item, piece of equipment, or product system, whether acquired commercially or off the shelf, modified, or customized, that increases, maintains, or improves functional capabilities of individuals with disabilities" (The Technology-Related Assistance for Individuals with Disabilities Act). For a list of adaptive or assistive technologies, see the University of Toronto's Adaptive Technology Resource Centre (ATRC) at http://www.utoronto.ca/atrc/reference/tech/techgloss.html.

The distinction between assistive or adaptive technologies and conventional technologies is blurring as more products are being designed for use by a greater number of individuals. A touch screen can be used as an alternative to the mouse by people with disabilities as well as by those without disabilities. For example, touch screens are often used in information booths at airports, in voting machines, and in amusement parks. Eventually, voice recognition may become the most common form of input for everyone, and the keyboard may disappear (Alliance for Technology Access, 2000; Bryant, Bryant, and Raskind, 1998).

Keyboard Modifications

The keyboard can be redesigned to meet the user's needs. There are many possibilities such as an alternative keyboard with greater space between the keys, a simplified arrangement, a keyboard with larger keys, left- and right-handed keyboards, or an on-screen keyboard. Disabling the repeat key helps students with less fine-muscle control; this way, users get one keystroke per character no matter how long the key is held down. For a user with difficulty pressing two keys simultaneously, the keyboard can be designed so that it has **sticky keys**—that is, certain keys that lock in place—allowing the student with a disability to use combination keystrokes without having to press keys simultaneously. A power strip can enable a user to turn on the computer equipment by pressing a single switch as opposed to three or four.

If modifying the keyboard does not work for the student, **keyboard emulators** (on-screen keyboards) may be used. An emulator presents a choice to the student in the form of a whole sentence, phrase, or character; the student then makes a selection with one movement. If a mouse is too difficult to use, a joystick can be used to control speed and direction. Emulators can be used to generate a sequence of keystrokes that can be recalled as sentences or words.

Many students who have disabilities cannot use a traditional input device such as a standard mouse, trackball, or keyboard. For these students, the computer industry has developed alternative devices such as a foot-controlled mouse, touch screens, onscreen keyboards, alternative keyboards, switches, touch tablets, voice-controlled devices, and word prediction software systems.

Touch-Free Switch

The **touch-free switch** is an input device that enables students to trigger a mouse click without applying any pressure. Edmark's touch-free switch is used in conjunction with a digital video camera and special software that enables the physically challenged student to interact with the camera. The digital camera recognizes almost any movement as a mouse click. It is placed on a monitor to see a head movement, on a student desk to recognize a hand movement, or on the floor to see a toe movement.

Discover Switch

Figure 13.5 Discover Switch

Madentec Limited of Alberta, Canada. Used with permission. www.madentec.com.

The **discover switch** is a talking computer switch for the classroom that attaches to the keyboard. With this switch, the computer user can do everything another user could do with a standard keyboard and mouse. A keyboard is displayed on the computer screen to provide choices for writing, using the mouse, or clicking the graphics in multimedia programs such as *Dr. Seuss* (The Learning Company). The choices are highlighted automatically, and students then press a switch to make their choice (Figure 13.5). In addition, the on-screen keyboard can speak words, phrases, and even sentences, offering nonspeaking students a way to communicate.

IntelliKeys Keyboard

IntelliKeys (IntelliTools) is for people with a wide range of disabilities who require a keyboard (Figure 13.6) with a changing face. The keyboard is compatible with Mac-

Figure 13.6
IntelliKeys

From Chime School, California.

intoshes or PC-compatible machines. *IntelliKeys* is packaged with six standard overlays including a setup overlay. Teachers or students can use these overlays with any software or word processing program with keyboard input. Teachers can also create their own custom overlays. Each standard overlay has a bar code that *IntelliKeys* recognizes. Students who use switches can choose from two built-in programmable switch jacks.

Also available are talking keyboards for the classroom, such as *Discover:Board*. The student presses *Discover:Board* keys for sounds and speech while doing work. Using this keyboard, the student can receive speech feedback with programs such as *Apple-Works, Co:Writer,* or *Kid Pix* as well as with the Internet and online services. It can be used with pictures, text, or just letters.

Touch Screen

The **touch screen** (Figure 13.7) is a pointing device on which users place their fingers to enter data or make selections. There are two types of touch screens: those designed with a pressure-sensitive panel mounted in front of the screen such as Edmark's *Touch Window* and those that require the use of special, touch-sensitive monitors such as the IBM *Info Window System.* The software program for the touch screen displays different

Figure 13.7 Touch Screen Panel

Used by permission of ArtToday.com, Inc.

options on the screen in a graphic button format. For example, in a multiple-choice exam, the student would touch the button for his or her selected answer, and the screen would change in response.

The touch screen offers a real advantage to students with disabilities because it is a fast and natural way to enter data, to make selections, and to issue commands. Despite these wonderful benefits, a touch screen is not useful for inputting large amounts of data or for pointing to a single character. Moreover, it is fatiguing to use for a long period of time, and the screen quickly gets finger marked. Lessons created on one variety of touch screen may not work on another because of software incompatibility.

Handheld Scanner

Wizcom Technologies offers a *QuickLink Pen* (Figure 13.8) that helps students with learning disabilities take notes. Students can use this device to scan printed text, printed Internet links, charts, tables, books, and magazines. The students can then transfer this information to their computers to aid them in writing reports.

Figure 13.8 *QuickLink Pen*

Reprinted by permission of Wizcom Technologies.

Portable Keyboards

AlphaSmart 3000 (AlphaSmart Company), previously discussed in Chapter 3, is a powerful portable tool for students with and without disabilities. Students can use this portable keyboard to learn keyboarding skills, write, take notes, and keep work organized. It can be used in the classroom (Figure 13.9), outside, or at home. The *AlphaSmart*

Figure 13.9 A Student Using an *AlphaSmart* Computer

3000 runs on three AA batteries and gives 700 hours of writing time. *AlphaSmart* also comes with sticky keys, **slow keys** (the computer recognizes only the key presses that are a certain length and disregards others), and auto-repeat control. There are four different keyboard layouts: QWERTY, Dvorak, left handed, and right handed. Students can use the keyboard to type their text, edit it, and then transfer it to a printer or directly to their computer for further modifications.

Building Design for the Special Education Student

When our education building was constructed, the doors were so heavy it was impossible for students with physical disabilities to push them open. Furthermore, the ramps were not adequate. The administration fixed both problems. They installed enlarged buttons that enabled people to open the doors automatically. In addition, they corrected the ramps so that students with wheelchairs could readily use them. Such modifications in school building design are essential so that students with disabilities can have the same access as those without disabilities. Classroom furniture must be modified. Light switches must be lowered. The furniture should be arranged so teachers and students can move easily around the room.

Software for the Special Education Classroom

Recommended Software
Programs for Students with Special Needs

For a listing of recommended software for students with special needs go to the Online Learning Center.

Today, many software programs help students with disabilities learn. The software ranges from tutorials to drill and practice. In recent years, there has been an emphasis on software that aids students who are diagnosed with reading problems to improve their proficiency. Because of this emphasis, many software programs focus on building vocabulary and developing phonetics skills and decoding skills. Let us now look at a selection of programs that are especially useful to the special education teacher.

Reading

Don Johnston offers a series of *Start-to-Finish Gold* books that motivate students who are struggling with reading. They are high-interest, controlled-vocabulary books that include abridged selections of classic literature, sports biographies, history biographies, original mysteries, and retellings of Sherlock Holmes mysteries. These books range from *The Red Badge of Courage* to the story of *Romeo and Juliet*. *Start-to-Finish* books help students who are two or more grades behind in reading or who are unsuccessful readers. They aid students with language disorders, students learning English as a second language, and those with spelling and writing difficulties. The program comes with a computer book, audiocassette, and paperback book. In Figure 13.10, a page from *Romeo and Juliet* is shown. The student has the option of listening to the book or reading silently. Students can use single switches to read the books by themselves. Don Johnston has expanded the series with the *Start-to-Finish Blue* books for more advanced students.

Along the same lines, Optimum Resources' *High School Reading Comprehension Series* reinforces reading comprehension, analysis skills, and evaluation abilities. This

Figure 13.10 *Start-to-Finish* Books

© Copyright Don Johnston, Incorporated. Used with permission.

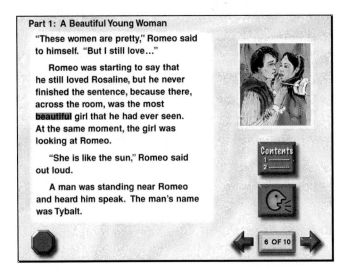

high-interest series features sound, music, and comprehension questions. One of the more popular topics included is fashion. Because of teenage interest in this topic, it encourages the reluctant teenage reader to read. In Figure 13.11, the reader answers a question about fashion and style.

Figure 13.11 *Fashion and Style*

© Optimum Resource, Inc. Used with permission.

Edmark Reading Program Level 1 and 2 (Riverdeep) is designed for students (K–Adult) who are struggling with basic reading skills. Using this program, students improve their sight recognition, learn the meaning of words, practice comprehension, and learn to use specific words in story content. The program uses short instructional steps, repetition, and positive reinforcement. Graphics can be turned off for the older student or adult. The management portion of the program is automatic so the individual student's progress is tracked. This program contains universal access features such as a touch window and single-switch compatibility. There is a choice of a standard interface or a simple interface for students who find it difficult to concentrate.

Simon S.I.O. (Sounds It Out), by Don Johnston, for pre-K to grade 2, is an interactive phonics tool designed to help students practice letter sounds. This program (Figure 13.12) features a helpful on-screen tutor, which is available for 31 levels of

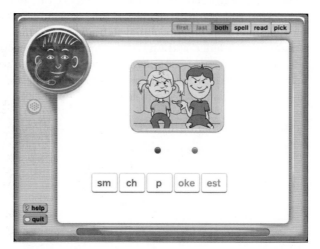

Figure 13.12 *Simon S.I.O.*

© Copyright Don Johnston, Incorporated. Used with permission.

sounds and words. Colorful graphics, digitized sound, and animation motivate and entertain the students during the learning process. *Simon S.I.O.* has a management component that enables the teacher to track the progress of multiple students and customize sound and word lessons. This product can be used with ESL students.

Word Processing Applications

Word processing is one of the most commonly used applications for students with learning disabilities (Holzberg, 1994). Students who have not written very much become motivated to write by word processing software. Talking word processors such as *Write:OutLoud* (Figure 13.13) can prove very beneficial for the student with learning disabilities. *Write:OutLoud* speaks letters, words, and sentences as they are typed. Students

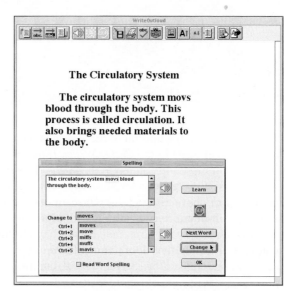

Figure 13.13 *Write: OutLoud*

© Copyright Don Johnston, Incorporated. Used with permission.

can then correct their writing. The word processor highlights text as it reads it. Students can include graphics in their writing or import graphics from other sources. On-screen tools with speech enable students to work without using menus. The word processor also comes with large font sizes to make the letters easier to read and a talking spell checker.

Another program that is helpful for writing is *Co:Writer 4000,* a writing assistant with word-prediction capabilities that will work with any word processor. A student simply types a letter, and *Co:Writer* suggests likely word choices and even reads the choices aloud (Figure 13.14). Students thus learn to make word choices. In addition, *Co:Writer* comes with built-in grammar prediction, which helps with such items as capitalization, spelling, and verb tense.

Figure 13.14
Co:Writer 4000

© Copyright Don Johnston, Incorporated. Used with permission.

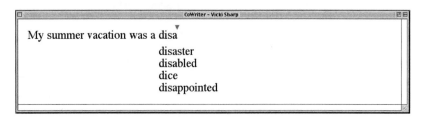

Clicker 4 is a writing and multimedia tool for students of all ability ranges. *Clicker* is a talking word processor that helps students write with pictures and words. After a student types a sentence, the sentence is spoken. Students also have the option of hearing each word said as they type it into the word processor. Students can also record their own speech. Figure 13.15 shows a *Clicker 4* screen. The top part of the screen is the

Figure 13.15 *Clicker 4*

© Crick Software Ltd. 2002. Courtesy of Crick Software.

Clicker Writer, and the bottom of the screen is the *Clicker Grid.* When the student types in a word, it appears in the *Clicker Writer.* If the student clicks on a word in the *Clicker Grid,* it is automatically entered in the *Writer.* This program offers great quality speech, and it is easy to customize for students with disabilities. It comes with a range of accessibility options for individuals who cannot use the mouse or keyboard. The program features built-in auditory scanning with access for students who use switches. When students use the *Clicker Grid,* they do not have to touch the keyboard to build simple sentences. If the student does not want to create anything, he or she can access ready-made free materials at the company's website (http://www.learninggrids.com). *Wordbar* is Crick's writing tool for older students.

Finally, the Rolls-Royce of the word processors is *Aurora 3.0* (Aurora Systems, Inc). The program is expensive at $395, but it comes with a whole array of features such as advanced word prediction, a talking spell checker, phonetic spell matching, and homonym selection tools. *Aurora* has been specifically designed for students with learning disabilities. The program reads the material as the student types, facilitating instant correction. For more information on this program, visit its website (http://www.aurora-systems.com/).

Math

Some programs use arcade-game formats to aid students in developing math skills such as adding and subtracting. These drill and practice programs are great ways of providing practice for students with learning disabilities. Some math tutorials give visual feedback to the student, and some simulation programs enable students to solve problems without personal risk. Two very fine programs are *Access to Math* (Don Johnston) and *Number Concepts 1 with Oshi the Otter* (IntelliTools, Inc.).

Access to Math is a talking math worksheet that aids students in learning addition, subtraction, multiplication, and division. This program gives students feedback on which problems are answered correctly, which need more work, and which are incorrect.

Number Concepts 1 with Oshi the Otter is a basic addition and subtraction program for very young students or those with disabilities, grades K–2. This program tutors the student on basic addition and subtraction. Oshi the Otter guides students working on beginning addition and subtraction problems at the tide pool, practicing counting with sea creatures, and helping an eel decide which school of fish is greater in number.

Drill and practice programs such as *Quarter Mile* (Barnum Software) and the *Math Blaster* series (Knowledge Adventure) are very useful for students with disabilities. These programs enable the students to work at their own pace and receive immediate feedback on math skills.

Science, Social Studies, and Miscellaneous Programs

There are many interesting programs in social studies and science. *Talking Walls* (Edmark), which was discussed in Chapter 12, helps students discover the stories behind some of the world's most interesting walls. Edmark's *Travel the World with Timmy! Deluxe* teaches students about people, places, and cultures. Students visit five different countries: Argentina, France, Japan (Figure 13.16), Kenya, and Russia. They learn stories,

Figure 13.16 *Travel the World with Timmy! Deluxe*

© Riverdeep Interactive Learning Limited.

When Dorothy got there, she watched sumo wrestling.

songs, crafts, and games and practice foreign language skills. Edmark's *Travel the World with Timmy! Deluxe* comes with a special talking picture dictionary and single-switch compatibility. When the program's scanning is turned on, a highlight goes from choice to choice, and the student uses a single-switch device to make a choice. Also, Edmark's *Virtual Lab Series* (Riverdeep) helps students build practical knowledge about light and electricity. These programs come with a built-in tutor and single-switch technology.

Multimedia

Inspiration (Inspiration), *BuildAbility* (Don Johnston), and *Visual Voice Tools* (Edmark) are three special programs that can help students with visual learning, multimedia authoring, and voice control. *Inspiration* is a powerful visual learning tool that helps students organize their thoughts (see Chapter 8). The students can visually map a story such as *Are You My Mother*? (Figure 13.17). In so doing they gain a greater understanding of the story's content.

Figure 13.17
Inspiration

Used by permission of Inspiration Software, Inc.

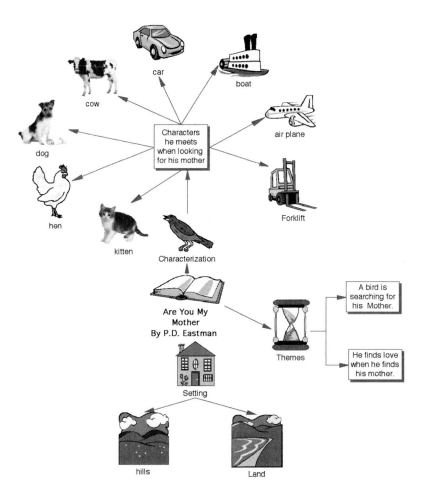

BuildAbility (Don Johnson) is unique multimedia authoring program designed for literacy activities and lessons. Teachers and students easily can build multimedia pages and storybooks. Teachers can use this tool to create instant lessons and books for the class. Students can use the one-click toolbar (Figure 13.18) to create their own multi-

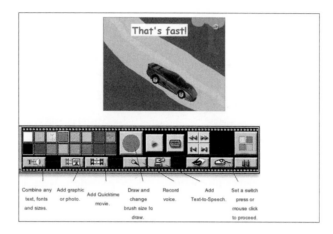

Figure 13.18
BuildAbility

© Copyright Don Johnston, Incorporated. Used with permission.

media productions. Students can add sound, text, movies, and pictures and even record sound. After the book is created the text is read aloud, and the words are highlighted to help the students with reading difficulties. Students with disabilities can use this program's single-switch options. Teachers and students have the option of creating a series of single-switch activities. Everyone can share his or her own book or activity using the *BuildAbility* player.

Finally, *Visual Voice Tools* is an assortment of tools that help students develop fine control over their voices. The program begins with simple sound awareness and progresses through multiple aspects of voice. The suggested users are students with a variety of speech disorders, hearing disorders, or physical problems that limit voice output.

On page 336 is a checklist to use when evaluating assistive/adaptive technology.

Laws Affecting Special Education

In 1949, no laws existed that required a school district to educate a student with special needs. If a student was diagnosed as having mental retardation, he or she usually was placed in a separate school or institution for children with disabilities. If there was no school or institution that could accommodate this student, the school district was not required by law to provide an education, and it was up to the parent or guardian to find a solution to the problem.

Assistive/Adaptive Technology Checklist*

Directions: Examine the following items and determine which ones you feel are important for your current teaching situation. Place an X on each line for which the technology meets your needs.

Hardware

_____ 1. Handheld devices

_____   a. Scans type and edits text

_____   b. Converts print documents into electronic format

_____   c. Has outlining and word prediction capability

_____   d. Exchanges files with PC and Palm applications

_____   e. Uploads to printer and computer

_____   f. Pronounces text, syllabication, spelling, and definitions

_____   g. Has built-in loudspeaker and earphone jack

_____ 2. Computer accessibility

_____   a. Displays large type, reverses print color, offers varying gray scale, and uses sound in place of visual output

_____   b. Alternative keyboard options include sticky keys and slow keys

_____   c. Has mouse options and touch-free or alternative input devices

_____   d. Is power activated with a single key

_____   e. Translates text on screen into Braille

_____   f. Prints out any size text or prints in Braille

_____ 3. Ease of use

_____   a. Memory requirements not too high

_____   b. Is software and hardware compatible

_____   c. Cost not too high

_____   d. Meets training requirements

Software

_____ 1. Reading programs

_____   a. Reads aloud individual words or whole passages

_____   b. Has comprehension and analysis checks

_____   c. Tracks progress of students and customizes lessons

_____   d. Offers voice and corrective feedback

_____   e. Creates personalized stories/movies

_____   f. Includes pictures, graphics, digitized sound, and animation

_____   g. Has high-interest stories with controlled vocabulary

_____   h. Has universal access features

_____   i. Has bilingual capabilities

_____ 2. Speech products and synthesizers

_____   a. Reads content from electronic documents/textbooks, word processors, and the Internet

_____   b. Is downloadable to MP3 or WAV formats

_____   c. Speaks Web page information and e-mail

_____   d. Has voice recognition to create documents, browse the Web, e-mail, and navigate the desktop

_____   e. Develops sound awareness and other aspects of voice

_____ 3. Writing programs and word processing applications

_____   a. Outlines and organizes writing

_____   b. Has visual tools to map ideas and stories

_____   c. Has speech/talking word processing capabilities

_____   d. Imports graphics from other sources

_____   e. Has word and grammar prediction capability

_____   f. Writes with pictures and words

_____   g. Has adjustable level of feedback and auditory support to help students self-correct

Rating Scale

Rate the tools by placing a check on the appropriate line.

Excellent_____ Very Good_____ Good_____ Fair_____ Poor_____

*Courtesy of Sarah Hall.

Parent groups organized in response to the fact that their children were not being given access to a general education, and a movement to educate the student with disabilities grew. At the same time, other factors contributed to the rise in the need for special education; these included changes in the economy, demographic shifts, changes in the family structure, and greater awareness of substance abuse and child abuse. As a result, laws were enacted to make sure that all students received optimal educational opportunities regardless of their disabilities.

Table 13.1 highlights a number of key pieces of legislation that were important in ensuring that all students receive the same educational opportunities regardless of ability.

A key component of IDEA 1997 was that preschool, elementary school, and secondary schoolchildren should receive a free appropriate public education (FAPE). For these students to receive a FAPE, schools are required to provide the students

Table 13.1 Equal Educational Opportunity Laws

Law	Accomplishment
Section 504 of the Rehabilitation Act of 1973 (PL 93–112)	This first piece of federal legislation addressing the civil rights of people with disabilities ensures that individuals with disabilities have equal opportunities in programs that receive federal funds.
The Education for All Handicapped Children Act (PL 94–142) (1975)	Signed by President Gerald Ford, this key piece of legislation mandates that there be appropriate and free education for students with disabilities.
The Education for All Handicapped Children Act Amendments of 1986 (PL 99–457)	This amendment expanded services for infants and young children who have disabilities or are at risk and for their families.
The Individuals with Disabilities Education Act (IDEA) (PL 101–476) (1990)	Known as the "Person First" law, this act changed the title of the special education law to the Individuals with Disabilities Education Act to emphasize the child first and then the disability.
The Americans with Disabilities Act (ADA) (PL 101–336) (1990)	Signed by President George H. W. Bush, this law provided major civil rights protection for people with disabilities by breaking down the barriers in areas of transportation, telecommunication, employment, and public accommodation.
The Individuals with Disabilities Education Act (IDEA) Amendments of 1997 (PL 105–17)	President William Jefferson Clinton signed these amendments into law on June 4, 1997. A focal point is to ensure access to general education curriculum for students with disabilities. These amendments placed more emphasis on the individualized education program (IEP), improving the student's progress and involvement in the general education curriculum. For a more complete explanation, visit the IDEA Practices website, sponsored by Idea Partnership (http://www.ideapractices.org).

with assistive technology (wheelchairs, switches, speech enhancement devices, etc., see http://www.ideapractices.org/law/regulations/index.php). Because of the enactment of these laws students with disabilities could no longer be separated from other students and still be considered to be treated equally. Students with disabilities are now required to be placed in the regular classroom whenever possible. Schools have tried to provide such equal access through collaboration, mainstreaming, and inclusion.

Collaboration

Collaboration is a group endeavor that involves students, families, educators, and community agencies. All these people work together, sharing resources, decision making, and skills for the student's good. The school district provides the resources and support so that these agencies and people can work cooperatively and focus on the student's needs. In some instances, the special education teacher works with the regular classroom teacher to help students with disabilities adjust to the regular classroom. The special education teacher might team-teach with the classroom teacher and modify the core curriculum to make it accessible to children with special needs.

Mainstreaming

After the passage of the 1975 Education for All Handicapped Children Act (PL 94–142), the term **mainstreaming** was adopted to refer to part-time and full-time programs that educated students with disabilities alongside their nondisabled peers. Students diagnosed with disabilities would be placed in regular classrooms all or part of the day. Students in mainstreaming programs might leave the general-education classroom for time in the resource room or for speech and language services. Special education teachers were in charge of these students, and the responsibility for their progress rested with them.

Special education services did not have to be provided in the regular classroom. Often, the decision to place a student in a mainstreamed class was based on the educator's assessment of the student's readiness. Students thus had to earn the right to be educated in a full-time general-education classroom. Mainstreaming was broadly interpreted, which led to many different implementations.

Inclusion

Inclusion grew out of mainstreaming and shares many of its goals. **Inclusion** is based on the concept of the least-restrictive environment (LRE). LRE requires that schools make every reasonable attempt to educate students with disabilities with their peers who do not have disabilities. *Inclusion* has all students attending regular classes unless the school can show a reason this is not feasible. *Full inclusion* requires that all students be educated in a regular classroom regardless of the severity of disability.

A successful inclusion program has a planned system of training and supports. Such a program usually includes the collaboration of a multidisciplinary team comprised of peers, classroom teachers, special educators, and family members. A disabled student is a full member of the classroom and receives special education within the regular classroom. For inclusion to be effective, teachers must be flexible and responsive to students' needs.

The CHIME Charter Elementary School, started by California State University's College of Education, is a national model for inclusive and accessible education. This school offers a free public education to its student population. It provides a fully inclusive setting where children of all abilities are educated together in a supportive and compassionate environment. Students who are deaf or hard of hearing and students without disabilities are all taught American Sign Language (ASL). The school is also a laboratory demonstration site for teacher preparation. Parents are very involved in the school, which is an important component of this inclusive setting. Because of the success of this school, CHIME opened a middle school August 7, 2003, at its sister campus.

Advantages of Inclusion. Some educational experts feel that **inclusive education**— regular classroom attendance regardless of disabilities—is very important to the well-being of the student with disabilities. The students in an inclusive classroom make academic progress comparable to and sometimes better than that of students who are segregated (Ryndak, Downing, Morrison, and Williams, 1996; Waldron and McLeskey, 1998; Cawley, Hayden, Cade, and Baker-Kroczynski, 2002; Rea, McLaughlin, and Walther-Thomas, 2002). One reason is that disabled students learn from watching the other students in the regular classroom. In an inclusive classroom students who do not have disabilities learn how to be more sensitive to students with disabilities and their needs. Students with disabilities become better acquainted with a wider range of people in their community, enabling them to manage more effectively their life outside of school.

Drawbacks to Inclusion. Even though there are many supporters of inclusion, they are also many opponents (Smith, Polloway, Patton, and Dowdy, 2001; Fuchs and Fuchs, 1994–1995). Schools have often disagreed with parents on the interpretation of special education laws. When students with special needs are placed in the regular classroom, the teacher may become overwhelmed and feel he or she cannot meet the needs of any of the students. The parents of nondisabled students may object because they feel that the special-needs students require too much attention. Also, attendance in a regular classroom does not guarantee that the student with disabilities will acquire the skills she or he needs to function in society. In addition, these laws put extra financial demands on school systems. For instance, when a school purchases software or hardware, according to law it must purchase adaptive equipment, such as discovery switches and voice recognition software, to make sure that the special education student can use the equipment. This equipment is far more costly than other technology resources. Schools with budget problems may hesitate to purchase equipment that will benefit only a small population of students. The speed with which technology changes hampers a school district's ability to keep abreast of the latest developments. Software and hardware compatibility issues and computer memory requirements are even greater for students with special needs.

There is also disagreement on how gifted students should be taught. Recently, there has been a trend to eliminate separate programs for the gifted student in favor of setting higher academic standards for all students. However, in 1998, a new legislative initiative called The Gifted and Talented Students Education Act provided grants to states to strengthen services for the gifted student (National Association for Gifted Children communiqué, 1998; http://www.nagc.org).

Inclusive education may lead parents to have unrealistic expectations for their children. Assistive technology is terrific and has helped many students, but it cannot suddenly "cure" students with severe physical and mental disabilities; it can only help them overcome and succeed in spite of the disabilities.

Adapting Classroom Lesson Plans for Students with Disabilities

By adapting classroom lessons, the teacher can meet the needs of the student with disabilities. The teacher should divide the class into small groups so that students can help each other. They then can work in pairs, complementing each other's strengths. Teachers can use a buddy system in which one student mentors another. If appropriate, teachers can use peer tutoring or cross-age tutoring. For any lesson, they can choose software that is auditory to help students who have trouble reading. The teacher can have someone read a written script to help with directions. Before writing a book report or composition, students might use a graphic organizer such as *Inspiration,* which visually represents the material and breaks it down into small steps. If the students need writing help, they can use a talking word processor or word prediction program.

Classroom Lesson Plans

I. USING FACE PUPPETS

Subject

Language Arts and Reading

Grade(s)

2–5

Objectives

Students will read a book, create a mask that portrays the main character in the story, and retell the story.

Standards

- NCTE English Language Arts Standards 3, 4
- ISTE NETS for Students 2, 3

Materials

You will need *MaskWorld* or a similar program.

Procedures

1. Arrange the class into pairs in which the strengths of one student complement the strengths of the other.
2. Assign a short story for each pair to read and discuss.
3. Have students use a mask-making program such as *MaskWorld* (Visions Technology in Education) to print out a mask to help illustrate their stories.
4. Next, have the students attach the faces to paper plates, sticks (Figure 13.19), or paper bags.

Figure 13.19
MaskWorld
Reprinted with permission of Visions Technology in Education™.
www.ToolsforTeachers.com.

5. Ask students to share their stories with the class by retelling them.

Adaptation

If students have reading difficulties, simply tape record the story. This way a student can stop the recording when he or she wishes. There are numerous free library audio-cassettes of books and short stories. Furthermore, Don Johnston has a collection of *Start-to-Finish* books that can be used for this activity. For this series, there are audio-cassettes, books, and CD-ROMs.

II. USING THE WEB TO DO HISTORICAL RESEARCH

Subject

Social Studies and History

Grade(s)

5–8

Objective

Using Internet sites such as *The American Civil War Homepage* (http://sunsite.utk.edu/civil-war/), students will learn about the Civil War.

Standards

- National Council for the Social Studies Curriculum Standards 2, 4, 5
- ISTE NETS for Students 4, 5

Materials

You will need an Internet connection and a word processing program.

Procedures

1. Arrange the class into pairs in which the strengths of one student complement the strengths of the other.
2. Have each group research some aspect of the Civil War. For example, a group could investigate the causes of the Civil War or contrast and compare the North and South.
3. Have the students search the Internet for information. Make sure they carefully document their research.
4. Ask students to use a word processor to create a paper explaining their findings.
5. Have the students discuss their papers in class.

Adaptation

If your students are visually impaired or blind, they can use a Web reader such as *Home Page Reader for Windows* (IBM). This program enables the student to open the Web page and listen to the page being read, including the text, data, and graphic descriptions. For students with visual impairments, teachers can print the material in big print. Teachers also can have students use keyboards with large-size letter stickers and software enlargement products.

III. WRITING STORIES

Subject

Language Arts and Writing and Planning

Grade(s)

2–6

Objective

Students will develop their language skills by writing a story.

Standards

- NCTE English Language Arts Standards 5, 12
- ISTE NETS for Students 2, 3

Materials

You will need a planner such as *Kidspiration* and a word processor such as *Write:Out-loud* or a combination word processor and planner such as *Writer's Companion.*

Procedures

1. Arrange the class into pairs in which the strengths of one student complements the strengths of the other.
2. Have students use an organizer, such as *Kidspiration,* to plan their stories.
3. Ask students to use a word processor to type their stories.

Adaptation

Use large print for students with vision limitations. *Kidspiration* comes with a speech and recording feature so the students can record sounds and hear their planner. Use a word processor with speech output such as *Write:OutLoud* so the students can hear their stories and see them.

IV. TRAVELING TO DIFFERENT COUNTRIES

Subject

Geography

Grade(s)

2 and Up

Objectives

Using the Internet, students will learn about a city, state, or region, and from this information create travel brochures.

Standards

- National Council for the Social Studies Curriculum Standards 3
- NCTE English Language Arts Standards 5, 12
- ISTE NETS for Students 3, 4

Materials

You will need an Internet connection and a print graphics program such as *Stationery Studio* (FableVision)

Procedures

1. Divide the class into small groups.
2. Have the students choose a city, state, or region.
3. Have the students pretend they are in charge of a tourist bureau for this area.

4. Ask students to research the region's geographic features, economy, restaurants, state capital, major attractions, hotel accommodations, camping facilities, and any other pertinent information. They can use the following Internet sites:
   a. State Report Information from Multnomah County Library in Portland, Oregon, http://www.multnomah.lib.or.us/lib/homework/statesch.html
   b. Sites with state facts information, http://www.multnomah.lib.or.us/lib/homework/state2hc.html#general
   c. Yahoo! Get Local, http://local.yahoo.com/
   d. Hometown USA, http://www.hometownusa.com
   e. Uscity.net, http://www.uscity.net/
   f. 411 Cities, http://www.411-cities.com/
   g. About.com's Cities/Towns, http://home.about.com/citiestowns/
   h. 2AccessAmerica.com, http://www.accessamer.com/
   i. Travel.excite.com, http://travel.excite.com/
   j. Travelfacts.com, http://www.travelfacts.com/
5. If the students do not want to limit themselves to these sites, have them use search engines to find other sites.
6. Have students in lower grades use a program such as *Stationery Studio* (FableVision) to create a mini book and students in upper grades use a program such as *Microsoft Word* to create a travel brochure.

Adaptation

If your students are visually impaired, they can use a Web reader such as *Home Page Reader for Windows* (IBM). You can print the material in big print. You can also have students use keyboards with large-size letter stickers and software enlargement products.

V. THE ALPHABET

Subject

Language Arts and English

Grade(s)

K–1

Objective

Students will develop their language skills by creating an alphabet book.

Standards

- NCTE English Language Arts Standards 3, 4, 7
- ISTE NETS for Students 2, 3

Materials

You will need a talking word processor.

Procedures

1. Divide the students into groups of two.
2. Tell each group to create an alphabet book.
3. Have each group use a talking word processor program such as *Write:OutLoud* to type a letter of the alphabet in a large font size. This word processor will speak the letter as it is typed.
4. Tell each group to find words to illustrate five letters of the alphabet. Students can look in books placed in the room.
5. When the students are finished, have them share the words they chose to illustrate the letters.

Adaptation

Students with handicaps may need an alternative keyboard with large numbers and letters such as *IntelliKeys* (IntelliTools). For students with learning disabilities, the computer should have speech output to read text. A tape recorder can be used to play the directions over and over.

VI. COMPARISON SHOPPING

Subject

Math and Problem Solving

Grade(s)

2–6

Objective

Students will learn how to shop by using a program such as *Ice Cream Truck* or *Hot Dog Stand* (Sunburst).

Standards

- National Council of Teachers of Mathematics Standards 6, 8
- ISTE NETS for Students 5, 6

Materials

You will need a program similar to *Ice Cream Truck*.

Procedures

1. Divide the class into small groups.
2. Have each group use *Ice Cream Truck* to assume the role of the owner and driver of an ice cream truck. Groups will begin with $500 (Figure 13.20) and try to make as much money as possible.

Figure 13.20 *Ice Cream Truck*

Reprinted by permission of Sunburst Technology.

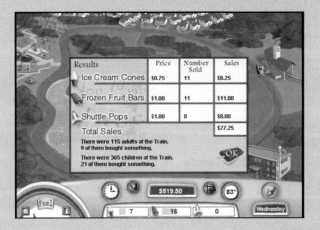

3. Have the groups decide where they want to sell the ice cream and how much they want to charge. These decisions are based on such factors as day of the week and temperature.
4. Ask the class to discuss strategies.
5. Have the students work on the project during the week.
6. At the end of the week, ask the students to discuss results.
7. To expand on the activities, have students conduct experiments to determine what type of ice cream adults and children prefer.

Adaptation

For students with low-vision problems, change the control panel to enlarge the text. The computer should have a voice synthesizer. Students with handicaps may need an alternative keyboard with large numbers and letters.

VII. BRUSHING YOUR TEETH

Subject

Science and health

Grade(s)

K and above

Objective

Students will learn how to create an instructional simulation.

STANDARDS

- National Science Education Standards F1
- ISTE NETS for Students 2, 3

Materials

You will need *PowerPoint* or a similar program, a computer with sound capabilities, and a digital camera.

Procedures

1. Divide the students into small groups.
2. Instruct each group to create an instructional simulation. For example, one group may want to show the class how to brush their teeth properly.
3. Have students take pictures of each step that is required to complete the assignment.
4. After they save their pictures, ask them to copy and paste them into *PowerPoint.*
5. Next have the groups record instructions for each slide. For example (Figure 13.21), students may start with "Place your toothbrush at a 45-degree angle against the gums" (ADA, 2003). If the class is advanced, they may enhance the recording by identifying the different types of teeth (molars, incisors, etc.).
6. Have students share their presentations.

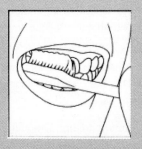

Figure 13.21 How to Brush

Image provided courtesy of the American Dental Association.

Adaptation

This activity can be used with students with developmental disabilities. However, the teacher should assemble the *PowerPoint* presentation. The students can take pictures and learn from the instructions. Wissick and Schweder (2001) wrote a creative article on making a grilled cheese sandwich. See the references for the complete citation.

Summary

The computer has been invaluable in helping special education students realize their potential. This chapter examined some of the key legislation affecting special education. We considered different ways of integrating technology into the classroom. In addition, we studied seven ready-to-use lesson plans for any student and how these lesson plans could be adapted for students with special needs. The chapter also reviewed some of the software and hardware that is available for these exceptional students. We explored terms such as *mainstreaming, inclusion,* and *collaboration* along with the problems and issues facing special education teachers, parents, and students. Be sure to review the annotated list of award-winning special education programs on the Online Learning Center.

Study and Online Resources

Go to Chapter 13 in the Student Edition of the Online Learning Center at **www.mhhe.com/sharp5e** *to* **practice with key concepts, take chapter quizzes, read PowerWeb articles** *and* **news feed updates** *related to technology in education, and* **access resources** *for learning about technology and integrating it into the classroom.*

Click on **Web Links** to link to the following websites.

About.com's Special Education Resources
This site is an encyclopedia of resources that covers topics such as adaptive P.E., autism, deafness, inclusion, intervention, gifted education, and special schools.

The Adaptive Technology Resource Centre from the University of Toronto

The Adaptive Technology Resource Centre provides descriptions of adaptive technologies with links to various products and their vendors.

The Adaptive Technology Resource Centre (ATRC)

The Adaptive Technology Resource Centre supports access to information technology by people with disabilities.

American Sign Language Browser

This site presents hundreds of ASL signs using *QuickTime* movies.

American Sign Language Finger Spelling

At this site, see any word you input signed to learn the ASL alphabet easily. Take the interactive quiz to learn how well you are doing.

Arc Home Page

Arc Home Page describes the nation's largest voluntary organization committed to the welfare of children and adults with mental retardation and of their families. The site offers many articles, especially with regard to advocacy, and related links.

Catalyst

The Catalyst is a quarterly newsletter on microcomputers and related technology for children and adults with any disability. It focuses mainly on special education and rehabilitation.

Center for Improvement of Early Reading Achievement

This site contains information about early literacy acquisition and effective strategies for teaching reading. CIERA publications offer solutions to persistent problems in learning and teaching beginning reading.

Children with Disabilities

This site offers information about advocacy, education, employment, health, housing, recreation, technical assistance, and transportation covering a wide array of developmental, physical, and emotional disabilities.

Closing the Gap

This site, owned and operated by Budd and Dolores Hagen, is a goldmine of information on the latest computer-related products available for people with special needs. It contains many tips on software and hardware for assistive technology. You can access many of its features without being a member.

Council of Exceptional Children

The Council of Exceptional Children's site contains publications, products, discussions and forums, a legislative action center, and links. There is a link to *Eric Clearinghouse on Dis-*

abilities and Gifted Education (http://ericec.org/), which has a searchable database and is rich in resources and links.

disAbility.gov

This comprehensive U.S. site provides a one-stop online access to disability resources, services, and information available throughout the federal government. Topics range from children and youth to tax credits and deductions.

Disability Resources, Inc.

Disability Resources is a nonprofit organization that publishes the online *Disability Resources Monthly (DRM).* The site includes the DRM WebWatcher, an easy-to-use guide to WWW resources, and Librarians' Connections, providing information about listservs, professional associations, and assistive technology to librarians who serve people with disabilities.

Education World: Special Education

This site contains lesson plans, information, and tools for the special education community and includes a special section for parents and teachers.

HandSpeak: A Sign Language Dictionary Online

HandSpeak is an animated dictionary of sign language. The signs are grouped alphabetically and by categories. A new sign is added daily. It is a great introduction to sign language, a review of vocabulary for the deaf, a quick tutorial for parents or teachers of hearing-impaired children, or just fun for anyone interested in the topic.

LD Online

LD Online, a service of the WETS PBS station, is an interactive guide to learning disabilities for parents, teachers, and kids.

Macomb Intermediate School District (MISD): Teacher Resources on the World Wide Web

This Macomb County school district in Clinton Township, of southeastern Michigan, provides a good collection of sites for assistive technology, curriculum planning, and other special education topics.

The National Information Center for Children and Youth with Disabilities

Developed by the National Information and Referral Center, this site provides information on issues and concerns related to disabilities for families and professionals. The focus of the information is on children and young adults.

National Institute for Urban School Improvement

The National Institute for Urban School Improvement, hosted by the University of Colorado at Denver, helps you stay abreast of new developments in urban education and inclusive schooling. Check out the Library for a searchable database that bridges the gap between research and practice in the overlapping fields of urban education and inclusive schooling. Updated monthly, it features over 425 annotated references to books, journal articles, videos, position papers, project reports, and a variety of other media.

Office of Special Education
This site from the Curry School of Education at the University of Virginia contains a Web-based collection of resources designed to serve parents, professionals, and others interested in special education.

The Parent–Educator Connection
This site provides information to families and educators of students and young adults with disabilities. The site has a wide variety of resources. Click on Disability Resources (http://www.aea267.k12.ia.us/ curriculum/speced.html) to find numerous links.

Parenting Special Needs
This About.com site provides information covering assistive technology, learning and mental disabilities, muscular dystrophy diseases, and other special education topics.

SchwabLearning.org—A Parent's Guide to Helping Kids with Learning Differences
SchwabLearning.org provides a roadmap to understanding learning differences and disabilities with over 200 pages covering everything from curriculum planning to family/social issues.

SCR*Tech www 4 teachers
SCR*Tech is rich with content that includes online journals, Internet technology lessons, special education links, a technology glossary, technology lessons, tutorials, assistive technology links, and portfolio assessment information. Click on Assistive Technology to learn more about assistive technology and how to locate assistive devices and find funding.

Secondary School Special Education Resources
About.com provides a resource center for secondary teachers covering everything from ADD to IEPs to visual impairment.

Silent Thunder Animations Page
Learn some common words in sign language at this animated site.

Special Education at the University of Kansas
The Department of Special Education at the University of Kansas provides a variety of Internet resources on disabilities and special education research projects, including 37 thematic units developed by elementary teachers.

Special Education Resources
TeachersFirst's E-Ready special education resource section provides a wealth of information on special education, specially targeted to the regular classroom teacher or those who may be working in special education for the first time. Included are a collection of lessons adapted or created for special education students. There is also a complete section for parents.

Special Education Resources on the Internet (SERI)
SERI is a collection of special education resources including information about general disabilities, legal and law issues, physical and health disorders, and learning disabilities.

Special Needs Education Network (SNE)
This site offers projects to aid parents and teachers of children with special needs as disparate as attention deficit disorder (ADD), autism, blindness, deafness, fetal alcohol syndrome, and many others. It is an invaluable "List of Lists" for links to services to aid these children, and it includes an SNEparentalk-L mailing list for discussing topics in the area of special needs education.

Sped Online
This site, created by a K–3 cognitive disabilities teacher at Mosinee Elementary School in Wisconsin, provides resources for those interested in special education issues.

Teaching Ideas for Early Childhood Special Educators
Linda's Teaching Ideas is a collection of teaching ideas for early childhood special education which range from making butter to making molding clay. There are numerous creative and fun ideas as well as a collection of worthwhile links.

Texas School for the Blind and Visually Impaired
This site includes an assortment of resources and instructional materials such as assessment resources for the visually and hearing impaired, instructional resources, adaptive technology resources, downloadable Braille materials, and information about eye diseases.

Yahoo! Directory: Special Education
These are resources indexed by Yahoo!

Chapter Mastery Test

To the Instructor: *Refer to the Instructor's Manual for the answers to the Mastery Questions. This manual has additional questions and resource materials.*

Let us check for chapter comprehension with a short mastery test. Key Terms, Computer Lab, and Suggested Readings and References follow the test.

1. How can the Internet be used to help students with special needs?
2. How does technology benefit students with special needs?
3. What is a *speech synthesizer*? What is the relationship between a speech synthesizer and voice input?
4. Distinguish among *mainstreaming, inclusion,* and *collaboration.*
5. Give two examples of output devices that help students with low vision or blindness overcome their disability.
6. What is *word prediction software* and why is it helpful for students with learning disabilities?
7. Why are the Individuals with Disabilities Education Act Amendments of 1997 (PL 105–17) important to students with disabilities?
8. What are some ways you can rearrange the computer equipment to make it easier for the student with special needs?
9. What is a *touch screen* and how can it be used to provide help to students with disabilities? List some advantages as well as disadvantages of this technology.
10. How can the computer enhance the development of reading skills for the child with learning disabilities?
11. Give two examples of input devices that help students with physical disabilities use the computer.

Key Terms

Adaptive or assistive technology   325–326
Collaboration   338
Discover switch   326
Exceptional children   321
Inclusion   338

Inclusive education   339
Keyboard emulators   326
Mainstreaming   338
Refreshable Braille display   324

Slow keys   328
Speech synthesis   323
Sticky keys   326
Touch screen   327

Touch-free switch   326
Voice recognition software   324

Computer Lab: Activities for Mastery and Your Portfolio

13.1 Using Computers in Special Education Read several scenarios and choose the technologies that will assist each child.

13.2 Use a multimedia program to develop a presentation for the class with special needs.

13.3 Using the computer, visit the White House site (http://www.whitehouse.gov). What are some of the advantages and disadvantages of this trip for a student with special needs over a real-life visit to the White House?

13.4 Using word processing software, write a story for the special needs class using students' names. Illustrate this story with pictures and sounds. Print the story and read it to the class.

Suggested Readings and References

Abbott, Chris. "Technology That Opens Doors." *Times Educational Supplement* 4206, no. 2 (February 7, 1997): 18.

Alliance for Technology Access. *Computer and Web Resources for People with Disabilities: A Guide to Exploring Today's Assistive Technology,* 3d ed. Alameda, Calif.: Hunter House, 2000.

Allington, R. L. "You Can't Learn Much from Books You Can't Read." *Educational Leadership* 603 (2002): 16–19.

Beigel, Andrew R. "Assistive Technology Assessment: More Than the Device." *Intervention in School and Clinic* 35, no. 4 (March 2000): 237.

Bender, Renet L., and William N. Bender. "Computer-Assisted Instruction for Students at Risk for ADHD, Mild Disabilities, or Academic Problems." Clearinghouse No. EC304880, February 20, 1996.

Brett, A. "Assistive and Adaptive Technology: Supporting Competence and Independence in Young Children with Disabilities." *Dimensions of Early Childhood* 24, no. 3 (1997): 14–15.

Bryant, B. R., and P. C. Seay. "The Technology-Related Assistance to Individuals with Disabilities Act: Relevance to Individuals with Learning Disabilities and Their Advocates." *Journal of Learning Disabilities* 31, no. 1 (1998): 4–15.

Bryant, D. P., B. R. Bryant, and Marshall U. Raskind. "Using Assistive Technology to Enhance the Skills of Students with Learning Disabilities." *Intervention in School and Clinic* 34, no. 1 (1998): 53–58.

Burke, Mack D., and Shanna L. Hagan. "Teaching Exceptional Children. What Curriculum Designs and Strategies Accommodate Diverse Learners?" *Teaching Exceptional Children* 31, no. 1 (September/October 1998): 34–38.

Castells, Manuel. *The Information Age: Economy, Society and Culture.* Boston: Blackwell, 1999.

Cavallero, Clara, and M. Haney. *Preschool Inclusion.* Baltimore: Paul H. Brookes, 1999.

Cawley, John, Shari Hayden, Elsa Cade, and Susan Baker-Kroczynski. "Including Students with Disabilities into the General Education Science Classroom." *Exceptional Children* 68, no. 4 (Summer 2002): 423–435.

Dacey, M., K. Eichleay, and J. McCauley. "The Student Access Map (SAM): Ensuring Access to the General Curriculum." *Closing the Gap* 11, no. 3 (2002): 1, 8–9, 23.

Dolan, B. "Universal Design for Learning." *Journal of Special Education Technology* 15, no. 4 (2000): 44–51.

Downing, June E. "Meeting the Communication Needs of Students with Severe and Multiple Disabilities in General Education Classrooms." *Exceptionality* 9, no. 3 (2001): 147–156.

Edyburn. D. L. "Reading Difficulties in the General Education Classroom: Taxonomy of Text Modification Strategies." *Closing the Gap* 21, no. 6 (2003): 1, 10–13, 30–31.

Edyburn, Dave L. "Assistive Technology and Students with Mild Disabilities." *Focus on Exceptional Children,* vol. 32, issue 9 (May 2000): 23–27.

Edyburn, Dave L. "Introduction to the Special Issue." *Remedial & Special Education* 24 issue 3 (May/June 2003): 130–132.

Edyburn, D. L. "Technology Integration Strategies: Universal Design and Technology Integration, Finding the Connections." *Closing the Gap,* 20, no. 1 (2001): 21–22.

Edyburn, Dave. "99 Essential Web Sites for Special Educators." *Special Education Technology Practice* (May/June 2002), 37–41.

Edyburn, Dave L. "2001 in Review: A Synthesis of the Special Education Technology Literature." *Journal of Special Education Technology* 17, no. 2 (Spring 2002): 5–24.

Freedman, Allen. *Computer Desktop Encyclopedia.* Point Pleasant, Pa.: The Computer Language Company, 2003.

Fuchs, L. S., and D. Fuchs. "Treatment Validity: A Unifying Concept for Reconceptualizing the Identification of Learning Disabilities." *Learning Disability Research and Practice* 13, no. 4 (1998): 204–219.

Fuchs, D., and L. S. Fuchs. "Sometimes Separate Is Better." *Educational Leadership* 52 (1994–1995): 22–24.

Hardman, Michael L., et al. *Human Exceptionality and Internet Guide,* 6th ed. Boston: Allyn and Bacon, 1999.

Heim, Judy. "Locking Out the Disabled." *PC World* 18, no. 9 (September 2000): 181.

Heward, William L. *Exceptional Children: An Introduction to Special Education,* 7th ed. Upper Saddle River, N.J.: Merrill, 2002.

Hitchcock, C., A. Meyer, D. Rose, and R. Jackson. "Providing New Access to the General Curriculum: Universal Design for Learning." *Teaching Exceptional Children* 35, no. 2 (2002): 8–17.

Holzberg, Carol S. "Technology in Special Education." *Technology and Learning* 14, no. 7 (April 1994): 18–21.

Howell, Richard. "Technological Aids for Inclusive Classrooms." *Theory into Practice* 35, no. 1 (Winter 1996): 58.

Kamp, Sue. "How Does 'Fair Use' Apply to Software Being Used in the Schools?" *Technology Connection* 5, no. 1 (1999): 19.

King, Thomas W. *Assistive Technology: Essential Human Factors.* Boston: Allyn and Bacon, 1999.

King-Sears. M. E. "Three Steps for Gaining Access to the General Educational Curriculum for Learners with Disabilities." *Intervention in School and Clinic* 37, no. 2 (2001): 67–76.

Koseinski, Susan, et al. "Computer-Assisted Instruction with Constant Time Delay to Teach Multiplication Facts to Students with Learning Disabilities." *Learning Disabilities Research Practices* 8, no. 3 (Summer 1993): 157–168.

Kusisto, Stephen. "Planet of the Blind Delta." *Journal of Developmental Disabilities,* December 29, 1998.

Lahm, Elizabeth A., and Beverly L. Nickels. "Assistive Technology Competencies for Special Educators." *Teaching Exceptional Children* 32, no. 1 (September/October 1999): 56.

Lauffer, Kimberly A. "Accommodating Students with Specific Writing Disabilities." *Journalism and Mass Communication Educator* 54, no. 4 (Winter 2000): 29.

Lewis, Rena B. "Changes in Technology Use in California's Special Education Programs." *Remedial and Special Education* 18, no. 4 (July/August 1997): 233.

Lewis, R. *Special Education Technologies: Classroom Applications.* Pacific Grove, Calif.: Brooks/Cole, 1993.

Lewis, Rena B., Tamarah M. Ashton, et al. "Improving the Writing Skills of Students with Learning Disabilities: Are Word Processors with Spelling and Grammar Checkers Useful?" *Learning Disabilities* 9, no. 3 (1999): 87–98.

Lewis, Rena B., Anne W. Graves, Tamarah M. Ashton, and Candace L. Kieley. "Word Processing Tools for Students with Learning Disabilities: A Comparison of Strategies to Increase Text Entry Speed." *Learning Disabilities Research and Practice* 13, no. 2 (1998): 95–108.

Lyman, Michael, and Mary Anne Mather. "Software for Special Needs." *Technology and Learning* 19, no. 4 (November/December 1998): 60.

Male, Mary. *Technology for Inclusion: Meeting the Special Needs of All Students.* Boston, Mass.: Allyn and Bacon, 2003.

Male, Mary, and Doug Gotthoffer. *Quick Guide to the Internet for Special Education.* Boston: Allyn and Bacon, 2000.

Mates, Barbara T., Doug Wakefield, and Judith M. Dixon. *Adaptive Technology for the Internet: Making Electronic Resources Accessible to All.* Chicago: American Library Association Editions, 2000.

McLeskey, James, and Nancy L. Waldron. "School Change and Inclusive Schools: Lessons Learned from Practice." *Phi Delta Kappan* 84, no. 1 (September 2002): 65–72.

McNaughton, David, et al. "Proofreading for Students with Learning Disabilities." *Learning Disabilities Research and Practice* 12, no. 1 (1997): 16–28.

Merbler, John B., Azar Hadadian, and Jean Ulman. "Using Assistive Technology in the Inclusive Classroom." *Preventing School Failure* 43, no. 3 (Spring 1999): 113.

Rea, Patricia J., Virginia L. McLaughlin, and Chriss Walther-Thomas. "Outcomes for Students with Learning Disabilities in Inclusive and Pullout Programs." *Exceptional Children* 68, no. 2 (Winter 2002): 203–222.

Robertson, Gladene, and Leonard P. Haines. "Positive Change Through Computer Networking." *Teaching Exceptional Children* 29, no. 6 (July/August 1997): 22.

Rose, D., and A. Meyer. *Teaching Every Student in the Digital Age.* Alexandria, Va.: ASCD, 2002. Available online at http://www.cast.org/teachingeverystudent/ideas/tes/.

Ryba, Ken, and Linda Selby. "Computers Empower Students with Special Needs." *Educational Leadership* 53, no. 2 (October 1995): 82.

Ryndak, D. L., J. E. Downing, A. P. Morrison, and L. J. Williams. "Parents: Perceptions of Educational Settings and Services for Children with Moderate or Severe Disabilities." *Remedial and Special Education* 17 (1996): 92–105.

Shiah, Rwey-Lin, et al. "The Effects of Computer-Assisted Instruction on Mathematical Problem Solving of Students with Learning Disabilities." *Exceptionality* 5 (1994–1995): 131–161.

Smith, Tom E., Edward A. Polloway, James Patlon, and Carol Dowdy. *Teaching Students with Special Needs in Inclusive Settings.* 4th ed. Boston: Pearson/Allyn and Bacon, 2003.

Stanovich, Paula J., and Anne Jordan. "Preparing General Educators to Teach in Inclusive Classrooms: Some Food for Thought." *Teacher Educator* 37, no. 3 (Winter 2002): 173–185.

Strong, William S. *The Copyright Book: A Practical Guide,* 5th ed. Cambridge, Mass.: MIT Press, 1999.

Trollinger, Gayle, and Rachel Slavkin. "Purposeful E-Mail as Stage 3 Technology." *Teaching Exceptional Children* 32, no. 1 (September/October 1999): 10.

United States Department of Education. *Twentieth Annual Report to Congress on the Implementation of the Individuals with Disabilities Education Act.* Washington, D.C.: U.S. Government Printing Office, 1998.

Waldron, N. L., and J. McLeskey. "The Effects of an Inclusive School Program on Students with Mild and Severe Learning Disabilities." *Exceptional Children* 64 (1998): 395–405.

Webb, Barbara J. "Planning and Organizing—Assistive Technology Resources in Your School." *Teaching Exceptional Children* 32, no. 4 (March/April 2000): 50.

Wehmeyer, M. L., D. Lattin, and M. Agran. "Achieving Access to the General Education Curriculum for Students with Mental Retardation." *Education and Training in Mental Retardation and Developmental Disabilities* 36 (2001): 327–342.

Wilson, Elizabeth K., and Margaret L. Rice. "Virtual Field Trips and Newsrooms: Integrating Technology into the Classroom." *Social Education* 64, no. 3 (April 2000): 152.

Wissick, Cheryl, and Windy Schweder. "The Grilled Cheese Project: Using Presentation Software to Ceate Functional Software for Your Classroom." *Special Education Technology Practice,* March/April 2001, 32–36.

Woodward, L., and R. Gersten. "Innovative Technology for Secondary Students with Learning Disabilities." *Exceptional Children* 58, no. 5 (March–April 1992): 407–421.

Zhang, Yuehua. "Technology and the Writing Skills of Students with Learning Disabilities." *Journal of Research on Computing in Education* 32, no. 4 (Summer 2000): 467.

Zorfass, J., P. Corley, and A. Remzl. "Helping Students with Disabilities Become Writers." *Educational Leadership* 51, no. 7 (1994): 62–66.

CHAPTER 14

Teacher Support Tools and Graphics Software

Integrating Teacher Support Tools into the Classroom

Some computer software programs are especially designed for teachers. These programs can make a teacher's school year easier. They help the teacher plan everyday activities; design notes, letters, labels, and newsletters; and track information. The teacher can utilize a variety of programs including grade-book programs, test makers, worksheet generators, crossword puzzle creators, certificate makers, and word searches. This chapter will explore how to use these software programs to help students better accomplish educational objectives. In addition, we will learn how the teacher and students can use graphics applications to improve students' performance in a variety of classroom situations. The chapter also will review Internet sites containing a rich assortment of lesson plans, online resources, and teacher utilities.

Objectives

Upon completing this chapter, you will be able to do the following:

1. Discuss the features of a variety of teacher support software packages.

2. Identify teacher support tools that help teachers and students be more productive.

3. Describe three types of graphics software programs and how they are used in the classroom.

Teachers Can

- create history or spelling crossword puzzles,
- create a slide show to teach about a country,
- use a grade-book program to keep track of students' scores,
- use a flash card maker to help students with math skills,
- use a story starter program to give the class help in writing, and
- create personal name tags for classroom trips.

Students Can

- prepare a portfolio using a presentation package such as *PowerPoint,*
- create a newsletter on a current event topic,
- use a print software tool such as *Stationery Studio* to write a book report,
- create a sign for special events or as a public service warning, and
- create a time line banner using a program such as *TimeLiner.*

What Are Teacher Support Tools?

Teacher support tools increase the classroom teacher's effectiveness (Moore, Orey, and Hardy, 2000). These programs are meant not for the student but for the teacher—to help in such tasks as recording grades, generating tests, making flash cards, generating puzzles and worksheets, and performing statistical analysis. These software tools save time and improve accuracy by assisting the teacher in chores that cannot easily be done otherwise. For example, a grade-book program can quickly weight students' grades, calculate means and standard deviations, assign grades, and alphabetize the student list.

A teacher using support tools to organize her classroom

Teacher Support Tools

When shopping for a utility program, determine whether the program fits your needs, saves time, and results in a more effective output.

Grade Books

Teachers have different options when it comes to keeping track of their grades. They can use the old-fashioned pencil-and-paper grade book, input the data using a spreadsheet, or use an electronic grade-book program specifically designed for keeping track of grades. A spreadsheet is more difficult to use than an electronic grade book, and it takes a longer time to set up. Although electronic grade books are less flexible than spreadsheets, they enable teachers to quickly print reports, generate graphs, create seating charts, and track attendance.

An obvious advantage of an electronic grade book is its potential for helping teachers quickly inform students, parents, and administrators about pupil performance in the classroom. Why spend hours recording and averaging grades when numerous grade-book programs on the market today can do this burdensome task for you? Some teachers feel that learning how to use an electronic grade-book program is too difficult. Because computers are not always accessible, many teachers feel that they still need to maintain a pencil-and-paper grade book in addition to an electronic one, which requires double entry.

A good grade book should enable you to enter students' names easily and quickly correct any errors. Once you have typed in the students' names, there should be an option for sorting the names alphabetically, numerically, or by class standing. The grade book should enable you to enter a large number of students for each class, record a sufficient number of grades, record absences, and flag the names of students with problems. For each score you enter, there should be a scaling factor to ensure that appropriate scores are figured in student or class averages. Furthermore, you should be able to assign weights according to the value of class assignments. The program should calculate pertinent statistics—such as the range, mean, and median scores—and should be able to save test information and produce a hard copy. Additionally, it should print out copies of easily generated graphs and tables depicting the performance of the students and showing comparisons with other class averages. You should also be able to include information in individual student reports, which have value in parent communication, and keep parents apprised of children's progress.

Some programs that are effective for the classroom teacher are *Grade Busters:Making the Grade* (Jay Klein Productions), *Gradebook Plus* (SVE & Churchill Media), *Grade Machine* (Misty City), *Easy Grade Pro* (Orbis Software), *Grade Quick* (Jackson Software), and *Gradekeeper* (shareware).

GradeQuick is an intuitive program created to look like a paper grade book (Figure 14.1). With this program you enter data directly into the grade-book spreadsheet

Recommended Software
Grade-Book Programs

For a listing of recommended grade-book software, go to the Online Learning Center.

Name	ID	Fiction	Poetry	Speech	Grammar			Total	Max	Avg	Grade
Long Name		Study of	Using Me	Shakespe	Subject						
Term		1	1	1	1						
Category		Test	Test	Quiz	Homework						
Date		3/5/00	3/12/00	4/1/00	5/15/00						
Possible		100	100	50	50						
1. Adler, Leslie	1	100	**	50.0	√			192.50	200	96.25	A
2. Boyd, Jerry	18	**	75.0	32.0	ok			144.50	200	72.25	C
3. Chang, Julia	5	94.0	97.0	49.0	Good			280.00	300	93.33	A
4. Cohen, Josh	6	100	100	X	√			242.50	250	97.00	A
5. Denton, Bill	14	90.0	81.0	48.0	A			266.50	300	88.83	B
6. Flaherty, Sarah	7	88.0	84.0	45.0	Fail			229.50	300	76.50	C
7. Gardner, Alex	4	92.0	76.0	50.0	NC			218.00	300	72.67	C
8. Guth, Michael	8	66.0	77.0	**	Good			183.00	250	73.20	C
9. Jackson, Martin	9	90.0	88.0	44.0	Pass			259.50	300	86.50	B
10. Johnson, Dave	2	NC	90.0	46.0	Fail			148.50	300	49.50	F
11. Lansing, Eva	10	70.0	88.0	30.0	A-			233.75	300	77.92	C
12. Lee, Thomas	13	97.0	55.0	38.0	Pass			227.50	300	75.83	C
13. Momac, Jennifer	17	72.0	60.0	25.0	√			199.50	300	66.50	D
14. Moran, Jim	19	77.0	50.0	29.0	Pass			193.50	300	64.50	D
15. Nelson, Chris	16	50.0	44.0	24.0	ok			155.50	300	51.83	F
16. Reisner, Nancy	15	86.0	78.0	38.0	A			249.50	300	83.17	B
17. Romero, Maria	3	82.0	89.0	49.0	B			262.50	300	87.50	B
18. Ryan, Patsy	20	83.0	88.0	49.0	X			220.00	250	88.00	B
19. Scott, Elizabeth	11	90.0	87.0	44.0	ok			258.50	300	86.17	B
20. Wilson, Lynn	12	93.0	88.0	42.0	√-			260.50	300	86.83	B

Figure 14.1
GradeQuick 5.0

© Jackson Software. All rights reserved. Reprinted with permission.

and display the information on one main screen. You can customize this main screen and view any item by just clicking the mouse. For example, you may want to display statistics or show personal student data fields in addition to student averages and test scores. You have control over the content, style, and layout of this program. There is a wide selection of ready-to-print reports. The program displays more than 30 statistics and will print them in any report. *GradeQuick* even comes with a seating chart feature that enables the teacher to display and print student pictures on the chart. With *Grade-Quick* you can post attendance records, homework assignments, and grades on the Web. More elaborate grade books display data as histograms or line graphs, report a wider range of statistics, and come with a variety of templates in English and Spanish for parent correspondence.

Grade Busters: Making the Grade (Macintosh and Windows) records 80 students, 320 assignments, 25 assignment categories, and 5 grading scales per class and displays the results graphically. Furthermore, it generates reports in English and Spanish.

Teachers are also using the Web to manage their grades, assignments, calendars, lessons, and attendance. For example, *ThinkWave Web Educator* (found at http://thinkwave.com/) handles these tasks easily. Using *ThinkWave*'s software, the teacher creates a grade book and selects the information to publish on the Internet. *ThinkWave* then creates student and parent accounts for each student in the teacher's class. Next, the teacher gives students and parents a start key and password so they can access the account. Students can log on to their accounts to see their individual class information. Parents can also log on to see their child's progress and communicate with the teacher.

Test Generators

A test-generating program resembles a word processor in that it comes with standard editing capabilities such as deletion and insertion. Many of these programs have font libraries from which you can select different typefaces. There are various test formats, including true/false, multiple choice, fill in the blank, short answer, essay, and matching. Some programs have graphics editors to help you integrate diagrams and pictures into your document. After entering your test questions, you can save them as a database file that can be retrieved on demand. Many programs enable you to randomize the order of the test questions and the arrangement of the possible responses to multiple-choice questions for makeup tests or alternate tests. The majority of programs enable you to print final copies of the tests along with answer sheets. Suitable test-making programs are *Test Designer Supreme II* (Super School Software), *Teacher's Tool Kit* (Teacher-Tools.com), *Teacher's Resource Companion Deluxe* (Visions Technology in Education), and *Test Creator* (Centron Software).

Test Designer Supreme II combines test creation, test taking, sound, graphics, and foreign languages. With this program, you can insert questions from a database into a test and use an overhead projector to give students a timed test on the computer. In addition, you can choose the test format you want and integrate graphics into it. An earlier version of this program, *Test Designer Plus*, was one of the first programs to integrate graphics into a test.

Programs such as *Teacher's Resource Companion Deluxe* also integrate graphics and offer a wide selection of options. *Teacher's Resource Companion Deluxe* (grades K–12) has an easy-to-use interface that many developers are following. This program enables you to create activity sheets, tests, and complete curricular packages. The formats include short essay, multiple choice, true/false, matching, fill in the blank, and word search

(Figure 14.2). You can create a database of your questions for review quizzes or to share with other teachers. The program even comes with 500 questions covering all curricu-

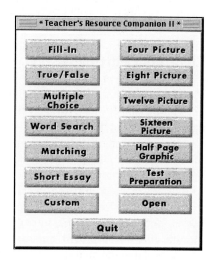

Figure 14.2 *Teacher's Resource Companion Deluxe*

Reprinted with permission of Visions Technology in Education™. www.ToolsforTeachers.com.

lar areas. You can use this program in all subject areas, including special education, ESL, foreign language, and geography.

Puzzle Makers

Puzzle makers motivate students studying potentially unexciting topics such as state capitals and parts of the body. You can use such programs to develop a crossword puzzle for reviewing Spanish, generate a geographical crossword for studying Europe, or create a math quiz in which equations are clues to a mystery. There are many noteworthy puzzle generators for the classroom, including *Crossword Companion Deluxe* (Visions Technology in Education), *Crossword Studio* (Nordic), *Word Bingo* and *Word Cross* (TeacherTools.com), *Crossword Creator* and *Puzzle Power* (Centron), and *Crossword Compiler* (shareware product, http://www.crossword-compiler.com/).

Figure 14.3 is a sample crossword puzzle generated from *Crossword Companion Deluxe.* This crossword puzzle maker is simple to use. The program enables you to

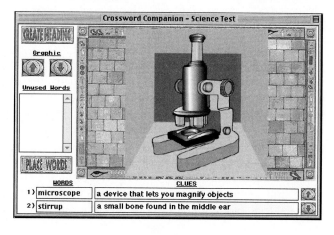

Figure 14.3
Crossword Companion Deluxe

Reprinted with permission of Visions Technology in Education™. www.ToolsforTeachers.com.

create your own crossword puzzles, and it automatically generates a variety of puzzles from the same word list. The product automatically creates clues and inserts a definition, synonym, or sentence selected from a 17,000-word dictionary. You can create picture clues using a variety of picture formats. You can even post your crossword puzzles on your website.

Electronic Portfolios

Profile tools such as the *Portfolio Builder for PowerPoint* (Visions Technology in Education) and *Grady Profile* (Aurbach & Associates) assist teachers in the design and management of performance-based portfolios. Portfolios constitute a valuable assessment tool for instructors.

A **portfolio** is an organized collection of documents that is used by a student to reflect his or her knowledge, skills, and learning accomplishments. An **electronic portfolio** is one created on computer. There are many different types of portfolios. For the purpose of this chapter we will classify these portfolios into three wide-ranging categories: personal, academic, and professional. **Personal portfolios** show a student's growth and development outside of school. The portfolio might include autobiographical data, information about hobbies and talents, awards, pictures, and goals. An **academic portfolio** shows the student's academic performance and achievement. This portfolio might include a collection of a student's work in all subject areas over time (Figure 14.4). The academic portfolio may include book report lists, computer-

Figure 14.4 *The Portfolio Builder for PowerPoint*

Reprinted with permission of Visions Technology in Education™. www.ToolsforTeachers.com.

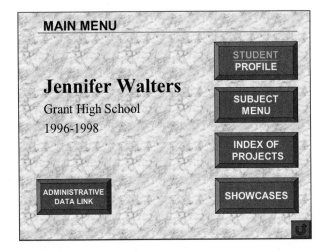

generated examples of student work or projects, paintings, collages, photos, timed writings, letters, poems, and short stories. Finally, the **professional portfolio** might contain samples of a student's work that meet graduation requirements for high school or college admission. This portfolio can also be used for employment seeking, reflecting only the student's best academic work. Preteachers can prepare such professional portfolios before launching a job search.

To create a portfolio, students import work created with other software applications into a portfolio builder. They can import graphics, text, scanned images, full-motion video, and sound clips into portfolio builders such as *Portfolio Builder for PowerPoint* (Visions Technology in Education) or authoring programs such as *HyperStudio* or

PowerPoint (see Chapter 8). In a program such as *PowerPoint,* they can manipulate the images and sound, even add animation, and save the work as a presentation. The presentation can then be burned on a CD-ROM, stored on a Zip disk or USB drive, or placed on a Web page. Refer to the Kailua High School website (http://kailuahs. k12.hi.us/portfolio_assignment/Index.html) to learn how to create an electronic portfolio as a Web page.

Many teachers find it helpful to use portfolio assessment as another means to keep track of a student's progress. They feel that testing only gives data on how well a student answers questions on a particular day in time. An electronic portfolio, on the other hand, gives the teacher insight into a student's personality and records his or her accomplishments over a period of time. Some teacher support tools such as *Learner Profile 3.0* (Houghton Mifflin) and *Grady Profile* (Auerbach) help provide the content and structure of a portfolio. This software assesses competencies on the basis of the work the instructor has collected from the student. Many of these software programs feature checklists, custom report forms, a place for comments, and the means to view and gather student work electronically. The *Teacher Profile* (Auerbach) was specifically developed for schools of education that require preservice teachers to maintain portfolios, for districts and schools with in-service teachers who want to keep portfolios, and for individual teachers who wish to maintain professional portfolios that represent their work. Every portfolio should be checked for the eight criteria shown in the checklist.

Portfolio Checklist

Is the portfolio
_____ 1. based on a standard or theme?
_____ 2. organized?
_____ 3. easy to read?
_____ 4. understandable?
_____ 5. interesting?
_____ 6. grammatically correct?
_____ 7. free of spelling and syntax errors?
_____ 8. one cohesive unit?

Worksheet Generators, Time Liners, Organizers, and Other Support Tools

Some programs, such as *Worksheet Magic* Plus (Teacher Support Software) and *Math Companion* (Visions Technology in Education), produce worksheets in a variety of formats. Other programs, such as *Make-a-Flash* (Teacher Support Software), make flash cards with vocabulary generated by a word processor. Still other programs produce labels, time lines (Figure 14.5), attendance charts, flowcharts, and lesson plans. The latest version of *TimeLiner 5.0* (Tom Snyder Productions) enables you to design, illustrate, and print out time lines of any length in Spanish or English. With *TimeLiner 5.0,* students can sequence events in chronological order. Teachers can print these time lines in any size to display the classroom. This new version of *TimeLiner 5.0* comes with 400 historical photographs as well as clip art. You can add movies and sounds to make a true multimedia time line. You can also import images from the Web to illustrate the time line,

Figure 14.5
TimeLiner 5.0

Used by permission of Tom
Snyder Productions.

and you can link to the Internet from any event in the time line. This utility enables you to convert time lines into slide shows. *TimeLiner 5.0* can be used in all curricular areas. There are even CD-ROMs with ready-made time lines for history, science, and social studies topics.

Report Writer Interactive (FTC Publishing) is a writing tool that teachers use to help a student or class create reports or presentations. The teacher introduces the class to a topic such as the dangers of smoking (Figure 14.6) and then encourages the class to fol-

Figure 14.6 *Report Writer Interactive*

Used with permission of FTC Publishing.

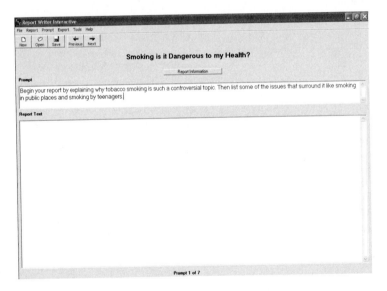

low the program's prompts and create their own reports. This program comes with 50 report templates in six subject areas. Each report has a short introduction followed by interactive writing templates. Teachers have the option of modifying existing templates or creating their own. Once the student has created the report the individual components can be put into a document, *PowerPoint* presentation, or *Microsoft Word* document.

Another delightful utility program from FTC Publishing for teachers is *PowerPak for PowerPoint: An Innovation Collection of Lessons and Game Templates*. This program enables the teacher to design lesson plans and supplemental games for the whole class. All the

work has been done for the teacher except for typing in the questions and answers. *PowerPak* covers all curriculum areas and includes 24 interactive game templates and dynamic lesson plans for a few students or an entire classroom. The theme templates range from *Academic Raceway 500* (Figure 14.7) to *Sunken Treasure.* These lessons can be great class reviews or test preparation material.

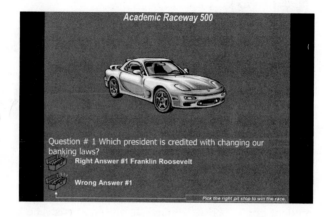

Figure 14.7
PowerPak for PowerPoint

Used with permission of FTC Publishing.

Teacher TimeSavers and *Research Assistant* (Visions Technology in Education) are two more utilities that lessen the teacher's workload. *Teacher TimeSavers* comes with assessment and time-saving templates. With the assessment templates, the teacher can keep records and calculate student percentages for different grade levels. The time-saving templates enable the teacher to print name tags, place cards, mailing labels, bookmarks, flash cards (Figure 14.8), and much more.

Figure 14.8 *Teacher TimeSavers Flashcard*

Reprinted with permission of Visions Technology in Education™.
www.ToolsforTeachers.com.

Inspiration (Inspiration Software), a powerful visual thinking tool, helps students and teachers organize ideas and information. In Figure 14.9, the student has created a character web to analyze Holden Caulfield, the protagonist of *Catcher in the Rye.* This program assists students in developing visual diagrams, flowcharts, and knowledge maps. It comes with an integrated outline view that helps students create concisely written proposals and reports. Students can plan speeches, and they can use

Figure 14.9
Inspiration Character
Web

Reprinted with permission of
Inspiration Software, Inc.

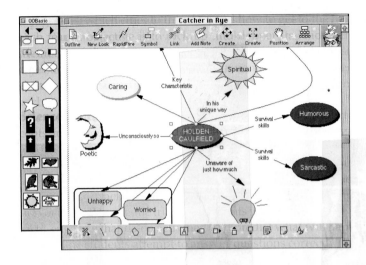

the program's checklist feature to complete tasks such as planning a multimedia presentation. Students are also able to brainstorm portfolios (Figure 14.10).

Figure 14.10
Inspiration Portfolio
Brainstorm

Reprinted with permission of
Inspiration Software, Inc.

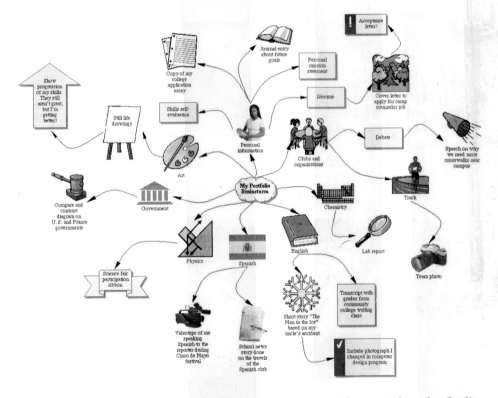

Using *Inspiration* teachers can compare two authors and then switch to the *Outline View* to show students how to create a report. They can use the program to help students gain a deep understanding of scientific concepts such as global warming. In social studies they can show cause-and-effect relationships in historical events such as the French Revolution. In math they can explain math concepts such as factoring, addition, and subtraction. *Inspiration* can help teachers plan lessons for the classroom, prepare research papers, and create reports. Finally, teachers can use the *Template Wizard* to create customized learning activities for all curriculum areas.

Statistical Programs

In the past, if you wanted to do statistical analysis, you had to do the work by hand or on a mainframe at a university. Today, many microcomputer programs help the classroom teacher make calculations and analyze statistics. Most of these programs handle the simplest statistics, such as mean and standard deviation, but the more complex programs also handle multilinear regression and factor/time series analysis. In a matter of seconds, you can compute a regression, an analysis of variance, or an unpaired t test.

Figure 14.11, from *SPSS* (SPSS), shows the calculation of an Anova test performed by simply selecting it in the menu. *SPSS* offers all the tools needed to analyze and present

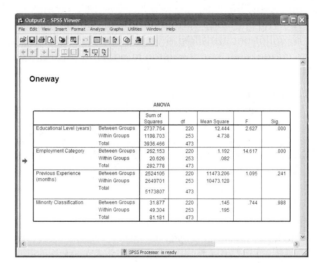

Figure 14.11 *SPSS*

Created with SPSS, Inc.
Copyright © 2003.

data in one application. Years ago, you had to enter data in a spreadsheet, perform manipulations, and then import the data into a statistical package for analysis. Next, you had to use another program to create graphs. Finally, you had to use a draw program to prepare tables and graphs for presentation. Today, the majority of statistical packages, including programs such as *GB Stat* (Dynamic Micro Systems), *NCSS Statistical Analysis* (Windows only), *Systat* (Systat Software, Inc.; Windows only), and *AcaStat Statistical* Software *DeltaGraph* (Red Rock Software), perform all of these functions. You will find links to other statistical packages at http://www.stata.com/support/links/stat_software.html. In most cases, you will not need an expensive statistical package because many spreadsheets or grade-book programs have sufficient statistics capabilities. However, if you are doing research or if your grade-management program does not provide statistics, then you will need this type of program.

Teacher Support Tools on the Internet

The Internet is a huge library where you can find teacher support tools and instructional material. There seems to be a limitless amount of resources available to the Web traveler. Many of these resources are free, and the ones that are subscription based usually have free resources for the teacher.

Blackboard is an excellent online course management tool with which teachers can communicate with students, post their grades, and send assignments back and forth. Teachers can use this site without having to create their own Web page (http://

www.blackboard.com). There are many teacher resources found at *T.H.E. Journal's Educators Road Map to the Web* (http://www.thejournal.com/highlights/roadmap/). This site covers all the content areas.

There are a tremendous variety of online references that a teacher can find by going to *Google* (http://www.google.com) and typing *reference sites* in its search engine. Especially good are *Refdesk* at http://www.refdesk.com/, the *University of Texas Library Online* at http://www.lib.utexas.edu/refsites/, *How Stuff Works* at http://howstuffworks.com (grades 8–12), and its companion site *How Stuff Works Express* (grades 4–8) at http://express.howstuffworks.com. At *Refdesk.com* a list of *Reference Resources* ranges from a *Facts Encyclopedia* to *Essential Reference Tools*. The UT (University of Texas at Austin) library has a list of useful reference sites ranging from online dictionaries to encyclopedias. Finally, *How Stuff Works Express* and *How Stuff Works* lets you learn about mechanisms and workings of technology, natural phenomena, and scientific concepts. The sites discuss a range of topics including MP3 files, hurricanes, United Nations, and computer viruses.

Clip Art Collections

Clip art are "canned" images that the teacher can insert into documents such as desktop publishing documents, presentation programs, word processing documents, authoring program files, or Web pages. For those of us who do not paint, these clip art libraries are an invaluable resource.

Using clip art saves the teacher or student the hours of time it would take to create images from scratch. At users' fingertips are hundreds of ready-to-use images. You can find clip art for any conceivable topic from a beautiful photograph of Crater Lake to a detailed drawing of the human body. Teachers can buy clip art from companies such as Corel, Adobe, and IMSI. Teachers can also discover a vast array of clip art that is free online such as *Barry's Clip Art* (http://barrysclipart.com/), which offers thousands of clip art images.

Teachers can also pay for an online subscription service such as *ArtToday* or *Clipart.com* (http://clipart.com), a site that has over 2 million downloadable images. If you want to use the clip art from commercial sites, see if there are any restrictions such as written permission or payment. The majority of clip art packages provide their pictures in file formats such as jpeg, gif, and eps, which makes them easy to insert in a variety of documents.

Individual Instructional Educational Plan (IEP) Generators

In the last couple of years politicians and the public have been calling for teacher and student accountability. This emphasis on accountability brings a need to track student progress and an increase in paperwork for the teacher. This has been especially true for the special education teacher with the enactment of the American Disability Act (see Chapter 13). This law requires that schools prepare an IEP (individualized education plan) for each special education student. To this end, teachers are purchasing IEP programs such as *IEP Writer Supreme II (SuperSchool), Teacher's Choice 2003* (db Education Solutions), and *IEP Software* (Tera Systems) to help them prepare their reports. For example, *IEP Writer Supreme* has tools that help you plan for IEP meetings and finish all the IEP forms on the computer. The program follows state standards and comes with planning tools, resources for classroom teachers, informal assessment tools, and a complete set of IEP forms.

At the end of this chapter is a list of IEP generators, instructional materials, tests, lesson plans, worksheet generators, test creators, puzzle makers, grade calculators, certificate makers, and clip art sites. The Teacher Support Tools Checklist is an assessment form to use when evaluating teacher support tools.

Teacher Support Tools Checklist*

Directions: Examine the following items and determine which ones you feel are important for your current teaching situation. Place an X on each line for which the software meets your needs.

Electronic Grade Books

_____ 1. Features

_____   a. Has screen views by category, student, and assignment

_____   b. Tracks attendance

_____   c. Has seating charts with pictures

_____   d. Sorts names alphabetically, numerically, or by class standing

_____   e. Enters large numbers of students and grades

_____   f. Flags students with problems

_____ 2. Statistical capabilities

_____   a. Averages grades

_____   b. Scales scores (selects scores for student or class averages)

_____   c. Weights grades according to value of assignments

_____   d. Calculates pertinent statistics (range, mean, median, and standard deviation)

_____   e. Compares individual students and class averages

_____ 3. Output capabilities

_____   a. Prints individual student and class reports

_____   b. Generates graphs and tables depicting student/class performance

_____   c. Saves information to disk

_____   d. Has templates/reports in different languages

_____   e. Posts information securely on the Web

_____ 4. Utility

_____   a. Is easy to set up and learn

_____   b. Is easy to use

_____   c. Saves time

_____   d. Is accessible at work, home, and on the Web

Test Generators

_____ 1. Features for test creation

_____   a. Has standard editing capabilities

_____   b. Has font libraries with different typefaces

_____   c. Integrates diagrams and pictures

_____   d. Randomizes order of test questions and responses

_____   e. Uses foreign languages

_____ 2. Test formats

_____   a. True/false

_____   b. Multiple choice

_____   c. Short answer

_____   d. Fill in the blank

_____   e. Matching

_____ 3. Storing/retrieval

_____   a. Items are saved in a database for easy retrieval

_____   b. Creates quizzes, activity sheets, and other curricular materials

_____   c. Prints final copies of tests and answer sheets

_____   d. Accesses questions from publisher's database

_____   e. Shares questions/tests with other teachers

Rating Scale

Rate the tools by placing a check on the appropriate line.

Excellent_____ Very Good_____ Good_____ Fair_____ Poor_____

Comments

*Courtesy of Sarah Hall.

What Is Graphics Software?

Pictures shape our perceptions and help us communicate. When a biology instructor discusses the anatomy of the body, he or she finds it helpful to show a labeled drawing on a model. The businessperson uses graphics to make important presentation points. The engineer creates a scale drawing to guide the builders of a bridge. The statistician creates charts from data. In our society, people use pictures to educate, to communicate ideas and feelings, and to persuade. A picture is indeed worth a thousand words.

The term **computer graphics** refers to "the creation and manipulation of picture images in the computer" (Freedman, 2003). When discussing computer graphics, we are referring to computer-generated pictures on a screen, paper, or film. Graphics can be as simple as a pie graph or as elaborate as a detailed anatomical painting of the human body. Graphics software can help teachers and students communicate with images.

Graphics Software

There are many excellent software programs that can be used by teachers and students. We will consider some of these programs organized by broad category.

Graphing and Charting Software

In Chapters 6 and 7, we discussed databases and spreadsheets and their applications. It is not difficult to create graphs and charts from such databases and spreadsheets to illustrate presentations. These graphs and charts can take many forms, such as a bar graph (Figure 14.12). Anyone quickly looking at this data can see that Clayton High

Figure 14.12 Bar Graph

Reprinted with permission of Visions Technology in Education™. www.ToolsforTeachers.com.

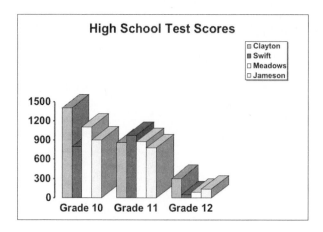

School has the highest test scores for grades 10 and 12, and Swift High School has the lowest test scores for grades 10 and 12.

Graphs show a relationship among categories of data. This bar graph compares the results for four different schools at three different grade levels, with each color bar representing a different school. Other types of graphs could have illustrated the same data in different ways. Figure 14.13 shows the same data displayed in a cone graph.

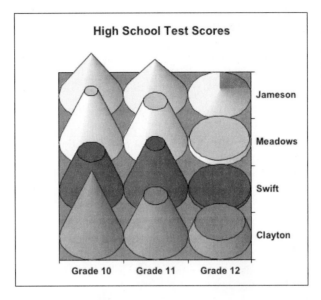

Figure 14.13 Cone Graph, *Excel Chart Program*

Screen shot of *Microsoft® Excel* used by permission of Microsoft Corporation.

You can use graphics to better understand a student's performance on a series of exams. In Figure 14.14, the teacher charts Jane Smith's scores on six math tests to grasp quickly the effect of an extreme score (10) on this student's performance.

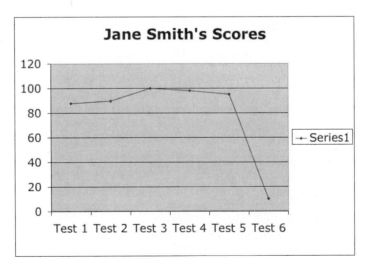

Figure 14.14 *Excel* Line Graph

Screen shot of *Microsoft® Excel* used by permission of Microsoft Corporation.

Graphing is a means of getting a clearer understanding of what the data represent. In education, graphing possibilities are unlimited. In science, students can graph the results of a series of plant experiments in which they alter variables such as temperature and water. In economics or social studies, the teacher might want the class to chart a stock's progress for a year or to graph voting trends. In English, the teacher can chart the incidences of certain words used in student writing to make a point about vocabulary.

Graphic programs such as *GraphPower* (Ventura Educational Systems) and *The Graph Club* (Tom Snyder Productions—Scholastic) are suitable for classroom use. If you do not want to buy a separate graphing program, you can use an integrated program such as *AppleWorks* (Apple) or *Microsoft Office,* which have graphing components.

With *GraphPower* (Figure 14.15), you can create a bar graph of the area of the continents, one example of the use of graphs to develop data analysis skills. In addition to

Figure 14.15
GraphPower

Used by permission of Ventura Educational Systems, Grover Beach, CA 93483-0425. www.venturaes.com.

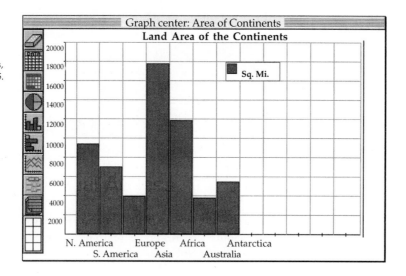

creating bar graphs, the program can create pictographs, line graphs, circle graphs, and box graphs. To use this program, you simply enter data in the *Data Center* and click on a graph icon to create a graph. After creating a graph, you can export it to a word processing or desktop publishing program. An online tutorial called the *Graph Tutor* helps you overcome problems. *GraphPower* not only shows how to read graphs, but also teaches the different functions of various graphs.

Another suitable graphing program is *The Graph Club,* which is appropriate for grades K through 4. Using this program to analyze data, students can create picture graphs, circle graphs, and bar graphs. *The Graph Club* has a library of over 150 fun pictures, and it includes an easy-to-use bilingual feature.

Presentation Graphics Programs

Presentation graphics programs have the capability of displaying charts, diagrams, special effects, predefined backgrounds, clip art, sound, transitions, and video in a computer-driven slide show. These slides are printable, but in most cases they are used to display material for a class or large audience. The teacher or students show their presentation on a regular monitor or a screen that is used in conjunction with a projector. An example of a presentation graphics program is *PowerPoint.* This program comes with art tools and templates that the user can incorporate into slide shows about everything from the anatomy of a heart (Figure 14.16) to the paintings of Van Gogh.

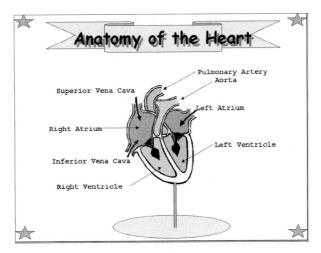

Figure 14.16 *Human Heart, PowerPoint*

Screen shot of *PowerPoint*® used by permission of Microsoft Corporation.

PowerPoint enables you to import content from other programs. At Microsoft's site (http://www.microsoft.com) you can download updated template and clip art. Refer to Chapter 8 for a discussion of presentation programs such as *Keynote* (Apple), *Hyper-Studio* (Sunburst), and *Leonardo's Multimedia Toolbox* (Riverdeep) and of programs with slide show capabilities such as *AppleWorks, Kid Pix Studio,* and *ImageBlender.*

Presentation graphics have become a substitute for the overhead projector. This software is replacing chalkboards and transparencies.

Print Graphics Programs

To create an award, a poster, a banner, a greeting card, or a certificate, you would use **print graphics** software. The best known program is *The Print Shop* (Riverdeep), which enables you to create a wide assortment of multicolored graphics. This classic program has won countless awards because it is easy to use and it saves hours of time and effort. Figure 14.17

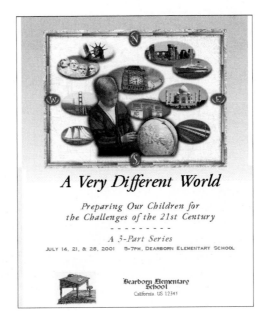

Figure 14.17 *The Print Shop Deluxe*

© 2004 Riverdeep Interactive Learning Limited, and its licensors.

shows a ready-made sign from *The Print Shop Deluxe.* Since the introduction of the original *Print Shop,* several versions have been produced. Although the concept remains the same, these programs vary in their capacity to produce color and graphics and work with a laser printer.

There are dozens of programs that can be used for print graphics. Some of the more popular are *Print Explosion Deluxe* (Nova), *Print Shop* and *Kid Pix Studio Deluxe* (Riverdeep), *Print Artist* (Sierra), *PrintMaster Platinum* (Mindscape), and *Stationery Studio* (FableVision). These programs produce attractive mini books, flyers, banners, and awards.

Stationery Studio (FableVision) is a perfect program for teachers or students in K–5. With this print graphic tool a student can print writing paper, templates for stories or reports (Figure 14.18), mini books, shape books, and much more. This program gives a

Figure 14.18
Stationery Studio

Reprinted with permission from FableVision.

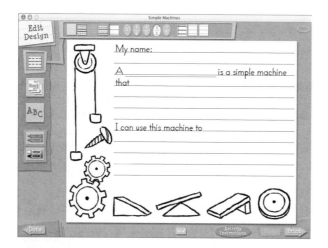

teacher more than 22 curriculum-themed shapes and borders to use. You can print the stationery in color or black and white, which students can then color in. Teachers can use the simple text tool to create story starters. *Stationery Studio* is capable of creating thousands of unique pieces of stationery.

Tom Snyder Productions produces a program called *Neighborhood MapMachine 2.0* (Scholastic). This program helps students create maps (Figure 14.19) and print them in

Figure 14.19
Neighborhood MapMachine 2.0

Used by permission of Tom Snyder Productions.

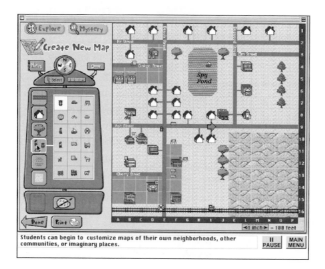

different sizes. In the process of creating these maps students learn about directions, scale, grid coordinates, symbols, and other geography concepts. Students can use these maps in slide shows that illustrate the history of a town or that gives a guided tour. The program comes with ready-to-use maps and activities that are correlated with state standards.

Culture World Diorama Creators (Visions Technology in Education) helps children explore other cultures on screen and then build and print paper dioramas. The students can join the Sioux as they hunt buffalo, build a small Ethiopian village, learn about the Alamo, join the isolated culture of medieval Japan, and find out about the Lewis and Clark expedition. For *Cultural World: Lewis and Clark,* the students assemble a diorama, print out figures to populate the diorama, and read an overview of the journey of Lewis and Clark (Figure 14.20).

Figure 14.20 *Culture World: Lewis and Clark*

Reprinted with permission of Visions Technology in Education™. www.ToolsforTeachers.com.

Print programs offer different templates, fonts, border designs, and clip art. These enhancement programs, designed for users with limited artistic talent, have far-reaching educational benefits. The teacher can produce attractive and interesting bulletin boards, announcements, awards, worksheets, and even transparency masters. Students can create mini books, maps, posters, fliers, banners, and letterhead stationery. After they create their letterhead, they can use it to communicate with each other by classroom mailbox.

Draw/Paint Programs

If you are having trouble finding a piece of clip art or a graphic, you may want to use a drawing or painting program to produce your own creation. Many of these programs are very sophisticated and expensive. They are wonderful to use, but unfortunately they do not give someone who is not talented in art the ability to draw or paint. You still must be artistically talented to produce a great work of art with these programs.

Drawing Versus Painting Tools. When using a **drawing program,** you create illustrations that consist of mathematically defined curves and line segments called *vectors.* **Vector graphics** "is a technique for showing a picture as points, lines, and other geometric entities" (Freedman, 2003). What this means is that all elements of the picture can be

Recommended Software

Print Graphics Programs

For a listing of recommended print graphics software, go to the Online Learning Center.

isolated, moved independently, and scaled separately from one another (Figure 14.21). Vector graphics can be displayed or printed at any resolution or degree of sharpness or

Figure 14.21 Vector-Based Drawing

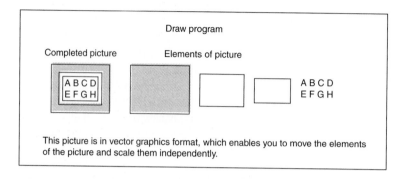

detail that a monitor or printer is capable of producing. Two popular drawing programs are *Adobe Illustrator* and *CorelDraw Graphics Suite.* With draw programs, students can draw geometric shapes, create designs, and construct miniature cities.

A **paint program** enables the student to paint on the screen with the use of a graphics tablet or a mouse. Paint programs are art oriented rather than design oriented. The paintings are made up of dots or pixels. Each pixel consists of data describing whether the pixel is white or black or what level of color it has. Unlike draw programs, paint programs do not permit images to be scaled and separated from one another (Figure 14.22). Editing groups of pixels can alter the pictures you create with this format. Because the bitmap images are resolution dependent, they will appear jagged and lose detail if you enlarge them.

Figure 14.22 Paint Program

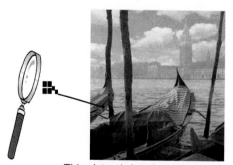

This picture's brush strokes are really made up of dots. The dots are called *raster graphics* or *bitmaps.*

The majority of paint programs mentioned in this book offer coloring and texturing capabilities. Most paint programs also feature brushes of different widths and shapes, drawing tools, a mirror-image function, different fonts, and an undo function.

There are significant advantages to using the computer for painting. If the artist makes a mistake, she or he can easily correct it. There is no mess to clean up because there are no real paints or watercolors to spill, drip, or smear. The painter simply clicks the mouse to change the color, enlarge an image, or move an object. There are also disadvantages, including a possible failure to connect with traditional art media and the loss of the opportunity to have a hands-on experience with paint, clay, and other media.

To create images with drawing or paint programs, students can use an input device, such as the keyboard, a mouse, a light pen with a graphics tablet, or a digitizer. The light pen (Figure 14.23), which handles exactly like a pencil, translates the students' drawings from the tablet into an electronic format so that they can be seen on screen.

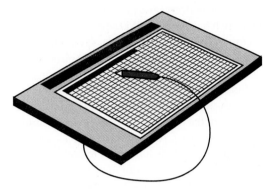

Figure 14.23
Graphics Tablet and
Light Pen

The more advanced teacher, student, or professional will find paint programs such as *Adobe PhotoShop*, *Painter 8* (Procreate), and *PaintShop Pro* (JASC Software) indispensable. For less-talented artists like myself, programs such as *Windows PaintBrush*, *Adobe PhotoShop Elements*, and *Disney's Magic Artist Deluxe* will create beautiful pictures or designs that can be used in word processing documents and desktop publishing documents. There are many good paint programs available today, including *Canvas* (Deneba Software) and *Painter* (Corel). An example of a paint program that is especially appropriate for elementary school children is *Kid Pix Deluxe 3* (Riverdeep). This program comes with 2,500 stamps, over 1,200 graphics, funny paintbrushes, and a collection of wacky tools, each with its own sound. *Kid Pix Deluxe 3* (Figure 14.24) includes a talking

Figure 14.24 *Kid Pix Deluxe 3*

© 2004 Riverdeep Interactive Learning Limited, and its licensors.

alphabet and six unique painting, drawing, and animation projects. Students learn shapes and practice motor skills by working with this program.

Older students can use the painting component of *AppleWorks* or *Canvas* to create a painting. A more advanced program is *Painter* (Corel), which comes with a variety of brushes, textures, canvas choices, and art materials.

Computer-Aided Design Applications

Computer-aided design (CAD) assists in the design of objects such as machine parts, homes, or anatomical drawings. You must have the proper CAD program to accomplish such tasks. With CAD software, you can easily change or modify designs without having to create actual models, saving time, money, and effort. *AutoCAD 2004 LT* (Autodesk) is a 2-D and 3-D drafting environment in which students create, view, manage, plot and output, share, and use drawings. Professional architects, engineers, and drafters can use this program. *AutoSketch 8* (autodesk) enables beginning users to create easily and quickly professional floor layouts, presentations, and home project plans.

Many of the programs in this field are simulations that show the use of created models. For instance, CAD software enables an engineer not only to design a car, but also to test it and even rotate it in space to see it from all sides. *Car Builder Deluxe* (Optimum Resource Software) is a simulation for education with which students construct, modify, and test cars. In the process of constructing a car, students must select the chassis length, the type and size of fuel tank, and the strength and size of the tires. When the mechanical selection is complete, students modify the body with data generated through a testing procedure that includes a wind tunnel and a test track. At the end of this testing session, students can save the specifications of the designed car on a disk (Figure 14.25).

Figure 14.25 *Car Builder Deluxe*

© Optimum Resource, Inc. Used with permission.

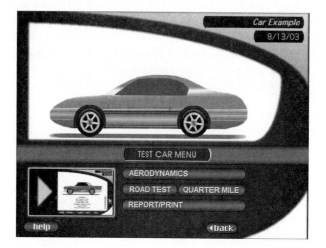

Sims and *SimCity 4* (Maxis/Division Electronic Arts) are popular design programs using principles of CAD. *Sims* is for younger students, and *SimCity 4* is for older students. Both programs are building games in which students create cities or neighborhoods. With *Sims,* students design homes, furnish them, build neighborhoods, and take control of them. In *SimCity 4,* students become planners, designers, and mayors of an unlimited number of cities. When using any type of simulation, students engage in problem solving. For example, in *SimCity 4* the students have to consider the consequences of placing police and fire protection in particular locations (Figure 14.26).

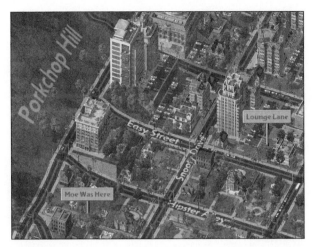

Figure 14.26
SimCity™ 4

Finally, *3D Railroad Concept & Design, Master 3D Railroad,* and *Train Engineer Deluxe* (Abracadata) are model railroad programs. With *3D Railroad Concept & Design* the student creates model railroad layouts, draws these layouts to any scale, and then views them. *3D Railroad Master* enables users to have complete control over trains. They select from a variety of rolling stock to build trains up to 100 cars long. In *Train Engineer Deluxe* students run trains as fast as they can across a background of realistic scenery.

Classroom Lesson Plans

I. PRESIDENTIAL ELECTION SURVEY

Subject

Social Studies

Grade(s)

2–8

Objectives

Students will learn how to do a survey and how to graph it using a bar graph and a pie graph.

Standards

- National Council for the Social Studies Curriculum Standards 3, 5
- ISTE NETS for Students 2, 3, 5

Materials

You will need a program that does graphics such as *GraphPower, The Graph Club,* or *AppleWorks* and one or more computers.

Procedures

1. Have the students work in teams to conduct a survey on the next presidential election.
2. Make sure they record information on socioeconomic level, education, voting preferences, and the like.
3. Have each team use the computer to create a bar graph of the results of its survey.
4. Finally, lead a discussion of the graphing results.

II. STATE DATA SHEET

Subject

Social Studies

Grade(s)

2 and up

Objectives

Students will read an almanac for information and learn how to graph their information using a bar graph and a line graph.

Standards

- National Council for the Social Studies Curriculum Standards 3, 5
- ISTE NETS for Students 3, 5, 6

Materials

You will need a graphing program such as *GraphPower* or *Excel* and one or more computers.

Procedures

1. Have each student select three states and research the annual rainfall of those states.
2. Ask the students to create bar graphs on the computer comparing the three states.
3. Have the students track down state rainfall statistics for three specific dates in the past.
4. Instruct students to construct line graphs showing the changes in the data for each state over a period of time.
5. Discuss with students what the graphs mean.

III. EDUCATIONAL SIGN—ABOUT DRUGS

Subject

English

Grade(s)

2–12

Objectives

Students will use a print graphics program to design a sign, learn about design and placement of objects, and discuss the reasons for not taking drugs.

Standards

- NCTE English Language Arts Standards 8, 12
- ISTE NETS for Students 1, 2, 3, 5

Materials

You will need *Print Shop Deluxe* or *Print Shop Explosion* and one or more computers.

Procedures

1. Discuss the reasons students should not take drugs.
2. Talk about placement and design with the students.
3. Instruct students to use a print graphics program to design a sign warning people not to take drugs.
4. After students have designed their signs, discuss what makes certain signs more appealing than others.

IV. MATH RIDDLE CARD

Subject

Math

Grade(s)

2–12

Objectives

Students will use a print graphics program to design a greeting card and practice solving math riddles.

Standards

- National Council of Teachers of Mathematics Standards 6, 8
- ISTE NETS for Students 5, 6

Materials

You will need *Print Shop Deluxe* or *Print Shop Explosion* and one or more computers.

Procedures

1. Give each student a riddle or have students find riddles in books.

2. Tell the students to design a greeting card, putting the riddle on the cover and the answer on the inside of the card. An example is shown in Figure 14.27.

Figure 14.27 *Print Shop Deluxe* Greeting Card Cover

Used with permission of Broderbund, Inc.

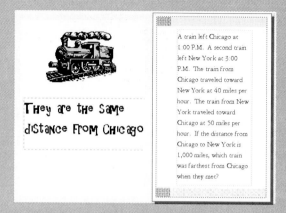

THeY are the SaMe distance FroM Chicago

A train left Chicago at 1:00 P.M. A second train left New York at 3:00 P.M. The train from Chicago traveled toward New York at 40 miles per hour. The train from New York traveled toward Chicago at 50 miles per hour. If the distance from Chicago to New York is 1,000 miles, which train was farthest from Chicago when they met?

3. Now distribute the greeting cards and have the students solve the riddles.

V. GEOMETRIC PATTERNS

Subject

Math

Grade(s)

K–3

Objectives

Students will use a paint program to make various geometric shapes, and they will learn about shapes.

Standards

- National Council of Teachers of Mathematics Standards 3, 8
- ISTE NETS for Students 1, 3, 4

Materials

You will need a paint program such as *Kid Pix Deluxe* and one or more computers.

Procedures

1. Teach the students about different geometric shapes.
2. Show the students how to use the paint program to create these shapes. Figure 14.28 shows an example.

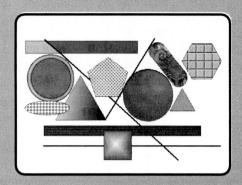

Figure 14.28 Shapes drawn in *KidPix*.

3. Explain how to fill the shapes with color and how to copy and paste shapes.
4. Have the students use the paint program to make abstract drawings without a fill pattern.
5. When they are finished, have them print out their shapes and color them, making sure all shapes of the same type are the same color.
6. Display these drawings on the bulletin board.
7. As a follow-up activity, have the students make collages with shapes or create faces.

VI. CELLS

Subject

Science

Grade(s)

5–8

Objectives

Students will use a draw program to illustrate the parts of an animal or plant cell and paste it in a report.

Standards

- National Science Education Standards C Life Science: The characteristics of organisms
- ISTE NETS for Students 1, 2, 3, 4, 5

Materials

You will need a drawing a program such as *Adobe Illustrator* or *AppleWorks* and one or more computers.

Procedures

1. Have students draw a cell on paper, labeling its parts.
2. Ask students to take turns using the computer to create their plant or animal cells.

3. Have students use a text tool to label each part of the cell.
4. Save this picture to disk.
5. Tell the students to prepare a report about animal cells or plant cells on the computer.
6. Have the students insert their pictures in their reports.
7. As a related activity, have the students draw the human body and label its parts.

Summary

Teacher support tools can make a teacher more effective. One of the most popular tools is the electronic grade book, which lessens the time a teacher spends entering grades, computing averages, and informing parents about students' progress. Other tools that save time and reduce effort are test and worksheet generators, organizers, puzzle makers, and statistical packages.

A good paint program or draw program enables the user to draw without the fear of making a mistake, and a print graphics program enables those who are not artistically inclined to create visuals, from awards to posters. CAD programs are useful in designing room layouts, machine parts, and cars; presentation graphics produce charts and graphs that show relationships among categories of data. At the end of the chapter, we examined six activities for integrating graphics and art into the classroom. The Online Learning Center offers an annotated list of award-winning teacher support tools and graphics sites.

 # Study and Online Resources

Go to Chapter 14 in the Student Edition of the Online Learning Center at www.mhhe.com/sharp5e *to **practice with key concepts, take chapter quizzes, read PowerWeb articles** and **news feed updates** related to technology in education, and **access resources** for learning about technology and integrating it into the classroom.*

Click on *Web Links* to link to the following websites.

Clip Art Sites

ArtToday (Clipart.com)

ArtToday is a subscription-based service with 2,600,000 downloadable images that range from pen-and-ink to wood-cut to nouveau retro.

Barry's Clip Art Server

This site offers thousands of animal pictures and other clip art images. If you cannot find what you need here, try the gallery at http://gallery.yahoo.com/.

Discovery Channel School's Clip Art Gallery

Discovery School offers hundreds of original clip art pieces, including animations. This site makes it easy to add graphics to your project.

Yahooligans! Teacher's Guide: Newsletters

Yahooligans provides clip art collections that you can use to teach a number of subjects. You can find icons for reports on politics, science, history, and mythology and teddy bears! Why not use these icons to decorate a newsletter? The site even offers borders to make your next project really snazzy!

Teacher Support Tool Sites

A+ Math

At this site, you can make your own flashcards, play *Matho* and *Hidden Picture* in the games room, use the homework helper tools to check solutions, or get worksheets for off-line practice.

Awesome Clipart for Kids: Worksheets & Puzzles Index

This site, updated weekly by 13-year-old Tom Brown and his family, provides free customizable worksheets, puzzles, and games for math, reading, spelling, holidays, and other seasonal topics.

Biological Science Worksheets

This site offers free printable worksheets covering the animal kingdom, cell chemistry, genetics, and other biology topics.

Calculate Your GPA

This site offers a simple spreadsheet template for calculating your GPA.

calculator.com

This site offers online calculators to help solve financial, science, cooking, health, and other everyday problems.

Convert It

Convert It features a wide range of calculators for currency rates, temperatures, time zones, measures, and weights.

DiscoverySchool.com: QuizCenter

QuizCenter enables you to create and correct online quizzes without any knowledge of HTML and automatically posts them on a server so they may be used by students. For a worksheet and generator and other online teaching tools from DiscoverySchool, visit the section on the left side of the page.

Discovery School's Puzzle Maker

Discovery School provides an easy-to-use puzzle generator for teachers and students, grades 3–12. You can create and print customized word search, crossword, and other puzzles using your word lists. You can also build a maze or print specially hand-drawn mazes with holiday and classroom topic themes.

Discovery School's WebMath

This site provides an array of math calculators giving step-by-step solutions to your math problems, from pre-algebra to calculus.

E.L. Easton: Exercises, Quizzes, Tests

This site includes hundreds of links to online exercises, quizzes, and test makers as well as a subject-arranged list of links to assessment tools.

FormSite.com

This site enables you to create an interactive form (with up to 30 fields) and collect data from parents, students, or other teachers.

FunBrain's Quiz Lab

FunBrain's Quiz Lab provides thousands of quizzes designed by teachers around the world. Teachers can create their own quizzes with its easy-to-use authoring tool and give their students quizzes over the Internet, at school or at home. You will get quiz results automatically via e-mail. The registration is free, and it is a snap!

iFigure

iFigure provides an extensive collection of online calculators and worksheets for help in planning, solving, and making decisions in daily life.

Quia Directory

The Quintessential Instructional Archive (Quia) Directory contains thousands of activities categorized into 50 subject areas. Using Quia's tools and templates, educators created all activities in the collection.

Quintessential Instructional Archive

This is another excellent test-maker site to support your curriculum.

School Express Free Worksheets

School Express provides over 5,000 free worksheets suitable for grades pre-K–8. Each printable worksheet has a separate answer sheet.

SuperKids: Educational Tools

SuperKids, owned and operated by Knowledge Share, provides a collection of easy-to-use, free worksheets for teachers to use in grades K–12. It includes a math worksheet generator teachers can use to customize printable worksheets for their students as well as vocabulary builders and classic problems that develop spatial reasoning.

University of Colorado at Denver GPA Calculator

This simple spreadsheet program calculates your GPA if you simply enter grades and the number of credits for each class. Another good calculator is owned by the University of California–Berkeley at http://www.aad.berkeley.edu/Meta-GPACalc.html.

Yahooligans!

Enter the word *worksheets* in the search engine to find hundreds of printable worksheets for your classroom.

Chapter Mastery Test

To the Instructor: *Refer to the Instructor's Manual for the answers to the Mastery Questions. This manual has additional questions and resource materials.*

Let us check for chapter comprehension with a short mastery test. Key Terms, Computer Lab, and Suggested Readings and References follow the test.

1. What is the difference between a presentation graphics program and a paint program? Describe the major features of each.

2. How has the availability of paint programs on the computer affected the traditional way of drawing and painting?

3. Define *CAD* and discuss its primary use.

4. What is a *teacher support tool program*? Explain how it can provide individualized instruction for a class.

5. What is a *print graphics program*? Discuss two uses for this program in the school curriculum.

6. Define *computer graphics* and explain its importance in today's world.

7. What are the advantages and disadvantages of using a grade-book program?

8. Explain how graphics programs can be beneficial for the classroom.

9. What is an *electronic portfolio* and why is it useful for measuring student performance?

10. Your school will let you purchase only one graphics program. Will you choose a print graphics, presentation graphics, paint, drawing, or computer-aided design (CAD) package? Explain and justify your selection.

Key Terms

Computer Lab: Activities for Mastery and Your Portfolio

14.1 Create an Applications Database   Create a basic database that can store a variety of information.

14.2 Practice Choosing Applications   Determine which kind of software you should use for a given scenario.

14.3 Use a presentation graphics program to graphically represent Jane Smith's grades of 50, 60, 70, 88, 97, and 100.

14.4 Use a print graphics program to produce (a) a riddle card, (b) a poster, (c) a calendar, and (d) letterhead stationery. Explain the educational value of each product.

14.5 Create a test for the class using a test-making program.

14.6 Evaluate three test-making programs, discussing their strengths and weaknesses.

14.7 Use one of the many puzzle utilities to create a product for class consumption.

14.8 Review three grade-book programs and talk about their differences and similarities. Explain why you would choose one over the others.

14.9 Create an electronic portfolio as a website.

Suggested Readings and References

Eiser, L. "Print It! 101 Things to Print with Your Computer." *Classroom Computer Learning* (April 1988), 76, 77.

Freedman, Allan. *The Computer Desktop Encyclopedia.* Point Pleasant, Pa.: Computer Language Company, 2003.

Friefeld, Susan. "Starry Night on Computer." *Arts and Activities* 122, no. 5 (January 1998): 25.

Guskey, Thomas R. "Computerized Grade Books and the Myth of Objectivity." *Phi Delta Kappan* 83, no. 10 (June 2002): 775–780.

Harris, Judith B. "What Do Freehand and Computer-Facilitated Drawings Tell Teachers About the Children Who Drew Them?" *Journal of Research on Computing in Education* 29, no. 4 (Summer 1997): 351–69.

Holzberg, Carol. "Print Creativity Packages." *Technology and Learning* 17, no. 7 (April 1997): 8–12.

Hostetter, Bryan. "CAD Essentials for the Classroom." *Tech Directions* 56, no. 6 (January 1997): 36.

Kilbane, Clare R., and Natalie B. Milman. *The Digital Teaching Portfolio Handbook: A How-to Guide for Educators.* New York: Allyn & Bacon, 2003.

Lindroth, Linda. "Blue Ribbon Software." *Teaching PreK–8* 33, issue 8 (May 2003): 24–28.

Mack, Warren E. "Computer-Aided Design Training and Spatial Visualization Ability in Gifted Adolescents." *Journal of Technology Studies* 21, no. 2 (Summer–Fall 1995): 57–63.

Martin, Joan, Mei-Hung Chiu, and Anne Dailey. "Science: Graphing in the Second Grade." *Computing Teacher* (November 1990), 28–32.

Moore, J. L., M. Orey, and J. V. Hardy. "The Development of an Electronic Performance Support Tool for Teachers." *Journal of Technology and Teacher Education* 8, no. 1 (2000): 29–52.

Rogers, Laurence T. "Computer as an Aid for Exploring Graphs." *School Science Review* 76, no. 276 (March 1995): 31–39.

Schrock, Kathleen, and Sharron L. McElmeel. "Newsletter Design to Make Them Take Notice." *Library Talk* 13, no. 1 (January/February 2000): 36.

Sharp, Richard, Vicki Sharp, and Martin Levine. *Best Web Sites for Teachers,* 5th ed, Eugene, Ore.: ISTE, 2002.

Sharp, Vicki, *Make It with Inspiration.* Eugene, Ore.: Visions Technology in Education, 2003.

Ursyn, Anna. "Computer Art Graphics Integration of Art and Science." *Learning and Instruction* 7, no. 1 (March 1997): 65–86.

PART IV

What Teachers Should Know About Educational Technology

CHAPTER 15

Issues and Research in Educational Technology

The Computer and the School

There are many issues surrounding the use of computers in the classroom. Many teachers, administrators, and parents must face the issue of having a single computer in a classroom of many students. Teachers in less-affluent neighborhoods, meanwhile, are lucky if they have even one computer in their classrooms. Software piracy, computer security, unequal access, and health risks are other important issues. Even computer research raises numerous issues, as does the role of the computer in our society. This chapter will explore all of these issues and review Internet sites that offer lesson plans and information on software piracy.

Objectives

Upon completing this chapter, you will be able to do the following:

1. List strategies for using one computer with 30 or more children in the math, science, social studies, and language arts areas.
2. Describe three factors related to software privacy.
3. Discuss three ways to lessen the chance of computer-related injuries.
4. List some practical ways a teacher can improve computer security.
5. Summarize the research findings on CAI and (a) gender differences, (b) science simulations, (c) word processing, (d) students with learning disabilities, (e) motivation, (f) attitudes, and (g) distance learning.

One Computer in the Classroom

The typical classroom used to have only one computer for 30 or more children. A recent survey, however, shows that the typical U.S. school today has one computer for every 3.8 students (*Market Data Retrieval*, 2002, http://www.schooldata.com/). Most of the time, however, these computers reside in a lab, and the classroom still offers only a single computer. Some teachers encase the one precious computer in plastic wrap and issue strict rules to govern its use, and others are afraid to use the computer at all. We will consider seven suggestions for better capitalizing on the computer's capabilities in the classroom: (1) select the software according to students' needs; (2) collect the appropriate equipment; (3) organize the classroom; (4) use the team approach; (5) know the software's time factor; (6) encourage group participation; and (7) integrate computer use into the curriculum.

Selection of Software

In any good instruction, you adapt the material to students' needs. This principle holds for software as well. Students have varied abilities, interests, and preferences that warrant different teaching considerations and strategies. For example, if a student does not know how to type, he or she will have to search for the keys on the keyboard, thus becoming easily frustrated with the computer. At a third-grade level, a teacher's first strategy may be to instruct students in keyboarding skills, starting with the return, escape, and arrow keys.[1]

Another strategy for introducing the keyboard is to create a large keyboard and place it at the front of the room. Next, arrange students in pairs to practice the letter and number locations on seat copies of the large-size keyboard. After students have had the experience of helping each other explore the keyboard, direct the whole class in finding designated keys. Eventually, have the children close their eyes and continue to practice finding keys.

Typing programs such as *Type to Learn Junior,* (K–2; Sunburst) and *Kid Keys 2.0* (Knowledge Adventure) provide excellent introductions to the keyboard. *Type to Learn Junior* features a learning tutorial and three interactive games to motivate early learners. One of the activities, *Cassie's Empty Nest,* emphasizes right-hand and left-hand placement. In Figure 15.1, a breeze is responsible for blowing different items out of

Figure 15.1 *Type to Learn Junior*

Reprinted by permission of Sunburst Technology.

Cassie's nest. The students type targets or letter combinations, in this case *mmm,* to help Cassie fill her nest again. *Kid Keys 2.0* has five activities that are designed to introduce young children to the keyboard. This program features on-screen helping hands that show correct finger position, multiple levels that enable students to advance at their own pace, and closed captioning for youngsters who are hearing impaired.

[1]One research scientist at SRI International recommends delaying the formal introduction of keyboarding until the third grade (Buckleitner, 2000).

Once the children are skilled in locating keys, they are ready to work with a typing program such as *Mavis Beacon Teaches Typing 15* (Riverdeep) and *Typing Tutor 10* (Knowledge Adventure). *Mavis Bacon Teaches Typing* teaches typing for age 8 to adult through personalized typing lessons that focus on the student's strengths and weaknesses. The content is age appropriate and so are the interesting activities. Teachers can personalize this program, adding custom content such as a vocabulary lesson, spelling words, or literature excerpts. There are eight different games that focus on accuracy, speed, and rhythm. *Typing Tutor 10* provides easy-to-use navigation and customized lessons based on students' needs. This program is well designed and effective in improving older students' (grade 5 and above) typing. Just click the *Lessons, Practice, Progress,* or *Games* buttons (Figure 15.2).

Figure 15.2 *Typing Tutor 10*

Used by permission of Vivendi Universal.

Furthermore, eight action-packed games motivate the learner. Once the students have achieved keyboard mastery, they can spend more time working with programs instead of working on the mechanics of finding keys.

If the students in the class need to improve their problem-solving abilities, a large range of programs are available. For example, **problem-solving software** such as *Where in the World Is Carmen Sandiego?* (Riverdeep) work effectively with middle-grade students in the social studies area, and *Science Seekers—Hidden in Rocks* (Tom Snyder Productions) works well for the same students in the science area. Using science seekers, students can collectively improve their critical thinking skills by taking notes, manipulating variables, analyzing the results, drawing conclusions, and offering solutions to problems (Figure 15.3).

If the class needs to study and research information about the United States, they can use a database software program such as *Access.* The students create information sheets, compose questionnaires, and collect appropriate data for computer entry. Each student might research two states and input information about each state's population, capital, number of representatives, and main crop. After information is entered into the database, students might search for a state in which the main crop is corn. When the state appears on the screen, the student at the computer calls out its name, and the other students shade the state on a blank seat map. After the students find all the applicable states and shade them, the class might study the maps and discuss

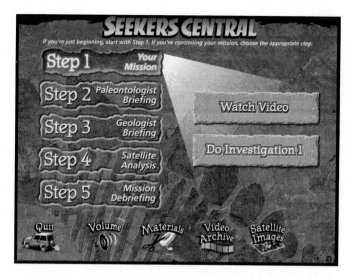

Figure 15.3 *Science Seekers—Hidden in Rocks*

Used by permission of Tom Snyder Productions.

where the corn-producing states are located. From this class discussion, the students could learn about the Corn Belt and why this region produces the most corn.

A teacher might use a drill-and-practice program such as *MindTwister* to improve students' math skills. This Math program can be used very effectively in a one-computer classroom. The teacher might organize students into groups of two or three and have the students compete with each other. For the example in Figure 15.4,

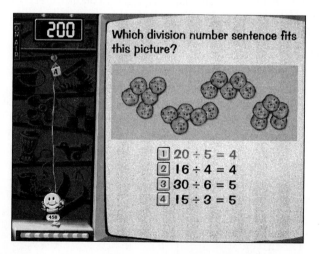

Figure 15.4 *MindTwister* Challenge Screen

© 2004 Riverdeep Interactive Learning Limited, and its licensors.

the player has to press the *A* key when he or she knows the answer and then press the correct answer, which is answer 1.

Collection of Equipment

When there is only one computer in the classroom, you need additional equipment to make the computer screen visible to the whole class. Projectors such as *InFocus* (Figure 15.5) display enlarged images from a personal computer onto a wall screen.

Figure 15.5 *LP130*
InFocus Projector
Courtesy of InFocus.

Another alternative is a portable **liquid crystal display (LCD) projection panel** or an overhead projector that uses the personal computer to display enlarged images on a screen. If the district cannot afford a projector or projection panel, there are less expensive alternatives. A T or Y adapter can split the signal coming from the class computer to display it on a larger television or monitor. A teacher can also use a **video scan converter** such as *TView Gold* to modify the personal computer or laptop output to display on a television or NTSC (National Television System Committee) monitor. (For a full explanation of these products, see Chapter 3.) Many Macintosh computers have video out ports; you simply plug into that particular port for large-screen television reception capability. In most cases, these computers are ready for use with an additional monitor.

When you are cramped for space, you can improve the situation by elevating a large television or monitor to increase visibility. You also can tape a transparency on the TV screen and use a grease pencil to write on the screen to illustrate a point. Furthermore, you can create practice sheets that duplicate a screen from a computer program so that students can work along with the presentation.

Classroom Organization

Ask yourself questions to determine the best seating arrangement for viewing the computer. Are the students going to be in their seats or on the floor? Will the class be divided into small groups for discussion purposes? Will students be traveling to different

Calahan Elementary School

learning stations in the room as they use manipulatives? Will they be using instruments such as a thermistor[2] to collect temperature data in different sections of the room?

Team Approach

Many students have been using computers since they were very young. If you have enough students who are familiar with the computer, organize them into a team. Under your tutelage, the team can practice giving directions, solving problems, and introducing new software. After the team is experienced, give the members identification badges and have them walk around the room answering questions on the current program. In addition to reducing the number of questions you will receive, this team method reaches a larger number of students.

Software Time Factor

For the computer program to be a success, you must know the program's time constraints. For instance, when the time frame is short, do not choose open-ended software, because the students will be unhappy when they have to stop prematurely. *The Oregon Trail V* (Riverdeep) takes at least 35 minutes to complete, and the students will object to quitting even though the program has a save function. *The Quarter Mile* (Barnum), on the other hand, is easier to stop and start with a class. Additionally, in selecting a program, check whether it saves the game or activity instantly or only at the end of a level. Software programs that require 15 or 20 minutes to finish a level might be inappropriate for some classroom situations.

Group Involvement

Your interactions with a class are very important and will determine how free your students feel to participate in class lessons involving computers. At the introduction of a lesson, explain that there are many acceptable answers and that often there is no one solution to a problem. Try to reduce the students' anxiety about evaluation. At first, involve the whole class in discussion; later, break the class up into smaller groups. Ask probing questions and ask students for their next move. Search for the reasons behind their answers and give them time to think. You should be a facilitator, letting the students do most of the talking and never imposing ideas on the class discussion. Try not to be judgmental in responding to the students; they will pick up even on your body language. Encourage the students to cooperate in order to promote learning and social skills. Advance the students' thinking by making comments such as "That seems like a good idea but expand on it."

Help the students practice problem solving by having them solve the same problem again, checking out their hypotheses and recording their collective answers. Give the students objects to manipulate at their desks to help them answer the questions that the software is posing. For example, *Puzzle Tanks* (Sunburst), a classic program, poses problems that involve filling tanks with Wonder Juice, Odd Oil, or Gummy Glue and moving this liquid over to a storage tank. At the simplest level, the program might ask the students to move 14 grams of Gummy Glue to a storage tank. For this problem, students are shown on the screen a tank that can hold 7 grams and another tank that can hold 1 gram. You can involve the whole class in this activity by distributing measuring cups

---

[2]A thermistor is a sensoring device that converts temperature into electrical impulses.

and beans to the students' desks. You might even divide the class into small groups that challenge each other to answer the most problems correctly. At the end of the day, have the students work on the computer in pairs, one partner using the computer and the other coaching and recording. This pairing encourages students to develop strategies for handling the problems inherent in the software. Organize the time the students spend at the computer with a schedule similar to the one in Figure 15.6. The students should

Figure 15.6
Computer-Use Chart

© 2004 Riverdeep Interactive Learning Limited, and its licensors.

PROGRAM: QUARTER MILE		
TIME	TEAMS	FINISHED
8:30-8:50	David Scott	✓
8:50-9:10	Bobbie Florence	✓
9:10-9:30	Jill Judy	

work on a program for a designated time interval. When their time is up, the next pair of students listed in the chart takes a turn. If a team is absent or busy, the next available partnership fills the void. This way the computer can be used by everyone in the class.

Integrating the Computer into the Classroom

How do you make the computer an integral part of the core curriculum? The software should not substitute for the standard curriculum but rather should complement it on a regular basis. We will look at four different software programs and how these programs can be included in classroom instruction. Then we will consider two methods for extending the reach of the computer in the schools: computer labs and wireless mobile labs.

Grolier Hollywood High. If you want to improve students' writing skills, you might use a program such as *Grolier Hollywood High* (Scholastic), which encourages creative writing and provides an opportunity for students to listen to their own written work and make revisions. When students use *Grolier Hollywood High* (Figure 15.7), they

Figure 15.7 *Grolier Hollywood High*

© Grolier Incorporated. All rights reserved.

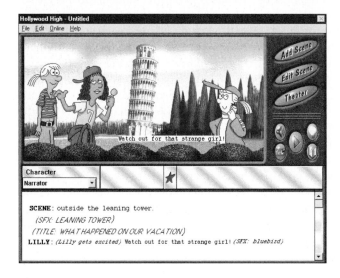

choose characters, expressions, and scenery for a play. They write scripts, add actions, edit the scripts, and then listen to and watch the characters perform. You can make suggestions for scripts that include recent events, historical occurrences, stories read, or class science experiments. Each student can work at his or her own desk to develop ideas for scripts, and the class can collectively brainstorm these ideas. Then you and the class can discuss the characters, plot, purpose, and climax. The class then can form small groups to write their own scripts, and these scripts can be translated to the computer and viewed by the whole class.

Mighty Math Calculating Crew. In math, you can use a **simulation** program such as *Mighty Math Calculating Crew* (Riverdeep) to help students improve their math problem-solving skills. This program invites students into an animated world of math adventure. They are given practice in handling topics such as multiplication, division, number lines, money, and 3-D geometry. Many of the activities contain virtual manipulatives, which help students make connections between concrete and abstract math. Using this program, the students experiment with geometry by rotating a 3-D solid or by changing a 2-D net to see the effect on the corresponding solid. They build spatial orientation skills, which enable them to recognize the same object when viewed from different angles, and spatial visualization skills, which allow them to mentally rotate a 3-D solid or imagine it in different configurations.

Crosscountry. For social studies, there is a truck-driving interactive simulation series entitled *Crosscountry* (Ingenuity Works), which includes such titles as *USA 2, Texas, Canada Platinum,* and *California.* The *Crosscountry* programs are effective for teaching map reading, geography, spatial relationships, and critical thinking skills. In *Crosscountry Canada Platinum,* (Figure 15.8) students discover the geography of Canada by

Figure 15.8
Crosscountry Canada Platinum

Used with permission from Ingenuity Works.

driving trucks to pick up commodities that the teacher or computer has selected from a list of 50 possibilities. These commodities are located in 79 Canadian cities. You could divide the class into two competing trucking companies and send them on their missions. (If one trucking company chooses to pick up only four commodities, its mission will require about 40 minutes.) You can customize the operation of the program so that both companies have to travel the same distance. Each team decides when to eat, sleep, and get gas; which cities to travel to; and how to get to the final destination. Obviously, each team's objective is to pick up and deliver its loads before the other team does. Members of the teams can record the trip routes, cities visited, population of those cities, locations, and other features. A winning team's strategy can be discussed, and each team can keep a journal of the journey.

Science Court. The *Science Court* series (Tom Snyder Productions) teaches science concepts to elementary and middle school students. The programs in the series cover, among other concepts and topics, sound, statistics, particles in motion, machines, the water cycle, fossils, and inertia. The program unfolds as a courtroom drama, and there are demonstrations and explanations as the lawyers battle over a case. In *Science Court—Fossils*, Jack Jenkins is accused of deliberately planting a fossil to halt construction of a café. During the trial, the students work in cooperative teams. They review the facts, engage in hands-on activities, and predict what will happen next. As the case progresses, the students attempt to answer questions correctly (Figure 15.9). After the case

Figure 15.9 *Science Court—Fossils*

Used by permission of Tom Snyder Productions.

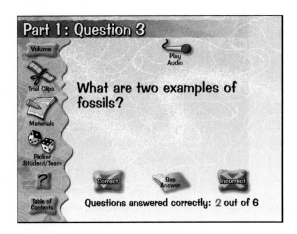

is presented, the students predict how the jury will vote. The teacher can lead interesting discussions about the trial. Members of the class can be encouraged to take notes and then share their notes with the class. During the course of the trial, the students learn about the different types of fossils and conditions for fossilization. They engage in experiments such as creating imprints of hands, feet, and teeth and then predict who made these imprints. Students also work as a team by listening and talking with others, sharing a goal, and becoming a member of a group. This series of programs is perfect for integrating the computer into the classroom.

In summation, you should select software that best satisfies the students' needs. You should also take time to collect the appropriate equipment, organize the room, and put the student experts to work. Learn the software, be aware of its time limitations, know how to integrate it into the classroom curriculum, and always encourage student participation by asking appropriate questions.

Computer Labs

With the paucity of computers in many classrooms and budget crunches, teachers may have to depend on computer labs. When setting up a computer lab the design is an important consideration. The computer lab's design is determined by the number of computers, room size, number of peripheral devices such as scanners and printers, and the instructor's teaching style. When the instructor demonstrates, it is important that students have an unobstructed view of the projection screen. If each computer station has a large desktop, students can work in pairs at each station. This is useful not only for collaborative activities, but also if some of the computers in the lab are not working.

There are many advantages to using a computer lab. A computer lab is invaluable for teaching students word processing, desktop publishing, math, science, CAD, multimedia production, and report preparation. The computer lab is the perfect place for the teacher to do classroom demonstrations. In a computer lab you can share resources, and the students can work on projects simultaneously.

There are some drawbacks to computer labs. The computer lab costs more because it must have a technical staff to maintain its operation. The lab administrators must be able to fix and maintain the machines and make sure the network is operating properly. Lab rules (no eating or smoking near equipment) must be established and followed, computer use must be scheduled, security must be maintained, and the equipment must be protected from viruses.

The Wireless Mobile Lab

Because schools want to integrate the computer into the classroom more easily, there is a trend away from the standard computer lab toward the **wireless mobile lab.** A typical wireless mobile lab has 16, 24, or 32 laptops locked inside the cart's wireless hub. (The hub is plugged into the school's network by a regular network cable.) Companies such as Dell and Apple (Figure 15.10) are currently selling these mobile wireless laptop labs. They usually have a printer, and the laptops have CD drives or DVD drives.

Figure 15.10 *iBook* Wireless Mobile Lab

Images courtesy of Apple Computers, Inc. and the photographer, Peter Belanger, www.peterbelanger.com.

Using this kind of setup, a school can then provide computer workstations when and where they are needed. Each computer has a card inside that gives the student wireless access to the Internet and the school's network. Teachers can sign up to use the cart when they need it, and they do not have to march students to a separate lab. Also, this type of lab takes up less space than a standard lab.

A problem with these wireless networks is security. Whenever you use a wireless network your data can easily be intercepted (Keizer, 2003; Brooks, 2002). Hackers can drive through your neighborhood, pulling access codes from your unsecured wireless network. It is easy to steal a person's Social Security number or banking account number and even place viruses on a network.

Security

One of the major issues related to computer use in the schools is security. Computer owners, including schools, must take steps to prevent theft and inappropriate use of their equipment. According to Safeware Insurance Agency, computer theft is the number-two cause of computer losses (Safeware, 2003; http://www.safeware.com/). Computer theft is a growing global problem costing billions annually (*PC Guardian*, 2003; http://www.pcguardian.com/portal/crimestats.html).

Today, most computer facilities have some sort of security system. These facilities have means of confirming the identities of persons who want to use the system so that unauthorized users do not gain access. Usually, authorized users are issued special cards, keys, passwords, or account numbers. In elementary schools and high schools, this identification system may consist of a simple list of names. Each person on this list has a key that provides access to a computer room with bolted-down machines. Unfortunately, some users lend their keys and share their passwords. Often, when computer users are allowed to choose their passwords, they choose easy-to-remember and easy-to-guess passwords.

One way to avert these problems is to assign access codes that are read by the computer from pass cards. The user does not have to remember this number, so the number can be complex. Even if the card is stolen, the code can be changed when the theft is reported. Recently, U.S. computer makers began offering **smart cards** as a security feature for laptop computers. A smart card can be used as an identification badge, consolidating different systems into one card. For example, an enabled smart card can be used for building access, network log-in, credit card, and remote and Web access. Figure 15.11 shows (A) the cardholder's picture, (B) the bar code, (C) the seal, and (D) the microchip.

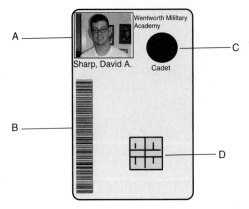

Figure 15.11 Smart Card

Courtesy of Vicki Sharp.

Another way businesses and schools are increasing security is by requiring every individual to enter a special code with his or her card. Experts advise going a step further by checking any available personal files for problems and restricting the number of people with access and the type of access they have to the computer. For instance, at most universities, students and professors use the same computer center, but they are not given the same access. Typically, the students have fewer privileges than the professors do.

Fingerprint recognition is another technology that can be used to control access to a computer or network. Before access is granted, the individual's fingers are scanned by a fingerprint reader and matched with the stored images of his or her fingerprints.

Another security problem concerns the protection of the operating system and data on the computer. It is essential that security measures protect all operating systems. Unscrupulous individuals have found ways to circumvent such systems to print out a list of users' passwords, to give themselves access rights they are not officially assigned, and to spread viruses. For these reasons, all sensitive data should be stored and locked up when not in use. Some large companies use data encryption to store data in a scrambled form, meaningless to anyone without a special data item called a *key*.

Computer labs are prone to abuse by students who may unintentionally or deliberately alter computer files, trash programs, and create all sorts of havoc. Teachers can safeguard their computers from tampering by purchasing desktop security programs such as *Fortres 101* (Fortres Grand Corporation) and *FoolProof* (SmartStuff Software, Figure 15.12). Developed for and by teachers, *FoolProof* ensures that students get the

Figure 15.12
FoolProof

© 2004 Riverdeep Interactive Learning Limited, and its licensors.

most beneficial use of their computer learning experience. *FoolProof* prevents users from deleting critical files and applications, making unauthorized changes to the desktop, saving unwanted programs, running disallowed programs, or corrupting the operating system, whether accidentally or maliciously.

Computers should also be safeguarded against natural disasters such as power surges, fires, and earthquakes. At the fundamental level, a good surge protector will rule out most power surges. If you have crucial data, a battery backup is essential because it gives you time to save your data. However, disks do wear out and fire destroys, so it is important even with battery backup to make backup disks and store them in a different location. Using USB Flash Drive and rewriteable CD-ROM's to store information.

From this discussion, it should be evident how important security is. How far one goes in implementing a system for security is related to cost. Usually, the more complicated the system, the more costly it is to carry out. Security will continue to be a problem because the number of computers and users continues to grow. Eventually, there will be a computer on each student's desk. The teacher's main job will be to determine how to use this technology as a powerful tool for education. The teacher will also have to provide appropriate security.

Software Piracy

Thomas Jefferson once said, "Some are born good, some make good, some are caught with the goods." Another issue related to computer use in the schools, besides an inadequate supply of computers and security concerns is software piracy. **Piracy**—the illegal copying of software—occurs by the thousands of incidents each year. A Business Software Alliance (BSA) study in 2002 showed that (1) in the United States there is a 23 percent piracy rate; (2) the United States suffered losses of $1.1 billion in 2001 from software pirates; (3) globally there is a $13.08 billion annual loss from software pirates; and (4) if you factor in the higher price of software, there has been a decline in piracy worldwide (http://global.bsa.org/usa/research/). We are gaining ground in the battle against software piracy, but we have not won the war.

Software copies work as well as the originals and sell for less money. Piracy is easy, and only the large piracy rings are caught. The SPA, a division of the Software and Information Industry Association (SIIA), reports finding many forms of software piracy on the Internet (SPA, 2003), and the Business Software Alliance reports an increase in Internet piracy (http://global.bsa.org/usa/research/). Internet sites offer pirated software for free downloading, and bulletin boards give links to these sites. For example, the well-known Pirates with Attitude (PWA) piracy ring was guilty of copyright infringement. PWA operated a website named *Sentinel*, which enabled members to download 5,000 copyrighted software programs for free. The website owner, Robin Rothberg, was arrested in February 2000, and a grand jury later indicted the other 16 members of the group (Software & Information Industry Association, http://www.siia.net/sharedcontent/press/2001/5-16-01.html).

The SIIA is the principal trade association of the software code and information content industry. SIIA represents more than 1,000 leading companies that develop and distribute software and electronic content for business, education, consumers, and the Internet. Hundreds of these companies look to SIIA antipiracy efforts to protect their intellectual property rights around the world. Visit the SIIA antipiracy home page at http://www.siia.net/piracy.htm.

In the 1980s, one of the most popular computer programs was a copy program that was able to duplicate protected software. It is speculated that 30 percent to 50 percent of a typical school's software has been illegally copied. Teachers discover this problem when they send illegally copied software to the software manufacturer for repair. People who would never think of stealing from a department store freely make illegal copies of software, justifying their dishonesty with the following rationalizations: (1) software developers receive free publicity for their products through illegal copies; (2) software is grossly overpriced and therefore fair game for piracy; and (3) the cost of copying software is borne by the developer and not the customer, and developers have money to spare. The truth is that software developers never condone illegal copying; they expect buyers to use the original copies of their products and make backups only as legally stipulated; software is very expensive to produce and market; and the cost of copying software is borne initially by the developers, but it is ultimately paid for by the legitimate buyer (Guglielmo, 1992).

The unauthorized duplication of software violates federal copyright law and deprives developers of the revenue they richly deserve. The law clearly states that "anyone who violates any of the rights of the copyright owner is an infringement of the copyright" (Federal Copyright Law, Section 501). Reproducing computer software without the proper authorization is a federal offense. The money paid for software represents a fee for one copy and does not give the user the right to copy freely. Civil damages for unauthorized copying can amount to as much as $150,000. Criminal penalties include jail and fines (Federal Copyright Law, Title 18, Section 2319[b]). Many bills have been introduced in Congress to strengthen the copyright laws and increase the penalties for illegal copying. The software piracy issue is certain to receive continued legal attention. The SPA has tried to help the software industry by creating a hotline for reporting software violations (1-800-388-7478). If the SPA finds a violation, it either works with the offending institution or petitions the federal court for a seizure order.

Software developers have produced elaborate copy protection schemes to combat the piracy problem. One method is to build instructions into the program that will override any command to copy the software. The problem with this method is that hackers can easily create a program that gets around the copy protection. Another method uses software fingerprints, an emerging protection method. Fingerprinting is a technique that examines a computer system's individual configuration to collect information that can be used as the system's unique identification. The data are selectively encrypted together to build a unique identifier that sets off a "time bomb" in the software program if the user does not pay, making the program erase itself along with any files that it created. Another method used is to program the software so it is linked to serial numbers inside the chips or logic board of the computer unit. Presently networks have serial numbers and there is electronic registration offered by almost every software house. Microsoft added the *Registration Wizard* to *Office 2000* so that you are forced to register your product. If you do not register the software, it will stop working after the 50th use (Wood, 2000). Yet for every scheme that is devised, a copy buster program is developed to override it.

Unfortunately, schools are a major culprit in educational software piracy. Why do schools copy illegally? Many schools and districts are eager to integrate the computer into the classroom. They have limited funds, and one copy for 32 students is not enough for group participation. Teachers want many copies so that they can have a group of students using the same software simultaneously. They view copying software as equivalent to photocopying teacher-made tests for their classrooms. They also justify the piracy as being for the greater good of students. In the end, the educator is the loser. Companies cannot make a profit selling educational software, so they divert their money to manufacturing products that are more economically lucrative. Software pirates ultimately drive smaller companies out of business.

What can school districts do to dissuade teachers or students from illegally copying software? They can warn teachers about illegally duplicating software and institute disciplinary action when violations occur. Furthermore, schools can keep software locked away in restricted areas and limit student and teacher access. They can appoint a person or committee to be responsible for keeping records on the software purchased and how it is being used. This person or committee would maintain a log of the software purchased and the machine on which the software resides. In addition, districts can require that teachers supervise students when they use software.

In the classroom, teachers can discuss recent criminal cases or related movies such as *War Games* to make students aware of the problems involved. Teachers can explain the federal and state laws and the differences between a felony, a crime punishable by a year in prison, and a misdemeanor, a crime punishable by a fine or a prison term. After the students have an understanding of the seriousness of computer crimes, they can devise a computer break-in policy for the school. The teacher can give each student a copy of this policy to read and study. The teacher can then present hypothetical cases concerning computer ethics breaches and ask the students what punishment according to the break-in policy they would recommend for the offender.

Teachers should find better ways to combat their budget constraints. Buying lab packs or multiple copies of software is one answer. A district can be encouraged to buy on-site licenses for selected programs, allowing the schools to make legal multiple copies and do multiple loadings of a program.[3] Schools should also move toward networking their machines, which enable them to run a networkable piece of software over multiple machines. Finally, teachers should involve students, parents, and the community in raising money for software. In the long term, it is better to purchase the software than to steal it because the legitimate buyer receives technical support and upgrades from the publisher. Most important, it is the honorable and ethical way to operate.

Presently, there is a trend for students to purchase their own computers for home use or to bring them to college. A student who does not have access to a computer is definitely at a disadvantage in this technological world. This leads us to the issue of computer access.

Unequal Access

Still another issue related to computer use in the schools and a major challenge to education in the 21st century is unequal access to computers. As it is often called, the **digital divide** "is the difference between those who have computers and high-tech gadgets in general and those who do not" (Freedman, 2003). Often, the divide runs along economic and racial/ethnic lines.

A computer gives a student the ability to search the Internet for the answers to questions or to use a word processing program to correct spelling and check grammar. Students can create better reports with graphics and sound; they can use computers to create electronic portfolios and multimedia presentations. With computer access students are more motivated to work harder in school, and they make greater strides in learning and developing technology skills. They can use distance learning to get an education from the privacy of their home. Unequal access to computers can widen the division between the wealthy and the poor. Cattagni and Farris (2001) showed that the ratio of students to computers with Internet access was higher for schools with the greatest poverty levels (6.8 to 1.0) than for other schools (4.5 or 5.6 to 1.0; National Center for Educational Statistics NCES, http://nces.ed.gov/pubs2002/internet/4.asp).

The Commerce Department report *Falling Through the Net: Toward Digital Inclusion* states that more and more individuals are using computers, but a digital divide still exists because digital access is still uneven. The report shows that the more money that a household earns, the higher the rate of computer access. Furthermore, the study shows that minorities, people with disabilities, and people with less education do not have as much access to computers. You can download the report from http://www.ntia.doc.gov/ntiahome/digitaldivide/.

By being aware of these problems of unequal access, the teacher can be more sensitive to the needs of the students. Teachers can use their expertise to integrate technology into the classroom more effectively. They can tell students who do not own

---

[3]*Multiple loadings* refers to the practice of loading a program from one disk onto several computers.

computers how to get access after school hours. They may want to be an advocate and raise money for more computers or talk to local businesses for help. There really is no easy answer to this issue in an era when the cost of education is increasing and budget cuts are too. Fortunately, private foundations have tried to alleviate this problem by donating computers to libraries. The Federal Commerce Commission offers a discounted price (e-rate) for Internet service, which applies to schools and libraries. There are many initiatives that are trying to make sure that all students have equal access to technology. In the years to come, ideally this situation will change, and the computer will be as commonplace as the telephone.

Health Risks Using Computers

Along with an inadequate supply of computers, security and piracy concerns, and unequal access is the issue of health risks. Every computer store offers a variety of injury-reducing equipment in the form of wrist pads, antiglare screens, and ergonomic keyboards and trackballs. Unfortunately, it is very easy to use computer equipment improperly to the point of damaging your body. **Repetitive strain injuries** are a serious medical problem. According to the Bureau of Labor Statistics (http://www.bls.gov/), computer monitors, like other electrical devices, generate electric and magnetic fields in a very low frequency. There is scientific debate over whether low-level electromagnetic emissions cause health problems such as cancer. Even though this debate is unresolved, the computer industry has moved to reduce these emissions. Most manufacturers support the guidelines known as MPR-II, which were established in 1990 by the Swedish Board for Measurement and Testing, or the stricter TCO guidelines, named after the Swedish office workers' union that developed them. Recently, school districts have begun to purchase liquid crystal display monitors instead of RGB monitors. The liquid crystal display monitor does not have emissions problems.

You can lessen the chances of computer-related injury by following these 10 suggestions:

1. Position yourself in front of the screen like a concert pianist, relax your shoulders, and keep your forearms and hands in a straight line. Make sure your lower back is supported and your thighs are horizontal to the ground. The top of the computer monitor should be slightly below eye level, and it should be positioned to prevent any type of glare. Finally, your feet should rest flat on the floor, and there should be clearance under the work area, between your legs and the desk (Figure 15.13).

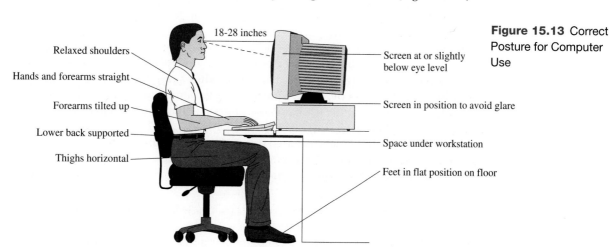

Figure 15.13 Correct Posture for Computer Use

2. Always work 18 to 28 inches from the monitor. Electromagnetic emissions from the front of any display should be negligible at 28 inches. Furthermore, the left side of the computer and the back usually generate the strongest emissions, so try to stay clear of these areas.

3. Avoid unnecessarily turning up the brightness on the monitor because you may be exposing yourself to higher emissions than the MPR-II guidelines allow.

4. Do not overwork. Take frequent breaks from the computer, at least once an hour. Move around and exercise your legs, arms, and neck. Do not stare at the monitor continually, but look around every 5 or 10 minutes. Remain relaxed.

5. Spend time finding a proper chair for your computer. Try it out and make sure you have ways of adjusting it to suit your individual needs.

6. The equipment you use most often should be close enough that you do not have to stretch to reach it.

7. Check to make sure the keys on your keyboard are not too difficult to press. The keys should give some tactile feedback; do not press too hard on the keyboard. Use function keys to help cut down on keystrokes.

8. Do not grip the mouse too tightly because it will increase the risk of injury. Additionally, choose a mouse that is comfortable for your hands.

9. Never brace your wrists against mouse pads when you are typing because this will eventually cause injury.

10. Finally, if you continually work with graphics, buy an appropriate input device such as a drawing tablet.

Computer-Assisted Instruction Research Findings

Computer-assisted instruction (CAI) has been used for over 25 years. CAI refers to applications specifically designed to teach a variety of subject areas to children and adults (Freedman, 2003). In CAI, students receive feedback from the computer, which controls the sequencing of the subject matter. Because of increased access to computers, teachers are concerned about the effects the computer has on instruction. The research literature contains many studies related to computer-assisted instruction, and this section will highlight some of these research findings.

Achievement

Numerous studies have compared the achievement scores of students using computer-assisted instruction with the achievement scores of students receiving regular instruction. Generally, the results indicate that CAI produces equal or greater achievement (Tsai and Pohl, 1978; Goode, 1988; Swan et al., 1990; Harrison and Van Devender, 1993; Kromhout and Butzin, 1993; Chambless and Chambless, 1994; Wenglinsky, 1998; Kuehner, 1999; Mann et al., 1999; Wong, 2001; Bayraktar, 2002).

Gene Glass (1976, 1977) introduced a technique called **meta-analysis**[4] in order to generate a clearer picture of the effects of computer-based treatments. Other researchers followed and compiled meta-analysis studies in the area of instructional

---

[4]Meta-analysis is a statistical technique that enables researchers to summarize the results of a large group of research studies and identify general effects.

computing. Kuliks's series of meta-analysis studies were the most comprehensive (C. C. Kulik, J. A. Kulik, and Cohen, 1980; J. A. Kulik, Bangert, and Williams, 1983; C. C. Kulik, J. A. Kulik, and Shwath, 1986; J. A. Kulik and Chen-Lin, 1987; C. C. Kulik, Chen-Lin, and J. A. Kulik, 1991). These studies showed that students who were taught using the computer scored higher on achievement tests than did those students who were taught using other methods. The Kulik studies also showed that this analysis produced different results, depending on the grade, ability level, and type of instruction.

Roblyer, Castine, and King (1988) summarized previous literature reviews on the educational effectiveness of instructional computing before they presented their meta-analysis of recent studies. Here is a brief rundown of their findings: (1) there are higher achievement results for college-age and adult students than for elementary and secondary students; (2) the computer produces the greatest achievement gains in science, with math, reading, and cognitive skills yielding about half the effect; (3) computer-assisted instruction software programs are all of approximately equal effectiveness; and (4) lower-achieving students show more gains with CAI than do students who are achieving at grade level, but these gains are not statistically significant.

Using a meta-analysis approach, Khalili and Shashaani (1994) reviewed 36 published studies to see how effective CAI was in improving students' academic achievement. They concluded that computers are very effective in improving academic performance and that length of computer usage is an important factor.

Using a meta-analytic technique over a 12-year span, Mann and Shakeshaft (1997) did a study that was commissioned by participating New York school districts to see if computer technology made a difference for the region's students, teachers, and schools. The study involved 1,722 elementary and secondary school students and 4,041 teachers. The researchers found that student achievement is higher in schools in which teachers believe that technology has a positive impact on learning. Moreover, overall gain from increased use of computer-related technology for students and teachers is statistically significant.

In a 1997 study, Christmann, Badgett, and Lucking compared the academic achievement of secondary students across academic areas. These students were instructed by CAI alone, by traditional methodology supplemented with CAI, or by traditional methodology alone. In addition, the study compared the recent results with earlier research findings. The meta-analysis study results showed that the average student receiving traditional instruction supplemented with CAI achieved higher academic achievement than did 57.2 percent of the students receiving traditional instruction alone. However, the effect of CAI on academic achievement showed a decline during the 12-year period; there was a very high correlation between the size of the effect and the number of years.

Sivin-Kachala (1998) did find an increase in achievement from pre-school through higher education for regular children and children with special needs. Schacter (1999) examined 700 studies on achievement and technology. He found that students who use CAI and other technologies show achievement gains on standardized tests, national tests, and constructed tests.

Finally, Bayraktar in his 2002 meta-analysis study reported how effective computer-assisted instruction is on achievement in secondary and college science education compared to traditional classroom instruction. The results he found showed positive effect for simulation and tutorial CAI instruction.

On the other hand, Clark's review of CAI in meta-analytical studies in 1985 was critical of the research and suggested that studies by the Kuliks and others overestimated CAI's benefits because uncontrolled instructional methods were embedded in the instructional treatments. Clark (1991, 1994) felt that the existing evidence did not indicate that computers yield learning benefits. In an eastern Canada high school study, Liu, Macmillan, and Timmons (1998) found computer integration produces no significant effect on achievement and there is no change in student attitude toward computers. Also, Rachal (1995) reviewed studies on adult reading achievement and CAI. He found that most of these studies did not show a significant difference between CAI and conventional approaches.

As you can see from this discussion, recent research findings on CAI suggest that CAI produces achievement equal to or greater than traditional teaching (Bayraktar, 2002; Wong, 2001, Kuehner, 1999; Mann et al., 1999; Schacter, 1999; Wenglinsky, 1998; Sivin-Kachala, 1998; Mann and Shakeshaft, 1997) even though there is still a lack of consensus among some researchers on the value of CAI.

Gender Differences

Most gender studies try to get at the reasons for males using the computer more than females. Collis and Ollila (1986) examined gender differences in secondary school students' attitudes toward writing on the computer. Females were significantly less positive than their male counterparts on every item that related to computers.

Swadener and Hannafin (1987) studied the gender similarities and differences in sixth graders' attitudes toward the computer. They found that boys with higher achievement levels in mathematics also had a high interest in computers. The boys with low scores had low interest in computers. This finding is completely opposite for females, with the low-achieving female students having the most interest in the computer.

Siann et al. (1988) studied gender stereotyping and computer involvement. They suggested there are some encouraging trends, but males still use computers more than females do.

Williams et al. (1994) examined the effects of factors such as past experience and sex-role stereotyping on computer-interaction tasks completed by 154 male and 223 female college students. The results of the study did support the pattern of male advantage, but they also highlighted the complex factors involved in computer interactions.

Makrakis and Sawada (1996) surveyed 773 ninth-grade students in Tokyo, Japan, and Stockholm, Sweden. They found that, regardless of the country surveyed, males reported higher scores on computer aptitude and enjoyment than females did. Whitley (1997) did a meta-analysis of studies of gender differences in computer attitude and found that males showed greater sex-role stereotyping of computer use, higher computer self-efficacy, and more positive attitudes toward computers than did females. The largest differences were found in high school students; most other differences were small. Liao (1999) did a meta-analysis on the effect of gender differences on attitudes toward computers. These results too suggest that male subjects have a slightly more positive attitude toward computers than female subjects.

Young (2000) used a student computer attitude survey with 462 middle and high school students. The results of the study showed greater confidence among male students in regard to the computer and the perception of computers as a male domain supported by males. Finally, in a study involving 104 first-year teacher education students in Brunei Darussalam, Swe Khine (2001) found that female students showed higher anxiety toward using computers as compared to their male counterparts.

The majority of studies on gender differences seem to point to males having a more positive attitude toward computers than females. There are many possible reasons:

(1) most of the computer games are violent and appeal to the male population; (2) computers are linked to math and science, fields that show an overrepresentation of males; (3) magazines and newspapers depict men using the computer more than women; (4) when women are associated with the computer it is in a secretarial role; and (5) many teachers encourage boys to use computers but discourage girls from doing so.

Science Simulations

Generally, students learn very well with science simulation software. Moore, Smith, and Avner (1980) found higher student achievement with computer simulations when students had to interpret the results of the experiments to make decisions. If the students only had to follow directions and calculate the results, there was no difference between the experimental and control groups. Summerville (1984) and Fortner, Schar, and Mayer (1986) noted similar findings. Linn (1986) conducted an experiment in which 8 eighth-grade science classes used computers as lab partners for a semester. The students learned to use the computer to collect and display data and save and print out their reports. They used tools such as temperature and light probes that were attached to the computer, and the results were displayed on their computer screens. Linn found that the students instructed in the microcomputer-based labs outperformed 17-year-olds who took a standardized test on scientific knowledge. In addition, these computer-taught students demonstrated a very positive attitude toward experimentation. Farynaiarz and Lockwood (1992) examined the impact of microcomputer simulations on environmental problem solving among community college students. The students showed a highly significant improvement in problem-solving skills after being exposed to three simulation models on lake pollution.

Kumar and Helgeson (1995) reviewed seven computer applications including simulation and found that simulation improved the quality and efficiency of record keeping and data analysis. Rueter and Perrin (1999) tested the effect of using a computer simulation to teach the concept of a food web to nonbiology majors in an introductory course. They concluded that the use of the simulation resulted in significantly better performance on an open-ended essay question for students using the software, and the average student generally scored higher. Finally, Shim, Park, Hyun-Sup Kim, Jae-Hyun Kim, Young-Chul Park, and Ryu (2003) did a study on virtual reality technology (VRT) learning programs for middle school students. Their study reported that VRT simulations increase the students' interest and understanding of scientific concepts. The results of the science simulation studies continue to be promising. Even a study that shows no significant difference between students who use the traditional method and students who use the computer is encouraging. Such a finding means that simulations can substitute for laboratory experiments, which is advantageous because science simulations are less dangerous, less time-consuming, and less expensive than actual lab work. They encourage student involvement in the learning process and enable teachers to give students access to situations that ordinarily would be impossible.

Word Processing

Many studies deal with word processing and its effect on the quantity and quality of student writing, but the evidence is contradictory (Bangert-Drowns, 1993). O'Brien (1994), Feldman (1984), Morehouse, Hoaglund, and Schmidt (1987), Jones (1994), and Owston and Wideman (1997) found evidence in favor of word processing. In 2001, Li and

Cumming did a study of adult male Mandarin speakers learning English as a Second Language (ESL). They studied whether using the computer for writing improved the quality of the revisions and the quality of the students' compositions. The results of the study showed that when the learners used the computer they stayed on task longer and they produced higher-level revisions. Owston and Wideman in 1997 did a three-year study (grades 3–5) of two groups of elementary school students and determined that writing quality improved in schools with high computer access, and word processors contributed to the improvement. Gupta (1998) compared Singapore students' composing behaviors using a spelling checker. He found that the spelling checker benefits those students whose writing ability is poor and who have trouble with the mechanical aspects of writing.

However, Daiute (1985) found that students wrote less with a word processor. Kurth (1987) found no differences in quality of writing or revisions between a secondary school group that used word processing for their writing and a secondary group that used pencil and paper. Seawel et al. (1994) compared the effects of computer-based word processing and writing by hand on third and fourth graders' attitudes and performance in writing. The third graders made more revisions and edits when using word processors, whereas the fourth graders made more changes in their hand-written drafts. Jackowski-Bartol (2001) investigated the impact of word processing on middle school students. Their study found that when students used the computer they had trouble with hand-thought coordination for typing, and that computer composition time exceeded that of traditional composition.

Roblyer, Castine, and King (1988) summarized the research and said that word processing did not appear to improve the quality of writing. Hawisher (1986) and Bangert-Drowns (1993) reviewed the research on word processing and noted that implementation differences among the various studies could affect their outcomes. Reed (1996) found that the type of word processor that is used affects the students. For example, younger students need more prompts, but older ones find this inhibiting. These criticisms highlight the problem, not only for word processing studies, but also for other research concerning computer applications. The inconclusive nature of these studies may be due to the difficulty of quantifying the assessment of writing.

Students with Learning Disabilities

Most research indicates that the learning disabled (LD) benefit from involvement with CAI. In 2002, Blair et al. studied 24 eighth-grade mildly dissabled students, and they found that these students improved their organization and writing performance with computer technology. During a one-month summer school remedial program, mildly disabled students were taught writing strategies using word processors and a visual planning software program called *Inspiration*. The students were tracked on their attitude toward writing and the quantity and quality of their writing compositions. As the students progressed, they engaged more in planning their writing, their objections to writing decreased, and positive attitudes toward writing increased. There was a slight increase in the quality of their writing and an increase in the amount of writing. Students enjoyed the computers and improved their keyboarding skills.

Zhang (2000) found similar results when he conducted a year-long research study involving 5 fifth-grade students with learning disabilities. He used a specially designed computer program as a writing tool to assist these students with weekly writing curriculum. The study showed that students had positive gains in their writing behaviors and their written products. Xin and Jitendra (1999), in a meta-analysis study on the effectiveness of instruction in word-problem solving for students with learning problems, found that computer-assisted instruction was most effective for group-design studies and long-term intervention effects. McNaughton et al. (1997) investigated the impact of integrated proofreading strategy training on LD secondary students. This training consisted of using a computer spelling checker and student strategies for proofreading. Students showed an increase in strategy use and percentage of spelling errors corrected on student compositions and proofread material. Every method improved writing accuracy. Shiah et al. (1994–1995) studied 30 elementary LD students and found that these students performed significantly better on mathematics tests when using a computer than they did using paper and pencil. The researchers found no differences among variations in computer-assisted instruction.

Koseinski et al. (1993) conducted a study with six male LD elementary school students. They were taught multiplication facts using computer software programs with a five-second constant time delay procedure. The results of the study indicated that this computer-assisted program was very effective and that the learning generalized with varying degrees of success. Carman and Kosberg (1982) showed a significant positive influence on attention-to-task behavior for emotionally disabled children. Other studies also support positive effects of CAI with learning disabled (Lally, 1980; Watkins and Webb, 1981; Hasselbring, 1982).

Motivation and Attitude

Teachers face the challenge of motivating students and fostering in them a positive attitude to improve their chances for success in school. For example, an essential element in improving students' spelling is keeping interest high (Ruel, 1977). Many studies report students' positive attitudes toward the computer and how computers motivate students and help them maintain high interest (Lim, 2002; Kosakowski, 2000; S. Hatfield, 1996; M. M. Hatfield, 1991; S. Clement, 1981).

In 2002, Glickman and Dixon studied community college intermediate algebra students. They found that students taught by CAI significantly outperformed on conceptual measures students taught with a lecture approach. Furthermore, they saw significant improvement in mathematics attitudes from the start to the finish of the semester.

Yildirim (2000) examined the changes in attitude of 114 preservice and inservice teachers toward computers after they participated in an educational computing class. The results indicated that the teachers' attitudes (anxiety, confidence, and liking) significantly improved after this computer literacy course. S. Hatfield (1996) examined the effective use of computer stations across the curriculum and found overall increased computer use and increased student motivation and interest. Terrell and Rendulic (1996) did a comparative study of elementary school students and found evidence that the use of computer-managed instructional feedback can have a positive effect on student motivation and achievement. Richman's (1994) study showed how innovations in educational technology contributed to motivation and achievement of at-risk students in the New York's Berkshire Union Free School District. Robertson (1978) found that children who had experienced failure in the past responded positively to computer-assisted programs. She concluded that the children involved in the study did not experience a sense of failure over an incorrect response.

In a departure from the other studies, McKinnon, Nolan, and Sinclair (2000) found that an increase in access to computers resulted in a decrease in favorable attitudes toward the computer. The findings seem paradoxical because the decrease in positive attitudes toward computers was accompanied by an increasingly positive attitude toward school and the integrated curriculum program in which computers were a major element. Mitra and Steffensmeir (2000) found that, if students did not have ready access to computers, their attitudes toward teaching and learning did not change. However, if these students had easy access through a networked institution, this fostered a positive attitude toward computers in teaching and learning. In a 1998 study, Liu, Macmillan, and Timmons found that there was no significant effect of computer integration on achievement, and there was no significant change in student attitude toward computers after the computer integration.

Generally, students perceived that using computers had a positive effect on their learning. Some researchers have tried to find out if students prefer computer-based methods simply because a computer is involved. Other research has focused on the computer's influence on student attitudes toward school and curriculum. Bracey (1982) found that students reacted favorably to computer use for instructional tasks. He reported that students who worked on the computer had a more positive attitude toward the machine than did those students who had not used the computer.

Generally, the CAI studies that focused on students' attitudes toward themselves and school learning were positive. However, the results are inconclusive on the effects of computer instruction on motivation and school achievement. One reason for this finding might be that achievement in school is not based on a simple set of variables but is the result of a complex set of factors.

Distance Learning Research

In the literature from the mid-1950s to the present there are numerous studies comparing distance learning with traditional learning. The majority of these studies found that there is no significant difference between distance learning and traditional classroom learning (Simonson, Smaldino, Albright, and Zvacek, 2003; Merisotis and Jamie, 1999; Russell, 1997). Even a finding of no significant difference between students who use the traditional method and students who use distance learning is optimistic. Such a finding means that distance learning can substitute for the traditional classroom experience. The research also shows that distance learners have a better attitude toward learning than do traditional learners. Distance learners feel they learn just as much as a traditional classroom learner (Simonson, Smaldino, Albright, and Zvacek, 2003; Bisciglia and Monk-Turner, 2002; Grenzky and Maitland, 2001; Inman, Kerwin, and Mayes, 1999).

Furthermore, a distance learner has greater satisfaction when there is more interaction between the teacher and the students. In distance learning the student must be able to communicate with the instructor (Simonson, 2000; Fulford and Zang, 1993; Westbrook, 1997). In a 1997 study, McHenry and Bozik found distance learners need a sense of community in order to be successful. If a distance learner perceives there is a decrease in interaction, this affects his or her coursework satisfaction. The research also shows that a successful distance learner is usually an abstract learner who is inwardly motivated (Osborn, 2001; Wang and Newlin, 2000; Song, Sang Ho, 2000; Bures, Abrami, Amundsen, 2000). Even with all this research on distance learning, there is a need for further research on distance learning's effect on K–12 students.

Problems with the Research

Although a considerable amount of research has been done since the early 1980s, the research is problematic. Many CAI studies were conducted before microcomputers were readily available. In addition, many studies are not thoroughly reported in the literature, so it is impossible to determine whether the conclusions drawn by the investigators are supported by the data. The meta-analysis that Roblyer et al. (1988) performed included 38 studies and 44 dissertations from a possible 200. The rest of the studies were eliminated because of reasons such as methodological flaws or insufficient data. A good portion of CAI research is anecdotal, based on experiences and not on experimental design.

Educators are now beginning to understand what role the computer could play in educating students. However, we still do not know if computers are the best way to foster learning. Studies have shown that students in most technologically advanced classrooms perform no better on standardized tests than their peers do (Trotler, 1997). There definitely is a need for higher-quality computer research to get substantive answers to our many questions.

Research Generalizations

Even with these problems, some relevant generalizations can be made from the research:

1. In science, the computer is a useful tool for simulations. The Army and Navy use war game simulations. Chemistry instructors can use computer-based simulations as substitutes for lab work. Flight instructors can use flight simulation software instead of putting novices at the controls of actual planes. A simulation program is generally less dangerous, less expensive, and less time-consuming than the real experience.
2. The computer is helpful for individualization. Students working with computers can progress at their own pace. If they need help with math facts, they can turn to the computer for individualized tutoring, freeing the teacher to work with other students or on other academic areas. This type of individualization spreads the range of abilities in a class and enables some students to move ahead.
3. The computer changes attitudes toward the computer, school, and school subjects. The computer does motivate children, and there is speculation that it might improve the dropout rate.
4. There is no strong body of evidence supporting the notion that a positive attitude toward the computer will result in improved achievement.
5. There is no significant difference between distance learning and traditional classroom learning.
6. Distance learners have a better attitude toward learning than do traditional learners.
7. Word processing motivates children to write. However, there is no difference between the quality of writing produced using a word processor and that generated with pencil and paper.
8. Gender studies have found that boys work more frequently with the computer than do girls. This finding appears to be a socially developed difference.

Summary

In this chapter, we explored how to integrate the computer into the curriculum, select software according to the needs of pupils, collect the appropriate equipment, organize the classroom, and employ the team approach. We discussed the teacher's use of computer labs and wireless mobile labs. We explore the issues such as computer security, software piracy, unequal access, and health risks. In discussing computer security, we explored data protection, unauthorized access, disk protection, and proper backup of computer files. We found out that software piracy is an issue that computer companies are still trying to resolve. Software houses offer alternatives to schools tempted to illegally duplicate software: on-site licensing, lab packs, and networkable discs. We also discovered that even though the computer is prominent in our society, there is still unequal access to computer technology. The research also shows that more and more individuals are suffering from health problems because of the computer. We examined safety guidelines to follow while using the computer. The chapter concluded with a brief rundown of some of the important research studies on computer-assisted instruction (CAI).

 # Study and Online Resources

*Go to Chapter 15 in the Student Edition of the Online Learning Center at www.mhhe.com/sharp5e to **practice with key concepts, take chapter quizzes, read PowerWeb articles** and **news feed updates** related to technology in education, and **access resources** for learning about technology and integrating it into the classroom.*

Click on *Web Links* to link to the following websites.

Arthur Levine: Creating an Education System for an Information Age

This site offers insight into the mind of Arthur Levine, an education leader. Levine believes that change is the biggest challenge that today's educators must face.

AT&T Learning Network

AT&T Learning Network offers the newest models and latest trends in education and professional development and support. The site provides information on cable in education, virtual academies, and other online services and resources.

California Instructional Technology Clearinghouse

California Instructional Technology Clearinghouse provides over 3,700 selected electronic learning resources that match the California content standards.

CDT's Resource Library

The Center for Democracy and Technology provides information on a number of civil liberties issues ranging from Internet filtering to privacy and security.

Computers and Society Social Issues Pages

Professor Judith A. Perrolle of Northeastern University in Boston addresses social issues in computing ranging from equity in access to ethics.

Electronic School

The *Electronic School* is an award-winning technology magazine for K–12 school leaders. This online edition of *Electronic School* provides articles from the print edition as well reviews, forms, and links.

SPA Software Publishers Association

The Software and Information Industry Association (SIIA) has brought together the leading companies of the software and information industry, expanding market opportunities and forging the way toward a stronger industry. SIIA is the only trade association with a global reach that provides a credible, unifying voice for all businesses that provide the software and information that underpin the digital economy.

Teaching in a Digital Age

The George Lucas Educational Foundation has launched a project called *Teaching in the Digital Age* that is designed to provide the impetus required to bring about change at the school, district, and system levels. Learn how one school benefited from this initiative.

21st Century Teachers Network

The 21st Century Teachers Network is a place where teachers can learn more about educational technology. Among the highlights are a library of lesson plans and activities that incorporate educational technology, a wide array of discussion groups, and a national event calendar.

Yahoo! Security and Encryption

Yahoo's directory offers information on a variety of computer security and encryption issues.

Chapter Mastery Test

To the Instructor: *Refer to the Instructor's Manual for the answers to the Mastery Questions. This manual has additional questions and resource materials.*

Let us check for chapter comprehension with a short mastery test. Key Terms, Computer Lab, and Suggested Readings and References follow the test.

1. Explain the conflict between the computer user and the software publisher.
2. What can ordinary persons do to protect their data from fire, theft, and storage media failure?
3. Discuss the findings of three research studies on CAI.
4. Does CAI research show that science simulations are more effective than laboratory experiences? Explain your answer.
5. Discuss three ways to reduce the risks of computer-related injuries.
6. Give three suggestions for using one computer with 32 students and explain each suggestion thoroughly.
7. Using one computer, how can the teacher increase group involvement in the learning process?
8. How can the teacher teach keyboarding skills effectively to young children?
9. How can the teacher utilize the computer to report scientific information?
10. Devise an organizational schedule for a classroom computer use.
11. What is the *digital divide* and why is it an important issue?
12. What is the major advantage and disadvantage of a wireless mobile lab? Explain your answer.

Key Terms

Digital divide   400
Liquid crystal display (LCD)
   projection panel   390
Meta-analysis   402

Piracy   398
Problem-solving
   software   388

Repetitive strain
   injuries   401
Simulation   393

Smart cards   396
Video scan converter   390
Wireless mobile lab   395

Computer Lab: Activities for Mastery and Your Portfolio

15.1 Ergonomics   Test your understanding of correct computer posture.

15.2 Using one of the research topics, write a paper discussing its implications for education.

15.3 Set up a security system for a hypothetical computer lab.

Suggested Readings and References

Allen, Mike, John Bourhis, Nancy Burrell, and Edward Mabry. "Comparing Student Satisfaction with Distance Education to Traditional Classrooms in Higher Education: A Meta-Analysis." *American Journal of Distance Education* 16, no. 2 (2002): 83–98.

Atan, H., F. Sulaiman, Z. A. Rahman, and R. M. Idrus. "Gender Differences in Availability, Internet Access and Rate of Usage of Computers Among Distance Education Learners." *Educational Media International* 39, issue 3/4 (September 2002): 205–211.

Atan, Hanafi, Nazirah A. Azli, Zuraidah A. Rahman, and Rozhan M. Idrus. "Computers in Distance Education: Gender Differences in Self-Perceived Computer Competencies." *Journal of Educational Media* 27, issue 3 (October 2002): 123–135.

Badgett, Christmann E. J., and R. Lucking. "Progressive Comparison of the Effects of Computer-Assisted Instruction on the Academic Achievement of Secondary Students." *Journal of Research on Computing Education* 29, no. 4 (1997): 325–337.

Bangert-Drowns, R. "The Word Processor as an Instructional Tool: A Meta-Analysis of Word Processing in Writing Instruction." *Review of Educational Research* 63, no. 1 (1993): 69–93.

Batchelder, John Stuart, and John R. Rachal. "Efficacy of a Computer-Assisted Instruction Program in a Prison Setting: An Experimental Study." *Adult Education Quarterly* 50, no. 2 (February 2000): 120–133.

Bayraktar, Sule. "A Meta-Analysis of the Effectiveness of Computer-Assisted Instruction in Science Education." *Journal of Research on Technology in Education* 34, no. 2 (Winter 2001–2002): 173–188.

Biner, P. M., R. S. Dean, and A. E. Mellinger. "Factors Underlying Distance Learning Satisfaction with Televised College-Level Courses." *The American Journal of Distance Education* 8, no. 1 (1997): 60–61.

Bisciglia, Michael, and Elizabeth Monk-Turner. "Differences in Attitudes Between On-Site and Distance-Site Students in Group Teleconference Courses." *The American Journal of Distance Education* 16, no. 1 (2002): 37–52.

Blair, Regina B., Christine Ormsbee, and Joyce Brandes. "Using Writing Strategies and Visual Thinking Software to Enhance the Written Performance of Students with Mild Disabilities." ERIC_NO: ED463125, 2002.

Bracey, G. W. "Computers in Education: What the Research Shows." *Electronic Learning* 2, no. 3 (1982): 51–54.

Brooks, Jason. "Wireless LAN Security Crackdown." *eWeek* 19, issue 18 (May 6, 2002): 45–47.

Buckleitner, Warren, ed. *The Complete Sourcebook on Children's Software.* Volume 8, New Jersey Active Learning Associates, 2000, page 5.

Bures, Eva Mary, Philip C. Abrami, and Cheryl Amundsen. "Student Motivation to Learn via Computer Conferencing." *Research in Higher Education* 41, no. 5 (October 2000): 593–621.

Carman, Gary O., and Bernard Kosberg. "Research: Computer Technology and the Education of Emotionally Handicapped Children." *Educational Technology,* February 1982, 32–36.

Cattagni, Anne, and Elizabeth Farris. "Internet Access in U.S. Public Schools and Classrooms: 1994–2000." *Education Statistics Quarterly* 3, no. 2 (Summer 2001): 54–61.

Chambless, Jim R., and Martha S. Chambless. "The Impact of Instructional Technology on Reading/Writing Skills of 2nd Grade Students." *Reading Improvement* 31, no. 3 (Fall 1994): 151–155.

Chang, Chun-Yen. "Does Computer-Assisted Instruction + Problem Solving = Improved Science Outcomes? A Pioneer Study." *Journal of Educational Research* 95, no. 3 (January–February 2002): 143–150.

Christmann, Edwin, John Badgett, and Robert Lucking. "Progressive Comparisons of the Effects of Computer-Assisted Instruction on the Academic Achievement of Secondary Students." *Journal of Research on Computing in Education* 29, no. 4 (Summer 1997).

Clark, Richard E. "Evidence for Confounding in Computer-Based Instruction Studies: Analyzing the Meta-Analysis." *Educational Communication and Technology Journal* 33, no. 4 (Winter 1985): 249–262.

Clark, Richard E. "Media Will Never Influence Learning." *Educational Technology, Research and Development* 42, no. 2 (1994): 21–29.

Clark, Richard E. "When Researchers Swim Upstream: Reflections on an Unpopular Argument About Learning from Media." *Educational Technology* 31, no. 31 (February 1991): 34–40.

Clement, Frank J. "Affective Considerations in Computer-Based Education." *Educational Technology,* April 1981, 228–232.

Collis, B., and L. Ollila. "An Examination of Sex Difference in Secondary School Students' Attitudes Toward Writing and the Computer." *Alberta Journal of Educational Research* 34, no. 4 (1986): 297–306.

Cope, Eric W., and Patrick Suppes. "Gifted Students' Individual Differences in Distance-Learning Computer-Based Calculus and Linear Algebra." *Instructional Science* 30, no. 2 (March 2002): 79–110.

Daiute, C. *Writing and Computers.* Reading, Mass.: Addison-Wesley, 1985.

Dvorak, John C. "One Child, One Laptop." *PC Magazine* 18, no. 20 (November 16, 1999): 83.

Elliot, Inman, Michael Kerwin, and Larry Mayes. "Instructor and Student Attitudes Toward Distance Learning" *Community College Journal of Research and Practice* 23, no. 6 (September 1999): 581–591.

Farynaiarz, Joseph V., and Linda G. Lockwood. "Effectiveness of Microcomputer Simulations in Stimulating Environmental Problem Solving by Community College Students." *Journal of Research in Science Teaching* 29, no. 5 (May 1992): 453–470.

Feldman, P. R. "Personal Computers in a Writing Course." *Perspectives in Computing,* Spring 1984, 4–9.

Fisher, G. "Where CAI Is Effective: A Summary of the Research." *Electronic Learning* 82 (November/December 1983): 84.

Flanagan, Patrick. "The 10 Hottest Technologies in Telecom." *Telecommunications* 31, no. 5 (May 1997): 25–28, 30, 32.

Fordahl, Matthew. "Seeking High-Tech Solutions for Seniors." *Los Angeles Times,* September 15, 2003.

Fortner, R., W. Schar, and J. Mayer. *Effect of Microcomputer Simulations on Computer Awareness and Perception of Environmental Relationships Among College Students.* Columbus, Ohio: Ohio State University, Office of Learning Resources (ERIC Document Reproduction Service No. ED 270–311), 1986.

Fulford, Catherine P., and Shuqiang Zhang. "Perceptions of Interaction: The Critical Predictor in Distance Education." *American Journal of Distance Education* 7, no. 3 (1993): 8-21.

Fulton, Mary. "The Data May Not Be Perfect. But If We Don't Start Somewhere and Have Something to Build on, We're Never Going Anywhere." *Education Week* 17, no. 11 (November 1997): 10–11.

Freedman, Allen. *The Computer Desktop Encyclopedia.* New York: American Management Association, 2003.

Garzella, M. F. "Using an Expert System to Diagnose Weaknesses and Prescribe Remedial Reading Strategies Among Elementary Learning Disabled Students." *Dissertation Abstracts International* 52/09-A (Order No. AAD92–07011), 1991.

"Gender Bias: Recent Research and Interventions." *New Jersey Research Bulletin,* no. 22 (Spring 1996).

Glass, G. V. "Integrated Findings: The Meta-Analysis of Research." In *Review of Research in Education,* ed. L. Schulman. Itasca, Ill.: Peacock, 1977.

Glass, G. V. "Primary, Secondary, and Meta-Analysis of Research." *Educational Researcher* 5 (1976): 3–8.

Gleason, Gerald T. "Microcomputers in Education: The State of the Art." *Educational Technology,* March 1981, 7–18.

Glickman, Cynthia L., and Juli Dixon. "Teaching Algebra in a Situated Context Through Reform Computer Assisted Instruction." *Research and Teaching in Developmental Education* 18, no. 24 (Spring 2002): 57–84.

Goode, M. "Testing CAI Courseware in Fifth and Sixth Grade Math." *T.H.E. Journal,* October 1988, 97–100.

Grenzky, Janet, and Christine Maitland. "Focus on Distance Education." *NEA Higher Education Research Center Update* 7, no. 2 (March 2001).

Guglielmo, Connie. "Managers Clamp Down on Software Piracy." *MacWeek* 6, no. 2 (January 13, 1992): 60–63.

Gupta, Renu. "Can Spelling Checkers Help the Novice Writer?" *British Journal of Educational Technology* 29, no. 3 (July 1998): 255–266.

Harrison, Nancy, and Evelyn M. Van Devender. "The Effects of Drill-and-Practice Computer Instruction on Learning Basic Mathematics Facts." *Journal of Computing in Childhood Education* 3, no. 304 (May 1993): 349–356.

Hasselbring, Ted S. "Remediating Spelling Problems of Learning-Handicapped Students Through the Use of Microcomputers." *Educational Technology,* April 1982, 31–32.

Hatfield, M. M. "The Effect of Problem-Solving Software on Students' Beliefs About Mathematics: A Qualitative Study." *Computers in the Schools* 8, no. 4 (1991): 21–40.

Hatfield, Susan. *Effective Use of Classroom Computer Stations Across the Curriculum.* ERIC Document No. ED396704 RIENOV96, Dissertations/Theses, Research Technical, June 30, 1996.

Hawisher, G. E. "The Effects of Word Processing on the Revision Strategies of College Students." Paper presented at the annual meeting of the American Educational Research Association, San Francisco (ERIC Document No. ED. 268–546), April 1986.

Haynes, Colin. *The Computer Virus Protection Handbook.* San Francisco: SYBEX, 1990.

Hess, Frederick M., and David L. Leal. "Computer-Assisted Learning in Urban Classrooms: The Impact of Politics, Race, and Class." *Urban Education* 34, no. 3 (September 1999): 370–388.

Hodges, Andrew. *Alan Turing: The Enigma.* London: Vintage Paper Back, Ranlon Century, 1992.

Hoffman, Patricia. *VSUM Database.* Santa Clara, Calif.: VSUM. (3333 Bowers Avenue, Suite 130, Santa Clara, CA 95054, (408) 988-3773, BBS (408) 244-0813), December 30, 1997.

Hulme, George V. "Networks Without a Safety Net." *Information Week,* issue 894, (June 24, 2002): 70–72.

Inman, Elliot, Michael Kerwin, and Larry Mayes. "Instructor and Student Attitudes Toward Distance Learning." Community College Journal of Research and Practice 23, no. 6 (1999): 581-591.

Jackowski-Bartol, Tillary R. "The Impact of Word Processing on Middle School Students," ERIC No. ED 453825, 2001.

Jessop, Deborah. "A Survey of Recent Advances in Optical and Multimedia Information Technologies." *Computers in Libraries* 17, no. 2 (February 1997): 53–59.

Jones, I. "The Effects of a Word Processor on the Written Composition of Second-Grade Pupils." *Computers in the Schools* 11, no. 2 (1994): 43–54.

Kassner, Kirk. "One Computer Can Deliver Whole-Class Instruction." *Music Educators Journal* 86, no. 6 (May 2000): 34.

Keizer, Gregg. "WLAN Security: Reducing the Risks." *TechWeb* April, 13, 2003, http://www.techweb.com/tech/mobile/20030407_mobile.

Khalili, A., and L. Shashaani. "The Effectiveness of Computer Applications: A Meta-Analysis." *Journal of Research on Computing in Education* 27, no. 1 (Fall 1994): 48–61.

Khine, Myint Swe. "Attitudes Toward Computers Among Teacher Education Students in Brunei, Darussalam." *International Journal of Instructional Media* 28, issue 2, (2001): 147–153.

Kosakowski, John. "The Benefits of Information Technology." *Educational Media and Technology Yearbook* 25 (2000): 53–56.

Koseinski, Susan, et al. "Computer-Assisted Instruction with Constant Time Delay to Teach Multiplication Facts to Students with Learning Disabilities." *Learning Disabilities Research Practices* 8, no. 3 (Summer 1993): 157–168.

Krein, T. J., and T. R. Mahollm. "CDT Has the Edge in a Comparative Study." *Performance and Instruction,* August 1990, 22–24.

Kromhout, Ora M., and Sarah M. Butzin. "Integrating Computers into the Elementary School Curriculum: An Evaluation of Nine Project CHILD Model Schools." *Journal of Research on Computing in Education* 26, no. 1 (Fall 1993): 5.

Kuehner, Alison V. "The Effects of Computer Instruction on College Students' Reading Skills." *Journal of College Reading and Learning* 29, no. 2 (Spring 1999): 149–165.

Kulik, C. C., C. Chen-Lin, and J. A. Kulik. "Effectiveness of Computer-Based Instruction: An Updated Analysis." *Computers in Human Behavior* 7 (1991): 75–94.

Kulik, C. C., J. A. Kulik, and P. Cohen. "Instructional Technology and College Teaching." *Teaching of Psychology* 7 (1980): 199–205.

Kulik, C. C., J. A. Kulik, and B. J. Shwath. "Effectiveness of Computer-Based Adult Learning: A Meta-Analysis." *Journal of Educational Computing Research* 2 (1986): 235–252.

Kulik, J. A., R. Bangert, and G. Williams. "Effects of Computer-Based Teaching on Secondary School Students." *Journal of Educational Psychology* 75 (1983): 19–26.

Kulik, J. A., and C. Chen-Lin. "Review of Recent Literature on Computer-Based Instruction." *Contemporary Education Psychology* 12, no. 3 (July 1987): 222–230.

Kulik, J. A., and C. C. Kulik. "Timing of Feedback and Verbal Learning." *Review of Educational Research* 58, no. 1 (1988): 79–97.

Kumar, David D., and Stanley L. Helgeson. "Trends in Computer Applications in Science Assessment." *Journal of Science Education and Technology* 41, no. 1 (March 1995): 29–36.

Kurth, R. J. "Using Word Processing to Enhance Revision Strategies During Student Writing Activities." *Educational Technology* 27 (1987): 13–19.

Lally, M. "Computer-Assisted Development of Number Conservation in Mentally Retarded Children." *Journal of Developmental Disabilities,* September 1980, 131–136.

Levy, Steven, and Brad Stone. "Hunting the Hackers." *Time Magazine,* February 21, 2000, 39–44.

Li, Jiang, and Alister Cumming. "Word Processing and Second Language Writing: A Longitudinal Case Study." *International Journal of English Studies* 1, no. 2 (2001): 127–152.

Liao, Cliff Yuen-Kuang. *Gender Differences on Attitudes Toward Computers: A Meta-Analysis.* ERIC No. ED 432287, Clearinghouse Number IRO19657, 1999.

Lim, Kee-Sook. "Impacts of Personal Characteristics on Computer Attitude and Academic Users' Information System Satisfaction." *Journal of Educational Computing Research* 26, no. 4 (2002): 395–406.

Linn, C. "Learning More—with Computers as Lab Partners." Paper presented at the annual meeting of the American Educational Research Association, San Francisco, April 1986.

Liu, Xiufeng, Robert Macmillan, and Vianne Timmons. "Assessing the Impact of Computer Integration on Students." *Journal of Research on Computing in Education* 31, no. 2 (Winter 1998): 189–201.

Lockee, Barbara, Mike Moore, and John Burton. "Old Concerns with New Distance Education Research." *Educause Quarterly* 24, no. 2 (2001): 60–62.

Luehrmann, A. "The Best Way to Teach Computer Literacy." *Electronic Learning* 3, no. 3 (April 1984): 37–42, 44.

MacArthur, C. A., J. A. Haynes, D. B. Melouf, and K. Harris. "Computer Assisted Instruction with Learning Disabled Students: Achievement, Engagement, and Other Factors Related to Achievement." Paper presented at the annual meeting of the American Educational Research Association, Washington, D.C., April 1987.

Machtmes, Krisanna, and J. William Asher. "A Meta-Analysis of the Effectiveness of Telecourses in Distance Education." *American Journal of Distance Education* 14, no. 1 (2000): 27–46.

Makrakis, Vasilios, and Toshio Sawada. "Gender, Computers and Other School Subjects Among Japanese and Swedish Students." *Computers and Education* 26, no. 4 (May 1996): 225–231.

Mann, D., and C. Shakeshaft. *The Impact of Technology in the Schools of the Mohawk Regional Information Center Area.* Technical Report, 1997. ERIC Document No. ED 405893, (800) 443-ERIC.

Mann, D., C. Shakeshaft, J. Becker, and R. Kottkamp. *West Virginia's Basic Skills/Computer Education Program: An Analysis of Student Achievement.* Santa Monica, Calif.: Milken Family Foundation, 1999.

Mayer, R. E., J. L. Dyck, and W. Vilberg. "Learning to Program and Learning to Think: What's the Connection?" *Communication of the ACM* 29, no. 7 (1986): 605–610.

McGrath, Diane, et al. "Multimedia Science Projects: Seven Case Studies." *Journal of Research on Computing in Education* 30, no. 1 (Fall 1997).

McHenry, Lynnea, and Mary Bozik. "From a Distance: Student Voices from the Interactive Video Classroom." *TechTrends* 42, no. 6 (1997): 20-24.

McKinnon, David H., C. J. Patrick Nolan, and Kenneth E. Sinclair. "A Longitudinal Study of Student Attitudes Toward Computers: Resolving an Attitude Decay Paradox." *Journal of Research on Computing in Education* 32, no. 3 (Spring 2000): 325–335.

McNaughton, David, et al. "Proofreading for Students with Learning Disabilities." *Learning Disabilities Research and Practice* 12, no. 1 (1997): 16–28.

McNeil, Barbara J., and Karyn R. Nelson. "Meta-Analysis of Interactive Video Instruction: A 10 Year Review of Achievement Effects." *Journal of Computer-Based Instruction* 18, no. 1 (1991): 1–6.

Merisotis, Jamie P. " 'What's the-Difference?' Debate." *Academe* 85, issue 5 (September/October 1999): 47–52.

Milbrandt, George. "Using Problem Solving to Teach a Programming Language." *Learning and Leading with Technology* 23, no. 2 (October 1995): 27–31.

Miller, Mark D., and William D. McInerney. "Effects on Achievement of a Home/School Computer Project." *Journal of Research on Computing in Education* 27, no. 2 (Winter 1994–1995): 198–210.

Mitra, Ananda, and Timothy Steffensmeier. "Changes in Student Attitudes and Student Computer Use in a Computer-Enriched Environment." *Journal of Research on Computing in Education* 32, no. 3 (Spring 2000): 417–433.

Moore, C., S. Smith, and R. A. Avner. "Facilitation of Laboratory Performance Through CAI." *Journal of Chemical Education* 57, no. 3 (1980): 196–198.

Morehouse, D. L., M. L. Hoaglund, and R. H. Schmidt. *Technology Demonstration Program Final Evaluation Report.* Menononie, Wis.: Quality Evaluation and Development, February 1987.

Nadeau, Michael, and Bram Vermeer. "Coming 'Soon': 3-GB CD-ROMs." *Byte,* October 1994, 4.

National Center for Education Statistics. *Distance Education at Postsecondary Institutions: 1997–98.* Washington, DC: U.S. Department of Education, NCES2000–013, 1999, 51.

O'Brien, P. "Working at Home." *PC Novice,* September 1994, 61.

Olsen, Florence. "Internet2 Effort Aims to Build Digital-Video Network for Higher Education." *Chronicle of Higher Education* 46, no. 33 (April 21, 2000): A49.

Osborn, Viola. "Identifying At-Risk Students in Videoconferencing and Web-Based Distance Education." *American Journal of Distance Education* 15, no. 1 (2001) 41-54.

Owston, Ronald D., and Herbert H. Wideman. "Word Processors and Children's Writing in a High-Computer-Access Setting." *Journal of Research on Computing in Education* 30, no. 2 (1997): 202–220.

Palumbo, David B., and Michael W. Reed. "The Effect of BASIC Programming Language Instruction on High School Students' Problem Solving Ability and Computer Anxiety." *Journal of Research on Computing in Education* 23, no. 3 (Spring 1991): 342–369.

Parker, Donn B. *Ethical Conflicts in Information and Computer Science Technology.* Wellesley, Mass.: QED Information Sciences, 1990.

Paul, Lawrence. "Keying Injuries Proliferate, Defying Clear Cut Remedies." *PC Magazine,* August 8, 1994, 81.

Pea, R. D. "The Aims of Software Criticism: Reply to Professor Papert." *Educational Researcher* 16, no. 5 (June/July 1987): 4–8.

Phelps, David. "SPA Reaches Settlement with Internet Software Pirates, Credits Teamwork with Internet Access Provider," http://www.spa.org, 1997.

Potter, Dianne. "Virus? Or Just a Hoax?" *Presentations Magazine,* November 2000, 24.

Rachal, J. R. (1995) "Adult Reading Achievement Comparing Computer-Assisted Instructional and Traditional Approaches." A Comprehensive Review of Experimental Literature. Reading and Research, and Instruction, 34, no. 3 (1995), 239–258.

Reed, W. M. "Assessing the Importance of Computer-Based Writing." *Journal of Research on Computing in Education* 28, no. 4 (1996): 418–437.

Richman, John A. "At-Risk Students: Innovative Technologies." *Media and Methods* 30, no. 5 (May–June 1994): 26–27.

Rittner-Heir, Robbin M. "One Student One Computer." *School Planning and Management* 39, no. 5 (May 2000): 10.

Robertson G. *A Comparison of Meaningful and Nonmeaningful Content in Computer-Assisted Spelling Programs.* Saskatchewan, Canada: Saskatchewan School Trustees Association Research Center, 1978.

Roblyer, M. D. "Technology and the Oops! Effect: Finding a Bias Against Word Processing." *Learning and Leading with Technology* 25, no. 7 (1997): 14–16.

Roblyer, M. D., W. H. Castine, and F. J. King. *Assessing the Impact of Computer-Based Instruction: A Review of Recent Research.* New York: Haworth Press, 1988.

Ruel, Alfred A. *The Application of Research Findings.* Washington, D.C.: National Education Association, 1977.

Rueter, John G., and Nancy A. Perrin. "Using a Simulation to Teach Food Web Dynamics." *American Biology Teacher* 61, no. 2 (February 1999): 116–123.

Russell, Ben. "Slow Achievement Causes Concern." *Times Educational Supplement* Issue 4219 (1997): 23.

Ryan, Bob. "Alpha Ride High." *Byte* (October 1994): 197–198.

Salerno, Christopher A. "The Effect of Time on Computer-Assisted Instruction for At-Risk Students." *Journal of Research on Computing in Education* 28, no. 1 (Fall 1995): 85–97.

Sarama, Julie, Douglas H. Clements, and Judith Day Seidel. "Using Computers for Algebraic Thinking." *Teaching Children Mathematics* 5, no. 3 (November 1998): 186.

Schacter, J. *The Impact of Education Technology on Student Achievement: What the Most Current Research Has to Say.* Santa Monica, Calif.: Milken Family Foundation, 1999.

Schroeder, Erica. "Voice Recognition Making Some Noise." *PC Week* 12, no. 20 (May 23, 1994): 7.

Seawel, Lori, et al. *A Descriptive Study Comparing Computer-Based Word Processing and Handwriting on Attitudes and Performance of Third and Fourth Grade Students Involved in a Program Based on a Process Approach to Writing.* ERIC Document EJ482040, 1994.

Shashaani, Lily. "Gender-Based Differences in Attitudes Toward Computers." *Computers and Education* 20, no. 2 (March 1993): 169–181.

Shashaani, Lily. "Gender-Differences in Computer Experience and Its Influence on Computer Attitudes." *Journal of Educational Computing Research* 11, no. 4 (1994): 347–367.

Shashaani, Lily. "Gender Differences in Mathematics Experience and Attitude and Their Relation to Computer Attitude." *Educational Technology* 35, no. 3 (May–June 1995): 32–38.

Shashaani, Lily. "Socioeconomic Status, Parents' Sex-Role Stereotypes, and the Gender Gap in Computing." *Journal of Research on Computing in Education* 26, no. 4 (Summer 1994): 433–451.

Shiah, Rwey-Lin, et al. "The Effects of Computer-Assisted Instruction on Mathematical Problem Solving of Students with Learning Disabilities." *Exceptionality* 5 (1994–1995): 131–161.

Shih, Y., and S. M. Allesi. "Mental Models and Transfer in Learning in Computer Programming." *Journal of Research on Computing in Education* 26, no. 2 (Winter 1993–1994): 154–175.

Shim, Kew-Cheol, Jong-Seok Park, Hyun-Sup Kim, Jae-Hyun Kim, Young-Chul Park, and Hai-Il Ryu. "Application of Virtual Reality Technology in Biology Education." *Journal of Biological Education* 37, issue 2 (Spring 2003): 71–75.

Siann, G., A. Durndell, H. Macleod, and P. Glissov. "Stereotyping in Relation to the Gender Gap in Participation in Computing." *Educational Research* 30, no. 2 (1988): 98–103.

Simonson, Michael, Sharon Smaldino, Michael Albright, and Susan Avacek. *Teaching and Learning at a Distance.* Upper Saddle River, N.J.: Merrill, Prentice Hall, 2003.

Simonson, Michael. "Myths and Distance Education: What the Research Says (And Does Not Say)." *Quarterly Review of Distance Education* 1, no. 4 (Winter 2000): 277–279.

Sivin-Kachala, J. *Report on the Effectiveness of Technology in Schools, 1990–1997.* Washington, D.C: Software Publishers Association, 1998.

Software Piracy. Software Publishers Association, white paper, 1992.

"Software Publishers Association Announces Settlement with College Student." http://www.spa.org/piracy/releases/puget.htm, 1997.

Software Publishers Association. News release, http://www.spa.org/, October 1995.

Software Publishers Association. Reports published on the World Wide Web, http://www.spa.org/, Fall 1996.

Soloway, E., J. Lockhead, and J. Clement. "Does Computer Programming Enhance Problem Solving Ability? Some Positive Evidence on Algebra Word Problems." In *Computer Literacy: Issues and Directions for 1985,* ed. R. J. Seidel, R. Anderson, and B. Hunter. New York: Academic Press, 1982.

Song, Sang Ho. "Research Issues of Motivation in Web-Based Instruction." *Quarterly Review of Distance Education* 1, no. 3 (Fall 2000): 225–229.

Stone, M. David. "One Computer, Many Users." *PC Magazine* 19, no. 2 (January 18, 2000): 135.

Stuart, Rory. *The Design of Virtual Environments.* New York: McGraw-Hill, 1996.

Summerville, L. J. "The Relationship Between Computer-Assisted Instruction and Achievement Levels and Learning Rates of Secondary School Students in First Year Chemistry." *Dissertation Abstracts International* 46, no. 3 (1984): 603a (University Microfilms No. 85–10891).

Swadener, M., and M. Hannafin. "Gender Similarities and Differences in Sixth Graders' Attitudes Toward Computers: An Exploratory Study." *Educational Technology* 27, no. 1 (1987): 37–42.

Swan, K., F. Gueerero, N. M. Mitrani, and J. Schoener. "Honing in on the Target: Who Among the Educationally Disadvantaged Benefits Most from What CBI?" *Journal of Research on Computing in Education* 22, no. 4 (1990): 381–404.

Tan, Soo Boo. "Making One-Computer Teaching Fun!" *Learning and Leading with Technology* 25, no. 5 (February 1998): 6–10.

Tatana M., and Robert A. Wisher. "The Effectiveness of Web-Based Instruction: An Initial Inquiry." *International Review of Research in Open and Distance Learning* 3, no. 2 (October 2002).

Teh, George P. L., and Barry Fraser. "Gender Differences in Achievement and Attitudes Among Students Using Computer-Assisted Instruction." *International Journal of Instructional Media* 22, no. 2 (1995): 111.

Terrell, Steve, and Paul Rendulic. "Using Computer-Managed Instructional Software to Increase Motivation and Achievement in Elementary School Children." *Journal of Research on Computing in Education* 26, no. 3 (Spring 1996): 403–414.

Tessler, Franklin N. "Safer Computing." *MacWorld,* December 1994, 96.

"The Tech Isn't Perfect, but Video Conferencing's Day Is Near." *Fortune: Winter 2001 Technology Guide* 142, no. 12 (2000): 242.

Thomas, Rex, and Elizabeth Hooper. "Simulations: An Opportunity We Are Missing." *Journal of Research on Computing in Education* 23, no. 4 (Summer 1991): 497–513.

Trosko, Nancy. "Making Technology Work for Your Students." *Technology Connection* 4, no. 2 (April 1997): 20–22.

Trotler, Andrew. "Taking Technology's Measure." *Education Week* 17, no. 11 (November 10, 1997): 6–13.

Tsai, San-Yun W., and Norval F. Pohl. "Student Achievement in Computer Programming: Lecture vs Computer-Aided Instruction." *Journal of Experimental Education* 46, no. 2: 66-70, W 78.

Wanat, Thomas. "Internet-Savvy Students Help Track Down the Hacker of an NCAA Web Site." *Chronicle of Higher Education* 43, no. 29 (March 28, 1997): A30.

Wang, Alvin Y., and Michael H. Newlin. "Characteristics of Students Who Enroll and Succeed in Psychology Web-based Classes." *Journal of Educational Psychology* 92, no. 1 (2000): 137-143.

Watkins, Marley W., and C. Webb. "Computer-Assisted Instruction with Learning-Disabled Students." *Educational Computer,* September/October 1981, 24–27.

Wenglinsky, H. *Does It Compute? The Relationship Between Educational Technology and Student Achievement in Mathematics.* Princeton, N.J.: Educational Testing Service Policy Information Center, 1998.

Westbrook, Thomas S., and Donald K. Moon. "Lessons Learned from the Delivery of a Graduate Business Degree Program Utilizing Interactive Television." *Journal of Continuing Higher Education* 45, no. 2 (1997): 25-33.

Whitley Jr., Bernard E. "Gender Differences in Computer-Related Attitudes and Behavior: A Meta-Analysis." *Computers in Human Behavior* 13, no. 1 (January 1997): 1–22.

Williams, Sue Winkle, et al. "Gender Roles, Computer Attitudes, and Dyadic Computer Interaction Performance in College Students." *Sex Roles: A Journal of Research* 29, no. 7–8 (June 1994): 515–525.

Wilson, Jan. "The Power of Distance Learning, Guest Editorial." *Education* 122, issue 4 (Summer 2002): 638–640.

Wong, Chi Kuen. "Attitudes and Achievements: Comparing Computer-Based and Traditional Homework Assignments in Mathematics." *Journal of Research on Technology in Education* 33, no. 5 (Summer 2001).

Wood, Christina. "Register Your Software—or Else!" *PC World* 18, no. 10 (October 2000): 35.

Woodward, L., and R. Gersten. "Innovative Technology for Secondary Students with Learning Disabilities." *Exceptional Children* 58, no. 5 (March–April 1992): 407–421.

Xin, Yan Ping, and Asha K. Jitendra. "The Effects of Instruction in Solving Mathematical Word Problems for Students with Learning Problems: A Meta-Analysis." *Journal of Special Education* 32, no. 4 (1999): 207–225.

Yildirim, Soner. "Effects of an Educational Computing Course on Preservice and Inservice Teachers: A Discussion and Analysis of Attitudes and Use." *Journal of Research on Computing in Education* 32, no. 4 (2000): 479–495.

Young, Betty. "Gender Differences in Student Attitudes Toward Computers." *Journal of Research on Computing in Education* 33, no. 2 (Winter 2000): 204–213.

Zellermayer, M., G. Salomon, T. Globerson, and H. Givon. "Enhancing Writing-Related Metacognitions Through a Computerized Writing Partner." *American Educational Research Journal* 28, no. 2 (1991): 373–391.

Zhang, Yuehua. "Technology and the Writing Skills of Students with Learning Disabilities." *Journal of Research on Computing in Education* 32, no. 4 (Summer 2000): 467–478.

CHAPTER 16

The Future

Schools of the Future

Future technology breakthroughs will make it easier to integrate the computer into the classroom. The majority of students will be distance learning, using wireless communication, using robots to aid them in the instructional process, working with virtual keyboards, downloading interactive books, and wearing their computers. Using virtual reality, students will visit museums, visit different countries, listen to chamber groups in concert, and learn how to fly airplanes, work in science labs, and engage in all sorts of exciting educational experiences. This chapter will look into the future of educational technology. The chapter includes the introduction from Janet Caughlin's and Tony Vincent's forthcoming book, *Handheld's for Teachers & Administrators,* and an essay by Dr. David Moursund, an expert on educational technology. We will conclude with a brief review of our lessons learned: What have we discovered about the computer in education over the course of this book?

Future Trends

Examining the research leads to some natural questions: What will the future bring? What are the trends for microcomputer development? Will we have more artificial intelligence applications? Will we have networking in every school? Will we have helper robots? Will there be an emphasis on distance learning and video conferencing? Will there be further developments in multimedia technologies? How will these new developments affect teaching? Let us use our crystal ball—an electronic one, of course—to try to answer some of these questions.

Computer Hardware

Recent developments such as the wireless computer and wireless computer network, distance learning, and flash memory chips will play a more prominent role in the computer's future. In a few years, the cathode ray tube (CRT) monitor will be replaced either by a large liquid crystal display, a plasma display, or a plastic screen called an OLED. An **OLED,** or **organic light-emitting diode display,** "is a thin-film, light-emitting device that typically consists of a series of organic layers between two electrical contacts (electrodes)" (Freedman, 2003). OLEDs are prepared using either low molecular-weight organic materials or polymer-based materials. An advantage of the OLED display is it will not break when dropped. Also, OLEDs generate their own light, and they save on energy. This cheap alternative to silicon will result in very tiny transistors, wall-size displays, or rolled-up pen displays. Eastman Kodak Company and Sanyo have a working color OLED as shown in Figure 16.1.

Figure 16.1 Kodak and Sanyo developed a prototype for a fifteen-inch flat panel display as far back as 2002.

Image courtesy © Eastman Kodak Company. KODAK is a trademark.

Future displays will feature poster-size screens as well as screens that can be hung on the wall or unfold from our pockets. Displays will evolve from two-dimensional displays into large three-dimensional displays.

If we want to access the Internet, we can use the pocket Net computer, a computer that fits in a pocket, to log on anytime from anywhere. Universal Display Corp has built a prototype of a pen (Figure 16.2) with a roll-up screen using OLED technology. This

Figure 16.2 OLED Roll-up Pen

Courtesy of Universal Display Corporation.

Figure 16.3 *Intelli-pen*

Reprinted by permission of Frog Design.

pen is so small you can easily slip it in your pocket. Another pen recently created by Motorola and Frog design is the *Intelli-pen* (Figure 16.3). This pen stores digital versions of what a person writes. Later the individual can use wireless technology to send their writing to the local network.

In the future our computer displays could come from an ordinary spray can. You could spray a video display from a can on any surface and be able to print it out.

Electronic Books

The electronic book, or **e-book,** may someday replace the traditional paper book or textbook. The e-book displays electronic versions of books, enabling you to set bookmarks, perform keyword searches, and make notes in margins. Already, many portable devices enable you to download books from the Internet: Palm handhelds, Pocket PCs, tablet PCs, portables, and readers such as the *Hiebook Reader* (eBookAd.com, Inc.) and *eBookMan* (Franklin). A number of excellent subscription-based websites enable you to download books ranging from the classics to popular nonfiction. For example, Palm Digital Media Inc. (www.palmdigitalmedia.com), and Lightning Source, Inc. (http://www.lightningsource.com) offer great classics collections. For a fee, students, teacher, and administrators have unlimited access to 500 e-books for a school year. The books are loaded on a school's website, from which users can download them to their portable devices.

By 2005, E Ink Immediate Technology will be producing paper-thin displays consisting of liquid ink embedded in paper-thin plastic sheets. E Ink is also creating electronic books with flexible plastic pages that can display downloaded text and then erase and reprint themselves. Each book will consist of hundreds of pages that a student can thumb through. Students then easily will attach the book to a PC and download whatever they want to read. At the Society for Information Display Exposition and Symposium in Maryland, E Ink and Philips recently showed a prototype of a paperlike display technology. The display (Figure 16.4) is high resolution (160 pixels per

Figure 16.4 Electronic Paperlike Display from E Ink

Photo courtesy of Philips Electronics.

inch) and easy to read. When this device is perfected, students may dispense with their backpacks loaded with books and instead carry only a lightweight electronic book. Visit the E ink site at http://www.eink.com/news/releases/pr69.html for further information.

Howard Strauss (2003) predicts that another alternative will be to have a textbook or novel stored in a standard format from which students can access it with a variety of pocket-size devices such as a wristwatch. The wristwatch will only require a small screen because it will be a text-to-speech device. The device will be capable of storing thousands of books that can be read to the wearer. The voices may be customized. To read the text, a student will connect it to a laptop or PDA.

Handhelds

Handhelds will continue to be popular in the classroom, because they are cheaper to buy than computers. Because of their lower price, these devices may make it possible for all children to have access to computers in the classroom. In the future *all* handheld computers will be easier to use and feature wireless Internet access, built-in cameras, virtual keyboards, and speech-recognition capabilities. Hewlett-Packard's *iPAQ 5450* has a fingerprint scanner that enables the owner to log on with a touch of a finger, and it features three types of wireless capabilities: IRA, bluetooth, and Wi-Fi.

Because of the popularity of handhelds in the classroom, many experts are writing about this topic. Among these experts are Janet Caughlin and Tony Vincent who just completed a book on handhelds. Janet Caughlin is well known for her *Workshop Books* series of technology books written specifically for educators and published by Tom Snyder Productions. Janet was a K–12 media specialist for 29 years while she taught graduate-level technology classes to teachers. Tony is a full-time 5th-grade teacher who is a whiz with technology and kids. He is nationally known for his expertise with handhelds. What follows is the introduction from their forthcoming book, *Handhelds for Teachers & Administrators:*

It has long been a goal of educators to get a computer into the hands of every student, teacher, administrator, and staff member in the school. This seemed like an unreachable goal until the advent of handheld computers. "Forget desktop and laptop computers in K–12; handheld computers are the only way each and every child is going to get his or her own personal computer—tomorrow!" says Elliot Soloway, a well-known expert on handhelds in education.

Judging by the schools we visited during the past year, educators in America agree with Dr. Soloway. Edward Bretzlaff, principal of West Hills Middle School in Bloomfield Hills, MI, assigned a handheld to every sixth grader last year. This year, those students will have their same handhelds, and the new sixth graders will get their own. Next year the new sixth graders will, again, get their own handheld. This will fulfill the goal that every student in Western Hills Middle School has his or her own computer 24/7. Could every student have gotten their own computer that soon without handhelds? "No," says Ed, "It's financially impossible at this time in education to find the money to do that."

Green Middle School in Uniontown, OH, doesn't have a handheld for every student, but they purchase class sets every year. "Look at this building; see how overcrowded it is?" said Paula Jameson, the Curriculum Technology Specialist. "If we had the money to buy more computers, where would we put them? We have room for handhelds, not computer labs. Besides, look at what you can do with handhelds! You can take them out to the pond with probes to do science experiments, you can access the Internet, they encourage the kids to work collaboratively—what more do you want?"

Jason Bartman, a programming teacher at South High School in Omaha, NE, is teaching students to program handheld computers. "They're teaching me as much as I teach them," says Jason. "We're learning together." As part of the Omaha South High Academy of Information Technology project, Jason's students meet with area educators and businesses to determine how they can create applications to help them meet their business goals.

Teachers, administrators, even the school's resource officer at South High School use handhelds to help them work more efficiently and model the use of technology. Roni Huerta, Ed.D., a curriculum specialist, is a visionary who has used handhelds since 1993 when she got her Apple Newton. Roni's vision is for anytime, anywhere technology. "I want the kids to be able to do their homework and have access to the Internet anywhere," says Roni. "I want them to be able to download at least three chapters of their textbook onto a handheld or tablet computer. They need to be able to highlight the text and take notes in the margins—do the college thing. I can't afford to provide single-use books for each student so they can do this. With textbooks on handheld or tablet computers we'd have a system that would help the kids fulfill their potential."

Every educator we talked to told us the same thing. "We can't believe how engaged the students are when they're using handhelds. They don't look up, they don't talk unless it has to do with the lesson, they go way beyond what we ask or expect of them. It's so inspiring!" Tony Vincent, a 5th grade teacher at Willowdale Elementary School in Omaha, NE, summed up another constant we found while talking to educators: "Handhelds have made teaching so much fun, both for us and for the students. They are learning more because they are so focused on the lessons." Dorothy Perry, a fifth grade teacher from Wichita, KS, says, "The kids are so focused when they are using handhelds. They are totally engaged! In fact, this level of engagement carries over in the non-handheld activities in those subjects."

Administrators are using them, too. Michael Soguero, Principal at Bronx Guild High School, in Bronx, NY, carries his handheld with him everywhere he goes. Like most administrators we talked to, Michael uses the calendar, address book, and task list applications found on every handheld to help him organize his day. Chuck Walker, the athletic director at South High School in Omaha, NE, uses a combination of his handheld and his desktop computer to schedule athletic events. He can schedule the entire season for this large high school in two to three hours. When he's finished, he synchronizes with his handheld and puts it onto HighSchoolSports.net so the community can access schedules and scores. Robert Nielsen, Ed.D., superintendent at Bloomington Public School in Bloomington, IL, is famous for pulling out his handheld whenever you ask him a question.

As you can see from this introduction on handheld computers, they have come a long way from simple task organizers and have evolved into devices for educational applications. Presently, many handhelds feature folded keyboards for data entry, built-in voice memo recorders, built-in cameras, and wireless connection to the Internet, and they are very portable. Using the handheld computer, you can easily enter and transfer information to and from your PC, using a wired connection to your PC or the handheld's wireless connectivity. These devices also have accessories that enable you to connect to your cell phone for transferring of data and voice. Students can take notes and start papers and reports that can be transferred to their desktop computers. They can also collect experimental data in the field and check sites on the Internet. They can use the device as a reference tool, a calculator, for drill and practice, and for graphing.

Computer Desktop Replacements

Displays. There is a trend toward smaller, faster, and easier-to-use computers. Earlier, we talked about OLED displays and how this technology will make it possible to have smaller computers. These displays will be incorporated into thin laptops that will replace desktop computers. Sony has developed a small prototype organic light-emitting diode (OLED) portable display computer (Figure 16.5) that is wafer thin.

Figure 16.5 Sony OLED Portable Display

Courtesy of Sony Electronics Inc.

Power. These future computers will not only be thinner and smaller; they also will be more powerful. Nanotechnology and quantum computing are two areas in which researchers are trying to supplant the silicon chip. These technologies use molecular or subatomic particles as logic components. A powerful microscopic computer that used the position of individual atoms or spinning electrons to calculate numbers would leave today's machine in the scrap bin.

Portability. Microscopic computing would require very little power, and it would be perfect for wearable computers such as wristwatches. Researchers predict that, in a few years, advances in such technologies could produce a powerful watch-size computer that would require minimum battery power. Resembling a Dick Tracy two-way wrist radio, this device would work with voice commands, feature wireless Internet access, and have holographic projection displays. Every child in the classroom could then have a personal computerized watch.

Xybernaut has produced wearable PCs, which enable people to perform a wide range of mobile tasks easily and safely. This wearable PC is small and lightweight, but it is powerful (Figure 16.6).

A monitor is mounted on an eyeglass frame. A handheld mouse and the CPU are located on a belt. Computers can be touch or voice activated. This computer enables users to surf, edit documents, and dictate while they are moving around.

Figure 16.6 Wearable Computer

Used by permission of Xybernaut Corporation.

In 2003, the Boston Public Schools received seven mobile/wearable computers codeveloped by Xybernaut Corporation and IBM. The *Mobile Assistant,* as the computer is called, is as powerful as a desktop computer and weighs only 2 pounds. The student easily can place it in a backpack or pocket. This wearable computer has a viewing screen that can be readable in any lighting situation, and it is touch sensitive. The computer comes with software specifically designed for education. It features voice-recognition applications, touch-activated icons, an onscreen keyboard, and handwriting recognition. This system is especially useful for the students with disabilities (Figure 16.7; http://www.xybernaut.com/Solutions/product/XyberKids_product.htm).

Figure 16.7 Student Using *Mobile Assistant*

IBM and Xybernaut Corporation.

Figure 16.8
Microdisplay Goggles

Reprinted by permission of Frog Design.

Other wearable computer prototypes come in the form of undetectable glasses and belt clips. Recently, a company called Microdisplay Goggles Company showed a prototype set of smashing dark goggles that simulates an 800 by 600–resolution display and features a digital camera, ear bud, and microphone for a cell phone. The glasses hide the fancy technology (Figure 16.8).

Plastics. Soon plastic transistors will change the way we see computing forever. Using plastics, engineers will be able to sew entire computer systems into a person's clothing. HP has even designed a yellow biodegradable computer made from corn-based plastic.

Speed. At the very least, plastic transistors will make computers smaller and faster. In 1994, DEC's *Alpha 21164* chip was considered the fastest microprocessor in the world. It could perform 600 transactions per second, and there was a 300 MHz version of this chip (Ryan, 1994). Every time we turn around, someone has introduced a new computer that is quicker and can run more complex programs. The speed keeps changing. Today machines run at a billion cycles per second; tomorrow machines could run at a trillion cycles per second.

Printers. Improved color inkjet printers will continue to figure prominently in the printing device market. Furthermore, color laser printers are becoming increasingly popular because of their superior printing capabilities and their reduced price.

Design. Apple Computer changed forever the design of new computers with its iMac. This computer is not bulky, and it houses the components of most desktop computers inside its base (Figure 16.9). The computer design will continue to change

Figure 16.9 Apple's 17-inch G4 iMac

© Hunter Freeman 2004. Images courtesy of Apple Computers, Inc.

and the next computer could have interchangeable parts. The next generation of computers may look like the PC shown in Figure 16.10 from Microsoft and Hewlett-Packard. This wide screen display includes a video camera and wireless handset. The flashing light tells when there is a new voice call or e-mail message. This wireless computer is referred to as the *Athens.* It communicates using *Bluetooth.*

Figure 16.10 *Athens PC*

Photo of *Athens* PC used by permission of Microsoft Corporation.

Memory. The memory needed to run different applications has increased. In the early 1980s, most microcomputers needed only 16K of random access memory (RAM) to run the available educational software programs. Today, it is not uncommon to see a machine with 8 GB of RAM, and in a few months this requirement will be much higher. Because of their large memory, new microcomputers are much more powerful and can perform a myriad of tasks. The price of the memory chip has decreased and will continue to do so in the next few years.

Storage. Not only has memory size increased, but storage devices have increased their capacity to store data. The 5 ¼-inch floppy disk faded into oblivion, and the 3 ½-inch disk has almost disappeared from sight. The hard drive capacity has increased, and many new machines have hard drives that hold 160 GB. Next year this will probably be the standard. Now online subscription storage depots such as *.mac* (http://www.mac.com/), *IBackup* (https://www1.ibackup.com/index.html), and *Xdrive* (http://www.xdrive.com/) provide online storage. This enables the user to store material quickly at one location and travel to another to retrieve it.

The 750-MB Iomega removable *Zip disk* has become a popular option for storage. The *USB flash drive,* which can hold as much as 2 GB (see Chapter 3), and the portable hard drive are just a few of the other options that are available. The trend is toward smaller disks that hold more information, such as the 1.8-inch disks already available for some portables. CD-ROM discs and laser discs are being replaced by DVD. The DVD is the same size as the CD-ROM, but it is capable of holding 17 GB of data with digital images equal to those of laser discs (see Chapter 3).

With their reduced price and faster access time, it is evident that erasable optical discs are a viable alternative to magnetic disks. These discs have the capacity to store gigabytes of information, and they do not wear out as floppy disks did. In addition to these features, optical discs offer the ability to reproduce high-quality color graphics, images, and animation.

Future storage might also occur in another dimension. Holographic storage disks, for example, could hold millions and millions of holograms, and the transfer rates could reach 1 GB per second. This technology holds promise for interactive video. These advances are just the tip of the iceberg—in the near future this huge amount of storage capacity will seem minuscule.

Input Devices. Along with the changes in storage devices are changes in input devices. The movement is away from the keyboard as the primary input device. Touch screens, optical pens, variations on the mouse, and virtual keyboards will replace the keyboard. The virtual keyboard projects an LED image of a keyboard on a flat surface such as a desk. An infrared motion detector senses the movement of the fingers on the keyboard. The *Canesta* virtual keyboard (shown in Figure 16.11) has mouse and touch-

Figure 16.11 *Canesta* Virtual Keyboard

Reprinted with permission from VKB Ltd.

pad controls. Companies such as BT Exact, part of British Telecommunications, are working on developing touch over the Internet. This new technology uses a 3-D scanner and special touch monitors (Figure 16.12), which could eliminate the need for monitors, keyboards, mice, and other peripherals.

Figure 16.12 Touch Monitor

© British Telecommunications plc. Reproduced with permission.

Wireless Networks in the Schools

In Chapter 9 we defined *wireless networking* and discussed its increased use in schools across the country. There are great possibilities for this technology in years to come. In the near future, we will probably see wireless wearable networks that are always in use. When you wake up in the morning, a panel that is installed in your house will tell you the time and alert you to the weather conditions outside. When you drive along the freeways, a device in your car will tell you the traffic conditions and immediately tell you the best route to travel. Microsoft Research has developed **Smart Personal Objects Technology (SPOT),** a technology that implants wireless connectivity that is always on in devices such as watches and necklaces (Figure 16.13).

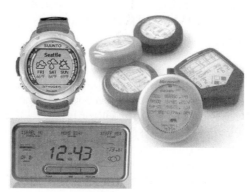

Figure 16.13
Microsoft SPOT
Wireless Technology

Photo of Microsoft® Spot Wireless Technology used by permission of Microsoft Corporation.

Each SPOT device has its own identifier so that your location can always update the watch or necklace with the local weather or time or traffic conditions (Kaplan, 2003). Using a low-bandwidth data channel on local radio, SPOT broadcasts data to receivers in your wearable gadgets. Presently, this system is one way, so it rules out the possibility of my checking on my teenage son's whereabouts.

The **mesh network,** funded by the Defense Advanced Research Projects Agency and named *Sensit,* is the next development in wireless networks. This network is built on thousands of tiny acoustic sensors that can distinguish sounds ranging from that of a falling ball to that of a shot fired by a soldier (Rupley, 2003). The *Sensit* wireless network is very reliable because it is not dependent on one central device. Soon, you will see the mesh network working in U.S. cars in the form of airbag sensors.

IBM Research is also working on a wireless communicator (Figure 16.14). This gadget, which has voice and text-to-speech capabilities, connects to a cell phone. Users can hear as well as see their e-mail messages.

Figure 16.14 Data Key Chain and Mobile Communicator

Used with permission from IBM Research and the photographer.

Voice Recognition Systems

In the future, we will no longer need a keyboard to communicate; we will use speech instead. **Voice recognition systems** have come a long way from the system introduced by Convox in 1991. The *Voice Master Key System II*, as it was called, could recognize only 64 words. Users typed in the words they wanted the system to listen for, spoke each twice, and then typed in the desired keyboard responses. After this programming, users only needed to say a command to direct the computer to execute it. This type of voice recognition was *discrete voice recognition* because it required a pause between each word.

From this type of voice recognition system we moved to *continuous-speech systems,* or systems that understand natural speech without pauses. The new voice recognition systems are speaker independent; that is, they do not require user training. These products are still not 100 percent accurate, but shortly we will see breakthroughs in speech recognition technologies.

In a few years, you will not have to speak a foreign language when you visit a foreign country. You will order meals easily or ask for directions with Yuqing Gao's *Multilingual Automatic Speech Translator* (MASTOR). Using a speech recognizer based on IBM's *Via Voice Gao,* a speech recognition expert at IBM Research's Watson Research Center has turned spoken words into text. A machine translator converts this text into a language, and a speech synthesizer converts it into audible words. Currently this program runs on a laptop, but soon it will run on a handheld computer (Metz, 2003). This will make communication between people of different countries easier (http://www.pcmag.com/article2/0,4149,1130938,00.asp).

Artificial Intelligence

Artificial intelligence (AI) is a range of computer applications that are designed to simulate human intelligence and behavior. For instance, with AI, a machine or robot can recognize pictures and sounds. In the future, we may be able to walk up to any computer or robot, ask it for help, and receive information useful in solving a problem.

In a short amount of time, the differences between a machine and an intelligent person will be reduced drastically. At UCLA and other universities, scientists are working on computer programs and, in some instances, on robots that will respond to conditions of animal life such as evolution. The computer ants program at UCLA is a product of an infant science called *artificial life.* David Jefferson, a computer scientist at UCLA, feels that the artificial ant colonies are a small step toward the creation of life itself. If these scientists are successful, electronic creatures capable of independent thought and action may emerge—a prospect both exciting and frightening. At Los Alamos National Laboratory, there exists a whole repertoire of self-reproducing computer codes. These are just variations of the computer viruses that have disrupted computer networks over the last few years.

AI systems designed for particular fields make evaluations, draw conclusions, and provide recommendations. They help doctors make diagnoses on diseases and treatments, they help drill oil wells, and they aid stockbrokers in making analyses.

This type of software will have a similar impact on education. Teachers are already demanding and using programs that have been made more interactive through artificial intelligence. The AI language will definitely increase the number of programs that respond in human ways. The software we will be using in the near future will tackle concepts and ideas. This software will accept a range of English-language commands and be easier to use. In the future, you will be able to converse with your average computer and ask for help. The computer will automatically bring up the appropriate application to aid you in solving your problem. We will see real AI as Alan Turning, the well-known mathematician, defined it: "A machine has artificial intelligence when there is no discernible difference between the conversation generated by the machine and that of an intelligent person" (Hodges, 1992).

Robots

Robotics is "the art and science of the creation and use of robots" (Freedman, 2003). A **robot** is a computer system that performs physical and computational activities. The robot can be created in a human form; however, industrial robots are not designed this way. The advantage of a robot is that it can perform many different human jobs often better than a person might perform them, or at least more efficiently or quickly. Robots are being designed with artificial intelligence features so they may respond more effectively to unusual situations. In the future, robots may be in the classroom serving as teachers' aides. Robots will spend time with the students, individually drilling them on math skills. In the chemistry lab, robots will handle dangerous chemicals. Robots will also help students with disabilities do their homework. Robots will be used to greet parents and show them around a school.

As the average age of the population increases, the need for and cost of assisted care will increase. Robots will escort patients to restrooms, to activity rooms, to meals, and on shopping outings. Robots can help people by carrying foods and drink and other items that they need for home care. Robots will reach items on top shelves, respond to voice commands, push wheelchairs, and walk dogs.

Robots already spray chemicals, chase birds, and serve as tour guides. There are robot vacuum cleaners such as *Roomba* and robot dogs for recreation. Jean-Claude Latombe, chairman of the computer science department at Stanford University, says, "One of the fastest-growing areas for robotics today is robot-assisted surgery." Stanford is doing brain surgery with robots. During radiation surgery for a brain tumor, the surgeon is not even in the same room with a patient. Instead, the doctor sits at a computer console in a nearby room and monitors what is happening during the operation (Kaplan, 1994). Robots are also being used as targets in weapons training. Dan Fetterly's remote-controlled robot can move like a human, run up to 9 miles per hour, carry 100 pounds, and spot any target (Dunn, 1998). K. G. Engelhardt, formerly manager of Robotics for the NASA Regional Technology Transfer Center and director for the Center for Human Service Robotics at Carnegie Mellon University, has been developing robots for 19 years. She has written a program that introduces teachers to robots. The *Teachers Corps* program utilizes robots and robotics-related technologies to teach scientific, biological, and engineering concepts (http://www-robotics.usc.edu/~behar/robot.html).

Robots in the Classroom. Students and teachers are programming robots such as *Roamer. Roamer* (Terrapin Software; Figure 16.15) is an easy-to-use robot that introduces kindergarten and first-grade students to Logo commands. *Roamer,* which is in the form of a turtle, contains a computer that is dedicated to Logo. Students can see, touch, and follow the Logo turtle as it moves around the room. *Roamer* has a very sturdy design with very few moving parts. Students can easily use the colored touchpad to give *Roamer* single-keystroke commands. *Roamer* is battery powered and lightweight, offering students hours of fun discovering Logo. *Roamer* can play music, and

Figure 16.15
Students Using *Roamer*
Robots

Reprinted with permission of
Terrapin Software.

it has accessories that enable users to customize it. For example, you can add a nose, ears, or tail and change its color. If you place a marker pen into the pen pack attachment, you can even watch *Roamer* draw designs. You can also connect *Roamer* to the computer and upload computer programs, as well as merge them with other programs. In addition, you can write programs on the computer and download them to the *Roamer* turtle. Sixteen story-based activities help students learn problem solving, programming, spatial concepts, and mapping. The activities integrate the *Roamer* floor turtle with the onscreen *Roamer* (http://www.terrapinlogo.com).

Using Lego kits, students can build machines in the form of a car, a camera robot, a tower (Figure 16.16), and a truck that includes motors, sensors, and gears. After these

Figure 16.16
Students Using *Lego*
Robots

Marianne Brooker's Class,
Calahan Elementary School.

machines are built, students connect them with an interface to a computer that speaks the proper dialect of Logo. Using a few simple commands, students write computer programs to control the machines. These commands turn the motors off and on and send them in various directions. These robotics construction kits are really a relic of the early days of Logo programming when the experimenters with Logo used a "floor turtle," a mechanical robot connected to the computer by a cord.

A Lego package usually includes an assortment of gears, wheels, motors, lights, and sensors. Students can send commands to Lego motors and lights and receive information from Lego sensors. *Terrapin Logo* can make a robot turn to the right or reverse direction when it touches a wall. Students can engage in all kinds of experimentation, and they can learn the importance of changing only one variable at a time. They can use the scientific method as they invent their machines, and when they have problems with their inventions, they can develop hypotheses and test them. When students use this computer-based system, they engage in data gathering, record keeping, and brainstorming.

MIT Artificial Intelligence Laboratory is working with robots called *Cog* and *Leonardo. Cog* is being designed to navigate unfamiliar places and interact with individuals. The researcher's goal is to make this robot have the thinking abilities of a 3-year-old. This requires a lot of programming. *Leonardo,* a furry mechanical animal created by Cynthia Brazeal, director of MIT Media Lab's Robotic Life Group, is roughly 2.5 feet tall, maintains eye contact, responds to touch, and shows a large repertoire of expression. *Leonardo* and *Cog* are two examples of the many experiments that are taking place with robots (Ulanoff, 2003).

As you can see, robots of the future will not just be doing repetitive tasks; they will also have personality and be able to think, hear, see, and communicate. Advances in face and object recognition and voice processing will make such robots a reality (Fordahl, 2003). They will not only take care of performing household chores such as vacuuming, lawn mowing, home protection, and dusting, but they also will be nannies, perform brain surgery, gather things from the ocean, teach, and help the elderly dress, wash, and take medicine.

Virtual Reality

Virtual reality (VR) is "an artificial reality that projects the user into a 3-D space generated by the computer" (Freedman, 2003). (See Chapter 8 for a more detailed explanation of virtual reality.) The future promises VR technological breakthroughs to help the student with disabilities function better in the classroom. VR technology enables the physically disabled student to interact with information being presented in all subject areas. Students can immerse themselves physically in different environments and experience life on a different intellectual plane.

VRML (virtual reality modeling language), a 3-D graphics language, is currently used on the World Wide Web. When you download one of the pages containing VRML, you see scenery and objects that you can rotate. Students can walk through simulated rooms such as a gallery in a museum of art.

At HP Labs Norm Jouppi developed a system called **eTravel** that enables a person to be in two places at the same time. The system is based on technology known as **mutually immersive mobil telepresence,** in which a robot substitutes for the individual. The robot is capable of moving from one room to another, viewing what is at the location, making eye contact with the people in the room, and whispering in people's ears. You can be in Rhode Island and see, hear, and talk to people in California. This robot device has cameras and microphones that provide a 360-degree video and audio view of a location. It displays the user's head on a flat panel display

(Figure 16.17; Janowski, 2003). The educational implications for this technology are endless. You could explore the Art Institute in Chicago while in a different location,

Figure 16.17 Mutually Immersive Mobile Telepresence

HP Labs.

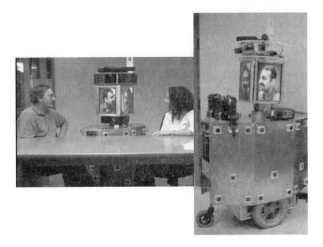

view an operation, and participate in a classroom when you are sick at home (http://www.hpl.hp.com/news/2003/jan_mar/norm_jouppi.html).

This technology surpasses current video conferencing. With this new technology, you become a part of the remote environment. What you see is lifelike, with colors that are vibrant. You can make eye contact with people at the remote location. As you participate, you can see physical nuances you might miss if you were just using video conferencing.

Computer Use by People with Disabilities

Many devices are currently available to aid the student with disabilities. These include Braille keyboards and computer-operated telephone devices for the deaf and screen reading programs for the blind. (Many of these devices were mentioned in Chapter 13.)

Screen reader programs such as *Job Access* (Henter-Hoyce, Inc., a division of Freedom Scientific) for Windows computers or *OutSPOKEN* (ALVA Access Group) for Macintosh computers enable the blind to surf the Web. Using speech synthesizers, the software reads text in a computerized voice and names the icons as the individual encounters them. The blind person then uses the keyboard to navigate, and the software interprets whether a user has tabbed to a button or graphic or other element. People can wear talking PDAs around their necks. Scotland's University of Glasgow introduced a talking computer mouse that was able to convey graphic shapes on a computer monitor.

Products for the speech-impaired such as *Speech Enhancer Spectrum VP* (Electronic Speech Enhancement, Inc.) use the latest voice processing technology to turn unclear speech into sound that can be understood by any person. Until this development, the only help for the speech-impaired was the amplifier, which did not improve voice clarity.

IBM's *Blue Eyes* research program is working on a face-recognition system. Using this technology, the computer can recognize faces, track gazes, and even sense moods. For gaze tracking, a computer camera is mounted on the user's computer display, and this camera follows the user's iris. Depending on where the person focuses his or her eyes, the monitor senses what information is wanted and calls it up. In addition, face recognition systems may be used for security. The keyboard locks out any unauthorized person who tries to use your computer.

Curtis Chong, Director of Technology of the National Federation of the Blind, predicts that handheld reading devices that convert text to speech by passing over a page will be available in the near future. *Jordy devices*, which have goggles with tiny screens that enable people with impaired vision to see clearly with their own eyes, will be commercially available in the next few years. Similarly the *Tactile Graphics Display* (TGD) will enable students who are visually impaired to feel an image. Using TGE, for example, a student could run his or her fingers over a picture of a bed of pins and feel pinpricks (Kushner, 2003).

Technology Classrooms

Smart Classrooms. The Hueneme School District, located in Ventura County, California, was one of the first to receive international recognition for its leadership in developing technology. According to superintendent Dr. Ron Rescigno, students have made marked improvement in their achievement.

The district offers technologically designed classrooms, called *Smart Classrooms,* organized by curriculum area. Each *Smart Classroom* is a state-of-the-art, completely furnished facility that follows unique design principles. The computer configuration of these classrooms facilitates seamless exchange of data, voice, and video; total integration of equipment; computer instruction; and in-service training. Electronic connections are concealed under desks but are easily accessed with a simple command. Color monitors are recessed underneath desktops, and keyboards are housed in drawers that pull out for each student.

The *Smart Classroom* design emphasizes student interaction and academic success. Students learn to use different applications such as desktop publishing programs, word processing programs, and databases while gaining knowledge in all curriculum areas. Students engage in observations, explore different scientific phenomena, perform manipulation activities, and assume responsibility for their own learning with self-administered quizzes and answer checks.

Each student has an individual workstation with access to a CD-ROM drive, printer, and laser disc player. Each teacher has a workstation with a color printer and color scanner. The teacher's workstation controls an overhead projection system mounted on the ceiling that projects to a motorized screen that could be used with a large group. Infrared electronic blackboards and conventional whiteboards are attached to the wall behind the teacher's desk. Furthermore, the lighting system is designed to eliminate glare.

Twenty-First–Century Learning Environments. Creative Learning Systems, of San Diego, California, has pioneered the whole-laboratory approach to technology education, introducing the *Technology Lab 2000* in 1987 as the first such system ever sold. This company currently provides custom and semicustom learning environments to middle and high schools under the trade names of *SmartLab, SmartStudio,* and *Creative Learning Plaza.*

Creative Learning Systems emphasizes the following core principles in its learning environments:

- a learning facilitation model, not stand-and-deliver teaching;
- learner-focused instruction, which engages young people and helps instill in them the love of learning that is so necessary to creating communities of lifelong learners;

- constructivist approaches, which allow learners to make meaning out of their experiences;
- portfolio-based assessment, not prescriptive "single-answer" testing;
- project work that requires collaboration;
- learning that is self-directed;
- cross-curricular project work (to better reflect the real world), rather than arbitrary separate subject matter; and
- a brain-based system of learning.

The educational program incorporated into *SmartStudio* uses a series of integrated curricular resources that challenge the student to discover the underlying principles of technology and apply them, through critical thinking, problem solving, and decision making. The scenario helps students acquire the skills and confidence needed to live and work in the technological environment of tomorrow.

Although *SmartStudio* incorporates an extensive collection of cross-platform computer equipment and peripherals, it is anything but another version of the computer classroom. Rather than dominate the instructional program, computers in these environments serve as the tools by which learners access the language and the images of a broader technological arena. The environment is a total integrated system of furnishings, equipment, computer-mediated instruction, software, and hands-on computer-based learning. The instructional resources are self-paced, interactive tutorials. The materials launch learners into a variety of technological experiences and support self-designed projects that expand students' understanding of technological phenomena. *SmartStudio* gives learners access to information in areas such as robotics, audio engineering, Web design, entertainment engineering, multimedia production, satellite technology, and lasers, to name just a few.

Figure 16.18 shows a floor plan of a *SmartStudio* for multimedia arts and science studies, a representative example of a Creative Learning Systems environment, of which there are in excess of 500 across the United States and Canada.

Figure 16.18
SmartStudio Floor Plan

Creative Learning Systems SmartLabTM. For more information contact Bob McIntosh at bmcintosh@learnscapesinc.com. Used by permission, Creative Learning Systems.

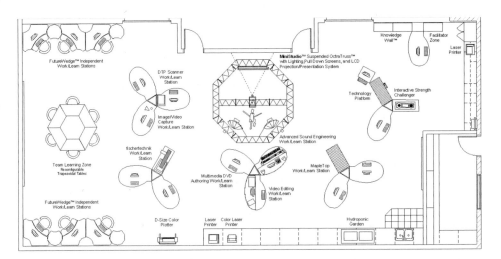

Islandlike arrangements of versatile, leading-edge laboratory furnishings form a series of activity zones within which students work and learn collaboratively. Each station is also reconfigurable to accommodate new activities or advanced explorations.

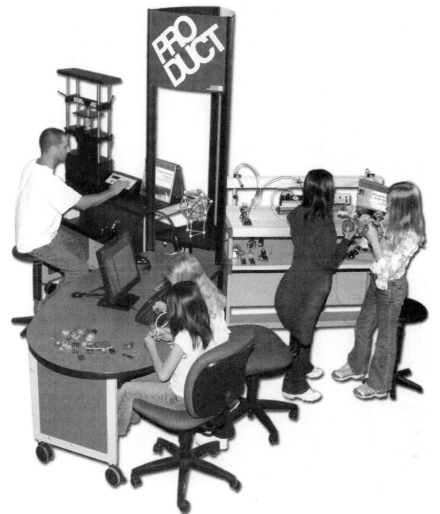

Figure 16.19 Team Workstation

Prototyping Technology Island, Creative Learning Systems. Used by permission, Creative Learning Systems.

Learner teams participate in computer-integrated enterprises in which all phases in the creation of a product are linked and interdependent.

Math, science, and technology-related areas of study are presented in an integrated curriculum. The power of the *SmartStudio* is realized when the vast array of activities are seen not as finite exercises, but rather as open-ended investigations, each leading to the next, linked by the common thread of curiosity.

One of the greatest changes in this new mode of learning is the teacher's role. The teacher is no longer the all-knowing instructor, but rather a facilitator of learning. The teacher-facilitator is freed to circulate, to facilitate creative contributions, and to help learners make connections and develop higher-order critical thinking skills.

Ventura Adult and Continuing Education. Students who attend the Ventura Adult and Continuing Education school can earn a high school diploma and receive preparation and testing for the General Education & Development (GED), for vocational education, and for much more. The programs at the Technology Development Center (TDC) are oriented toward employment in tomorrow's world. TDC covers a wide range of disciplines, including computer systems technology, medical programs, business, digital multimedia, TV production, and computer-aided design (CAD). Because of this modern orientation, this center has the most up-to-date technology. Over 90 percent of the students attending this school work with computers. The students are expertly trained to survive in today's digital world. The students have access to high-end Apple multimedia computers and state-of-the art drafting tools. They are trained to produce digital music videos in a multimedia class. This school responds to what employers want, upgrading to the best technology. According to Denise Mc Millan, principal of Ventura Adult Education, the goal of the school is to "provide a caring, nurturing environment where all students feel valued and accepted." TDC has a very high success rate.

Furthermore, students at this school have access to a stunning new technology called *rapid prototyping*. Using this technology, they can print three-dimensional objects. Student projects include chess figures, tiny human skulls with sinus cavities and brains, and complex interior displays. The items on the table in Figure 16.20 were the result of

Figure 16.20
Computer-Aided
Design Drafting Class
Products

a computer-aided design drafting class. To produce these items, the student feed digital images into a machine that looks like a photocopier and that costs $55,000. It "combines a glue-like binder with corn starch or gypsum power and proceeds to grow spectacularly intricate objects" (Arlow, 2002). Even though the school accepts more students with severe disabilities than other schools of its kind, it still has a 70 percent placement rate overall (Tronstad, 2003).

Software

Software manufacturers are producing high-quality multimedia programs that follow sound educational principles. The *JumpStart Series* (Knowledge Adventure; designed especially for children from kindergarten through grade 6), Scholastic's *Why Mosquitoes Buzz in People's Ears* (pre-K to grade 2), Edmark's *Talking Walls Series* (Riverdeep) (grades 4–8), and *Body Voyage* (Time Warner Electronic Publishing; designed for junior high school students to adults) are examples of innovative multimedia programs. Prices for educational software and computers are now reduced, and parents are taking advantage of these lower prices by buying more computers and software.

Today, students interact with computer programs differently because of developments in artificial intelligence. Programs such as *Crosscountry USA Deluxe* (Ingenuity), *Math Mind Benders* (Critical Thinking Books & Software), and Apple's *Gnu Chess* (Figure 16.21) contain elements of artificial intelligence. Publishing houses are mov-

Figure 16.21 *Gnu Chess*

Images courtesy of Apple Computers, Inc.

ing in the direction of integrating software with state-adopted texts and national standards. Lab packs and networkable products are now available as well. In the future, every textbook will come with a supplemental disk. Programs such as *World Book*—which combines sound, still sequences, animations, and full-motion video, photographs, and simulations—will be the norm. Virtual reality is also being integrated into every software package through *QuickTime VR* (see Chapter 8 for a full discussion).

Thoughts on the Future of Computers in Education

For this edition of *Computer Education for Teachers,* Dr. David Moursund was asked to share his thoughts on the future of computers in education. Dr. David Moursund, a leader in technology, has authored or co-authored more than 30 books and numerous articles on information technology in education. He is well known as the founder of the International Society for Technology in Education (ISTE). He served as editor-in-chief of *Learning and Leading with Technology,* the flagship publication of ISTE, from 1974 to 2001. In June 2000 Dr. Moursund and others founded the Oregon Technology in Education Council. He currently works as a professor in the College of Education at the University of Oregon (moursundoregon.uoregon.edu, http//darkwing.uoregon.edu/~moursund).

Dr. David Moursund wrote the following insightful response to my question.

Computers in Education: The Next 10 Years by David Moursund

Over the next decade we will likely see improvements in computer speed, fast computer memory, mass computer memory, and connectivity by a factor of 25 to 50 or more. We will see significant progress in developing software that is specifically designed for educational use, as well as software that will be used in education but is not specific to education.

The future of computers in education lies in the education-oriented problems that computers can help solve and the education-oriented tasks that computers can help accomplish. Here is a sample list of such problems and tasks that will continue to prove quite important. Each item is followed by a short paragraph discussing the types of progress likely to occur over the next decade. Undoubtedly you can think of other candidates for inclusion on this list.

1. *Basic goals of education:* The goal is to improve significantly our ability to accomplish the basic goals of education.

    In the United States we have approximately 4 million students at each of the K–8 grade levels. At these grade levels, Intelligent Computer-Assisted Learning (ICAL) is making significant progress and is economically viable. The next decade will see a steady use in ICAL products that can produce better learning (on average) than can an average teacher working with a classroom full of students. At the higher grade levels, a merger of ICAL and Distance Learning will provide courses and units of study that are more cost effective than traditional classroom instruction. Although many students will make use of such courses outside of the traditional classroom, the majority of use will occur within a traditional school setting and/or under close supervision of teachers in traditional schools.

2. *Learning problem solving:* The goal is to have students gain knowledge and skills in solving complex problems and accomplishing complex tasks and in transferring this learning so they can deal with novel problem-solving and task-accomplishing situations they will encounter in the future.

    Each academic discipline can be defined by the types of problems and tasks it addresses, its tools and methodologies, and its accomplishments. Problem solving and critical thinking are key components of each discipline. Our educational system is placing increasing emphasis on such higher-order knowledge and skills, and this trend will continue. Computers are now important aids to solving problems and accomplishing tasks in each academic discipline. Over the next decade we will see a steadily increasing integration of computers into each K–12 course and unit of study because of the steadily increasing power of computers as an aid to problem solving.

3. *Learning to learn:* The goal is to help all students become independent and self-sufficient lifelong learners who take steadily increasing responsibility for their own learning as they progress through school.

    The science of teaching and learning has made substantial progress in the past two decades. Researchers and practitioners know a lot about the theory and practice of how to teach better and how to learn better. This science is gradually being incorporated into teacher preservice and inservice education and into curriculum materials, instructional processes, and assessment. For example, the Web can be thought of as a huge and steadily growing global library that students can access now and throughout their future lives. We know how to help students gain some of the knowledge and skills of a research librarian, and we are gradually implementing such instruction and use throughout the curriculum. The next decade will see significantly increased emphasis on students learning to learn and taking more responsibility for their own learning in learning environments that include the Internet, Web, and Distance Learning.

4. *Computer content in noncomputer disciplines:* The goal is to help all students gain substantially increased understanding of computer and information science as part of the core content of each discipline they study.

   Computer-based content topics are now important components of the content of art, business, language arts, music, mathematics, all of the sciences, and a number of other subject areas taught at the K–12 levels. For example, reading and writing interactive multimedia is an important component of language arts. Modeling, simulation, and microcomputer-based laboratory are important components of all of modern science. Computers are now routinely used in the composition and performance of music. The next decade will see continuing progress in integrating such computer knowledge into the everyday K–12 curriculum.

5. *Computer knowledge and skills:* The goal is for all students to develop a broad-based fluency in computer tool knowledge and skills as well as introductory knowledge and skills in the discipline of computer and information science.

   Our educational system places great emphasis on students developing a relatively high level of fluency in reading, writing, and arithmetic (basic math). For example, in reading the goal is for students to learn to read well enough so that they can read to learn and so that reading can be a routine component of the learning process in many different courses. The past decade has seen some signs of schools beginning to understand that a similar type of student fluency is needed in using basic computer tools. The next decade will see an increased pace of acceptance of this idea and of the routine integration of computer tool use throughout the curriculum.

   At the current time, relatively few K–12 students are receiving any formal instruction in the discipline of computer and information science. The typical student has not learned very much about procedural thinking, software engineering, computer hardware engineering, artificial intelligence, and the other components of this important field of science and engineering. This situation is unlikely to change significantly over the next decade.

6. *Teachers:* The goal is for all preservice and inservice teachers to become competent in appropriate use of computers in facilitating and accomplishing goals 1–5 and in carrying out their other professional work.

   Progress toward achieving this goal has been spotty. For example, the International Society for Technology in Education has developed National Educational Technology Standards for Teachers that cover some of topics 1–5. However, relatively few preservice and inservice teachers meet the ISTE standards. Some of the professional societies for the various K–12 discipline areas have addressed some of goals 1–5 in their "standards" documents. By and large, however, they have not done an adequate job of addressing goal 4 nor of stressing the routine integration of computer use in coursework for their disciplines.

   Preservice and inservice teacher education are faced by rapidly moving targets in goals 1–5. Although progress is occurring, the pace of change of computer technology is faster than the pace of this progress. It is not likely that this difficulty will be overcome during the next decade.

Notice that no specific pieces of computer hardware, software, or connectivity are mentioned in the previous discussion. We began with a forecast of continued very rapid pace of change in computer hardware and connectivity. It is difficult to comprehend the meaning of this current pace of change. A change by a factor of 2 over a period of time means that the amount of change during this time is equal to all of the change that has ever occurred before then.

We now have the technology to build a portable computer device with a wide range of capabilities for potential use in education. The following bulleted list contains some of the features that such a *Communicator* might have. The next decade will see the mass production and sale of such a Communicator to the general public at a price that makes it possible for every student to have one. It will be interesting to see the effects of this on our educational system and our society.

- The Communicator weighs less than a pound, runs on long-life rechargeable batteries or a built-in fuel cell, and has a color display screen.
- It contains a global positioning system that determines its location on earth within a few meters and displays maps of its location.
- It contains a digital color camera and an audio recorder.
- It contains a cell phone.
- It provides wireless connectivity to the Internet (for example, for e-mail and the Web).
- It provides wireless radio-based connectivity to other nearby Communicators.
- It has sufficient storage capacity to store a full-length movie or many thousands of still pictures, many hours of recorded audio, an address book, and lots of other data.
- It includes a clock that displays the time in the time zone you are in. This clock automatically adjusts as you move to a different time zone and is self-correcting so that it provides the time correct to the nearest .01 second.
- It uses voice input and voice output.
- It accurately processes handwritten input.
- It includes a built-in arithmetic, graphing, and equation-solving calculator.
- It uses a combination of fingerprint identification, voiceprint identification, and password protection to help guard against unauthorized use.
- It can be used as a "Smart Card" to store and spend electronic money and/or to make credit card and debit card purchases.
- It has a modest but useful level of capability to translate among a number of different languages, using its voice input and output.
- As an add-on feature, a special pair of eyeglasses will receive signals from the ICT Communicator and project images onto the user's retina, thus producing the equivalent of a large screen display.
- Another add-on feature is a hearing aid type of device that receives stereo broadcast radio signals from the Communicator and that can also act as a hearing aid if the user needs one.
- Another add-on feature is a scanner that can scan and process text, pictures, and bar codes.

Concluding Thoughts

We would all like to see technologically advanced computer labs such as *SmartStudio 2003*. Furthermore, we want every student in our classrooms to have a computer that is connected to a wireless network. If a robot aide could decrease our workload, most of us would order one tomorrow. Many of the items on our wonderful wish lists may never materialize. Unfortunately, schools do not have the money to buy the equipment to implement a technology-based program. The more sophisticated computer equipment will be found primarily at the college and university level. Elementary and secondary schools will not be able to afford this costly hardware. But there is another problem: the lack of teachers trained to manage this new technology. Still, most states now require that teachers complete a computer course for certification. Because of this requirement, eventually there will be more trained teachers who can integrate the computer in the classroom.

What does the future hold? Computer use will increase, and the computers will be smaller, faster, more efficient, and less expensive. More emphasis will be placed on computer ethics, and the Internet will be available to all schools and children. Multimedia software will be even more sophisticated, offer speech recognition, be less expensive and more transparent, and will be menu and icon based. Computer storage capacity will be improved, and optical drives will enable teachers and students to access software more easily. More networkable machines will be available; advances in networking will lead to better communication among classrooms, schools, and school districts. One classroom will be networked with another classroom on a national or state database. Eventually, classrooms will be networking with classrooms in other countries. Students and teachers will commonly use desktop video conferencing and publishing programs as well as scanners, digital cameras, and fax machines to import pictures and graphic images into their documents.

Teachers will be "teaching" less because the computer will have a more prominent role in the classroom. Computers will enable teachers to assume the role of facilitators, designing learning experiences and individualizing instruction. There will be less drill and practice and more problem solving and real, meaningful learning activities. Many more of our universities will offer virtual degree programs, giving classes via the Internet. Books are still going to exist but maybe as a supplement to technologies such as the Internet. There may be only electronic books in our future, with the traditional book disappearing forever. Ahead of his time, one Illinois state superintendent of schools wanted laptop computers in his school instead of books. The computer is a remarkable invention. Its possible impact on the curriculum is staggering, but it needs to be given a chance to show what it can do for children in the schools. It is up to educators to inspire, motivate, and excite students and colleagues about this remarkable instrument for learning.

Lessons We Have Learned

We have learned quite a few things from our experiences with the computer. History has taught us that technology will not solve all our educational problems. Programming or networked computers do not offer quick answers to the question of how to educate students. The computer is an especially useful tool when applied to students with learning disabilities (see Chapter 13). We are living in a society where technology is constantly changing and the skills that students need to compete are ever changing. These skills differ according to a student's needs and competencies.

Educators generally want technology integrated into the classroom, but there are no firm guidelines for accomplishing this task. Stand-alone computers and networked computers each have their advantages and disadvantages. Networked computers enable teachers to standardize material across schools, districts, and classrooms. Stand-alone systems enable teachers to individualize the curriculum and control scheduling. We have learned that teachers usually do not have the time to develop computer materials or curricula. Distance learning has enabled people to attend class and conferences online, without having to travel to other locations. However, there is still something wonderful about face-to-face instruction.

From the history of educational computing we can see that technology is developing faster than teachers can keep abreast of these changes. Teachers can no longer use the same handouts, homework, worksheets, or lecture notes. Educators must continually change to take advantage of technological advances. Finally, even in this new technology world, teachers will always be essential, and their understanding of how to use this technology in the classroom is indispensable.

Summary

Computers are not just a passing fancy; they will be with us for a long time. They have made life both easier and more complicated. We can accomplish a great deal more by using a computer, but we have to work harder to keep up with the technology. In the end, we must consider the future of this exciting technology. We will definitely have smaller, faster, easier-to-use, and more powerful computers. Future software and hardware will accommodate multimedia, be networkable, include voice recognition, be based on artificial intelligence, and involve robots. Education will integrate computers into the curriculum as much as possible, but problems with funding and a lack of adequately trained teachers may limit what is accomplished in classrooms. We can only speculate on what will happen in the future. What we do know is that the coming years will be exciting!

Study and Online Resources

Go to Chapter 16 in the Student Edition of the Online Learning Center at www.mhhe.com/sharp5e *to **practice with key concepts, take chapter quizzes, read PowerWeb articles** and **news feed updates** related to technology in education, and **access resources** for learning about technology and integrating it into the classroom.*

Chapter Mastery Test

To the Instructor: *Refer to the Instructor's Manual for the answers to the Mastery Questions. This manual has additional questions and resource materials.*

Let us check for chapter comprehension with a short mastery test. Key Terms, Computer Lab, and Suggested Readings and References follow the test.

1. What are two lessons we have learned from our experiences with educational technology?
2. Why is the voice recognition system the wave of the future?

3. Define *artificial intelligence* and speculate on how it could be used in the classroom.
4. How can the computer help children with disabilities?
5. What has slowed the use of computers in the schools? How can these obstacles be overcome?
6. Explain how computers in the classroom will change the traditional roles of teachers, students, and parents.
7. What are some future directions for computer use in the classroom? Defend your choices.
8. Explain what the OLED display is and why it would be valuable in the classroom.
9. Explain what the mesh network is and why it is important.

Key Terms

Artificial intelligence
(AI)   428
E-book   420
eTravel (mutually immersive
mobil telepresence)   431

Mesh network   427
Organic light-emitting
diode display
(OLED)   418

Robot   429
Smart Personal
Objects Technology
(SPOT)   427

Virtual reality (VR)   431
Voice recognition
systems   428

Computer Lab: Activities for Mastery and Your Portfolio

16.1 Keeping Abreast of the Future   Find out how you can
keep up with the constant changes in technology.

Suggested Readings and References

Apicella, Mario. "Robots Are Marching Toward a More Intelligent and More Mobile Future." *InfoWorld* 22, no. 47 (November 20, 2000): 72.

"The Best of What's New." *Popular Science,* December 1997, 44–81.

Bork, Alfred. "The Future of Computers and Learning." *T.H.E. Journal* 24, no. 11 (June 1997): 69–77.

Bramscum, Deborah. "Monitors and Health." *MacWorld,* December 1994, 175–176.

Crawford, Walt. "Faster, Better, Cheaper: A Decade of PC Progress." *Online* 21, no. 1 (January–February 1997): 22–26, 28–29.

Crawford, Walt. "Jargon That Computes: Today's PC Terminology." *Online* 21, no. 2 (March–April 1997): 36–41.

DuBois, Grant. "Membership Swells for the E-Book Club." *EWeek* 17, no. 41 (October 9, 2000).

Dunn, Kate. "Inventor's Robot Is a Big Hit on the Shooting Range." *Los Angeles Times,* April 27, 1998, D7.

Dvorak, John C. *Dvorak Predicts: An Insider Look at the Computer Industry.* New York: Osborne McGraw-Hill, 1994.

Ediger, M. "Computers at the Crossroads." *Educational Technology* 28, no. 5 (May 1988): 7–10.

Freedman, Alan. *Computer Desktop Encyclopedia.* Point Pleasant, Pa.: Computer Language Company, 2003.

Hodges, Andrew. *Alan Turning: The Enigma.* London: Vintage Paper Back, Ranlon Century, 1992.

Hof, Robert D. "The Quest for the Next Big Thing." *BusinessWeek.* August 18–25, 2003, 91–94.

Hogan, Mike. "PC of Tomorrow." *IDG,* January 1998, 132–142.

Howard, Bill. "2001: The Future Is Now." *PC Magazine,* January 2, 2001, 99.

Janowski, Davis D. "Silicon Photonics." *PC Magazine,* July 2003, 100.

Jerome, Marty. "The Fastest PCs in the World." *PC Computing,* August 1997, 183–188.

Kaplan, Jeremy. "Microsoft SPOT." *PC Magazine,* July 2003, 102.

Kaplan, Karen. "Robots Roll up Their Sleeves." *Los Angeles Times,* March 10, 1994, 1D.

Knowles, John. "E-Bombs." *PC Magazine,* July 2003, 86–88.

Kushner, David. "They Give Sight to the Blind." *Los Angeles Times: Parade,* September 7, 2003, 6–8.

Leeds, Matthew. "Desktop Videoconferencing." *MacWorld,* November 1994, 87–92.

Levine. "OLED Displays." *PC Magazine,* July 2003, 98.

McDonald, Glenn, and Crotty Cameron. "The Digital Future." *PC World,* January 2000, 116–134.

Metz, Cade. "Carbon Nanotubes." *PC Magazine,* July 2003, 83–84, http://www.pcmag.com/.

Metz, Cade. "Plastic Transistors." *PC Magazine,* July 2003, 94.

Neel, Dan. "Wearable PC Goes to Work." *InfoWorld* 22, no. 47 (November 20, 2000): 10.

Port, Otis. "Cheap, Pliable, and Powerful." *Business Week,* August 15, 2003, 104.

Robertson, S., et al. "The Use and Effectiveness of Palmtop Computers in Education." *British Journal of Educational Technology* 28, no. 3 (July 1997): 177–189.

Roblyer, M. D., and M. Cass. "Virtual Reality in Special Education: Still More Promise Than Potential." *Learning and Leading with Technology* 36, no. 8 (1999): 51–53.

"The Tech Isn't Perfect, but Video Conferencing's Day Is Near." *Fortune Winter 2001 Technology Guide* 142, no. 12 (2001): 242.

Rupley, Sebastian. "Mesh Networks." *PC Magazine,* July 2003, 104.

Strauss, Howard, "Reflections: Another Look at Education Technology." *Syllabus,* April 2003, 41–42.

Ulanoff, Lance. "Cognitive Machines." *PC Magazine,* July 2003, 118–120.

Viscusi, Vance. "21st Century Classroom." In *Computers in Education,* 8th ed. New York: Dushkin/McGraw-Hill, 2002, 31–33.

Willis, William. "Speech Recognition: Instead of Typing and Clicking, Talk and Command." *T.H.E. Journal* 25, no. 6 (January 1998): 18–22.

Withrow, Frank B. "Technology in Education and the Next Twenty-Five Years." *T.H.E. Journal* 24, no. 11 (June 1997): 59–62.

Williams, Peter E. "Will a Digital Textbook Replace Me?" *T.H.E. Journal* 30, no. 10 (May 2003): 25–26.

Appendix A

Directory of Selected Software Publishers

A.D.A.M. Software, Inc.
1600 RiverEdge Parkway, Ste. 800
Atlanta, GA 30328
800/408-2326
404/980-0888
404/955-3088 (fax)
www.adam.com/

Addison-Wesley, Boston office
75 Arlington Street
Suite 300
Boston, MA 02116
617/848-7500
www.aw.com/

Adobe Systems, Inc.
345 Park Avenue
San Jose, CA 95110-2704
800/833-6687
408/537-6000 (fax)
www.adobe.com/products/main.html

AIMS Multimedia
9710 DeSoto Avenue
Chatsworth, CA 91311
800/367-2467
818/773-4300
818/341-6700 (fax)
http://www.aimsmultimedia.com

AlphaSmart
973 University Ave
Los Gatos, CA 95032
888/274-0680
408/355-1000
408/355-1055 (fax)
www.alphasmart.com/

Apple Computer, Inc.
1 Infinite Loop
Cupertino, CA 95014
800/767-2775
408/996-1010
www.apple.com

AppleWorks
1 Infinite Loop
Cupertino, CA 95014
800/MY-APPLE (Apple Store)
408/996-1010
www.apple.com/appleworks/

Aurbach & Associates, Inc.
9378 Olive Street Road, Suite 102
St. Louis, MO 63132
800/774-7239
314/432-7577
314/432-7072 (fax)
www.aurbach.com/

Barnum Software
5191 Morgan Territory Road
Clayton, CA 94517
800/553-9155
650-610-9034 (outside Canada)
800-553-9156 (fax)
www.thequartermile.com/

Baudville
5380 52nd Street S.E.
Grand Rapids, MI 49512
800/728-0888
616/698-0888 (Technical Support)
616/698-0554 (fax)
www.baudville.com/

Blue Squirrel (ForeFront)
686 E 8400 South
Sandy, UT, 84070
800/403-0925
801/352-1551
www.bluesquirrel.com

Bytes of Learning
60 Renfrew Drive, Suite 210
Markham, Ontario, Canada L3R 0E1
800/465-6428
905/475-8650 (fax)
www.bytesoflearning.com/

Classroom Connect
8000 Marina Boulevard, 4th Fl.
Brisbane, CA 94005
800/638-1639
310/536-9574 (fax)
650/351-5100
650/351-5300 (fax)
www.classroom.net/

Clearvue/eav
6465 North Avondale Avenue
Chicago, IL 60631
800-CLEARVU (253-2788)
773-775-9433
800-444-9855 (fax)
www.clearvue.com/

Cognitive Technologies Corporation
Math Realm
4884 Cloister Dr.
Rockville, MD 20852
800/335-0781
301/581-9653 (fax)
www.cogtech.com/

CompassLearning (formerly Josten)
9920 Pacific Heights Boulevard
San Diego, CA 92121
800/422-4339
www.compasslearning.com/

Compu-Teach, Inc.
PMB 137
16541 Redmond Way, Ste. C
Redmond, WA 98052
800/448-3224
425/885-0517
425/883-9169 (fax)
www.compu-teach.com/

Corel Corporation
1600 Carling Avenue
Ottawa, Ontario, Canada K1Z 8R7
800/772-6735
613/761-9176
www.corel.com

Crick Software
50 116th Ave S.E., Ste. 211
Bellevue, WA 98004
866/332-7425
425/467-8245 (fax)
www.cricksoft.com

Critical Thinking Books & Software
P.O. Box 448
Pacific Grove, CA 93950
800/458-4849
831/393-3288
831/393-3277 (fax)
www.criticalthinking.com/

Discovery Channel Multimedia
800/889-9950
multimedia.discovery.com/

Disney Interactive
800/328-0368
818/846-0454 (fax)
disney.go.com/DisneyInteractive/

DK Publishing, Inc.
(See *Global Software Publishing* for DK's CD-ROMs.)
375 Hudson St.
New York, NY 10014
800/788-6262

212/213-4800 x220
212/689-4828 (fax)
800/227-9604 (fax)
us.dk.com/

Don Johnston, Inc.

26799 West Commerce Drive
Volo, IL 60073
800/999-4660
847/740-0749
847/740-7326 (fax)
www.donjohnston.com

Edmark Corporation (See Riverdeep)

Electronic Arts

866-543-5435
www.ea.com/

Encore Software

16920 South Main Street
Gardena, CA 90248
800/507-1375
310/768-1800
310/768-1822 (fax)
www.encoresoftware.com

Equilibrium

307 Bedford Street
Lexington, MA 02420
415/892-3700 x204
www.equilibrium.com/

FableVision

44 Pleasant Street
Watertown, MA 02472
888-240-3734
617/926-1231
www.fablevision.com/

FileMaker, Inc.

5201 Patrick Henry Drive
P.O. Box 58168
Santa Clara, CA 95052-8168
800/325-2747
www.filemaker.com/

FTC Publishing Group

P.O. Box 1361
Bloomington, IL 61702
888/237-6740
www.ftcpublishing.com/

Global Software Publishing

(DK Multimedia)
535 West 34th Street
New York, NY 10001
info@gspna.com
www.learnatglobal.com/

Grolier Interactive (See Scholastic)

Hi Tech of Santa Cruz (TeacherTools.com)

89 Munroe Street
Somerville, MA 02143
info@teachertools.com
646-365-2450 (fax)
teachertools.site.yahoo.net/

Humongous Entertainment (Atari)

3855 Monte Villa Parkway
Bothell, WA 98021
425/486-9258
www.funkidsgames.com/

IBM Software

New Orchard Road
Armonk, NY 10504
(888/SHOP-IBM) 888-746-7426
800/246-6329 (fax)
www-306.ibm.com/software

Ingenuity Works, Inc.

1123 Fir Avenue
Blaine, WA 98230-9702
800/665-0667
604/484-8053
604/484-8096 (fax)
www.ingenuityworks.com/

Inspiration Software, Inc.

7412 S.W. Beaverton Hillside Highway, Ste. 102
Portland, OR 97225-2167
800/877-4292
503/297-3004
503/297-4676 (fax)
www.inspiration.com/

Intellectum Plus, Inc.

66 Crescent Drive
Gatineau, Sector Aylmer
Quebec, Canada J9H 1T1
819/682-5494
www.intellectum.com

Jackson Software

361 Park Avenue, Suite B
Glencoe, IL 60022
800/850-1777
847/835-1992
847/835-4926 (fax)
www.jacksoncorp.com/

Jay Klein Productions, Inc.

2850 Serendipity Circle West, Suite 202
Colorado Springs, CO 80917
719/599-8786
719/380-9997
www.gradebusters.com/

Knowledge Adventure

6060 Center Drive, 10th Floor
Los Angeles, CA 90045
800/545-7677
310/258-0744 (fax)
www.knowledgeadventure.com/

Lawrence Productions

1800 S. 35th Street
Galesburg, MI 49053
800/421-4157
264/665-7075
269/665-7060
www.lpi.com/

The Learning Company (See Riverdeep)

www.riverdeepinet/learningcompany/

Logo Computer Systems, Inc. (LCSI)

P. O. Box 162
Highgate Springs, VT 05460
800/321-5646
514/331-1380 (fax)
www.lcsi.ca/

Mainstay

1320 Flynn Road, Suite 401
Camarillo, CA 93012
800/362-2605
805/484-9400
805/484-9428 (fax)
www.mstay.com/

McAfee.com

3965 Freedom Circle
Santa Clara, CA 95054
888/VIRUSNO
800/SNIFFER
801/772-1891
www.mcafee.com

McGraw-Hill Children's Publishing

3195 Wilson Drve NW
Grand Rapids, MI 49544
800/417-3261
www.mhteachers.com/

Microsoft Corp.

1 Microsoft Way
Redmond, WA 98052-6399
800/426-9400
206/882-8080
www.microsoft.com/

Milliken Software

11643 Lilburn Park Road
St. Louis, MO 63146
314/991-4220
800/325-4136
314/991-4807 (fax)
www.millikenpub.com/

MindPlay

440 S. Williams Blvd, Suite 206
Tucson, AZ 85711

520/888-1800
520/888-7904 (fax)
www.mindplay.com/

Neufeld Learning Systems

7 Conifer Crescent
London, Ontario, Canada N6K 2V3
866-429-Math
519/657-9334
519/657-3220 (fax)
www.neufeldmath.com/

Nordic Software, Inc.

P.O. Box 5403
Lincoln, NE 68505
800/306-6502
402/489-1557
402/489-1560 (fax)
www.nordicsoftware.com/

Opcode Systems, Inc.

309 Plus Park Blvd.
Nashville, TN 37217
800/444-2766 ext. 2367
615/889-5509 (fax)
www.opcode.com/

Optimum Resource, Inc.

18 Hunter Road
Hilton Head Island, SC 29926
888/843-689-8000
843/689-8008 (fax)
www.stickybear.com/

Pearl Software

64 East Uwchlan Ave, Suite 230
Exton, PA 19341
800/732-7596
www.pearlsw.com

PLATO Learning

10801 Nesbitt Avenue South
Bloomington, MN 55437
800/869-2000
952/832-1000
952/832-1270 (fax)
www.plato.com

The Princeton Review

2315 Broadway, 3d Fl.
New York, NY 10024
800/738-4392
800/Review 2
212/874-8282
212/874-0775 (fax)
www.princetonreview.com/

Riverdeep, Inc.

500 Redwood Boulevard
Novato, CA 94947
888/242-6747
415/763-4700
800/825-4420
877/278-7456 (fax)
www.riverdeep.net

ScanSoft, Inc.

9 Centennial Drive
Peabody, MA 01960
978/977-2000
408/395-7000
www.scansoft.com/

Scholastic, Inc.

557 Broadway
New York, NY 10012
800/541-5513
800/724-6527
212/343-6100
www.scholastic.com/

Sierra, Inc.

3060 139th Avenue S.E., Ste. 500
Bellevue, WA 98005
425/649-9800
www.sierra.com/

SmartStuff's Foolproof Security (See Riverdeep)

Sunburst Technology

1550 Executive Drive
Elgin, IL 60123-9979
800/321-7511
888/800-3028 (fax)
www.sunburst.com/

Super School Software

1857 Josie Avenue
Long Beach, CA 90815-3432
562/594-8580
www.superschoolsoftware.com/

Symantec Corp.

20330 Stevens Creek Boulevard
Cupertino, CA 95014
800/441-7234
541/984-8020 (fax)
www.symantec.com/

Teacher Support Software (Gamco)

325 North Kirwood Road, Suite 200
St. Louis, MO 63122
888/726-8100
314/984-8063 (fax)
www.tssoftware.com

Tech4Learning, Inc.

10981 San Diego Mission Rd., Suite 120
San Diego, CA 92108
877/834-5453
619/563-5348
619/283-8176 (fax)
www.tech4learning.com/

Terrapin Logo Software

955 Massachusetts Ave.
Cambridge, MA 02139
800/774-LOGO
617/923-3533
800/776-4610 (fax)
www.terrapinlogo.com/

Tom Snyder Productions (Scholastic)

80 Coolidge Hill Road
Watertown, MA 02172-0236
800/342-0236
617/926-6000 ext. 276
800/304-1254 (fax)
www.teachtsp.com/

True Basic, Inc.

P.O. Box 501
Hartford, VT 05047-0501
800/436-2111
802/296-2715 (fax)
www.truebasic.com/

Ventura Educational Systems

P.O. Box 425
Grover Beach, CA 93483-0425
800/336-1022
800/493-7380 (fax)
www.venturaes.com/

Videodiscovery

920 N. 34th Street, Suite 300
Seattle, WA 98103
800/548-3472
206/285-5400
206/285-9245 (fax)
www.videodiscovery.com/

Visions Technology in Education

2095 Laura Street, Ste. H
Springfield, OR 97477
800/877-0858
800/816-0695 (fax)
www.toolsforteachers.com

Appendix B
Recommended Mail-Order and Online Software Sources

Amazon.com, Inc.

www.amazon.com/

Attainment Company (special education)

504 Commerce Parkway
P.O. Box 930160
Verona, WI 53593-0160
800/327-4269
800/942-3865 (fax)
www.attainmentcompany.com/

CCV Software

P.O. Box 6724
Charleston, WV 25362-0724
800/843-5576 (East)
800/541-6078 (West)
800/321-4297 (fax—East)
800/457-6953 (fax—West)
www.ccvsoftware.com

ClassroomDirect.com

P.O. Box 830677
Birmingham, AL 35283-0677
800/599-3040
800/628-6250 (fax)
www.classroomdirect.com/

Educational Resources

1550 Executive Drive
P.O. Box 1900
Elgin, IL 60121-1900
800/624-2926
www.edresources.com/

Education Technology, Inc. (ETI)

2102 N.E. 30th Street, Ste. A
Tacoma, WA 98403

800/677-6221
253/474-5200
253/474-3550 (fax)
www.edtech.com/

Education Works Inc.

http://shop.store.yahoo.com/educationworks/

Education Software Cooperative

www.edu-soft.org/escmembers.shtml

Educational Software Directory.net

www.educational-software-directory.net/

Egghead Software (Powered by Amazon)

www.egghead.com/

eToys.com

www.etoys.com/

Funschool

www.funschool.com/

Goggle Directory

www.shop.store.yahoo.com/educationworks/

Interact CD-ROM Store

www.interactcd.com/

KBkids.com

1099 18th Street, Ste. 1000
Denver, CO 80202
877/452-5437
303/228-9000
www.kbkids.com/soft/

Kids Click
www.kidsclick.com/

Kids Domain
www.kidsdomain.com/

Learning Services
P. O. Box 1036
Eugene, OR 97440
800/877-9378 (West)
541/744-2056 (fax—West)
800-815-5154 (fax)
www.learningservicesinc.com

MacConnection
730 Milford Road
Merrimack, NH 03054-6002
800/800-2222
www.macconnection.com

MacMall
2555 W. 190th Street
Torrance, CA 90504
800/622-6255
www.macmall.com

MacWarehouse (CDW)
200 N. Milwaukee Avenue
Vernon Hills, IL 60061
800/348-3636
www.CDW.com/mac

MacZone
707 South Grady Way
Renton, WA 98055-3233
800/248-0800
www.maczone.com

MicroWarehouse (PCs) (CDW)
200 N. Milwaukec Avenue
Vernon Hills, IL 60061
800/463-4239
www.cdw.com/

PC Connection
730 Milford Road
Merrimack, NH 03054
800/800-5555
www.pcconnection.com

PCMall
2555 W. 190th Street
Torrance, CA 90504
800/555-6255
www.pcmall.com

PCZone
707 South Grady Way
Renton, WA 98055-3233
800/419-9663
www.zones.com

Smart Kids Software
888/881-6001
www.smartkidssoftware.com/

Software Express, Inc.
4128-A South Boulevard
Charlotte, NC 28209
800/527-7638
704/522-7638
704/529-1010 (fax)
www.swexpress.com

Softwareoutlet.com
www.softwareoutlet.com/

SuperKids
www.superkids.com/

Surplus CD-ROM Family Software
www.surpluscdrom.com/

TigerDirect.com
7795 W. Flagler Street, Ste. 35
Miami, FL 33144
800/879-1597

305/415-2200
305/415-2202 (fax)
www.tigerdirect.com/

Tucows

800/371-6992
416/531-5584 (fax)
www.tucows.com/

Tukids

800/371-6992
416/531-5584 (fax)
download.tucows.com/perl/TUKIDS.html
cyberlynk.tukids.tucows.com/

Yahoo! Shopping: Internet Marketing Associates

877/275-9955
813/571-7631
http://shop.store.yahoo.com/meter/
http://search.yahoo.com/bin/
search?p=educational+software

ZDNET Reviews (Ziff Davis Software Library)

www.zdnet.com/products/stories/reviews/
0,4161,2611159,00.html

Glossary

Abacus An ancient calculating device consisting of beads strung on wires or rods that are set in a frame.

ABC An abbreviation for the Atanasoff-Berry Computer, the first electronic digital computer.

Academic portfolio Shows the student's academic performance, and achievement.

Access time The time a computer needs from the instant it asks for information until it receives it.

Acoustic coupler A type of modem that enables the user to insert the telephone handset into a built-in cradle that sends and receives computer signals through telephone lines.

Active matrix A screen, generally used in portable computers, in which each pixel is controlled by its own transistor.

Ada A high-level programming language developed in the late 1970s and named after Augusta Ada Byron, Countess of Lovelace and daughter of Lord Byron.

Adaptive technology (also referred to as assistive technology) Refers to using technology to provide equal access for students with disabilities.

Algorithm Generally a set of instructions for a person to follow in order to solve a problem. A computer program is an algorithm that tells the computer what to do in a step-by-step manner—in a language that it comprehends.

Analog device A mechanism that handles values in continuous variable quantities such as voltage fluctuations.

Analytical engine A sophisticated mechanical calculating machine designed by Charles Babbage in 1833. Conceived before the technology was available, it was to have been capable of storing instructions, performing mathematical operations, and using punched cards for storage.

Applet In Java, a small program that is embedded in a Web page and, when downloaded, is started by the browser.

Application program or software A program written for a certain purpose, such as word processing.

Archie server Finds files stored at an anonymous FTP site.

Arithmetic logic unit (ALU) The central processing unit component responsible for the execution of fundamental arithmetic and logical operations on data.

Artificial intelligence (AI) Use of the computer to simulate the thinking of human beings.

ASCII The American Standard Code for Information Interchange, a standard computer character set that facilitates efficient data communication and achieves compatibility among computer devices.

Assembler A computer program that converts assembly language programs into executable machine language programs.

Assembly language A low-level programming language that uses mnemonic words and in which each statement corresponds directly to a single machine instruction.

Assistive technologies Equipment that increases, maintains, or improves the capabilities of individuals with disabilities.

Authoring language A computer language used to create educational software, such as drill-and-practice lessons.

Authoring system A program requiring little knowledge, used to create computer-based lessons and tests.

Backup disk A second copy of a program or document.

Bandwidth The amount of data that can be transmitted through a communication network.

Bar code reader An input device that scans bar codes and converts the bar codes into numbers that are displayed on the screen.

BASIC Beginner's All Purpose Symbolic Instruction Code, one of the most commonly used high-level programming languages.

Baud rate The speed at which a modem can transmit data.

Binary notation The number system a computer uses. It has only two digits, 1 and 0.

Bit An abbreviation for *binary digit*, either 1 or 0 in the binary number system.

Bookmark manager A software program that enables you to organize and collect Uniform Resource Locators (URLs) in a hierarchical manner.

Boolean algebra Devised by George Boole, a system of algebra that uses the operations of informal logic.

Booting the system The process of starting the computer.

BPS An abbreviation for *bits per second,* the measurement of data transmission speed. Presently, the fastest modem transfer over phone lines is 56 kilobits per second (kbps).

Broadband Refers to high bandwidth that transmits 1.5 Mps over fiber optic cables.

Browser Software that enables users to surf the World Wide Web. *Netscape Navigator* and *Internet Explorer* are the two most popular browsers.

Bug A mistake or error in a computer program.

Bulletin board system (BBS) A computer that serves as a center for exchange of information for various interest groups.

Bus network A network with a single bidirectional cable or bus line that carries messages to and from devices. Each workstation can access the network independently.

Buttons "Hot spots" that are clicked to initiate an action.

Byte A unit of computer storage that consists of eight binary digits (bits). A byte holds the equivalent of one character, such as the letter C.

C A computer language developed by Bell Labs for the Unix operating system.

Cable modem A modem that uses a cable TV service to provide high speed access to the Internet.

Card A rectangular box on the screen that contains text, graphics, sound, and animation. A bunch of cards are referred to as a stack.

Cathode ray tube (CRT) The basis of the television screen and the typical microcomputer display screen.

CD-ROM (compact disc–read only memory) A means of high-capacity storage (more than 600 megabytes) that uses laser optics for reading data.

Cell In an electronic spreadsheet, the intersection of a row and column.

Central processing unit (CPU) The "brains of the computer," where the computing takes place. The CPU is also called the *processor.* It is made up of a control unit and the arithmetic logic unit.

Chat room A real-time Internet discussion on some topic.

Circuit board A board onto which electrical components are mounted and interconnected to form a circuit.

Clipboard A temporary memory storage area where text or graphics can be copied from a document and stored until pasted elsewhere in a document.

Clock speed (clock rate) Refers to the speed that the computer performs basic operations.

COBOL Common Business-Oriented Language, a high-level programming language used for business applications.

Compiler A program that translates the source code of a program written in a higher-level language such as BASIC into a machine-readable, executable program.

Composite color monitor A monitor that accepts an analog video signal and combines red, green, and blue signals to produce a color image.

Computer A machine that accepts information, processes it according to a set of instructions, and produces the results as output.

Computer chip A piece of semiconducting material, such as silicon, with transistors and resistors etched on its surface. The formal name for a computer chip is integrated circuit.

Computer conferencing Communication between two or more computers in real time.

Computer graphics Using the computer to create and manipulate pictures.

Computer literacy The basic knowledge that one needs to work independently with the computer.

Computer-aided design (CAD) Use of the computer for industrial design and technical drawing.

Computer-assisted instruction (CAI) Use of the computer as an instructional tool.

Computer-managed instruction (CMI) A computerized record-keeping system that diagnoses a student's progress, provides instruction, and analyzes progress.

Connect time The time spent online between logging on and logging off.

Constructivism A learning theory emphasizing experience-based activities.

Control unit The component of the central processing unit that receives programmed instructions and carries them out.

Cookie A text file that a server writes to a person's hard drive without his or her knowledge. The purpose is to track the individual's computer usage.

Copyright The laws that protect people who own creative works such as music, art, text, software, and other products of this nature.

CPS An abbreviation for *characters per second,* a term used to describe the number of characters printed per second by the printer.

Cursor The blinking light that shows the user where he or she is working on the computer screen.

Cyberspace The use of computer technology to create virtual space.

Daisy-wheel printer An impact printer that produces a typewriter-quality print. This printer has its type characters set around a daisy wheel, similar to a wagon wheel minus an outer ring.

Database A collection of information organized according to some structure or purpose.

Database management system Application software that controls the organization, storage, and retrieval of data in the database.

Debug To find the errors in a computer's hardware or software.

Delete To remove information from a file or disk.

Demodulation Used in telecommunication, the process of receiving and transforming an analog signal into its digital equivalent, which can be used by the computer.

Desktop A computerized representation of a person's work as if he or she were looking at a desk cluttered with folders.

Desktop publishing (DTP) The use of the personal computer in conjunction with specialized software to combine text and graphics to produce high-quality output on a laser printer or typesetting machine.

Desktop publishing software Programs such as *Microsoft Publisher, Adobe PageMaker,* and *QuarkXpress.* These applications enable the computer to be a desktop publishing workstation.

Desktop video conferencing Refers to using a personal computer to do video conferencing.

Digital camera A portable camera that records images in a digital format.

Digital computer A computer that operates by accepting and processing data that has been converted into binary numbers.

Digital divide A term that refers to the gap between those who have access to computer technologies and those who do not have access.

Digital subscriber line (DSL) A digital technology that offers high-speed transmission over standard copper telephone wiring.

Digitizer A device that translates analog information into digital information for computer processing. Examples include scanners and digital cameras.

Discover switch An "intelligent" switch that enables people with physical disabilities to use a variety of software programs that feature single-switch scanning.

Display The representation of data on a screen in the form of a printed report, graph, or drawing.

Distance education The delivery by institutions or instructors of knowledge via telecommunication or remote capabilities. (See *Distance learning.*)

Distance learning The receiving of training from a remote teaching site via TV or computer. The same as *distance education.*

Documentation The set of instructions, tutorials, or reference materials that is required for the computer program to run effectively. Documentation can be in the form of online help or printed material.

DOS (disk operating system) A program that enables the computer to control its own operation. This program's major task is to handle the transfer of data and programs to and from the computer's disks.

Dot pitch The smallest dot that a computer monitor can display. The smaller the dots, the higher the resolution.

Dot-matrix printer An impact printer that produces characters and graphic images by striking an inked ribbon with tiny metal rods called *pins.*

Download The process of sending information from a larger computer to a smaller one by means of a modem or network.

Drag-and-drop A technique that uses the mouse to drag objects on the computer screen.

Drawing programs Programs that use vector graphics to produce line art.

Drill and practice A type of computer instruction that enables students to practice information with which they are familiar in order to become proficient.

DVD-RAM (digital video disc–random access memory) The read/write version of DVD-ROM.

DVD-ROM (digital video disc–read only memory) Similar to CD-ROM in appearance, this disc format has the capacity to hold 17 gigabytes.

E-book A handheld computer, similar in size to an organizer, that displays electronic versions of books, enabling users to set bookmarks, do keyword searches, and make notes in margins.

Educational technology Technology that aids the teaching and learning process.

Electronic mail, e-mail A system of transmitting messages over a communication network via the computer. *Pine* is an e-mail service most commonly used at universities, and *Eudora Lite* is a mail application used most often by the general public.

Electronic portfolio A representative collection of an individual's work that shows his or her talents and is presented electronically by a presentation program or displayed on a website.

Electronic whiteboard A device that is connected to a teacher's computer that enables users to see what the instructor writes and that captures the information that is written into a computer file.

E-mail address A name and a computer location (often referred to as a *host*). An example is vicki.sharp@csun.edu, in which vicki@sharp is the name and csun is the location.

Encryption The process of coding information so that it cannot be understood unless decoded.

Encyclopedia database (see *Free-form database*)

Ergonomics The science of designing computers and furniture so that they are easy and safe to use.

Ethernet One of the most popular types of local area network connections.

Execute To carry out the instructions given in machine language code.

Expansion slot A slot inside the computer that accepts boards that add to the computer's capabilities and features.

Fair use The part of the copyright law that tells when it is legal to copy another's creative work.

FAQs (frequently asked questions) Files found at Internet sites that answer frequently asked questions. It is a good idea to check for FAQs and read them.

Fax machine An input/output device that enables the user to transmit text and images between distant locations.

Fiber optics A medium consisting of glass fibers that transmit data using light.

Field A record location in which a certain type of data is stored.

File A collection of related records.

File server A powerful computer that stores information and programs that users share.

Filtering software A program that tries to prevent the user from accessing adult material on the Internet.

Finger server Finds out information about another Internet user, including the name of the person behind the user identification name.

Firewall A security system that protects a network against threats from hackers from other networks.

FireWire A high-speed serial bus that connects up to 63 peripheral devices such as digital cameras and printers.

Flame An argumentative posting of an e-mail message or newsgroup message in response to another posting.

Flat file database A simple database that works with only one data file at a time, with no linking to other data files.

Floppy disk Covered with magnetic coating, such as iron oxide, the mass storage device used primarily with microcomputers.

Flowchart A graphical representation of the flow of operations that is needed to finish a job. It uses rectangles, diamonds, ovals, parallelograms, arrows, circles, and words to represent different levels of operations.

Font A group of letters, numbers, punctuation marks, and special characters with the same typeface, style, and weight.

Footer In word processing, repeated text such as a title that appears at the bottom of a page.

Format To prepare a disk so the user can store information on it. During the formatting process, the computer's disk drive encodes a magnetic pattern consisting of tracks and sectors.

FORTRAN FORmula TRANslator, one of the oldest high-level programming languages, suited for scientific and mathematical applications.

Frame In desktop publishing, a movable and resizable box that holds graphics and text.

Free-form database A database that enables the user to enter text without regard to its length or order.

Freeware Software that is given away at no charge.

FTP (File Transfer Protocol) The basic Internet function that enables files to be transferred between computers. It can be used to download files from a remote host computer as well as to upload files from a computer to a remote host computer.

Function key A key located on the keyboard that the user programs to perform a specific task.

Gigabyte A unit of measure that equals approximately 1 billion (1,073,741,824) bytes.

Gopher A program that enables the user to browse the Internet using menus.

Graphic organizer A visual communication tool that enables users to organize their ideas using symbols.

Graphical user interface (GUI) An interface that differs from a character-based computer interface such as MS-DOS. An example of a popular graphical interface is the Macintosh operating system.

Graphics tablet A plotting tablet that the user draws on to communicate with the computer.

Gutenberg, Johannes The inventor of movable type.

Hacker A computer expert; sometimes one who illegally accesses and tampers with computer programs and data.

Handheld computer A small mobile computer that enables the user to write on-screen with a stylus. This device provides tools for everyday use such as a notepad, word processor, appointment calendar, address book, and fax modem.

Hard copy Computer output that is on paper, film, or another permanent medium.

Hard disk One or more disk platters coated with a metal oxide substance that enables information to be magnetically stored.

Hard drive The computer's main storage device.

Hardware The physical components of the computer system, which include the computer, monitor, printer, and disk drives.

Header In word processing, repeated text such as page numbers that appear at the top of the page.

Hierarchical database A database that stores items in a top-to-bottom organizational structure.

High-level language Language that is further away from the machine's operation and approximates human language. Low-level language is nearer the machine's operation.

Home page The main page in a website, at which you find hyperlinks to other pages.

Host The computer that serves as the beginning point and ending point for data transfer when accessing the Internet.

Hub A central connecting device in a computer network that joins communication lines together on the network.

HyperCard An authoring tool that enables the user to organize information and retrieve on-screen cards that contain text, graphics, sound, and animation.

Hyperlink A graphic, an icon, or a word in a file that, when clicked, automatically opens another file for viewing.

Hypermedia A system nearly synonymous with *hypertext* (however, it emphasizes the nontextual components of hypertext) that uses the computer to input, manipulate, and output graphics, sound, text, and video in the presentation of ideas and information.

HyperTalk The programming language that is used with *HyperCard.*

Hypertext Nonsequential associations of images, sound, text, and actions through which the user can browse, regardless of the order. An example of hypertext is a computer glossary from which a user can select a word and retrieve its definition.

Hypertext Markup Language (HTML) The basic language that people use to build hypertext electronic documents on the Web.

Identity theft The illegal gathering of information about a person and its use for the successful impersonation of this person by mail, over the telephone, in person, or online.

Inclusion or inclusive education Education of students with disabilities with their peers who do not have disabilities.

Initialize See *Format.*

Inkjet printer A nonimpact printer that uses a nozzle to spray a jet of ink onto a page of paper. These small, spherical bodies of ink are released through a matrix of holes to form characters.

Instant messaging A service that tells users when their friends are online and enables them to exchange information in real time.

Integrated circuit (IC chip) (see *Chip*)

Integrated learning system (ILS) A central computer with software consisting of planned lessons in various curriculum areas.

Integrated program An application program like Microsoft Works that combines several tasks such as word processing and database management in one package and facilitates the free interchange of information among applications. These applications do not offer as much capability as a single application.

Interactive video A system consisting of a computer, videodisc player, videotape, and software that provides the student with immediate feedback. It includes management features so lessons can be customized to specific student needs.

Interface The place at which a connection is made between two elements so they can work together harmoniously. In computing, different interfaces occur, ranging from user interfaces, in which people communicate with programs, to hardware interfaces, which connect devices and components in a computer.

Internet A system of worldwide networks that enables a user to send electronic mail, conduct research, chat, and participate in newsgroups.

Internet 2 The second generation of the Internet designed primarily to exchange multimedia data in real time at high speeds.

Internet appliances Low-cost devices that handle e-mail and Web browsing and perform this job faster than an ordinary modem connection.

Internet relay chat (IRC) A real-time Internet service that enables users to do conferencing all over the world.

Internet service provider (ISP) An organization that charges a fee for users to dial into its computer for an Internet connection.

Interpreter A high-level program translator that translates and then executes each statement in a computer program. It translates a statement into machine language, runs it, then proceeds to the next statement, translates it, runs it, and so on.

ISDN (Integrated Services Digital Network) A telecommunications standard that offers digital service from a person's residence to a dial-up telephone network.

Java A programming language designed by Sun Microsystems to write programs that can be downloaded from the Internet with a Java interpreter. Many World Wide Web pages on the Internet use small Java applications, or applets, to display animations.

JavaScript A scripting language for Web publishing.

Joystick A small, boxlike object with a moving stick and buttons used primarily for games, educational software, and CAD systems.

Kbps An abbreviation for *kilobits per second,* a computer modem's speed rating, measured in units of 1,024 bits. This is the maximum number a device can transfer in one second under the best of conditions.

Kerning In typography, the adjustment of space between pairs of characters, as in "B A," to enhance the appearance of the type or to enhance readability.

Keyboard An input device similar to a standard typewriter but with extra keys, such as function keys and a numeric pad.

Keyboard emulator A device exists inside a computer or is connected to a computer that imitates the computer keyboard's performance.

Kilobyte (K) A unit of measure for computers that is equal to 1,024, or 2^{10}, bytes.

Laser disc A large-sized optical disc that utilizes laser technology for the purpose of video.

Laser printer A printer that produces high-quality text and graphic output by tracing images with a laser beam controlled by the computer.

Leading In typography, the vertical spacing between lines of type that is measured from baseline to baseline.

Light pen An instrument, used in conjunction with a video display, with a light-sensitive, photoelectric cell in its tip that sends an electrical impulse to the computer, which identifies its current location.

Light-emitting diode (LED) When charged with electricity, a semiconductor diode that gives off light.

Linotype machine The first successful automated typecasting machine.

Liquid crystal display (LCD) A display that uses a liquid compound, positioned between two sheets of polarizing material squeezed between two glass panels.

Liquid crystal display projection panel A projector that receives computer output and displays it on a liquid crystal screen placed on an overhead projector. The projector displays on a large screen the program that the computer generates.

Local area network (LAN) A network that provides communication within a local area, usually within 200 or 300 feet, as found in office buildings.

Logo A high-level programming language designed for children that contains many functions found in LISP.

Low-level language A programming language, like assembly language, that is close to the machine's language.

Machine language A programming language composed of a pattern of 0s and 1s that is far removed from the language understood by human beings. This is the only language that computers understand.

Macro A group of routines or commands combined into one or two keystrokes.

Magnetic disk A device that stores data magnetically in circular tracks that are divided into sectors.

Magnetic ink character recognition (MICR) A character recognition system that reads text printed with a special magnetic ink. All the checks issued by banks are coded with this special ink and characters so that an MICR unit can read them.

Magnetic tape A reel of tape that is usually around ½ inch wide that can store about 25 megabytes of data magnetically in a linear track.

Mail merge A word processing feature that prints customized form letters.

Mainframe computer A high-level computer designed for sophisticated computational tasks.

Mainstreaming In partial and full-time programs the education of students with disabilities with their nondisabled peers.

Mark I An electromechanical calculating machine designed by Howard Aiken at Harvard University and built by IBM.

Megabyte (MB) A unit of measure that equals approximately 1,048,576 bytes.

Megahertz (MHz) A measure of frequency equal to 1 million cycles per second.

Memory The circuitry inside the computer that enables it to store and retrieve information. Generally, *memory* refers to the semiconductor storage (RAM) that is directly connected to the microprocessor.

Mesh network An Internet-like communication network that has at least two pathways to each node. In a completely meshed network every node has a direct connection to every other node.

Microcomputer system A computer that uses a single chip microprocessor, one that is less powerful than that of a minicomputer.

Microprocessor chip A chip that contains the central processing unit of the computer.

Microworld The Logo environment in which a child freely experiments, tests, and revises his or her own theories in order to create a product.

MIDI (Musical Instrument Digital Interface) A protocol that enables individuals to exchange musical information between musical instruments, computers, and synthesizers.

Millisecond (ms) Equivalent to 10^{-3}, or one-thousandth, of a second.

Minicomputer A midlevel computer whose capabilities are between those of a mainframe and a microcomputer.

Modem Short for MOdulator/DEModulator, a device that enables two computers to communicate with each other via telephone lines.

Modulation In telecommunication, the means that a modem uses to convert digital information sent by computer to its analog form, so that the information can be sent over telephone lines.

Monitor A video display that resembles a television set, designed to handle a wider and higher range of frequencies.

Morphing A special effect that changes one image into another image.

Mouse A popular input device that is used instead of the keyboard to make menu selections.

MPEG Audio Layer 3 (MP3) A Moving Pictures Experts Group (MPEG) audio format that produces CD quality audio using a 12:1 compression rate.

Multimedia A subset of hypermedia that combines graphics, sound, animation, and video.

Nanosecond (ns) Equivalent to 10^{-9}, or one-billionth, of a second.

Napier's rods A device used for multiplying large numbers, invented by John Napier, a Scottish mathematician, in 1617.

Netiquette The etiquette used in cyberspace.

Network Computers that share storage devices, peripherals, and applications. A network can be connected by telephone lines, satellites, or cables.

Network database Works the same as a hierarchical database except that a record can belong to more than one main group.

Newsgroups Electronic bulletin boards where you can read messages that others have written and contribute to the discussion.

Online The status of a computer interacting with an online service or the Internet.

Online help The capability of a program to display onscreen guidance while an individual uses the computer.

Online service Any commercial service such as *America Online* (AOL) that gives access to electronic mail, news services, and the Web.

Operating system See *DOS*.

Optical character recognition (OCR) A device that recognizes printed or typed text.

Optical disc A round platter that has information recorded on it with laser beam technology. It is capable of storing large amounts of information.

Optical mark reader (OMR) A device that reads penciled or graphic information on cards or pages. Lamps furnish light reflected from the card or paper; the amount of reflected light is measured by a photocell.

Organic light-emitting diode display (OLED) A technology pioneered by Kodak. This display typically consists of a series of organic layers between two electrical electrodes. The display is brighter than the current liquid crystal displays.

Output After processing, the information that is sent from the computer to a peripheral device.

Page layout In desktop publishing, the process of arranging text and graphics on the page.

Paint programs Graphics programs that enable individuals to simulate painting on the computer screen with the use of a mouse or graphics tablet. Paint programs create raster graphic images.

Pascal A high-level structured programming language, designed by Niklaus Wirth in the late 1960s.

Peripheral The devices that are connected to the computer under the microprocessor's control, such as disk drives, printers, and modems.

Personal data assistant (PDA) A small, handheld computer that accepts input on the screen from a stylus.

Personal portfolios Show a student's growth and development outside of school.

Piracy The act of copying software illegally.

Pixel Short for *picture element*, a linear dot on a display screen. When this dot is combined with other dots, it creates an image.

Plagiarism The taking of the graphic representation, writings, or ideas of another person and using them as one's own.

Plasma display A display produced by a mixture of neon gases between two transparent panels, giving a very sharp, clean image with a wide viewing angle.

PLATO Programmed Logic for Automatic Teaching Operations, an early computer system developed by the University of Illinois and Control Data Corporation and designed for instructional use.

Plug-ins Programs built to extend a browser's capabilities. Plug-ins enable users to see and hear video, audio, and other kinds of multimedia files.

Portal A website that acts as a starting point to the Internet, usually on a specific subject area.

Portfolio An organized collection of documents that is used by a student to reflect the student's knowledge, skills, and learning accomplishments.

Predetermined functions Ready-made formulas that enable the user to solve problems quickly.

Presentation graphics Combining text and images, software that produces and displays graphic screens.

Print graphics Has many of the same characteristics as presentation graphics: clip art, image manipulation; however, its focus is on creating products for print out.

Printer A device that produces computer output.

Problem-solving software Computer-assisted software that helps students develop critical thinking skills with the intent that these skills will transfer to other areas of the curriculum.

Professional portfolio Could contain samples of students' work that meet graduation requirements for high school or college admission.

Program A series of instructions designed to make a computer do a given task.

Protected and hidden cells A spreadsheet program feature that protects a group of cells from being altered or erased.

Public domain software Software that is not copyrighted and can be copied freely and distributed without payment or permission.

QuickLink pen A device that scans printed text, printed Internet links, charts, tables, books, and magazines. The students can then transfer this information to their computers to aid them in writing their reports.

QuickTime A program designed by Apple to show small movies on the computer screen.

QuickTime VR An extension of *QuickTime* that enables the user to view on-screen movies in 3-D space.

Quicktionary Reading Pen A device that scans printed words, displays them in large characters, pronounces them aloud, and defines them at the touch of a button.

Random access memory (RAM) Volatile memory. Whenever the computer is turned off, information stored in RAM is lost.

Raster graphics or bit-mapped graphics Images made up of a pattern of pixels or dots. These images are limited to the maximum resolution of the computer display or printer.

Read only memory (ROM) Memory that retains its contents when the power supply is turned off. Often referred to as *hardwired, internal memory,* it cannot be altered or changed.

Real time The immediate processing of data as it becomes available. In telecommunication, a person online can be connected to others who are online at the same time.

RealAudio A plug-in that enables users to listen to live or prerecorded audio transmissions on the World Wide Web.

Record A collection of related fields that are treated as a single unit.

Red, Green, and Blue (RGB) monitor A CRT (cathode ray tube) monitor that uses three electronic guns to generate red, green, and blue.

Refreshable Braille display A device that is added to a computer system to translate text on the screen into Braille.

Relational database Links files together which enables the user to work with more than one file at a time.

Repetitive stress or strain injury An injury caused by the repeated use of muscles, ligaments, tendons, tendon sheaths, and nerves, often during computer use.

Representational portfolio A portfolio that contains only a student's best work and that can be used for employment purposes.

Resolution The clarity or degree of sharpness of a displayed character or image, expressed in linear dots per inch.

Ring network A group of computers that communicate with each other in a ring, without a file server.

Robotics A branch of engineering that is concerned with the training and creation of robots.

Router A device that forwards data packets from one network to another.

Satellite data service Uses a satellite dish to connect to your computer.

Scanner A device that digitizes photographs or line art and stores the images as a file that can be transferred into a paint program or directly into a word processor.

Search engine A program that enables a user to find information on the Internet.

Shared-bus network A network where a single bidirectional cable carries messages to and from devices.

Shareware Copyrighted software that is distributed free but must be paid for if the customer is satisfied.

Simulation Software that approximates the conditions of the real world in an environment in which the user changes the variables.

Site licensing A software licensing system in which a person or organization pays a set fee to run copies of a program on a large number of computers.

Slow keys Enable the computer to recognize only the key presses that are a certain length and disregard others.

Smart card A credit card with an embedded microprocessor that provides information about its user's identity.

Software A program that instructs a computer to perform a specific job.

Software suite A collection of programs that are usually sold individually (e.g., *Microsoft Office*).

Sorting An operation that reorders data in a new sequence, usually alphabetically or numerically.

Spam Unsolicited messages sent via the Internet.

Speech recognition A computer program that can decode human speech into text.

Speech synthesizer An output device that generates sound. This chip gives the computer the ability to search for words and their pronunciations in a database.

Spider programs Automated electronic software programs that follow the links on a page and put all the text into one huge database.

SPOT A technology that implants wireless connectivity that is always on in devices such as watches and necklaces.

Spreadsheet A computerized version of a manual worksheet, with a matrix of numbers arranged in rows and columns, that facilitates calculations.

Star network A communications network in which all the computers are connected to a file server or host computer.

Sticky keys Certain keys that lock in place—allowing a user with a disability to press combination key strokes without having to press multiple keys simultaneously.

Streaming audio Compressed audio that is sent in real time via the Internet.

Streaming video Compressed movies that are sent in real time via the Internet.

Style sheet A file that contains instructions that apply character, paragraph, and page layout formats to desktop publishing and word processing documents. Style sheets include settings such as tabs, margins, columns, and fonts.

Supercomputers The largest and fastest of the mainframe computers with the most advanced processing abilities.

Surge suppressor Also known as a *surge protector,* a device that protects the computer from damaging electrical surges.

Switch A network device that forwards traffic at very high speeds.

SYSOP Acronym for SYStem OPerator, the person who runs a bulletin board.

System disk The disk that contains operating software and can also be used to boot the computer.

Teacher-directed approach A learning theory that emphasizes that the teacher is the manipulator of the class environment and the student is the receptacle.

Telecommunication The electronic transmission of information, including data, television pictures, sound, and facsimiles.

Telnet A commonly used protocol on the Internet that enables users to log onto a remote computer to run a program.

Template A predesigned document that includes text or formulas that are needed to create a standard document.

Terabyte A unit of measurement equal roughly to 1 trillion bytes (actually 1,099,511,627,776 bytes).

Thermal printer A printer that uses heated wires to burn dots into a costly special paper.

Time bomb A computer virus that is programmed to go off on a specific day and time.

Touch screen A display that has a pressure-sensitive panel mounted in the front. The user makes choices by touching the screen in the correct location.

Touch-free switch An input device that enables users to trigger a mouse click without applying any pressure.

Trackball A movable ball that moves the cursor on the screen as it is manipulated.

Trackpad or touchpad A pressure-sensitive pad that is smaller and more accurate than the trackball.

Transistor An electronic gate that bridges the gap between two wires and enables the current to flow.

Tutorial Similar to a tutor, a program that explains new material and then tests the student's progress.

Uniform Resource Locator (URL) A site address on the World Wide Web. For example, the URL for the California State University home page is http://www.csun.edu.

UNIX Originally developed by AT&T Bell laboratories, an operating system used on different types of computers that supports multitasking.

Upload Transfer of information from one computer to a remote computer.

USB drive (pen drive) A flash memory card that plugs into the user's USB port.

Usenet A leading network system of bulletin boards that services more than 1,500 newsgroups.

User friendly A term that means "easy to learn and use."

User group A group of users of a specific type of computer who share experiences to improve their understanding of the product.

Utility programs Programs that perform a variety of housekeeping and control functions such as sorting, copying, searching, and file management.

Vector graphics Images made of independent objects that can be sized, moved, and manipulated.

Video RAM (VRAM) A chip used to transfer and hold an image on the computer screen.

Video scan converter A device that changes personal computer or laptop output so it can be displayed on a television monitor.

Video-conferencing A multiuser chat in which the live images of the users are displayed on each participant's computer screen.

Videodisc A read-only optical disc that uses an analog signal to store and retrieve still and moving pictures, sound, or color.

Virtual reality (VR) A computer-generated world in which a person is able to manipulate the environment. The user generally wears a head-mounted device and special sensor gloves.

Virus A program that infects computer files by duplicating itself.

Voice recognition software or system A system that converts the spoken word into binary patterns that are computer recognizable; it understands human speech.

Warping A process similar to morphing, involving the altering and manipulation of a single image.

Weblog A method of expressing oneself using a personal online diary.

Web page An HTML document that displays information on the World Wide Web.

WebQuest Bernie Dodge defines a WebQuest as "an inquiry-oriented activity where most or all of the information that the students use comes from the Web."

Website A collection or related Web pages on the Internet that contains information about instructional material, services, products, and so on.

Wide area network (WAN) A network that uses long-distance communication or satellites to connect computers over greater distances than a local area network does.

Wildcard character A character such as an asterisk that is used to represent one or more characters.

Window An onscreen frame in which users can view a document, database, spreadsheet, or application program.

Windows A graphical interface developed by Microsoft Corporation for IBM and IBM-compatible computers.

Wireless communication A method of linking computers with radio waves or infrared. There are no interconnecting cables or wires.

Wireless network A network that enables users to transmit information by infrared, microwave technology, or radio waves instead of by wire.

Wizard A small program that enables the user to input information to create a customized template.

Word processor A software program designed to make the computer a useful electronic writing tool that can edit, store, and print documents.

Word wrap In word processing, when words go beyond a margin, the process of automatically pushing them to the beginning of the next line.

World Wide Web (WWW) An Internet service that enables users to navigate the Internet using hypertext documents.

Worm A program that can run by itself and replicate a full working version to other computers. After the worm is finished with its work, the data are usually corrupted and irretrievable.

Index